AMERICAN POLITICS   Changing Expectations

AMERICAN POLITICS

D. Van Nostrand Company

New York   Cincinnati   Toronto   London   Melbourne

Changing Expectations

RONALD E. PYNN

University of North Dakota

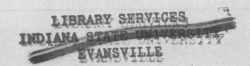

Cover photo: © Pete Turner/The Image Bank.

Chapter opening photos: Chapters 2, 3, 5, 6, 8, 9, 10, 11, 12, 13, 14—
Stan Wakefield; Chapters 1 (Reagan), 4, 7—United Press International;
Chapter 1 (Carter) Mary Anne Fackelman, the White House

D. Van Nostrand Company Regional Offices:
New York   Cincinnati

D. Van Nostrand Company International Offices:
London   Toronto   Melbourne

Copyright © 1981 by Litton Educational Publishing, Inc.

Library of Congress Catalog Card Number: 80-52352
ISBN: 0-442-25865-8

Published by D. Van Nostrand Company
135 West 50th Street, New York, N. Y. 10020

10   9   8   7   6   5   4   3   2   1

Preface

American Politics: Changing Expectations, which follows the traditional topical outline of an American politics text, is also a thematic text: the theme of change is used here as a means for organizing and understanding American politics, for capturing the differences between our political system in 1960 and our political system now.

In teaching American government for a dozen years, I have been struck by the extent of the changes in the American electorate and in American politics. These changes are deep, and perhaps when they have run their course they will be looked upon as revolutionary. But they are really an evolution: the principles, behaviors, and institutions that have marked America for two hundred years are still at work.

The change is in our attitudes toward these principles and institutions and our expectations of them and perhaps of ourselves. Three events from the 1960s and 1970s are particularly relevant in explaining the changing expectations toward American politics: the Great Society, Vietnam, and Watergate. All profoundly affected the consensus forged in the 1930s, the image of America and Americans that all of us held with a certain pride.

The future, on the eve of the 1960 presidential election, looked bright: there was peace; Europe was recovering; there was prosperity and technological progress at home. The election was almost a cause for celebration, and the victory of John F. Kennedy a sign of a new and wonderful era. In 1980, by contrast, the mood was sober and sometimes angry, because so many promises seemed not to have been kept, so many dreams to have turned into illusions.

The election of Ronald Reagan in 1980 was in part an expression of frustration with government and its inability to find solutions. Americans want no more of the same. They want answers; they want change. If President Reagan can deliver the promised answers, there exists the opportunity to renew Americans' faith in their government and to shape the course of politics for future decades.

THE TEXT: AN OVERVIEW

The book is intended for those to whom the study of American government is new. It provides basic information as well as analysis and interpretation. Chapter 1 sets the stage for the study of American government by introducing the theme of changing expectations. Chapters 2 and 3 describe the historical foundations of American politics, the Constitution and the federal system. Chapters 4 and 5 deal with individual liberties and equality, the two principles central to an understanding of how ideals and reality combine to produce policy. Chapters 6 and 7 describe the role of public opinion and interest groups, vital parts of the American process. Chapter 8 deals with the political parties as systems in themselves and with their functions. Their role in the electoral process and the changes in voting patterns over time are the subject of Chapter 9. The next four chapters, 10, 11, 12, and 13, survey the basic institutions of our government: the presidency, the bureaucracy, Congress, and the courts. The final chapter is devoted to a look at the future and at what the effect of the changing expectations on which the book is focused may mean for our system as a whole.

SPECIAL FEATURES AND STUDY AIDS

To sharpen the focus on change, to make basic concepts and issues clear, and to help bring American government alive in terms familiar from daily newspapers or TV news, the book contains a number of special features.
At the end of each chapter:

- A **Summary** lists the main points covered.
- **Key Terms** are listed for ready review.
- Three or four **Research Projects** give the student an easy opportunity to enhance understanding.
- An annotated **Bibliography** gives suggestions for further reading.

Throughout the text:

- **Fact Files.**   The fact files contain basic data related to the content of the chapters.

- **Public Policy Essays**   Every chapter presents a view on public policy—revenue-sharing, social welfare, national security. Together, these views form a coherent outlook on the policy process and how it works.
- **Changing Consensus**   In order to further highlight the changes in the American consensus, particular events and issues are presented in terms of the consequences of the change for real policies.
- **Practicing Politics**   These features provide practical information for the active, involved citizen: how juries are selected, where information on members of Congress can be found, how a voting machine works.
- **Illustrations**   Drawings and photographs are used throughout to illustrate and clarify events, issues, and concepts.

At the end of the book:

- A **Glossary** of all the terms in the book.
- The two major documents of American politics, the Declaration of Independence and the Constitution, both annotated by the author.

In addition to the text itself, there are several other aids to teaching and learning:

- The **Instructor's Manual,** by Joan Flynn contains summaries of chapter contents, teaching objectives, discussion questions, quiz questions, and additional reading sources.
- A separate **Test File** contains over 800 essay, multiple choice, true-false, and fill-in questions.
- The **Student Learning Guide,** by Murray Fishel of Kent State University, includes chapter summaries, learning objectives, key terms with extensive definitions, review outlines, self-review tests, and annotated lists of suggested readings and resources.

WITH THANKS

The study of American politics is important, and it ought to be enjoyable. The point of this book, and of the special features and aids, is to return to that study some of the excitement and the sense of participation in an extraordinary enterprise that has always been so much a part of American life, and of being an American citizen.

Although this point of view and this endeavor are mine, many people have participated in making the book. I am indebted to Boyd Wright, who read and commented on earlier drafts of the text, and contributed much to the final manuscript. Reviewers made valuable comments that strengthened the book: Ross Baker of Rutgers; Andrew Cowart of SUNY at Stony Brook; Larry Elowitz of Georgia College; Murray Fishel of Kent State University; Benjamin Hourani of

Eastern Michigan University; Donald Johnson of the University of Iowa; K. Robert Keiser of San Diego State University; H. L. Nieburg of SUNY at Binghamton; James Pierson of the University of Pennsylvania; Sandra Schwartz of Douglass College, Rutgers; Joseph Tucker of Ohio University; and Dale Vinyard of Wayne State University.

At D. Van Nostrand Company, Judith Joseph, Publishing Director, first sensed that my view of change in the political system could become the basis for a new college text. Her encouragement and support are most warmly appreciated. Only in writing a book can one appreciate competence in editing and agreeableness in an editor. Harriet Serenkin, Executive Editor, had both.

And finally my wife, Scharlene, and my children, Suzanne, Stephen, and Karen, from whom I stole a good deal of time, not to mention the dining room table, gave a great deal of care and understanding while this new member of the family was being born.

Contents

1 The Anguish of Change

2 The Constitution

34

3 Federalism

78

4 Individual Liberty and the First Amendment 116

5 Equality, Due Process, and the Fourteenth Amendment 150

6 Public Opinion

7 Interest Groups

Political Parties   262

The Changing American Voter and the Electoral Process   304

The Presidency

11 Bureaucracy   412

12 Congress   454

13 The Judiciary   **510**

14 The Future of American Politics 555

Public Policy

The making of public policy and selected policy issues are treated in the following essays:

AMERICAN
POLITICS   Changing Expectations

Chapter

1

The

Anguish of Change

The political world of two generations of Americans, that fashioned by Franklin Delano Roosevelt out of the Depression and World War II and continued in the post-World War II era, is changing—and in a rapid and sometimes frightening way.

In the 1930s through Roosevelt's New Deal, government had promoted industrial growth and economic security. The National Industrial Recovery Act gave business a badly needed boost while maintaining the free enterprise system. The Social Security Act in 1935 was to provide retirement security for the elderly. With the Employment Act of 1946, Keynesian economics became the theory of the day: Government must do the spending to support the economy if private enterprise will not or can not.

The political process had realigned into a new Democratic majority supporting the presidency of Franklin D. Roosevelt. The power of the presidency was greater than ever before, and Roosevelt, elected to an unprecedented fourth term in 1944, was one of the most popular presidents.

In the period after World War II, America had been the victorious liberator of Europe and Asia, with no rival for power except Russia. The Marshall Plan had aided in the recovery of Europe. The North Atlantic Treaty Organization (NATO) was created in 1949 by the United States and the nations of Western Europe as a mutual protection against attack, and in the hope of containing Russia and Soviet communism. At home, Americans were prosperous and content.

But by the 1960s, American politics were in a state of disarray. The coalition fashioned by Roosevelt was disintegrating. The power of the presidency was under attack. The Keynesian economic system was not working. Government had grown—in size and cost—but Americans did not feel better for it. In fact, the people felt that they were worse off than at any time in their history.

Three events from the 1960s and 1970s bring into focus the depth of the change in our political process. These three were the Great Society program, Vietnam, and Watergate.

CHANGING EXPECTATIONS: THE RECENT PAST

THE GREAT SOCIETY PROGRAM

The Great Society had begun as a bold program in social engineering. President Johnson announced a war on poverty; Congress passed the first major civil rights legislation in nearly a hundred years; Medicare was added to the social security system; and food stamps were provided for the unemployed and disadvantaged. Housing and urban mass transit were to be revitalized. In short, as President Johnson described the Great Society, it "rests on abundance and liberty for all. It demands an end to poverty and racial injustice—to which we are totally committed."

But by 1968 guns and butter became increasingly difficult to obtain; federal government policies accelerated the drift from the Great Society to military commitment in Vietnam. The Johnson administration budgeted $79 billion for the military in 1968 and $15 billion for the Great Society—including $2 million for the school lunch program and $40 million for rat extermination in the city slums. Only two years earlier the defense budget was $56 billion, or 7.9 percent of the Gross National Product (GNP). In 1968 it was 9.1 percent of GNP.

Whether because of the escalation of Vietnam or poor planning or simple shortsightedness, the Great Society failed to meet expectations. Programs were badly designed: Frequently they were funded by categorical grants without coordination with other programs and agencies responsible for similar concerns. Legislative victory appeared to be more important than administrative implementation. But more critically, the Great Society raised the hopes of millions of Americans with the pledge of racial justice, jobs for the unemployed, medical care for the elderly, housing for slum dwellers, and the eradication of poverty. It created a climate of rising expectations, but left promises unfulfilled. It represented a departure from the New Deal. The New Deal distributed money and provided regulation, relatively easily achievable goals within the framework of governmental administration. The Great Society asked for fundamental reallocation of resources and values. It asked for social change and required governmental social engineering.

President Lyndon Johnson signing a piece of Great Society legislation. (National Archives)

VIETNAM

What began in the 1950s and early 1960s as technical assistance to the South Vietnamese government became, under Lyndon Johnson, full-scale military combat by U.S. forces in support of the South Vietnamese. Vietnam became for America an unwanted, undeclared, and socially devastating war. The Cold War was fading: The claim of communist containment in Asia seemed remote and unconvincing. For many Americans, Vietnam was a civil war and not a conflict where America's national interest was at stake.

Of grave concern for students of American government were the legal and political processes behind the conduct of the war. Clouds hung over the 1964 Gulf of Tonkin Resolution, in which Congress authorized the president "to take all steps necessary, including the use of armed forces," to protect areas seeking American assistance, "in defense of its freedom." On the basis of a North Viet-

American soldiers in Vietnam. The buildup of American troops in Vietnam began in 1964 and lasted until the U.S. withdrawal of troops in 1973. (The Bettmann Archive, Inc.)

namese attack on a U.S. ship, the U.S.S. Maddox—some critics say staged attack in order to secure the Resolution—the Johnson Administration escalated and sustained the war effort in Vietnam. In 1970 President Nixon announced to the nation that he had ordered the bombing of Cambodia—secretly and without the advice or consent of Congress.

The Vietnam war was divisive. Students and other Americans were demonstrating in opposition to it; opinion was polarizing between ''doves'' and ''hawks.'' The Cambodian bombing touched off a wave of new and violent social protest. At Kent State University, four students were killed by National Guardsmen attempting to quell the protests. The Democratic party had split over the war, Eugene McCarthy challenged Lyndon Johnson for the nomination in 1964, and George McGovern won the nomination in 1972. Both were outspoken critics of the war. The members of Congress felt isolated and uninvolved in policymaking. They had abdicated their responsibilities in the Gulf of Tonkin Resolution and, in 1973, faced a defiant President Nixon who threatened to disobey a congressional resolution to halt the bombing or to withdraw from Vietnam by a certain date.

The war in Vietnam had taken a terrible toll. It sapped the resources of the Great Society, leaving hopes and promises unfulfilled. It created a credibility gap between government and its citizens; support for the war and for government was ebbing. It remained a presidential war: Congress was ignored, even lied to. Critics said presidential power had been imperialized; the personality and prestige of the president were more important than national policy.

WATERGATE

The third event was Watergate. Orginally labeled a "third-rate burglary," the illegal break-ins, dirty tricks, coverup and conspiracy to obstruct justice we call Watergate eventually touched America to the roots of its constitutional and democratic processes. As the revelations implicated the White House and finally the president himself, questions were raised about the unprecedented growth of presidential power and the constitutional mechanism for checking that power. The dirty tricks, illegal campaign contributions, and abandonment of party politics raised questions regarding the future of political parties.

The American people's confidence in their public officials and political system was at an all-time low. The mood on August 9, 1974, when Richard Nixon stepped down from the presidency, was one of gloom. The president himself had participated in the coverup and conspired to obstruct justice. The office of the presidency had been disgraced.

The political process was little better off. Reform of the Democratic party had facilitated McGovern's nomination; Richard Nixon, nominated by the Republicans, had established his own separate reelection organization. The whole process had been denigrated by money: $130 million was raised by the presidential candidates, much of it from large contributors and some from illegal corporate contributions. Voters were disgusted; party loyalties were weakening; people were splitting their ballots and fewer and fewer were going to the polls.

Watergate signaled disaffection with the political process. The political system had been severely tested. With the resignation of Richard Nixon, Gerald Ford became president pledging to "put Watergate behind us." The nation heaved a sigh of relief; the nation seemed safe, but the costs had been high. The presidency was in disrepute. Americans had grown cynical toward their government. Political parties were crumbling and the electoral process was facing the challenge of reform in the wake of "dirty tricks" and rising costs. For two years the nation had been in the grip of Watergate; now its political leaders would seek to govern again. Gerald Ford gave Richard Nixon a pardon for his part in Watergate. Jimmy Carter came to the presidency in 1976 pledging to restore faith in government and to get on with the business of governing the nation.

The events of the 1960s and 1970s precipitated the decline of postwar politics. Through these events we are coming to a better understanding of the extent of the change wrought in our political process. As Theodore H. White observed, "the postwar world was dead and awaited burial." But there were other forces of change within American society as well.

Richard Nixon bids farewell to his staff. Nixon resigned the presidency in August 1974 due to the scandal called Watergate. (United Press International)

THE AGENDA FOR CHANGE

Expectations toward politics are much changed as a result of the three events of the Great Society, Vietnam, and Watergate. We must understand, however, that the agenda for these changed expectations had been fashioned by the thrust of social policy in America over several decades and most recently since the New Deal.

We have witnessed throughout the twentieth century the increased activity of government in social and economic policies. The public sector of American life has added new responsibilities in response to demands as American life changed. Government has become responsible for cushioning the impact of change—both intended and unintended. The net result is that governmental policy now affects every citizen in very real and personal ways.

CHANGE IN SOCIETY

One of the easiest, yet most fundamental reasons for the changed agenda is that American life has changed dramatically in the twentieth century. We see the changes of American life reflected in the shifting population, employment, and income patterns.

Population.   By 1900 America had ceased being a rural nation. More citizens had come to live in metropolitan cities than on farms or in rural towns. This trend has continued until where, today, three out of four Americans live in an urban environment (see Figure 1.1).

Not only has our population grown, but the composition of the population has changed internally. The well noted post-World War II "baby boom" produced

Figure 1.1

A population map of the United states showing how the United States might look if the states were relatively as large in size as they are in population. (*National Journal,* March 29, 1980)

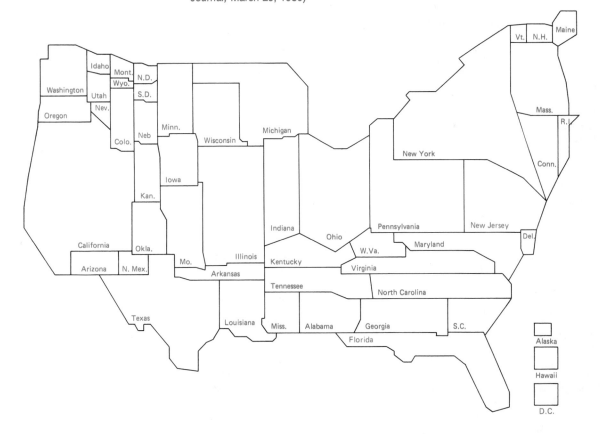

FACT FILE

A POPULATION PROFILE OF THE STATES[a]

	Population Total (millions)	Urban	Age 18–25	65 +	Median voting age	Racial composition White	Black	Employment White collar	Blue collar
Alabama	3.7	58.4%	18.9%	14.7%	42.8	73.4%	26.4%	40.6%	42.7%
Alaska	0.4	48.7	26.0	3.8	33.9	78.8	0.3	64.8	35.2
Arizona	2.4	79.6	19.5	14.2	41.9	90.6	3.0	51.1	32.3
Arkansas	2.2	50.0	17.2	18.7	45.5	81.2	18.6	64.8	35.2
California	22.3	90.9	19.0	13.5	41.6	89.0	7.0	54.4	30.7
Colorado	2.7	78.5	21.1	13.0	40.2	95.7	2.9	53.8	28.3
Connecticut	3.1	77.4	16.8	14.3	43.7	93.5	6.0	52.4	36.2
Delaware	0.6	72.2	18.7	12.4	41.4	85.1	14.2	51.0	34.4
D.C.	0.7	100.0	21.3	13.2	40.2	27.7	71.1	73.6	26.4
Florida	8.6	80.5	16.0	21.1	46.5	84.1	15.5	49.8	32.0
Georgia	5.1	60.3	20.6	12.4	40.4	73.8	26.0	43.6	39.9
Hawaii	0.9	83.1	22.9	8.9	38.3	38.8	1.0	49.9	31.3
Idaho	0.9	54.1	12.5	9.5	43.2	98.0	0.3	46.7	33.2
Illinois	11.2	83.0	17.4	14.9	43.3	86.4	12.8	49.1	36.6
Indiana	5.4	64.9	18.7	14.7	42.5	92.8	6.9	42.0	42.7
Iowa	2.9	57.2	17.2	18.9	45.1	98.5	1.2	42.8	30.8
Kansas	2.3	66.1	18.9	17.7	44.0	94.5	4.8	47.8	30.6
Kentucky	3.5	52.3	19.3	16.0	43.0	92.3	7.5	40.1	41.2
Louisiana	4.0	66.1	20.4	13.5	41.5	69.7	29.9	45.2	36.1
Maine	1.1	50.8	17.7	17.6	44.5	99.3	0.3	40.6	44.1
Maryland	4.1	76.6	18.7	11.7	41.2	81.4	17.9	55.8	31.0
Massachusetts	5.8	84.6	18.2	16.6	44.1	96.3	3.1	52.7	34.2
Michigan	9.2	73.8	19.0	13.3	42.2	88.3	11.2	44.8	40.7
Minnesota	4.0	66.4	18.5	16.8	43.2	98.2	1.0	48.5	30.9
Mississippi	2.4	44.5	19.8	16.1	43.2	62.8	36.8	38.6	41.0
Missouri	4.9	70.1	17.3	17.9	44.6	89.3	10.3	46.9	35.6
Montana	0.8	53.4	18.0	15.5	43.6	95.5	0.3	45.3	28.3
Nebraska	1.6	61.5	18.1	18.7	44.5	96.6	2.7	44.4	28.3
Nevada	0.7	80.9	17.3	9.7	40.5	91.8	5.7	47.1	26.2
New Hampshire	0.9	56.4	18.4	16.1	43.2	99.4	0.3	44.5	42.1
New Jersey	7.3	88.9	15.8	14.5	44.1	88.6	10.7	52.7	36.2
New Mexico	1.2	69.8	20.4	11.5	40.1	90.1	1.9	51.4	39.9
New York	17.7	81.7	16.5	15.8	44.1	86.8	11.9	55.1	30.8
North Carolina	5.6	45.0	21.1	12.4	40.8	76.6	22.4	38.5	45.8
North Dakota	0.7	44.3	19.3	16.9	43.9	97.0	0.4	42.4	21.0
Ohio	10.7	75.3	18.2	14.4	42.9	90.6	9.1	45.4	40.8
Oklahoma	2.9	68.0	18.1	17.3	44.2	88.9	7.0	47.8	33.2
Oregon	2.4	67.1	17.7	16.2	44.1	97.2	1.3	48.2	34.2
Pennsylvania	11.8	71.5	16.4	16.0	45.2	91.0	8.6	45.0	41.5
Rhode Island	0.9	87.1	19.8	16.0	44.1	96.6	2.7	45.1	42.3
South Carolina	3.0	47.6	22.1	11.6	40.1	69.3	30.5	37.3	46.8
South Dakota	0.7	44.6	18.3	18.9	45.2	94.7	0.2	41.0	22.3

A POPULATION PROFILE OF THE STATES[a] (Continued)

	Population Total (millions)	Urban	Age 18–25	Age 65+	Median voting age	Racial composition White	Racial composition Black	Employment White collar	Employment Blue collar
Tennessee	4.4	58.8	18.7	14.7	42.6	83.7	16.1	41.4	42.2
Texas	13.0	79.7	19.8	13.7	41.4	86.6	12.7	48.4	34.2
Utah	1.3	80.4	23.3	12.1	39.2	97.4	0.6	51.8	32.2
Vermont	0.5	32.1	19.7	16.4	42.8	99.6	0.2	46.2	34.3
Virginia	5.1	63.1	20.8	11.9	40.5	80.8	18.6	48.9	36.2
Washington	3.7	72.6	19.5	14.2	42.3	95.4	2.1	50.7	32.9
West Virginia	1.9	39.0	17.3	16.6	45.2	95.6	4.2	40.4	45.2
Wisconsin	4.7	65.9	18.4	16.6	43.7	96.4	2.9	43.2	37.2
Wyoming	0.4	60.5	18.0	14.2	42.7	97.2	0.8	46.3	30.2

a. Population—1978; other data—1970.

SOURCE: *National Journal,* October 20, 1979, p. 1772.

a record number of children, 4.3 million, in 1957. Since then the number of births has declined annually. This has had two important consequences. First, we have reached and exceeded "zero population growth." Fewer babies are being born annually than are needed to keep the U.S. population constant. If this trend continues at its present rate, the population of the United States will decline about 17 percent per generation.[1] Second, the population trend represents the "graying of America" as more and more of the population falls into the over 65 age category. These are citizens past their prime income earning years and for whom income maintenance is a major concern. Both trends have enormous consequences for government funding in the future years.

The ethnic composition of the population has also changed. Black Americans constitute 11.5 percent of the total population today. However, they constitute 30 percent of the population of central cities with populations 2 million or over, and blacks are a majority in several urban cities of America. The fastest growing ethnic group in American are Hispanic Americans: They now number some 12 million people, increasing nearly 15 percent in the past five years.

Employment.   Changing populations also means a changing labor force. The increases in technology have altered the nature and skills necessary for employment. Figure 1.2 shows that white collar employees number nearly 50 percent of the labor market; industrial blue collar employees continue to decline as our economy and technology change. Seventeen percent of the work force now represents employment by government. Today a service economy has relocated and dispersed employment.

The changing labor force has also demanded specialized skills and training.

1. *Congressional Quarterly, Weekly Report,* January 27, 1979, p. 114.

TABLE 1.1
Population of the United States (in millions)

	1790	1820	1860	1900	1950	1960	1970	1980	2000(Projected)
Total population	4	9.5	31	76	151	180	204	222	260.4
Urban	0.2	0.7	6.2	30	97	126	149	NA	NA
Rural	3.7	9	25	46	54.5	54	54	NA	NA
White	3.2	8	27	67	135	159	179	191.5	219
Nonwhite	NA	2	4.5	9	16	20.5	25	30.5	41.5
Under 20			16	34	51	69	67.5	70.5	77
20–64			13.5	39	88	94.5	117.5	127	151.5
65–over		0.5	1.5	3	12	16.5	20	25	31.8
Male	NA	5	16	39	75	89	100	108	126.5
Female	NA	5	15	37	76	91	104	114	134
In school			65	17	28.5	42	51.5	57.3	NA
In college			0.05	0.25	2	3.5	8	12	NA

SOURCE: Historical Statistics of the United States: Colonial Times to 1970. 1980 and 2000 data from Bureau of the Census, Population Estimates and Projections, Series P-25, Number 704.

There has been a constant press for education. In 1940, 25 percent of the population had a high school education and 5 percent a college degree; by 1980, 68 percent of the population had a high school diploma and 16 percent were college educated.

We also see a continual rise in women as part of the labor force: They now constitute 50 percent of the labor force. The greatest influx of women into the labor market today are married—they now total 25 million—as the women's movement and a worsening economy continue to cause more and more women to seek employment.

Income.   There has been a continual and constant increase in personal and family income over the years. As society and life-styles changed, Americans' incomes have risen, although since the mid-1970s inflation has taken a heavy toll on increased earning power. The median income has risen from $12,000 in 1973 to $19,684 in 1980. There has been growth, for whites and blacks, in the percent of families earning $25,000 or more (see Figure 1.3).

Yet the figures belie the income problems many Americans continue to face. Inflation erodes earning power. The purchasing power of the 1967 dollar was 67 cents in 1975. Inflation in 1974 and 1979 jumped the consumer price index 12 and 13 percents, respectively. Particularly hard hit are the retired and others on fixed income.

Blacks and minorities continue to struggle for economic parity. There remain 26 million Americans with income levels below the officially defined level of poverty. Blacks make up 31 percent of the total, 13 percent are elderly, and 47 percent are families with female heads of households.

Unemployment remains a serious concern for Americans. In the face of

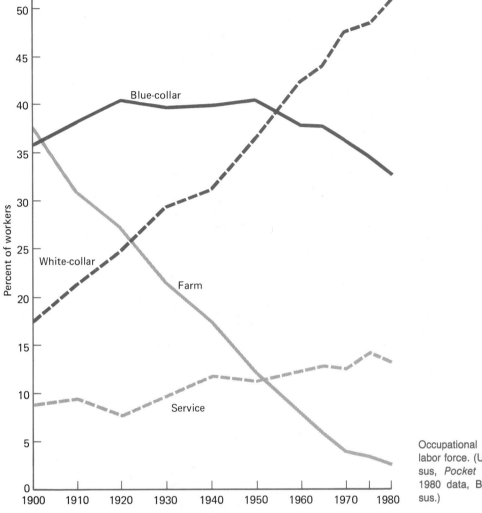

Figure 1.2

Occupational distribution of the labor force. (U.S. Bureau of Census, *Pocket Book Data*, 1976; 1980 data, Bureau of the Census.)

technology, we have had to live with a continuing unemployment rate of seven or eight percent when three to four percent unemployment was considered permissible in past times of economic growth and prosperity. As for the unemployed, one in five is under 20 years of age, one in five is nonwhite, two in five are female, and almost half are blue-collar workers.

CHANGE IN GOVERNMENT

The changed agenda for government represents more than the growth of government, it represents a redefined goal for government policy. With the New Deal, government came to play increasing roles in economic and social affairs.

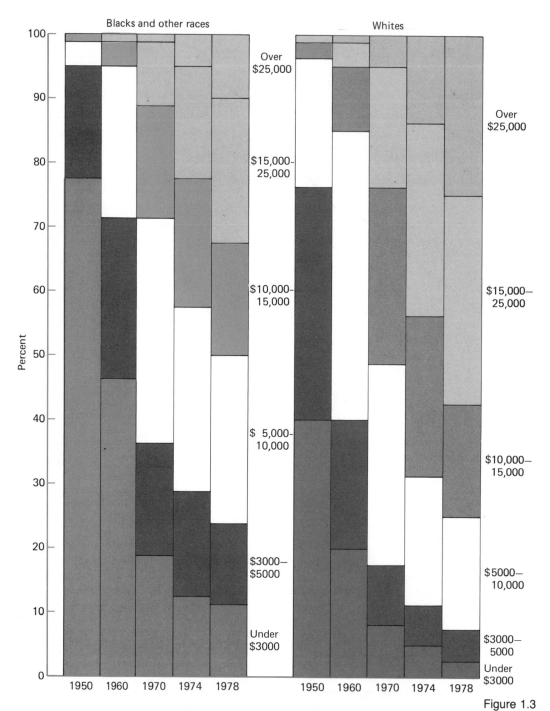

Figure 1.3

Family income levels. (U.S. Bureau of the Census, *Statistical Abstracts*, 1962 and 1979)

There grew substantial amounts of money dedicated to programs—as social security, debt retirement—committing future governments to spend. Government expenditure became a powerful incentive as a tool of public policy. Today all levels of government spending represent 33 percent of the GNP.

There are three ways we can measure this change in government. First by the growth in public employment, second by the growth of the federal budget, and finally by the changing nature of expenditures.

Public Employment.   One measure of the increased role of government is to note the increases in public employment to deal with the increased activity of government. Public employment has increased approximately 40 percent in 20 years. But what is most clearly revealed by Figure 1.4 is the growth in public employment at the state and local levels. In fact, federal public employment has shown a slight decline in recent years. The real growth in federal employment came earlier in the wake of the New Deal. The recent increases in state and local public employment illustrate the growth of public services and the need for employment at the local and state levels to deliver those services.

The increased demand for public services, hence employment, is a direct response to the changing complexion of society. The changes in population and income have mandated personal and social protection policies as well as economic regulation. Public employees are needed to implement these increased and changed activities.

Federal Budget.   Public spending by the federal government surpassed one-half a trillion dollars in 1980. While government spending has been constantly on the rise, the dramatic growth in expenditures came in 1974. Throughout

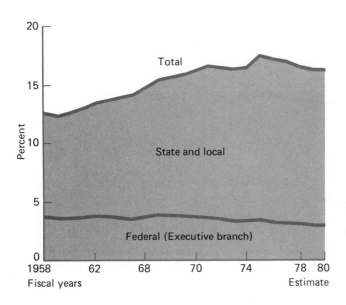

Figure 1.4

Growth in government civilian employment as a percent of total civilian employment. (Government Civilian Employment, *Weekly Report,* Congressional Quarterly, January 27, 1979, p. 147)

the 1960s and early 1970s, federal outlays as a percent of GNP remained constant, but with 1975 federal spending rose to 23 percent of the GNP. But these recent budget increases largely reflect the impact of inflation on the American dollar (see Figure 1.5).

The spiraling growth in the federal budget is principally caused by the nature of programs and spending, the so-called **uncontrollables.** Presently 75 percent of the federal budget is uncontrollable. Uncontrollables are the dedicated and entitled programs such as social security, Medicare, interest payments on the

Figure 1.5

Growth in Federal expenditures. In terms of current dollars, President Carter's fiscal 1980 budget shows a huge increase in spending over previous years. But inflation accounts for much of the increase, as the budget shown in constant (1972) dollars indicates. Note that the increase over 1979 spending is 7.7 percent in current dollars but only 0.7 percent in constant dollars. (*National Journal,* January 27, 1979, p. 125)

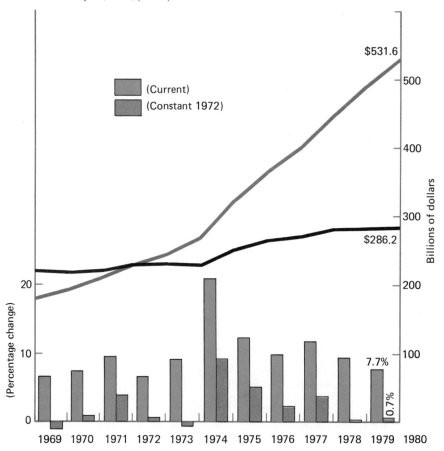

debt, revenue sharing, and so on, not subject to annual action by Congress. They are, in effect, permanent appropriations of Congress.[2] Such programs and expenditures, therefore, become part of a permanent government.

Expenditures.   Perhaps the best means to illustrate the changed agenda is to note the changing areas of expenditures within the federal budget. As a result of the changes in society—the increased social welfare policies and personal protection programs—the distribution of federal expenditures has changed.

Figure 1.6 shows that the major change in expenditures has been in national defense and veterans benefits which during the late 1960s required 45 percent of the budget. In 1973, however, these functions were overtaken by welfare, health and income protection. In 1980 defense and veterans benefits were 25 percent of the budget; health, education, and income security rose to 50 percent of the budget. The effects of a changed environment were making themselves felt through the budget priorities of the national government.

Figure 1.6

Portion of the Federal budget by selected expenditures. (U.S. Bureau of the Census, *Statistical Abstracts,* 1962 and 1979. 1980 data from 1980 budget, Office of the Treasury)

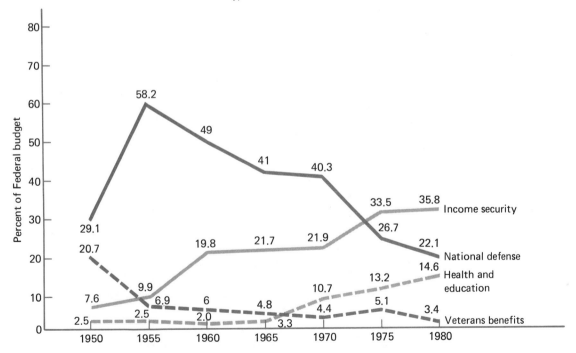

2. Committee for Economic Development, *Redefining Government's Role in the Market System* (New York: Committee for Economic Development, July 1979), p. 53.

CHANGING EXPECTATIONS AND GOVERNMENT

The agenda for change produced a change both in the size and scope of government. Not only has the budget grown but so has the scope of governmental policy. Two unmistakable trends stand out. First, government has become a major component of the nation's economy. Government is a major consumer of economic goods. The delivery of services and the size of increases in government spending do much to affect the state of economic health in America. Government is also a chief regulator of economic activity. The level of government spending stimulates or slows private business activity; government regulation sets the boundaries for doing business as well as mandating standards and wages. Government policy now seeks to regulate economic activity as a means to control inflation and keep employment high.

The second trend is closely linked to the first. The achievement of the nation's economic goals is intertwined with the nation's social goals. We have seen increased government activity in response to shifting populations and income levels. Increasingly, government has sought to intervene on behalf of citizens to promote social values, frequently using its economic resources to achieve those social policies. Two examples are pollution abatement to protect the environment and affirmative action hiring practices to assist minority employment. Government has come to take prime responsibility for the maintenance of the democratic values of equality and justice. In many diverse areas as housing, health, transportation, prison reform, and so forth, government policy seeks to promote equality and fairness for all citizens. More recently, government has intervened on behalf of its citizens to buffer the forces of change—often from the consequences of unintended changes, as in the case of high energy costs resulting from OPEC (Organization of Petroleum Exporting Countries) oil. Income security is the major budgetary consequence of this kind of policy.

As a consequence of these changes, we have become accustomed to government activism in order to deal with the enormous social and economic complexities that face our nation. The forces of change have transcended individual lives and individual control. We need the support of government. The events of the last two decades, however, leave Americans skeptical and unsettled regarding the use of political power. Changing expectations toward politics have created a tension in American politics—we expect government intervention in the issues facing the nation, but we fear the continued growth of government and the potential abuse of so much power. Everett Ladd, as shown in Figure 1.7, has captured well the confused and conflicting mood of the American people.[3] Citizens think government too powerful, that it spends to excess, yet the people look to government for help in resolving virtually every problem they face.

Americans have been brought up to believe in their political system, that the democratic process benefits everyone, that the values of a democracy make it the best form of government in the world. There is liberty and equality, a system

3. Everett Ladd, "What the Voters Really Want," *Fortune,* December 18, 1978.

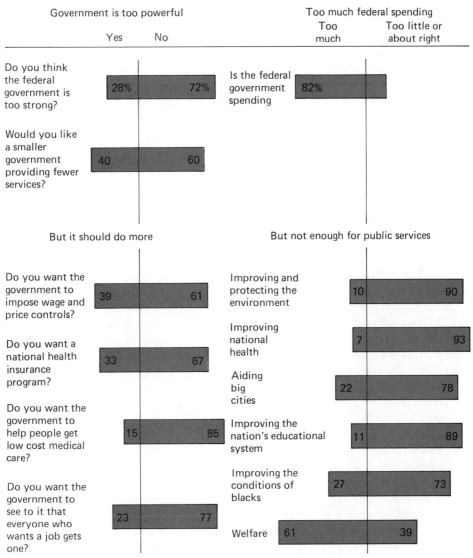

Figure 1.7

The feeling of Americans toward government and federal spending. (Based on a chart from Everett Ladd, "What the Voters Really Want," originally appearing in *Fortune Magazine,* December 18, 1978)

of majority rule, and justice for all—along with a free-enterprise economic system that seeks to harmonize individual initiative and mass efficiency. Americans had believed their society capable of infinite progress and prosperity.

Hence, it is because American democracy promises so much that failure to achieve has led to uncertainty and disillusionment. Ultimately, changing expec-

The Study of Public Policy

The study of public policy is the study of what government does. It involves a purposive course of action to be followed by government bodies and public officials in dealing with a problem, a matter of concern.[1] Public policy seeks to distinguish between what governments intend to do and what in fact they achieve. It is a process and not simply decision making, although decisions are frequently made among policy alternatives. There are several components to the policy process that form a sequential pattern of activity:

1. *Agenda setting.* How does an issue come before government? How does it becomes a public problem? How does an issue get placed on the government's agenda for recognition as a significant problem for society?
2. *Policy formulation.* What are the alternatives being developed to solve the problem? Who participates in the proposal of solutions? What is the range of permissable alternatives?
3. *Policy adoption.* What policy is finally adopted and analysis of the process for its adoption? What goals and participants gain legitimacy? How is support achieved for adopted policies?
4. *Policy implementation.* How is policy carried out? What are the resources necessary to achieve the policy objectives? What impact, including changes in behavior, does the policy have?
5. *Policy evaluation.* How effective was the policy in achieving its goals? Who assesses policy impact and what happens as a result of that assessment?

There are several ways to examine public policy. It can be examined by subject-matter—such as, education, tax, welfare; or by the institutions adopting policy—legislature, bureaucracy, or judiciary. But the most useful typology is that developed from Theodore Lowi on public policy's impact on society and the participants involved[2]:

1. *Distributive policy.* The distribution of services and benefits to specific private groups and individuals in society. Governmental funds and benefits are provided to particular segments of society to subsidize their private activities. It is believed that such governmental support benefits all of society and the policies produce benefits without direct costs to other specific groups. Hence there is no competition for public funds, and distributive policy normally has short-term consequences.
2. *Regulatory policy.* Restricting or limiting the permissible range of activity for groups or individuals in society. Regulatory policy involves the competitive allocation of goods and services. One side wins, one side loses in the competition for the delivery of goods and services. Some activities and policies are deemed appropriate and permissible while others are declared illegitimate and not permissible. Regulatory policies determine, for example, what television stations can broadcast in a city or the amounts of pollution industries can discharge into the air or water.
3. *Self-regulatory policy.* Like regulatory policy, this policy involves restrictions and controls. It seeks to establish general rules and policies; however, it does

this by the regulated group's direct involvement and support in the formulation of policy as a means of protecting and promoting the group's interests and activities. A classic example of self-regulatory policy is professional licensure.

4. *Redistributive policy.* The reallocation of wealth and benefits among broad classes or groups of people in society. Such policies aim at a massive shift in wealth or rights enjoyed by groups so that significant changes in position in society are accomplished. Since groups are generally unwilling to give up their wealth or power, redistributive policies are difficult to achieve and involve the broadest range of values and issues.

1. James E. Anderson, *Public Policy Making,* 2nd edition (New York; Holt, Rinehart & Winston, 1979), p. 3.
2. Theodore J. Lowi, "American Business, Public Policy, Case Studies, and Political Theory," *World Politics* 16 (June 1964).

---

tations require us to reexamine and assess once again the fundamental principles of democracy. First, let us examine briefly the changing expectations, the public's mood, and how the organs of government try to formulate public policy in such an environment.

ELECTIONS AND VOTING

The battle for the ballot has been one of the longest and most symbolic struggles in American history. The right to vote symbolizes the democratic nature of the political process; the opportunity for people of all races, occupations, and religions to meet on an equal plane and select the candidates of their choice. Yet today public officials are not held in high esteem: They are viewed as captured by money and special interest groups. Many citizens see the electoral process as denigrated by the high cost of campaigning; they see elections as bought and sold.

Increasingly over the past two decades, voter disaffection can be seen by their decreased turnout at the polls. Throughout the twentieth century the proportion of the electorate going to the polls had been increasing steadily until 1960. From 1960 to the present, however, there has been an uninterrupted decline. In 1980 there was the lowest turnout, 52.3 percent of eligible voters, for a presidential contest since 1948.

PARTY DISARRAY

Political parties are considered an indispensable ingredient of democracy because they provide the vehicle for competition and free choice at elections. Without parties, there would be no free elections. The great political vehicles of the New Deal era, however, are in a state of disarray. In 1968 George Wallace received a surprising 13.5 percent of the vote in his third-party presidential campaign. George McGovern challenged the Democratic party in 1972 and won the nomination for president. In that same election Richard Nixon, the Republican nominee, shunned the party by setting up his own reelection organization—The Committee to Re-Elect the President—Jimmy Carter campaigned in 1976 on the slogan of restoring confidence in government by downplaying political parties and promising reform. In 1980 Ronald Reagan built upon the unfulfilled promises of Carter in 1976 as well as a large anti-Carter sentiment in the electorate to capture the presidency.

Voters have sensed this mood of party confusion. Confidence in parties has declined; more and more voters refuse to align themselves with either party. Party identification is at an all-time low. Even for those still identifying with political parties there is growing reluctance to support party candidates. McGovern may have won the Democratic nomination, but 44 percent of Democratic party identifiers voted against him. This trend is becoming more prevalent. Split-ticket voting, where party identifiers vote for some candidates of the opposing party on the election ballot, has become a significant trend. The results from 1980 were striking. A conservative Republican, Reagan, pulled approximately *one-half* of his support from traditional Democratic party identifiers while an Independent, John Anderson, won 7 percent of the vote.

TRUST

Ultimately, the strength of any government can be measured by the degree of confidence its citizens have in their government. They need to feel—and know—that government is working for them. Ordinary people, whose lives are shaped in many ways by what government does or does not do, have to feel they have the power to understand and control the issues; that politicians listen; that government is responsive to their needs.

Presently trust and confidence in government is in eclipse. A large number of Americans feel that politics is too complicated, that politicians care more about their own welfare than serving the public, that the bureaucracy is wasteful and impersonal, and that government costs too much. Certainly Vietnam, Watergate, and inflation have given citizens reason to be skeptical. Since its peak in 1960, confidence in politics and government has been systematically eroded.

This feeling of powerlessness has been accompanied by a growing mistrust and cynicism toward government. Mistrust of the federal government has markedly increased in the 1960s and 1970s. By 1976 America had produced the most cynical generation of citizens in its history.[4] Only 10 years before, a significant majority of Americans trusted their government and its officials.

4. "A Crisis of Confidence in Institutions." *Public Opinion Magazine* Oct./Nov., 1979, p. 30.

THE PRESIDENT

Traditionally, the president has enjoyed a high rating with the American people; but Vietnam, Watergate, and growing conflicts with Congress have left people bewildered, skeptical, and shaken in their confidence. Popularity polls for the president have dramatically declined in the 1960s and 1970s from those of Franklin D. Roosevelt and John F. Kennedy. When Lyndon Johnson made his announcement not to seek reelection in 1968, he was at his lowest popularity rating of 35 percent; on the eve of his resignation, Richard Nixon's approval rating was only 27 percent. Jimmy Carter, pledging to restore confidence and trust in government, had, in 1980, an approval rating of only 23 percent.

The president has also had difficulty with Congress. The War Powers Act and Budget and Impoundment Control Act in 1974 significantly curbed the autonomy of the chief executive. Since then Congress has more often refused to acquiesce to presidential wishes, as the debate over SALT (Strategic Arms Limitation Treaty) II illustrates.

Critics have been frustrated at the imperialization of the presidency, at extending the limits of executive power and accountability often at the expense of Congress and the courts. The chief complaint is that the array of laws and powers is more than any one person can exercise or control. We have continually expanded the presidency in order to facilitate presidential control; Americans now wonder if that much power is wisely placed in one person.

CONGRESS

If Congress is enjoying a resurgence in the post-Watergate era, there remain lingering doubts regarding the ability or resolve of Congress to influence public policy. Americans continue to hold Congress in low regard. Popular support for Congress fell throughout the early 1970s but climbed back to a 33 percent level in 1976. Nonetheless, the American people remain discontented with the performance of Congress, and Koreagate did not help matters. In the wake of Watergate came the testimony of Korean businessman Tongsun Park that he bribed some Congressmen in the late 1960s and early 1970s for their continued support for U.S. economic and military aid to Korea. Then, in 1980, came OPERATION ABSCAM, the revelation that FBI agents posing as Arab representatives bribed several Congressmen.

The plight of the presidency does not mean that Congress automatically becomes more powerful. Some critics charge that the seniority system and committee process make Congress slow and inefficient, that it is incapable of responding to a crisis, or the president. Legislators seem more concerned with reelection than with their constituents. Congress retains an image of a stuffy, unrepresentative body that would rather talk than fight.

Until very recently, most Americans would have agreed with Harry Hopkins' idea of what government should do: "We will spend and spend, and tax and tax, and elect and elect." Hopkins, one of Franklin Roosevelts's closest advisers, caught in these words the essence of the New Deal—that government should be as active in directing the economy and dealing with people's problems as it was in foreign affairs and national defense. Another part of the New Deal consensus was that government should promote equality—that government should use its power to tax to redistribute wealth.

For nearly forty years, the system seemed to work. Government at every level grew and grew, as did the number of services it provided. But then, with the end of American involvement in Vietnam, came stagflation, the combination of inflation and stagnating production. Money began to be worth less, and government needed to collect more and more to keep up with the demand for services. People began to grumble—and then, in California in June 1978, they revolted. By a margin of 2 to 1, California voters passed Proposition 13, which required cutting property taxes by 57 percent and mandated that no local tax thereafter could increase by more than 2 percent a year.

What had happened? The oil crisis of the early 1970s added to inflation, escalating prices and causing the dollar to be worth less and less. Government, like any consumer, needed more and more money to pay for the goods and services it had to buy in order to administer a constantly growing number of programs. Yet people complained that they got little in return; and when local property taxes, which are used to pay for such basic services as schools, police, and sanitation, began to rise sharply and continuously, the economic blow to the middle-class homeowner was direct and devastating. The situation was made worse because with soaring prices for homes and soaring interest rates for mortgages, people could neither sell their expensive home nor find others to buy at prices and taxes they could afford.

The result? One of the bases of government—the power to tax—is being undermined, along with the whole set of attitudes and ideas that had supported the expansion of government into the lives of all the people. Americans are saying, in effect, that the contract between government and people has been violated, and that they are no longer willing to abide by it.

What this break in the American consensus will mean for the future is not yet clear, but the issue is a difficult one. For a generation, government at all levels has been taking over functions once performed by the family or by individuals for themselves. What happens if these services are suddenly stopped? What about the services and aid to minority groups so that they can begin to experience equality of opportunity? Do we suddenly abandon this commitment? And if government payrolls are cut, where do all those workers find new jobs? As of 1980, governments—state, federal, local—employed nearly half the American workforce. And yet to raise taxes so high that people lose their homes or are unable to maintain a decent standard of living is political suicide. It is a dilemma for government and people alike, and there appear to be no obvious or easy solutions.

BUREAUCRACY

The symbol of big government, the bureaucracy has grown to employ 15 million people; 3 million federal, 3.3 million state, and 8.8 million local government employees. The 3 million federal employees administer a budget of over $600 billion, and overall public employees spend over $1 trillion annually! Spending that much money is seen as waste and inefficiency; the bureaucracy has become a hideaway for inefficient and overpaid officials. President Carter himself complained that government is remote and caught up in red tape—it takes forever to get anything done. Citizens wonder what the bureaucrat does with his or her time, and the taxpayers' money.

The costs of government have risen dramatically. The Great Society added new and expensive programs to the federal budget, often with little or no attention to their administration. As society has become more mobile and technologically sophisticated, government has assumed many of the functions once considered private only a few years ago. This has produced a myriad of regulations, agencies, and bureaucrats. To the average citizen—and sometimes the public official—the bureaucracy seems an impenetrable maze.

"OH, YOU WOULDN'T BE
INTERESTED IN THE OTHERS."
From *Herblock's State of the Union* (Simon & Schuster, 1972).

Watergate, too, contributed to the problems of the bureaucracy. White House personnel were placed in agency positions in order to report on progress in implementing presidential objectives. The IRS was asked to harrass political enemies by auditing their tax returns; the CIA was supposed to participate in the Watergate coverup. To the bureaucracy's credit, most of these efforts were resisted, but this too causes concern. Can the bureaucracy be autonomous? To whom is it responsible?

DEMOCRACY AND THE PROCESS OF CHANGE

Democracy in the United States has never been a simple process. The Framers of the Constitution had been careful to distinguish consent of the governed, for which there was widespread approval as the original source of political power, from democracy, which the Framers took to mean direct government by the people and in which they had little confidence. They declared the new government to be a republic, a governmnet founded on the consent of the governed but whose power was carefully circumscribed by a written Constitution.

Democracy as a word comes to us from Greece, where the power of rule *(kratia)* by the people or populace *(demos)* literally meant people power—rule by the people. As used by the Greeks, particularly the Athenians, democracy was treated unkindly as blind, ignorant rule by the populace—almost mob rule. This the Greeks contrasted to rule by an enlightened few (aristocracy) or rule based on military achievements (timocracy).

Americans have brought forth the principle that power originates with the people. Except for the New England town meetings and a few colonial efforts, however, Americans have not seriously tried to involve all citizens directly in lawmaking. We are not a pure or direct democracy. That was limited to the Greek city-state of a few thousand citizens, not a nation of four million in 1790 and of 220 million people today. We prefer the term republic, in which the people do not govern directly but consent to **representatives** who make and administer the laws *for* the people. We can call the United States a **representative democracy.**

Public officials are selected by the people to make public policy, and although not all officials are elected, we hold them accountable for the exercise of their power. The Framers of the Constitution combined democracy and constitutionalism. Democracy refers to the representational process by which public officials are selected and maintained in office; constitutionalism refers to how authority is conferred and limited. We established a system of governmnet in which public officials must receive and re-receive the consent of the people in order to govern. But we have added the safeguard of specific, recognized limits on the power of any officeholder.

Democracy has within it two components. There exists a procedural process by which the consent of the governed confers legitimacy on public officials, thereby making representation a real and meaningful concept. The heart of pro-

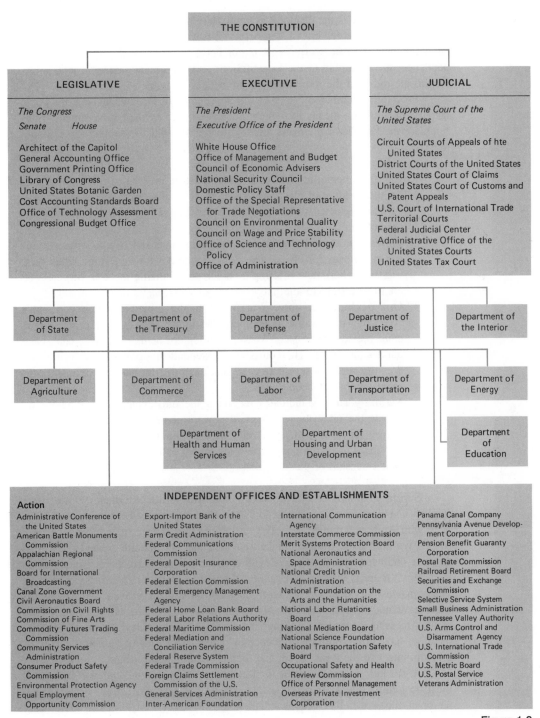

Figure 1.8
The government of the United States of America.

cedural democracy is the electoral system. Here the majority rules. But there also exists a substantive feature of democracy inculcating certain values that are desired for their intrinsic worth. This is our heritage from the Declaration of Independence, the Preamble to the Constitution, and the Emancipation Proclamation. Herein the rights of the individual are protected.

Procedural democracy stresses the importance of the mechanisms for popular government, the means by which citizens consent to their government. Elections are the key. Four elements are said to be essential for democratic elections to exist:

1. **Regular, periodic elections.** There must be prescribed times and places for the conduct of elections. These must be at regular and frequent intervals. All elected public officials are required to stand for election and reelection.

2. **Political competition.** Citizens or groups must be free to organize and run candidates for office. The right to vote has little meaning when there exists no alternative offering a choice or criticizing those in power. Voters have a right to alternative points of view, to all the information.

3. **One person, one vote.** We believe in the principle that one person's vote counts the same as another, that in the secrecy of the ballot box, bank president and steel worker, millionaire or unemployed, each casts but a single vote. The courts have extended this principle to include the drawing of electoral districts so that each district has approximately the same number of people.

4. **Majority rule.** Candidates receiving the most votes win. Whether we endow the majority with special powers or merely find it an expedient excuse for power, majority rules. Losing candidates are obligated to follow the will of the people, and legitimacy is conferred as an expression of the consent of the governed.

Substantive democracy has been part of our political heritage. Out of their English and European past, the colonists shaped and molded the values we associate with American democracy. The line of the Declaration of Independence still rings "We hold these truths to be self evident, that all men are created equal; that they are endowed by their Creator with certain inalienable rights."

First, there is a belief in equality, the unique claim of each individual to be treated as an individual whose worth does not have to be proved. Clearly Americans have not always practiced this in the past, or present, as the plight of the black American or the native American graphically illustrates. Nor does equality mean all have equal political influence or power. This idea of equality, rather, is a commitment to the basic worth and dignity of the human person.

A second important value is freedom. Americans believe the individual must be free to select his or her goals, not be coerced into action. Self-determination is the word. Innovation and progress are associated with the spontaneity and variety that are products of freedom. We accept certain rights as basic to our freedom. Such rights as free speech, press, religion and assembly in the 1st Amendment, as well as the right to work and live where and how we choose, make freedom a preferred value. Finally, the idea of individualism is basic to democracy. The individual is supreme in democracy. Society exists for no other purpose than to serve the individual. Individual dignity, worth, and value are the premises on which the structure of democracy is erected.

Our democracy is far from perfect, as our recent past shows. The visions of a Great Society remain largely that—a vision. Vietnam reminds us that a president can commit thousands of Americans to their death in an undeclared war. Inflation robs millions of lower- and middle-class Americans of their dreams, and of financial security. Watergate and Koreagate left a citizenry skeptical and distrustful of politics and public officials. Our democracy is a flexible one, however; reports of the death of American democracy are greatly exaggerated. But there is no doubt that our expectations are changing. The processes of democracy will have to adjust; the values of democracy will have to be renewed.

SUMMARY

1. The theme of this textbook centers on the changing expectations in American politics. The political behavior and government activity formed from two generations of Americans has changed greatly. Three historic events dramatized these changing expectations in politics: the Great Society programs, the Vietnam War, and Watergate.

2. Change has some longer standing implications as well. Population patterns pose political problems for America by placing strain on the federal budget and on the social fabric. Employment demands increased education to cope with the increased technology. And while incomes rise, inflation seriously erodes such increases to incomes, notably for the retired and minority groups.

3. Changes in government have doubled the number of public employees in the past two decades. Federal spending also increased, representing almost one-quarter of the total value of all goods and services in America. The priority for government expenditure has changed also. Where national defense once dominated, income security programs now take the largest portion of the budget.

4. The result of changing expectations in politics has produced a citizenry dependent on government action but suspect and cynical toward government power. The American people want government programs but are fearful of the growth of government.

5. Democracy is composed of a procedural process and a substantive commitment to the values of equality, freedom, and individuality. The procedural process depends on the mechanisms of regular elections, political competition, equality of the vote, and majority rule.

democracy   26
graying of America   11
the Great Society   4
Gulf of Tonkin
   Resolution   5–6
income protection   17
Keynesian economics   3
procedural
   democracy   26

republic   26
service economy   11
substantive
   democracy   28
Vietnam   5–6
Watergate   7
zero population
   growth   11

**RESEARCH
PROJECTS**

1.1 Vietnam War. How was the war in Vietnam different from previous wars? Read and study some books on World War II and Korea; compare these with works on Vietnam. Good books on Vietnam include Francis Fitzgerald, *Fire on the Lake* (Little, Brown, 1972); Townsend Hoopes, *The Limits of Intervention* (David McKay, 1969); and William Westmoreland, *A Soldier Reports* (Doubleday, 1976). You might interview some veterans from the World War II era, Korea, and Vietnam. How do they feel regarding their military service? Finally, review the process of intervention in Vietnam, the conduct of the war, and the decision to withdraw.

1.2. Constitutional issues of Watergate. Watergate is a broad term for several events, including campaign illegalities, the abuse of presidential power, and the coverup itself. What constitutional issues were raised with Watergate? There were two major Supreme Court cases that raised constitutional questions; another question was raised in the House Judiciary Committee. Make a list of the issues and the relevant sections of the Constitution. You might wish to consult *Congressional Quarterly, Chronology of a Crisis (Congressional Quarterly,* 1975); Leon Jaworski, *The Right and the Power: The Prosecution of Watergate* (Readers Digest Press, 1976); and Philip Karland, *Watergate and the Constitution* (University of Chicago Press, 1978).

1.3. The Federal Budget. Secure some copies of the federal budget for different years; examine how the budget has increased and what functions receive a smaller percentage of funds over time. You can usually find the federal budget in your college or city library; the *Budget in Brief* is an easy way to review the data. You can also find the data in *Statistical Abstract* or reported in *Congressional Quarterly* or *National Journal.*

BIBLIOGRAPHY

Galbraith, John K. *The New Industrial State*. New York: Signet Press, 1978.

Galbraith is a readable economist, though not a typical apologist for free enterprise. This work examines American economic life as the product of large organizations—private and public. This, Galbraith says, obscures, even surpresses, capitalism.

Ginzberg, Eli, and Robert Solow (eds.). *The Great Society*. New York: Basic Books, 1974.

A series of essays that provide a critical evaluation of Great Society programs. The topics of health, education, income, housing, manpower, and civil rights are analyzed by authors in response to a decade of criticism over these basic social programs.

Halberstam, David. *The Best and the Brightest*. New York: Random House, 1972.

A journalist's account of how the United States became involved in Vietnam. Halberstam's extensive study reveals how bright and capable people get caught up in bureaucracy and policy.

Harris, Louis. *The Anguish of Change*. New York: W. W. Norton, 1973.

A discussion of the results of Harris' surveys over a thirteen-year period. The work illustrates the dramatic changes in public opinion, over that period of time, which Harris feels have not been adequately appreciated by the leadership in America.

Hoopes, Townsend. *The Limits of Intervention*. New York: McKay, 1969.

A discussion of the decision to escalate the war in Vietnam by one who was on the periphery of that decision as Under Secretary of the Air Force. The book demonstrates a sensitive grasp of military and political events and their larger implications.

Levitan, Sam, and Robert Taggert. *The Promise of Greatness*. Cambridge, Mass.: Harvard University Press, 1976.

A fairly comprehensive review of the programs of the Great Society and their impact on the 1970s. The authors are fairly sympathetic to the policies and programs of the Great Society.There is much data and information included in their analysis.

Lipset, Seymour (ed.). *The Third Century: America as a Post-Industrial Society*. Stanford, Calif.: Hoover Institution, 1979.

A group of sixteen scholars seek to look into the future on a wide range of social and political topics. The essays start with the theme of America as a postindustrial society and examine the media, education, ethnic groups, courts, the presidency, and so on.

Lipson, Leslie. *The Democratic Civilization*. New York: Oxford University Press, 1964.

A broad study of democracy, its origins, development, and contemporary dimensions. Lipson centers on the social context, the political and institutional arrangements, and the philosophical ideas of democracy.

Lowi, Theodore. *The End of Liberalism*. New York: W. W. Norton, 1979.

Lowi grasps better than most the profound interconnections between politics and economics and social well being. His work questions the value of interest group liberalism as a theory of politics.

The Pentagon Papers. Senator T. Gravel (ed.). New York: Beacon Press, 1971.

The "secret" Department of Defense study on the history of our involvement in the Vietnam War. Included are many documents and memos casting American policy in less than favorable light. The papers were first published in the *New York Times* and *Washington Post*.

Pynn, Ronald E. *Watergate and the American Political Process*. New York: Praeger, 1974.

.A collection of essays on Watergate that examine the impact of Watergate on the political process and the institutions of government. The essays look to the larger implications of Watergate.

Schlesinger, Arthur S., Jr. *The Imperial Presidency*. Boston: Houghton Mifflin, 1973.

An examination of the Nixon presidency and the history of presidential power by a leading contemporary historian of the presidency. While focusing on foreign policy, Schlesinger also discusses domestic developments expanding presidential control.

Chapter 2

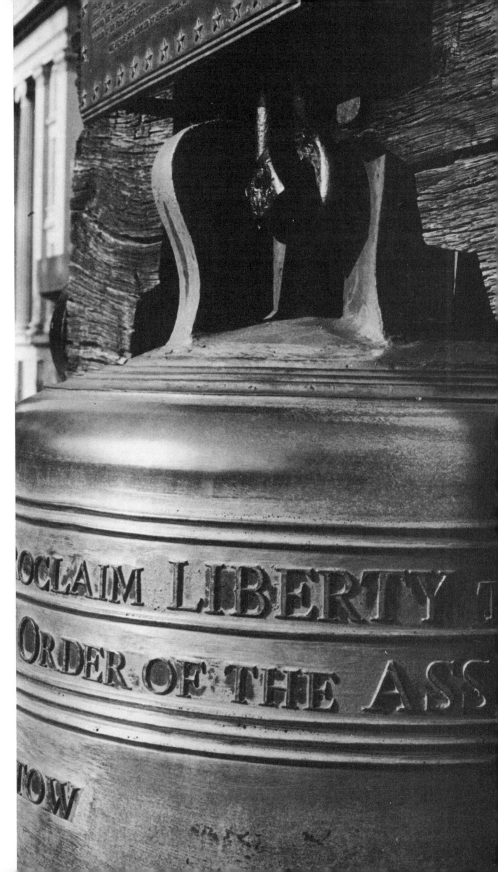

The Constitution

The tall ships sailed into the harbor, past the Statue of Liberty and on up the Hudson River. They had come from around the globe to help America celebrate its bicentennial—200 years since the signing of the Declaration of Independence. We are now close to the bicentennial of the Constitution. It is the oldest constitution in the world; it has survived the vicissitudes of politics: the establishment of the new republic and westward expansion, slavery and the Civil War, social and economic progress, depression and world wars, and more recently, Watergate. The Constitution, of course, has not solved all our problems but it has provided a framework for the government of a federal state for nearly two centuries.

The Constitution could not have survived these 200 years had it not been a flexible set of rules. The particular genius of the American Constitution is its broad, general grants of authority, open to interpretation and change as social, economic, and political conditions changed. The Constitution established the basic structure of American government and provided a framework of authority within which government could operate. It contains only a small proportion of the laws, customs, traditions, and political decisions of a nation; however, there are volumes of statutes and judicial opinions adapting the Constitution to new problems and situations. Ultimately, its strength rests with the people, with their ability and desire to uphold and defend this symbol of their community and form of government.

THE POLITICAL FOUNDATION

THE ENGLISH TRADITION

The Constitution grew out of the English political heritage and government practice in American colonies. The first arrivals in the New World brought with them the experience and tradition of English politics. But they began, almost immediately, to shape those practices into a uniquely American set of ideas and patterns of government.

From England the colonists brought with them English law and the traditions of common law and contract. The common law was a major part of the English system. The common law in England emerged from customary practices and standards of reasonable behavior that judges applied to settle local disputes. Over a period of time the practices and standards evolved into a series of legal rules which became commonly applied. From the common law came the ''rights of Englishmen.'' The Magna Carta, signed at Runnymede in 1215, affirmed for

King John signing the Magna Carta, affirming that the King's authority is limited by law. (The ·Bettmann Archive, Inc.)

Englishmen that the power of their king was not absolute, and merged the tradition of higher law into the common law. From the writings of Sir Edward Coke, Americans came to believe in judicial review and kingly, or executive, authority as "under the law." Coke argued the common law was superior to the will of the king, indeed any political authority, and judges were bound to review and uphold the law against government abuse. From Sir William Blackstone's *Commentaries on the Laws of England*, widely hailed in the colonies and used as a legal text, came defense of parliamentary sovereignty, civil liberty, and reason.

A second tradition from England was that of contract—the idea that those who govern are responsible to those who are governed. The power of government is limited by the higher law, the constitutional tradition and customs of the people. Power, to be legitimate, needs the consent of the people.

John Locke's *Second Treatise on Civil Government* presented the analogy of free and equal citizens in a state of nature binding together to form a civil society. In this state of nature individuals possessed certain natural and inalienable rights, among them the rights of life, liberty, and property. These rights, however, were not secure. To make them so, people freely consent to put themselves under the authority of government. This was the social contract—the express consent of the governed binding themselves to a political authority in return for the secure enjoyment of their liberties.

Finally the colonists brought with them a concept of mixed government, or republicanism. Historically this evolved as a means for different social classes to share power, a balancing of interest within the society: It was a blend of the continuity of the monarchy, the strength of the aristocracy, and the vitality and support of the people necessary to maintain civil authority. Republicanism then was a balancing of interests and power. By mixing democracy and aristocracy with monarchy, the danger to political power from any one form of government would be balanced by forces pulling in the opposite direction by the other forms. "Only through this reciprocal sharing of political power by the one, the few, and the many, could the desirable qualitites of each be preserved."[1] To James Harrington, a seventeenth century English republican, a mixed form of government would preclude men from having either an interest or a power to subvert government.

The colonists found a means to express their understanding of mixed government through the concept of a commonwealth, where separation of interest and function merged with separation of office. Hence, the colonists emphasized, freedom was best protected when the mixed or republican principle operated, where the best men were recruited to government. To this the colonists added the more mechanical separation of powers whereby no branch of government representing a class of interests could exercise all the powers or activities of government. Each branch of government would be independent and equal. It was largely through

---

1. Gordon S. Wood, *The Creation of the American Republic, 1776-1787* (New York: W. W. Norton & Co., 1969), p. 198.

the work of the French theorist Montesquieu that the colonists absorbed the doctrine of the equilibrium of legislative, executive, and judicial powers of government. Even the wise were not to be trusted with too much power. Where power was separated, liberty was most secure.

COLONIAL PATTERNS

The colonial experience with government left a mark on American political thinking and institutions. The first settlements were of three types: those founded by merchant capitalists seeking raw materials and trade; those founded by religious leaders seeking freedom of worship; and those founded by royal favorites given grants of land by the Crown.

Commercial expansion in the New World was facilitated when the Crown granted **joint-stock** charters to English trading companies with a monopoly over area trade. Virginia and Massachusetts Bay, for example, were both founded as joint-stock ventures, and their governments were patterned after the joint-stock company. A governor was appointed by the company to administer the affairs of the colony. Gradually, colonial legislatures emerged with some lawmaking authority in order to stimulate local interest in the colonial venture. But the joint-stock enterprise in America did not prove successful; both Virginia, in 1625, and Massachusetts, in 1684, had their charters revoked and were made royal colonies. Governors were appointed by the king and laws passed by the legislative assemblies could be annulled by him; nevertheless, a pattern of government—a framework of legislative and executive authority—had been established.

Compact colonies were established in New England—in Plymouth, Connecticut, and Rhode Island—as a result of ideas borrowed from religious theory. Separatists were accustomed to basing church authority on compact or mutual consent. Now they had a unique opportunity to extend that theory of organization to society and their political institutions. By **compact** (mutual consent of the adult males), they drafted their own basis for government. The Mayflower Compact in 1620 was the most famous of many such covenants. The compact operated as a constitution and provided for the necessary agencies of government. The pattern was a legislature elected by all free men in the colony, which in turn selected the governor. Here were America's first efforts at local self-government. The compact became the colonial symbol for self-government, an instrument created by general agreement and binding on governors and governed alike.

Maryland, New York, New Jersey, Pennsylvania, the Carolinas, and Georgia emerged from royal land grants. These **proprietary colonies,** as they were called, were autonomous principalities. The proprietor was given complete control over the affairs of the colony. Some of the proprietors, such as Lord Baltimore and the Duke of York, at first insisted on exercising complete authority through a locally appointed governor. Others, such as William Penn, moved to establish greater colonial authority with local assemblies. In both cases, the proprietary grants proved awkward. As financial ventures they were largely unsuccessful; and their feudal organizations were unwieldly and out-of-date. The colonial trend toward parliamentary authority was more than the proprietors cared to, or were able to, resist. In fact, the proprietary experience in America probably promoted the colonists' commitment to parliamentary institutions.

By the close of the seventeenth century, most colonial governments were becoming similar in structure. Most colonies were to become royal colonies (Virginia in 1625, Massachusetts in 1684, and New York in 1685). The colonies had similar legislative, executive, and judicial systems, with some measure of local authority. All were increasingly subject to regulation from England. This common experience of the colonies promoted the development of democracy in the colonies. Several distinct elements were clearly visible. There were bicameral legislatures where local interests were represented; separate executive authority, both in office and function; judicial appeal to the Privy Council from local courts of law; regular and frequent elections; and an abiding faith in constitutionalism in the conviction that free government requires written limits and prohibitions to political power.

TOWARD INDEPENDENCE

By the middle of the eighteenth century, the interests of England and the colonies were diverging. England still viewed the colonies as subordinate political units governed by Parliament and the Crown; the colonies had begun to see themselves differently. The Sugar and Stamp Acts of 1764 and 1765 illustrated the colonies' growing separation from England. The colonial cry of "Liberty, Prop-

The Stamp Act touched off a storm of protest in the American colonies. It caused colonists to become increasingly aware of their differences with Great Britain. (The Bettmann Archive, Inc.)

erty and No Stamps'' grew out of England's effort to levy a duty of threepence per gallon of molasses imported into the colonies as well as to place levies on such imported goods as sugar, coffee, calico, and indigo. The purpose of the acts was to raise revenue—''defray the expenses of defending, protecting, and securing the colonies.'' England had long imposed tariffs on the colonies to regulate trade, but a tax affecting commerce and industry would impair colonial prosperity. James Otis declared the acts void for being ''against the fundamental principles of the British Constitution'' in his pamphlet, *The Rights of the Colonists Asserted and Proved.* Natural rights and the British Constitution had been violated by a tax levied by a Parliament in which the Americans had no representation. To the colonists, England had begun the revolution.

The removal of the French from Canada had relieved the military dependence on England. The population was growing, and pressure for westward expansion was increasing. Cultural and economic interests had established themselves and in many respects were considerably unlike English customs and practices. This growing awareness contributed, however subtly, to the ''breakdown in sympathy, respect and understanding between the colonists and the mother country.''[2]

The Townshend Acts, named for Charles Townshend, chancellor of the exchequer, proved that America and England were irreconcilably drifting apart. Townshend fashioned a series of taxes on glass, lead, tea, and paper imported into the colonies. The measures were disguised to take advantage of the supposed colonial distinction between external and internal taxation. Internal taxation designed to collect revenue and regulate internal matters was rejected, as the Stamp Act crisis demonstrated, but external taxation to regulate trade throughout the empire was legitimate.

But it was soon obvious that the Townshend Acts were as much designed to raise revenue as the Stamp Tax had been. Colonial reaction was swift and intense. John Dickinson's *Letters of a Pennsylvania Farmer,* which ran in several colonial newspapers, had immediate appeal. Parliamentary sovereignty over the colonies was limited; Parliament could regulate commerce, but it could not tax the colonies. To England, which had always viewed the empire as a single community under parliamentary authority, the distinction Dickinson and the colonists now drew was absurd. If Parliament's authority over the colonies could be denied for ''one instance,'' then it must be denied for ''all instances.''[3]

The controversy died down with the repeal of the Townshend Acts in 1770 (except for the tax on tea), but Americans were coming more and more to question Parliament's authority over the colonies. James Wilson in 1774 found it difficult to draw the line between colonial authority and parliamentary authority: ''such a line does not exist; and there can be no medium between acknowledging

2. Alfred Kelly and Winfred Harbison, *The American Constitution,* 4th Edition (New York: W. W. Norton and Co., 1970), p. 64.
3. William Knox, *The Controversy Between Great Britain and Her Colonies Reviewed.* (London, 1769), pp. 50-51.

Poor old England endeavouring to reclaim his wicked American Children: *Anon.*

Reprinted by permission of G.P. Putnam's Sons from *The Cartoon History of the American Revolution* by Michael Wynn Jones. Copyright © 1975 by Michael Wynn Jones.

and denying that power in all cases.''[4] The result was a shift in American thinking. By 1774, the colonists were rejecting parliamentary sovereignty. The colonial tie with England rested with the king; colonial legislatures were independent of parliamentary regulation. As the debate moved forward, the colonists began to set the machinery of revolution in motion. The First Continental Congress met in 1774 to deal with the imperial problem. For a time it considered a plan of union giving the colonies dominion status, but this was tabled in favor of the Declaration and Resolves of the First Continental Congress declaring the states ''entitled to a free and exclusive power of legislation.''

War broke out in 1775, and a Second Continental Congress was called for May 1775. It took up the task of raising an army and abandoned any hope of reconciliation with Great Britain. Tom Paine's *Common Sense* which appeared in January 1776, greatly inflamed the public and urged revolution by attacking loyalty to the king. By the spring of 1776 Congress had declared American ports open to foreign trade, and on May 10, 1776, Congress called for the states to create regular governments. On June 7, 1776, Richard Henry Lee, acting on instructions from Virginia, offered the following resolution to Congress:

4. James Wilson, *Considerations on the Nature and Extent of the Legislative Authority of the British Parliament. The Works of James Wilson,* James Andrews, ed. (Chicago: Callaghan & Co., 1896), Vol. II, p. 506.

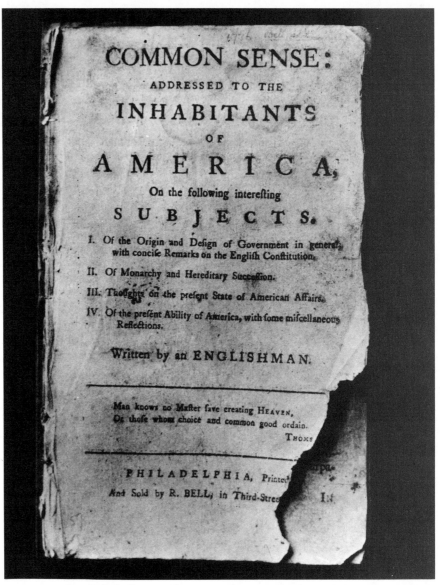

Tom Paine's *Common Sense* served as a catalyst for revolutionary arguments in the thirteen colonies. (The Bettmann Archive, Inc.)

Resolved, that these United Colonies are, and of right ought to be, free and independent states, and that they are absolved from all allegiance to the British Crown, and that all connection between them and the state of Great Britain is, and ought to be, totally dissolved.

A committee of five was appointed to prepare a "declaration to the effect of the said resolution."

On July 1 the committee reported back a declaration written by Thomas Jefferson. On July 2 a resolution of independence was adopted by a vote of 12 states. (New York was undecided and did not vote.) Finally, on July 4, 1776, a unanimous Continental Congress adopted the document we now know as the Declaration of Independence.

The Declaration of Independence was an eloquent appeal to the eighteenth-century symbols of constitutional democracy—natural rights, compact, popular sovereignty, and the right of resistance. Separation was achieved, but not independence.

THE ARTICLES OF CONFEDERATION

The Revolutionary War had just begun and would last until 1783. In the meantime, the states had to govern themselves. Virtually all adopted new state constitutions. The Second Continental Congress, in accepting Richard Henry Lee's resolution for independence, also accepted his resolution to draft a constitution for the "United Colonies." The principle of a national government was not entirely new. Benjamin Franklin, at the Albany Conference in 1754, had proposed a scheme for greater colonial cooperation on common problems that amounted to a plan for a federal government. The First Continental Congress in 1774 saw a need for planning and collective action. Franklin again moved, in 1775, a plan for a "league of friendship" uniting the states under a national Congress. The federal pyramid of local, state, and national governments was becoming visible. But the system set up by the Articles of Confederation, which were submitted to the states in 1777, maintained the revolutionary arrangement under the Continental Congress and did not solve the problem of sovereignty.

The Article placed full authority for the new national goverment in Congress while retaining the revolutionary principle of state sovereignty. The organization of the government under the Articles of Confederation is presented in Figure 2.1. Article Two of the Articles, added by Thomas Burke of North Carolina, stated: "Each state retains its sovereignty, freedom and independence, and every power, jurisdiction, and right, which is not by this confederation expressly delegated to the United States, in Congress Assembled." Burke's addition made the Articles of Confederation a "league of friendship" rather than the basis for a strong national government.

Congress was given the power to make war and peace, to enter into treaties and alliances, to equip an army, to request money from the states, to regulate trade with the Indians, and to establish a postal system. The important matters before Congress—war, foreign relations, and money—required the assent of nine states. Amendments to the Articles required unanimous consent. No national executive or court system was created, but two vital powers, taxation and regulation of commerce, were denied Congress. These had been central to the dispute with England, and the colonists were not about to encourage centralized authority again. The Confederation, forced to rely on the colonial levy system, came to the

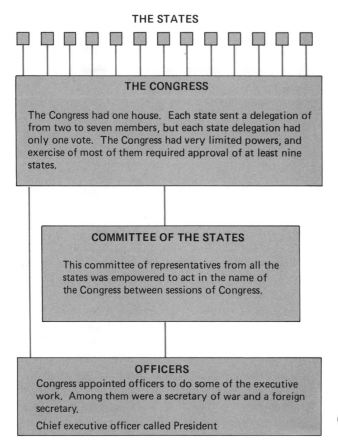

Figure 2.1
Government under the Articles of
Confederation.

verge of bankruptcy. Another weakness was the absence of any enforcement mechanism; the government was obliged to fall back on the states to enforce and carry out the functions of the central government. There was no judiciary, so when questions of authority arose or states needed coercion to enforce policy, no agency existed. Finally, the necessity for nine states to assent to legislation frequently proved an obstacle to legislation. Unanimous consent for amendments was impossible, none were ever ratified.

Under the Articles a degree of union was achieved, but problems mounted in the 1780s. The financial difficulties were especially severe. States were not meeting their financial assessments to finance the war; Congress had borrowed heavily from the French and Dutch governments and was unable to pay back even the interest. There were problems in foreign affairs. Commercial treaties could not be negotiated because Congress lacked the power of enforcement. Those treaties that were negotiated were ignored. Britain closed the West Indies to American trade. States quarreled with one another. New York levied duties on commerce from New Jersey, which in turn taxed commerce from New York.

States ignored Congress and issued their own paper money, so that trade and commerce became increasingly difficult. Credit and money were either impossible to get or worthless. In Massachusetts, in 1786, the paper money advocates, debtors and small farmers, rebelled in what is known as Shays' Rebellion. The mob, led by Revolutionary War Captain Daniel Shas, closed courts in Massachusetts, thus preventing them from foreclosing mortgages on farms. They threatened to attack Boston proper if easier money was not made available. The fear of violence in Massachusetts and the worsening economic and political situation heightened the movement for constitutional revision.

Calls for revision of the Articles of Confederation had been heard as early as 1780, before the Articles even had been ratified. Alexander Hamilton proposed that Congress call a convention to prepare plans for a "general confederation." In 1781, Congress itself formed a committee to examine the deficiencies of the Articles, but it was left for the Annapolis Conference in 1785, formed to consider interstate commerce problems, to move the colonies toward constitutional revision. The Annapolis meeting was a failure, only five states sent delegates, and no trade policy emerged. But Alexander Hamilton of New York and James Madison of Virginia sensed the opportunity and issued a call for a new convention, to meet in Philadelphia the next year, to revise the Articles of Confederation.

THE CONSTITUTIONAL CONVENTION

The delegates assembled in the "large room" of the State House in Philadelphia on the second Monday in May 1787. There were not enough delegates present to represent a majority of states, so the meeting adjourned. On May 25 delegates from nine states opened the Constitutional Convention. By the end of June, delegates from 11 states were in attendance.

THE DELEGATES

Of the 74 delegates appointed, only 55 appeared. The real work of the convention was done by less than 20 delegates, all eminent men. The gathering included many of America's leading political figures, bankers, merchants, and landowners. They were men well versed in the literature of politics.

But it was a different mood from that before the Revolution. As Oliver Ellsworth of Connecticut observed, "a new set of ideas seemed to have crept in since the Articles of Confederation were established." Only eight delegates had signed the Declaration of Independence; approximately half had fought in the war for independence. Many of the noteworthy figures of the Revolution were not delegates to the Philadelphia convention. Thomas Jefferson was serving as minister to France; John Adams as minister to Great Britain. Patrick Henry had been selected a delegate, but "smelt a rat" and declined to participate. Not selected as delgates were such famous figures as Thomas Paine, Samuel Adams, and Richard Henry Lee.

Table 2.1

The Federal Convention 1787 and Ratification

The Federal Convention 1787	
May 14–24	Preliminary meetings
May 25–28	Organization
May 29	Proposal of Randolph (Virginia) Plan and Pinckney Plan
May 30–June 11	Debate on the Randolph Plan, ending in adoption of its main provisions
June 15	The Paterson (New Jersey) Plan; revolt of the "small state" delegations
June 15–30	Two weeks of debate over the two plans
June 30	The Compromise Committee is appointed
July 5	Report of the Compromise Committee proposing popular representation in the lower house, equal representation in the upper, and origin of all money bills in the lower house
July 5–16	Debate on the Connecticut Compromise
July 16	The Compromise is adopted
July 17	Agree to a judicial negative of unconstitutional state acts
July 23	Adopt the provision for per capita voting in the Senate
July 26	Agree upon a single executive: a President to be chosen for a term of seven years and ineligible for re-election
August 8–10	Agreement upon qualifications of voters and representatives and upon the regulation of elections.
August 15–23	Debate on the powers of Congress (Article I, Sections 8 and 9)
August 24–25	Debate on the powers of the President
August 28	Adopt restrictions upon the states
August 29	The "three-fifths" clause; the slave trade; and the commerce clause
August 30	Agree upon the provisions for admission of new states
September 6	Agree to election of the President by electors in the states and with no restrictions upon re-election
September 7–8	Agree upon the annexation of the Senate in the appointive power and in the treaty-making power
September 10	Provision for amendments to the Constitution
September 12	Report of the Committee of Style
September 17	Signing of the Constitution and Adjournment
Ratification	
Delaware	Thirty members ratified unanimously December 7, 1787
Pennsylvania	Ratified by a vote of 46 to 23, December 12, 1787
New Jersey	Thirty-nine delegates ratified unanimously December 18, 1787
Georgia	Twenty-six delegates ratified unanimously January 2, 1788
Connecticut	Ratified by a vote of 128 to 40 on January 9, 1788
Massachusetts	Ratified by a vote of 186 to 168, February 16, 1788
Maryland	Ratified by a vote of 63 to 11, April 26, 1788
South Carolina	Ratified by a vote of 149 to 73, May 23, 1788
New Hampshire	Ratified by a vote of 57 to 47, June 21, 1788
Virginia	Ratified by a vote of 89 to 79, June 25, 1788
New York	Ratified by a vote of 30 to 27, July 26, 1788
Rhode Island	Ratified by a vote of 34 to 22, May 29, 1790
North Carolina	Rejected 193 to 75, August 4, 1788; finally ratified November 21, 1789

SOURCE: David Smith, *The Convention and the Constitution.* New York: St. Martins Press, 1965, pp. 33–34.

Virginia sent a distinguished delegation. George Washington, the war hero, commanded respect and had the confidence of the delegates. This undoubtedly was a factor in his being elected president of the convention. James Madison, aged 36, was a strong advocate for the establishment of a national government and largely drafted the Virginia Plan. For this he has been called the ''Father of the Constitution.'' Madison was a driving force at the convention. It is from his notes of the proceedings that much of the convention's activities have been reconstructed. Also present from Virginia was the governor, Edmund Randolph, who introduced the Virginia Plan to the convention.

Pennsylvania's delegation was equally distinguished. Benjamin Franklin, second only to Washington in reputation and respect, was the oldest delegate at 82. A renowned statesman and philosopher, Franklin took little active part in the convention. His presence and spiritual support added credibility to the deliberations, however, and made compromise easier. James Wilson was the scholar of the convention. A legal theorist, Wilson had argued the colonies' case during the revolution. At the convention, he supported strong central government and direct popular election of the president. (Washington was later to appoint him Associate Justice of the Supreme Court.) Another supporter of national government from

Thomas Paine.
(National Archives)

FACT FILE

		LIST OF DELEGATES[a] *Age at signing*	
New Hampshire	*John Langdon*	46	*signed*
	(John Pickering)		
	Nicholas Gilman	32	*signed*
	(Benjamin West)		
Massachusetts	*(Francis Dana)*		
	Elbridge Gerry	43	
	Nathaniel Gorham	49	*signed*
	Rufus King	32	*signed*
	Caleb Strong	42	*(approved of)*
Rhode Island	*No appointment*		
Connecticut	*William Samuel Johnson*	59	*signed*
	Roger Sherman	66	*signed*
	Oliver Ellsworth	42	*(approved of)*
	[Erastus Wolcott was elected but declined to serve.]		
New York	*Robert Yates*	49	
	Alexander Hamilton	32	*signed*
	John Lansing, Junior	43	
New Jersey	*David Brearley*	42	*signed*
	William Churchill Houston	41	
	William Paterson	42	*signed*
	(John Neilson)		
	William Livingston	63	*signed*
	(Abraham Clark)		
	Jonathan Dayton	26	*signed*
Pennsylvania	*Thomas Mifflin*	43	*signed*
	Robert Morris	53	*signed*
	George Clymer	48	*signed*
	Jared Ingersoll	38	*signed*
	Thomas Fitzsimons	46	*signed*
	James Wilson	44	*signed*
	Gouverneur Morris	35	*signed*
	Benjamin Franklin	82	*signed*
Delaware	*George Read*	53	*signed*
	Gunning Bedford, Junior	40	*signed*
	John Dickinson	54	*signed*
	Richard Bassett	42	*signed*
	Jacob Broom	35	*signed*
Maryland	*James McHenry*	33	*signed*
	Daniel of St. Thomas Jenifer	64	*signed*
	Daniel Carroll	56	*signed*
	John Francis Mercer	28	
	Luther Martin	39	
	[Charles Carroll of Carrollton, Gabriel Duvall, Robert Hanson Harrison, Thomas Sim Lee, and Thomas Stone were elected but declined to serve.]		

LIST OF DELEGATES[a] (Continued).
Age at
signing

Virginia	George Washington	55	signed
	Edmund Randolph	34	
	John Blair	55	signed
	James Madison, Junior	36	signed
	George Mason	62	
	George Wythe	61	(approved of)
	James McClurg	41	(approved of)
	[Patrick Henry, Richard Henry Lee, and Thomas Nelson were elected but declined to serve.]		
North Carolina	Alexander Martin	47	
	William Richardson Davie	31	(approved of)
	Richard Dobbs Spaight	29	signed
	William Blount	38	signed
	Hugh Williamson	51	signed
	[Richard Caswell and Willie Jones were elected but declined to serve.]		
South Carolina	John Rutledge	48	signed
	Charles Pinckney	29	signed
	Charles Cotesworth Pinckney	41	signed
	Pierce Butler	42	signed
	(Henry Laurens)		
Georgia	William Few	39	signed
	Abraham Baldwin	32	signed
	William Pierce	47	(approved of)
	(George Walton)		
	William Houstoun	32	
	(Nathaniel Pendleton)		

a. Those whose names are in parentheses did not attend.

SOURCE: Max Ferrand, *The Records of the Federal Convention of 1787,* Volume 3 New Haven, Conn.: Yale University Press, 1966.

Pennsylvania was Gouverneur Morris, an eloquent debater whose ideas found their way into the final draft of the constitution.

From New York came Alexander Hamilton, John Lansing, and Robert Yates. Hamilton, at 32, had achieved national prominence by the time of the convention. Yet his support for a strong national government was continually frustrated, in part by his insistence on a constitutional monarchy, in part by Lansing and Yates, who outvoted him to support weak government. All three left the convention before it had finished its work.

The small states also had their advocates. William Paterson, author of the New Jersey Plan, argued for weak central government and equal representation of states. Also supporting the small states was John Dickinson of Deleware, who had achieved fame during the revolution and by drafting the Articles of Confederation. The most vocal champion of states rights, however, was Luther Martin of Maryland. A brilliant lawyer and Attorney General of Maryland, Martin was an outspoken critic of centralized authority and nationalistic tendencies. Martin would leave the convention in disgust before the Constitution was signed by the delegates.

Other delegates deserve mention. Oliver Ellsworth of Connecticut, who had served in Congress, was now Chief Justice of his home state's Supreme Court and was to become Chief Justice of the United States. Rufus King of Massachusetts became a strong force for national government and won respect as a speaker. Also from Massachusetts was Elbridge Gerry, who would refuse to sign the finished product as a ''monarchial'' document. Another who refused to sign was George Mason of Virginia. Mason, a friend of Thomas Jefferson, saw the Constitution as too aristocratic. John Rutledge of South Carolina, an important southerner, argued for stronger national authority.

By the end of May the Convention had organized and settled its preliminary business. Washington was unanimously elected to preside, each state would have an equal voice in voting, and all meetings would be secret. Many of this assembled body had already distinguished themselves in public service, and more would distinguish themselves under the new government. Their average age was slightly over 43 years.

THE VIRGINIA PLAN

On May 27, 1787, the convention met. Edmund Randolph opened the session with the Virginia Plan. The convention, on its very first day of business, had not a plan to revise the Articles, but an entirely new plan of Union. As John Roche has suggested:

> Its (Virginia Plan) consequence was that once business got underway, the framework of discussion was established on Madison's terms. There was no interminable argument over agenda; instead the delegates took the Virginia Resolutions—''just for purposes of discussion''—as their point of departure. And along with Madison's proposals, many of which were buried in the course of the summer, went his major premise; a new start on a Constitution rather than piecemeal amendment.[5]

The Virginia Plan occupied the delegates for more than two weeks. It was a nationalistic plan for strong central authority and more than remedied the weaknesses of the Articles. Congress could legislate where ''the separate states are incompetent, or where the harmony of the United States may be interrupted.'' A national executive was provided for. A Council of Revision had veto power over

5. John P. Roche, ''The Founding Fathers: A Reform Caucus in Action,'' *American Political Science Review,* Vol. 55 (December 1961), p. 803.

both national and state legislation, and Congress could negate any law passed by the states.

It appeared that the Virginia Plan would be adopted. The Articles had been discarded; debate centered on the method of electing representatives to Congress and apportioning them among the several states. Apparently the delegates accepted the principle of a two-house legislature, popular elections, strong executive authority, a national judiciary, and a national veto power. The small states preferred state representation and state control of the legislature; they also would have liked equal representation of states. The large states favored the Randolph proposals but were prepared to compromise—one chamber could be selected by state legislatures. Having secured a compromise on state control of elections for the Senate, the small states acceded.

A plan for ratification was outlined on June 10, 1787. The convention adjourned so that "leisure might be given" to thoughts on securing ratification; but now the small state delegates—Paterson, Martin, Elbridge Gerry, and others—realized their situation. They used the recess to declare the new Constitution unacceptable, as pushing too far beyond the Articles. William Paterson of New Jersey was then asked to draft a "purely Federal" plan that might serve as an alternative.

THE NEW JERSEY PLAN

The New Jersey Plan was little different from the Articles of Confederation, although it did remedy some of its defects. It would establish a "supreme tribunal," but with little enforcement power. A plural executive would be given only limited authority. The rights to tax and regulate commerce were added to the powers of Congress. But the New Jersey Plan was truly a federal plan: the states selected the representatives to Congress, Congress would be a single chamber, and states would be equally represented. The New Jersey Plan was voted down, but for two weeks the merits of the two plans were debated. The debate droned on, and tempers shortened. At the center was the growing schism over state sovereignty and nationalism. And the nationalists knew the convention would not succeed without support from the small states.

THE GREAT COMPROMISE

A majority of the states remained committed to proportional representation; small state delegates were equally determined to fight for equal representation. A compromise was necessary. When the delegates voted to accept proportional representation in the lower house at the end of June, moderates on both sides saw their opportunities: proportional representation for the lower house, equality for the upper chamber. A committee of eleven was quickly appointed, and on July 5 it recommended:

A scene from the Constitutional Convention in 1787. (National Archives)

- That in the lower house each state be allowed one member for every 40,000 inhabitants.
- That all bills for raising or appropriating money originate in the lower house, and not be amended by the upper.
- That each state have an equal vote in the upper house.

This was the Great Compromise, or the Connecticut Compromise, named after Roger Sherman of Connecticut, who had been the first to suggest the solution. From then on, the convention made steady progress. There was no more talk of adjournment, and the outline of the Constitution began to take shape. The issue of federalism would occupy and divide the convention for better than a month, with sectional rivalries clearly in evidence; but the solutions came. The admission of new states and the disposition of western lands was one problem. The East had few such lands and was suspicious of cheap land for farmers. Easterners were more interested in federal power to regulate trade and commerce. The South, joined by a few northern states, opposed Congress' monopoly on trade and its power of direct taxation. These issues brought to the surface the issue of slavery. With the arguments over trade, the issue of slavery and the slave trade could no longer be avoided. The delegates sifted the issues, and ultimately a series of compromises was fashioned:

1. There would be a unified national power to regulate commerce, with the

promise that there be no state taxation of imports or federal taxation of exports.

2. Direct taxation would be apportioned according to population and all excises would be uniform.

3. The slave population would be counted at three-fifths, both for taxation and representation.

4. Congress was empowered to impose conditions for the admission of new states.

5. The slave trade would continue until 1808 (for 20 years).[6]

The problem of federalism was also visible in the debate over the executive and the judiciary. Both sides recognized the lack of an executive under the Articles. One side wanted a weak executive, responsive to the legislative will. The other side, the convention's nationalists, argued for a national executive possessing independent authority. The conflict focused on the mode of the election. The Randolph Plan called for election by Congress; the nationalist position was ambigious. James Wilson called for direct election, but most delegates rejected this proposal as too democratic and foreign to American experience. The solution, of course, was the Electoral College—people in the various states would choose electors, who in turn would elect the president. Each state could choose electors "in such a manner as its legislature may direct." Yet the electors were independent: they might be popularly elected, and if no candidate received a majority, the House of Representatives would elect the president.

The debate over the judiciary went to the heart of the federal question. Here the problems of the Articles of Confederation were obvious: state enforcement of national policy, and interpretation of the jurisdictions of the states and the national government. The Virginia Plan empowered a national government to legislate directly. A Council of Revision would have authority to suspend acts of the states. Congress, in turn, presumably would interpret the limits of its authority since it had, under the Virginia Plan, the authority to negate any law contravening the Articles of the Union. The net result was that Congress would have to review every act passed in every state in order to determine if it contravened federal legislation or the Constitution. This criticism, along with the objection that laws contrary to the Union would not be recognized by the courts, led the convention to abandon the proposal.

But what should replace it? Luther Martin suggested a phrase from the New Jersey Plan. After a short debate, the convention unanimously accepted Martin's suggestion. It read as follows:

This Constitution, and the Laws of the United States which shall be made in pursuance thereof; and all treaties made, or which shall be made, under the authority of the United States, shall be the supreme Law

6. David G. Smith, *The Convention and the Constitution* (New York: St. Martins, 1965), pp. 50–51.

of the Land and the Judges in every state shall be bound thereby, anything in the Constitution or Laws of any state to the contrary notwithstanding.

From this came the second paragraph of Article VI of the Constitution.

The delegates also removed Congress' right to contravene laws contrary to
the Constitution. Some delegates felt that power rightly belonged with the court;
others disagreed. James Wilson, Elbridge Gerry, and Gouverneur Morris spoke in
favor of the federal judiciary declaring federal law unconstitutional. John Dickinson, on the other hand, stated that ''no such power ought to exist.'' The Committee on Detail's resolution setting forth the jurisdiction of the Supreme Court
was amended, extending the Court's jurisdiction to ''all cases arising under the
Constitution and laws of the United States.'' Madison records the delegates as
generally agreeing that the jurisdiction ''was constructively limited to cases of a
judiciary nature.'' But in outlining the jurisdiction of the federal judiciary, the
delegates inserted no provision for judicial review. If the delegates intended the
courts to pass on the constitutionality of laws, they did not say so in Article III
of the Constitution.

By early September, only 42 delegates remained at the convention. A Committee on Style was appointed to draft and edit the final document, with Gouverneur Morris doing most of the writing. The draft was accepted almost without
alteration. On September 17, 1787, 127 days after convening, 39 delegates
stepped to the table at the head of the long room in the State House in Philadelphia and affixed their signatures to the Constitution.

RATIFICATION

If one drew a line the length of America from Maine to Georgia 50 miles
in from the sea, it would quite accurately separate the tidewater Federalist supporters of the Constitution from the inland anti-Federalist opposition (Figure 2.2).
Merchants, shippers, bankers, and landowners, primarily residing on the seacoast,
were in favor of a government that would protect commerce and establish a sound
national economy and financial system. The interior was inhabited by small farmers, trappers and traders, and frontiersmen who cared little for commerce or land
speculation. To them, the Constitution meant the end of paper money and easy
access to land for settlement.

Ratification was not only an economic dispute. People of all economic
classes in Delaware, Virginia, and Pennsylvania supported the Constitution. The
cities of New York and Philadelphia favored the new Constitution, as did predominately rural New Jersey. At the center was a serious political issue: The Constitution took sovereignty away from the states; the Articles of Confederation had
been discarded. The Framers even ignored state legislatures for the purpose of
ratification.

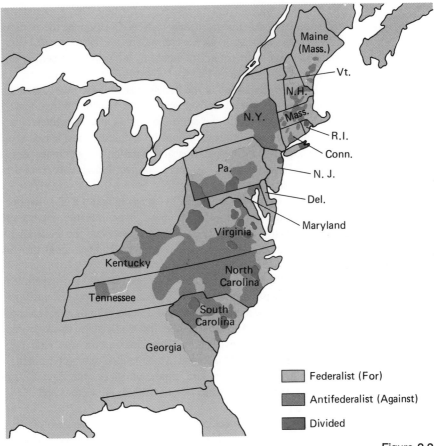

Figure 2.2
Support for the new constitution.

The Convention had declared the Constitution ratified when approved by "popularly elected conventions in nine of the thirteen states." In a sense, the method was illegal. The Articles of Confederation required that amendments be submitted to state legislatures and approved by all thirteen states. This, the delegates knew, would be almost impossible to secure. Many delegates also felt that popular approval in the states would enhance the Constitution's national appeal.

THE DEBATE

The debate over ratification was public. Newspaper articles, pamphlets and speeches were plentiful on both sides. The most circulated piece of anti-Federalist literature was Richard Henry Lee's *Letters From a Federal Farmer*. The Federalist position was set out in a series of articles by Alexander Hamilton, James Madison, and John Jay published in New York under the pseudonym Publius. In all, 85 essays appeared; they were known as *The Federalist* and they remain the clearest and most articulate statement of the principles behind our system of government.

Some of the issues in the debate were trivial; others went to the heart of the Constitution. **Anti-Federalists** questioned whether a national government with centralized power could govern a large and culturally diverse nation. They feared that local and state interests would be ignored. They feared the increased power of the national government was an invitation to depotism. And, of course, they noted there was no Bill of Rights to protect individuals from a powerful national government.

The **Federalists** countered by stressing that a Bill of Rights was unnecessary because the new government was one of enumerated powers. The addition of a Bill of Rights was a bargaining point, however; the Federalists pledged, in the ratification conventions, to adopt a Bill of Rights should the convention support ratification.

After 10 months, the process was coming to an end. Five states ratified quickly and with little opposition, but in four others the vote was close, and in two states (New Hampshire and Rhode Island) the Constitution was at first rejected. New Hampshire became the ninth state to ratify on June 21, 1788, when a second vote was held. The Constitution was now the supreme law of the land. Still, New York and Virginia had not yet ratified, and without the largest and strategically most important states, the new Constitution had little chance of success. Virginia soon ratified, however, and New York ratified a month later.

Ratification was achieved in large measure because of the political skills of the Federalists. They were astute politicians who used the addition of a Bill of Rights to their advantage and left their opponents with only one choice: ratify the Constitution or keep the Articles, and political chaos and economic ruin. The Federalists had stressed the federal nature of the Union and the republican basis of authority. The Constitution was not perfect, but it was the best available remedy; it was the work of the best minds the nation had to offer.

THE CONSTITUTIONAL FRAMEWORK

Benjamin Franklin was approached one day as the convention was drawing to a close and asked "Well Doctor, what have we got—a republic or a monarchy?" "A Republic," replied the Doctor, "if you can keep it." The "patchwork of compromises" sent to the states for ratification had become the basis for a new and "more perfect" union based on republican principles.

REPRESENTATION

The delegates at Philadelphia were committed to wise and virtuous representation. They believed not in majority rule, but in representatives for the people as the most efficient solution for problems and the best defense of liberty. Madison noted that a republic differs from a democracy only in that a republic is "a government in which the scheme of representation takes place." We commonly use the phrase **democratic republic,** meaning that our representatives are chosen by the democratic principle of majority rule. The Framers were distrustful of direct democracy. John Adams distrusted its instability; Elbridge Gerry remarked to the Convention during the debate over election procedures for Congress "that the decline in virtue is caused from the excess of democracy."

The cure for the excesses of democracy was the republican principle. Madison particularly argued for republicanism. His Federalist No. 10 was a classic statement on the nature of republicanism. A republic could ensure representation of the people through the franchise. Yet in a country as large and diverse as America, representation would discourage the formation of a majority. Madison fervently believed that in the "extended republic," among the great variety of interests, parties, and sects within America, no majority could form. Coalitions would have to form in order to govern. This process of coalition formation would temper majorities and in turn democratic processes would function freely.

NO TITLES OF NOBILITY

It was fairly clear from the outset on the debate over representation that the delegates wished to abolish hereditary titles of nobility and hereditary offices. The trend had begun in the states and was carried to the convention. Every citizen ought to be judged on merit. The people have a right to pass judgment on their public officials at the polls: "No qualification of wealth, of birth, of religious faith, or of civil profession is permitted to better the judgment or disappoint the inclination of the people," declared the Federalist No. 57.[7] Only through an open electoral process could public officials earn the esteem and confidence of the citizens.

PERIODIC ELECTIONS

It was assumed from the outset that regular and periodic elections were the way to ensure the consent of the governed. The Federalist No. 52 explained it this way:

7. Alexander Hamilton, James Madison, John Jay, *The Federalist Papers,* editor Clinton Rossiter (New York: The New American Library, 1961), p. 351.

As it is essential to liberty that the government in general should have a common interest with the people, so it is particularly essential that the branch of it under consideration should have an immediate dependence on, and an immediate sympathy with, the people. Frequent elections are unquestionably the only policy by which this dependence and sympathy can be effectually secured.[8]

TENURE IN OFFICE

A prime means of preventing majorities or demagogues from abusing their office was to establish, for different offices, differing terms and differing modes of election. The term for the House of Representatives was fixed at two years, the Senate at six years, and the presidency at four years; judges would serve for life. In addition, the House was to be directly elected by the people. The Senate was indirectly elected; state legislatures would fix the mode of selection. The president would be indirectly elected through the Electoral College. The Framers' purpose was not to prevent popular control; indirect election is admittedly less democratic, but it is still a representative system.

SEPARATED POWERS

Madison put the issue of power directly in the Federalist No. 37: "[we must combine] the requisite stability and energy in the government with the inviolable attention due to liberty and to the republic form."[9] The delegates labored long and hard to set up a government that could rule effectively and yet not oppressively. The nationalists wanted a strong central authority; the small states demanded protection for states rights.

The Constitution tried to balance the power of the central government against that of the states—to unite a national government and thirteen separate states within a federal system. The Constitution also balanced the powers of the national government into three separate but related branches of government—legislative, executive, and judicial.

Federalism.   The Constitution did not solve the problem of sovereignty: states rights would always be a problem. What the Constitution did was to expand the powers of the national government and give it authority to operate directly on the people. At the same time, the states' authority to legislate their affairs was reserved to them. This was a masterpiece of political engineering: from two contradictory positions of authority the Framers fashioned a workable compromise.

8. Hamilton, Madison, Jay, *The Federalist Papers,* p. 327.
9. Hamilton, Madison, Jay, *The Federalist Papers,* p. 226.

Separation of Powers.   Federalism had been a compromise thrust on the delegates because of the debate over sovereignty. Separation of powers, on the other hand, was a seventeenth- and eighteenth-century political theory designed to protect liberty and prevent tyranny. From the writings of John Locke, and from the French writer Montesquieu's *The Spirit of the Laws* (1748), the colonists took the idea of dividing the power of the national government into three distinct branches: the legislative, executive, and judicial. The delegates wanted power to be separated so that no one branch could take over the powers and responsibilities of the other branches.

Separation of powers gives constitutional authority to each of the three branches of the national government (See Figure 2.3). None is dependent on the others for the source of its authority; yet none of the three can operate without sharing authority. The Framers made sure there would be **checks and balances** to authority by overlapping the domains of the branches. For example, the legislature passes laws, but the laws become valid only after the president signs them. It is the chief executive who conducts foreign affairs and makes treaties with foreign countries, but he does so with the advice and consent of the Senate. The courts act as a ''watch dog'' over the Constitution, exercising the power of judicial review to declare acts of Congress or of state legislatures unconstitutional. Supreme Court judges are appointed by the president and confirmed by two-thirds vote of the Senate.

LIMITED AUTHORITY

It is often said that we are a government of laws, not people. Article VI declares that the Constitution, and the laws and treaties of the United States, are the supreme law of the land. The Constitution both grants and limits political authority. The Framers of the Constitution enumerated and limited power wherever they felt it was necessary. In Article I, the delegates enumerated the powers of the new Congress. They also placed some specific prohibitions on the powers of Congress in Section 9 of Article I, while in Section 10, they placed limitations on the states. Years of change and interpretations by courts and Congresses have significantly altered this framework. But the principle remains: power should be limited.

The power of the judiciary was likewise restricted in Article III. It was to hear only ''cases and controversies,'' and then only where federal law or parties of different states were concerned. The Supreme Court was not to make policy. In a most real sense, then, constitutionalism means limited government.

Legislative Prohibitions.   Article I, Section 9, of the Constitution placed some specific restrictions on the powers of Congress. Among these were some basic English rights that the Framers felt government may not violate. Foremost was the right to a *writ of habeas corpus* which Congress was prohibited

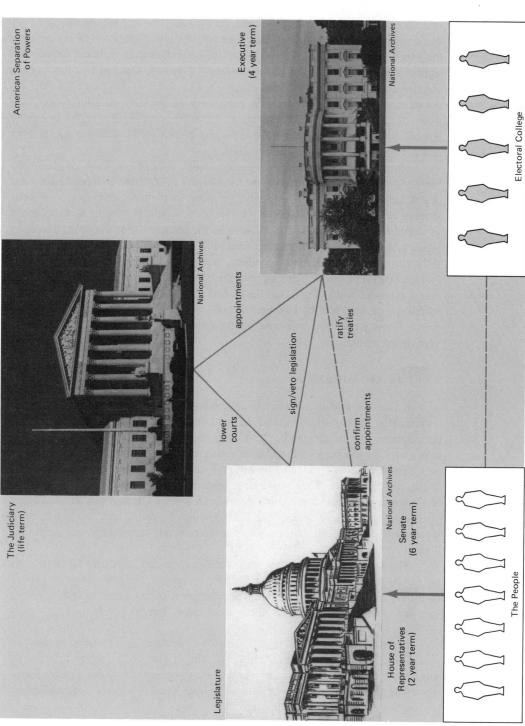

Figure 2.3a

American separation of powers.

British Division of Powers

Judiciary

Bettmann Archive, Inc.

The Monarchy

Bettmann
Archive, Inc.

Prime Minister
Cabinet

UPI

Parliament

House of Lords
House of Commons

Bettmann Archive, Inc.

The people

Figure 2.3b

British division of powers.

from suspending unless compelled by rebellion or invasion. The writ of habeas corpus is a basic citizen right to a judicial order directing an official holding a person in custody to show cause why that person can be legally detained. Congress was also prevented from passing a *bill of attainder*. A bill of attainder was a legislative declaration of guilt naming the individual, crime, and punishment without benefit of trial. Finally Congress was denied the right to make *ex post facto* laws. Such laws are retroactive criminal statutes which declare actions a crime after they have been committed and permit punishment.

THE BILL OF RIGHTS

Added to the Constitution shortly after ratification, the Bill of Rights protected individuals' rights against the power of the national government. The first ten amendments to the Constitution form the Bill of Rights. They were a distillation of rights under English law and state constitutions growing out of the American Revolution.

The First Amendment freedoms of religion, speech, press, assembly, and petition are designed to protect the individual and insure a democratic political process. The Second and Third Amendments (keep and bear arms, quartering troops) are largely eighteenth century protections little applied to twentieth century problems. The Fourth Amendment (search and seizures), Fifth Amendment (grand jury indictment, double jeopardy, self-incrimination) and Sixth Amendment (jury trial and confront witnesses) are procedural guarantees of fairness and due process when citizens confront the law. The Seventh Amendment extends jury trials to civil matters, and the Eighth Amendment prohibits excessive bails and cruel and unusual punishment. These latter two are known as substantive guarantees. The Ninth Amendment was designed to protect emerging rights not enumerated in the Constitution. No thought was that all rights could be listed or anticipated. The Tenth Amendment is a protection for the states and the people of the states so as to reserve powers to them not delegated to the national government. Taken together the Bill of Rights stand as an impressive statement of individual liberty against a possibly oppressive government.

THE QUESTION OF MOTIVES

Perhaps because Americans have so venerated the Constitution, it becomes somewhat difficult to interpret the motives behind its formulation. Early on, critics of national power such as Thomas Jefferson and John C. Calhoun would construct a constitutional theory defending states rights and restricting national power. After the Civil War, the age of "Constitution worship" began. John Fiske's *The Critical Period in American History, 1783–1789,*[10] argued that the

10. John Fiske, *The Critical Period in American History, 1783–1789* (New York: Houghton, Mifflin Co., 1888).

nation, under the Articles of Confederation, was on the verge of economic chaos and political disunion. The Constitution warded off anarchy and tyranny, yet preserved liberty and popular government through a republican process of government. The Constitution had saved the Union. In the twentieth century, the Framers' motives were challenged. J. Allen Smith and especially Charles Beard, in his *An Economic Interpretation of the Constitution,* questioned the Framers portrayal as patriots. Beard's charge was the strongest and most influential: the Constitution was "an economic document drawn with superb skill by men whose property interests were immediately at stake."[11] Beard cast the convention in an altogether different light. The Articles of Confederation were adversely affecting the economic interests of certain classes. The men who met in Philadelphia to draft the Constitution were the ones adversely affected under the Articles. Beard argued that they drafted the Constitution to protect their own personal economic interests.

Generations of scholars have argued over Beard's thesis. Robert E. Brown[12] attacked it: he held that the Framers lost economically as much as they gained by ratification of the Constitution. Forrest McDonald[13] argued that ratification of the Constitution in the states did not come as Beard would have predicted. The states whose economic interests were promoted did not overwhelmingly favor adoption. The Constitution's democratic character was also challenged. J. Allen Smith drew this conclusion:"We are trying to make an undemocratic Constitution the vehicle of democratic rule."[14] Smith, and later Vernon Parrington,[15] stressed the aristocratic character of the delegates and their disdain for democracy.

None of these criticisms and interpretations is totally accurate; yet they serve a useful purpose. They help us to see the delegates not as gods or saints, but as eighteenth-century politicians with all the shortcomings of human beings, fashioning a government with the tools at hand.

THE EVOLVING CONSTITUTION

John Marshall, the great Chief Justice of the Supreme Court from 1801 until 1835, said of the Constitution in *McCulloch* v. *Maryland:*

This is a Constitution intended to endure for ages to come, and consequently, to be adapted to the various crises of human affairs. To have prescribed the means by which government should in all future time,

11. Charles A. Beard, *An Economic Interpretation of the Constitution of the United States* (New York: Macmillan, 1960), p. 188.
12. Robert E. Brown, *Charles Beard and the American Constitution* (Princeton: Princeton University Press, 1956).
13. Forrest McDonald, *We The People: The Economic Origin of the Constitution* (Chicago: University of Chicago Press, 1958).
14. J. Allen Smith, *The Spirit of American Government* (New York: Macmillan, 1907), p. 31.
15. Vernon L. Parrington, *Main Current in American Thought* (New York: Harcourt, Brace, 1930).

execute its powers, would have been to change entirely the character of the instrument, and give it the properties of a legal code. It would have been an unwise attempt to provide, by immutable rules, for exigencies which . . . can be best provided for as they occur.[16]

The Framers were generally agreed that the Constitution would have to be changed from time to time, that changing conditions would necessitate alteration. They provided, in Article V of the Constitution, a formal method for changing it. But one of the reasons the Constitution has been formally amended so little has been because of the informal ways to change it. The Constitution has been changed by congressional and presidential actions that have defined and given substance to its vague language. Finally, and most significantly, the Constitution has been kept up-to-date by the courts continually interpreting action and events in accordance with its principle.

FORMAL AMENDMENT

Formal amendments may be proposed by two methods: by a two-thirds vote of both houses of Congress, or by a national convention called by Congress at the request of the legislatures of two-thirds of the states.

The national government initiates the process. Congress would call for a national convention at the request of the legislatures of two-thirds of the states. Is Congress obligated to call such a convention upon receipt of a petition from two-thirds of the states? The language of Article V of the Constitution would imply that this was so: "The Congress . . . *shall* call a convention. . . ." But the language of Article IV for returning fugitives charged with a crime is equally imperative: A person fleeing from justice and found in another state "*shall* on demand of the executive authority of the state from which he fled, be delivered up. . . ." Yet the courts have ruled they lack any enforcement powers to compel a governor to comply. Could the courts compel Congress to call a constitutional convention? How would they enforce such a decree? Furthermore, would the subject matter necessarily be limited to the topic proposed by the states in the petition? One must remember the only constitutional convention ever convened did not limit its work to "amending the Articles of Confederation."

Nearly 400 petitions for constitutional conventions have been filed with Congress over the years; only one, however, has come close to obtaining the consent of the required number of state legislatures. Between 1963 and 1971, 33 states (one short of the required two-thirds) petitioned Congress to call a convention to reverse a Supreme Court decision requiring state legislatures to be reapportioned on the basis of population. No such convention was ever called. Presently, the National Taxpayers Union is leading a campaign in which 30 state legislatures have petitioned Congress for a convention to balance the federal

16. *McCulloch* v. *Maryland,* 4 Wheat. U.S. 316 (1819).

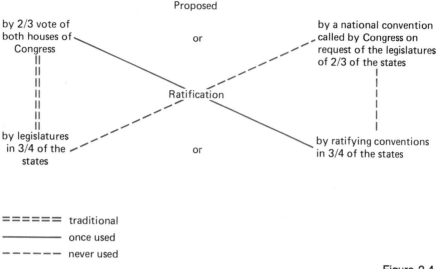

Figure 2.4
Amending the Constitution.

budget. But to date Congress shows no signs of using this method to propose amendments to the Constitution.

Amendments that are proposed are ratified by the states in one of two ways: by the legislatures of three-fourths of the states, or by special ratifying conventions in three-fourths of the states. Congress determines which of the two methods is to be used (Figure 2.4).

Of the 26 amendments that have been passed, only the Twenty-first, repealing prohibition, was submitted to ratifying conventions. States normally have seven years in which to ratify, although Congress determines what times will be provided. Where unspecified, the courts have concluded that seven years is reasonable. Congress has generally followed this practice, although with the proposed Equal Rights Amendment, ratification was extended for 39 months beyond the seven-year period.

A state may ratify an amendment after first having rejected it. But the question of undoing ratification is less settled. Some states have voted to rescind their ratification of the Equal Rights Amendment; but is that valid? State ratification is now monitored by the General Services Administration (GSA), which certifies the ratification and keeps the count of states. Previously, the Secretary of State performed this duty. The Supreme Court has stayed away from the dispute. Presumably Congress or the GSA will have to decide whether or not a state can rescind ratification. There have been odd occurrences in the past: North Dakota ratified the Twenty-fifth Amendment thinking it was the thirty-eighth state, only to find that it was thirty-seventh. North Dakota then sought to withdraw ratification. Min-

Policy Formulation and the
Separation of Powers

The Founding Fathers contemplated the formulation of public policy as a structural process wherein each of the three branches of the national government would have delegated powers and functions. The primary responsibility for formulating policy was vested with Congress as Article I, Section 8 sought to articulate the range of policy areas. The President could veto legislation, otherwise he was to administer the formulated policy. The court would interpret policy and rule on its constitutionality.

The distribution of power and necessary cooperation, however, has changed greatly over 200 years. Today the policy process is the result of the shifting balance of power within separation of powers. A contemporary review of the policy-making process must make note of the following relevant factors:

1. *Bureaucracy.* There is now almost universal recognition that bureaucracy is significantly involved in public policy. The administration of policy includes discretionary authority. The implementation of policy requires rule making.

2. *Subgovernment phenomenon.* A broad range of policy making and implementation is conducted by subgovernments. The most relevant subgovernments are influential congressmen and subcommittees, administrative agencies with policy jurisdiction, and affected interest groups. The subgovernment is normally involved with routine administration, hence prerogatives become established that are difficult to alter.

3. *Courts.* Judicial review has given the courts great influence over policy in the United States. They are frequently called upon to interpret statutes and to legitimate courses of action. More and more groups and individuals are turning to the courts to enjoin government or private actions or, conversely, to prompt government action in a policy area.

4. *Interest groups.* As the source of much demand for policy adoption, interest groups represent interests before government and provide criticism for policy implementation. There has been a proliferation of interest groups concerned with public policy in the 1970s, much of it focusing on narrow, single issue policy concerns.

The change in the policy process necessitates close interaction between official and unofficial participants. Subgovernment dominance in policy areas creates a need for this close interaction, and the influence of government and nongovernment participants changes with the interaction and policy areas.

A useful basis for classifying policy formulation is that which identifies the nature of decision making. Three types of policy formulation are:

1. *Incrementalism.* This is a congruent process where decisions are patterned after previous decisions. There is no reformulation of policy, and decisions only incrementally differ from existing policies. A well-established base exists, therefore, from which to predict policy consequences. Subgovernment participation is strongest in this type of formulation.

2. *Imitative.* Problems of government are treated by analogy. What has worked in

the private sector, particularly business, can be imitated for the public sector. Cost-benefit analysis and management by objectives are examples. The executive, courts, and interest groups are likely participants.

3. *Innovation.* New policies are proposed that have no tradition or equivalence in the private sector. They suggest new directions for solutions of problems of public policy. True innovative policies are uncommon and typically face opposition. Hence their adoption is uncertain. The Chief Executive normally dominates this area.

---

nesota then ratified after North Dakota, thinking it was the thirty-eighth state, and was followed in short order by Nevada. North Dakota's withdrawal apparently was successful, for Minnesota was declared the thirty-seventh state and Nevada the thirty-eight state to ratify the amendment.[17]

Changes in the Constitution have occurred through formal amendments. We might categorize these changes as follows:

1. **Authority of Government.** The Eleventh Amendment removed from federal court jurisdiction suits against a state by citizens of another state or a foreign citizen. The Thirteenth Amendment abolished slavery and empowered Congress to legislate its enforcement. The Sixteenth Amendment empowered Congress to levy a graduated income tax. The Eighteenth Amendment prohibited the manufacture, sale or transportation of alcoholic beverages. The Twenty-first Amendment repealed the Eighteenth and empowered states to regulate alcohol.

2. **Power to the Citizen.** The Fourteenth Amendment made the former slaves citizens of the state wherein they resided and extended to them the "privileges and immunities" of citizenship as well as "due process of law" and "the equal protection of the law." The Fifteenth Amendment barred prohibitions to voting on the basis of race, color, or previous condition of servitude. The Seventeenth Amendment gave citizens the direct vote for election of U.S. senators. The Nineteenth Amendment assured women the right to vote. The Twenty-fourth Amendment abolished the poll tax as a prerequisite for voting. The Twenty-sixth Amendment extended the franchise to all persons eighteen years of age and older. If ratified, the Twenty-seventh Amendment will extend equality of rights on the basis of sex.

3. **Structural Changes.** The Twelfth Amendment provided for the separate election in the Electoral College of the president and vice-president. The Twentieth, or lame duck amendment, changed the dates on which terms

17. Robert E. Cushman and Robert F. Cushman, *Cases in Constitutional Law* (New York: Appleton-Century-Crofts, 1968), p. 8.

of office for Congress and the president began. The Twenty-second Amendment limited a president to two terms. The Twenty-third Amendment expanded the Electoral College by adding three votes for the District of Columbia. The Twenty-fifth Amendment on presidential succession and disability clarified the procedure and succession when a vacancy or disability occurs in the presidency. A proposed amendment before Congress would extend representation in Congress to the District of Columbia.

INFORMAL MEANS

The Constitution, as a frame of government, cannot provide for every situation. It has to be adapted to the crises of the moment as they occur. In fact, the body of constitutional law is primarily the result of informal changes, of applying the Constitution to the various legal, economic, social, and political problems the nation has encountered. These informal changes are basic to the American constitutional system.

Congress, in acting on the authority specified in the Constitution, frequently fills in the details of the Constitution. In 1789 Congress passed the Judiciary Act, which established the basic lower court structure we have today. The federal bureaucracy is the result of Congress authorizing the organizations and functions for a very unspecific executive branch established in Article II.

In 1974 Congress moved to fill in the meaning of "high crimes and misdemeanors" when the Judiciary Committee of the House of Representatives undertook Articles of Impeachment against President Nixon as a result of Watergate. The Committee did not believe impeachable offenses had to be criminally indictable offenses. It voted three articles of impeachment: obstruction of justice in the Watergate coverup, abuse of power in the misuse of governmental agencies and violating the oath of office, and contempt of Congress in willfully disobeying congressional subpoenas. We do not know what might have happened since Richard Nixon resigned his office prior to a full congressional vote.

Presidential practice has defined the power of the chief executive. There have been no changes in the formal powers of the president since 1789, yet the office and its powers have changed remarkably over the years. World war, the growth of a world economy, and a host of other events have modified the Constitution as the presidency has grown with the changing national and international environment.

In the Watergate debate over the confidentiality of presidential conversations, President Nixon claimed executive privilege for presidential conversations, tapes, and documents. *U.S.* v. *Nixon*[18] required the president to turn over the material but also formally, for the first time, recognized the principle of executive privilege as rooted in the Constitution. Here is a presidential practice going back

18. *United States* v. *Nixon* 418 U.S. 683 (1974).

as far as Thomas Jefferson being accepted as presidential practice under the Constitution (subject to review by the courts, however, as *U.S.* v. *Nixon* made plain).

Custom and practice over the years have also established a number of other procedures. The clearest example is the presidential nominating convention. The Constitution made no mention of how candidates were to be nominated. Over the years, political parties developed and gradually devised the convention method for nominating candidates. In 1972, George McGovern was soundly defeated for the presidency, but no one disputed his right to challenge Richard Nixon. He had secured the Democratic endorsement and therefore had won the right to challenge Mr. Nixon.

JUDICIAL REVIEW

Judicial interpretation has continually updated the Constitution. Charles Evans Hughes said the Constitution is "what the Supreme Court says it is." The greatest amount of change has actually come through judicial interpretation. Since the wording of the Constitution is ambiguous, courts play an important role in translating its language to deal with modern political events and problems. In *Brown* v. *Board of Education* (1954) the Supreme Court held that the language of the Fourteenth Amendment required desegregation of public schools. In 1896,

John Marshall. Fourth Justice of the United States from 1801 until 1835. (The Bettmann Archive, Inc.)

The New Deal put in motion, and the Supreme Court's 1954 *Brown* decision seemed to crystallize, a new consensus on the need for politicians to do more than merely preach equality of opportunity: Government was to promote actively equal opportunity for the nation's long-disadvantaged minorities by a variety of means. Some of these means were spelled out in the 1964 Civil Rights Act, which in its Title VI prohibits discrimination against any person "on the grounds of race, color, or national origin" in "any program or activity receiving federal financial assistance." Another way of promoting equal opportunity is the principle of *affirmative action,* the idea that we as a society must make up for past discrimination by offering members of minority groups special access to education, training, and employment. Affirmative action has been promoted by the federal government in all projects and programs in which there is federal funding; and it has been one of the government's major weapons in changing university admissions' policies.

From the 1960s to the early 1970s the policy seemed to be working: People who might not otherwise have had a chance were able to get jobs, enter training programs, and go to college and to law or medical school. But there was some protest.

In 1972 Bakke, a white man in his midthirties, sought admission to medical school at the University of California at Davis, which followed an affirmative action policy and used a special Task Force and a quota system for the admission of minorities. Although he scored high on all the tests, had a solid background, did well on the personal interview, and should have been admitted easily despite his age, an illness in his family delayed his completing the application. Later, when he was ready to apply for admission there were not enough places left, and he was refused. Bakke tried again, this time threatening legal action, and was again refused. He then sued the University of California in the state courts and won. The university, fearing its authority over admissions policies might be destroyed, appealed the decision to the U.S. Supreme Court. The Court accepted the case in 1977. In July 1978 it handed down a decision in favor of Bakke's admission but also allowed universities to continue to use race or minority status as a criterion of admission. It thus gave Bakke his admission while at the same time upholding the principle of affirmative action.

The Court was split down the middle in the case: The decision was 5 to 4, and the justices wrote six different opinions that were revised three times before finally being printed. Sixty-one *amicus curiae* (friend of the court) briefs were filed by interested groups—a record in the history of the Court. Clearly the decision had been extremely difficult, since both sides appeared to be in the "right" on the issues. *Reverse discrimination,* the charge critics level against affirmative action, can indeed sometimes result in injustice; but there are also generations of discrimination against minorities, and the need exists to help these groups improve their position in society. We simply cannot afford so many wasted lives, so many talents unused because of prejudice or fear of competition.

But the problem remains: how to make up for past injustice without creating what some have called new and different injustice.

the Court had ruled that same language did not require desegregation, and had held that separate but equal facilities were adequate.

The Framers gave the courts no express power of judicial review, although there is some evidence they considered it and some, at least, approved of it. This power was added by the Court in *Marbury* v. *Madison* in 1803. In 1800 Thomas Jefferson was elected to the presidency; the Federalist era was over. John Adams and the Federalists did not take the defeat well. A lame duck Congress that did not adjourn until March 1801 created several new federal judgeships, and Adams eagerly filled them with loyal Federalists. One such appointment went to William Marbury as Justice of the Peace for the District of Columbia. Working right up to the change of office on March 3, Adams signed the appointments and turned them over to his Secretary of State, John Marshall, to seal and deliver. Not all, however, could be delivered by the next day, and the new president had no intention of filling the posts with Federalists. Jefferson ordered his Secretary of State, James Madison, not to deliver the 17 remaining undelivered appointments.

Marbury sued to recover his appointment. Under Article 13 of the Judiciary Act of 1789, the Supreme Court had been given original jurisdiction to issue *writs of mandamus*. Such a writ directs a public official to act in a certain way or perform some duty. Delivery of a properly authorized and approved judicial appointment was suitable for a writ of mandamus. Marbury sued Secretary of State Madison for delivery of the Justice of Peace appointment for the District of Columbia, and the case came before the Supreme Court on original jurisdiction.

Jefferson said plainly he would not have the appointment delivered. Could the Court compel Jefferson to comply? Could the Court interfere with the executive? The Supreme Court issued its opinion on February 24, 1803. Speaking for the Court, Chief Justice John Marshall, a lame duck appointee himself to the Supreme Court by John Adams, reasoned that the appointment was proper and Marbury was entitled to the commission. Marshall also held that a writ of mandamus was the proper judicial remedy for a ministerial function unperformed by a public official. But, he concluded, the Supreme Court could not issue such a writ. Article 13 of the Judiciary Act of 1789 enlarged the original jurisdiction of the Supreme Court in Article III of the Constitution. This was contrary to the Constitution, for the Supreme Court had original jurisdiction only in cases affecting an ambassador or a foreign minister, or in which a state is a party. Marbury was none of these. The case was dismissed.

What Marshall had done was to avoid direct confrontation with President Jefferson. Marbury did not get his post but Marshall made it clear that Marbury had been entitled to the appointment. Marshall then went on to declare that the courts have the power of **judicial review,** the power to make authoritative interpretations of the Constitution:

> It is emphatically the province and duty of the judicial department to say what the law is. Those who apply the rule to particular cases, must

of necessity expound and interpret that rule. If two laws conflict with each other, the courts must decide on the operation of each.[19]

Today we can fully appreciate the magnitude of this power of the courts. The president and the Court had disagreed on an interpretation of the Constitution, and the Court clearly declared that judges—not the executive—interpret the law: "If two laws conflict with each other, the court must decide on the operation of each." Marshall had been shrewd: in a masterpiece of judicial reasoning, he had disarmed a potential constitutional crisis of the first magnitude, and maintained the integrity, and power, of the judiciary.

TOWARD THE THIRD CENTURY

The future of our constitutional structure poses some interesting and important questions. What are some of the major problems government is going to have to confront?

1. **Limited Growth.** The allocation of scarce resources will be a major concern. The depletion of nonrenewable resources as coal, oil, and gas, and the damage to the environment in securing and using these resources, will have to be weighed against the need for jobs and industrial growth. Can the nation continue to use the growth of GNP as the measure of progress? The problem of redistribution of resources is equally troubling. Food, population, and human services all demand attention. How do we bring the problems under control, and yet protect individual liberty? Problems of regulation and distribution involve the issues of separation of powers and big government.

2. **The Postindustrial Society.** The postindustrial society is an advanced industrial society dominated by sophisticated technology, a service economy, and rapid change—and it is the projection for America in the future. Government will be increasingly important as a provider of social benefits. An educated society will be mobile and service-oriented. The tendencies for meritocracy and social stratification confront theories of democracy. In a service economy, new property and new income depend on governmental policy and spending. The individual needs protection from himself. Government regulation becomes social policy. Public planning becomes a necessity. New groups and clienteles are emerging, and the old politics will have to give way and accommodate new realities.

3. **International Relations.** The multinational corporation and global economic policies already temper our political process. The demands for

19. *Marbury* v. *Madison*, 1 Crunch 137 (1803).

new policies, for Congress and the president to work together to coordinate foreign and domestic policies, is an emerging imperative. OPEC already alters our domestic economy. National security and secrecy, human rights, and international cooperation are all values to be judged within the context of the international environment. The need for governmental accountability in foreign affairs is perhaps the most important change that is needed.

4. **Political Values and Ideas.** Whether the postindustrial society is a reality or not, American political values are already changing. Americans are distrustful and cynical of government. They are fearful of increased taxes. Political alignments are polarizing within both parties. (There are already strains on the political process because of the open convention system and disarray of the parties.) Single-issue voting is increasing. The traditional values of an open, pluralistic political system stand in contrast to the growing resistance of interest groups to governmental regulation, voluntary wage controls, and affirmative action practices. The growth in the size and complexity of government may produce veto groups that will destroy separation of powers.

5. **Mass Communication.** From a political standpoint, we are already seeing the effects of mass communication. Presidential candidates no longer need political parties; elections are conducted through the media, and candidates' advertising budgets have soared. Issues have been shaped and dramatized by the media; much of what Americans learn and know about political issues is what the media presents. There is growing concern about an opinion-shaping ideological bias in mass communications.

6. **Violence.** In the 1960s and early 1970s violence became a national political problem. The assassinations of President Kennedy, Robert Kennedy, and Martin Luther King; the killings at Kent State; and terrorist violence abroad and racial protest at home all seemed indicators of a trend toward settling problems by means of violence. There was a tendency for small groups to pressure public authority by the use of hijackings and kidnappings. Street crime increased. The obligations of society toward victims of violence became a major new area of law and civil liberties. How to keep the political process open and peaceful, yet accommodating, is a major issue that will test the flexibility of our constitutional system.

SUMMARY

1. America's political heritage is the result of English political traditions—the common law and republicanism—and colonial political experience, notably legislative authority, free elections, and constitutionalism.

2. The Articles of Confederation were the United States' first attempt at

national self-government. They established a weak central government and left real power to the separate states. The Constitution was a new plan for national government where national power operated directly upon the people.

3. The Constitution represents some basic American political principles. Representation requires decision makers to stand for election by the people. Power is separated so that no institution or officeholder is entrusted with too much power. Limited authority prevents abuse to political office. Over the years, however, our thinking on limited authority has changed. Finally, individual liberty is protected by a Bill of Rights added to the Constitution.

4. There has been a continuing debate over the Constitution, over the motives of the Founders drafting the Constitution, and over the distribution of power between the national government and the states. The Constitution has been made adaptable to meet the changing expectations of the American people.

5. The Constitution is shaped and will continue to be shaped by the important political problems America faces. While these problems will test the ability of constitutional government to respond, the Constitution is likely to endure—as it has for nearly 200 years.

TERMS

anti-Federalists 56
Articles of
   Confederation 44
bill of attainder 62
common law 36
compact colony 38
contract 37
ex post facto law 62
federalism 58
Federalist 54
Great
   Compromise 51–52

joint-stock colony 38
judicial review 71
post-industrial society 72
proprietary colony 38–39
New Jersey Plan 51
representation 57
republicanism 37
separated powers 59
tenure in office 58
Virginia Plan 50-51
Writ of habeas
   corpus 59–62

RESEARCH PROJECTS

2.1. A New Constitution. The present constitution is approaching 200 years old. If a new constitutional convention were to be held, what changes would you propose for the convention? Write out some new articles or amendments for the constitution. If you have no changes to propose, why is the present document adequate? There are some interesting efforts discussing redrafting the constitution you may wish to consult. Rexford Tugwell, *The Emerging Constitution* (Harper's Magazine Press, 1974) and Leland Baldwin, *Reframing the Constitution* (ABC–Clio, 1972).

2.2. Ratification of the Constitution. Debate over ratification of the Constitution was between Federalists and anti-Federalists. Write an essay describing the struggle for ratification. Include such things as (a) what kind of people were the Federalists and anti-Federalists; (b) how were the delegates to state conventions selected; (c) what was the geographical distribution of Federalists and anti-Federalists; (d) what issues emerged over the constitution; and (e) how did the states vote on ratification. Would you conclude the struggle to have been a profound or a minor struggle, fast or slow, ratification easy or difficult to achieve?

2.3. The Frameworks for Government. Line off four columns on a sheet of paper and compare item by item the Articles of Confederation, the Virginia Plan, the New Jersey Plan, and the Constitution. Compare such things as structure and representation in Congress, delegation of power to Congress, Presidential power, mode of electing the President, structure of the courts, court jurisdiction, admission of new states, enforcement.

BIBLIOGRAPHY

Bailyn, Bernard. *The Ideological Origins of the American Revolution*. Cambridge, Mass.: Harvard University Press, 1967.

An excellent discussion of the sources and ideas from the eighteenth century with which the American colonists fashioned the revolution. Bailyn looks at the revolution through its ideas and intellectual development.

Becker, Carl. *The Declaration of Independence*. New York: Vintage Press, 1942.

A now classic study on the ideas and events surrounding the Declaration of Independence. Following the trend of ideas, Becker sees the Declaration as a culmination of dominant eighteenth century thought.

Corwin, E. S. *The Constitution and What it Means Today*. Harold Chase and Craig Ducat (eds.) Princeton, N.J.: Princeton University Press, 1978.

A section by section discussion of the Constitution in the light of contemporary Supreme Court decisions and political practices. A useful book to the understanding of the present interpretation or meaning of the Constitution, article by article.

Farrand, Max. *Records of the Federal Convention*. New Haven, Conn.: Yale University Press, 1937.

The most extensive and indexed record of the debates of the federal convention. Farrand has reconstructed, largely from Madison's notes, the debates and results of the constitutional convention. The best source on the constitutional convention.

Hamilton, Alexander, James Madison, and John Jay. *Federalist Papers*. New York: New American Library, 1961.

As close as America comes to original political theory, the *Federalist Papers* seek to explain and justify the new constitution. Many of the original essays give valuable insight into the philosophy of the Constitution and the delegates who penned it.

Jensen, Merrill. *The New Nation: A History of the United States During the Confederation*. New York: Alfred A. Knopf, 1958.

The foremost scholar on the period of the confederation, Merrill Jensen focuses on the events and conflicts between the Revolution and the Constitution. Jensen examines America's first efforts to govern the new nation and the problems the nation faced.

Kelly, Alfred, and Winfred Harbison. *The American Constitution*. New York: W. W. Norton, 1970.

A well-written treatment of constitutionalism in America from its earliest origins up to the present. Kelly and Harbison present excellent discussions of early issues and conflicts and the legal precedents surrounding them. These then are carried forward as constitutional history.

Peltason, Jack. *Understanding the Constitution*. Hinsdale, Ill.: Dryden Press, 1976.

An excellent discussion of the Constitution, its origins and present meaning. Peltason is a readable source book for understanding any article or section of the Constitution and for understanding present construction of the Constitution.

Rossiter, Clinton. *The Seedtime of the Republic*. New York: Harcourt, Brace, & World, 1953.

A masterful history of colonial and revolutionary America. Rossiter provides a very readable account of colonial life—social life, economics, government, and revolutionary thought—the men and ideas that influenced the revolution. Rossiter seeks to describe the environment in colonial and revolutionary America.

Rossiter, Clinton. *1787, The Grand Convention*. New York: Macmillan, 1976.

Rossiter provides a well-written, lively account of the constitutional convention and struggle for ratification. The book contains much useful and interesting information on the convention deliberations as well as on its delegates.

Wills, Gary. *Inventing America*. Garden City, N.Y.: Doubleday, 1978.

A fresh look at the events surrounding the Declaration of Independence. Much of the book is devoted to Jefferson's draft of the Declaration, seeking to explain Jefferson's meaning and how it differs from other interpretations of the Declaration.

Wood, Gordon S. *The Creation of the American Republic*. Chapel Hill, N.C.: University of North Carolina Press, 1969.

A scholarly examination of the ideology of the American revolution, state governments, and politics until the constitutional convention. Wood methodically discusses the creation of an American science of politics prior to 1787.

Chapter
3

Federalism

The history of federalism is a history of intergovernmental cooperation and tension. The Framers had no grand design; their novel experiment in shared sovereignty would necessarily adapt to the changing environment of the nation and the states. Federalism is as much an attitude—a pragmatic, decentralized approach to problem solving—as it is a legal-constitutional arrangement for separated powers between a national government and component states. An Englishman, M. J. Vile, described federalism this way:

> Americans have a "federal attitude" towards government which colours their whole approach to governmental problems, which insures that the solutions found to these problems will be within a particular pattern. This attitude is . . . vague and meandering, and contains contradictory elements. It is a way of thinking which enables considerable changes necessary in order to adapt to new conditions, changes which can be brought by compromises, the elements of which are easy to find in the rich and varied ideas of American history.[1]

Federalism has its origins in shared decision making and a decentralized party system as much as in the Philadelphia Convention. Morton Grod-

1. M.J.C. Vile, *The Structure of American Federalism* (New York: Oxford University Press, 1961), p. 39.

---

zins spoke of federalism not as a layer cake with each level a neat, separate sphere of decision-making authority, but rather as a "marble cake" in which the functions of government transverse all levels of government, each of which shares in making public policy.[2] There are no separate or distinct federal, state, or local functions. From the Northwest Ordinances, in which states set aside federal land to finance education as a condition for settlement, to the new Department of Education, the school lunch program, or New York's request for federal aid, "the history of the American governments is a history of shared functions."[3]

As a system of authority, federalism is a method of dividing powers between the central, or national, government and the constituent units, or states, that gives substantial and independent authority to each (see Figure 3.1). No level of government is dependent on another for its authority or is in a position to change the distribution of power. The attributes of federalism can be summarized as follows:

1. There is a constitutional division of governmental functions such that each level is autonomous in at least one sphere of action;
2. Each government is final and supreme in its constitutionally assigned area;
3. Both levels act directly on citizens (unlike a confederation, where only the regional units act directly on the citizens, while the central government acts only on the regional governments);
4. Both levels derive their powers from the "sovereign" (that is, the people or the Constitution), rather than from one another;
5. Therefore, neither can change the relationship unilaterally;
6. The regional divisions (that is, states) exist as of their own rights.[4]

Formally, then, federalism can be distinguished from a **unitary system** of government. A unitary system derives all authority from the central government, and all local governments exist at the pleasure of the central government. The central government may delegate authority and functions to local governments as it chooses. This is the case in Great Britain, and it is the relationship between American states and their cities and countries. A **confederation,** on the other hand, places legal authority in the hands of constituent governments, which in turn may choose to create and delegate authority to a central government. The central government does not have authority to regulate individuals directly; it operates at the direction of the states and acts upon them. This was the system under the Articles of Confederation in 1783. Figure 3.2 shows the system of government under the confederation and the federation.

2. Morton Grodzins and Daniel Elazar, "Centralization and Decentralization in the American Federal System," in Robert A. Goldwin, ed., *A Nation of States* (Chicago: Rand McNally, 1963).
3. *Ibid.*, p. 7.
4. From the New Federalism by Michael Reagan. Copyright © 1972 by Oxford University Press, Inc. Reprinted by premission.

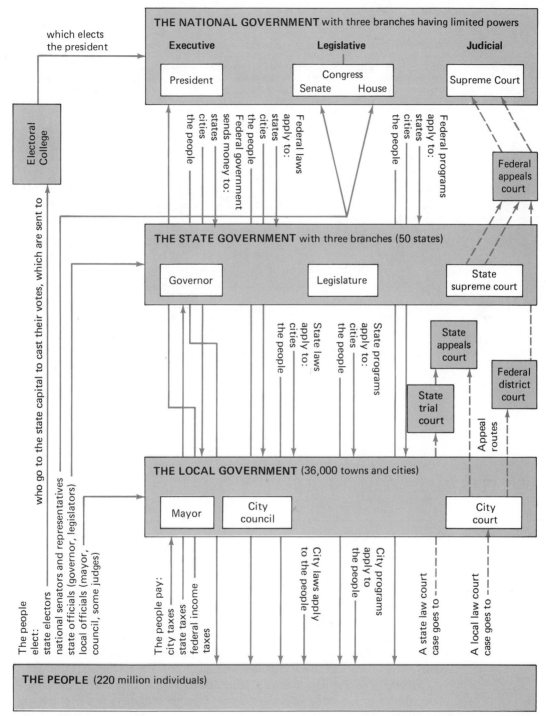

Figure 3.1
The Federal structure of government.

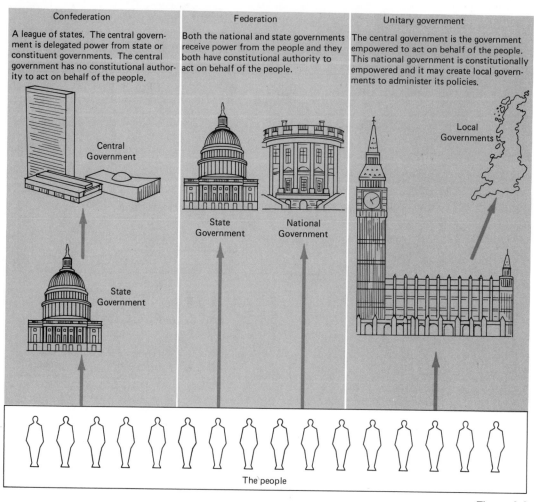

Confederation

A league of states. The central government is delegated power from state or constituent governments. The central government has no constitutional authority to act on behalf of the people.

Central Government

State Government

Federation

Both the national and state governments receive power from the people and they both have constitutional authority to act on behalf of the people.

State Government

National Government

Unitary government

The central government is the government empowered to act on behalf of the people. This national government is constitutionally empowered and it may create local governments to administer its policies.

Local Governments

The people

Figure 3.2
The Confederation and the Federation.

As a legal theory, federalism stresses the independence of each level of authority; the Constitution grants exclusive authority to each level of government. But in fact the real genius of federalism rests with its shared responsibilities. Federalism is a dynamic relationship allowing for decentralized authority and joint activity. It provides a relatively efficient method of problem solving.

Whether the Framers intended federalism to be a cooperative problem-solving device or a contractual, constitutional division of powers is a question of some dispute. States rights lawyers are likely to argue for the latter; but much of the discussion of federalism revolves around problem solving. Part and parcel of our changing expectations toward federalism is increased intergovernmental co-operation in managing our problems. From clean air to recreational facilities, to saving New York City, people want efficient and effective solutions to problems.

THE HISTORY OF FEDERALISM

The American experience with federalism began with the colonies and the Articles of Confederation. Working out an acceptable relationship between central and state authorities was a familiar problem for the delegates at Philadelphia.

EARLY COOPERATION AND CONFLICT

By 1765, when the British abandoned their policy of "salutary neglect," colonial self-government was well intrenched. Foreign affairs and trade were commonly recognized as under the Crown, but in domestic matters local legislatures had developed the habit of governing for themselves. Stephen Hopkins, the brilliant governor of Rhode Island, compared the British Empire to a federal state in 1765. Parliament could legislate such things as commerce, money, and credit, but "each of the colonies hath a legislature within itself, to take care of its interests." In the Albany Plan, Benjamin Franklin had proposed a "grand council" to which the colonies would delegate the power to raise military forces, to legislate, to make war and peace with the Indians, and to levy taxes and collect customs duties. Earlier still, in 1643, Massachusetts Bay, Plymouth, Connecticut, and New Haven formed the Confederation of New England. Motivated by fear of the Indians, the Dutch, and the French, confronted with common problems and religious interests, they signed the Articles of Union, which provided for two representatives from each colony and gave them power to declare war, make peace, and settle boundary disputes.

The Articles of Confederation were a "league of friendship," with the states retaining final authority. They failed in important ways to give Congress sufficient authority to legislate; they were cumbersome and impossible to amend. Yet the Articles displayed the growing federal character of the new nation and were an attempt to provide a national government with powers to meet common problems.

The constitutional convention took up where the Articles left off. The Virginia Plan created a national government, and while it recognized the states, it left little authority to them. The New Jersey Plan was more in accord with the Articles, more what the small states felt the convention ought to draft. Out of the debate over these two plans emerged the final federal form. Actually, it was a series of compromises between the large and small state delegates, between the nationalists and the states righters. Over the question of representation in Congress, and in matters of federal supremacy, court jurisdiction, congressional authority, and the Electoral College, the delegates fashioned a series of compromises. They found a middle ground between a unitary government and a confederation, a way of building on their experience with dividing power between two levels of government. This middle ground was federalism.

CHANGING EXPECTATIONS

The Framers had fashioned a series of compromises based on their experience. Federalism had been a means to solve the problem of Union, but, as we have seen, this cooperative venture had built-in tensions. The small states wanted state equality and state sovereignty. They remained concerned that the new federal venture could not maintain the diversity of interests and localism necessary to good and free government. Madison and Hamilton argued in the *Federalist* that the states, rather than the national government, would have the upper hand. Over the years, the language of the Constitution and our attitude toward federalism have changed considerably; we still have a federal system, but it is far different from what the Framers imagined it would be.

The early years of the country were ones of adjustment between the national and state governments. Instead of operating on the states, the national government operated directly on the people; its power derived from the Constitution, not the states. This view was most obviously put forth by a Supreme Court heavily weighted with Federalists who successfully sought to extend the powers of the national government at the expense of the states. The competitive federalism of the early years was the result of an effort to identify "proper spheres of governmental jurisdiction" and to define boundaries of authority as clearly as possible. It was also a period of national growth. The Supreme Court expanded national authority in interstate commerce in *Gibbons* v. *Ogden* (1824), giving Congress exclusive and broad powers to regulate interstate commerce. In *McCulloch* v. *Maryland* (1819) implied powers broadened the enumerated powers in Article One. The sequence of Constitutional amendments after the Civil War worked against the states: the Reconstruction Amendments required states to protect the rights of blacks; the income tax (Sixteenth Amendment) dramatically increased the taxing power of the national government; and the Seventeenth Amendment removed the election of senators from state legislatures.

The effort to define jurisdictions led, in the late nineteenth century, to the concept of **dual federalism.** This was an effort to modify the conflict between national and state governments, to redress the balance of power by recognizing a duality of power between the national government and states, each level with its own sphere of authority and distinct jurisdiction. Dual federalism fit the constitutional theory of federalism; each level of government would handle separate domains, both having derived their authority from the Constitution, and one need not infringe upon the other. Dual federalism existed during a period of industrial growth, and the laissez-faire economic policies it produced worked to keep federal regulation at a minimum.

But in reality, there are no dual and separate domains. In fact, even during the period of dual federalism (until World War I) cooperative ventures continued. The idea had simply proved convenient for economic and industrial growth. But the marble cake intermingling of authority could not be denied, and by the first decade of the twentieth century, dual federalism had given way to cooperative federalism. By this time, America was much changed. Industrial growth had created economic interdependence; urbanization and the elimination of the frontier made great changes in American life. Government was growing. Technological developments placed strains on the social and economic systems. The Sixteenth Amendment enabled the national government to raise tremendous amounts of revenue and funnel it back to the states. The Agricultural Extension Service established a state aid program, the federal highway program was begun, and by 1930 the government was moving toward a permanent grant-in-aid system. In 1935 came the Social Security Act, the landmark legislation that first made the federal government responsible for the welfare of Americans.

In cooperative federalism there was no effort to maintain a clear distinction between powers and jurisdictions. There was a sharing of powers for the purpose of joint problem solving. Much of the movement toward cooperative federalism came with the national government's entry into areas previously the domain of

Federal aid to states increased as a result of the Depression. Here a WPA work program improves city streets in 1935. (The Bettmann Archive, Inc.)

the states, such as education, public welfare, and health care. The Depression of the 1930s hastened the process. The development of cooperative federalism also came without any formal change in the Constitution.

The economic crash in 1929 forced the national government and the states to cooperate to solve the mounting economic crisis. Grants-in-aid were a favored technique. Federal money was made available to states and localities for specific projects, and during the Depression these included welfare, employment, health care, housing, and school lunches. By 1933, aid totaled a half-billion dollars, or 13 percent of federal expenditures. In 1935, at the height of the Depression, federal support totaled $2 billion, or almost 50 percent of all state revenues. From World War II through the 1960s, federal programs continued to proliferate, the 1960s being the decade when grant programs grew extensively. Hospitals, urban renewal, clean air, crime control, rat control, and aid to depressed areas were all federal grant programs to finance specific functions. By 1971, some $30 billion was being spent for federal grants-in-aid, quadruple the amount a decade earlier.

Richard Nixon used the phrase the "new federalism" to describe the changed direction for the 1970s. In fact, the phrase suits our changing expectations. As Michael Reagan, a contemporary student of federalism, explains, "New style federalism is a political and pragmatic concept, stressing the actual interdependence and sharing of functions between Washington and the states, and focusing on the mutual leverage that each level is able to exert on the other."[5] Federalism today is a pragmatic, flexible constitutional arrangement to meet human needs and solve problems. The Constitution can be interpreted and applied differently at different times to achieve the nation's goals. With shifts in power or availability of resources, accommodations can be made to address the needs of the nation and its states.

THE DISTRIBUTION OF POWERS AND RESPONSIBILITIES

The Constitution has been correctly described as a living document, one whose provisions change with interpretations to keep it abreast with the times. And since we accept change more readily when the names remain the same, we are likely to continue to think of federalism as a distribution of power between the national government and the states. As we shall see, however, that distribution is much changed.

THE POWERS OF THE NATIONAL GOVERNMENT

The powers of the national government are largely outlines in the first three Articles of the Constitution establishing the three branches of the national government—legislative, executive, and judicial. First, there are the **enumerated pow-**

5. Reagan, *The New Federalism*, p. 3.

ers, the powers of the national government specifically provided for and listed. The powers of Congress in Article I include the power to coin money, to establish post offices, to promote the progress of science, and to regulate commerce. In addition, the Constitution and the courts allow for **implied powers** that can be inferred from the enumerated powers. The Constitution gives Congress the power to make all laws "necessary and proper" to execute the enumerated powers. This is the "elastic clause" of the Constitution that has allowed government to meet all kinds of new demands.

The third kind of national government power is **inherent power.** This power flows not from the Constitution itself, but from the fact that the United States is a government. Every nation must deal with other countries. In matters of war and peace, exploration, and occupation of territory, the national government has power "as necessary concomitants of nationality." The Supreme Court made this position clear in *U.S.* v. *Curtis-Wright Export Corporation* (1936). The national government would have powers to make war and peace, enter into treaties, and maintain diplomatic relations with foreign countries even if the Constitution did not enumerate or confer them.

THE POWERS OF THE STATES

The powers of the states are generally referred to as **reserved powers,** meaning that states retain all powers not granted by the Constitution to the national government or prohibited to them. The Tenth Amendment to the Constitution is the source of the reserved powers. Today it is also the source of misunderstanding. The common assumption is that enumerated powers of a national government and reserved powers for states provide a clear, common line of separation between national and state powers. Nothing is further from the truth. The Tenth Amendment does not seriously restrict national power; rather, the courts view the Tenth Amendment as a truism, "that all is retained which has not yet been surrendered."[6]

Powers not denied the states or exclusively given the national government may be exercised as **concurrent powers** by both national and state governments (Table 3.1). Article VI of the Constitution states that there can be no conflict between national and state law; national law is supreme. Yet the structure of federalism is largely erected on the ability of states and the national government to concurrently exercise power. For example, both the national government and the states levy taxes, regulate commerce, and protect the welfare of citizens.

Much of the history and growth of federalism has been the expansion of the national government into intergovernmental affairs without preempting state activity. The great sharing of responsibility has continued even while the national government has grown. This defies the neat separation of functions idea and yet it illustrates the strength of federalism: the ability to meet changing

6. *U.S.* v. *Darby,* 312 U.S. 100, [1941].

Table 3.1

A Continuum of National–Local Relationships

One-way beneficial	Mutually cooperative	Competitive	One-way coercive
U.S. Coast and Geodetic Survey provides geodetic controls for land surveys and mapping	Agricultural Extension Service gathers and diseminates agricultural information	FBI versus local police or sheriff	Department of Justice enforce's Voting Rights Act
U.S. Army quells local disorders	U.S. Public Health Service cooperates with county health department to contain spread of contagious disease	Atomic Energy Commission site approval versus local zoning opposition	HEW enforces school desegregation
U.S. Department of Labor arbitrates dispute between a city and its garbage collectors	U.S. Civil Service Commission and local personnel agency exchange experts under Intergovernmental Personnel Act	U.S. Department of Transportation versus local departments of parks, environment, and zoning over route of interstate highway	Environmental Protection Agency forces local adherence to air quality standards

SOURCE: Reprinted by permission of Parris N. Glendening and Maris Mann Reeves, *Pragmatic Federalism,* Pacific Palisades, Calif.: Palisades Publishing, p. 272.

expectations without destroying the Constitution or precipitating a crisis over jurisdictions.

This is not to say there are no conflicts over or restrictions on the power of the states. The Constitution places certain restrictions on the states: They may not make treaties, grant letters of marque and reprisal, coin money, emit bills of credit, pass a bill of attainder or ex post facto law, impair the obligation of contracts, grant any title of nobility, lay duties on imports or exports, keep troops in peacetime, or enter into an agreement with another state without the consent of Congress. State regulation cannot become an ''undue burden'' on the powers of the national government. What constitutes an undue burden and who decides the issue? Ultimately, it is the courts who decide.

THE SUPREME COURT AS UMPIRE

Federalism is a mutually accommodating system, but not without conflicts that need resolution. The Supreme Court plays the role of umpire in the federal system, partly by design and partly by the twists of history. Under a system of rule by law, it is principally by lawsuit that our system of power is challenged. This necessarily involves the Court in the political thicket of federal–state relations. Yet these legal issues disguise a political struggle for power and problem solving. The Supreme Court recognizes its role in modernizing the Constitution and keeping the nation "armed" constitutionally to keep abreast of social problems. As a branch of the national government, the Court has often been charged with favoring national power over state and local control. The Court's history would appear to bear this out. Maryland could not tax the national bank in order to interfere with its operation in the nineteenth century, and New York could not ban the SST from landing or taking off at its airports in the twentieth century. The federal system needs a way to maintain peaceful accommodation, however, and the Supreme Court is the "least dangerous" branch because it does not initiate policy or carry it out.

OBLIGATIONS TO THE STATES

The Constitution imposes some national obligations toward the states. Article IV contains a set of guarantees to the states that require the national government to:

1. Guarantee to every state in the Union a republican form of government.
2. Protect each state against invasion and domestic violence.
3. Provide for the admission of new states and protect the jurisdiction of present states.

The guarantee of a republican form of government has never been clearly outlined except to say that enforcement is a congressional responsibilty. When the initiative and referendum were challenged in the states as violating the republican principle, the courts have refused to hear the cases stating the question was one for

The SST Concorde jet was the center of a federal-state dispute over landing rights and noise pollution levels at airports in 1976. (The Bettmann Archive, Inc.)

Congress to decide. The national government is also obligated to protect states against invasion or domestic violence. Congress, or the president, to whom Congress has delegated authority, can send troops to quiet disturbances at the request of a state. At the height of the 1967 Detroit riot, President Johnson, at the request of Michigan's Governor George Romney, sent in federal troops to help state and local officials stop the violence.

Congress may also provide for the admission of new states. No territory has a right to statehood; granting it is a discretionary power of Congress. Congress normally provides for an "enabling act" preparing the way, and when the people draft a constitution for the state, Congress must approve it. Congress can place restrictions on a territory as a condition for admission as a state—provided, of course, they not impair the jurisdiction of existing states without their consent. Utah, for example, as a condition for statehood in 1894, was obliged to provide for religious toleration in the state and to prohibit polygamous marriages. In 1910, Arizona was denied the power to recall judges as a condition of admission. After admission, however, the Arizona constitution was promptly amended, and Congress could do nothing about it; Arizona was now a state with all the powers of a state.

HORIZONTAL FEDERALISM

Article IV of the Constitution imposes on the states certain obligations in their relationships with one another.

The **full faith and credit** clause requires states to accept the laws, records, and court decisions (in noncriminal cases) of another state. Although there are several technicalities in this clause, in practice it means that the civil court judgments of one state are honored in another state. Should a court in New York render a verdict for a landlord for back rent and the tenant moves to Illinois, the landlord does not have to bring suit again in Illinois. Illinois courts are to give full faith and credit to the New York verdict without retrying the case. Divorce is a common example: Couples who are divorced in one state and then move to different or separate states are to be recognized as single under full faith and credit. The technicalities emerge if we change the example a bit. If the couple go to another state for a divorce—say Nevada with its short residency—and return to their home state, are they legally divorced? Not necessarily. The courts have held that the state of residence may, under specific circumstances, rule that the divorce-granting state lacked jurisdiction.

States are to extend to citizens of other states the **privileges and immunities** of citizens of that state. This means citizens of other states are entitled to the full protection of the laws of the state, to the use of the courts, and to nondiscriminatory treatment. The speed limit is the same for all motorists, not 55 mph for residents and 45 mph for nonresidents. State tax rates are the same for residents and nonresidents alike. Unfortunately, this clause is also fraught with ambiguity and technicality. For example, tuition to attend college or a university can be set at a higher rate for out-of-state students and not violate the privileges and immunities clause. Out-of-state fishing and hunting licenses are also acceptable. And privileges and immunities do not extend to political rights, such as voting or serving on juries.

Third, the Constitution states that a state shall deliver up a fugitive from justice to the state wherein the crime was committed when requested to do so by that state. **Extradition** means the governor of the state shall return such fugitives to the state in which they are accused of the crime. Normally governors comply with such requests. Despite the word ''shall,'' however, there have been noteworthy examples where governors have refused to comply with requests, and courts have said there are no enforcement mechanisms for the extradition clause.

Finally, the Constitution permits states to enter into **interstate compacts** with the consent of Congress. Of little importance prior to the twentieth century, these compacts are increasingly being used to solve metropolitan and multistate problems. They are legal and binding agreements on all states signing the compact. The Port of New York Authority is the result of an interstate compact between New York and New Jersey. Thirty-three states are signatories to an interstate oil compact to avoid federal control over oil.

THE GROWTH OF NATIONAL GOVERNMENT

On all levels, government has expanded into new fields and taken on additional functions. This has meant more intergovernmental cooperation and frequent interaction between states and the national government. Some commentators claim the growth of the national government as a victory for nationalism over states rights. From a constitutional perspective this view is correct, but it ignores the purpose and cooperative nature of federalism. The growth of the national government should be viewed, rather, as a changed expectation to solve problems that once were local in nature but now are national.

McCULLOCH v. MARYLAND

The growth of national powers was early advanced by the Supreme Court in the famous case of *McCulloch* v. *Maryland* (1819). The ruling of Chief Justice John Marshall laid the cornerstone for the implied powers doctrine of enumerated powers and strongly curtailed state authority to interfere with the national government.

The case involved the Bank of the United States, Alexander Hamilton's idea of some years earlier. The Bank had been created to handle the government's monetary and financial problems, in the hope of stabilizing credit and fostering commerce. Yet by 1819, a Second National Bank had neither checked speculation nor improved financial conditions. Some branches of the bank were badly managed and a few even engaged in fraud. The branches were becoming increasingly unpopular in several states. Among these was Maryland, whose legislature in 1818 placed a heavy tax on the Baltimore branch. Maryland demanded that James W. McCulloch, cashier of the bank, pay the $15,000 annual tax. McCulloch refused, and Maryland brought suit. The Maryland court upheld the Maryland law, and the Bank appealed the case to the Supreme Court. Daniel Webster and William Pinckney argued the case for the Bank, while Luther Martin defended Maryland. After three days of argument, a unanimous Supreme Court handed down its verdict on March 6, 1819. Congress had the constitutional power to charter a national bank; the Court denied Maryland's right to interfere with its operation, thereby declaring unconstitutional Maryland's law taxing the bank.

The first issue disposed of by Chief Justice Marshall in rendering the verdict was that of the power to incorporate a bank. Using the doctrine of national sovereignty, Marshall held that the federal government derived its power directly from the people. He admitted authority was divided between the states and national government but said that, though limited, the national government's power ''is supreme within its sphere of action.'' Marshall then set forth the broad construction of implied powers. Creating the Bank was admittedly not one of the enumerated powers of Congress, but the Constitution also gave Congress powers to carry out and execute its enumerated powers. The creation of a national bank was implied by the enumerated power to coin and regulate money. As Marshall argued, ''it can never be to their [the people's] interest and cannot be presumed to have been their intention, to clog and embarrass its execution, by withholding the

A National bank. The national banking system was first created by Alexander Hamilton and Congress in 1791. (National Archives)

most appropriate means." Marshall was following the principle laid down by Hamilton in 1791: "Let the end be legitimate, let it be within the scope of the Constitution and all means which are appropriate, which are plainly adopted to that end, which are not prohibited, but consistent with the letter and spirit of the Constitution, are Constitutional."[7]

The second question in the case was Maryland's constitutional right to tax the Bank, an issue of dual federalism. Using the principle of federal supremacy, Marshall ruled that the "power to tax involves the power to destroy." Since the Bank was a legal instrument of federal authority, an act of Congress must supersede any state effort to control or limit the Bank's functions. The supremacy clause in Article VI made the laws and treaties of the United States the supreme law of the land; therefore, the Maryland law was unconstitutional.

At a very early point in the nation's history, the stage was set for the broad interpretation of national powers. Two additional constitutional provisions have supported national growth and adaptability: the power to regulate interstate commerce, and the authority to tax and spend for the general welfare.

THE COMMERCE CLAUSE

The interstate commerce clause was interpreted broadly to include all "intercourse" between the states, not merely the buying and selling of goods.[8] John Marshall again, using the same approach he had five years earlier in *McCulloch* v. *Maryland,* ruled that the operation of boats on New York waters constituted interstate commerce because they were passenger vessels engaged in "intercourse" between states.

The commerce clause has also been used to support legislation that has nothing to do with commercial affairs. The 1964 Civil Rights Act prohibiting discrimination in public accommodations was upheld by the Supreme Court because of the disruptive effect racial discrimination has on interstate travel.[9] The principle is whether the activity affects commerce, not whether it is interstate commerce. A recent exception is a 1976 Supreme Court decision declaring unconstitutional the 1974 amendments to the Fair Labor Standards Act extending minimum wages to state and local employers. This, the Court said, violated the state sovereignty guaranteed in the Tenth Amendment.[10]

The Court, charge critics, including some Supreme Court justices, has strained the commerce clause. It is not a judicial function to fix congressional authority under the commerce clause, but a political issue for Congress itself. Three justices dissenting in the 1976 case *(National League of Cities* v. *Usury)* asked for congressional restraint in the commerce power and held that such restraints lie "in the political process and not in the judicial process." The fact is

7. *McCulloch* v. *Maryland* 4 Wheaton 316 (1819).
8. *Gibbons* v. *Ogden,* 9 Wheaton 1 (1824).
9. *Heart of Atlanta Motel* v. *United States,* 379 U. S. 241 (1964).
10. *National League of Cities et al.* v. *Usury* (1976).

that the commerce clause has been adapted to our changing economic and social life: The lives of city dwellers are affected by the feed a Colorado rancher uses for his cattle. It is this growing interdependence that determines the growing scope of the regulation.

THE POWER TO TAX AND SPEND

The taxing and spending powers of the national government have also helped national authority to grow. This power raises the question of whether Congress can tax and spend for the general welfare or whether that power has to be related to its enumerated powers. The Supreme Court has concluded that Congress may tax and spend to promote the general welfare, to provide for functions it would otherwise be unable to legislate. The Supreme Court does not inquire into the motive behind an appropriation. Congress may use taxation as a means of regulation. In fact, Congress frequently attaches regulations to appropriations measures, thus legislating while it is spending. Nor does the Court make judgments or place conditions on the general welfare clause of the taxing and spending power. The conditions for taxing and spending are to be set by Congress.

In fact, until recently Congress could tax and spend for the general welfare as it saw fit, attaching whatever conditions or regulations it deemed appropriate. Taxpayers or states could not challenge that power in the courts.[11] But in 1968[12] the Supreme Court modified this stand slightly to allow taxpayers to bring suits based on a specific constitutional challenge. The courts have cautioned as recently as 1974, however, that they are not a haven for taxpayers to make "generalized grievances" against government.[13]

THE POLITICS OF FEDERALISM

The growth of the national government points to one overriding development: a nationally dominated system of shared powers and shared functions.[14] The growth of the national government has been facilitated by constitutional interpretation; it has come to have the major responsibility for providing services and regulating activities. Much of the growth in federal activity came as a result of the Depression and Franklin D. Roosevelt's New Deal. The states then had neither the financial resources nor the jurisdiction to respond; the federal government did. Since that time, in increasing areas from social security and unemployment assistance to law enforcement, resource management, civil rights, and consumer protection, the federal government has maintained its increased level of activity. The continued growth of the bureaucracy illustrates this increased activity of the

11. *Frothingham* v. *Mellon,* 262 U. S. 447 (1923); *Massachusetts* v. *Mellon,* 262 U. S. 447 (1923).
12. *Flast* v. *Cohen,* 392 U. S. 83 (1968).
13. *United States* v. *Richardson,* 418 U. S. 166 (1974).
14. Reagan, *The New Federalism,* p. 145.

federal government: Health and Human Services, Housing and Urban Development, Transportation, Energy, and Education are all new or reorganized cabinet-level departments.

But the rise of the national government points to another unmistakable trend: the increased activity of government at all levels. State and local governments are providing more services and spending more money than at any time in the past. Table 3.2 shows the relative growth in spending for all three levels of government in the twentieth century.

Table 3.2

Government Spending
(in billions of dollars)

	1902		1922		1932		1940		1950		1960		1970		1974		1980	
	$	%	$	%	$	%	$	%	$	%	$	%	$	%	$	%	$	%
Federal	0.6	35	3.6	39	4	32	9.2	44	42.4	60	90.3	60	18.5	55	254.4	53	561.3	61.6
State	0.1	6	1.1	12	2	16	3.6	18	11.9	15	22.2	15	56.2	17	86.2	18	140.5	15.4
Local	1	59	4.6	49	6.4	52	7.7	38	17	24	38.8	25	92	28	139.5	29	210	23

SOURCE: Bureau of the Census, *Pocket Data Book;* 1980 data from Bureau of the Census, preliminary estimates.

The increases and changes are closely related to key events of the twentieth century. The Depression, coupled with military spending during World War II, accounted for the great increase in federal spending in the 1930s and 1940s. That increased level of spending continued on through the 1950s and into the Great Society of the 1960s. The greatest decline has come in local expenditures as a percentage of the total. At one time local spending accounted for over half of the total expenditures; now, local spending is only one-quarter of the total public money spent. States have continued to maintain their share, which has increased somewhat in the last 30 years. Table 3.2 illustrates the growing nationalization of America's problems and the sustained activity of the national government in problem solving.

FISCAL FEDERALISM

Walter Heller, former chairman of the Council of Economic Advisers under President Kennedy, said "Prosperity gives the national government the affluence and the local governments the effluence,"[15] and it is precisely this juxtaposition

15. Walter W. Heller, *New Dimensions of Political Economy* (Cambridge: Harvard University Press, 1967), p. 129.

of federal resources and local problems that creates the need for increased federal assistance. There is a fiscal mismatch. The national government can readily increase tax revenues yearly, while state and local governments cannot. Yet the demand for services and problem solving is primarily heard at state and local levels. The result, Michael Reagan argues, is that "state–local ability to meet public demands goes down, while their dependence on federal funds and their indebtedness both increase."[16] For the state and local governments to raise sufficient revenues in the coming decades to meet their needs would not only bankrupt them but, as Congressman Henry Reuss (D. Wisc.) explains, would be socially undesirable and politically improbable, since state taxes are "inequitable and inflexible."[17] State and local taxes are inequitable because they are based primarily on regressive taxes that hit lower-income groups proportionately harder than higher-income groups, and because resources are not equal from state to state. State and local taxes are inflexible because they are commonly based on authorized limits fixed by law or state constitutions. Taxpayers are now moving to established authorization limits where none exist as a means of venting their anger over rising taxes. So only federal taxes have the progressiveness to equalize resources and the flexibility to adapt to shifting, multistate problems.

The three major categories of taxes—income tax, sales tax, and property tax—each serve as the primary source of tax revenue for a different level of government. Income taxes are the primary source of tax revenue for the federal government, accounting for 80 percent of revenues in 1978; the general sales tax is the primary tax of states, constituting 52 percent of tax income in 1978; for local governments the property tax is the backbone of revenues, making up 80 percent of the total in 1978. Collectively, for 1978, income taxes provided 60 percent of all tax revenues. Since the income tax serves as the national government's primary taxing source, it is no surprise that the national government dominates the revenue picture. This is the primary cause of our current system of fiscal federalism—grants-in-aid, categorical grants, block grants, and revenue-sharing.

Grants-in-aid are a form of money payments from the national (or state) government to state (or local) governments for specified programs under whatever conditions the granting authority wishes to impose. The actual administration of the programs for which money is received is the responsibility of the state or local government. The conditions depend in large measure on the kind of grant. The traditional categorical grants were designed for specific and narrowly defined purposes, leaving state and localities little flexibility in administering them. Block grants, on the other hand, are broad grants in some area (health or education) that leave unspecified the specific purposes for which money can be spent. These give local officials more discretion in setting goals and spending money. Closely related, but different again, is revenue-sharing. General revenue-sharing means fed-

16. Reagan, *The New Federalism*, p. 34.
17. Henry S. Reuss, *Revenue Sharing: Crutch or Catalyst for State and Local Governments?* (New York: Praeger, 1970), p. 39.

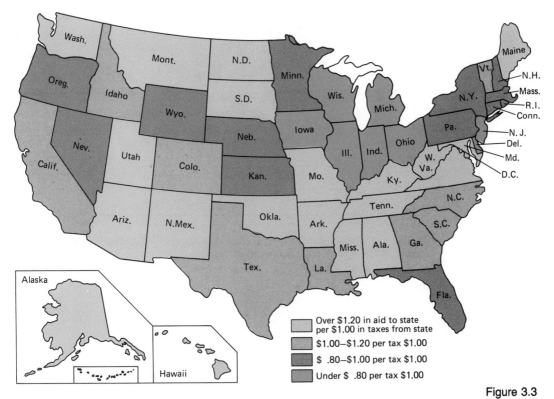

Figure 3.3
Federal aid to the states in 1976.

eral money is returned to state and local governments without prior specification of purpose and without conditions attached to its spending. The money may be spent by state and local governments as they think wisest, no strings attached.

GRANTS-IN-AID

The best proof that there is shared responsibility in federalism is the grant-in-aid system, which uses a fiscal federal relationship as its basis for cooperation. This system embodies the marble cake principle of federalism suggested by Morton Grodzins.

The Advisory Commission on Intergovernmental Relations estimated that in 1974 there were a total of 530 grant-in-aid programs. The Office of Management and Budget figures another 279 programs were added between 1974 and 1980. The number of grants is matched only by the amount of money appropriated by the grant programs. Appropriations for grants-in-aid have risen almost tenfold since 1960. The figures in Table 3.3 show the remarkable growth in federal grants-in-aid to state and local governments.

Table 3.3
Federal Grants-in-Aid, 1950-1980
(in billions)

1950	$ 2.5
1960	7.0
1965	11.0
1970	24.0
1975	49.8
1980	88.9

SOURCE: U. S. Bureau of the Census, *Statistical Abstract 1979;* 1980 Figure from Office of Management and Budget, 1981 budget.

CATEGORICAL GRANTS

Until the Depression, federal grants totaled less than $100 million annually. The major areas were for agricultural extension, highways, and vocational education. But the Depression added 14 new programs and the New Deal brought federal supervision and conditions to the grant process. Faced with a mounting urban crisis in the 1960s, Congress expanded grants almost fourfold and set up the **categorical grant** system. Congress determined the programs and provided funds. States seeking to participate in a program must commit a certain percentage of state money to match the federal funds, create a state agency to administer the program, submit written plans for administering and spending the money, and be willing to be reviewed periodically by federal officials.

State and local governments have some role in shaping the administration of the programs, although it is Congress that determines the programs and their conditions. This allows Congress to set priorities and determine needs. In 1965-66 alone there were 67 new programs: 21 in health, 17 in education, and the rest in resource development, employment, urban affairs, and economic programs. The expansion in the Great Society years saw federal aid go directly to local governments and to nongovernmental agencies such as community action groups, professional associations, and private businesses. Under Medicare, Congress has contracted with insurance companies to process the claims and, with professional associations, to determine the eligibility of participating institutions.

Until 1972, almost all grants-in-aid were categorical grants—there were 500 such programs. A major issue was the setting of priorities. To receive money, states had to apply to Washington, get approval, follow the conditions laid down

The interstate highway system is the result of categorical grant monies provided states by the national government. (The Bettmann Archive, Inc.)

by Congress, and match with some of their own money. This, critics argued, gave Washington too much control. The system not only affected the budget priorities of states and local governments, but the federal "strings" controlled the state's goals and added regulatory purposes tangential to the grant's intent.

The proliferation of grants also gave rise to the criticism that there were too many programs to administer efficiently. The federal government often threatened to withhold funds if agencies did not comply with federal regulations. Often programs would be competing and jurisdictions would overlap. Water and waste treatment grants, for example, were available from four departments: Interior, Commerce, Housing and Urban Development, and Agriculture. Coordination was weak, and delays in granting approval were common.

BLOCK GRANTS

The mounting pressure for reform of the grant system led President Nixon in the 1970s to propose consolidating many categorical grant programs into **block grants.** These are grants to state and local governments for broadly defined purposes within which local officials have discretion on the specific programs to be operated. They permit greater state control, and there are fewer conditions and increased flexibility in spending. States typically submit only a master plan for approval. The Crime Control and Safe Streets Acts of 1968 provided the first block grant money to states and cities to fight crime. In the 1970s most of the consolidation to block grants occurred in the areas of health care, law enforcement, manpower training, and education.

FACT FILE

GEOGRAPHIC DISTRIBUTION OF FEDERAL FUNDS, 1979[a]

Comparison of federal funds made by major federal organizations and ranked by states

Federal dollars spent in states (in millions)	25,059 Agriculture		3,643 Commerce		108,758 Defense		11,790 Energy		181,021 Health, Education & Welfare		6,749 Housing & Urban Development		5,826 Interior		1,704 Justice		15,178 Labor	
State	Rank	%	Rank	%	Rank	%	Rank	%	Rank	%	Rank	%	Rank	%	Rank	%	Rank	%
Alabama	28	1.5	17	1.0	19	1.6	30	.3	20	1.6	19	1.7	43	.4	30	.9	20	1.5
Alaska	43	.5	16	1.1	34	.6	42	.0	51	.1	50	.1	4	6.7	45	.2	38	.6
Arizona	38	.9	36	.4	22	1.4	43	.0	32	1.0	35	.7	3	8.1	12	1.9	23	1.4
Arkansas	23	1.7	27	.5	38	.5	45	.0	31	1.0	32	.9	41	.5	32	.5	33	.9
California	2	7.0	6	4.6	1	17.1	3	8.6	2	9.7	2	7.7	2	10.0	2	11.3	1	11.7
Colorado	19	2.0	9	3.0	23	1.4	17	2.4	35	.9	30	.9	5	6.0	17	1.5	29	1.2
Connecticut	41	.8	31	.4	8	3.7	28	.3	25	1.4	20	1.6	46	.2	25	1.1	26	1.3
Delaware	50	.1	46	.2	45	.2	49	.0	48	.2	47	.2	49	.1	50	.2	47	.3
District of Columbia	20	1.8	2	12.3	17	1.8	11	3.3	22	1.6	8	4.3	1	10.2	1	18.6	4	5.0
Florida	8	2.9	12	1.7	5	4.0	24	.6	4	5.1	11	2.8	22	1.3	7	3.8	10	3.4
Georgia	10	2.4	23	.7	13	2.4	32	.1	16	1.9	13	2.1	15	1.7	8	2.5	13	2.0
Hawaii	45	.3	32	.4	25	1.3	41	.0	42	.3	42	.3	44	.3	39	.4	41	.5
Idaho	37	1.1	44	.2	48	.2	16	2.4	45	.3	46	.2	9	2.6	46	.2	44	.4
Illinois	6	3.3	25	.6	18	1.8	10	3.5	5	4.8	4	5.3	35	.6	5	4.0	6	4.1
Indiana	27	1.5	15	1.2	20	1.5	35	.1	14	2.1	21	1.6	39	.5	19	1.4	15	1.9
Iowa	7	3.2	45	.2	42	.4	34	.1	26	1.3	29	.9	45	.2	37	.4	34	.7
Kansas	11	2.4	38	.3	27	1.1	48	.0	33	1.0	31	.9	31	.7	21	1.3	36	.6
Kentucky	26	1.6	26	.5	30	1.0	9	3.8	24	1.5	24	1.4	34	.6	18	1.5	25	1.3
Louisiana	17	2.1	3	10.4	28	1.0	5	7.4	23	1.5	22	1.6	33	.7	27	1.1	21	1.5
Maine	44	.4	30	.5	35	.5	47	.0	37	.5	37	.5	47	.2	38	.4	40	.5
Maryland	34	1.2	1	12.8	10	3.1	8	4.2	15	2.1	17	1.8	27	.8	20	1.3	18	1.6
Massachusetts	36	1.1	13	1.6	9	3.3	23	1.0	10	3.2	7	4.5	24	1.0	15	1.8	11	3.2
Michigan	18	2.1	19	.8	16	1.9	29	.3	8	4.2	9	3.6	28	.8	9	2.3	7	3.9
Minnesota	4	4.1	33	.4	29	1.0	33	.1	19	1.7	18	1.8	21	1.3	22	1.3	27	1.2
Mississippi	21	1.8	18	.9	26	1.2	38	.1	30	1.1	28	1.0	29	.8	36	.5	32	.9
Missouri	14	2.3	21	.8	6	3.8	18	2.0	11	2.2	12	2.4	25	.9	10	2.3	16	1.9
Montana	30	1.4	34	.4	47	.2	27	.4	43	.3	44	.3	13	2.2	42	.3	42	.4
Nebraska	5	3.4	49	.2	39	.4	50	.0	36	.6	39	.5	40	.5	43	.3	45	.3
Nevada	51	.1	42	.2	43	.3	13	2.8	49	.2	48	.2	14	1.9	41	.3	43	.4
New Hampshire	47	.2	43	.2	37	.5	44	.0	41	.4	41	.3	50	.1	49	.2	49	.2

	412		16,632		11,685		5,332		3,306		4,725		21,177		46,749		
	State		Transportation		Treasury		Environmental Protection Agency		General Services Administration		National Aeronautic Space Administration		Veterans Administration		All Other		Total State Funds
Rank	%	Rank	%	Rank	%	Rank	%	Rank	%	Rank	%	Rank	%	Rank	%	States	Mil-lions
																Total	
23	.1	25	1.3	24	1.2	30	1.0	17	.9	6	4.5	17	2.0	17	1.9	Alabama	7,419
	.0	22	1.5	44	.3	44	.4	26	.3	38	.0	51	.1	49	.2	Alaska	1,932
21	.1	29	1.0	29	.9	25	1.3	21	.5	19	.4	26	1.5	27	1.0	Arizona	5,539
36	.0	32	.9	35	.7	43	.4	39	.2	47	.0	25	1.5	35	.7	Arkansas	3,958
6	2.4	3	6.1	3	10.1	2	7.5	6	5.3	1	39.5	1	9.5	3	8.1	California	52,534
28	.0	15	2.1	28	1.0	28	1.1	10	2.4	14	1.3	30	1.3	24	1.2	Colorado	6,211
18	.2	28	1.1	26	1.0	31	1.0	38	.2	9	2.1	35	1.0	29	.9	Connecticut	8,268
30	.0	48	.3	47	.2	45	.4	32	.3	39	.0	48	.3	50	.2	Delaware	1,029
1	65.5	1	10.3	1	12.3	3	5.9	1	24.1	13	1.5	12	2.5	6	4.8	Dist. of Columbia	15,435
12	1.0	7	4.2	10	2.6	7	3.7	19	.8	2	9.4	4	5.2	8	3.7	Florida	19,648
16	.4	12	2.7	12	2.4	20	1.7	9	2.9	25	.2	10	2.7	16	2.0	Georgia	9,727
32	.0	39	.7	40	.4	38	.6	45	.1	31	.1	46	.3	39	.4	Hawaii	2,659
44	.0	45	.4	43	.3	39	.5	40	.2	48	.0	44	.3	45	.3	Idaho	1,838
14	.8	4	5.9	6	4.2	8	3.7	3	5.9	23	.3	7	3.6	1	11.0	Illinois	20,785
9	1.2	23	1.4	22	1.5	21	1.6	15	1.1	21	.4	22	1.7	20	1.4	Indiana	7,934
41	.0	34	.8	32	.9	32	1.0	41	.2	29	.1	32	1.2	30	.9	Iowa	4,650
37	.0	33	.9	36	.7	37	.6	36	.2	33	.0	34	1.1	28	1.0	Kansas	4,731
43	.0	27	1.3	20	1.6	29	1.0	27	.3	37	.0	24	1.6	18	1.6	Kentucky	6,604
24	.1	24	1.3	18	1.6	24	1.3	35	.2	8	2.8	21	1.7	26	1.0	Louisiana	7,500
46	.0	43	.4	38	.5	35	.7	44	.1	42	.0	38	.6	40	.4	Maine	2,263
5	2.9	14	2.4	17	1.6	15	2.3	11	2.3	4	8.4	27	1.4	11	2.7	Maryland	11,649
15	.7	8	4.0	9	3.0	10	3.2	13	2.1	16	1.1	8	3.0	13	2.3	Massachusetts	13,711
10	1.2	16	2.0	7	3.4	9	3.6	2	20.1	22	.3	9	2.8	15	2.0	Michigan	14,328
13	.9	17	2.0	21	1.5	16	2.1	29	.3	24	.2	20	1.8	22	1.3	Minnesota	7,314
25	.1	35	.8	27	1.0	27	1.1	31	.3	18	.6	29	1.3	31	.9	Mississippi	5,036
22	.1	18	1.9	13	2.1	18	1.8	4	5.6	26	.1	15	2.2	14	2.1	Missouri	11,923
48	.0	42	.5	42	.3	47	.4	34	.2	50	.0	43	.4	42	.3	Montana	1,754
45	.0	40	.6	37	.5	49	.3	42	.1	46	.0	36	.7	33	.8	Nebraska	3,314
42	.0	41	.6	46	.2	40	.5	43	.1	36	.0	45	.3	46	.3	Nevada	1,673
33	.0	47	.4	45	.2	36	.7	50	.1	34	.0	42	.4	44	.3	New Hampshire	1,667

GEOGRAPHIC DISTRIBUTION OF FEDERAL FUNDS, 1979[a] (Continued).

Comparison of federal funds made by major federal organizations and ranked by states

| | 25,059 | | 3,643 | | 108,758 | | 11,790 | | 181,021 | | 6,749 | | 5,826 | | 1,704 | | 15,178 | |
| Federal dollars spent in states (in millions) | Agriculture | | Commerce | | Defense | | Energy | | Health, Education & Welfare | | Housing & Urban Development | | Interior | | Justice | | Labor | |
State	Rank	%	Rank	%	Rank	%	Rank	%	Rank	%	Rank	%	Rank	%	Rank	%	Rank	%
New Jersey	32	1.4	11	1.9	14	2.1	19	1.8	9	3.4	10	3.5	37	.5	11	1.9	9	3.7
New Mexico	39	.8	37	.3	33	.7	4	7.6	39	.5	38	.5	6	5.9	35	.5	35	.7
New York	1	7.6	4	6.1	4	5.1	14	2.8	1	10.0	1	11.9	20	1.4	4	7.0	2	8.9
North Carolina	13	2.3	14	1.4	15	2.0	39	.0	13	2.1	14	1.9	30	.7	23	1.2	19	1.6
North Dakota	24	1.7	47	.2	44	.3	36	.1	46	.3	45	.2	23	1.1	47	.2	48	.2
Ohio	16	2.1	24	.6	12	2.5	7	5.5	7	4.4	5	5.0	26	.8	13	1.9	5	4.2
Oklahoma	33	1.2	35	.4	24	1.4	22	1.1	27	1.2	26	1.2	18	1.5	26	1.1	31	1.0
Oregon	9	2.7	20	.8	41	.4	20	1.3	28	1.1	33	.8	7	4.1	31	.7	28	1.2
Pennsylvania	12	2.3	5	5.2	7	3.7	15	2.5	3	6.0	3	6.2	16	1.6	6	3.8	3	5.8
Rhode Island	49	.2	39	.3	40	.4	46	.0	38	.5	36	.7	48	.2	44	.3	39	.5
South Carolina	35	1.2	28	.5	21	1.4	12	3.0	29	1.1	27	1.0	36	.6	33	.5	30	1.0
South Dakota	31	1.4	48	.2	49	.2	40	.0	44	.3	43	.3	17	1.6	48	.2	46	.3
Tennessee	15	2.3	22	.7	31	.9	1	11.5	17	1.8	16	1.9	42	.4	28	1.0	22	1.5
Texas	3	6.7	7	3.2	2	7.9	21	1.1	6	4.7	6	4.9	19	1.5	3	8.2	8	3.9
Utah	40	.8	40	.3	32	.8	26	.4	40	.4	40	.3	8	2.9	40	.3	37	.6
Vermont	48	.2	50	.1	51	.1	51	.0	47	.2	49	.2	51	.1	34	.5	50	.2
Virginia	29	1.4	8	3.0	3	6.1	2	9.6	18	1.8	15	1.9	10	2.5	16	1.7	17	1.6
Washington	25	1.6	10	2.5	11	2.9	6	6.6	21	1.6	25	1.3	12	2.3	14	1.8	14	2.0
West Virginia	42	.6	41	.2	46	.2	31	.2	34	.9	34	.7	32	.7	29	1.0	12	2.7
Wisconsin	22	1.7	29	.5	36	.5	37	.1	12	2.2	23	1.5	38	.5	24	1.2	24	1.4
Wyoming	46	.3	51	.1	50	.1	25	.5	50	.1	51	.1	11	2.4	51	.1	51	.2

a. The organizational units were chosen as traditionally tabulated items of general interest which are the agency categories similar to those shown in the federal budget.

SOURCE: Community Services Administration, Executive Office of the President.

Yet block grants, too, have been controversial. Members of Congress and federal officials are reluctant to give up control. They fear a "waste" of money if state and local governments control priorities. Congress also worries about satisfying constituents and interest groups if it lacks control over spending. Many beneficiaries of categorical grants also raised objections. Civil rights and welfare groups have been particularly outspoken critics of the consolidation. Law enforcement officials objected that the 1968 Crime Control Act gave too much money to

State		Transportation		Treasury		Environmental Protection Agency		General Services Administration		National Aeronautic Space Administration		Veterans Administration		All Other		States	Total State Funds
412		16,632		11,685		5,332		3,306		4,725		21,177		46,749			
Rank	%	Rank	%	Rank	%	Rank	%	Rank	%	Rank	%	Rank	%	Rank	%		Millions
																Total	
8	1.2	10	2.8	11	2.5	11	3.1	16	1.0	15	1.2	16	2.2	12	2.5	New Jersey	12,629
19	.2	36	.7	39	.4	48	.3	25	.4	20	.4	37	.7	38	.5	New Mexico	3,894
2	11.4	2	6.8	2	10.4	1	9.1	5	5.4	12	1.5	2	7.1	2	8.8	New York	37,112
7	1.9	21	1.6	14	1.7	6	4.0	23	.4	30	.1	11	2.6	21	1.4	North Carolina	9,035
50	.0	46	.4	50	.2	51	.2	46	.1		.0	47	.3	48	.2	North Dakota	1,580
17	.3	9	3.0	8	3.2	4	5.8	18	.8	7	4.0	6	3.9	9	3.1	Ohio	16,576
39	.0	19	1.7	34	.8	33	.8	33	.3	35	.0	23	1.6	23	1.3	Oklahoma	5,892
27	.0	31	1.0	31	.9	19	1.7	20	.5	32	.1	31	1.2	32	.8	Oregon	4,828
11	1.0	5	5.2	5	4.6	5	5.2	14	1.6	10	2.1	5	4.6	7	4.6	Pennsylvania	22,351
35	.0	51	.2	41	.3	34	.8	49	.1	40	.0	40	.5	41	.4	Rhode Island	1,927
29	.0	37	.7	25	1.1	26	1.2	37	.2	41	.0	28	1.4	34	.7	South Carolina	5,378
49	.0	44	.4	48	.2	46	.4	47	.1	44	.0	41	.5	47	.2	South Dakota	1,549
34	.0	20	1.6	15	1.7	22	1.6	22	.4	28	.1	14	2.3	4	5.8	Tennessee	10,418
3	3.1	6	4.4	4	4.8	12	2.8	8	3.5	3	9.2	3	6.7	5	5.5	Texas	26,232
38	.0	38	.7	30	.9	41	.5	24	.4	11	1.5	39	.5	37	.6	Utah	2,849
40	.0	50	.3	49	.2	42	.5	51	.1	45	.0	49	.3	51	.2	Vermont	918
4	2.9	13	2.6	19	1.6	14	2.3	7	4.3	5	4.8	13	2.5	10	3.0	Virginia	15,079
20	.2	11	2.8	23	1.2	13	2.6	12	2.2	17	.9	18	1.9	19	1.6	Washington	9,920
31	.0	30	1.0	33	.9	17	2.1	28	.3	49	.0	33	1.1	36	.7	West Virginia	3,545
26	.0	26	1.3	16	1.6	23	1.5	30	.3	27	.1	19	1.8	25	1.1	Wisconsin	6,835
47	.0	49	.3	51	.1	50	.3	48	.1	43	.0	50	.2	43	.3	Wyoming	954

suburban police departments and too little to urban forces who dealt with far more crime. Mayors were unhappy as money was channeled to states rather than localities; they felt urban problems were not receiving enough attention or support.

The result has been that only some programs have been shifted over to block grants. The political struggle between a Democratic Congress and President Nixon in the 1970s prevented further consolidation. For the Administration, it was a matter of efficiency and local autonomy to consolidate categorical programs. When Congress resisted, President Nixon **impounded** funds; that is, he refused to spend money appropriated by the Congress for the programs he most disliked. For liberal Democrats in Congress, Mr. Nixon's effort to consolidate or eliminate categorical programs was an attack on governmental assistance and public welfare programs for blacks and minorities, those most in need of support. The net result was that some programs were consolidated, and others were left as categorical grants. Both critics and proponents then turned their attention to revenue-sharing.

REVENUE-SHARING

When Richard Nixon proposed revenue-sharing in 1969, he said it was time to stop the expansion of the national government. Revenue-sharing, Mr. Nixon argued, "marks a turning point in federal–state relations, the beginning of decentralization of governmental power, the restoration of a rightful balance between the state capitals and the national capital."

Revenue-sharing, or returning a portion of the federal tax revenues back to state and local governments to spend as they see fit with no conditions or requirements, is not new. Andrew Jackson once distributed a federal budget surplus among the states. In 1958, Melvin Laird, then a Republican congressman from Wisconsin and later secretary of defense for President Nixon, proposed returning tax money to the states. In 1960, Walter Heller, who was to become chairman of the Council of Economic Advisers under Presidents Kennedy and Johnson, presented a plan. But neither proposal received much attention or support. By 1967-68, however, there were over 100 bills with some 30 variations of revenue-sharing introduced into the Congress.[18] Congressmen and senators were coming to endorse the idea; both presidential candidates in the 1968 election supported the proposal.

Soon after his inauguration in 1969, Mr. Nixon proposed the "New Federalism," which was designed to rebalance the federal-state relationship. Central to the New Federalism was revenue-sharing. The president proposed that the federal government turn back tax revenues to the states to spend, with only the stipulation that states "pass through" a portion of the money to the cities and local governments.

In 1972, Congress passed the State and Local Fiscal Assistance Act, authorizing a sum of $30.2 billion to be returned to state and local governments over a five-year period, with one-third of the funds for states and two-thirds of the funds to be distributed to local governments. There had been considerable opposition. Democrats were suspicious; Wilbur Mills, then chairman of the powerful House Ways and Means Committee, was flatly opposed. Organized labor had been opposed. Mayors were fearful because they worried that states would

18. Reagan, *The New Federalism,* p. 90.

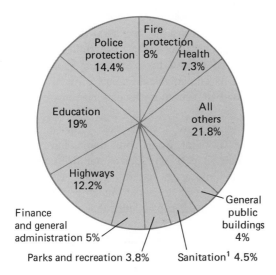

Figure 3.4

Reported use of the revenue-sharing dollar, 1979. (U.S. Treasury Department, Office of Revenue Sharing)

eat up the funds and cities would receive little aid; so Congress had delayed. Then Vietnam was over, however, and revenue-sharing did not threaten existing programs; the categorical grants-in-aid were to remain. A substantial percentage of money would go to local and urban governments, thus pacifying the mayors. As the president had requested, there were relatively few strings attached to use of the funds: money could be spent for needed services, whatever they were.

The Office of Revenue Sharing in the Treasury Department began to distribute the money, more than $6 billion, in 1972. The entitlement of each government was calculated by a formula that included population, tax effort, and per capita income. Despite suspicion and uncertainty, revenue-sharing has proved relatively successful. Most public officials appear satisfied. A survey in 1973 reported that 75 percent of local public officials were satisfied with revenue-sharing and only 10 percent were really dissatisfied with it.[19] The support figure has fallen since, but it remains high.

How has revenue-sharing money been spent? Figure 3.4 shows that in 1979 state and local governments were spending revenue-sharing money for public safety, education, and transportation. There have been some differences in spending patterns between state and local governments. The major areas of expenditures for local governments have been public safety (39 percent) and capital outlays for buildings and construction projects (33 percent), followed by public transportation (9 percent), environmental protection (6 percent), and health services (5 percent).[20] States report spending over half of their money for education. (Local

19. David A. Caputo and Richard Z. Cole, "Initial Decisions in General Revenue Sharing," *Municipal Year Book,* 1974, p. 99.
20. Parris N. Glendening and Mavis Mann Reeves, *Programatic Federalism* (Pacific Palisades, Calif.: Palisades Publishing 1977), p. 175.

governments were forbidden by the 1972 act from using their funds for education.) One must be careful in measuring the fiscal impact of revenue-sharing on spending patterns, however, because of the **"fungibility"** of money. A community may report earmarking general revenue-sharing money for police and fire protection, and then transfer an equivalent amount of local tax receipts out of the police and fire budgets and allocate those funds for an entirely different program, say road maintenance.

There has been some move toward—and criticism of—using revenue-sharing funds to provide tax relief. Some communities have placed general revenue-sharing money in their budgets to reduce or stabilize taxes, thus reducing the strain on local sources and appeasing taxpayer groups. However, there has been no strong trend toward using revenue-sharing funds for tax relief. A study by the National Science Foundation in 1976 concluded that

> (1) The principal impact of the program was to expand the capital outlays of local governments, and to extend the transfer payments of state governments; (2) more revenue-sharing funds were used to maintain or expand operating programs; and (3) both at the local and state levels, GRS funds appear to have been used primarily to support ongoing activities, with only modest amounts of revenue-sharing monies going to activities that would be appropriately characterized as innovative.[21]

In the Fall of 1976, Congress extended the revenue-sharing program until September 1980, and $25.5 billion was appropriated for a 45-month period. All the essential features of the earlier program were continued. Two-thirds of the money goes to local general-purpose governments and one-third to states. The formula for distribution was retained, with a limit of $6.85 billion a year as the maximum amount of money to be distributed. The only changes in the 1976 extension were stronger provisions against discrimination and for greater public participation in deciding how the funds are to be used. Public meetings must be held and they must be publicized in the newspapers before any decision on budgeting the money can take place. The secretary of the treasury and the attorney general have been given authority to ensure compliance with the antidiscriminatory civil rights provisions. In addition, the law requires state and local governments to report more fully on where the money is being spent, but no accounting procedures are required.

The debate over revenue-sharing continues. President Carter, originally reluctant to recommend reauthorization, has proposed continuation of revenue-sharing for the 1980s; supporters argue that it combines the best of cooperative sharing: the federal tax dollar expands the public sector, yet the return places no undue burden on state and local governments. The result, they say, has been to increase the authority of state and local governments, to bring problem solving

21. *Ibid.*

back to the people closest to the problems. Supporters also argue that revenue-sharing has relieved some of the financial strain on local and state governments. It gives government the flexibility to finance essential services without having to raise taxes.

Opponents continue to emphasize national goals and the need for Washington to have control over programs on natural resource management, poverty and low income protection, health care, and civil rights if these programs are to be real national priorities. If local governments continue to determine how funds are spent, revenue-sharing will hurt blacks, low-income families, and other disadvantaged groups. To counter the argument, Congress in 1976, passed **countercyclical revenue-sharing,** emergency federal grant funding to communities where the unemployment rate reaches 6.5 percent or more. Since such communities are adversely affected by the general revenue-sharing formula, countercyclical aid provides an anti-recessional financial boost to areas facing severe economic and fiscal problems. President Carter has recommended extending countercyclical aid. Another charge of the critics is the inability of states and local governments to plan to spend the money wisely. State legislatures meet infrequently, are filled with generalist citizens, and often are unsympathetic to social problems. There is little accountability for the use of funds. Some would prefer that the funds be given directly to specialists, such as welfare agencies, educational administrators, and chiefs of police. The political control, critics contend, leads to politically expedient decisions, foolish spending, and tax reductions that reduce the effectiveness of the program's purpose.

THE FUTURE OF FEDERALISM

The debate over federalism is by no means over. For 200 years we have experimented with a federal arrangement. The Constitutional Convention did not settle the issue. If anything, it heightened its potential for conflict. Historical events have often focused attention on the federal basis of the Union. Some settled issues of federal-state relations are: court decisions on commerce, federal supremacy, and taxing authority; the Civil War and the question of slavery. Still other issues have dramatized the failure of the federal system to simply or clearly distribute power and solve problems: The Depression, civil rights, urban living, poverty, environmental regulation, and urban bankruptcy have all altered our thinking on federalism.

Revenue-sharing had its measure of success, but it has proved no panacea. It amounts to only 11 percent of the federal revenue shared with state and local governments. Newer reforms are likely to alter the balance of power between Washington and the states. The problems facing America in the 1980s transcend the simplistic conceptualizations of federalism as a neat tripartite division of power among three layers of government. For a nation spending three-quarters of a trillion dollars annually, political life is much too complex for this to work.

Revenue Sharing and Public Policy

Revenue sharing has been part of the federal partnership for almost a decade. Whether the impact of revenue sharing was intended to be distributive or redistributive as a policy is a source of debate. Some feel the program had redistributive potential as part of new federalism but has evolved into a distributional program of funding states, cities, and counties. What are the public policy implications of revenue sharing?

Richard Nathan has suggested three ways to evaluate the policy effects of revenue sharing on state and local governments: distributional, fiscal, and political.[1]

The distributional effects of revenue sharing concern the formula for distributing $6 billion annually. One-third of the money goes to states, two-thirds to local governments. The formula distributes money based on population, urbanization, per capita income, state income taxes, and general tax effort. Population appears to be the critical variable. Since the need for federal funds is most acute in America's urban centers, the population variable would favor urban cities. The formula, however, places a ceiling of 145 percent on the per capita entitlement of revenue-sharing funds. The distribution of federal funds and needs of urban areas is becoming more of a concern. As of 1980, 45 states showed budget surpluses—32 of them in excess of revenue sharing funds received.[2] Several policy alternatives emerge.

1. *Elimination of the state's one-third share.* Either as a means to provide more funds for local government or as a means of reducing federal expenditures to balance the budget, there is growing support for this option. President Carter supports the proposal.

2. *Threshold eligibility requirements.* The vast majority of local government recipients are New England and midwestern townships and counties under 5,000 persons. Many could be eliminated by establishing population thresholds or minimal funding levels in order to qualify for revenue-sharing funds.

3. *Additionl formula factors.* In order to compensate for urban hardships, additional formula factors could be added for cities. Such items as population density and age of housing units would directly benefit urban areas.

The second policy effect of revenue sharing concerns the impact of funds upon the finances of state and local governments. The largest issue is whether revenue sharing has facilitated new programs for governments, assisted in social service areas, or has been a tax fund replacement. The Brookings study on the use of revenue sharing categorizes spending of revenue sharing accordingly:

Public sector impact
1. new spending
   a. new captial uses
   b. expanded operations
   c. increased pay and benefits
2. maintained spending
   a. program maintenance
   b. federal aid restoration

Private sector impact
1. tax reduction
2. tax stabilization
   a. stabilization
   b. avoidance of borrowing[3]

In general the Brookings people found little funding for social service programs, but all governments did spend a close majority of funds in new spending areas.

The political impact of revenue sharing raises three policy issues. The first issue is decentralization. Revenue sharing was part of new federalism allowing states and localities more discretionary authority. Its strongest supporters stress the shift in policy making from Washington to state and local governments. The second issue, which is closely allied, is dependency on the federal government for collecting and dispensing tax revenues. Some analysts suggest this promotes fiscal irresponsibility in states, leaving taxation to the federal government. The final issue is growing awareness of the use of revenue sharing resulting in a competitive politization of budget making by local governments.[4] The influx of discretionary federal funds, and its visibility, brings interest groups and public officials into conflict over shares of the money in local budgets and how they should be spent.

1. Richard P. Nathan, "Methodology for Monitoring Revenue Sharing," *Public Policy Making in a Fderal System,* eds., Charles O. Jones and Robert D. Thomas (Beverly Hills, Calif.: Sage Publications, 1976), p. 65.
2. *National Journal,* April 19, 1980, p. 638.
3. Richard P. Nathan and Associates, *Revenue Sharing: The Second Round* (Washington, D.C.: Brookings Institution, 1976), p. 32.
4. Nathan, "Methodology for Monitoring Revenue Sharing," p. 76.

The future of American federalism will continue to be intimately related to the future of national politics. The continual shifts in population, both growth and migration, will affect the resources of states as well as the nature of their problems. Economic development and social conditions in the nation generally are reflected in the individual states. Employment, urban blight, and technology are all problems that must be faced. The plight of the cities means more federal assistance. Demands for services and support for disadvantaged citizens conflict with those of overburdened taxpayers unhappy with the spiraling cost of government services. The future is apparent. Centralization of federal financial assistance will continue. States and localities will become more and more dependent on the federal dollar. Revenue-sharing is likely to continue, but it will not redress the balance between the states and the national government. Categorical grants will remain a part of fiscal federalism. But if national financing is to play a central role, services will continue to be shared. It seems improbable that the federal government will take over or control more services. "New Federalism" points in the opposite direction.

The trend of the future is probably toward multistate regionalism. This seems a midpoint between federal control and the untenable position of state and local programs extending beyond local legal boundaries. It is a recognition that crime, pollution, energy development, and transportation transcend localities. Regional organizations promote interstate cooperation and aid in solving interstate conflicts. They enable a group of states to pursue solutions within an area without concern for established jurisdictions. They are also a means to decentralize administrative decision-making and improve coordination. Organizations have been

New York Mayor Edward Koch testifying before Congress on the need for more federal money for New York City. (United Press International)

successful in the past. The Tennessee Valley Authority works to provide power, irrigation, and water management to the Tennessee Valley; the Delaware River Basin Commission manages water resources and prevents pollution in the Delaware basin (which affects New York, New Jersey, Pennsylvania, and Delaware), and the Appalachian Regional Commission administers special financial assistance programs for the depressed regions of 13 states constituting the Commission. More pressing is the need for metropolitan organizations to address the problems affecting urban America. The ability of cities and states, backed by federal resources, to launch coordinated programs will be a major priority in the future.

Finally, pragmatic federalism as a variation of cooperative federalism is likely to remain. The constitutional issues are likely to win some supporters and do continue to shape federalism by enabling the system to undertake and cooperate in problem-solving. It has become clear, however, that the demands of citizens for government to meet new needs and solve problems form an institutional imperative. The people want problems solved, not jurisdictional stalemates; what works, whatever the authority or level, is the essence of pragmatic federalism. The faith of a people in their government is at stake. People are pessimistic and cynical. Taxpayers revolt, demanding efficiency and economy in government. Yet the essence of federalism is the system's ability to adjust and to adapt to new situations. The movement throughout the 1970s has been for more state and local autonomy in spending federal funds. Should the 1980s require greater national control of priorities and problem solving, the federal system is flexible enough to provide it, and our attitude toward federalism is pragmatic enough to allow it.

SUMMARY

1. Federalism, as a system of divided authority between the national government and the states, has its origins in shared decision making to solve common problems.

2. The history of the nation–state relationship changed with the development and growth of the nation. From early efforts to define separate boundaries, to more recent cooperative ventures, federalism has proven a flexible set of standards. There has been very little concern over constitutionally separated power.

3. In the distribution of power, the national government has enumerated powers while the states retain reserved powers. Interpretation of the powers of the national government, however, has greatly broadened those powers. Yet states remain strong and viable entities in the federal scheme.

4. Fiscal federalism illustrates the dependence of state and local governments on federal government spending as federal aid has been pumped into communities as a means of maintaining the federal partnership. State and local governments are likely to remain heavily dependent on the federal dollar in support of public programs.

5. Revenue-sharing seeks to provide federal money to states and localities without specifying how or where it should be used. Supporters like revenue-sharing because it prompts local autonomy yet keeps the federal dollars coming. Critics argue for the need to establish national goals, not allowing states or communities to spend for brick and mortar or reduced taxes.

block grants   99
categorical grants   98
confederation   80
concurrent powers   87
cooperative
   federalism   85–86
countercyclical revenue-
   sharing   107
dual federalism   84
enumerated
   powers   86–87
extradition   91
federalism   80
fiscal federalism   96

full faith and credit   90
fungibility   106
horizontal
   federalism   90
implied powers   87
impoundment   104
inherent power   87
interstate compact   91
new federalism   86
privileges and
   immunities   90
reserved powers   87
revenue-sharing   104
unitary government   80

**RESEARCH
PROJECTS**

3.1. Multiple Governments. How many government jurisdictions are there in your city or area? First make a list of government units you are aware of without consulting any reference source. Next take the phone book to see if you can locate any more. Finally consult the *Blue Book* for your state and the *Census of Governments–Govermental Organization* published by the Bureau of the Census to find a complete listing of government units. (Hint: Don't forget school districts, park districts, airport authorities, and water management districts.)

3.2. The Federal Dollar. How much federal money does your state and city or town receive? The most complete source to find this is the *Geographical Distribution of Federal Funds* published each year by the Community Services Division of the Executive Office of the President. Other good sources are the *Census of Government–Compendium of Government Finances* published by the Bureau of the Census and the *Book of the States* printed each year by the Council of State Legislatures.

3.3. Revenue-Sharing. In examining federal funds in your state and city, you can find how much federal revenue-sharing money your state and town receives. The *Statistical Abstract* will also provide this data. How does your local government use these funds? Is the money being spent for new programs, capital improvements, or to keep the cost of local taxes down? You might interview some local public officials—

mayor, council members, auditor—to see their views toward revenue-sharing and its use.

3.4. National Priorities. Do national issues take precedence over state or local matters? Is the national government the center of our attention? Watch a local television newscast (not national news) and compare numbers of stories on national, state, and local affairs. Do the same for a local or state newspaper (*The New York Times* would *not* be a good example) to examine coverage of events on the national, state, and local levels. You might have to do this for more than one day as unique news events may prejudice the results.

BIBLIOGRAPHY

Elazer, Daniel. *American Federalism: A View From the States*. New York: Thomas Y. Crowell, 1972.

A basic work on federalism. Elazer approaches federalism as a partnership, and he discusses federalism as it has changed over the years. Much of the book looks at federalism from the states' viewpoint. Elazer has much good information on the states, including their political culture.

Glendening, Parris, and Mavis Reeves. *Pragmatic Federalism*. Pacific Palisades, Calif.: Palisades Publishers, 1977.

A very good treatment of federal–state relations with particular attention to the political environment within which it operates. The view here is that federalism is an evolving, pragmatic effort to work out solutions to issues as they arise.

Goldwin, Robert (ed). *A Nation of States*. Chicago: Rand McNally, 1963.

A collection of essays on federalism. Some essays examine the history and intent of federalism, while others defend or criticize the national government's role in federalism.

Grodzins, Morton. *The American System*. Chicago: Rand McNally, 1966.

An extensive history of federalism from the perspective that federalism has always meant shared·responsibility. Grodzins' is a valuable source book that provides an indispensible understanding of federalism and the various areas of shared authority.

Nathan, Richard, *et al. Monitoring Revenue Sharing*. Washington, D. C.: Brookings Institution, 1975.

A major work that provides an in-depth study of revenue-sharing. The work looks at how cities and states use their revenue-sharing money. There is a great deal of data, and the authors seek to assess what groups most benefit from the use of revenue-sharing.

Reagan, Michael. *The New Federalism*. New York: Oxford University Press, 1972.

A sharp and insightful discussion of federalism. Reagan is critical and politically astute. New Federalism is intergovernmental relations where policy expands government largely through federal grants-in-aid. This, Reagan says, alters our understanding and approach toward federalism.

Riker, William. *Federalism: Origins, Operation, Significance*. Boston: Little, Brown, 1964.

Riker provides the most critical assessment of federalism. The book, however, seeks to develop a theory of federalism by examining federal governments in Europe and elsewhere as well as in America.

Sanford, Terry. *Storm Over the States*. New York: McGraw-Hill, 1967.

Sanford provides a first-hand look at federal–state relations (Sanford was Governor of North Carolina from 1961 to 1965). His effort is to set forth the most urgent problems facing states, examining how the federal government has and has not helped, and to give some suggestions for change.

Sharkansky, Ira. *The Maligned States*. New York: McGraw-Hill, 1978.

A defense of states; Sharkansky feels state autonomy and flexibility in dealing with problems has considerable merit. While noting differences between states, on balance, state accomplishments to provide services and deal with social problems has been good.

Wright, Deil. *Understanding Intergovernmental Relations*. Cambridge, Mass.: Duxbury Press, 1978.

A very good study of intergovernmental relations. Wright provides a strong measure of analysis to accompany his description and discussion of intergovernmental relations. Much of the volume focuses on finances and attitudes toward intergovernmental activities.

Chapter

4

Individual Liberty and the First Amendment

"The preservation of the sacred fire of liberty, and the destiny of the republican model of government, are justly considered as deeply, perhaps as finally, staked on the experiment entrusted to the hands of the American people." So said George Washington at his first inaugural. Washington was voicing the eternal problem of individual liberty and authority vested with a community. Liberty and authority are difficult to balance, and particularly so in a democratic society. A constitutional republic was a government of limited and enumerated powers emanating from a written constitution. It was devised to protect individual liberty. At the convention, Charles Pinckney said of the Constitution: "Our true situation appears to me to be this— a new, extensive country containing within itself the materials of forming a government capable of extending to its citizens all the blessings of civil and religious liberty, capable of making them happy at home."

James Madison saw the problem clearly in *Federalist* No. 51: "In framing a government which is to be administered by men over men, the great difficulty lies in this: you must first enable the government to control the governed; and in the next place, to control itself." The Supreme Court has understood the issue in exactly this way; it has been a staunch defender of civil liberties. The rule of law that the justices are sworn to uphold is the substance and sustenance of civil liberty. As Mr. Justice Black wrote: "The worst citizen no less than the best is entitled to equal protection of the laws of his state and his nation."[1]

1. *Bell* v. *Maryland,* 378 U. S. 226 (1964).

FUNDAMENTAL FREEDOMS

Democratic government is created for the well-being of its citizens. Constitutional government must protect civil liberties and rights. But how? And which were to be considered basic and inviolable, an individual's fundamental liberties? Mr. Justice Cardozo spoke in *Palko* v. *Connecticut* (1937) that there were two categories of rights: those implicit in the concept of ordered liberty and those which were not. Those liberties not implicit in ordered liberty would have to be enumerated, as in a Bill of Rights, to be protected; but the freedoms within ordered liberty need not be listed to be protected, they flow from a "principle of justice so rooted in the traditions and conscience of our people as to be ranked as fundamental."[2] The differentiation of fundamental freedoms was to recognize that some freedoms are indispensible for liberty and justice, that courts were to give closer judicial protection for these civil liberties than other parts of the Constitution. Unfortunately, Mr. Justice Cardozo or the Supreme Court have never articulated a list of fundamental freedoms. The Court has refused to say all liberties within the Bill of Rights are fundamental freedoms. In recent years, however, the Court has spoken of rights as abortion, racial equality, free speech, and criminal justice as preferred rights.

Yet it was to the first ten amendments, the Bill of Rights, that Mr. Justice Cardozo was speaking. These amendments were added to the Constitution in 1791, thus fulfilling the promise of the Founders to add protection for civil liberties in order to secure ratification. Various states already had Bills of Rights in their state consititutions, and the absence of such basic protections in the national Constitution caused distrust and fear of centralized power. The Bill of Rights was directed at the national government, and in an early nineteenth century case, the Supreme Court held that the Bill of Rights applied only to the national government and not to the state governments.[3]

Can the liberties of the Bill of Rights be labeled as fundamental and thereby obligate the states as well as the national government? Justice Cardozo thought so, but the Supreme Court refuses to bind states by declaring freedoms fundamental. The Court has, however, used the Fourteenth Amendment, which does apply to states, to impose on the states many of the freedoms in the Bill of Rights. In fact, today, much of the Bill of Rights has been interpreted as applying to limit state governments. Using the due process clause of the Fourteenth Amendment, the Supreme Court began a gradual process of *selective incorporation*. *Gitlow* v. *New York,* in 1925, is the landmark case: For the first time the Court held that a provision of the Bill of Rights—the First Amendment right of free speech and press—could not be impaired by states any more than it could by the national government. The decision said: "[These] are among the fundamental personal rights and liberties protected by the due process clause of the Fourteenth Amendment from impairment by the states." Since 1925, the Supreme Court has moved

2. *Palko* v. *Connecticut*, 302 U. S. 319 (1937).
3. *Barron* v. *Baltimore*, 7 Peters 243 (1833).

How to get a passport

If you are unmarried and over the age of 13, you must have a passport in your own name to travel abroad. Here is how to go about obtaining one.

1. Have your picture taken by a passport photographer, who will give you prints of the required size and quality. Two 2 × 2 inch photographs, front view and full face in ordinary street dress, are needed. They may be black and white or color. Sign your name on the back of each.

2. You need your birth certificate (original, certified copy) or other evidence to prove you hold U.S. citizenship.

3. You will need proof of your identity such as a previous passport or a driver's license (a credit card or a social security card are not acceptable).

4. You must appear personally at a U.S. passport agency, before a clerk of any federal court or state court of record, before a judge or clerk of any probate court accepting applications, or at a post office designated to accept passport applications. U.S. passport agency offices are located in Boston, Chicago, Detroit, Honolulu, Houston, Los Angeles, Miami, New Orleans, New York, Philadelphia, San Francisco, Seattle, Stanford, and Washington, D.C.

5. Obtain and fill out the application, submit your documents, and pay the necessary fees. If all is in order, you will receive your passport in the mail, usually within two weeks.

6. U.S. passports are valid for five years from the date of issue. The passport will contain a list of countries for which it is not valid; this list changes depending on the international situation.

---

to include more provisions of the Bill of Rights as fundamental personal rights protected from impairment by states under the due process clause of the Fourteenth Amendment. The Court has been unwilling to say that the language of the Fourteenth Amendment incorporated the entire Bill of Rights, but today virtually all of its provisions (including the right to privacy) have been applied to the states. Many of the fundamental personal rights and liberties are contained within the First Amendment to which we now turn our attention. The First Amendment protects the freedom of religion, speech, press, assembly and other forms of expression.

FIRST AMENDMENT FREEDOMS

FREEDOM OF RELIGION

It is not surprising that the first right mentioned in the First Amendment is freedom of religion. Puritan colonists had come to America to escape religious persecution, and freedom of religion was for them a necessity. Thus the first

FACT FILE

THE PROCESS OF SELECTIVE INCORPORATION

Provision	Amend-ment	Year	Case
"Public use" and "just compensation" conditions in the taking of private property by government	V	*1896 and 1897*	*Missouri Pacific Railway Co. v. Nebraska, 164 U.S. 403, 17 S. Ct. 130; Chicago, Burlington & Quincy Railway Co. v. Chicago, 166 U.S. 226, 17 S. Ct. 581*
Freedom of speech	1	*1927*	*Fiske v. Kansas, 274 U.S. 380, 47 S. Ct. 655; Gitlow v. New York, 268 U.S. 652, 45 S.Ct. 625 (1925) (dictum only); Gilbert v. Minnesota, 254 U.S. 325, 41 S.Ct. 125 (1920) (dictum only)*
Freedom of the press	1	*1931*	*Near v. Minnesota, 283 U.S. 697, 51 S.Ct. 625*
Fair trial and right to counsel in capital cases	VI	*1932*	*Powell v. Alabama, 287 U.S. 45, 53 S. Ct. 55*
Freedom of religion	I	*1934*	*Hamilton v. Regents of Univ. of California, 293 U.S. 245, 55 S.Ct. 197 (dictum only)*
Freedom of assembly, and, by implication, freedom of association	I	*1937*	*DeJonge v. Oregon, 299 U.S. 353, 57 S.Ct. 255*
Free exercise of religious belief	I	*1940*	*Cantwell v. Connecticut, 310 U.S. 296, 60 S.Ct. 900*
Separation of church and state; right against the establishment of religion	I	*1947*	*Everson v. Board of Educ., 330 U.S. 1, 67 S.Ct. 504*
Right to public trial	VI	*1948*	*In re Oliver, 333 U.S. 257, 68 S.Ct. 499*
Right against unreasonable searches and seizures	IV	*1949*	*Wolf v. Colorado, 338 U.S. 25, 69 S.Ct. 1359*
Exclusionary rule as concomitant of unreasonable searches and seizures	IV	*1961*	*Mapp v. Ohio, 367 U.S. 643, 81 S.Ct. 1684*
Right against cruel and unusual punishments	VIII	*1962*	*Robinson v. California, 370 U.S. 660, 82 S.Ct. 1417*
Right to counsel in all felony cases	VI	*1963*	*Gideon v. Wainwright, 372 U.S. 335, 83 S.Ct. 792*

THE PROCESS OF SELECTIVE INCORPORATION *(Continued)*

Provision	Amend-ment	Year	Case
Right against self-incrimination	V	1964	*Malloy* v. *Hogan, 378 U.S. 1,84 S.Ct. 1489; Murphy* v. *Waterfront Com'n, 378 U.S. 52, 84 S.Ct. 1594*
Right to confront witnesses	VI	1965	*Pointer* v. *Texas, 380 U.S. 400, 85 S.Ct. 1065*
Right to privacy	*Various*	1965	*Griswold* v. *Connecticut, 381 U.S. 479, 85 S.Ct. 1678*
Right to impartial jury	VI	1966	*Parker* v. *Gladden, 385 U.S. 363, 87 S.Ct. 468*
Right to speedy trial	VI.	1967	*Klopfer* v. *North Carolina, 386 U.S. 213, 87 S.Ct. 988*
Right to compulsory process for obtaining witnesses	VI	1967	*Washington* v. *Texas, 388 U.S. 14, 87 S.Ct. 1920*
Right to jury trial in cases of serious crime	VI	1968	*Duncan* v. *Louisiana, 391 U.S. 145, 88 S.Ct. 1444*
Right against double jeopardy	V	1969	*Benton* v. *Maryland, 395 U.S. 784, 89 S.Ct. 2056*
Right to counsel in all criminal cases entailing a jail term	VI	1972	*Argersinger* v. *Hamlin, 407 U.S. 25, 92 S.Ct. 2006*

Other Incorporated Provisions

Provision	Amend-ment		
Right of petition	I	*Included by implication of other First Amendment incorporations*	
Right to be informed of the nature and cause of the accusation	VI	*Included by implication of other Sixth Amendment incorporations*	

	Amend-ment	*Provision(s) Not incorporated*
	II	*All*
Provisions of the First Eight Amendments Not Incorporated	III	*All*
	V	*Right to indictment by grand jury*
	VII	*All*
	VIII	*Right against excessive bail; right against excessive fines*

SOURCE: Harold Chase and Craig Ducat, *Constitutional Interpretation,* 2nd ed. St. Paul, Minn.: West Publishing Co.

Churches dot the American landscape. Freedom of worship is a basic tenet of the American heritage. (National Archives)

words of the First Amendment are clear and emphatic: ''Congress shall make no law respecting an establishment of religion, or prohibiting the free exercise thereof.''

The Establishment Clause.   This clause prevents the federal government or any state from setting up a church. Nor can any government pass laws to aid any religion, or prefer one religion over another.[4] Some critics argue that the establishment clause was never intended to prevent government support for religion, only favoritism for a particular religion or religions. But this *no preference*

4. *Everson* v. *Board of Education*, 330 U. S. 1 (1947).

position has not been accepted by the Supreme Court: It has adhered to the idea of a "wall of separation between church and state," as set forth by Mr. Justice Black in a 1947 decision, *Everson* v. *Board of Education*. It was on this basis that the Court struck down prayer in schools as "wholly inconsistent with the Establishment Clause,"[5] and outlawed Bible reading as a daily requirement in public schools.[6]

The wall of separation doctrine has drawn considerable opposition, particularly on the prayer and Bible-reading decisions. It is equally true that the distinction between church and state cannot be drawn easily; the Court has walked a very fine line at times. Not every law that confers an "indirect" or "incidental" benefit to religion, the Court said, is necessarily invalid.[7] For example, after having apparently laid down its narrow interpretation of permissible support in *Everson,* the Court went on to hold that reimbursement to parents for transportation to and from parochial schools was not a violation of the wall of separation principle. This was not aid to religion, but rather had to do with the child's welfare and safety.

The Court sought to clarify the establishment clause by creating a three-part test for any program: it (1) would have to have a clear secular purpose; (2) it must neither advance nor inhibit religion; and (3) it must avoid causing "excessive government entanglement with religion."[8] In the case, Chief Justice Burger declared for the majority that property tax exemptions for churches have a secular purpose and provide only incidental aid to religion, thereby meeting the threefold test.

A year later in 1971, however, the Court found two state attempts to subsidize the costs of parochial school education to be unconstitutional.[9] Here the attempt to supplement teachers' salaries in private schools was held to cause excessive administrative entanglement, even though the Court found acceptable the program's secular purpose of promoting the education of young children. In 1973 the Court added income tax credits and tuition reimbursements to parents of students enrolled in parochial schools as violations of the establishment clause.

Over the years, the relationship between financial aid to parochial schools and the establishment clause has been a knotty problem. In *Everson* v. *Board of Education,* while laying down its wall of separation doctrine, the Court held that aid to parochial education did not, in itself, violate that doctrine. Where the primary benefit was to the child, state aid would not necessarily be invalid. The "child benefit" theory has survived as the Court has struggled to determine when aid was primarily secular in purpose and benefited the child, and when it violated the three-part test of *Walz* and was public support to religion. The Court has rejected direct subsidies for salaries or tuition reimbursements as unconstitutional;

5. *Engel* v. *Vitale,* 370 U. S. 421 (1962).
6. *Abington School District* v. *Schempp,* 374 U. S. 203 (1963).
7. *Committee for Public Education and Religious Liberty* v. *Nyquist,* 413 U. S. 756 (1973).
8. *Walz* v. *Tax Commission,* 397 U. S. 664 (1970).
9. *Lemon* v. *Kurtzman,* 403 U. S. 602 (1971).

it has accepted the use of tax funds to purchase textbooks, provide diagnostic health services, reimburse parents for bus transportation, administer state prepared tests, and support recordkeeping and reporting activities.

State support for religious schools is another issue. Very little state aid may go to parochial elementary and secondary schools without violating the establishment clause. The Supreme Court has ruled that these schools are permeated with religious teaching. At the college and university level, however, the Supreme Court has been more generous in allowing state support for nonpublic education. There still cannot be support for religion, and a two-part test has been devised to judge such aid. The test says: (1) the institution's secular function must not be permeated with a religious atmosphere, and (2) there must be assurances by the college or university that the aid will not be used for religious teaching or activities. On this basis in 1976 the Court approved, for the first time, annual grants to religious colleges in Maryland to support their operation.[10]

Because of the establishment clause's wall of separation, prayers and Bible reading have been outlawed in the public schools. No official sponsorship or approval of religious beliefs is permitted.[11] Even nondenominational prayers are included.[12] Released time for religious instruction may be permissible, provided the instruction is not given on school premises during the school day. Bible study is permissible if it is presented as an academic subject.

The Free Exercise Clause.   If the First Amendment prohibits the establishment of religion, it also protects the individual's right to worship freely. This means people are free to worship or believe what they will, or even to hold no religious beliefs. Government is absolutely prohibited from proscribing any religious belief, and is also required to make some accommodations for the practice of religion. Government may not burden an individual or confer any benefits upon an individual because of religious beliefs. The Constitution itself prohibits any religious tests as a condition for office in the federal government. In 1961, the Supreme Court invalidated state laws that required a religious oath as a condition for state employment.[13] Yet governmental accommodation to religious beliefs does not mean that the practice of one's religion is not subject to limitation. The profession of faith is absolute; the practice of one's faith is not. In 1879, Mormons were prohibited from practicing polygamy. The Supreme Court held that Congress was free to prohibit any action, regardless of its religious implication, provided it did not prohibit a belief.[14]

The free exercise clause and government regulation through its police powers have had to strike a balance. Sunday closing laws have been upheld, when challenged by Orthodox Jews, as having a secular purpose of setting aside a day

10. *Roemer* v. *Maryland Public Works Board,* 426 U. S. 736 (1976).
11. *School District* v. *Schempp,* 374 U. S. 203 (1963).
12. *Engel* v. *Vitale,* 370 U. S. 421 (1962).
13. *Torcaso* v. *Watkins,* 367 U. S. 488 (1961).
14. *Reynolds* v. *United States,* 98 U. S. 145 (1879).

Church and State: A Judicial Thicket in Lower Federal and State Courts

The First Amendment's freedom of religion continues to perplex courts in spite of Supreme Court rulings. The Supreme Court sought to provide a policy for lower courts and public officials to follow in implementing permissible forms of activity. In *Walz* the Court established its three-part test for church–state relations. Yet in the past two years courts have been pressed with church–state issues, often resulting in conflicting applications. Here are some of the issues lower federal and state courts have been faced with regarding church–state relations.

Figurines in nativity scene. A Colorado U.S. District Court said the display of a creche along with Santa Claus, his sleigh and reindeer, and an elves' toy shop violated the First Amendment. The nativity scene is an "affirmation of and support for the tenets of the Christian faith." *Citizens Concerned for Separation of Church and State* v. *City and County of Denver*, 12-79.

Ten Commandments in the Classroom. Posting the Ten Commandments of the Christian faith is unconstitutional in North Dakota (*Ring* v. *Grand Forks Public School District No. 1*. N.D. U.S. District Court, 1-80), but constitutional in Kentucky. Apparently in Kentucky the placards with the Commandments were financed by voluntary contributions and were no more religious than the Preamble to the Kentucky Constitution. Kentucky Supreme Court, *Stone* v. *Graham*, 4-80.

Smoking marijuana. Members of the Coptic church may be prevented from smoking marijuana as part of their religious worship. The Florida Supreme Court said the state's interest in public health and safety outweighed the free exercise of their religion. *Town* v. *Florida*, 11-79.

Transcendental Meditation. The inclusion of "Science of Creative Intelligence/ Transcendental Meditation" courses as electives in New Jersey high schools violates the First Amendment. Transcendental Meditation is a religious activity says the Court of Appeals for the Third Circuit. *Malnak* v. *Yogi*, 2-79.

Christmas Carols. Public schools may sing Christmas carols or otherwise use music, art, literature, or drama with religious themes. These religious symbols are part of our heritage and have a secular purpose according to the Court of Appeals for the Eighth Circuit. *Florey* v. *Sioux Falls School District*, 4-80.

Christian Virtues. School officials in Florida may be directed to inculcate Christian virtues in their students, as ruled by the Court of Appeals for the Fifth Circuit. *Meltzer* v. *Board of Public Instruction of Orange County, Fla.*, 7-78.

Interracial romance. A private fundamentalist Christian school's expelling of a white female student believed to be having a romantic relationship with a black male classmate violated the female student's rights. The Court of Appeals for the Fourth Circuit could find no official church doctrine opposing interracial romance; therefore, as no valid religious belief had been called into question, it was not necessary for the court to decide if the student's rights were more important than the church's doctrine. *Fiedler* v. *Marumsco Christian School*, 10-80.

for rest, recreation, and tranquility.[15] School vaccinations and medical treatment may be administered over the religious objections of parents or other individuals.[16] In 1972, however, the Supreme Court held that a state could not compel Amish children to attend public school beyond the eighth grade.[17] Nor could Jehovah's Witness children be required to salute the flag or participate in any public ceremony that offended their religion.[18] In fact, New Hampshire was prevented from levying a fine on a Jehovah's Witness citizen who covered over the license plate motto "Live Free or Die."

Persons claiming an exemption from government regulation must demonstrate that such regulation burdens the practice of their religion. In this area, there are several recurring problems. One is exemption from military service on religious grounds. The Selective Service Law permitted exemption from combat for persons belonging to "well recognized" religions whose creeds prevent them for participating in war. This was interpreted as requiring belief in a Supreme Being. The Supreme Court broadened the exemption to all whose nontheistic beliefs occupied the place of a religion in their lives,[19] or whose sincere beliefs required them to refuse to participate in war.[20] The Vietnam war brought a greater challenge, however, as critics of the war sought to argue that their religion required them to refrain from participation in "unjust" wars. The Supreme Court rejected the argument, holding that the exemption applied only to persons opposed to participation in any war.[21] The other recurring problem is in health and medicine. Court decisions have permitted vaccinations, medical treatment of children, or blood transfusions over religious objections. Modern medical techniques, life support devices, and the "right to die" present serious free exercise clause issues that have not been resolved by the Court, at least not on the free exercise of religion grounds.

FREEDOM OF SPEECH

Freedom of speech is basic to democracy. As Mr. Justice Holmes once observed, "It is not free thought for those who agree with us, but freedom for the thought that we hate" that makes this freedom so important. Democratic government depends on free expression: Public elections, the power of the press, interest groups, congressional investigations, and public entertainment all depend on the substantive guarantees in the First Amendment for a free and open society. Yet free speech also provokes controversy. President Nixon claimed that the Vietnam war protesters aided and comforted the enemy and impaired the American war

15. *Braunfeld* v. *Brown,* 366 U. S. 599 (1961).
16. *Jacobson* v. *Massachusetts,* 197 U. S. 11 (1905).
17. *Wisconsin* v. *Yoder,* 406 U. S. 205 (1972).
18. *Board of Education* v. *Barnette,* 319 U. S. 624 (1943).
19. *United States* v. *Seeger,* 380 U. S. 163 (1965).
20. *Welsh* v. *United States,* 398 U. S. 333 (1970).
21. *Gillette* v. *United States,* 401 U. S. 437 (1971).

Oliver Wendell Holmes. Associate Justice of the Supreme Court from 1902 until 1932. (The Bettmann Archive, Inc.)

effort. Today, many people feel obscenity and pornography have been protected, to the detriment of American life. Public officials complain that freedom of information and sensational journalism prevent them from receiving frank opinions and making strong decisions because of the "fish bowl" environment they must operate in.

These challenges to free speech grew louder in the 1960s as courts expanded the umbrella of protection for free expression, notably in the area of obscenity and protest against the Vietnam war. There is a surprisingly low level of support for free expression among the American public; as one moves from abstract concepts to specific situations, the American people exhibit little tolerance for Mr. Justice Holmes' "marketplace of ideas."[22] Government and the courts frequently do place limits on free expression. This in itself is the source of some controversy, since the courts apply different tests and take different attitudes in different cases.

22. See for example James W. Prothro & Charles Grigg, "Fundamental Principles of Democracy: Bases of Agreement and Disagreement," *Journal of Politics,* 22 (Spring 1960); Herbert McClosky, "Consensus and Ideology in American Politics," *American Political Science Review,* 58 (June 1964); Robert Erickson, Norman Luttbeg & Kent Tedin, *American Public Opinion,* 2nd Edition, (New York: John Wiley & Sons, 1980), pp. 84–88.

Balancing Interests.   The strongest position for freedom of expression was taken by Mr. Justice Black, who argued that free speech was an absolute right, that this was what the Framers intended by 'Congress shall make *no law* . . . abridging the freedom of speech.'' Justice Black would allow no law abridging freedom of speech or press, including laws for slander and libel. For him, First Amendment rights enjoyed a *preferred position,* not to be "balanced away whenever a majority of [the] Court thinks that a State might have an interest sufficient to justify abridgment of those freedoms.'' Yet Justice Black was never able to persuade a majority of the Court to adopt the preferred position or absolutist view. The Court has consistently looked for some means, or test, to *balance* the constitutional protection of individual expression with the requirements of public order and safety.

The balancing approach resulted from a series of opinions and dissents written by Justices Holmes and Brandeis early in the twentieth century. With what was called the "clear and present danger'' test, the Court sought to restrict freedom of expression for the benefit of society only when such expression constituted a clear and present danger to society. The two cases arose out of the Espionage and Sedition Acts of 1917 and 1918, when some Socialists were arrested and convicted for mailing out leaflets protesting the draft.[23] The convictions were upheld; the Supreme Court saw the leaflets as an immediate threat to national security. Writing in *Schenck* v. *United States,* Justice Holmes expounded the clear and present danger doctrine:

> [The] character of every act depends upon the circumstance in which it is done. . . . The most stringent protection of free speech would not protect a man on falsely shouting fire in a theater and causing a panic. It does not even protect a man from an injunction against uttering words that may have all the effect of force. . . . The question in every case is whether the words used in such circumstances are of such a nature as to create a clear and present danger that they will bring about the substantive evils that Congress has a right to prevent. It is a question of proximity and degree.[24]

In the *Abrams* case, the majority of the Court found that criticism of the war effort produced a "bad tendency'' and that speech could be prohibited as it tended to bring harmful results. In *Gitlow* v. *New York*[25] the Court went further and adopted the bad tendency test to balance state regulation of seditious activity. In this case, the Court upheld a New York law prohibiting the advocacy of violent overthrow of the government.

By the 1940s, the Court had begun to use the clear and present danger test to examine free expression. The Justices began to look at Justice Black's reason-

---

23. *Schenck* v. *United States,* 249 U.S. 47 (1919); *Abrams* v. *United States,* 250 U.S. 616 (1919).
24. *Schenck* v. *United States,* 249 U.S. 47 (1919).
25. *Gitlow* v. *New York,* 268 U.S. 652 (1925).

ing that the "substantive evil" that follows as a result of the speech "must be extremely serious and the degree of imminence extremely high before utterances can be punished."[26] This trend has continued until now; the Court has focused on protecting the advocacy of unpopular ideas and the printing of allegedly prejudicial pretrial material or classified documents in the press. In *Watts* v. *United States,* the Supreme Court reversed the conviction of a man protesting the draft. Watts had said that, if drafted and forced to carry a rifle, the first man he would aim the rifle at would be the President. The Court viewed this as "symbolic speech" and not a threat to incite violence.[27] It also refused to allow the conviction of a Ku Klux Klan member for advocating political violence and the teaching of political violence.[28] The Court now appears to be saying that clear and present danger must provoke incitement to violence, imminent lawless action, or a court determination of the objective meaning of the speaker's words before free speech can be limited. This provides fresh and strong protection for the First Amendment freedom.

26. *Bridges* v. *California,* 314 U.S. 252 (1941).
27. *Watts* v. *United States,* 394 U.S. 705 (1969).
28. *Brandenburg* v. *Ohio,* 395 U.S. 444 (1969).

A rally by members of the Ku Klux Klan. (United Press International)

The Burger court has demonstrated that it is equally serious with regard to protection for free speech. It has refused convictions for disorderly conduct for a speech that did not result in imminent lawless behavior.[29] It struck down, as unconstitutionally overbroad, a Massachusetts law allowing the conviction of a person wearing the American flag on the seat of a pair of blue jeans.[30] It has also added *commercial speech,* advertising of professional services, to the constitutional protection of the First Amendment.

Prior Restraint.   Prior restraint of free expression is considered by the courts to be equally or more serious than actual impairment to freedom of expression. Although not all forms of prior restraint are unconstitutional, notably where obscenity is involved, "the government carries a heavy burden of showing justification for the imposition of such a restraint."[31] These include the public forum for speeches, motion pictures, use of the mail, press reporting at trials, and, of course, the press.

The most famous case of prior restraint in recent years was the Pentagon Papers case, in which the United States government sought to prevent *The New York Times* and *Washington Post* from publishing a classified report on the history of policymaking in Vietnam. The Supreme Court, in a 6 to 3 decision producing nine separate opinions, ruled that the prohibition sought by the government was an unconstitutional example of prior restraint. Justices Black and Douglas were of the opinion that any and all forms of prior restraint were unconstitutional, that limiting the publication of news would make a shambles of the First Amendment. The majority opinion, however, declared that there were situations in which the government might legitimately seek restraint for the publication or expression of material. The government bore a "very heavy burden, " however, to demonstrate the publication would cause "immediate and irreparable damage" to the nation. In this case the majority held that the publication of the Pentagon Papers posed no such threat to the security of the nation.[32]

In *Nebraska Press Association* v. *Stuart* (1976), the Supreme Court extended the principle of prior restraint to the publication of materials relating to criminal proceedings in a trial court. The Nebraska Press Association had sought to publish confessions made by a defendant in a murder trial. It was restrained from doing so by the trial court because the statements were "strongly implicative" of the accused. A unanimous Supreme Court held the order invalid. Again, prior restraint was a formidable barrier. As Chief Justice Burger said, due process and a fair trial may be reasons for such restraint, but the deprivation of a fair trial does not necessarily come about from publicity surrounding sensationalized crimes.[33]

29. *Hess* v. *Indiana,* 414 U.S. 105 (1973).
30. *Smith* v. *Goguen,* 415 U.S. 566 (1974).
31. *Organization for a Better Austin* v. *Keefe,* 402 U.S. 415 (1971).
32. *New York Times Company* v. *United States,* 403 U.S. 713 (1971).
33. *Nebraska Press Association* v. *Stuart,* 427 U.S. 539 (1976).

FREEDOM OF THE PRESS

It is difficult to separate freedom of speech and freedom of the press. Both are forms of expression; both are protected under the First Amendment. In fact, in this era of electronic journalism and instant communications, it is primarily through newsprint and television that information is broadcast. The tradition of a free press is basic to the democratic tradition. As early as 1735 in the John Peter Zenger trial, freedom of the press was upheld as a freedom from oppression and persecution. Zenger was acquitted of charges of libeling the royal government in a New York newspaper.

Freedom of Information.   Freedom of the press, however, does not guarantee the right to broadcast or televise what may be spoken or published elsewhere. The airways are regulated; the right of the listening or viewing public is paramount, not the rights of broadcasters. There is no First Amendment right to a radio or television license; the Federal Communications Commission (FCC) may deny licenses in the public interest and not violate freedom of speech.[34] The privilege of an operating license also involves responsibility. What standards of fairness must a broadcaster follow in exercising the right of free speech? The Court has ruled that the FCC may require stations operating under an FCC license to follow the "fairness doctrine" and provide time for replies in cases of personal attack and political editorials.[35] The Court also ruled, however, that this doctrine does not require stations to provide air time to groups seeking to make known their views on controversial issues. Unlimited access to the public airways does not best serve the public interest, and there exists no such right to access under the First Amendment.[36] The same principle has been applied to newspapers. The Supreme Court has rejected legislative efforts to apply the fairness doctrine or the right of access to newspapers. In *Miami Herald Publishing Co.* v. *Tornillo* (1974), the Court struck down as violating the First Amendment a Florida law requiring newspapers to provide free space to political candidates whom the newspaper had criticized. The First Amendment erects a "virtually insurmountable barrier" between the critical process of editorial judgment and government regulation of the print media.[37]

Free Press and Fair Trial.   Freedom of the press meets its most serious challenge when it comes into conflict with another basic right, the right to a fair trial. When the details of a crime, and the subsequent arrest and trial of a suspect are reported by the media, the right to a fair and unbiased trial is jeopardized. Juries may find it impossible to separate fact and trial evidence from rumor and

34. *National Broadcasting Co., Inc.* v. *United States,* 319 U.S. 190 (1943).
35. *Red Lion Broadcasting Co.* v. *Federal Communications Commission,* 395 U.S. 367 (1969).
36. *Columbia Broadcasting System* v. *Democratic National Committee,* 412 U.S. 94 (1973).
37. *Miami Herald Publishing Co., Inc.* v. *Tornillo,* 418 U.S. 241 (1974).

sensational reporting. In the celebrated Sam Sheppard murder trial, the conviction of Dr. Sheppard for the murder of his wife was overturned because the court failed to protect the defendant, the jurors, and the witnesses from the overwhelming and oftentimes prejudical publicity.[38] Courts have routinely, as a result, resorted to protective orders, ''gag rules,'' to prevent the printing of information that might violate the rights of a defendant or prejudice a prospective jury. As we have already seen in the *Nebraska Press Association* case, one such order was overturned as a form of prior restraint. Nonetheless, courts are expected to provide remedy to ensure the fair trial of defendants. In 1979 the Court held that the Sixth Amendment can be used to prevent press and public from having access to pretrial hearings; avoiding pretrial publicity outweighs the press and the public's right of access.[39] But in 1980 the Supreme Court forthrightly put the issue to rest by declaring the public and press have a First Amendment right to attend criminal trials, apparently including pretrial hearings. Chief Justice Burger wrote: ''we hold that the right to attend criminal trials is implicit in the guarantees of the First Amendment; without the freedom to attend such trials, which people have exercised for centuries, important aspects of freedom of speech and of the press could be eviscerated.''[40]

Journalists and reporters also have no constitutional right to withhold confidential information or protect confidential sources. Reporters have long argued for this right, but in 1972 the Supreme Court ruled otherwise. It said that requiring newspaper reporters to appear and testify before state or federal grand juries does not abridge the freedom of speech and press guaranteed under the First Amendment.[41]

Libel.   Libel is another form of speech not protected under freedom of speech and press. Traditionally, courts have made it exceedingly difficult to prove libel with respect to public officials. The Supreme Court has held that to libel a public official, one must prove that the statements were made with ''malice.'' That is, that the statements were made with the knowledge that they were false or with reckless disregard of whether they were false or not.[42] The category of ''public official'' has been broadened to include ''public figures,'' those who are candidates for public office and even other persons involved in public affairs or events of general public interest.[43]

Recently, however, the Court has redefined the standard for libel. First, any controversy of interest to the public is not necessarily a public controversy.[44] In the case, *Time* v. *Firestone,* the Supreme Court awarded libel damages to Mrs.

38. *Sheppard* v. *Maxwell,* 384 U.S. 333 (1965).
39. *Gannett Co., Inc.* v. *De Pasquale,* 443 U.S. 368 (1979).
40. *Richmond Newspapers* v. *Virginia,* ___ U.S. ___ (1980).
41. *Branzburg* v. *Hayes,* 408 U.S. 665 (1972).
42. *New York Times* v. *Sullivan,* 376 U.S. 254 (1964).
43. *Curtis Publishing Company* v. *Butts,* 388 U.S. 130 (1976); *Rosenbloom* v. *Metromedia,* 403 U.S. 29 (1971).
44. *Time, Inc.* v. *Firestone,* 424 U.S. 448 (1976).

One of our fundamental freedoms has always been that guaranteed by the First Amendment—freedom of speech and of the press. And until recently, the notion that a reporter's sources of information were confidential and that reporters could not be called into court to testify was part of the consensus about how the First Amendment works. But that consensus seems to have changed. In 1978, for example, the Supreme Court ruled that government agents seeking criminal evidence can get a warrant to search a newsroom and examine files and that in criminal investigations officials may gain secret access to reporters' and newspapers' long-distance telephone records.

In the same year, Myron Farber, a reporter for *The New York Times,* went to jail in New Jersey for refusing to turn over to the judge in a murder trial notes he had made in the course of investigative reporting that had led to the indictment in the first place. The trial was that of a New Jersey physician accused of murdering three patients in the 1960s at a New Jersey hospital with overdoses of curare. The reporter held that the information he had gathered and the sources he had used were protected under the First Amendment. The defense attorney held that under the Sixth Amendment his client was entitled to have access to this information. After a series of actions before state and federal courts, Myron Farber was cited for contempt of court and spent 39 days in jail. He was released only because the defendant was acquitted. And his paper, *The New York Times,* paid $285,000 in fines.

The Farber case happening at all—and the lengths to which all the participants went—is a reflection of several recent Supreme Court decisions that have attempted to change, or at least call into question, the traditional idea that the First Amendment is a blanket protection that cannot be subjected to "balancing tests" against other rights and freedoms. The Court has held that persons are entitled to freedom of speech and that the press is entitled to protection; it has also held that an accused person is entitled to a fair trial, to access of facts of evidence, and that when both rights are in question, the courts should apply a balancing test on a case by case basis.

The result of these cases has been to muddy the consensus on what freedoms such as those guaranteed by the Bill of Rights mean. How can the press be free if confidentiality is not allowed? When investigative reporting is directed at the government, can the government protect itself—and prevent the people from knowing—by prosecuting reporters and newspapers? A changing consensus in this area of American life can affect much of what we take for granted as citizens of a free and democratic country.

Firestone for *Time's* reporting that her husband was divorcing her on grounds "of extreme cruelty and adultery." Second, nonpublic figures suing for libel need not prove actual malice in establishing the basis for libel.[45] Third, the "public official" protection does not extend to activities of public officials outside the performance of their official responsibilities.[46] Senator William Proxmire could be sued for libel in awarding his "Golden Fleece" award. Fourth, a reporter's "state of mind," may be probed in a libel trial to discover his or her thoughts, opinions, and conclusions during the editorial process in order to establish evidence of reckless or knowing disregard for the truth.[47]

The Court explained there is no First Amendment protection that keeps a person from inquiring of those who write, edit, or produce information if they knew or suspected the publication was in error.

Restricting Freedom of the Press.   The actions of the Burger Court, in conjunction with decisions on Sixth Amendment fair trial cases and First Amendment freedom issues, have eroded the power of the press to pursue information:

1. Journalists have no special right to withhold the identity of confidential sources before grand juries. (*Branzburg* v. *Hayes*, 1972).
2. Court hearings may be closed to the press and public for pretrial testimony. Defendants need not be public figures. (*Gannett Co., Inc.* v. *DePasquale*, 1979).
3. The court narrowed the ability of the press to defend itself from libel suits by allowing questions to uncover a journalist's state of mind in writing an editorial. (*Herbert* v. *Lando*, 1979).
4. The Court broadened the public's right to sue for invasion of privacy. (*Wolston* v. *Readers Digest Association*, 1979; *Hutchinson* v. *Proxmire*, 1979).
5. Newsrooms may be searched without prior notice for "third party" evidence, evidence of a crime believed to have been committed by others. (*Zurcher* v. *Stanford Daily*, 1978).

FREEDOM OF ASSEMBLY AND ASSOCIATION

The First Amendment protects the right of people "peaceably to assemble and to petition the government for a redress of grievances." This right, the Supreme Court has said, is as "equally fundamental" as the other First Amendment freedoms. Speech, association, assembly and petition are all considered to be part of the constitutionally protected right of free expression under the First Amend-

45. *Wolston* v. *Readers Digest Association*, 443 U.S. 157 (1979).
46. *Hutchinson* v. *Proxmire*, 442 U.S. 111 (1979).
47. *Herbert* v. *Lando*, 441 U.S. 153 (1979).

ment. The courts have long recognized the right to use public places to assemble peaceably and petition.[48] This includes the right of labor organizations to hold meetings and picket,[49] civil right groups to march and demonstrate,[50] and of the Communist party to hold political rallies.[51]

The right of assembly is not an unlimited right, however. The assembly must be conducted in a law-abiding, peaceful manner. Cities and states may require licenses for parades and demonstrations. A group is not free to block traffic, incite riot, or otherwise disrupt the public or public buildings. The government may make regulations concerning the manner in which such an assembly may occur, although it may not use its regulatory power to interfere with the lawful right of a people to assemble. The line is a thin one. The Court has upheld laws prohibiting picketing near a courthouse as an undue influence on a judge, juror, or witness that would interfere with the trial.[52] The American Nazi party was allowed to parade through Skokie, Illinois, the home of many Jews who had survived Nazi concentration camps. Freedom of association is closely allied with freedom of assembly. The Court ruled in *Bates* v. *Little Rock* that a list of names of individuals participating in an assembly does not have to be furnished to governmental authorities. This is an unnecessary infringement of personal liberty.[53] Under freedom of association, the right of student organizations to exist has been upheld regardless of their parent organization's previous record;[54] the NAACP may assist individuals with civil rights grievances;[55] and union officials may aid members in labor disputes with an employer.[56] But the major issues of association have centered on loyalty and security questions.

The clash results from including advocating the overthrow of the government in free expression and the need to protect the nation's peace and security. The major tests have come from the perceived Communist threat in the 1950s and at time of war or dangerous international situations. During and after World War II, the Soviet Union was viewed as pressing for world domination; groups expounding socialist or revolutionary ideas were frequently viewed as ''fronts'' for the Soviet Union. Senator Joseph McCarthy (R-Wis.) is infamous for his efforts in the 1950s to root out Communists and Communist sympathizers in the federal government. It was Senator McCarthy's campaign that caused Americans to recognize that First Amendment rights were being trampled in the name of national security. Nevertheless the courts have long recognized that the government does have a legitimate right to protect national security and regulate subversive activity.

48. *David* v. *Massachusetts*, 167 U.S. 43 (1897).
49. *Thomas* v. *Collins*, 323 U.S. 516 (1945).
50. *NAACP* v. *Alabama*, 356 U.S. 449 (1958).
51. *DeJonge* v. *Oregon*, 299 U.S. 353 (1937).
52. *Cox* v. *Louisiana*, 379 U.S. 559 (1965).
53. *Bates* v. *Little Rock*, 361 U.S. 516 (1960).
54. *Healy* v. *James*, 408 U.S. 169 (1972).
55. *NAACP* v. *Button*, 371 U.S. 415 (1963).
56. *Brotherhood of Railroad Trainmen* v. *Virginia*, 377 U.S. 1 (1964).

The Smith Act of 1940 made it a crime for anyone to advocate the violent overthrow of the United States government. In 1951, the Supreme Court upheld the constitutionality of the Smith Act, thus allowing the conviction of 11 Communist party leaders for advocating "overthrow of the government."[57] Subsequently, however, the Court restricted the interpretation of the Smith Act to persons actively intending to overthrow the government. No longer would mere advocacy of an abstract doctrine of revolution (i.e., Marxism) be adequate for prosecution under the Smith Act.[58] It was, however, still a crime to be a member of the Communist party, as the Smith Act provided.

The anticommunist campaign was stepped up during the Korean conflict with the passage of the McCarran Act, which required Communists and communist organizations to register with the Subversive Activities Control Board as communist agents or communist front groups. At first the power of the board was upheld by the Supreme Court, and the Communist party could be compelled to register as a communist action organization. But then, in 1965, the Supreme Court ruled that to require individual Communists to register violated their Fifth Amendment right against self-incrimination.[59] Subsequent decisions have further restricted the use of the McCarran Act.

In the 1950s, loyalty oaths had become a common practice in public employment. The Court at first upheld the oaths on the basis that employment was a privilege and not a right. But by the 1960s the oaths were more and more being invalidated, though more often than not on the grounds that they were too vague. Finally, in 1967 the Court struck down loyalty oaths for both state and federal employment as a form of guilt by association that violated the First Amendment. Political affiliation could no longer be a condition for public employment.[60] In 1980 the Supreme Court added, in *Branti* v. *Finkel,* that political party affiliation alone was insufficient cause to remove an appointee from public office. Here the Court argued that belonging to a different political party than the employer—even in patronage public positions—was protected under the First Amendment.[61]

OTHER FORMS OF SPEECH

Symbolic Speech.   So far, we have been treating nonverbal behavior as a form of free expression. Generally the Court has been willing to look upon this as free expression covered by the First Amendment, but whenever there is a question of action rather than just verbal speech, the problem of reconciling individual liberty with social needs for peace, order, and security becomes more

57. *Dennis* v. *United States,* 341 U.S. 494 (1951).
58. *Yates* v. *United States,* 354 U.S. 298 (1957).
59. *Albertson* v. *Subversive Activities Control Board,* 382 U.S. 70 (1965).
60. *Keyishian* v. *Board of Regents,* 385 U.S. 589 (1967); *United States* v. *Robel,* 389 U.S. 258 (1967).
61. *Branti* v. *Finkel,* _____U.S. _____(1980).

significant. The Supreme Court has wrestled with the issue, trying to distinguish between speech and action and balancing the interests of each. Draft card burning was held to be a form of action, not "symbolic speech," and hence the individual could be prosecuted. Yet public school children could not be compelled to salute the flag. Civil rights protesters and antiwar demonstrators have argued that their rights to assemble and demonstrate are rights under the First Amendment.

Symbolic speech as a consitutionally protected form of free expression under the First Amendment was recognized as early as 1931. It was not, however, until the civil right campaigns and Vietnam that symbolic speech was put to the test. In 1963 civil rights demonstrators had their conviction for breach of peace overturned when they demonstrated on the grounds of a state capitol. The demonstrators had been peaceful and, the Court reasoned, they did not impede pedestrian or vehicular traffic.[62] Three years later, the Court upheld a sit-in by blacks in a library protesting segregated facilities, even though the sit-in extended beyond the normal activities of a library.[63] In *Tinker* v. *Des Moines School District,* the Court said school officials could not expel or punish students for wearing black armbands to protest the war in Vietnam. The Court reasoned this was a symbolic "silent, passive expression of opinion" that in no way disrupted the operations of the school.[64] The Court has also permitted desecration or alteration of the flag under certain circumstances as a constitutionally protected form of free expression.[65] Finally, the Court has ruled for a motorist's right to obscure the license plate motto "Live Free or Die" as symbolic speech.[66]

Commercial Speech.   Up until 1975, advertising was not protected from governmental regulation as free speech. In *Bigelow* v. *Virginia,* however, the Supreme Court ruled that if an activity is legal, the state cannot prohibit advertising it.[67] The *Bigelow* case involved the newspaper advertising of abortions. The Court ruled that the advertisement was of interest to the public and extended the First Amendment freedom to cover such advertisements. The Court was careful to point out that it was sanctioning the advertising of a legal activity—the constitutional right to an abortion—and not illegal abortions. Subsequently, the Supreme Court has added the advertising of prescription drug prices,[68] "for sale" signs on homes in racially integrated communities,[69] contraceptives,[70] and legal fees for attorneys.[71] It is now clear that the Court intends commercial speech to be a constitutionally protected First Amendment freedom.

62. *Edwards* v. *South Carolina,* 372 U.S. 229 (1963).
63. *Brown* v. *Lousiana,* 383 U.S. 131 (1966).
64. *Tinker* v. *Des Moines School District,* 393 U.S. 503 (1969).
65. *Street* v. *New York,* 394 U.S. 576 (1969); *Spence* v. *Washington,* 418 U.S. 405 (1974).
66. *Wooley* v. *Maynard,* 430 U.S. 705 (1977).
67. *Bigelow* v. *Virginia,* 421 U.S. 809 (1975).
68. *Virginia State Board of Pharmacy* v. *Virginia Citizens Consumer Council, Inc.,* 425 U.S. 748 (1976).
69. *Linmark Associates, Inc.* v. *Township of Willingboro,* 431 U.S. 85 (1977).
70. *Carey* v. *Population Services International,* 431 U.S. 678 (1977).
71. *Bates* v. *State Bar,* 433 U.S. 350 (1977).

Thus, although the Court has declared commerical speech to be constitutionally protected by the First Amendment, it has reaffirmed the state's authority to regulate the place and conditions under which the speech may take place, so long as it does not impair the content of the speech. Furthermore, illegal, deceptive, or untruthful commercial advertising is not protected.

Political Speech.   Political campaigning is, of course, basic to our democratic process, and candidates have the "untrammeled right of free speech." The competition for votes requires an environment in which candidates can freely express an opinion and voters can learn about the candidates and their platforms. Political campaigning and advertising, however, are subject to increased regulation by the states. The Court has ruled that military bases may prohibit political rallies and the distribution of campaign literature, since the principal function of a military base is the training of soldiers.[72] The Court has also ruled that a municipal transit system can refuse to sell political advertising space even though it sells commercial advertising on its buses. The bus is not a public forum and the riders are a captive audience.[73] We have already noted the Court ruling not requiring newspaper editors to provide space for replies to critical editorials. Nor do broadcasters have to sell broadcast time to candidates or parties for political advertising. But informing the public on controversial issues of the day does not depend upon the identity of the source—even when a corporation. The Court, in 1980, permitted public utility firms to advertise and to place bill inserts in their mailings to promote their position on controversial issues of public policy.[74]

Obscenity.   Obscenity is not a constitutionally protected form of free speech. In *Roth* v. *United States* (1957), the Supreme Court held that obscenity is not protected by the First Amendment, saying, in part, "implicit in the history of the First Amendment is the rejection of obscenity as utterly without redeeming social importance."[75] The principle of *Roth* still governs obscenity cases today: The question is not constitutional protection for obscenity, but what constitutes obscenity. No issue before the Court has caused it more difficulty in recent years. Changing standards of morality and changing expectations for state regulation of individual sexual behavior have produced an array of court cases dealing with the issue of obscenity and sexually explicit material. From Erskine Caldwell and D. H. Lawrence a generation ago, to the more recent movie *Deep Throat* and *Hustler* publisher Larry Flint, the standards and bounds of permissible expression have continually been tested. It was Justice Brennan, writing in 1973, who said: "No other aspect of the First Amendment has, in recent years, commanded so substan-

72. *Greer* v. *Spock,* 424 U.S. 828 (1976).
73. *Lehman* v. *City of Shaker Heights,* 418 U.S. 298 (1974).
74. *Consolidated Edison Co. of New York, Inc.* v. *Public Service Commission of New York,* _____ U.S. _____1980; and *Central Hudson Gas and Electric Corp.* v. *Public Service Commission of New York,* _____U.S. _____(1980).
75. *Roth* v. *United States,* 354 U.S. 476 (1957).

tial a commitment of our time, generated such disharmony of views, and remained so resistent to the formulation of stable and manageable standards.''

The *Roth* case declared obscenity not within the area of free speech or press, but went on to say that material, to be obscene, must be ''utterly without redeeming social importance.'' Therefore, any ideas having the slightest redeeming social importance must have the full protection of the First Amendment. It was Justice Brennan, writing for the majority, who outlined the test for judging material as obscene. Material could be declared obscene and without constitutional protection, Brennan stated, if such material appealed to the prurient interest in sex; had no serious literary, artistic, or political merit; and on the whole, was offensive to the average person under contemporary community standards.

In the abstract, the Court had set guidelines for judging obscenity. In practice, they did not help much; and the court would be faced with specific questions and circumstances. The language in *Roth* did not help. How was one to establish an appeal to prurient interest using some contemporary community standard as understood by the average person? Subsequent cases sought to clarify the various elements of the test. The Court held, in a case involving the book *Fanny Hill,* that all elements of the test must be applied independently and the work must fail all three parts to be obscene. *Fanny Hill* may, under community standards, appeal to the prurient interest in sex, but it was not ''utterly without redeeming social value.''[76] The meaning of ''contemporary community standards'' was never agreed upon by the Justices. For some it meant local standards; for others, it meant a national standard.

As a result of the tentativeness in interpreting the language of *Roth* and applying it to specific circumstances, subsequent cases had the effect of removing the more prohibitive restrictions on sexually explicit material. Adult bookstores sprang up in almost all metropolitan centers. More sexually explicit movies began playing in neighborhood theaters. Nudity in movies, magazines, and night clubs became more common. As a result of *Memoirs* v. *Massachusetts,* which limited obscenity to material without redeeming social value, many argued not even hardcore pornography could be outlawed by the state.

In 1973 the Supreme Court addressed the issue again. It abandoned the direction of *Memoirs,* which had required the state to prove the negative—that material was utterly without redeeming social value. Consequently, when the California restaurant manager opened Marvin Miller's sexually explicit solicitation to purchase four books, the Court was ready to abandon the ''utterly without redeeming social value'' test and allow states greater latitude in regulating obscenity. In *Miller* v. *California* (1973), Marvin Miller's conviction was upheld in a narrow 5 to 4 vote, and the Court set a new test for obscenity: (a) whether the average person, applying contemporary community standards, would find that the work, taken as a whole, appeals to the prurient; (b) whether the work depicts or de-

76. *A Book Named ''John Cleland's Memoirs of a Woman of Pleasure''* v. *Attorney General of Massachusetts,* 383 U.S. 413 (1966).

"THAT'S TO TAKE CARE OF OBSCENITY CASES"

From *Herblock on All Fronts* (The New American Library, 1980).

scribes, in a patently offensive way, sexual conduct specifically defined by the applicable state law; and (c) whether the work, taken as a whole, lacks serious literary, artistic, political or scientific value.[77]

77. *Miller* v. *California*, 413 U.S. 15 (1973).

The Court had said that local communities should apply their own "community standards" to judge obscenity. Although a national standard never commanded a majority of the Court, adherence to a national standard seemed to inhibit the applicability of any local standard. Now the Court specifically faced that issue and rejected a national standard in favor of local community standards. Note too that the negative proof and language of *Memoirs* was absent in Miller: "utterly without" is replaced with "serious," and "redeeming social value" changed to read "literary, artistic, political or scientific value." The decision was intended to pave the way for greater efforts by state and local authorities to exercise their judgment in controlling the stream of sexual publications and films.

Yet, only one year later, the Supreme Court warned local communities that, although they are to apply community standards to judge obscenity, local juries do not have "unbridled discretion" in determining what is patently offensive.[78] The Court here overturned a state conviction which had found the movie *Carnal Knowledge* obscene. Their own viewing of the film convinced the Justices that it was not obscene. Subsequent decisions have reinforced the "unbridled discretion" limitation on local efforts to ban movies and activities as obscene. Drive-in movies could not ban movies with nudity per se.[79] The musical *Hair* could not be banned without a proper judicial hearing.[80]

The Court has further made it clear that normal criminal procedures must be followed in prosecuting for obscenity. In 1980 the high court overturned convictions for obscenity because such procedures were not followed. A Texas statute, which enjoined movie theaters from showing films suspected of being obscene on the basis that the theaters had been found to show obscene films in the past, was invalidated. This was an unconstitutional form of prior restraint.[81] Also, the Court would not permit the conviction for obscenity where twelve cartons of obscene material were mistakenly delivered to the wrong person and subsequently turned over to the FBI. The use of the evidence by the FBI amounted to a warrantless illegal search and seizure. The proper addressees on the packaging label had every right to expect their privacy to be protected.[82]

The intent of *Miller* was the elimination of hard-core pornography, although some people question whether that happened as special cases have developed to be considered along with the *Miller* decision. The private possession of obscene materials is not a crime,[83] but the state can prohibit their transportation, even for private use.[84] Also, the state may prohibit the use of the mail as a means of receiving obscene material.[85] In *Young* v. *American Mini Theaters, Inc.* the Court

---

78. *Jenkins* v. *Georgia*, 418 U.S. 153 (1974).
79. *Erznoznik* v. *City of Jacksonville*, 422 U.S. 206 (1975).
80. *Southeastern Promotions, Ltd.*, v. *Conrad*, 420 U.S. 546 (1975).
81. *Vance* v. *Universal Amusement Co., Inc.*, 445 U.S. 308 (1980).
82. *Walter* v. *United States*, ___ U.S. ___ (1980).
83. *Stanley* v. *Georgia*, 394 U.S. 557 (1969).
84. *United States* v. *Orita*, 413 U.S 139 (1973).
85. *United States* v. *Reidel*, 402 U.S. 351 (1971).

accepted the use of zoning ordinances to regulate the location of adult movie theaters.[86] In short, the state is not without recourse to control the location or distribution of obscene material.

THE RIGHT TO PRIVACY

The right to privacy may well be "the most comprehensive of rights and the right most valued by civilized man."[87] It has been associated with personal freedom and limited government in democratic theory. Constitutionally, it has been associated with protection from unreasonable searches and seizures and the protection of private property. Justice Brandeis defined the right to privacy as the right to be left alone—a protection for the individual, in private matters, from governmental intrusion.

The right to privacy is not specifically mentioned in the Bill of Rights. It was first raised as a constitutional protection in 1890 by Louis Brandeis and Samuel Warren in a law review article in which they suggested that individuals ought to have their private affairs protected from publication in newspapers.[88] As a Supreme Court Justice, Mr. Brandeis held the view that government may not violate the "privacy of the individual" under the Fourth Amendment to the Constitution. A majority on the Supreme Court, however, did not come to this view until 1965. In *Griswold* v. *Connecticut,* the Court recognized, or created, the right to privacy as a constitutionally protected freedom.

PENUMBRAS

The case arose over a Connecticut law that forbade the use of contraceptive devices or the dispensing of medical advice on the use of such devices. Griswold, an M.D. and the executive director of the Planned Parenthood League, was convicted of providing medical advice and information to married couples on means of birth control. The Supreme Court reversed the conviction. Justice Douglas, writing for the Court, found that the law impermissibly limited the right to privacy of married couples. To ground the right to privacy in the Constitution, Justice Douglas turned not to the Fourth Amendment, which prohibited unreasonable searches and seizures, nor to the Ninth Amendment, which provided for the enumeration of additional rights not specifically provided for in the Bill of Rights, but to "penumbras," zones of privacy emanating from several provisions in the Bill of Rights, particularly the First Amendment.

---

86. *Young* v. *American Mini Theaters, Inc.,* 427 U.S. 50 (1976).
87. Justice Brandeis, dissenting in *Olmstead* v. *United States,* 277 U.S. 438 (1928).
88. See Louis Brandeis and Samuel Warren, "The Right to Privacy," *Harvard Law Review,* 193 (1890).

>Specific guarantees in the Bill of Rights have penumbras, formed by
>emanations from those guarantees that help give them life and substance
>. . . various guarantees create zones of privacy.[89]

The First Amendment freedom of association created a zone of privacy, the right
to educate a child in a parochial school; the right of an organization to protect its
membership list. The Third, Fourth, and Fifth Amendments created penumbras
protecting the individual from intrusions by government. Justice Douglas noted
the historical basis for recognizing the right to privacy as supporting the Court's
decision in ruling invalid the Connecticut statute: "We deal with a right of privacy
older than the Bill of Rights—older than our political parties, older than our
school system," he said.

Justice Goldberg concurred, but he reasoned that the due process clause of
the Fourteenth Amendment also embraced fundamental personal rights. Thus
states would be barred from infringing on the concept of liberty, including the
right of marital privacy, even though the right is not mentioned in the Constitution. This rationale was supported by the intent of the Framers as evidenced in
the Ninth Amendment where, Justice Goldberg argued, the Court can find support
for its activity in broadening personal rights not enumerated in the Constitution.

Seven years later, the Court held that there was no legitimate way to distinguish between married and unmarried couples as to the use of contraceptives. In
Eisenstadt v. *Baird,* the Supreme Court ruled invalid a state law prohibiting the
distribution of contraceptive devices to unmarried persons as a violation of equal
protection. Justice Brennan wrote for the majority, saying: "If the right to privacy
means anything, it is the right of the individual, married or single, to be free from
unwanted governmental intrusion into matters so fundamentally affecting a person
as the decision whether to bear or beget a child."[90] In 1977, the Court held
invalid a law restricting the sale of contraceptive devices by licensed pharmacists
to persons over the age of 16.[91] The Court, without a majority opinion, apparently
reasoned that the denial of contraceptives to children did not deter them from
sexual activity.

ABORTION

Undoubtedly the greatest, and by far the most controversial, extension of the
right of privacy came in the 1973 ruling that extended the right of privacy to
include the right to an abortion. In two cases, *Roe* v. *Wade* and *Doe* v. *Bolton,*
the Supreme Court declared "this right to privacy, whether it be founded in the
Fourteenth Amendment's concept of personal liberty and restrictions upon state
action, as we feel it is, or . . . in the Ninth Amendment's reservation of rights

89. *Griswold* v. *Connecticut,* 381 U.S. 479 (1965).
90. *Eisenstadt* v. *Baird,* 405 U.S. 438 (1972).
91. *Carey* v. *Population Services International,* 413 U.S. 678 (1977).

The right to privacy includes the right to an abortion. This issue has proved controversial as supporters rally in defense of the Court's interpretation. (United Press International)

to the people, is broad enough to encompass a woman's decision whether or not to terminate her pregnancy."[92]

The Court skirted the issue of the fetus as a person from conception. It found no *legal* basis for such a conclusion, but did not rule it out on religious or philosophical grounds. Rather, the Court focused on the interests of the mother as the compelling issue controlling legislation on abortions.

The Burger Court has shown no reluctance to extend the right to abortion as part of the right of privacy. In *Planned Parenthood* v. *Danforth,* the Supreme

92. *Roe* v. *Wade,* 410 U.S. 113 (1973).

Court ruled that a state could not require parental or spousal consent for a legal abortion.[93] Nor could a state make maturity or competence a judicial criterion for women under eighteen to obtain an abortion.[94] The court did note in *Maher* v. *Roe* that the right to an abortion meant only freedom from governmental interference in exercising the right; it did not include the right to have government pay for a nontherapeutic abortion.[95]

The most controversial extension of this principle was the Hyde Amendment wherein since 1976, Congress sought to limit Medicaid funds to pay for therapeutic abortions. The Hyde Amendment prohibited federal funds for abortions except in situations necessary to save the woman's life or for cases of rape or incest. The Amendment had been challenged in federal court as violating the Due Process Clause of the Fifth Amendment and the Religious Clause of the First Amendment. In 1980 the Supreme Court upheld the constitutionality of the Hyde Amendment. The Court reasoned the Amendment placed no government obstacles in the path of women choosing to terminate their pregnancies, only that there was no constitutional entitlement to the financial resources of the federal government in order "to realize all the advantages of that freedom."[96]

THE RIGHT TO DIE

Does a person have a personal right to choose to die? Is such a right to die covered by the right of privacy? In the Quinlan case, argued before the New Jersey Supreme Court in 1976, the contention that self-determination and the right of privacy are synonomous was put forth. The court avoided the issue by holding the question to be one of a guardian making a decision for an incompetent adult. It held that Karen Quinlan's father could act in her best interests, including removal of life-support devices, based on his religious beliefs. It appears likely that it will be only a matter of time before this question will have to be confronted by the Supreme Court.

SUMMARY

1. Civil liberties are basic to a democratic government. Some individual rights are fundamental freedoms which must be protected. Originally interpreted to apply to the national government only, the Bill of Rights containing our basic civil liberties has been gradually extended to cover the states as well.

2. Freedom of religion prohibits government intrusion into religious worship. This does not mean there is no government support or regulation

93. *Planned Parenthood* v. *Danforth*, 428 U.S. 52 (1976).
94. *Bellotti* v. *Baird*, 440 U.S. 904 (1979).
95. *Maher* v. *Roe*, 432 U.S. 464 (1977).
96. *Harris* v. *McRae*, ___ U.S. ___ (1980).

of religious activity, only that the Supreme Court has been very careful to keep government activity to a minimum.

3. Freedom of speech is not an absolute right but must be balanced against the eminent threat to public order. There is a long history of protection, however, for this basic right. Democracy is dependent on the freedom of speech as well as the other First Amendment freedoms.

4. Newer forms of expression today also receive protection under the First Amendment. These include symbolic speech, commerical speech, and political speech.

5. Obscenity has never been protected as a form of expression within the First Amendment. The Supreme Court, however, has never satisfactorily arrived at a definition of obscenity. Presently, the Court allows communities to define obscenity for themselves, although within circumscribed boundaries.

6. The right of privacy has emerged as the most recent fundamental freedom to receive protection under the First Amendment and the entire Bill of Rights. It may well be the most important right for it protects individuals from unnecessary government invasion into their lives. This includes the right of women to choose an abortion.

TERMS

bad tendency   128
balancing doctrine   128
civil liberties   117
clear and present
  danger   128
commercial speech   137
community
  standards   141
establishment
  clause   122
fairness doctrine   131
free-exercise clause   124
freedom of
  information   131
fundamental
  freedoms   118

gag rule   132
libel   132
no preference   122-123
obscenity   139
penumbra   142
political speech   138
preferred position   128
prior restraint   130
privacy   142
seditious speech   136
symbolic speech   136-
  137
selective
  incorporation   118
wall of separation   123

RESEARCH PROJECTS

4.1. Brief a Supreme Court case. Try to digest an important Supreme Court decision. In the library there will be several books on constitutional law that contain Supreme Court cases. Pick an interesting case. In one or two pages, summarize the case. You should follow a common format: (a) state the facts of the case—who did or said what, first court verdict on what grounds; (b) constitutional issue—what constitutional principles are in question; (c) decision—what did the Supreme Court rule; (d) reasoning—outline the logic of the Court's basis for making its ruling; and (e) precedent—what broader implication does the ruling hold?

4.2. Support for the First Amendment Freedoms. Construct a brief questionnaire on first amendment rights to ascertain the level of support for these basic freedoms. You can give this questionnaire to some of your college friends and acquaintances. Then you might also give it to neighbors or friends of your parents—any differences in the responses of the groups? Here are some questions you could ask:

- Should people be allowed to vote even if they can't do so intelligently?
- Do you agree that we do not have to allow known communists to speak because they do not believe in the American system?
- Is it true that no one has a right to treat the flag or other symbols of our country with disrespect?
- Should we respect a person's freedom of worship even if we do not like their religion?

4.3. Obscenity. What is the availability of "adult literature," material with a sexual appeal? For example are R- or X-rated movies shown, are there adult bookstores, and how and where are adult magazines such as *Hustler, Playboy, Oui,* and *Playgirl* displayed? Is there any effort to control this by the use of zoning laws? You might wish to interview city officials on their views of the nature of the problem and efforts to zone areas in order to control obscenity.

4.4. Press Coverage and Fair Trial. Try to find a pending trial case and examine the press coverage surrounding the case. Now put yourself in the place of a juror. Do you think you could render an impartial verdict? What parts of the press coverage might be labeled sensational? If you were the newspaper editor, what parts of the story might not have been printed and yet protect the people's right to know?

BIBLIOGRAPHY

Abraham, Henry. *Freedom and the Court.* New York: Oxford University Press, 1977.

A standard work that discusses civil rights and liberties including freedom of speech, religion, race, and due process. The book is current and sufficiently detailed to provide an excellent survey of rights and liberties as interpreted by the Court.

Emerson, Thomas. *Toward a General Theory of the First Amendment*. New York: Random House, 1966.

Emerson takes the approach that the First Amendment confers an absolute right of free speech on citizens. Nevertheless, Emerson raises several issue areas and relates Supreme Court decisions to those areas that makes for lively reading.

Krislov, Samuel. *The Supreme Court and Political Freedom*. New York: Free Press, 1968.

A reasoned discussion of political freedoms as the Supreme Court has attempted to unravel some of the thorny issues. Rather than concentrate on case law, Krislov looks for standards or reasoning by the court to establish principles for political freedoms.

Mason, Alpheus T. *The Supreme Court: Palladium of Freedom*. Ann Arbor, Mich.: University of Michigan Press, 1962.

Mason views an important role of the Supreme Court to be the protection of minority rights. Mason provides a nice historical discussion of the Supreme Court in dealing with political freedoms.

Morgan, Richard. *The Supreme Court and Religion*. New York: Free Press, 1975.

An overview of church–state relations, Morgan looks at the sources of conflict and the groups involved in the conflicts. Only some attention is given to law and court decisions on church–state matters.

Sigler, Jay. *American Political Policies*. Homewood, Ill.: Dorsey Press, 1975.

A discussion of the First Amendment policies as developed by the Supreme Court. There is an especially good analysis of implementing rights. The work affords a good overview of political rights, including the rights of groups such as women, Indians, and the handicapped.

Sorauf, Frank. *Wall of Separation*. Princeton N.J.: Princeton University Press, 1976.

The best and most extensive treatment of the First Amendment right to freedom of religion. Analyzes not only the issues and parties to church–state suits but also the political and legal context for such suits. Makes use of empirical data.

Sunderland, Lane. *Obscenity*. Washington, D.C.: American Enterprise Institute, 1974.

A review of major court decisions pertaining to obscenity and legislative proposals relating to obscenity. The first chapter presents a nice overview of present and previous obscenity decisions.

Young, J. B. (ed). *Privacy*. New York: John Wiley, 1978.

A sophisticated collection of articles on privacy, the first sections seek to examine the role and value of privacy while the remainder of the articles look at privacy and social policy. Includes topics on government, law enforcement, media, and several professions.

chapter
5

Equality, Due Process, and the Fourteenth Amendment

The Fourteenth Amendment to the Constitution produced a civil revolution. It changed the way America acts and thinks. The Amendment says that no state shall deny to any of its citizens the equal protection of the laws. No other phrase in the Constitution has meant more for the protection of the civil rights and personal liberty of individuals. The Fourteenth Amendment has been the vehicle for securing racial justice. It has been the source for support for aid to the poor and the minorities. The Fourteenth Amendment also serves as the basis for women to challenge sex discrimination.

The principle of equality is important to Americans—yet, in practice, equality remains elusive. The Fourteenth Amendment introduced into our concept of equality the specific requirement that states treat individuals equally with respect to the law. This constitutional guarantee has been extended to apply to both the states and the national government.

RACIAL JUSTICE

The most dramatic use of the equal protection clause of the Fourteenth Amendment has been to secure racial justice. The Court's application of it has produced a revolution in public education, and it has been further used to secure voting rights, jobs, and housing. Because of the impact of the

Fourteenth Amendment, things have changed, yet no one can say that racial discrimination has ended. There continues to be severe problems: racial tension often runs high; unemployment for black Americans runs well ahead of the average for white workers; the educational level for blacks is below that of their white counterparts; their median income is lower; and infant mortality is higher. Housing conditions for blacks remain substandard. Yet, were it not for the Fourteenth Amendment, there would be little constitutional basis for attacking any of these situations.

SEPARATE BUT EQUAL

The Reconstruction Amendments were ratified shortly after the end of the Civil War. The Thirteenth Amendment, ratified in 1865, abolished the institution of slavery. The Fourteenth Amendment, proposed in 1866 and ratified in 1868, extended citizenship to the freed slaves and included the rights and privileges pertaining thereto. The last of the three amendments, the Fifteenth, was ratified in 1870 and gave the black American citizen the right to vote in federal and state elections.

Yet "Jim Crow" and segregation were not gone. The Constitutional amendments abolished slavery and declared equal protection of the laws, but they said nothing about personal association and treatment. For example, in 1882, the Supreme Court ruled valid a state law that provided for more stringent penalties for adultery and fornication if the couple were of opposite races than if they were of the same race.[1] In 1883, the Supreme Court ruled that the Fourteenth Amendment did not prohibit discrimination by private individuals, only state actions that were discriminatory.[2] And then, in 1896, the Court adopted the constitutional position that public accommodations could legally be separate if they were equal.

Louisiana railways were required by law to maintain "separate but equal accommodations." Homer Plessy, one-eighth African, boarded one such train, sat in a coach reserved for whites, would not move when asked, and was arrested. The Supreme Court in *Plessy* v. *Ferguson* refused to deny the arrest as a violation of the Fourteenth Amendment. In short, the Louisiana statute of "separate but equal accommodations" was compatible with the Constitution. "It [the Fourteenth Amendment] could not have been intended to abolish distinctions based upon color, or to enforce social, as distinguished from political equality, or a commingling of the two races upon terms unsatisfactory to either."[3]

Justice Harlan was the lone dissenter. His view was that the Civil War amendments had made the Constitution "color-blind." To impose a categorical distinction of "separate but equal" was to perpetuate and protect "classes among citizens." In time, Justice Harlan prophesied, the decision will "prove to be quite

1. *Pace* v. *Alabama,* 106 U.S. 583 (1882).
2. Civil Rights Cases, 109 U.S. 3 (1883).
3. *Plessy* v. *Ferguson,* 163 U.S. 537 (1896).

as pernicious as the decision made by this tribunal in the *Dred Scott* Case'' (the decision to force a runaway slave in a free state to be returned to his owner).

It would not be until 1954, however, that the Court would rectify its decision. The Court really never took equal accommodations seriously. It allowed the closure of black schools for ''purely economic reasons'' and the merger of black children into overcrowded schools,[4] and extended the concept of separate but equal educational facilities to races other than blacks, thereby prohibiting their admission to white schools.[5] It was in public education particularly that the separate but equal doctrine was most consistently applied. And it was in public education that the revolution in racial justice was begun.

The Revolution in Public Education.   In 1954 the Supreme Court, in *Brown* v. *Board of Education of Topeka, Kansas,* overturned the ''separate but equal'' doctrine, declaring simply: ''in the field of public education the doctrine of separate but equal has no place.''[6] The Court argued that segregated facilities were not and could not be equal. It was not the tangible signs—buildings, teachers' salaries, books, and so forth—that were inequitable, it was the effects of segregation on the children directly and presently. ''We cannot turn the clock back to 1868 when the Amendment was adopted, or even to 1896 when *Plessy* v. *Ferguson* was written. We must consider public education in the light of its full development and its present place in American life throughout the nation.''

The Court asked itself this question: ''Does segregation of children in public schools solely on the basis of race, even though the physical facilities and other tangible factors may be equal, deprive the children of the minority group of equal educational opportunities?'' The Court was unanimous that it did. Separate educational facilities were inherently unequal; segregated facilities deprived citizens of the equal protection of the laws guaranteed by the Fourteenth Amendment.

Technically, the *Brown* decision only applied to public educational facilities. The Supreme Court moved swiftly and resolutely, however, to extend the desegregation principle to buses, public parks, golf courses, restaurants, municipal auditoriums, and the like. Such cases merely cited *Brown* to strike down ordinances that segregated facilities on a ''separate but equal'' basis.

Yet it was one thing to desegregate public facilities and quite another to order their integration. In *Brown* v. *The Board of Education,* 1955 *(Brown II)* the Court had to consider the scope and timing for its previous decision. The Court ruled that public schools should proceed with ''all deliberate speed'' to desegregate their facilities.[7] But events in the South, and elsewhere, indicated just how slow and difficult a process that was going to be. In 1957, President Eisenhower had to send in federal troops to quell a disturbance and help escort black students as they sought to attend high school in Little Rock, Arkansas. In 1962, the Uni-

4. *Cummings* v. *Board of Education,* 175 U.S. 528 (1899).
5. *Gong Lum* v. *Rice,* 275 U.S. 78 (1927).
6. *Brown* v. *Board of Education of Topeka, Kansas,* 347 U.S. 483 (1954).
7. *Brown* v. *Board of Education (Brown II),* 349 U. S. 294 (1955).

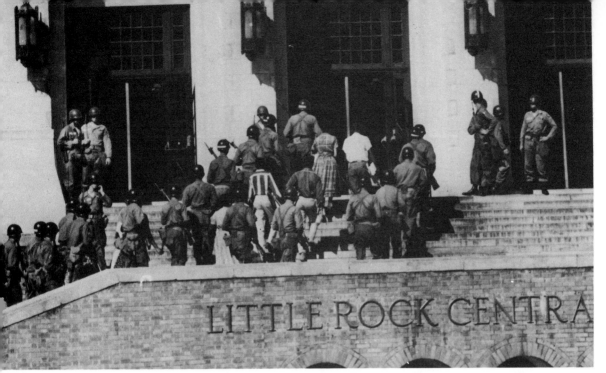

Desegregation of education would not be swift nor easy. Here federal troops escort black students to high school in Little Rock, Arkansas. (United Press International)

versity of Mississippi was integrated only after rioting on campus had claimed the lives of two men. A year later, the Governor of Alabama, George Wallace, physically blocked black students from entering the University of Alabama.

The Court was growing impatient. It recognized the need for time in desegregating school facilities, but it would not tolerate unnecessary delay and certainly not direct and open violation of its rulings. In 1964, the Court ruled "the time for mere deliberate speed has run out."[8] In *Green* v. *County School Board*, the Court not only repeated its statement about prompt action, but required the school board to put forward a plan that would work, "and promises realistically to work now."[9] More and more school systems would have to take action to eliminate racial discrimination.

BUSING

No affirmative action proposals have caused more controversy than the court-ordered remedy of forced busing to overcome intentional discrimination against racial minorities. In 1971, *Swann* v. *Charlotte-Mecklenburg Board of Education* established the readiness of the Court to impose judicial remedy for

8. *Griffin* v. *Prince Edward County Board of Education*, 377 U. S. 218 (1964).
9. *Green* v. *County School Board*, 391 U. S. 430 (1968).

The yellow school bus, the contemporary symbol surrounding racial integration in education. (Stan Wakefield)

school systems perpetuating a dual, or segregated, system. Where a federal court found intentional discrimination, where de jure (legal) segregation was present and no adequate plan for desegregation existed, the court was authorized to provide specific remedy.[10] What the Supreme Court did in this case was to order an extensive program of two-way busing of students between Charlotte and Mecklenburg County to break up segregated schools. Students would be bused out of their neighborhood schools, to schools some distance from home if necessary, to break the pattern of segregation.

District courts around the country were quick to follow suit. A federal District Court judge in Detroit, Michigan, ordered area-wide busing in the fall of 1971. Richmond, Virginia, was ordered to bus students across city and county lines in 1972. Judge Garrity of Boston ordered blacks bused into South Boston and Charlestown in 1974. By 1975, Lousiville, Kentucky, had been added to the list. And in 1978, after several delays, the city of Los Angeles undertook the most massive busing of students to date.

Court-ordered busing of schoolchildren has produced strong criticism and even violence. But the Court has not backed down. In 1979 Columbus and Dayton, Ohio, were required to bus students. A resolute Court said that the affirmative duty to disestablish dual school systems "is beyond question."[11] Busing is now a well-established tool for judicial relief to provide Fourteenth Amendment rights of equal protection of the law where intentional legal segregation exists in public education.

10. *Swann* v. *Charlotte-Mecklenburg Board of Education,* 402 U. S. 1 (1971).
11. *Columbus Board of Education* v. *Penick;* 441 U. S. 903 (1979) and *Dayton Board of Education* v. *Brinkman;* 441 U. S. 903 (1979).

DESEGREGATION IN PUBLIC FACILITIES

The revolution produced by the *Brown* decision spread quickly. Throughout the last half of the 1950s, racial barriers began to fall. The Court invalidated segregation in parks, buses, athletic contests, restaurants, auditoriums, and the like. But the change was not easy. Demonstrations, boycotts, sit-ins, and protests occurred throughout the South. To end segregation on bus lines, Martin Luther King, Jr. organized a boycott in Montgomery, Alabama, in 1956. Sit-ins occurred at several segregated restaurants and lunch counters in the early 1960s. And in 1963 Dr. King organized a massive demonstration against segregation in Birmingham, Alabama. The demonstrators were met in that city by fire hoses, well-protected police officers, and police dogs. The resulting scenes of violence and brutality touched the conscience of a nation. Two hundred thousand people jammed the Mall in Washington, D. C., in August 1963 to participate with Dr. King in his "March on Washington." Civil rights for black Americans was a national concern; America would have to respond.

Congress had not passed a meaningful civil rights act bill in nearly a century when President Kennedy sent in a comprehensive civil rights bill in 1963. President Johnson, upon the death of President Kennedy, urged Congress to act swiftly. The bill was passed and signed into law by President Johnson on July 2, 1964. It proceeded to make it a federal crime to discriminate on the basis of race, color, religion, national origin, or sex in places of public accommodation, including hotels, motels, restaurants, gas stations, theaters, sports arenas, movie houses, or other places of entertainment involved in interstate commerce. It also

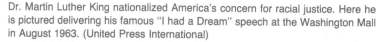

Dr. Martin Luther King nationalized America's concern for racial justice. Here he is pictured delivering his famous "I had a Dream" speech at the Washington Mall in August 1963. (United Press International)

forbade discrimination in employment. It prevented differing standards being applied with respect to voting. It empowered the attorney general to bring suit to enforce the desegregation of public accommodations, and it permitted the executive branch to cut off federal funds to those agencies or organizations continuing to practice discrimination.

VOTING RIGHTS

By 1964, the civil rights movement was turning its attention to the political process. The Fifteenth Amendment was meant to sweep away racial barriers to voting, yet the percentage of eligible black voters remained low throughout the twentieth century. No more than 15 percent of black voters were registered to vote as of 1948. Southern states had devised means to prevent blacks from voting: The "white primary" excluded blacks from voting not in a general election, but in the primary. This was declared unconstitutional in 1944. The poll tax as a condition for voting was eliminated by Court action in 1966 and became the Twenty-fourth Amendment to the Constitution. Literacy tests were used to disqualify voters unable to read or write. Grandfather clauses sought to restrict voting to descendants of eligible voters a generation earlier. And if these measures failed, there was always outright intimidation.

The battle for the ballot was long and legal. Under the leadership of the Supreme Court, qualifications were being swept away, but on a case-by-case basis. In 1965 Congress passed the Voting Rights Act. Instead of outlawing discriminatory practices as the 1964 act had done, the act impowered federal officials to register voters and to supervise the conduct of elections. Literacy tests were suspended, and heavy fines were set for intimidation of voters or interfering with voting rights. In 1980 the Court affirmed the 1965 Act as preventing Rome, Georgia, from altering its electoral system from a plurality electoral system to a majority vote for members of the city commission because it had the effect of being racially discriminatory even though the purpose of the change was nondiscriminatory.[12]

The results were immediate and direct: Eligible black voter registrations increased dramatically. By 1971, over half the eligible voters in the South were registered. And for the first time since Reconstruction, blacks were candidates for public office. By 1970, close to 500 blacks had been elected to public office.

The Voting Rights Act has twice been extended, each time broadening the scope and power of the law. In 1970 the act was broadened by suspending all literacy tests. Residence requirements to participate in federal elections were reduced from the traditional six months to two years to thirty days. In 1975 Congress acted to incorporate other minorities under the provisions of the law, including the printing of election materials in bilingual form for those not speaking English.

12. *City of Rome, Ga.* v. *United States,* _____U.S. _____(1980).

PUBLIC ACCOMMODATIONS, EMPLOYMENT, AND HOUSING

The urban migration of blacks from the South to the cities of the North in the 1940s and 1950s produced black ghettos. Unemployment, poverty, and substandard housing left millions of Americans hopeless and desperate.

Public Accommodations.   The 1964 Civil Rights Act had attacked private discrimination in places of public accommodation. Title II of the 1964 Act made it a federal offense for a person to discriminate on the basis of race, color, religion, or national origin in places of public business or occupancy. The law specifically included inns, hotels, motels, and public boardinghouses. It also listed businesses serving the public: restaurants, gasoline stations, and any place serving food or selling products that have moved through interstate commerce. Also included were those places of public occupancy open to a public moved in interstate commerce: motion picture houses, theaters, concert halls, sports arenas, and other forms of entertainment. The attorney general was empowered to bring suit to effect desegregation as well as intervene in cases brought by individuals.

The major provisions of the Act were quickly challenged, notably the authority of Congress to use the interstate commerce clause to desegregate public accommodations. In 1964, a unanimous Supreme Court upheld the constitutionality of the act in the *Heart of Atlanta Motel* v. *United States.*[13] The result has been the effective desegregation of public facilities.

Employment.   Title VII of the 1964 Civil Rights Act made it an unfair labor practice for any employer engaged in interstate commerce to discriminate on the basis of race, color, sex, religion, or national origin. Congress created an Equal Employment Opportunity Commission (EEOC) to enforce the fair employment portions of the Act, and it has been further strengthened with the passage of the Equal Employment Opportunity Act of 1972. The EEOC works primarily to aid disadvantaged groups seeking employment opportunities.

Discrimination in employment and the work of the EEOC have been supplemented by Executive Order 11246 in 1965 (as amended by Executive Order 11375 in 1967 to include sex), which prohibits discrimination in employment by employers doing business with the federal government. Under the threat of withholding federal funds—or debarment from federal grants—employers, contractors, and public universities have been required to adopt affirmative action plans to redress the past effects of discriminatory practices. Recruitment plans, salary schedules, retirement programs, and fringe benefits are all screened to ensure compliance with federal rules and law.

Housing.   President Kennedy ordered the federal government to stop allowing federal money to be used for housing projects operated on a segregated basis. That was 1962. In 1968, Congress passed the Civil Rights Act of 1968, which prohibited discrimination in the sale or rental of private property listed

13. *Heart of Atlanta Motel* v. *United States,* 379 U.S. 421 (1964).

through a real estate agent. The legislation covered the bulk of housing in the nation. Private individuals selling their own homes were exempted, but real estate brokers and public housing projects were all included. The Act forbade discrimination in the sale of private property; it also forbade the discriminatory advertising of homes for sale.

The Supreme Court also moved to outlaw discrimination in the sale of private homes. In *Jones* v. *Mayer Co.*, the Court upheld an 1866 Civil Rights Act that prevented discrimination in the sale of private property. This did not involve state action and therefore could not be held unconstitutional under the Fourteenth Amendment. Rather, the 1866 Act was upheld as banning private acts of discrimination under the Thirteenth Amendment. Private discrimination constituted a "badge of slavery" and was impermissible under the Thirteenth Amendment.[14] The amendment, the Court reasoned, allowed Congress to outlaw not only indentured servitude, but also "badges of slavery." Private acts constituted "badges" of slavery, and Congress could pass legislation to eliminate them.

Under the Fourteenth Amendment, state action was necessary in order for the Court to strike down state law as violating equal protection of the laws. Congress could act only in its areas of competence, such as interstate commerce, but here the Court was allowing Congress to attack purely private discrimination under the Thirteenth Amendment. In *Runyan* v. *McCrary,* the Supreme Court extended the reasoning of *Jones* to prohibit private, nonsectarian schools from denying admission to students because of their race.[15] The private school had violated the contractual rights of blacks by not offering services equally to white and nonwhite students. Although the Court has not extended this reasoning to every situation—a private social club can limit membership on the basis of race and yet not lose its liquor license[16]—the authority of Congress to legislate under the Thirteenth Amendment to attack private as well as public acts of discrimination is established.

EQUAL PROTECTION OF THE LAWS

The thrust of the Supreme Court's reading of the Fourteenth Amendment as well as its reviews of congressional acts has been to examine laws that distinguish or classify people by race. The Court has never held that laws cannot classify by race (or for that matter by sex or age). What the Court has said is that such laws cannot *unreasonably* classify people. An unreasonable classification is one that bears no relationship between the classes of people created and the legitimate goals of government to be advanced. There must be some "compelling state interest" to permit classification of people by race. The Court treats such laws with great suspicion and subjects them to rigid scrutiny before sustaining them. Race has become the most suspect classification, but the category of laws is being extended for classifications based on sex, age, and physical disability.

14. *Jones* v. *Alfred H. Mayer Co.*, 392 U.S. 409 (1968).
15. *Runyan* v. *McCrary*, 427 U.S. 160 (1976).
16. *Moose Lodge No. 107* v. *Irvis*, 407 U.S. 163 (1971).

Race: The Road from Newark to Miami

In the long hot summer of 1967, 25 persons were killed in racial violence in Newark, New Jersey, 43 persons died in Detroit race rioting, and Martin Luther King, Jr., was assassinated in Memphis, Tennessee. At that time civil rights was an urgent national priority. President Johnson formed a Presidential Commission on Civil Disorders to examine the cause of racial violence. Its report in March 1968 said, ''What white Americans have never fully understood—but what the Negro can never forget—is that white society is deeply implicated in the ghetto. White institutions created it, white institutions maintain it, and white society condones it.'' Their conclusion was stark: We are moving toward two societies, one white, one black, separate and unequal.

The rioting in Miami in May 1980 left 17 dead. We were once again reminded that racial justice must be on the policy agenda of the nation. But the broader issue raised by the rioting in Miami was whether racial policy as presented by the Commission on Civil Disorders had been implemented during the decade of the 1970s. The Commission had raised three levels of policy issues; in priority they were:

First level
  ● police practices
  ● unemployment and underemployment
  ● inadequate housing
Second level
  ● inadequate education
  ● poor recreational facilities
  ● ineffectual grievance mechanisms
Third level
  ● disrespectful white attitudes
  ● discriminatory justice
  ● inadequate federal programs

Since 1968, except for Miami in 1980, there has been little racial violence or national attention on racial justice. Does this mean that rioting served its purpose in moving race to the governmental agenda and subsequent policy adoption? Can we call the decade of the 1970s a healing decade?

While it is clear that race no longer occupies a premier place in American public opinion as a pressing social concern, there is little evidence that real progress has been achieved toward racial justice.

Many cities remain geographically segregated and many school systems remain predominately black. The economic status of blacks has not changed appreciably. Over the decade of the 70s real progress was made in education in that the median years of education has climbed steadily for blacks: to 11.9 years for blacks as compared with 12.5 years for whites. The percent of black and white students going on to college has become almost identical: 31.5% for blacks and 32.2% for whites. But in income and employment blacks have lost ground relative to whites. The median income of blacks in 1978 was $10,900 compared with $18,400 for whites. This represents a greater disparity than at the start of the decade ($6,300 for blacks and $10,200 for whites). There were more unemployed blacks relative to unemployed whites; in fact, a 50% increase in the gap for the decade. As of 1976 12.2% of blacks were unemployed compared with 5.1% of whites.

How then do we react to Miami? Was it an isolated phenomenon for the 1980s? There appears little evidence that the government agenda produced policy changes. Rather than healing, racial justice seems to have been pushed from the governmental agenda to have become the forgotten agenda issue.

Reverse Discrimination.   A more interesting problem arises for laws that promote benign racial classification—laws that use classifications to benefit or promote a racial or ethnic minority. The recent affirmative action plans, racial balance programs in education, and "quotas" for employers and contractors all have raised questions regarding equal protection of the laws. Should these laws be viewed as suspect as well, or is there a "compelling state interest" in overcoming the social, political, and economic effects of past discrimination?

The issue first arose in the *De Funis* case; Marco De Funis was denied admission to law school in favor of some minority applicants screened by separate standards. A trial court in Washington ordered him admitted. The state supreme court reversed the decision, holding that the setting aside of seats for minority students was a compelling state interest in promoting racial equality and integration. De Funis appealed to the Supreme Court. Justice Douglas stayed the Washington Supreme Court order until the full court could consider the merits of the case. But this never happened: De Funis was in his last year of law school by then, and the Supreme Court dismissed the case without discussing the merits of benign classification.[17]

But the issue could not long be avoided. In 1973 and 1974 Allan Bakke had been denied admission to the University of California–Davis medical school in favor of some minority applicants under Davis' special admissions program to increase the proportion of "disadvantaged" students in medical school. In both years, disadvantaged applicants were admitted with lower scores on admission tests than those achieved by Bakke. Bakke sued, charging the special admissions program excluded him from medical school because of his race, thereby denying him the equal protection of the laws guaranteed by the Fourteenth Amendment. He charged "reverse discrimination." The Supreme Court agreed, but on narrow grounds and in a divided opinion.

Alan Bakke was to be admitted to medical school. The explicit use of quotas (setting aside a specific number of seats for disadvantaged students) was a violation of the Fourteenth Amendment. "It tells applicants who are not Negro, Asian, or Chicano that they are totally excluded from a specific percentage of the seats in an entering class." Indeed, this was the fatal flaw in the Davis admission program. Justice Powell wrote for the Court that race can be taken into consideration as a factor for admission. It may be deemed a "plus" in an applicant's file, yet it does not isolate the individual from all other candidates. Furthermore, a program based solely on race does not promote the state's interest in ethnic diversity; yet the Court found ethnic diversity a worthwhile educational objective.[18] Schools may use race as a factor, but they cannot make it the sole factor. The Court was walking a fine line. Affirmative action was to continue: "The state has a legitimate and substantial interest in ameliorating, or eliminating where feasible, the disabling effects of identified discrimination." Yet the use of quotas was not

17. *De Funis* v. *Odegaard,* 416 U.S. 312 (1974).
18. *University of California Regents* v. *Bakke,* 438 U.S. 265 (1978).

The case of Alan Bakke's admission to medical school challenged the policy of affirmative action. Supporters of affirmative action urge the Supreme Court not to overturn the policy. (United Press International)

permissible. In *Steelworkers and Kaiser Aluminum* v. *Weber* (1979), the Court specifically confronted positive programs to recruit minority personnel for union and private industry trainee openings. The Court found no objection. This was a private, voluntary plan; no state action was involved. Here affirmative action did not violate equal protection of the laws.[19]

The Court also upheld the "minority business enterprise" provision of the Public Works Employment Act of 1977 which required at least 10 percent of federal funds used for local public works projects to be set aside for minority businesses. Congress, the Court noted, seeks to overcome the effects of prior discrimination by ensuring that minority business enterprises are not denied equal

19. *Steelworkers and Kaiser Aluminum* v. *Weber*, 440 U.S. 954 (1979).

opportunity to participate in federal grants to state and local governments and that racial and ethnic criteria are valid means to accomplish Congress' objective. In pressing for the goal of equality of economic opportunity, the ''Congress has necessary latitude to try new techniques such as the limited use of racial and ethnic criteria to accomplish remedial objectives.''[20]

SEX AND AGE DISCRIMINATION

Until recently the courts never looked seriously at sex discrimination as a violation of the Fourteenth Amendment. Men and women were treated differently under the law, and married women in particular were subject to several limitations. Women were discriminated against in employment, inheritance, ownership of property, and even jury duty.

By 1971, that began to change. For the first time, in *Reed* v. *Reed,* the Supreme Court offered equal protection guarantees against sex discrimination under the Fourteenth Amendment.[21] At issue was an Oregon statute that gave mandatory preference to a male in the selection of an administrator for an estate. The Supreme Court ruled unanimously that the arbitrary preference for males could not be justified under the Fourteenth Amendment.

The decision stopped short of declaring sex a suspect category; it did not question a legislature's power to use gender as a basis for classification. It simply stated: ''To give a mandatory preference to members of either sex over members of the other, merely to accomplish the elimination of hearings on the merits, is to make the very kind of arbitrary legislative choice forbidden by the Equal Protection Clause of the Fourteenth Amendment.'' But in 1973 Justice Brennan found sex to be a suspect class, though not in the same manner as race is viewed as suspect.[22] Such a declaration will have to await the outcome of the proposed Equal Rights Amendment.

In subsequent decisions, the Supreme Court has struck down laws that exempted women from jury duty,[23] provided for social security benefits based on the earnings of the deceased husband differently from the earnings of a deceased wife,[24] created differing ages of majority for males and females in cases of support,[25] favored alimony for women,[26] set gender-based Aid to Families with Dependent Children (AFDC) unemployment benefits,[27] or discriminated in the sale of beer.[28] The Court has been willing to sustain sex distinctions in law with regard

---

20. *Fullilove* v. *Klutznick,* _____U.S. _____(1980).
21. *Reed* v. *Reed,* 404 U.S. 71 (1971).
22. *Frontiero* v. *Richardson,* 411 U.S. 677 (1973).
23. *Taylor* v. *Louisiana,* 419 U.S. 522 (1975); *Duren* v. *Missouri,* 439 U.S. 890 (1978).
24. *Weinberger* v. *Wiesenfeld,* 420 U.S. 636 (1975).
25. *Stanton* v. *Stanton,* 421 U.S. 7 (1975).
26. *Orr* v. *Orr,* 440 U.S. 268 (1979).
27. *Califano* v. *Westcott,* 440 U.S. 944 (1979).
28. *Craig* v. *Boren,* 429 U.S. 190 (1976).

"MARRIED COUPLES SUING FOR RAPE, UNMARRIED COUPLES SUING FOR ALIMONY, THE DIVORCE RATE IS SOARING, ILLEGITIMATE BIRTHS ARE UP..... HONESTLY! SOMETIMES I WONDER WHATEVER BECAME OF THE NORMAL FAMILY UNIT, DEAR."

1979—*The Cincinnati Enquirer* Jim Borgman ©

to property tax exemptions for widows, however, since they are more likely to face an unsympathetic job market.[29] The Court allowed a male naval officer passed over for promotion to be discharged while retaining in service a female passed over for promotion,[30] and it permitted greater social security benefits to women "to compensate women for past economic discrimination."[31] It would, however, not allow workmen's compensation to deny benefits to men unless they were actually dependent on deceased wife's earnings, while widows need not prove dependence on husband's earnings.[32]

Of particular concern has been the status of maternity leaves. In 1974 the Supreme Court ruled that mandatory leaves for teachers violated due process.[33] Mandatory leave placed a heavy burden on a woman in matters of marriage and

29. *Kahn* v. *Shevin,* 416 U.S. 190 (1976).
30. *Schlesinger* v. *Ballard,* 419 U.S. 498 (1975).
31. *Califano* v. *Webster,* 430 U.S. 313 (1977).
32. *Wengler* v. *Druggists Mutual Insurance Co.* __ U.S. __ (1980).
33. *Cleveland Board of Education* v. *LaFleur,* 414 U.S. 639 (1974).

family, matters that were personal. Using the same logic, the Court struck down a statute that exempted pregnant women from employment leave benefits due to the pregnancy.[34] But the Court has allowed the exclusion of pregnancy from the disability benefits allowed employees.[35]

In 1979 the Court provided an additional avenue for women to redress sex discrimination in education. The Supreme Court ruled in *Cannon* v. *University of Chicago* that the Title IX regulations for the Educational Amendments of 1972 created a right to a private course of action.[36] Rather than limiting Title IX to administrative action, the Court found a benefit conferred on persons and legislative intent permitting individuals to bring private lawsuits.

THE EQUAL RIGHTS AMENDMENT

The Equal Rights Amendment (ERA), currently before the states for ratification, would prohibit sex-based classifications. Section One of the Amendment reads:

> Equality of Rights under the Law shall not be denied or abridged by the United States or by any state on account of sex.

34. *Turner* v. *Department of Employment,* 423 U.S. 44 (1975).
35. *General Electric Co.* v. *Gilbert,* 429 U.S. 125 (1976).
36. *Cannon* v. *University of Chicago,* 441 U.S. 677 (1979).

Supporters of the Equal Rights Amendment celebrate Congress' extension of the ratification deadline for the Amendment. (United Press International)

It appears that sex classifications will be treated like race if the amendment passes, and if the logic of treating suspect classifications through Constitutional language is a proper analogy. The congressional debates on ERA suggest that the intent is to treat men and women equally, including eliminating laws giving women preference over males. There would be some logic for differential treatment, though narrowly drawn, on personal rights and common sense.

AGE DISCRIMINATION

Like laws on race and sex, those that discriminate on the basis of age are increasingly coming under attack. Although age discrimination is not itself an unreasonable or arbitrary distinction, an increasing number of laws and administrative rules prohibit discrimination on the basis of age. The 1967 Age Discrimination in Employment Amendment to the 1964 Civil Rights Act added age to the list of prohibited bases for discrimination that constituted an unfair labor practice. The Older Americans Act of 1975 extended the protections against "unreasonable discrimination" based on age by permitting the federal government to withhold federal funds from any program that unreasonably discriminates or withholds benefits because of age. The act empowered the United States Commission on Civil Rights to identify such programs and report them to the Secretary of Health, Education, and Welfare.

More recently, Congress extended the mandatory retirement age from 65 to 70 years of age for most nonfederal workers. The law passed in 1978 extends protections of the 1967 Age Discrimination Amendment to include those between 65 and 70 years of age. In effect, this prohibits forced retirement before 70. The law also eliminated age ceilings for federal employees who previously had to retire at 70 years of age.

The physically disabled are treated like any other category of people. There can be no unreasonable discrimination of the physically handicapped. The Vocational Rehabilitation Act of 1975 barred discrimination under any program receiving federal funds. The 1978 Disabilities Act extended the provisions to include executive-operated agencies. Health and Human Services (formerly HEW) is charged with promulgating regulations to implement nondiscrimination against the physically handicapped. Affirmative action, however, is not required under these statutes. The Court ruled that a hearing disability was sufficient grounds to exclude an applicant from a nursing program.[37] Programs do not have to be modified if modifications would substantially lower standards. But the Court cautioned, "identification of those instances where a refusal to accommodate the needs of a disabled person amounts to discrimination against the handicapped continues to be an important responsibility of HEW."

---

37. *Southeastern Community College* v. *Davis*, 442 U.S. 397 (1979).

In the America of a generation ago, for most women, whether they worked before marriage or not, their wedding day was also the day of their retirement from the salaried workforce. This generally posed no problem, for marriages were stable. According to the social consensus, a woman who spent her life as a homemaker could expect to be supported throughout her life. Whether or not to consider homemaking a career and what one's prospects might be in the labor force outside the home simply were not issues.

Today, the circumstances are quite different. A woman left without support because of death of a spouse or divorce when she is in her late forties or fifties is a person completely outside the system. She is not yet eligible for social security benefits (which in any case are tied to her husband's years of work and earnings); social agenices can offer her little. She is not eligible for unemployment insurance, and the job market is a nightmare. When a recently widowed fifty-year-old woman walks into an employment agency looking for a job, she finds herself quickly shuffled out with the suggestion that she do volunteer work. Even if she held a job for a few years before her marriage, that experience is no longer considered relevant. And it is almost impossible for her to get training: Training programs—even the federally funded CETA—are for those who will be working for years and so will repay an employer's investment in them. She is a nonperson by virtue of her age, sex, and life history.

What makes this discrepancy between the American dream and reality so poignant is that as of the 1974 census, 37 percent of American women over forty have no husbands, and more than a million widowed or divorced women under sixty are out of the labor force. In addition, more than six million are married homemakers— but the fact is that one out of every three marriages ends in divorce.

These changes—and the obviously changed consensus on marriage and a woman's giving up a career or a place in the labor force in exchange for lifelong support—are part of the ferment that has brought a revitalized women's movement, the organization of older people into such groups as the Gray Panthers, and an attempt to pass federal legislation to provide job training and the development of special community service positions for older women. And perhaps because discrimination issues are so closely tied to the reality of economic survival, as well as to the American ideal of justice and opportunity for all, a new consensus may be emerging. If it is not, we may soon be forced to forge one, for our population is aging, and statistically American women outlive men.

DUE PROCESS

Political power involves a trust that can easily be abused. The Founding Fathers were well aware of the danger of concentrating too much power in the hands of the government. In addition to the Bill of Rights, they wrote due process protections into the Constitution. Article I, section nine, outlined specific guarantees, while the Fifth Amendment provided the broader guarantee that no person could be deprived of life, liberty, or property without due process of law. **Due process** is of two kinds, procedural and substantive. **Procedural due process** refers to the fairness with which laws are enforced. **Substantive due process** deals with the reasonableness of the law itself.

SUBSTANTIVE DUE PROCESS

Substantive due process is an ancient concept: There have always been some rights that government could not violate, rights considered basic natural rights of free people.

In the early part of the twentieth century, substantive due process was needed to protect freedom of contract—that is, the Supreme Court would strike down almost any law that impaired economic liberty. The right of property was almost inviolable. The Court would not accept minimum wage laws, price controls, regulations for working hours, or working conditions as legitimate state interests. It argued that the right of contract could be impaired only where legislation has some reasonable relation to a legitimate end of government. Only when the health and safety of the public was at stake could the Court be convinced to sustain legislation.

With the Great Depression and the New Deal in the 1930s the Court began to abandon this view. Today the Supreme Court will no longer apply the liberty of contract view of substantive due process to economic legislation. It prefers to think that the reasonableness of the use of property and economic regulations is a legislative responsibility. As long as it can find some relationship between legislation and public welfare, the Court will not interfere.

The Court has now turned its attention to the protection of fundamental constitutional rights. The Court will use the equal protection clause and the due process clause to limit *any* government from interfering with the fundamental constitutional rights of citizens. Once a right has been given the status of a fundamental right, it requires a compelling state interest before the Court will sustain legislation limiting that right. The Court has proceeded cautiously in lengthening the list, but there is no reason to believe its attitude toward the protection of fundamental rights, such as the right to vote, will change.

One technique citizens may use to protect fundamental constitutional rights is to bring a **class action suit.** This is a lawsuit brought by a group of persons with a common legal concern who are willing to share the costs of bringing suit. The Supreme Court has held that parties to the suit must have some personal interest in the suit, not any general interest in the outcome for a third party. Most commonly used by taxpayers and public interest groups, women have sued to prevent sex discrimination in employment and retirement benefits, while doctors have successfully prevented restrictions to the doctor–client relationship. But the Court is not eager to encourage general challenge to laws. Taxpayers were not allowed to challenge the secrecy of the Central Intelligence Agency since they suffered no injury, nor can citizens bring suit to unseat members of Congress. Furthermore, members of a class action must demonstrate some substantial personal interest, at least $10,000 individually (the group cannot total all losses to arrive at $10,000).[38]

PROCEDURAL DUE PROCESS

The language of the Fifth and Fourteenth Amendments, which prohibit the national and state governments from depriving citizens of life, liberty, or property without due process of law, is the basis for procedural due process. This requires that the government be fair in providing a process to consider a person's interests when it acts to deprive someone of life, liberty, or property. In other words, the government must give the individual his or her "due."

It is in the area of criminal justice that procedural due process is most evident and criticized. An accused citizen must be afforded all rights guaranteed by the Bill of Rights as well as be given a fair hearing. There are rules by which evidence may be used against a defendant. The government must prove beyond any "reasonable doubt" that a crime was committed. The primary sources of procedural due process rights in the Constitution are the Fourth, Fifth, and Sixth Amendments to the Constitution.

DUE PROCESS AND THE CRIMINAL JUSTICE SYSTEM

Figure 5.1 (pp. 170–71) gives an overview of our criminal justice system.

Searches and Seizures. The Fourth Amendment protects persons against unreasonable searches and seizures. All searches and seizures are not unconstitutional, but persons are to be "secure in their persons, houses, papers, and effects against unreasonable searches and seizures." It is this definition of unreasonable, however, that has produced what Justice Lewis Powell called a "twilight zone."

In general the Fourth Amendment requires a search warrant, issued by a judicial officer on the basis of "probable cause," for a search to be constitutional. There are two main procedural requirements: First the warrant is to be issued by a nonpolice officer, who has a neutral and detached outside view of the issue; second, the place to be searched and the person or things asked to be seized are to be specifically described.

---

38. *Zahn* v. *International Paper Co.,* 414 U.S. 291 (1973).

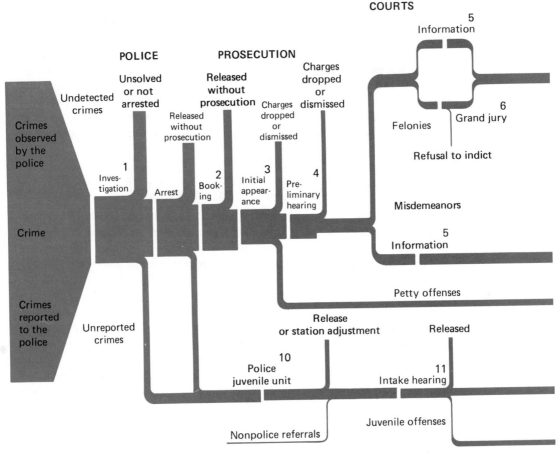

1 May continue until trial.
2 Administrative record of arrest. First step at which temporary release on bail may be available
3 Before magistrate, commissioner, or justice of peace. Formal notice of charge, advice of rights. Bail set. Summary trials for petty offenses usually conducted here without further processing.

4 Preliminary testing of evidence against defendant. Charge may be reduced. No separate preliminary hearing for misdemeanors in some systems.
5 Charge filed by prosecutor on basis of information submitted by police or citizens. Alternative to grand jury indictment: often used in felonies, almost always in misdemeanors
6 Reviews whether government evidence sufficient to jusitfy trial. Some states have no grand jury system; others seldom use it.

CORRECTIONS

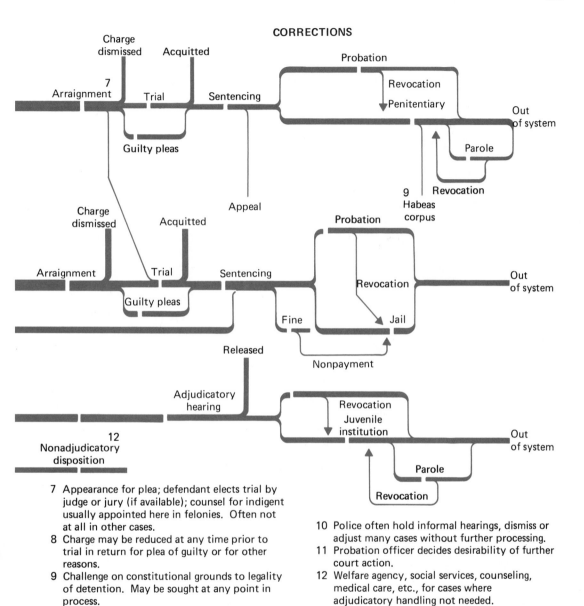

7 Appearance for plea; defendant elects trial by judge or jury (if available); counsel for indigent usually appointed here in felonies. Often not at all in other cases.

8 Charge may be reduced at any time prior to trial in return for plea of guilty or for other reasons.

9 Challenge on constitutional grounds to legality of detention. May be sought at any point in process.

10 Police often hold informal hearings, dismiss or adjust many cases without further processing.

11 Probation officer decides desirability of further court action.

12 Welfare agency, social services, counseling, medical care, etc., for cases where adjudicatory handling not needed.

Figure 5.1

An overview of the criminal justice system, showing the movement of cases through the criminal justice system. Procedures in individual jurisdictions may vary from the patterns shown here. The differing weights of the lines indicate the relative volumes of cases disposed of at various points in the system, but this is only suggestive since no nationwide data of this sort exist. (*The Challenge of Crime in a Free Society.* Report by the President's Commission on Law Enforcement and Administration of Justice, Government Printing Office, 1967, pp. 8–9)

The Court has held that the Fourth Amendment and the Fifth Amendment right against self-incrimination prevent authorization of the seizure of "mere evidence" to establish a criminal charge against someone because this amounts to a seizure that compels self-incrimination. In other words, a court cannot authorize a "fishing expedition" by issuing a warrant to search a house in order to see if something can be found that would allow bringing charges against the individual. In *Dunaway* v. *New York,* the Court forbade taking a suspect into custody without probable cause for purposes of interrogation in the hope that "something might turn up."[39] The "mere evidence" rule seems to preclude any self-incriminating evidence, including taking fingerprints or a drunk-driving test, but this is not the case. The Supreme Court, in *Schmerber* v. *California,* ruled that taking blood samples to introduce as evidence to prove drunk driving did not violate the right to be protected against self-incrimination.[40] The Court read the Fifth Amendment as not requiring an individual to bear witness against himself, but it did not prohibit the introduction of physical evidence as the object of a reasonable search and seizure. The "mere evidence" rule has been sufficiently modified to allow evidence aiding in the apprehension and conviction of those accused. In *Warden* v. *Hayden,* the Court said: "There must, of course, be a nexus—automatically provided in the case of fruits, instrumentalities or contraband—between the item to be seized and criminal behavior. Thus in the case of 'mere evidence,' probable cause must be examined in terms of cause to believe that the evidence sought will aid in a particular apprehension or conviction."[41]

What then is subject to seizure? Generally speaking, it must be evidence relating to proof that a crime was committed or is about to be committed, and it must be described plainly and adequately in the search warrant. Police officers can seize other property if that property is related to the property described in the warrant or if it is contraband. They cannot, however, use as evidence property unrelated to the property described in the warrant, such as shotgun shells found in a locked trunk when the warrant was for alcohol. The courts do allow "plain view" evidence as an exception: If in the process of a legitimate search the police inadvertently come across a piece of incriminating evidence, they may seize the evidence under the prior justification for which the warrant was issued.[42] But the Court has cautioned: "The plain view doctrine may not be used to extend a general exploratory search from one object to another until something incriminating at last emerges."

As a general rule, searches and seizures conducted without a warrant are unreasonable, but there are important exceptions. Most arrests are made without a warrant, and an arrest is a seizure under the Fourth Amendment. A police officer may make an arrest without a warrant if a crime was committed in the presence of the officer or if the police officer has probable cause to believe a

---

39. *Dunaway* v. *New York,* 442 U.S. 200 (1979).
40. *Schmerber* v. *California,* 384 U.S. 757 (1966).
41. *Warden* v. *Hayden,* 387 U.S. 294 (1967).
42. *Collidge* v. *New Hampshire,* 403 U.S. 443 (1971).

felony has been committed and that the accused committed the felony. The Supreme Court recently reaffirmed this position in not requiring warrants for felony crimes in pressing situations. A postal inspector was allowed to arrest a suspect without a warrant upon the probable cause that he possessed stolen credit cards.[43] It would not, however, accept the right of the Occupational Safety and Health Administration (OSHA) to make warrantless inspections of businesses and industries because it "devolves almost unbridled discretion upon executive and administrative officers, particularly those in the field, as to when to search and whom to search.[44] There must be some assurance that the search is reasonable and for some purpose. On this basis, the Court accepted as valid "third party" warrants. It upheld the right of law enforcement officials in California to secure a warrant to search student newspaper offices at Stanford University for pictures of demonstrators who had assaulted police at a demonstration. The Fourth Amendment did not prevent a state from issuing a warrant simply because the owner or occupant of the place searched was not suspected of criminal activity. The significant element in a reasonable search is that there exists reasonable cause to believe evidence is located on the premises to be searched.[45]

The Court has moved, more recently, to restrict police officers without a warrant from entering private homes to make routine felony arrests. It was often common practice for police, acting with probable cause, to enter private homes in order to effect an arrest. The Court held it was a basic principle of the Fourth Amendment that searches and seizures inside a home without a warrant are presumptively unreasonable. This was the intent of the Framers, and it constitutes an invasion of the sanctity of the home. "In terms that apply equally to seizures of property and to seizures of persons, the Fourth Amendment has drawn a firm line at the entrance to the home. Absent exigent circumstances, that threshold may not reasonably be crossed without a warrant." Henceforth police officers are forbidden from entering homes to make warrantless arrests and have only limited authority to enter homes to make arrests when they do have an arrest warrant and probable cause.[46]

No issue seems to have presented more problems than lawful searches. Courts permit the search of automobiles without a warrant if police have probable cause to believe the automobile contains evidence relating to a crime. For a routine stop in traffic, a search can extend to cover visual evidence in "plain view" but not to the trunk of a car. Stop and frisk, however, is under attack. In 1979 the Court said police cannot randomly stop automobiles under the guise of checking operator's license or vehicle registration in order to "aggressively patrol" high-crime districts.[47] Police officers may "stop and frisk" a suspect on the street if they have reason to believe the individual is armed and dangerous. But the stop-

---

43. *United States* v. *Watson*, 423 U.S. 411 (1976).
44. *Marshall* v. *Barlow, Inc.*, 436 U.S. 307 (1978).
45. *Zurcher* v. *The Stanford Daily*, 436 U.S. 547 (1978).
46. *Payton* v. *New York*, ___ U.S. ___ (1980).
47. *Delaware* v. *Prouse*, 440 U.S. 648 (1979).

ping of pedestrians without reasonable suspicion of criminal activity violates the Fourth Amendment.[48] Even patrons in a bar being investigated with a search warrant cannot be searched without probable cause.[49] In short, the police need probable cause—some reasonable basis—to stop a motorist or a pedestrian to interfere with their lives.

Under the Fourth Amendment, the courts have only one device to ensure protection against unreasonable searches and seizures, and that is to exclude from evidence material unconstitutionally obtained as the result of an illegal search and seizure. This is known as the **exclusionary rule.** In *Mapp* v. *Ohio,* the Supreme Court extended the exclusionary rule to state criminal proceedings.[50] The intent was to deter police from violating the constitutional rights of citizens. In the process, critics have charged that criminals go free. The Burger Court has been sensitive to this charge and has since cut back on the scope of the exclusionary rule. In 1974 the Court ruled that the exclusionary rule does not extend to grand jury proceedings, at which witnesses may be required to answer questions from illegally obtained evidence.[51] And in 1976, the Court restricted the right of federal courts generally to review state court convictions where questions of improper evidence had been raised.[52] If the state court considered the question and rejected the contention of illegal evidence, federal courts were not free to order a new trial on the basis of the exclusionary rule. In 1980 the Court permitted the use of illegally obtained evidence to impeach a defendant's false statements as long as the testimony was in response to proper cross-examination reasonably suggested by the defendant's direct examination.[53]

More importantly, in 1980, the Supreme Court made two rulings that significantly restricted the exclusionary rule. It overturned the ''automatic standing'' rule that gave defendants standing to challenge searches and seizures in crimes of possession. The Court also greatly restricted federal courts' ability to apply the exclusionary rule. In *United States* v. *Salvucci* the Supreme Court declared that the *Jones* rule (*Jones* v. *United States,* 362 U.S. 257 (1960)) had outlived its usefulness in giving automatic standing to challenge the legality of a search in cases involving crimes of possession without regard to whether they (defendants) had an expectation of privacy. The Court now declared defendants ''may only claim the benefits of the exclusionary rule if their own Fourth Amendment rights have in fact been violated.'' Police had seized, with warrant, stolen mail from the home of the mother of one of the defendants. The Court said the defendants had no legitimate expectation of privacy in the area of the mother's home. Hence the automatic standing rule was overturned as ''the doctrine now serves only to afford a windfall to defendants whose Fourth Amendment rights have *not* been violated.''[54]

48. *Brown* v. *Texas,* 440 U.S. 903 (1979).
49. *Ybarra* v. *Illinois,* 444 U.S. 85 (1979).
50. *Mapp* v. *Ohio,* 367 U.S. 643 (1961).
51. *United States* v. *Calandra,* 414 U.S. 338 (1974).
52. *Stone* v. *Powell,* 429 U.S. 874 (1976); and *Wolff* v. *Rice,* 429 U.S. 874 (1976).
53. *United States* v. *Havens,* ___ U.S. ___ (1980).
54. *United States* v. *Salvucci,* ___ U.S. ___ (1980).

The second case involved the flagrantly illegal search of a bank officer's briefcase by IRS officials in order to obtain evidence against a third party charged with income tax evasion. A U.S. District Court set aside the conviction when it learned the evidence had been obtained by the illegal search. The Supreme Court reversed the decision saying that the defendant charged with income tax evasion lacked standing to challenge the conviction because his privacy rights had not been violated (only those of the bank officer). But more importantly the Supreme Court ruled the supervisory power of the federal courts (use of the exclusionary rule) does not permit it to suppress otherwise admissible evidence. "Our Fourth Amendment decisions have established beyond any doubt that the interest in deterring illegal searches does not justify the exclusion of tainted evidence at the instance of a party who was not the victim of the challenged practices."[55]

Complicated questions arise now because of new technology and the wide availability of sophisticated listening devices and recording equipment. The Founding Fathers thought in terms of physical objects—homes, papers, and documents—when drafting the Fourth Amendment. Indeed, early in the twentieth century, the Supreme Court held that the Fourth Amendment applied only to physical objects or physical entry into a home.[56] But by 1967 the full thrust of the new technology could not be ignored. The issues of electronic eavesdropping and wiretapping, the right to privacy, and security under the Fourth Amendment could no longer be avoided. In *Katz* v. *United States,* the Supreme Court said conversations captured electronically were subject to search and seizure rules under the Fourth Amendment.[57] The seizure of a telephone conversation without a warrant violated Fourth Amendment rights. Said the Court, "wherever a man may be, he is entitled to know that he will remain free from unreasonable searches and seizures."

The *Katz* decision meant that warrants would be required for wiretapping, and that courts would now have to contend with the issue as a search and seizure question. The Omnibus Crime Control and Safe Streets Act of 1968 helped somewhat. It required federal agents to secure a warrant from a federal judge before doing any wiretapping and outlined a broad range of potential crimes for which wiretapping warrants might be issued. The act similarly allowed state officials, namely the attorney general, to apply for warrants to wiretap in state situations where a crime has been or is about to be committed. The Act set up a procedure by which the attorney general of the United States would grant permission for wiretapping after securing the necessary warrant. Richard Nixon's attorney general, John Mitchell, interpreted the law as allowing him, *without* court approval, to sanction electronic surveillance in cases involving a threat to the internal security of the United States. In the only case to emerge on the question, the Supreme Court rejected Mr. Mitchell's contention and ruled that the law did not include the right to authorize surveillance for domestic conspiracy.[58] The Court left

55. *United States* v. *Payner,* ___ U.S. ___ (1980).
56. *Olmstead* v. *United States,* 277 U.S. 438 (1928).
57. *Katz* v. *United States,* 389 U.S. 347 (1967).
58. *United States* v. *United States District Court for the Eastern District of Michigan,* 407 U.S. 297 (1972).

open the possibility of electronic surveillance of foreign agents for purposes of national security, but stated directly: "The danger to political dissent is acute when the government attempts to act under so vague a concept as the power to protect domestic security." In the wake of Watergate and the subsequent revelations regarding past presidents and warrantless wiretapping, Congress has been considering legislation that would prohibit all government wiretapping, for any reason, unless undertaken with a judicial warrant.

Rights of the Accused.   The Fifth and Sixth Amendments are the foundation of the procedural guarantees affording due process of the law to persons standing accused of a crime. The Supreme Court has played a prominent role in extending these rights, particularly from federal courts to state courts. Its liberalization of the rights of the accused in the 1960s produced public criticism that the courts were "coddling criminals" and ignoring the rights of law-abiding citizens. Nonetheless, the Court's aim has been to extend the ancient and sacred principles of innocence and burden of proof to all persons standing before the bar of justice.

The Fifth Amendment protects citizens by requiring the government to present evidence to a grand jury to determine if it is sufficient to justify a criminal trial. It also protects citizens from having to incriminate themselves: the burden of proof rests with the state. The Sixth Amendment provides for a jury trial for all criminal prosecutions; the right to be informed of charges, to be confronted with witnesses, and to have the assistance of counsel are also Sixth Amendment rights in federal prosecutions.

In federal prosecutions, it has always been a principle that persons accused of a crime are protected against self-incrimination. Coerced confessions are not permitted as evidence; an individual has the right to remain silent. It was not until 1936 that the principle was extended to include state prosecutions, although these cases dealt with the trial stage and said little about pretrial interrogation and custodial treatment. Rule 5 of the Federal Rules of Criminal Procedure requires the accused to be presented "without unnecessary delay" before a committing officer. Confessions obtained during an unlawful detention are inadmissible. Rule 5 (b) states:

> [The Commissioner] shall inform the defendant of the complaint against him, of his right to retain counsel and of his right to have a preliminary examination. He shall also inform the defendant that he is not required to make a statement and that any statement made by him may be used against him.

The Supreme Court has used this rule to give it supervisory powers over lower federal courts on the admissibility of evidence. The rule was applied in *Mallory* v. *United States,* when the Court overturned a rape conviction on the basis that the confession was exacted with an undue delay in arraigning the defendant.[59]

59. *Mallory* v. *United States,* 354 U.S. 449 (1957).

This still left open the question of at what point during a police interrogation counsel must be provided and a suspect informed of the right against self-incrimination. In *Escobedo* v. *Illinois,* the Court voided a murder conviction because the defendant was denied counsel and not told of the right to remain silent during police interrogation.[60] The full range of those rights was then made clear in *Miranda* v. *Arizona,* in which the Court detailed the principles governing interrogation:

> Prior to any questioning, the person must be warned that he has a right to remain silent, that any statement he does make may be used as evidence against him, and that he has a right to the presence of an attorney, either retained or appointed. . . . If he indicates in any manner and at any stage of the process that he wishes to consult with an attorney before speaking, there can be no questioning.[61]

Chief Justice Warren made it clear there would be no federal or state convictions if defendants were denied the due process of law from the moment they were taken into custody or otherwise deprived of their freedom.

The *Miranda* decision extended the scope of protection from the trial to the point of origination of custody, for both federal and state criminal proceedings. The decision also produced strong protests from law enforcement officials. They claimed their job was difficult enough without further impeding their ability to arrest and convict criminals. Citizens groups protested the protection afforded criminal defendants and the apparent lack of concern for the victims of crimes.

The appointment of Warren Burger to the Supreme Court in 1969, and the subsequent appointments of four new members, has produced a Supreme Court decidedly more cautious in protecting the rights of the accused. It began early in 1971 to restrict the extent of the *Miranda* ruling. In *Harris* v. *New York,* the Court allowed statements to impeach testimony given to police who had not followed *Miranda* guidelines. (The statements, however, would not be admissible as evidence for the prosecution.)[62] In *Michigan* v. *Tucker* (1974), the Court further restricted *Miranda* by applying it only to the defendant's own testimony, not to incriminating statements made by a friend whom the defendant voluntarily named to police.[63] In *Michigan* v. *Mosley* (1975), it allowed a conviction based on a confession to a crime when the defendant had been interrogated and informed of his rights for a separate crime.[64] The right to remain silent and be informed of that right does not prejudice prosecution for another crime. In 1979 the Court further restricted *Miranda* when it held that explicit waiver of the right to counsel was not necessary once the *Miranda* rights have been made known to a defendant.[65] In 1980 the Court said that interrogation within the meaning of *Miranda*

60. *Escobedo* v. *Illinois,* 378 U.S. 478 (1964).
61. *Miranda* v. *Arizona,* 384 U.S. 436 (1966).
62. *Harris* v. *New York,* 401 U.S. 222 (1971).
63. *Michigan* v. *Tucker,* 417 U.S. 433 (1974).
64. *Michigan* v. *Mosley,* 423 U.S. 96 (1975).
65. *North Carolina* v. *Butler,* 441 U.S. 369 (1979).

applies to express questioning and not a suspect's susceptibility. *Miranda* comes into play whenever police question or say or do things they should know to be incriminating. It does not extend to routine conversation or off-hand remarks between police not intended to invite a response from a suspect. Here suspect susceptibility to make self-incriminating responses was not limited by the *Miranda* principles.[66]

Nevertheless, if the Court has seen fit to restrict *Miranda*, it has not indicated any readiness to discard the ruling. The *Innis* case expands the meaning of "interrogation" beyond express questioning. The Court refused to restrict *Miranda* to direct questioning but included "any words or actions on the part of police . . . that the police should know are reasonably likely to elicit an incriminating response from the suspect." Hence, included under *Miranda* are those things which are the "functional equivalent" of express interrogation. In 1975, in *Doyle* v. *Ohio* and *Wood* v. *Ohio* the Court ruled that the exercise of *Miranda* rights could not be used against a defendant as evidence in a trial; the state cannot use silence as an indication of guilt.[67] Finally, in 1977 the Court said a confession of murder given while the suspect was being transported was inadmissible as evidence, because the questions of locating the body for a "Christian burial" amounted to interrogation and *Miranda* rights were not observed.[68] The case drew nationwide attention when the Court held as inadmissible information obtained to locate the body of a ten-year-old child who had been raped and murdered. The police officer transporting the defendant accused of the crime appealed to the defendant's Christian principles to allow the parents to give the child a "Christian burial." The officer did not ask the defendant the location of the body, but when the defendant led the officer to the place, the fact of the knowledge was admitted into evidence. This the Court said amounted to custodial interrogation and required *Miranda* rights, which the defendant was not given.

The Right To Counsel.   Closely related to the right against self-incrimination and, indeed, part of the *Miranda* ruling, is the right to counsel. As originally stated in the Sixth Amendment, the right to have "the assistance of counsel" extended only to the right of the accused to employ counsel; the state had no obligation to provide that counsel. Furthermore, the Court made it clear in *Betts* v. *Brady* (1942) that the Fourteenth Amendment requirement of due process did not include the Sixth Amendment right to counsel in state criminal proceedings.

All that changed in 1963. The landmark decision of *Gideon* v. *Wainwright* required everyone accused of a serious crime to have the opportunity to be assisted by counsel. If the defendant could not afford to employ counsel, the state was obligated to provide such assistance.[69] The Court said: "Any person haled into court, who is too poor to hire a lawyer, cannot be assured a fair trial unless counsel is provided for him." The ruling applied to all felony proceedings, both

---

66. *Rhode Island* v. *Innis*, ___ U.S. ___ (1980).
67. *Doyle* v. *Ohio* and *Wood* v. *Ohio*, 423 U.S. 823 (1975).
68. *Brewer* v. *Williams*, 431 U.S. 925 (1977).
69. *Gideon* v. *Wainwright*, 372 U.S. 335 (1963).

PRACTICING POLITICS   5.1

Your Due Process Rights

If you are legally placed under arrest for a misdemeanor or a felony, the arresting officer will read you the Miranda warning, which is a statement of your due process rights. This is a copy of the actual form used by the Grand Forks Police Department:

MIRANDA WARNING

1. You have the right to remain silent.
2. Anything you say can and will be used against you in a court of law.
3. You have the right to talk to a lawyer and have him present with you while you are being questioned.
4. If you cannot afford to hire a lawyer one will be appointed to represent you before any questioning, if you wish one.

If you are detained by the police, you have the following due process rights:

1. *Detention for investigation.* The degree and length of detention for investigation, for which there must be probable cause and not mere suspicion, is unclear. However, this is considered custodial interrogation, and your Miranda rights apply.
2. *Arrest.* If you are placed under arrest, you have the right to know the charges. Police must bring you for arraignment on specific charges or release you. (These charges are not binding; it is the prosecutor who decides the charge.) If you are acquitted or the charges are dismissed, it may be possible to have the arrest expunged from the record. The case law varies, but it can and has been done.
3. *Arraignment.* Within a period of time (it varies from state to state), police must bring you before a judicial officer in order to determine whether the arrest was lawful and if sufficient evidence exists to charge you with a crime. At this point you are either formally charged with a crime or set free. If you are charged, usually a preliminary hearing is held to test the evidence. You (your lawyer) can challenge the probable cause for the charges, and charges can be dropped or reduced.
4. *Bail.* For all but the most serious charges—murder or treason—you are eligible for bail once you are booked and arraigned. Bail is based on the presumption of innocence since you have not yet been proved guilty. The amount of bail required depends on the seriousness of the charges, the evidence, your employment, financial resources, character, and past criminal record.

---

federal and state. The Court expanded on the *Gideon* decision in 1972 when it extended the right to counsel to include not only felony cases, but also misdemeanors or so-called lesser offenses.[70] The Court felt that deprivation of liberty— even for short periods of time—was a serious matter and that lack of legal assis-

70. *Argersinger* v. *Hamlin,* 407 U.S. 25 (1972).

tance impinged on due process. In 1979 the Court ruled that the right to counsel did not extend to persons charged with state crimes who are not sentenced to jail, even though they stand charged with crimes punishable by jail sentences.[71]

In 1978 the Court overturned a state conviction for three defendants because they were not each afforded counsel after repeated requests to be separately represented. The Supreme Court ruled that each defendant was entitled to separate counsel to insure adequate assistance and to prevent a potential conflict of interest.[72] The Court reiterated its position in *Bounds* v. *Smith* when it held that prison inmates not only have a fundamental constitutional right of access to the courts, but prison authorities have an obligation to assist inmates in their right of access.[73] This includes allowing inmates to file writs and other legal motions, making available adequate legal library resources, and providing competent legal counsel.

Trial by Jury.   The Sixth Amendment also protects the oldest and most treasured right in the Constitution: trial by jury. Jury trial is guaranteed in Article III of the Constitution as well as in the Sixth Amendment. Article III, Section 2 reads:

> The trial of all crimes, except in cases of impeachment, shall be by jury; and such trial shall be held in the state where the said crimes shall have been committed.

The Sixth Amendment reads:

> In all criminal prosecutions the accused shall enjoy the right to a speedy and public trial, by an impartial jury of the state and district wherein the crime shall have been committed.

Trial by jury has been falling into disuse, however; courts have traditionally held that petty offenses do not require trial by jury. And, of course, an individual may waive the right to trial by jury, subject to approval of the court.[74] Several states have reduced the number of jurors from the traditional 12 or altered the unanimity requirement for conviction. In 1970, the Supreme Court ruled that a state need not provide a 12-person jury to fulfill the Sixth Amendment trial by jury provision. A jury conviction for robbery and a subsequent sentence of life imprisonment was upheld even though Florida provided only a six-person jury.[75] Ruled the Court: "The fact that the jury at common law was composed of precisely 12 is an historical accident, unnecessary to effect the purpose of the jury system and wholly without significance 'except to mystics.' " There must be at

71. *Scott* v. *Illinois,* 440 U.S. 367 (1979).
72. *Holloway* v. *Arkansas,* 435 U.S. 475 (1978).
73. *Bounds* v. *Smith,* 430 U.S. 817 (1977).
74. Rule 23(a), Federal Rules of Criminal Procedure; *Singer* v. *United States,* 380 U.S. 24 (1965).
75. *Williams* v. *Florida,* 399 U.S. 78 (1970).

least six, however; the court ruled that a five-person jury was too small.[76] The number six will also satisfy the Seventh Amendment requirement of a jury trial in civil suits.[77]

States have also reduced the requirement of unanimity for juries to reach a verdict for conviction. Oregon's Constitution permitted guilty verdicts in criminal cases, except first-degree murder, where 10 of the 12 jurors so voted. The Supreme Court upheld the provision.[78] As in *Williams,* the Court said: "After considering the history of the 12-man requirement and the function it performs in contemporary society, we concluded that it was not of constitutional stature. We reach the same conclusion today with regard to the requirement of unanimity." But unanimity is necessary for 6-person juries. Six is the minimum number necessary for juries and for convictions without violating the Sixth and Fourteenth Amendments.[79]

Cruel and Unusual Punishment.   Derived from the English Bill of Rights, the Eighth Amendment protection from "cruel and unusual punishments" sought to regulate both the manner of punishment and its severity. Supposedly the Framers had in mind such practices as drawing and quartering, burning at the stake, crucifixion, or tarring and feathering; but more recently the Eighth Amendment has been invoked to overturn a California statute making it a misdemeanor for a person to "be addicted to the use of narcotics." And in 1980 the Court said mandatory life imprisonment for convictions on three nonviolent property crimes (total value: $229) was not cruel and unusual punishment.[80] The major issue in recent years, however, has been that of capital punishment.

As early as 1879 the Supreme Court ruled that capital punishment did not violate the Eighth Amendment as long as the death penalty was carried out without unnecessary cruelty. In this century citizen groups have waged campaigns to abolish capital punishment. In the 1950s and 1960s several states did abolish the death sentence, but the goal of these groups has been to get the Supreme Court to make an authoritative ruling. The question of capital punishment has sparked lively debate over the years. Opponents argue that the death penalty is a cruel and unusual punishment that has no effect in deterring crime. The function of sentencing ought to be rehabilitation, not punishment. Proponents respond by noting the rising crime rate and the need to provide the criminal justice system with the tools adequate to meet the challenge. They argue that swift and sure justice is the best cure for rising crime.

The Court finally answered its critics in 1972 in *Furman,* when it ruled that the death penalty, as presently administered by the states, did constitute cruel and

---

76. *Ballew* v. *Georgia,* 435 U.S. 223 (1978).
77. *Colgrove* v. *Battin,* 413 U.S. 149 (1973).
78. *Apodaca* v. *Oregon,* 406 U.S. 404 (1972).
79. *Burch* v. *Louisiana,* 441 U.S. 130 (1979).
80. *Rummel* v. *Estelle,* ___ U.S. ___ (1980).

unusual punishment.[81] By a 5 to 4 vote, the Court ruled that the death sentence had been applied in a wanton and capricious manner, discriminated against the poor and minorities, and left too much discretion to juries. Only two justices argued that the death sentence was cruel and unusual punishment in itself, however; the rest of the majority were speaking specifically about the handling of the death sentence.

States were left in a quandary. Did *Furman* ban the death sentence as unconstitutional, or would states have only to tighten the discretionary elements in the law? Most states felt it prudent to suspend the death sentence until the Court had an opportunity to review the issue. That opportunity came in 1976, when the Supreme Court reviewed the laws of five states: Georgia, Texas, Florida, North Carolina, and Louisiana. Two of the state laws that provided for a mandatory death sentence were ruled unconstitutional. The remaining three laws were upheld, however, because they provided for proper discretionary power of imprisonment or death as a separate decision once guilt had been established.[82]

Gregg v. *Georgia* clearly stated that capital punishment itself was not unconstitutional as a form of cruel and unusual punishment: "We hold that the death penalty is not a form of punishment that may never be imposed, regardless of the circumstances of the offense, regardless of the character of the offender, and regardless of the procedure followed in reaching the decision to impose it." The Court did, however, indicate that there must be careful review and use of the death sentence only for certain specified crimes. In *Coker* v. *Georgia,* the Court ruled that capital punishment for rape was cruel and unusual punishment because the sentence was excessively disproportionate; there was no loss of life to the victim.[83] In *Godfrey* v. *Georgia* the Court overturned a Georgia statute as being unconstitutionally vague because it permitted the death penalty for murder when the murder was "outrageously or wantonly vile, horrible or inhumane in that it involved torture, depravity of mind, or an aggravated battery to the victim."[84] While in *Beck* v. *Alabama* the death penalty was overturned because the jury was not given the opportunity to consider a verdict of guilty to a lesser included, noncapital offense.[85]

PROTECTION FOR VICTIMS AND WITNESSES

The Burger Court has shown more inclination to protect society's rights than the Warren Court before it. In numerous areas of the criminal justice system, the Court has accorded protection for society against the individual. The actions of the Court appear to be consistent with the thrust of public demands for a response to the rising crime rate and for protection. President Ford, in a message

81. *Furman* v. *Georgia,* 408 U.S. 238 (1972).
82. *Gregg* v. *Georgia,* 428 U.S. 153 (1976), and four other cases.
83. *Coker* v. *Georgia,* 433 U.S. 584 (1977).
84. *Godfrey* v. *Georgia,* — U.S. — (1980).
85. *Beck* v. *Alabama.,* — U.S. — (1980).

to Congress in 1975, stated: ''For too long, the law has centered its attention more on the rights of the criminal than on the victim of the crime. It is high time we reversed this trend and put the highest priority on the victims and potential victims.'' Victims are often persons in the criminal justice system. Rape victims, for example, were subjected to enormous pressure on the witness stand to recount the details, and were often faced with the accusation that they had somehow encouraged the defendant. Witnesses for the prosecution were often bullied into testifying by police, and then given no protection from threats by a defendant. The system offered little sympathy and even less compensation for the disruption caused victims and bystander witnesses.

With the 1970s came a wave of programs to assist witnesses and the victims of crime. Funded largely from the Law Enforcement Assistance Administration (LEAA), the new services have included:

> Referring victims to social services; assisting victims in obtaining benefits; supplying information, such as advice about residential security measures, the status or disposition of the criminal case in which the victim is involved, and the rights of victims to insurance, restitution, compensation, or other benefits; comforting or counseling the victim after the crime; advising the victim as to what he or she can expect as a witness; assisting in obtaining witness fees; providing transportation or sitting services for witnesses; providing a special witness notification system designed to prevent unnecessary trips to the courthouse; ensuring that witnesses have their property returned once it has been used as evidence; providing lounges in courthouses; and arranging for victim-offender confrontations designed to allay victim fears and improve the offender's chances for rehabilitation.[86]

The one area attracting the greatest interest now is compensation and restitution for victims of crime. Over a dozen states now have initiated such programs. **Restitution programs** require the offender to make reparation to the victim; in **compensation programs,** the state compensates the victim just as an insurance company pays a damage claim.

SUMMARY

1. The Fourteenth Amendment to the Constitution has been the basic constitutional device by which equal rights and due process of law are extended to citizens in states. Most effectively used to secure rights for black Americans, the Amendment is also used by the poor, American Indians, and women.

2. The struggle for racial justice has been long and incomplete. Attacked in

---

86. This excerpt is adapted from ''Criminal Justice and the Victim: An Introduction'' by William McDonald and is reproduced from *Criminal Justice and the Victim* (*Sage Criminal Justice System Annuals* Volume 6), William McDonald, editor, copyright 1976, pp. 17–55 by permission of the publisher, Sage Publications, Inc. (Beverly Hills/London).

the courts, segregation was declared unconstitutional in 1954. Yet it would take another decade for advancements in voting, housing, and employment. Even today blacks lag behind whites in most all of these areas.

3. Today the issue of racial justice turns from eliminating laws that bar equality to more active governmental support for racial integration, such as affirmative action in redressing past discriminatory practices.

4. Sex and age discrimination are increasingly coming under attack. Yet, to date, the Supreme Court has not put these discriminatory practices in the same suspect category as racial discrimination.

5. We recognize two forms of due process protection for citizens: procedural due process requiring fairness in enforcing laws, and substantive due process which requires law itself to be reasonable.

6. In the criminal justice system citizens are not to be subject to unreasonable searches and seizures. Persons may not be arrested or detained without cause or knowledge of their rights. In short, government may not interfere with citizens' lives without justifiable reason.

7. The principle issue in the Eighth Amendment ban on cruel and unusual punishment has been the death penalty. The Court has said that the death penalty per se is not a form of cruel and unusual punishment.

TERMS

RESEARCH PROJECTS

5.1. Equal Employment Opportunity. Undoubtedly your college or university has a set of rules and procedures for Equal Employment Opportunity, likely mandated by the federal government. Find out what those rules and procedures are, find out where they came from—that is, if they were locally developed or adopted from federal rules and regulations. Who monitors their implementation? You might wish to compare this with the Bureau of National Affairs, *The Equal Employment Act of 1972,* or the *Supervisors EEO Handbook* published by Executive Enterprise Publications.

5.2. Capital Punishment. Write an essay on capital punishment setting forth the arguments pro and con for capital punishment. Does your state use capital punishment? If it does, what procedures are followed in its implementation? How do local lawyers and prosecutors feel on the subject?

5.3. Black Civil Rights. Analyze the progress made by black Americans in the United States since 1960. Compared with their white counterpart note the comparative levels for blacks on income, education, employment, housing. Much of this data can be found in the *Statistical Abstract* or *Social Indicators* published by the Bureau of the Census. A useful reference work is Levitan and Taggart, *Still a Dream* (Harvard University Press).

5.4. *Miranda* Rights. After reviewing and listing the *Miranda* rights and how the courts have recently interpreted these rights, go to your local police department and interview some police officers on the effect of *Miranda* rights on the performance of their responsibilities. Be sure to explain to the police department what you are doing and why. Could you sense any confusion or hostility toward these rights or the courts?

5.5. ERA. What is the status of the Equal Rights Amendment in your state—ratified, efforts to rescind ratification? What is the level of support for ERA in the state? What groups provide support or opposition? Do a short survey of how people would vote if ERA were put to a popular vote. What kind of people support/oppose ratification?

BIBLIOGRAPHY

Fellman, David. *The Defendants' Rights Today*. Madison, Wis.: University of Wisconsin Press, 1977.

A basic and extensive work that treats the defendant's rights from beginning to end. Arrest, preliminary hearing, and basic trial rights are discussed in a fairly nontechnical manner. The procedures are clearly presented.

Franklin, John H. *From Slavery to Freedom*. New York: Knopf, 1974.

The standard work on the history of the black struggle in America. The volume provides excellent coverage of slavery and colonial life as well as reconstruction and emergence into the twentieth century.

Freeman, Jo. *The Politics of Women's Liberation*. New York: David McKay, 1975.

A quite complete analysis of the women's liberation movement in terms of its political impact. Freeman provides history, contemporary activities, and policy impact of the women's movement.

Levitan, Sar, William Johnson, and Robert Taggart. *Still a Dream*. Cambridge, Mass.: Harvard University Press, 1975.

This book addresses the status of blacks since 1960. Utilizing considerable data, the authors examine black progress in income, employment, education, health, housing, family areas, and so on.

Lewis, Anthony. *Gideon's Trumpet*. New York: Random House, 1964.

The gripping story of Clarence Gideon and his efforts to be represented by counsel. Anthony Lewis is the Supreme Court reporter for the *New York Times* and wrote the absorbing account of the Supreme Court case culminating in a landmark decision.

Kluger, Richard. *Simple Justice*. New York: Vintage Books, 1976.

A fascinating and detailed study of the history of school desegregation and the *Brown* decision. For its length, the book is not overly technical or complicated, rather it reviews the history and drama surrounding that historic case.

Sindler, Allan. *Bakke, De Funis, and Minority Admissions*. New York: Longman, 1978.

A discussion of recent court decisions on reverse discrimination and affirmative action. Provides considerable supplementary information surrounding the two cases.

Spurrier, Robert L. *To Preserve These Rights: Remedies for the Victims of Constitutional Deprivations*. Port Washington, N.Y.: Kennikat Press, 1977.

A fairly technical work, the book examines constitutional remedies for persons accused of crimes. Included are such things as the exclusionary rule, suits against arresting officers, and victim compensation.

Wilson, James Q. *Thinking About Crime*. New York: Basic Books, 1975.

A series of essays written by Wilson, they seek to understand crime and the way society deals with crimes. Wilson is not very content with the way criminologists and politicians have dealt with crime; he offers some suggestions for improvement.

Wise, David. *The American Police State*. New York: Vintage Books, 1978.

A journalistic, but documented account of how government agencies with police powers abuse their powers. Focuses on the activities of the FBI, CIA, and IRS.

Chapter 6

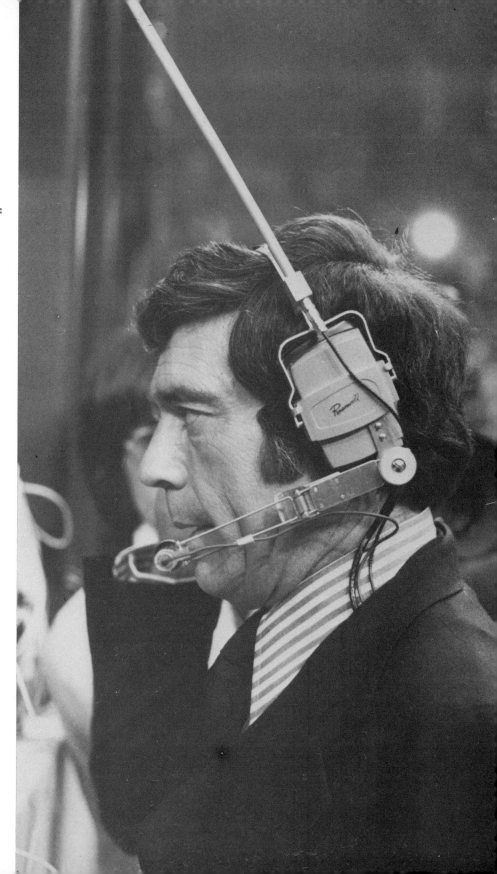

Public Opinion

Throughout America, there is a growing, widespread dissatisfaction with politics. Old patterns of opinions and consensus are deteriorating; new patterns of cynicism and distrust are creating a disquieting environment. Political parties are weak, and elections bring declining voter participation. Members of Congress and the president are unable to raise their reputations with the public. The public is concerned with nothing less than the traditional assumptions of democratic politics. As a contemporary student of public opinion has been led to conclude, "Much that has been said in the recent past about stability, orderliness, legitimacy, efficaciousness, and widespread consensus in American political life has come to appear quite vulnerable."[1] The 1950s and 1960s produced some fundamental alterations in public opinion; the last decades of the twentieth century will see politics quite unlike that of the previous generation, according to Nie, Verba, and Petrocik:

> In the 1950's the public was only mildly involved in politics, was relatively content with the political process, and had long-term commitments to one or the other of the major parties. Today it is more politically aroused, more detached

1. Richard E. Dawson, *Public Opinion and Contemporary Disarray*. (New York: Harper & Row, 1973), p. 1.

from political parties than at any time in the past forty years, and deeply dissatisfied with the political process.[2]

The basic fabric of public opinion has changed. Professor Dawson cites three conditions in contemporary American political life that helped shape the current sense of political malaise.[3] First, the past few decades have witnessed a growing disquiet and sense of frustration among people. The coalitions of the New Deal and the Democratic and Republican parties are disintegrating; the Great Society represented a significant political and social departure from the goals of the New Deal, and the social and political coalitions it created now seek recognition and power. Second, the disquiet and disarray have altered the forms of political concerns: ''There have been changes in the types of issues that are most salient to the public and in the socioeconomic conditions and groupings that struc-

2. Norman Nie, Sidney Verba, and John Petrocik, *The Changing American Voter*. (Cambridge, Mass.: Harvard University Press, 1976), p. 1.
3. Dawson, *Public Opinion and Contemporary Disarray,* p. 3.

Activism and protest in the 1960s changed the fabric of public opinion. (United Press International)

ture political outlooks and consequently political conflict and consensus.''[4] Third, these changes in issues and political outlook have made it difficult for political institutions to respond clearly and effectively to what the people are most concerned with. Political leaders find it increasingly difficult to address the concerns of citizens.

The patterns of contemporary disarray are easily discernible. The period of the Great Society, democratic reform, and taxpayer revolution have seen the emergence and politicization of groups such as blacks, minorities, women, welfare recipients, blue collar workers, and middle income taxpayers. These groups have come to dominate the new issues, expressing frustration and disaffection with the political process. Second, there is the decline in Americans' attachment to their political process. Turnout in presidential elections has been declining steadily since 1960. The public opinion polls have also reported the decline in political party identification. Fewer and fewer people adhere to a partisan label, and among young voters independents outnumber partisan identifiers altogether. The same opinion polls show the decline in confidence in public officials. Congress and the presidency have labored, with little success, to raise their reputations. The bureaucracy has borne the brunt of protest by taxpayers and become a symbol of waste and inefficiency. Courts and law enforcement officials also have not been immune from the erosion of confidence. A third pattern of contemporary public opinion has been the shift in issue saliency. The newer issues are not dividing the population into traditional patterns, nor are the newer patterns exhibiting the stability characteristic of the traditional issues. The issues of fiscal accountability, governmental responsibility, and abortion have produced new groups that are being politicized due to the saliency of the issues. Single-issue politics dominate. For such groups, traditional issues of economic welfare, governmental intervention, or civil rights appear less salient than in prior decades.

WHAT IS PUBLIC OPINION?

Public opinion is a rich mix of opinions from the diverse segments and political groups comprising American society. There is the general, mass distribution of opinion, often broken down into ''special publics'' to identify patterns of conflict or consensus within the opinion expressed by the American people. Students of public opinion also have found it useful to separate out the opinions of political leaders and media representatives—that is, elite opinion (see Figure 6.1). The characteristics of elites or opinion leaders have particular relevance in shaping and protecting the opinions of the public. Finally, the impact of institutions on opinions must be examined. Opinions are formed and shaped through the mediating influence of the family, the school, elections, interest groups, and governmental institutions. These institutions mediate between public opinion and elite opinion.

4. *Ibid.*

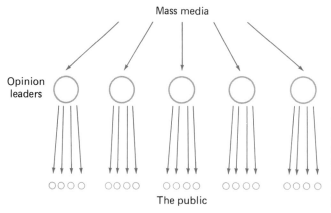

Figure 6.1

The two-step flow of communication and public opinion. (D. Hill and N. Luttbeg, *Trends in American Electoral Behavior*, F.E. Peacock Publishers, Inc., Itasca, Illinois, 1980, p. 11. Reproduced by permission of the publisher.)

Public opinion is important in a democracy, for it forms the basis of political life. Yet we cannot assume that government can or even ought to find, let alone act, on the basis of public opinion. Public opinion varies in stability and intensity, and not all opinions are relevant to politics. V. O. Key once defined public opinion as "those opinions held by private persons which governments find is prudent to heed." We are concerned with those opinions that relate to and affect the policies and practices of politics.

Public opinion is the assembling of individual attitudes, whether these attitudes are individually generated or formed as a result of interest group or party affiliation. Individual attitudes on political matters differ in several important ways.

Salience.   People differ over which issues are important for politics. Salient issues are those issues that people feel are important to their lives. For the homeowner, the most pressing political problem may be property tax relief; the assembly line auto-worker might worry over unemployment and inflation. The more closely the issue is viewed as affecting the life of a citizen, the more likely the issue will be salient to that citizen.

Salience differs with individuals; it also differs with time. For a majority of Americans in the 1930s, employment, income, and economic security dominated politics. In the 1940s and 1950s, war and Communist aggression were salient concerns. Social issues such as racial justice, poverty, and Vietnam moved to the fore in the 1960s. By 1980, Americans were again personally aroused over jobs, inflation, and income security as various forces worked to threaten their standard of living.

Stability.   While some opinions change rapidly, there are opinions that resist change and endure for long periods of time. Americans with consistent political values and continuous interest in an issue maintain a stable pattern of opinions which does not change with time. People who remain in the same job, reside in the same locality, and associate with the same circle of friends have the most stable opinions. For a generation, partisan preference and group identification were stable opinions. And they were easily identifiable with job, income, and ethnic factors. We could reliably predict that groups of people would behave in consistent ways. Now these factors are changing. Democrats do not necessarily vote Democratic, nor do they always believe that more government is helpful.

Intensity.   The most elusive aspect of public opinion is its intensity. People vary greatly in the strength of the opinions they hold. Some may mildly agree with a position, say more stringent penalties for crimes. Others can be violently opposed. Then, of course, there are those who have no opinion. It is not always easy to equate intensity with the general character of public opinion. Intensity can be short-lived or of long duration; people may hold intense feelings on particular concerns, or an individual may be just "letting off steam." Public officials must move cautiously around the question of intensity of public opinion.

Consistency and Knowledge.   Public opinion is often formed from low levels of knowledge. Students of public opinion prefer to distinguish "mass public opinion" from attentive or "elite public opinion." Even with the increase in issue concern, many Americans regularly pay little or no attention to politics. Opinion formation is often personal and emotional, and this low level of knowledge can lead to unstable and inconsistent public opinion: "The point here is that if a person lacks opinions on many issues, for whatever reason, then it will be impossible for him to demonstrate any consistent ideological pattern of thinking."[5] Free and Cantril, for example, distinguish between "operational" liberals and "ideological" liberalism–conservativism.[6] Operational liberals are persons indicating approval for specific programs involving government policy and power (compulsory medical insurance; low rent housing). Two-thirds of the public were counted as operational liberals by Free and Cantril. On measures of ideological liberal–conservative such as general attitude toward governmental power, local control, and individual initiative, 50 percent were opposed to government and national control—that is, they *thought* conservative. According to the authors, "For a large proportion of the American people, there is clearly not only a separation of but a conflict between their attitudes toward practical governmental operations and programs, on the one hand, and their ideological ideas and abstract concepts about government and society, on the other."[7]

5. Alan D. Monroe, *Public Opinion in America* (New York: Dodd, Mead & Co., 1975), p. 162.
6. Lloyd Free and Hadley Cantril, *The Political Beliefs of Americans* (New York: Simon and Schuster, 1968).
7. *Ibid.*, p. 46.

MEASURING PUBLIC OPINION

There are several reasons why we measure public opinion. First, people are curious about how other Americans feel on issues of public concern. In newspapers and magazines and on television, journalists report public attitudes on everything from presidential popularity to the length of skirts and the price of hamburger. Second, market polls are used by industry and politicians to test attitudes towards products, including political candidates. Business will test market a product to assess public acceptance; political candidates test public response to campaign activity, including how and where to campaign. Third, there is scientific opinion polling. The results of this research provide information for political scientists and other scholars to better understand public opinion. Results of scientific polling have given us, for example, knowledge of the relationship between beliefs and partisanship.

The measurement of public opinion is done through the survey method. We ask people to register their opinion, or their preference. Can we get an accurate representation of American public opinion this way?

There are two major issues in opinion polling: the sample used and the wording of questions. First, it is necessary to know that we have a representative sample. Pollsters cannot—nor do they need to—sample everyone. A representative sample can give a relatively accurate picture of the whole body (with usually 3 percent error either way). It is necessary, however, that the sample number truly be representative of the population to be surveyed. A **random sample,** where the people surveyed are selected completely at random, is best. In some cases, a **quota sample** is adequate. As long as the people surveyed fall within the percentage for age, sex, income, occupation, and so on, of the larger population, we can assume the sample to be reasonable. Professional pollsters have developed

TRAVELS WITH FARLEY

their skill to the point where a few thousand, or even as few as 1,500 people, can give an accurate picture of public opinion.

In addition, we know that the way we ask questions will, in large measure, determine the answers we get in return. It is difficult to write a question that does not affect the respondent's answer. The words must convey a clear meaning but without prejudicing the response. For example, in asking a question on abortion, use of the phrase "unborn child" implies that the fetus is a person and abortion is murder. If we ask people to agree or disagree with a statement, this does not necessarily give the respondent a fair range to express an opinion. This can be avoided by using a multiple choice response. If we ask open-ended questions (where the respondent supplies all information for the answer), we get a better reflection of opinion but have difficulty summarizing and tabulating answers. Such questions also assume the respondent has enough information or interest to be able to answer. Forced answers, however, give a false sense of knowledge and saliency. In short, measurement of public opinion is tricky business. How people come to have political opinions, however, is now a fairly clear process.

POLITICAL SOCIALIZATION

Political opinions are formed early in life, and much of what children learn about politics shapes their later attitudes. Political socialization is the process through which persons acquire political orientations and patterns of behavior.[8] Awareness begins in the preschool years, and a fairly concrete set of opinions and partisan preferences emerges in the primary school years. In other words, most of our political attitudes and behaviors are learned. The "agents" most responsible for transmitting political values and opinions are, by and large, the same agents responsible for nonpolitical socialization: family, school, peer groups, and the mass media.

THE LEARNING OF POLITICAL ORIENTATIONS

The partisan awareness that begins in the early school years follows closely the identifiable partisanship of the parents. By grade 6 all but 4.5 percent of students in one study had some appreciation of the party labels Democrat or Republican, although the authors pointed out that the label "Democrat" or "Republican" is a vague one which students "root for." Fewer than 20 percent of third grade students could identify the president's party.[9]

The early awareness of politics is limited to vague symbols; apparently chil-

8. David Easton and Jack Dennis, *Children in the Political System* (New York: McGraw-Hill, Co., 1969), p. 7.
9. Robert D. Hess and Judith V. Torney, *The Development of Political Attitudes in Children* (Chicago: Aldine, 1967), p. 278.

dren view government as a person. Easton and Dennis report that in the early grades, students view the president as the government. Only gradually do the more differentiated symbols, such as Congress or voting, expand the meaning of government.[10] Yet even by the eighth grade the president remains a dominant, benevolent symbol, "the person who helps you and your family most."

The first attitude of a child toward politics is a positive sense of trust and support for the government. Reported Easton and Hess, "the sentiments of most children with respect to their political community are uniformly warm and positive throughout all grades, with scarcely a hint of criticism or rate of dissatisfaction."[11] This sense of trust and support remains with children throughout grade school, though it diminishes slightly with age. Easton and Dennis report finding 72 percent of fourth graders feeling the president rarely or almost never errs; that dipped to 51 percent for eighth graders.[12]

We do know that political changes in the past few years are having an effect on these positive preadult attitudes. There is a growing disaffection with political authority. A study of Watergate's impact on political authority found a growing disaffection with the president. F. Christopher Arterton discovered that concern for Watergate closely followed party identification.[13] In their study of preadult attitudes and Watergate, Marjorie Hershey and David Hill found that concern for Watergate increased with age, interest in politics, and partisanship. The more salient Watergate appeared to the student, the less benevolent the president was thought to be. This was particularly true for partisans; Democratic children were particularly likely to see Watergate as important and the president as less responsive to their concerns. Yet "young children—those for whom Watergate is associated with sharpest decrease in attachment to the President—are also least likely to consider Watergate an important problem."[14] In short, it seems Watergate or other dramatic events may affect the positive attitudes of preadults toward the political system, but the feelings may be true of only a small number of children, and for relatively short periods of time.

Party identification is an acquired belief, coming primarily from the parents. By age 7 or 8, a majority of children identified with one or the other of the two major political parties. Reported Easton and Hess, "a strong majority in each grade from two (age 7–8) through eight (age 13–14) state that if they could vote they would align themselves with [one] of the two major parties in the United States."[15]

10. Easton and Dennis, *Children in the Political System*, p. 116.
11. David Easton and Robert D. Hess, "The Child's Political World," *Midwest Journal of Political Science*, Vol. 6 (1962), pp. 236–237.
12. Easton and Dennis, *Children in the Political System*, pp. 179–181.
13. F. Christopher Arterton, "The Impact of Watergate on Children's Attitudes Toward Political Authority," *Politcal Science Quarterly* (June 1974), pp. 269–288.
14. Marjorie R. Hershey and David B. Hill, "Watergate and Preadults' Attitudes Toward the President," *American Journal of Political Science* 19 (November 1975), pp. 703–726.
15. Easton and Hess, "The Child's Political World," p. 245.

By adolescence, children come to have developed a fairly clearly defined political orientation. They possess a sense of partisanship; they are developing opinions and ideological stances on issues. By age 14, children approach a level of political opinion that will change little with adult life.[16] Their attitudes toward politics and government are well established. "All of this suggests that the 13-year-old is almost as much a political man as he will become. Armed with the party identification he typically borrows from his parents, a sense of civic duty, and a positive orientation remaining from his early impressions of political actors, he changes little thereafter."[17]

AGENTS OF POLITICAL SOCIALIZATION

The Family.   The family is the most pervasive socializing agent, and it shapes the child's political orientation in fundamental ways. We have already noted the inheritance of party labels. Jennings and Niemi report overwhelming adoption of partisanship from the family among high school seniors; only 7 percent differed in party identification from the parents. Even more striking was the finding that, as adults, two-thirds of those surveyed continued to identify with the political party they inherited from the parents. Only 10 percent had changed parties; the remainder called themselves independents.

Table 6.1
Parent and Child Agreement in Party Identification

Students	Parents			
	Democratic	Independent	Republican	
Democrat	66%	29%	13%	(43%)
Independent	27	55	36	(36%)
Republican	7	17	51	(21%)
Total	100%	100%	100%	
Marginals[a]	(49%)	(24%)	(27%)	100%

a. The marginal totals present the proportion of parents and students that hold a particular party preference. For example, looking at the column marginals we can see 49 percent of the parents are Democratic. Looking at the row marginals we can see that 43 percent of the students in the sample are Democratic.

SOURCE Adapted from M. Kent Jennings and Richard G. Niemi, *The Political Character of Adolescence: The Influence of Families and Schools* (Copyright © 1974 by Princeton University Press): Table 2.2, p. 41. Reprinted by permission of Princeton University Press.

16. Herbert Hyman, *Political Socialization* (Glencoe, Ill.: The Free Press, 1959), p. 59.
17. Robert S. Erickson & Norman R. Luttbeg, *American Public Opinion* (New York: John Wiley & Sons, Inc., 1973), p. 129.

The transmission of political values other than party identification from parent to child was far weaker. There was only meager parental influence in the comparison of political attitudes of parents and children on policy issues, political activity, and political cynicism.[18] Children were quite likely to be in disagreement with parents on issues of governmental activity, voting, political efficacy, and feeling toward groups in society. The reasons for this differ considerably. Jennings and Niemi found that frequency of political communication within a family affects parent–child agreement. This in turn is affected by the degree of consistency on issue orientation among the parents. Apparently adolescent rebellion is not a cause of political disagreement. Lane and Sears concluded: "Rebellion against parental beliefs does not play a large role in determining the political opinions of American voters. . . . The rebelling adolescent is much more likely to rebel in terms which are more important to his parents, such as in his dress, his driving, his drinking, his obedience to the law, his sexual behavior and so forth. Only in rather rare instances does it have political effects as well."[19]

The School.   Education plays a significant role in the political socialization of children. In school, children learn the values of the political system: they memorize the pledge of allegiance, sing patriotic songs, and learn about great leaders, notably presidents like George Washington, Abraham Lincoln, and John Kennedy. In later grades, they receive formal instruction in civic education and democracy. The environment the teacher creates in the classroom is a "political environment" that students learn from or accept. Teachers report giving considerable attention to citizen duties in the classroom. In fact, the teacher is a most salient agent in the socialization of the school child. Hess and Torney, for example, reported finding an evolutionary trend from the second to eighth grades of compatibility of beliefs between student and teacher.[20]

School, then, is an important socializing agent. It transmits information on substantive issues to the child, and teaches the duties and responsibilities of citizenship. School is not responsible for the affective domain of trust and loyalty, nor for partisanship. In fact, there is no reliable trend toward any party with increased education.[21] But teachers do have an appreciable effect on the political beliefs of their students. Students expect to be taught in school, so there is fairly high receptivity to messages; however, civics courses—the course specifically designed to instruct students in politics and democracy—have only a marginal impact on political attitudes. Langton and Jennings found the number of civics courses almost unrelated to attitudes, political knowlege, sense of efficacy, or

18. M. Kent Jennings and Richard G. Niemi, "Transmission of Political Values From Parent to Child," *American Political Science Review,* 62 (March, 1968), pp. 177–179.
19. Robert Lane and David Sears, *Public Opinion* (Englewood Cliffs, N.J.: Prentice-Hall, Inc., 1964), p. 25.
20. Hess and Torney, *The Development of Political Attitudes in Children,* pp. 200–202.
21. Eleanor E. Maccoby, Richard E. Mathews and Anton S. Morton, "Youth and Political Change," *Public Opinion Quarterly,* Vol. 18 (1954), p. 37.

levels of toleration. There was only one major exception, black students.[22] For the black student, there was a significant increase in political knowledge, efficacy, and tolerance after taking civics courses. For blacks, civic education presents new material; but for white students, civic education is redundant.[23]

The Peer Group.   We have long known that groups with which we identify influence our thinking. Therefore, it is not surprising that children are influenced by their peers, although the extent of the influence is difficult to sort out. Children are politicized when friends the same age report talking about politics. In the school years it is difficult to disentangle the effects of family, school, and peer group influences because these are mutually reinforcing sources. What peer groups seem to do is reinforce already formulated political attitudes.

Friendship has been found to be a major component in peer group political socialization. Substantial political agreement occurred between people designated as best friends. This was even more true for girls than boys, an indication that girls are more sensitive than boys to the views of those around them.[24] With age and a career, some stability and homogeneity in the social environment results. Social class, work associates, and ethnicity affect political attitudes. Some time ago, Berelson, Lazarsfeld, and McPhee found that relationships with those who held similar political beliefs increased with age.[25] After the late twenties there was a marked stability and settling down into a homogeneous opinion environment.

The Mass Media.   We have come to accept the ability of the media to sell commercial products and shape the taste, preferences, and life-styles of Americans, so it is not surprising that the mass media shape political opinions as well. The impact of the media on children is uncertain. The child is clearly exposed to politics through the media, and television is the primary source of this exposure. For younger children, television dominates; as the child grows older, newspapers come to be an increasingly important source of information. Among the poor, television remains the dominant medium. Figure 6.2 shows the sources of most of our news.

It is difficult to document direct media influence on political attitudes, although recent studies are finding the mass media to be a principal source of political information for young children. N. Hollander labeled the media "the new parent" in recognition of the role they play in transmitting political learning to

22. Kenneth P. Langton and M. Kent Jennings, "Political Socialization and the High School Civics Curriculum in the United States," *American Political Science Review,* 62 (September, 1968), pp. 852–877.
23. *Ibid.*
24. S. K. Sebert, M. K. Jennings, and R. Niemi, "The Political Texture of Peer Groups," in Jennings, M. K. & Niemi, R., *The Political Character of Adolescence* (Princeton, N.J.: Princeton University Press, 1974).
25. Bernard R. Berelson, Paul F. Lazarsfeld, and William N. McPhee, *Voting* (Chicago: University of Chicago Press, 1954), p. 97.

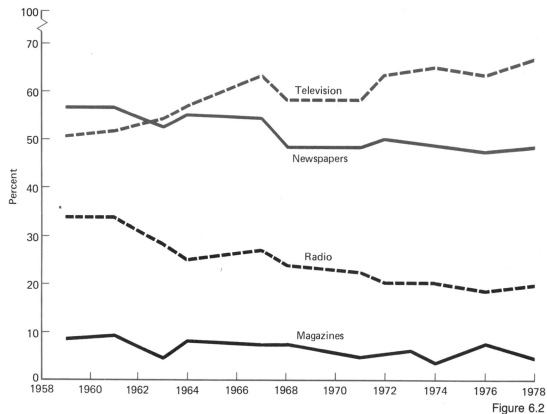

Figure 6.2

Where people usually get most of their news about what is going on in the world. Multiple responses per respondent. (Survey by the Roper Organization for the Television Information Office, latest that of December 1978. "And That's the Way it is Today," *Public Opinion Magazine,* August/September 1979, pp. 30–31)

the child. Children report the media as being influential; S. H. Chaffee reported students rating the media as the most important source of opinion influence, over parents, teachers, and friends.[26]

THE PATTERNS OF PUBLIC OPINION

CONFLICT AND CONSENSUS

Most political commentators have viewed the past two decades as a period of change. Whether one uses the label "revolution" or "crisis," the changes in economic life, race relations, foreign affairs, and family life have been pro-

26. S. H. Chaffee, L. S. Ward and L. P. Tipton, "Mass Communication and Political Socialization," *Journalism Quarterly,* 47 (1970), 647–659.

Table 6.2

The Public's View of Television and Newspapers, 1959–1978

Question: First, I'd like to ask you where you usually get most of your news about what's going on in the world today—from the newspapers or radio or television or magazines or talking to people or where?

Source of most news:	1959	1961	1963	1964	1967	1968	1971	1972	1974	1976	1978
Television	51%	52%	55%	58%	64%	59%	60%	64%	65%	64%	67%
Newspapers	57	57	53	56	55	49	48	50	47	49	49
Radio	34	34	29	26	28	25	23	21	21	19	20
Magazines	8	9	6	8	7	7	5	6	4	7	5
People	4	5	4	5	4	5	4	4	4	5	5
Don't know/ no answer	1	3	3	3	2	3	1	1	—	—	—

Question: If you got conflicting or different reports of the same news story from radio, television, the magazines, and the newpapers, which of the four versions would you be most inclined to believe—the one on radio or television or magazines or newspapers?

Most believable:	1959	1961	1963	1964	1967	1968	1971	1972	1974	1976	1978
Television	29%	39%	36%	41%	41%	44%	49%	48%	51%	51%	47%
Newspapers	32	24	24	23	24	21	20	21	20	22	23
Radio	12	12	12	8	7	8	10	8	8	7	9
Magazines	10	10	10	10	8	11	9	10	8	9	9
Don't know/ no answer	17	17	18	18	20	16	12	13	13	11	12

Note: In April 1979, the Gallup Organization asked respondents to indicate their confidence in ten key institutions. Newspapers ranked fifth with 51% indicating "a great deal/quite a lot of confidence." Television followed in seventh place with 38% indicating "a great deal/quite a lot of confidence."

SOURCE: *Public Opinion Magazine,* August/September 1979, pp. 31–32. Published bimonthly by the American Enterprise Institute for Public Policy Research.

nounced. Government has had difficulty adjusting and responding to new attitudes and changing demands.

Patterns of conflict and consensus are important if a government is to represent a people. The distribution of opinions helps government decide if it should or should not act and in what direction (see Figure 6.3). The long-term stability of opinions in an area lends legitimacy to governmental policy. It also affords policymakers a fair measure of predictability in contemplating policy changes. By 1968, however, those traditional patterns were breaking down. And as yet, a new stability has not formed.

Television has become a pervasive force with its instantaneous means of communication. (Stan Wakefield)

Domestic Welfare and Economic Issues.   Domestic welfare and economic issues have long been a focal point in politics. Since the Depression and the New Deal, government has been deeply involved in domestic welfare and economic policies. And this involvement has been the source of an enduring and stable conflict. Democrats, labor, minorities, and low-income groups supported government involvement in general, and welfare and economic regulation specif-

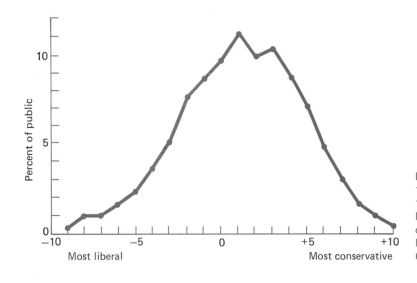

Figure 6.3

Distribution of public opinion over 10 issues, 1976. (SRC/CPS, 1976 election data. R. Erickson, N. Luttbeg, and K. Tedin, *American Public Opinion*, 2nd ed., New York: John Wiley, 1980, p. 65)

ically. Republicans, business, and the higher income groups were generally opposed.

The New Deal coalition is crumbling, however; there is an increasing fragmentation of the American public over domestic welfare and economic issues. Note Harry Holloway and John George: "The original coalition was thought to draw potentially from six somewhat overlapping groups: the poor, blacks, the unions, Catholics and Jews, the white South, and the central cities. . . . But by the late 1960s neither the poor nor the South were firm elements of the coalition. . . . By 1976 other changes were evident. Blacks and labor supported Carter, but the Carter coalition differed in its appeal to Protestants, to the suburbs, to rural areas, and to a biracial South."[27]

The fragmentation of domestic issues results from the intrusion of new people and new issues into politics. We have already noted the changing population patterns and further noted the shifting coalition base for the political parties. The result may be nothing short of a generational realignment of the American public.[28] The new social issues divide America and do it in ways that cross the older, established economic and class divisions.

If they do not necessarily prefer small government, Americans are divided over adding new programs such as wage and price controls, a national health insurance program, or a guaranteed job program. The guaranteed annual income and national health insurance are important new domestic issues generating conflict. Neither has anything approaching a consensus in favor of their enactment. Yet their surfacing on the agenda of domestic public opinion issues may mean eventual acceptance; Social Security and aid to cities were also controversial issues at one point.

The social issues that have emerged now have to do with abortion, gay rights, pornography, and divorce. We see from the sampling of opinion in Table 6.3 that the public exhibits far less tolerance on these issues. While there has been some movement on the issues over the decade of the 1970s, they continue to be the source of bitter disagreement between large numbers of Americans.

Foreign Affairs.   Traditionally foreign policy, war, and the threat of communism have been major focuses of concern for Americans. All during the Cold War years of the Eisenhower administration and into the early 1960s foreign affairs was *the* dominant concern. With the end of the post-World War II world, however, the domestic emphasis of Lyndon Johnson, and subsequent economic and inflationary problems in the 1970s, the public's concern for foreign affairs as a pressing problem has dropped from a high of 63 percent in 1962 to 10 percent.

From World War II through the 1960s, Americans readily accepted active involvement with other parts of the world. Three-fourths of the American people viewed favorably our direct concern with foreign affairs. From 1956 through the

27. Harry Holloway & John George, *Public Opinion* (New York: St. Martins, 1979), pp. 25–26.
28. Nie, Verba, Petrocik, *The Changing American Voter* (Cambridge, Mass.: Harvard University Press, 1976), especially Chapter 5.

FACT FILE

WHAT THE AMERICAN PUBLIC IS WORRIED ABOUT

As far as the American public is concerned, no problem facing the nation is more important than the state of the economy. And that has been true since 1974, according to samples of the public taken at least twice a year by the Gallup Organization, Inc.

Between 51 and 82 percent of respondents have singled out the economy as public problem No. 1 since October 1974. Since 1955, when Gallup began asking the public what it finds troubling, respondents have never been so consistently united over the nation's chief concern. Foreign affairs rose to a level of 63 percent in 1962, the year of the Cuban missile crisis, and 60 percent during the escalation of the Vietnam war in 1966. Social problems—including race relations, crime, urban unrest, college disturbances—hit peaks of 52 percent in 1963 and 56 percent in 1970.

Since 1955, Gallup has asked this question (or one with slightly different wording): "What do you think is the most important problem facing this country today?" The responses are listed in the following table (totals exceed 100 percent because some respondents named more than one problem):

	The economy	Foreign affairs	(Vietnam[a])	Social problems	Govt. malper-formance	Energy	Others	Don't know
Oct.–Nov. 1955	10%	49%	—%	2%	—%	—%	28%	17%
Sept. 1956	17	51	—	20	—	—	21	10
Aug.–Sept. 1957	24	43	—	16	—	—	8	13
Sept. 1958	19	44	—	9	—	—	20	8
Sept. 1959	21	51	—	5	—	—	15	8
Feb. 1960	18	59	—	9	1	—	19	7
Feb. 1961	37	59	—	7	—	—	4	6
April 1962	18	63	—	9	—	—	10	9
Sept. 1963	13	25	—	52	—	—	13	5
Sept. 1964	10	46	—	35	4	—	17	7
Sept. 1965	8	53	(19)	37	—	—	12	5
May 1966	20	60	(45)	14	—	—	11	2
Oct.–Nov. 1967	16	50	(50)	21	—	—	—	13[b]
May 1968	12	42	(42)	43	—	—	9	3
June–July 1968	12	52	(52)	44	—	—	6	1
Aug. 1968	10	51	(51)	41	—	—	12	2
Jan. 1969	12	40	(40)	40	—	—	16	2
May 1970	10	36	(22)	56	—	—	16	2
Feb. 1971	29	40	(28)	28	—	—	15	2
June 1971	27	40	(33)	37	—	—	14	1
Nov. 1971	41	23	(15)	28	—	—	19	4
April 1972	30	41	(29)	29	2	—	12	2
June 1972	30	40	(32)	17	1	—	13	3
July 1972	28	30	(25)	28	2	—	16	2
Sept. 1972	30	37	(27)	23	3	—	13	3
Feb. 1973	39	10	(3)	32	3	—	20	9
May 1973	48	9	(3)	26	14	2	8	3
Sept. 1973	69	7	(1)	16	14	3	11	3
Jan. 1974	30	6		7	22	46	7	3
May–June 1974	48			11	26	6	19	4
Oct. 1974	82			3	11	3	15	2
Feb.–Mar. 1975	80	5		15	7	7	18	3

WHAT THE AMERICAN PUBLIC IS WORRIED ABOUT (continued)

	The economy	Foreign affairs	(Vietnam[a])	Social problems	Govt. malper- formance	Energy	Others	Don't know
July 1975	72	—		10	12	5	20	2
Jan. 1976	70	5		12	4	3	25	3
April 1976	62	5		18	17	2	25	3
Oct. 1976	78	6		9	10	1	23	4
July 1977	51	10		14	6	15	17	8
Oct. 1977	61	7		13	5	18	14	3
Feb. 1978	57	9		9	5	23	11	4
Feb. 1979	66	18		6	3	14	8	3
May 1979	62	5		6	3	33	8	2

a. Vietnam percentages are included in the foreign affairs totals
b. Others and don't know combined in 1967

SOURCE: *National Journal,* October 20,1979, p. 1730.

Table 6.3
Opinion Distribution on Social Issues

		"Liberal"	"Conservative"
Divorce:	Should divorce in this country be easier or more difficult to obtain than it is now? (NORC, 1977)	Easier, 31%	More Difficult, 51%
Marijuana:	Do you think the use of marijuana should be legal or not? (Gallup, 1977)	Yes, 28	No, 66
Pornography:	Do you think the standards of this community regarding the sale of sexually explicit material should be stricter than they are now, not as strict, or kept as they are now? (Gallup, 1977)	Not as strict, 6	Stricter, 45
Abortion:	Would you favor [a constitutional amendment] which would prohibit abortions or would you oppose it? (Gallup, 1976)	Oppose, 49	Favor, 45
Gay Rights:	Do you think homosexual relations between consenting adults should or should not be legal? (Gallup, 1977)	Should, 43	Should not, 43

SOURCE: **Robert S. Erickson, Norman R. Luttbeg, and Kent L. Tedin.** *American Public Opinion.* 2nd Edition (New York: John Wiley & Sons, 1980).

Table 6.4

Right to get involved in Vietnam

Right to get involved?[a]	1964	1968	1970
Yes, we did the right thing	60%	36%	38%
Depends (other)	2	2	
No, we should have stayed out	39	62	62

a. Wording of question: "Do you think we did the right thing in getting into the fighting in Vietnam or should we have stayed out?"

SOURCE: Data from SRC surveys, 1964, 1968, 1970. Richard E. Dawson, *Public Opinion and Contemporary Disarray* (New York: Harper & Row, 1973). Copyright © 1973 by Richard E. Dawson.

"That's the worst set of opinions I've heard in my entire life."

Source: Drawing by Weber; © 1975 The New Yorker Magazine, Inc.

late 1960s, support for foreign affairs consistently increased. Vietnam changed that consensus. From the beginning of our active involvement in Vietnam until the negotiated withdrawal of American troops in 1973, public opinion made a complete change. Table 6.4 illustrates the change that took place in the 1960s. Very few issues in American history have produced so dramatic a change in opinion in such a short time.

The 1980s again bring foreign affairs into focus for the American people. The Panama Canal Treaty was attacked as an "American giveaway." SALT II has increased worry over military strength and preparedness vis-a-vis the Soviet Union. The Soviet invasion of Afghanistan in 1979 raised questions about our

Public opinion concerning Iranians developed quickly with seizure of the U.S. embassy in Iran. Here police drag away an Iranian student demonstrating in support of Iran. (United Press International)

ability to contain the Russians and protect our interests around the globe. The extended crisis in Iran, where 50 Americans have been held hostage in the U.S. Embassy, has further prompted Americans to reemphasize foreign policy and military affairs.

Opinion on foreign affairs is closely tied to attitudes toward expenditures for military preparedness or defense. The Cold War years saw strong, general support for the military budget. With Vietnam, new conflict arose over the portion of the federal budget being devoted to military expenditures. By 1973, the proportion of people who thought we were spending too much for defense reached a majority. Today, people are again thinking we need to spend more for defense in order to fulfill our obligations around the globe.

Civil Rights.   Concern for race relations has been an enduring issue since the late 1950s. After two decades of protests, demonstrations, and legal battles, the issue of black America still is not settled in the minds of many Americans. There are conflicts over the rights of blacks and other minorities, including the role of government in supporting those rights, and then there are deep cleavages within racial groups.

Over the years, public support for government intervention in the racial integration of jobs, schools, and public accommodations has been divided. The percentage supporting government activity is more than a majority, and the proportions have varied very little over the years. Yet many Americans refuse to openly embrace desegregation as a position. The most common response is something in between. Many Americans also apparently feel that civil-rights leaders are pushing too fast for change, while only a handful think the process of change has been too slow. Two newer areas of conflict to emerge over civil rights are busing and affirmative action plans. There is widespread disagreement over the desirability of either. A 1979 poll showed that 80 percent of the American people opposed busing children across town for interracial education, and 75 percent of whites thought that blacks are "entitled to no special consideration and must make it strictly on merit."

DEMOCRATIC VALUES

It may be recalled that democracy is based on some fundamental principles. In particular we spoke of individual freedom, equality of opportunity, majority rule, and open political participation. Can we assume that these are values all Americans believe in and support?

Studies conducted over the years reveal a strikingly consistent pattern: On the level of abstract generality, the American people are united and supportive of basic American values; on the level of application of those principles to specific situations, they are far less supportive and are divided in their support. James Protho and Charles Grigg found in 1960 that Americans could agree on and support such statements as "Every citizen should have an equal chance to influence government policy," and "People in the minority should be free to try to win majority support for their opinions." When these same citizens were asked how they felt regarding statements applying the principles to concrete situations, however, the agreement quickly melted away. There was very little support for the statements on application. On ten statements concerning items such as barring blacks from office, allowing only taxpayers to vote, permitting antireligious speeches, or allowing Communist speeches there were only three statements on which 75 percent or more of those polled could agree. The percentage was somewhat higher for people with more education, but even here half the questions left the educated in disagreement.[29]

Herbert McClosky found much the same results in his 1964 study. McClosky sampled the general electorate, as well as a group of delegates to the national party nominating conventions; these he labeled "influentials." He asked both groups—electorate and influentials—a series of questions on the democratic rules of the game and social and political equality (see Table 6.5). On the rules of the game, McClosky found that the general public could not reach consensus (75 percent or more in agreement) on any of the questions asked. When the same questions were put to the influentials, consensus was achieved on 8 of the 12 questions. For the values of democracy, McClosky asked a series of questions that translated social, political, and economic equality into specific situations. Again the pattern of responses was similar (see Table 6.6). The general public could achieve consensus (75 percent agreement) on none of the areas; the rate for the influentials was not much better. They achieved consensus on only a few questions, though they did score closer to the needed 75 percent on many more questions than the electorate. McClosky concluded, "American politics is widely thought to be innocent of ideology, but this opinion more appropriately described the electorate than the politically active minority. . . . The evidence suggests that it is the articulate classes rather than the public who serve as the major repositories of the public conscience and as the carriers of the Creed. Responsibility for keeping the system going, hence, falls most heavily upon them."[30]

GROUP DIFFERENCES AND PUBLIC OPINION

The consequences and impact of public opinion can be readily and meaningfully assessed when we understand the groupings that differentiate mass public opinion. At the outset we said that public opinion was a rich mix of opinions from the diversified groups comprising society. In fact, one may argue there is no

29. James Protho and Charles Grigg, "Fundamental Principles of Democracy: Basis of Agreement and Disagreement," *Journal of Politics* 22 (1960), p. 282.
30. Herbert McClosky, "Consensus and Ideology in American Politics," *The American Political Science Review,* 58 (1964), 369.

Table 6.5
Democracy's "Rules of the Game"[a]

Items	Political Influentials (N = 3020)	General Electorate (N = 1484)
	% Agree	
There are times when it almost seems better for the people to take the law into their own hands rather than wait for the machinery of government to act.	13.3	26.9
The majority has the right to abolish minorities if it wants to.	6.8	28.4
We might as well make up our minds that in order to make the world better a lot of innocent people will have to suffer.	27.2	41.6
If congressional committees stuck strictly to the rules and gave every witness his rights, they would never succeed in exposing the many dangerous subversives they have turned up.	24.7	47.4
I don't mind a politician's methods if he manages to get the right things done.	25.6	42.4
Almost any unfairness or brutality may have to be justified when some great purpose is being carried out.	13.3	32.8
Politicians have to cut a few corners if they are going to get anywhere.	29.4	43.2
People ought to be allowed to vote even if they can't do so intelligently.	65.6	47.6
To bring about great changes for the benefit of mankind often requires cruelty and even ruthlessness.	19.4	31.3
Very few politicians have clean records, so why get excited about the mudslinging that sometimes goes on?	14.8	38.1
It is all right to get around the law if you don't actually break it.	21.2	30.2
The true American way of life is disappearing so fast that we may have to use force to save it.	12.8	34.6

a. Since respondents were forced to make a choice on each item, the number of omitted of "don't know" responses was, on the average, fewer than one percent, and thus has little influence on the direction or magnitude of the results reported.

SOURCE: Herbert McClosky, "Consensus and Ideology in American Politics," *The American Political Science Review,* 58 (June 1964).

public opinion, only the opinions of many subpublics. In other words, we break down public opinions into categories, or groupings, that we think are politically relevant. The usual divisions are formed from social class, income, age, race, religion, and sex. In this way, social scientists can look for clusters of opinions within mass public opinions that command a consensus in a specific group or segment of American society. The focus on group differences is helpful in understanding conflict and consensus within American society. It is particularly helpful

Table 6.6
Application of Democracy to Social, Political, and Economic Equality

Items	Political influentials (N = 3020) % Agree	General electorate (N = 1484)
Political equality		
The main trouble with democracy is that most people don't really know what's best for them.	40.8	58.0
Few people really know what is in their own best interest in the long run.	42.6	61.1
"Issues" and "arguments" are beyond the understanding of most voters.	37.5	62.3
Most people don't have enough sense to pick their own leaders wisely.	28.0	47.8
It will always be necessary to have a few strong, able people actually running everything.	42.5	56.2
Social and ethnic equality		
We have to teach children that all men are created equal but almost everyone knows that some are better than others.	54.7	58.3
Just as is true of fine race horses, some breeds of people are just naturally better than others.	46.0	46.3
Regardless of what some people say, there are certain races in the world that just won't mix with Americans	37.2	50.4
When it comes to the things that count most, all races are certainly not equal.	45.3	49.0
The trouble with letting certain minority groups into a nice neighborhood is that they gradually give it their own atmosphere.	49.8	57.7
Economic equality		
Labor does not get its fair share of what it produces	20.8	44.8
Every person should have a good house, even if the government has to build it for him.	14.9	28.2
I think the government should give a person work if he can't find another job.	23.5	47.3
The government ought to make sure that everyone has a good standard of living.	34.4	55.9
There will always be poverty, so people might as well get used to the idea.	40.4	59.4

SOURCE: Herbert McClosky, "Consensus and Ideology in American Politics," *The American Political Science Review,* 58 (June, 1964).

in understanding changing opinions as new issues and new people come to the fore.

The traditional stability of opinion groupings is changing. New polarities by race, age, and education are emerging. This is true for party support and for a number of other issues as well. We will briefly examine four groupings that have relevance for the 1980s: (1) the persistence of ethnic or racial divisions; (2) the decline of class and economic differences; (3) the growth of a generation gap caused by differences of age and education; and (4) the reemergence of religious differences.

RACIAL DIFFERENCES

It has been noted several times that America came out of the 1970s more polarized along racial lines than at the start of the decade. Racial divisions persist. Concludes Alan Monroe: "For whatever reason, the difference between black and white opinions on issues is the greatest of any social cleavage. This cleavage in opinion is reinforced by several factors. Individuals are aware of being black or white and, what may be important, they know that others are aware."[31]

The depth of racial divisions is evidenced in opinions on political issues. The differences are even more pronounced when the issues are pointed toward race. On desegregation, Erickson, Luttbeg, and Tedin report finding different attitudes on desegregation. From data gathered by the Survey Research Center at the University of Michigan in 1976, black and white responses were markedly different when asked whether they favored desegregation, strict segregation, or something in between. Three out of four blacks favored desegregation as compared with two out of five white respondents; 50 percent of the whites favored something in between while only one-quarter of the blacks said so. Furthermore, blacks are far less convinced that desegregation has moved along fast enough (45 percent said not fast enough), while whites think desegregation is proceeding about right or too fast (44 percent said too fast).[32] On the more volatile issue of busing, blacks are much more likely to approve (75 percent in 1974 Gallup Poll), while whites equally strongly disapprove (72 percent).

Ethnic differences persist on all issues. Blacks are more likely to take liberal positions on issues of public policy, such as spending, the guaranteed annual income, and government medical care.[33] Electorally, blacks remain firm in their support for the Democratic party. Their support for Lyndon Johnson and then Hubert Humphrey in 1968 was overwhelming. By 1972 whites were fleeing the Democratic party; blacks remained solid. The 1976 election saw blacks less enthusiastic but nonetheless voting Democratic; whites were evenly divided.

CLASS AND ECONOMIC DIFFERENCES

With the acceptance of the policies of the New Deal, economic and class differences have declined. On economics, most Americans see themselves as middle class. As incomes have increased, the traditional disputes over wages and tax

31. Alan Monroe, *Public Opinion in America,* p. 93.
32. Robert S. Erickson, Norman R. Luttbeg, and Kent L. Tedin, *American Public Opinion,* 2nd Edition (New York: John Wiley & Sons, 1980), pp. 168–169.
33. Erickson, Luttbeg, & Tedin, *American Public Opinion,* p. 169.

policies have diminished. The welfare state notion no longer evokes strong protest. This is not to say economic issues and unemployment are not concerns for Americans. In 1979, 75 percent of Americans rated inflation and economic health as the most serious problems facing America. The point is that differences of opinion are not breaking along economic or class lines.

On noneconomic social issues, class or social status are affected by other factors, such as education or race. We find, for example, greater intolerance of civil rights or rights of the accused among lower-income groups. But whether this is a function of class status or low education is unclear, since most lower-income people have lower education levels. Lower socioeconomic groups also take a more "isolationist" view of foreign policy, opposing foreign aid or trade with Communist nations. These opinions are commonly cited to prove a "working-class authoritarianism." The problem is that a similar attitude is not in evidence on social-welfare issues or even in a careful analysis of foreign policy issues. State Erickson, Luttbeg, and Tedin: "The accumulation of survey evidence indicates that economic status has virtually no impact on the aggressiveness of one's foreign policy stance."[34]

In short, class divisions seem to be declining. Postwar affluence has eroded the meaningful distinctions based on class status, and there is a consensus on governmental and social goals. What conflicts do occur are largely the result of ethnicity, age, or other factors. The distinctions of class remain, but the impact is limited.

EDUCATION AND AGE

Education is a relevant variable for public opinion, but as educational level increases throughout the nation, the differences diminish. Recent events have also blurred educational distinctions. Traditionally, college-educated persons are more tolerant and support dissent. Yet support for Nixon and criticism of the Watergate investigation were highest among the better educated. Education makes some difference in opinions, but we are cautioned by students of public opinion to "put aside stereotypes of the less educated as authoritarians ranked against the enlightened college-educated elites."[35]

Age appears to be a very salient variable for opinion differences. It is readily apparent from Table 6.7 that a "generation gap" does in fact exist. On all ten items, young people take the more liberal position; on seven of the ten items, the differences are dramatic. Particularly on marijuana and obscenity, young adults take a strikingly more permissive position. Politically, the differences by age are most evident in the refusal of young voters to take partisan labels. In 1976, half the voters under 25 called themselves independents. If this trend continues or accelerates in the 1980s, the generational impact could cause a partisan realignment or seriously undermine political parties altogether.

34. Erickson, Luttbeg & Tedin, *American Public Opinion*, p. 162.
35. Holloway & George, *Public Opinion*, p. 106.

Table 6.7

Age and Opinions on Selected Political Issues

Opinion[a]	Percent support among opinion holders		
	21–29 Years old	50 Years or older	Difference
The use of marijuana should be made legal. (Gallup, 1977)	52	11	−41
Oppose stricter community standards regarding sale of sexually explicit materials. (Gallup, 1977)	67	32	−35
Red China should be admitted to the United Nations. (Gallup, 1970)	60	34	−26
Do not disapprove of all protest marches that are permitted by the local authorities. (SRE, 1968)	59	34	−25
The government in Washington should make every possible effort to improve the social and economic position of blacks and other minority groups. (CPS, 1976)	56	35	−21
Women should have an equal role with men in running business, industry, and government. (CPS, 1976)	79	58	−21
The government in Washington is paying too much for national defense. (Gallup, 1977)	37	18	−19
Oppose the death penalty for persons convicted of murder. (Gallup, 1976)	37	27	−10
The government in Washington should see to it that every person has a job and a good standard of living. (CPS, 1976)	43	37	− 6
Favor a government insurance plan which would cover all medical and hospital expenses. (CPS, 1976)	53	51	− 2

a. For Gallup data, percentages may be in error by about one percent, since they were recalculated from original tables in which nonopinion holders were included in the percentage base.

SOURCE: Robert S. Erickson, Norman R. Luttbeg, and Kent L. Tedin. *American Public Opinion.* 2nd Edition (New York: John Wiley & Sons, 1980).

RELIGION

Religion has been a historic factor in differences of opinion. Yet in the 1960s religious differences did not widen or become significant political divisions for the American people. Religious differences in political party support were evident then and remain today, but on a whole range of social issues—capital punishment, Vietnam amnesty, defense spending, or busing—religious differences were not significant.

By 1976, however, a "religious renewal" had surfaced. A "born again" Christian was elected president, religious groups and cults spread across college campuses and the nation, and new social issues divided opinions along religious lines.

Fundamentalist religious movements have become intensely political. In 1980 the Moral Majority was formed to back conservative Christian candidates for public office—including presidential winner Ronald Reagan. The Moral Majority is predominately protestant, white, and middle class, an outgrowth of video evangelist Jerry Falwell. Several additional Christian groups formed Christian PACs to influence the election. Such groups no longer shun preaching politics from the pulpit, the establishment of voter registration desks in backs of churches or the creation of "Christian hit lists." These largely evangalical Christian groups actively campaigned and contributed money for or against candidates they targeted on moral and religious grounds. (This aided in the defeat of several liberal senators and congressmen in 1980.)

THE MEDIA AND PUBLIC OPINION

The impact of the mass media on public opinion appears immense. Over 60 million newspapers are sold daily; nearly 10,000 weekly, semimonthly, and monthly periodicals are published; and 95 percent of American homes contain at least one television set. The mass media reach a wide audience as shown in Figure 6.4, and yet social scientists remain uncertain of the role the media actually play in shaping public opinion.

Nearly two-thirds of Americans report television as the prime source of most of their information, followed by newspapers (50 percent) and radio (20 percent). Television remains the most believable of the news media, with 43 percent citing television as most believable in 1976 to 21 percent for newspapers. Less educated and lower-social-status individuals tend to rely on television exclusively; with more education, there is a tendency to use multiple sources of information. Those who read newpapers with strong reputations were found to be more politically informed than readers of less notable newspapers.[36]

Do the media influence opinions? There is little question that the media do

36. Erickson, Luttbeg, & Tedin, *American Public Opinion,* p. 134.

Public Opinion and Agenda-Setting for Policy

We are constantly reminded that public opinion forms the boundaries for a democratic government. Individuals and groups are continually placing demands upon government, and these demands help shape the policy agenda for democratic government. Yet we also recognize that much public opinion is uninformed and unorganized. A great many of the policy decisions made, as V. O. Key said, are where "extremely small proportions of the general public have any awareness of the particular issue, much less any understanding of the consequences of the decision."[1] There is a great volatility to public opinion of which policy makers must be keenly aware. In measuring the impact of public opinion on public policy, two features of opinions must be borne in mind: the type of policy agenda involved and the character or organization of public opinion.

1. Roger Cobb and Charles Elder have identified two types of policy agendas:

    Systematic agenda.   All issues commonly perceived by members of the political community as meriting public attention.
    Governmental agenda.   Those problems to which public officials give serious and active attention.[2]

2. The character or organization of public opinion is concerned with the question of how issues are raised from the systematic agenda to the governmental agenda. A typical characterization of the public is as follows:

    Mass public.   The great bulk of citizens who possess only rudimentary political information and interest. While they may vote, they remain passive observers of politics. They comprise 80 percent of the public.
    Attentive public.   Persons who regularly concern themselves with political issues and communicate those ideas among persons with whom they are associated. They comprise 15 percent of the public.
    Mobilized public.   Persons who not only concern themselves with political issues but who also seek to mobilize support in behalf of those issues by first hand contact with public officials. They comprise 5 percent of the public.[3]

It is to the attentive, and more specifically to the mobilized, public that the agenda-setting function of public opinion falls. "For all practical purposes the attentive public is the public between elections."[4] While we cannot suggest that governmental agendas are determined by attentive publics (a great deal of public policy precedes independently of what public opinion holds or may be mobilized to do), the attentive and mobilized publics do make important contributions to the policy process. James Rosenau suggests three policy roles for the attentive public to perform as a form of citizenship between elections.

Attentive public as unorganized audience. As a sounding board for policy debate, governmental and nongovernmental leaders carry on discussion and argumentation leading to policy choice. The attentive public provides the boundaries for acceptable choices.
Attentive public as organized groups.

This may be viewed as support building activities for which publics have become mobilized into pressing their attitudes and demands upon governmental officials. This helps to reinforce or diminish the preference for policy positions on the part of policymakers.

Attentive public as surrogate electorate. Because of the first two roles, the attentive public provides continual evidence of what may happen at the next election. This serves to link public opinion and the attentive public back to the mass public. They expose public officials to currents of thought and provide them a measure of their political vulnerability.[5]

1. V. O. Key, *Public Opinion and American Democracy* (New York: Knopf, 1961), p. 14.
2. Roger W. Cobb and Charles D. Elder, *Participation in American Politics; The Dynamics of Agenda-Building* (Boston: Allyn and Bacon, 1972), p. 85.
3. James N. Rosenau, *Citizenship Between Elections* (New York: Free Press, 1974), p. 106.
4. *Rosenau,* p. 4.
5. *Rosenau,* pp. 6–16.

influence what issues are important; they perform what is called the agenda-setting function. Television is particularly adept in performing this function. The evidence is that the presentation and focus on events in the media controls the political agenda and establishes the issues people perceive as critical or important. But if the media can set the agenda for a nation, can they direct public opinion? Here the evidence is far less clear. There has been a high correlation between newspaper endorsement and electoral success. This was even more true where there was a long ballot and voter information was low.[37] Yet Thomas Patterson and Robert McClure's *The Unseeing Eye* found little evidence of the public being taken in by television ads. Viewers were not "duped" by political ads; if anything, they became more knowledgeable: "To put it bluntly, spot political commercials educate rather than hoodwink the voters."[38] Michael Robinson's study of military news reporting put the impact negatively: Broadcast reports give rise to cynical and negative attitudes toward the issue. There was growth in negative feelings toward the political system, an attitude Robinson labeled "video-malaise."[39]

In recent years, more charges of biased reporting have surfaced. Harris surveys in early 1970 found sympathy for Spiro Agnew's attack on the media; respondents felt he "was right to criticize the way TV networks cover the news." Yet the criticisms apparently proved short-lived. Within two years, Roper polls were reporting a restored level of confidence in the media. Surveys of the televised Watergate hearings found that partisanship was a good predictor of opinion. Republicans who voted for Richard Nixon in 1972 tended not to watch the hear-

37. John E. Mueller, "Choosing Among 133 Candidates," *Public Opinion Quarterly,* 34 (Fall 1970), pp. 395–402; Michael Hooper, "Party and Newspaper Endorsement as Predictors of Voter Choice," *Journalism Quarterly,* 43 (Summer 1969), pp. 302–5.
38. Thomas Patterson and Robert McClure, *The Unseeing Eye* (New York: G. P. Putnam's Sons, 1976), p. 23.
39. Michael J. Robinson, "Public Affairs Broadcasting and the Growth of Political Malaise: The Case of the Selling of the Pentagon," *American Political Science Review,* 70 (June 1976).

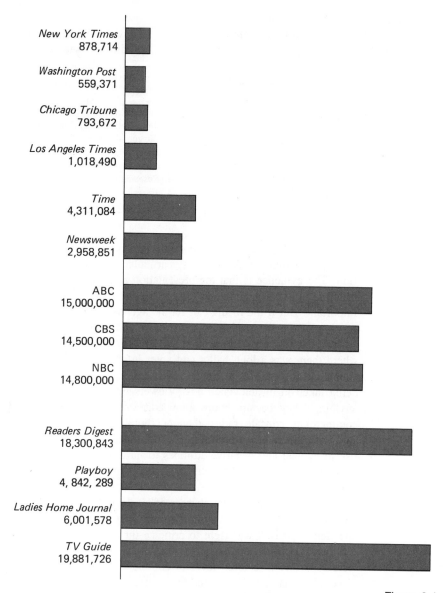

Figure 6.4

Audience reached by selected media. (*Ayer Directory of Publication,* Philadelphia, Pa.: Ayer Press, 1979. *Advertising Age,* October 15, 1979, p. 114.)

Table 6.8

Changing Issue Priorities of the American Public, 1965–1970

Problem (in order of change in concern)	1965	1970	Change
Reducing pollution of air and water	17%	53%	+36%
Reducing the amount of crime	41	56	+15
Improving housing, clearing slums	21	27	+ 6
Beautifying America	3	5	+ 2
Helping people in poor areas	32	30	− 2
Reducing racial discrimination	29	25	− 4
Improving highway safety	18	13	− 5
Conquering "killer diseases"	37	29	− 8
Reducing unemployment	35	25	−10
Improving public education	45	31	−14

SOURCE: *Gallup Opinion Index*, June 1970, p. 8. Given in Robert Erickson, & Norman Luttbeg, *American Public Opinion* (New York: John Wiley & Sons, 1973), p. 147.

ings and felt they "weren't good for the country." Those who voted for George McGovern in 1972 were most likely to watch the hearings.[40] What is evident here is a self-selection process based on preformed perceptions.

In fact, what takes place is a good deal of selective perception. People focus on issues that are salient to them; and issues that appear to affect them personally are most likely to be salient issues. They also selectively perceive the content of the news. People focus on issues and facts that support their own concerns and biases. The "facts" are related by the individual according to his or her cognitive screen. We select out the points that support our positions. The difference between what is presented and what is heard can be startling.

Yet the impact of the various media cannot be ignored; they have the power to change opinion and change it dramatically. Television particularly has an immediacy and directness the print media cannot match. This same advantage, however, provides ample opportunity for misuse. The dramatization of events may make them appear more critical than they are. The selection of events or comments can be out of context and convey inaccurate impressions. Such was the case at the 1980 Republican national convention when, pressed for news, the networks centered on Reagan's discussions with Gerald Ford for the vice-presidency. It was the respected CBS anchor Walter Cronkite who coined the phrase "co-presidency" to characterize the discussions; a term used by neither Ford or Reagan.

Studies indicate that television does not appear to create a bandwagon effect—that is, reporting an election result from the East before the polls have

40. Lang and Lang, "Televised Hearings: The Impact Out There," *Watergate and the American Political Process,* ed. Ronald E. Pynn (New York: Praeger, 1974), p. 75.

Television reaches a vast number of persons. From its early years, television news has become an important source of information for the American public. (The Bettmann Archive, Inc.)

closed in the West does not change results in the West. William Glaser's study of television's impact on voter turnout concluded that people who rely on television for campaign information are no more likely to vote than any other citizens.[41] The major influence of television has been a change in the way we conduct campaigns. It has removed campaigning from the party professionals and party activists. Candidates now rely on the media rather than the party to reach more people, more quickly, and more dramatically. Now media managers create an image, market a candidate, and use media campaigns, based on market research, to maximize votes much in the same manner Ford spurs sales of its automobiles.

PUBLIC TRUST

Ultimately, the test of public opinion may be measured by the confidence a people express in their political system. In a democracy, where consent of the people is so vital, the erosion of confidence is of serious concern. How serious a malaise is the decline in public confidence today? Some suggest that the loss of confidence impairs effectiveness, gives rise to instability, and even threatens the survival of democratic government. Whether we go this far or not, public confidence does indicate public satisfaction with government.

Public satisfaction with government and American institutions is not high

41. William A. Glaser, "Television and Voting Turnout," *Public Opinion Quarterly,* 29 (Spring 1965), pp. 71–86.

PRACTICING POLITICS   6.1

Joining a local community or block association

Many people prefer to participate in politics at the local level and devote their time and energy to solving community problems. There are thousands of local organizations all over the country. Here are some ways to go about locating and joining those in your area.

1. Check bulletin boards at local shops and supermarkets; specialty bookstores in particular often serve as information clearinghouses for a local area.
2. Talk to friends, neighbors, and local community leaders.
3. Check your local library: often there is a community bulletin board, and often too the librarians will know about local groups. The *Encyclopedia of Associations,* a standard reference work in most libraries, contains profile listings of organizations and projects, including when the group was founded, size of membership, staff, activities, and publications. Regional and local directories may also be available; ask the reference librarian.

Once you have located the organization(s) that seem to suit your needs and talents, find out all you can about them. Go to the office or to a meeting and volunteer. If you have an idea for a project that is not on the group's agenda, find out why and offer to carry it out if the group approves.

today. Over the past decade, manifestations of distrust and cynicism have reached epidemic proportions. Trust and responsiveness indicators have declined sharply in the past decade; over half of all Americans are now expressing distrust of and cynicism toward national institutions. Directed primarily toward politics, the erosion of confidence throughout the 1970s has affected the president, Congress and

Table 6.9

Erosion of Public Trust and Confidence

	1966	1973	1974	1975	1976	1977	1978	1979	1980
Televisions news	25%	41%	31%	35%	28%	28%	35%	37%	31%
Medicine	73	57	50	43	42	43	42	30	—
Military	62	40	33	24	23	27	29	29	—
Press	29	30	25	26	20	18	23	28	22
Organized religion	41	36	32	32	24	29	34	20	—
Major companies	55	29	21	19	16	20	22	18	19
Congress	42	29	18	13	9	17	10	18	11
Executive branch	41	19	28	13	11	23	14	17	18
Organized labor	22	20	18	14	10	14	15	10	—
Average	43	33	28	24	20	24	25	23	—

SOURCE: *Public Opinion* magazine. October–November, 1979. Published bimonthly by the American Enterprise Institute for Public Policy Research. 1980 data, American Enterprise Institute for Public Policy Research.

the courts. But the waning of support is not limited to politics: all major institutions have suffered. There is also a decline in political efficacy. In the 1960s Americans shared a consensus that public officials cared about people, that people have a say in what government does. By 1970 that consensus was shaken; the public was almost evenly split over its ability to affect government or even be heard by public officials.

The public is frustrated and angered by events making it more difficult for government to respond. And the future is unclear. Let us hope that Jack Citrin's analysis is correct: "Political systems, like baseball teams, have slumps and winning streaks. Having recently endured a succession of losing seasons, Americans boo the home team when it takes the field. But fans are often fickle; victories quickly elicit cheers. And to most fans what matters is whether the home team wins or loses, not how it plays the game."[42]

SUMMARY

1. Much of what we know about public opinion is changing. Old patterns of opinion and consensus are deteriorating. New people and new issues are producing new patterns of political conflict.

2. Political socialization explains much of what a person believes about politics by examining how people acquire their political attitudes. By adolescence a child has a well developed set of political attitudes. The influence of family, peers, education, and media comingle to produce a political picture that remains fairly stable through adult life.

3. Traditional social and economic conflicts, which divided Americans for two generations, are finding resolution today. The expanded role for government policy has won approval from most Americans. Newer social issues such as abortion, gay rights, and pornography have surfaced to divide the people.

4. We can take little confidence that the American people are united in their support of democratic values. On abstract generalities the people are supportive, but on the application of values to particular settings and people, there is little commitment to democracy. This is one reason we differentiate between elite and mass opinion.

5. Public opinion groupings dramatize the social cleavages in America. Race continues to be a persistent and deep division, while social class has diminished in importance. Newer cleavages by education and age are growing in importance. These trends are likely to continue in the coming years.

6. The media exert a persuasive influence for Americans. The source of

42. Jack Citrin, "The Political Relevance of Trust in Government," *American Political Science Review,* 68 (September 1974), p. 987.

most political information, the media—particularly television—set the agenda for important political issues. The instantaneous technology has the capacity to inform and educate; when abused, it also has the ability for irreparable harm.

TERMS

agenda setting 215
elite opinion 193
ideology 193
intensity 193
isolationism 213
mass opinion 193
operational liberal 193
political socialization 195

quota sample 194
random sample 194
salience 192
selective perception 219
single-issue politics 191
stability 192–93
video malaise 217
working-class
    authoritarianism 213

RESEARCH PROJECTS

6.1. Political Socialization. Has the process of socialization into politics for you and your friends been similiar to that reported in the text? Ask yourself and some of your friends, say five to ten, some questions and compare with the results from the studies on political socialization
- What is your party affiliation?
- What was your father's/mother's party affiliation?
- What is your degree of interest in politics?
- How often did your parents talk about politics with you?
- What political events stand out in your mind? How do you feel about these events?
- How do your parents feel about those events?
- Name three close friends. Can you describe their party identification and attitude toward politics? Similiar to yours?

6.2. Public Opinion Poll. Conduct your own public opinion poll. You could poll a class you are taking, do the neighborhood where you or your parents reside, or if the school has a little money, mail a questionnaire to city residents by randomly selecting them from the telephone book. Ask persons to agree or disagree with statements on relevant, contemporary issues; for example:
- We should use force, if necessary, to achieve the release of the hostages in Iran.

- All women should be permitted to have an abortion if they want.
- The government has become too large and wasteful to be effective.
- Blacks and minorities should be given preference for employment and admission to colleges and universities.
- No one has the right to advocate the violent overthrow of the American government.

You will want to examine the results by social–economic characteristics, so include a couple of questions on age, sex, race of respondent. Carefully examine the results. Do they differ from other studies? Why? Was your sample scientifically drawn? How could this account for the differences?

6.3. Trends in Public Opinion. The Gallup Poll puts out the monthly *Gallup Opinion Index;* there are also volumes of Gallup Polls, *The Gallup Poll, 1935–1971,* and *The Gallup Poll, 1972–1977.* Trace the changes in opinion on major issues over time. Many of the polls break down the answers by social–economic characteristics. Note how the responses differ by age, income, race, and sex. You can select one or two issues and trace it over the years; you can also select a more recent issue and analyze the results. What are the demographic patterns? What is the conclusion on stability and change toward issues by the American public?

6.4. The Media. Does the media set the agenda of issues for the American public? Compare and analyze national circulation newspapers—*The New York Times* and *Washington Post,* a national network TV newscast, and a state or local newspaper. What stories are covered? Are they the same? Do lead TV stories have front page stories in the papers? What priorities are events given and how much overlap between media sources is there?

BIBLIOGRAPHY

Dawson, Richard. *Public Opinion and Contemporary Disarray.* New York: Harper and Row, 1973.

One of the first works to sense the change in public opinion over the past two decades. Provides a fresh and insightful treatment to public opinion.

Dawson, Richard, Kenneth Prewitt, and Karen Dawson. *Political Socialization.* Boston: Little, Brown, 1977.

An excellent summary of the findings on political socialization. Contains a discussion of the process of political socialization, integrating the results of studies to that process.

Erickson, Robert, Norman Luttbeg, and Kent Tedin. *American Public Opinion*. New York: John Wiley, 1980.

The most complete and up to date study of public opinion. There are several good chapters covering public opinion and ideology, democracy, differences, elections, parties, and pressure groups.

Free, Lloyd, and Hadley Cantril. *The Political Beliefs of Americans*. New York: Simon and Schuster, 1968.

A basic work that looks at the beliefs of Americans along liberal–conservative dimensions. Free and Cantril provide a good insight into the value process of forming and expressing opinion.

Holloway, Harry, and John George. *Public Opinion*. New York: St. Martins, 1979.

An excellent text on public opinion that examines coalitions of opinions and their impact on elites in society. There is extensive coverage of the opinion grouping of mass opinion.

Jennings, M. Kent, and Richard Niemi. *The Political Character of Adolescence: The Influence of Families and Schools*. Princeton, N.J.: Princeton University Press, 1974

A basic work on political socialization which underscores the importance of family and schools as agents of socialization. Explains the process of socialization, what family values are brought with students, and how school alters those beliefs.

Monroe, Alan D. *Public Opinion in America*. New York: Dodd, Mead, 1975.

A text in public opinion that gives a survey of findings on public opinion. Seeks to find patterns of stability in public opinion.

Patterson, Thomas, and Robert McClure. *The Unseeing Eye*. New York: G.P. Putnam's Sons, 1976.

Television may not be the all powerful generator of public opinion. Patterson and McClure seek to explain the impact of television on public opinion, notably candidates and election issues. They find the impact less than overwhelming.

Shaw, Donald, and Maxwell McCombs. *The Emergence of American Political Issues: The Agenda Setting Function of the Press*. St. Paul, Minn.: West, 1977.

A collection of essays on the role of the press in establishing the priority of issues for Americans. It discusses how issues are prioritized from news and how susceptible people are to the influence of the press.

Chapter
7

Interest Groups

Two hundred twenty-two million Americans live in metropolitan centers, urban ghettos, suburban tracts, rural towns, and on farms and ranches: The population is a vast mix of backgrounds and cultures. No matter how we look at America, the picture is always one of diversity. This same diversity is reflected in its groups and organizations.

Americans have always been inclined to divide into groups. James Madison called these groups "factions" and felt their source was the unequal distribution of property. In the 1830s, Alexis de Toqueville, traveling in the United States, was impressed with the number and assortment of interest groups: "Americans of all ages, all conditions and all dispositions constantly form associations." De Tocqueville called America a society of joiners. Today, his assessment still holds true. In 1976, 57 percent of Americans reported being active in a voluntary association.[1] There are some 15,000 groups and associations. Some are ethnic and cultural, others are formed on the basis of economic and occupational status, still others are generated by issues of concern to citizens. Figure 7.1 shows how people join groups based upon the amount of education they have. Individuals seek the support

1. Samuel H. Barnes, "Some Political Consequences of Involvement in Organizations," paper delivered at the American Political Science Association Annual Meeting, 1977.

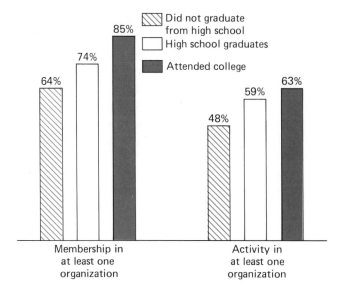

Figure 7.1

Membership and activity in organizations by Americans with different amounts of education. (Samuel H. Barnes, "Some Political Consequences of Involvement in Organizations," paper presented at the 1977 annual meeting of the American Political Science Association)

and resources of others to achieve common goals. When the purpose of any group includes pressuring government to enhance the group's objectives, it becomes a political pressure group, and something of interest to the study of American politics.

Political pressure groups, once felt to be a "normal" and healthy part of the American political process, have recently come under attack along with other institutions. A 1973 study by the Senate Committee on Government Operations found three out of four Americans felt that "special interests get more from the government than the people do." A 1975 Harris Poll recorded 72 percent of Americans thinking that Congress was too much under the influence of special interest lobbies. Americans see the political processes dominated by special interest groups, and government as serving the purposes of a few big interests, not those of the general public.

The decline of trust and confidence in the political system has deeply affected interest groups. "Politicians captured by special interest" and "big business running the country" are common charges. Many feel the present malaise in government can be laid at the feet of interest groups. Former lobbyist Robert Winter-Berger writes, "Without the lobbyists, corruption in government would be minimal, simply because the efforts to corrupt would be so disorganized, so diffuse."[2]

---

2. Robert Winter-Berger, as cited by Carol S. Greenwald in *Group Power* (New York: Praeger Publishers, 1977), p. 324.

INTEREST GROUPS AND PUBLIC POLICY

The public sees interest groups as powerful brokers dominating and controlling the political process. Yet students of interest groups are far from agreed on their influence. According to Lewis Dexter, "Washington representatives would no more bribe or threaten government officials than a professional author would bribe or threaten editors. . . ."[3] And Lester Milbrath, summarizing his interviews with lobbyists, concluded: "The weight of the evidence . . . suggests that there is relatively little influence or power in lobbying per se."[4] Others who have traced the lobbying efforts of an organization or followed a particular issue find considerably more evidence of power and influence.[5]

The problem stems, in part, from the nature and functions of interest groups. Some people see interest groups as the key variable in political activity. David Truman saw politics as the interaction of groups in American society. He defined an interest group as "a shared-attitude group that makes certain claims upon other groups in the society through any of the institutions of government."[6] Whether one goes so far as to call public policy the result of competing group interaction, it is clear that interest groups are important, active, and influential in the policy process.

WHAT IS AN INTEREST GROUP?

We have noted David Truman's definition of an interest group; Carol Greenwald offers another: "An interest group is a combination of individuals who seek to pursue shared interests through a set of agreed upon activities."[7] Any group becomes a political pressure group when a combination of individuals seek to pursue shared interests by attempting to influence decisions within the policy-making system.

Table 7.1, which lists voluntary organizations in the United States, shows that economic, social welfare, health, and education groups dominate. Many of these organizations make use of the political process when it suits their needs and goals. They differ on where to apply pressure on the political process, and their goals lead them to take different forms of action. Agricultural groups may find commodity exchange policies set by the executive branch and a sympathetic Department of Agriculture a logical place to lobby if they seek to influence policy.

3. Lewis Anthony Dexter, *How Organizations Are Represented in Washington* (Indianapolis, Ind.: Bobbs-Merrill Co., Inc. 1969), p. 7.
4. Lester Milbrath, *The Washington Lobbyist* (Chicago: Rand McNally, 1963), p. 353.
5. See Robert Engler, *The Politics of Oil* (Chicago: University of Chicago Press, 1967); Mark Nadel, *Corporations and Political Accountability* (Lexington, Mass.: D. C. Heath, 1976); and Russell Warren Howe and Sarah Hays Trott, *The Power Peddlers: How Lobbyists Mold America's Foreign Policy* (New York: Doubleday and Co., 1977).
6. David B. Truman, *The Governmental Process* (New York: Knopf, 1951), p. 37.
7. Greenwald, *Group Power,* p. 15.

Table 7.1

Types of Voluntary Organizations in the United States

Category	Number	Percent
Trade, business, and commercial	3033	21.6
Cultural organizations	1337	9.5
Health and medical	1336	9.5
Scientific, engineering, and technical	981	7.0
Public affairs	949	6.8
Education	932	6.6
Social welfare	879	6.3
Hobby and avocational	866	6.2
Religious	782	5.6
Agricultural	658	4.7
Legal, government, public administration, and military	493	3.5
Athletic and Sport	472	3.4
Fraternal, foreign interest, nationality, and ethnic	437	3.1
Greek letter, and related	316	2.3
Labor unions, associations, and federations	226	1.6
Veterans, hereditary, and patriotic	204	1.5
Chambers of Commerce	102	0.7

SOURCE: Nancy Yakes and Denise Akey, Coeditors, *Encyclopedia of Associations,* 14th Edition (Detroit, Mich.: Gale Research Co., 1980).

Social welfare groups may find new legislation necessary to further their goals. They might lobby Congress and the appropriate committees to write legislation enhancing the mission of their groups. Fraternal organizations may be concerned about other matters such as tax-exempt status. Very few organizations, however, are totally committed to political activity.

INTEREST GROUP FUNCTIONS

Interest groups perform several functions, three of which are worth looking at in detail: material, social, and political functions. The most common function associated with interest groups is material reward and benefits. Groups work to promote their own material self-interest. Labor organizations strive to push up wages to keep earning power ahead of inflation. General Motors opposes tougher emission standards for automobiles because they drive up the cost of automobiles and thereby have the potential to reduce sales and profits. In a less political way, groups provide material benefits to their members directly. Belonging to the American Association of Retired Persons qualifies people for low-cost, generic drug and vitamin purchases. Consumers Union tests and rates brand name merchandise for its members so that they can get the best value for their dollar.

Groups may also perform social functions. These can have both intrinsic worth for individual members as well as extrinsic worth for the group. Membership in a group may be undertaken to reinforce one's self-identification. For example, the National Organization of Women (NOW) and Association of Retired Persons provide such self-identification. By stressing women's concerns, members of NOW can feel that women share common problems and they can work to assert their own identity. The Association of Retired Persons, on the other hand, argues that life does not end at 60, but rather that retired persons can lead active and full lives. The social function also works to promote social solidarity and rapport within the group. Like-minded people join together to collectively advance their interest. The Right to Life Association was formed as a direct result of the Supreme Court's decision on abortion. The Sierra Club and the Audubon Society are made up of individuals dedicated to protecting the environment and maintaining wilderness areas. These people join together in the hope of collective success in situations where individuals would be less powerful.

The political function interest groups perform is essentially a linkage function. They are the primary means by which social issues and demands can be formulated and articulated to government in a more or less systematic manner. What individuals alone cannot achieve, groups stand a realistic chance of securing. Groups fill a void by representing interests to government, thereby providing legislators and other public officials with a sense of what segments of the American public think about major issues before them.

INFLUENCE

Political observers disagree on the influence of groups on politics, and there is no easy way to measure it. Rising medical costs do not necessarily mean that doctors or hospital groups are influential in preventing government agencies from regulating costs. A visit with a member of Congress does not equal influence peddling. And all groups are not equal. An association of independent dry cleaners does not possess the resources or opportunities of General Motors or of IT&T. In fact, General Motors may not need to lobby in the traditional sense of the term; a news release, a phone call to an old friend, or a plant closing can produce the desired effect. Many means of influence are simply not visible.

Robert Presthus has sought to understand interest-group influence—looked at as the ability of an interest group to make good its demands upon government. He distinguishes between "objective" behavioral influence deriving from direct personal contact with political officials, and "subjective" or reputational judgments of the behavior and legitimacy of groups.[8] In general, groups with the most experience and resources committed to lobbying government are the most suc-

8. Robert Presthus, *Elite Accommodation in Canadian Politics* (New York: Cambridge University Press, 1975), p. 173. Compare with his "Interest Group Lobbying: Canada and the United States," *Annals of the American Academy of Political and Social Science* (May 1974).

PRACTICING POLITICS   7.1

How to join a women's group

If you want to focus your political activity on achieving opportunities and rights for women, here are some national organizations you can contact for information about the groups and activities in your area.

Groups active on all issues related to women:

Center for the American Woman and Politics. A nonpartisan research and educational center. Eagleton Institute of Politics, Rutgers University, New Brunswick, New Jersey 08901.

League of Women Voters. A long-established group dedicated to nonpartisan political action and education; state and local branches throughout the country. 1730 M Street NW, Washington, D.C. 20036.

National Organization for Women. A group dedicated to using politics, education, and legal resources as a means to improve the status of women. 425 Thirteenth Street NW, Suite 101, Washington, D.C. 20004.

Women's Lobby, Inc. Collects information on and monitors the progress of legislation affecting women.

Groups focused on electing women to office:

National Women's Educational Fund. Provides information and technical training for women who want to seek political office. 1532 Sixteenth Street NW, Washington, D.C. 20036.

National Women's Political Caucus. Provides information and training for women candidates. 1921 Pennsylvania Avenue NW, Washington, D.C. 20006

Women's Campaign Fund. A nonprofit group that raises money to support women candidates for national and state office. Box 24145, Washington, D.C. 20024.

cessful. Groups actively engaged in lobbying were more successful than groups that were not. The more interaction between lobbyists and public officials, the higher the level of influence.[9]

CATEGORIES OF INTEREST GROUPS

Groups can be categorized in countless ways. Here we will classify them as occupational, issue-oriented, and ethnic and religious groups.

OCCUPATIONAL GROUPS

Since a principal function of interest groups is material benefits for its members, it is logical that occupational groups should be the largest category. Occupational groups are dominated by business and labor, but there are agricultural and professional associations as well.

9. Presthus, ''Interest Group Lobbying. . . .'' especially pp. 49–50.

Business.   Business groups form the oldest, largest, and most heterogeneous category of groups.[10] The National Association of Manufacturers, founded in 1895, represents some 14,000 firms throughout the nation. It is a leading spokesman for big business, actively opposes labor, and promotes free enterprise. In addition, many large corporations maintain their own lobbyists. Most corporations prefer to retain a Washington law firm specializing in lobbying to look after the company's interests. Many small businesses belong to trade associations or join together to employ a law firm in Washington. Business groups focus on regulatory activities and the federal bureaucracy as much or more than they do on Congress.

Since World War II the National Association of Manufacturers has suffered a decline in membership and come more and more to represent "big business." But, report Norman Ornstein and Shirley Elder, "a diminishing membership has been accompanied by a growing aggressiveness in political affairs."[11] The U.S. Chamber of Commerce, with a broader membership, represents some 4,000 local chambers of commerce with individual, trade association, and business memberships of over 70,000. The total membership for the U.S. Chamber of Commerce stands at 4.5 million. Its budget of $16 million is chiefly raised from membership dues. The Chamber uses standing committees to initiate policy positions. Then its professional staff, working with the committees, seeks to lobby government to implement those policies. Recent issues have included common site picketing, tax laws, and government regulation.

In more recent years, the Business Roundtable, founded in 1972, has become a vocal organization defending business interests. Composed of corporate chief executives from nearly 200 of America's largest and most prestigious corporations, the Roundtable was established because of dissatisfaction with the efforts of the other business lobbies. Since the Business Roundtable is composed of corporate chiefs, it prefers to work through members and not lobbyists or law firms; a major corporate executive is far more likely to have direct personal contact with a senator or departmental secretary than a hired representative. The Roundtable addresses major areas of concern to business such as the Arab boycott, Consumer Protection Agency proposals, and antitrust legislation.

The energy crisis has increased the number of energy lobbying groups. After 1974, for example, over 50 petroleum interest groups registered as Washington lobbyists.[12] The oil industry is represented by its trade association, the American Petroleum Institute, but many separate industry associations also exist. Almost all the major oil companies maintain Washington lobbyists. The American Gas Association represents pipeline and distributing companies, and the International Natural Gas Association represents interstate pipeline companies and the

10. V. O. Key, Jr., *Politics, Parties and Pressure Groups* (New York: Thomas Y. Crowell Co., 1958), p. 82.
11. Norman J. Ornstein and Shirley Elder, *Interest Groups, Lobbying and Policymaking* (Washington, D.C.: Congressional Quarterly Press, 1978), p. 38.
12. Greenwald, *Group Power*, p. 29.

gas transportation industry.[13] Several individual gas-producing firms also register as lobbyists, as do electric utility companies. In fact, almost every gas and electric utilities company has some sort of lobby representation in Washington. The number of citizen groups lobbying on energy matters has also grown. There are more than 20 such groups lobbying in Washington, including the Consumer Energy Council of America, Critical Mass Energy Project, the Energy Committee of America, Solar Lobby, and Friends of the River.

Labor.   Dominated by the AFL–CIO, organized labor is often seen as a single interest group. In fact, the AFL–CIO (American Federation of Labor/Congress of Industrial Organizations) is an umbrella for 106 separate affiliate unions whose 14 million members are a diverse assortment of laborers, teachers, and white collar workers. In addition, organized labor includes other individual unions such as the United Auto Workers, the United Mine Workers, and the Teamsters.

It is the AFL–CIO that sets the tone for organized labor, however; it is a powerful force in American politics. The president (George Meany from 1955 until his death in 1980) presides over the Executive Council, composed of him and affiliate union presidents. The union maintains a separate legislative depart-

13. Ornstein and Elder, *Interest Groups, Lobbying and Policy Making,* pp. 40–41.

George Meany, longtime president of the AFL-CIO until 1980, addresses a rally of labor members. (United Press International)

ment with eight professional lobbyists. In addition, there are lobbyists employed by the affiliate unions. The most potent political arm of the AFL–CIO, however, is its political department, COPE (The Committee on Political Education). COPE employs seven professionals, fifteen assistants, and eighteen field representatives. COPE's primary responsibilities are fund raising, voter registration drives, political party support, and electioneering. COPE spends more than a million dollars in a federal election supporting House and Senate candidates that the AFL–CIO endorses.

In recent years, the AFL–CIO has adapted to the political realities of post-partisan politics. It concentrates less on party and more on issues and candidates sympathetic to labor. It continues to mobilize resources and voters to support its lobbying efforts. To use George Meany's term, the AFL–CIO is a "political machine".[14]

But organized labor, even the AFL–CIO, cannot speak for all workers. The American labor movement has never been united. Walter Reuther and his United Auto Workers split with the AFL–CIO in 1968 and became an independent union, with a membership of 105 million. The Teamsters, with 1.8 million members, are another large and separate group. Farm workers have begun to organize under the militant Cesar Chavez. Public employee unionization has been growing and labor has been divided over their striking and disrupting essential services.

Agriculture.   American farmers represent a large interest group. Nearly 4 million are members of farm organizations. They are a clientele group, long recognized as vital to the nation. The Department of Agriculture was established in 1862 to support and work with farm and agri-business interests. Yet the farmer remains an independent political actor. Farm groups have never unified and spoken with one voice.

The largest of the three national farm organizations is the American Farm Bureau, with approximately 3 million members. The Farm Bureau has a close association with the Department of Agriculture: Bureau and Agricultural Extension agents work closely on farming techniques and crop and livestock productivity. With its strength primarily in the Midwest, the Farm Bureau has come to oppose government regulation in agriculture and supports the free market economy. It opposes the price-support program for crops.

The Farm Bureau generally speaks for the larger, more successful producer; the National Farmer's Union, however, with a membership of 250,000, draws from the smaller, less profitable farmers, primarily in the Upper Midwest and Western states. Calling itself the champion of the dirt farmer, the Farmer's Union supports high levels of price supports for crops and livestock. In more recent years, the Farmer's Union has supported efforts to protect migrant farm workers. The oldest of the national farm groups, founded in 1867, is the National Grange.

14. Harry Holloway, "The Political Machine of the AFL–CIO," *Political Science Quarterly,* 94 (Spring 1979), p. 132.

GOOSEMYER   by parker and wilder

Goosemeyer by Parker and Wilder. © 1980 Field Enterprises, Inc. Courtesy of Field Newspaper Syndicate.

It has a membership today of some 600,000, with primary support in New England and the Mid-Atlantic states. Historically, the Grange has been a social organization concerned with the welfare of the farm family, but in more recent years the Grange has adopted the more political approach of supporting price supports for farmers.

Recently, we have witnessed a growing militance among farm interests. The National Farmer's Organization (NFO) calls for withholding produce from the market to increase the price paid to producers. The 1978 "tractorcade" to Washington sought to dramatize the plight of the farmer caught between low prices for products and the high costs of farming. The United Farm Workers won a five-year boycott against grape growers in California in 1970. To organize lettuce field workers, Chavez's National Farm Workers has again called for a nationwide boycott, this time of iceberg lettuce.

Professional Associations.   There are currently hundreds of professional groups operating in the United States. Many maintain registered lobbyists in Washington; others are involved in politics in other ways.[15] Two of the best established and most powerful groups are the American Bar Association and the American Medical Association. Beyond the control these groups exercise over lawyers and doctors through licensing and training standards, both are active on political issues. The American Bar Association rates all judicial candidates as to their fitness to serve on the federal bench. The American Medical Association has recently opposed national health care insurance and efforts to further regulate the

15. There are several interesting and revealing case studies of these Associations and their political activities. Robert Alford, *Health Care Politics: Ideological and Interest Group Barriers to Reform* (Chicago: University of Chicago Press, 1975); Stephen Bailey, *Education Interest Groups in the Nation's Capital* (Washington, D.C.: American Council of Education, 1975); Joel B. Grossman, *Lawyers and Judges: The ABA and the Politics of Judicial Selection* (New York: Wiley, 1965); Richard Harris, *A Sacred Trust* (Baltimore: Penguin Books, 1969).

health care industry. There are also professional associations for bankers, teachers, bureaucrats, historians, political scientists, and any number of other groups. They are not regularly or constantly active, but they do lobby when an issue affects them.

ISSUE-ORIENTED GROUPS

Issue groups are those formed in direct response to a public controversy. The Right to Life Association was founded after the 1973 Court decision permitting abortion; Environmental Action, Inc., was founded to protest a threatened environment on Earth Day, 1970. Issue groups may, of course, take a broader focus on political issues or be directed toward narrower or single-issue politics. More recently, public interest groups have emerged. A public interest group is one that seeks a goal that "will not selectively and materially benefit the membership or activists of the organization."[16] Figure 7.2 shows distribution of membership in various groups.

Environmental Groups.   With rising concern for the environment, there has been a proliferation of environmental interest groups. Ecology has become a concern for many citizens. There was a rapid rise in the number of groups following the oil embargo in 1973, and recent air pollution incidents and oil spills. Some of the groups are older, well-established organizations. The Sierra Club, founded in 1892, has a membership over 150,000. It lobbies for clean air, clean water, and opposes construction activity that spoils scenic areas. The National Wildlife Federation has 3.5 million members and a budget of more than $24 million. These groups tripled their membership in the decades of the 1960s and 1970s. Newer groups include Friends of the Earth Inc., Environmental Action, Inc., and the Wilderness Society. These groups have memberships ranging from 15,000 to 100,000; their budgets run up to $1 million, and they are activist, direct-action-oriented, political pressure groups. Currently some 500 environmental–ecology–energy issue groups hold meetings, disseminate information, and lobby.[17]

Public Interest Groups.   Jeffrey Berry's 1972-73 study of public interest groups identified 83 such groups in areas ranging from the environment, general politics, consumerism, church, and poverty-civil rights, to peace groups.[18] Much of the public interest activity can be traced to Ralph Nader and his efforts to protect the American consumer. Nader, with the aid of some law students and lawyers (dubbed "Nader's Raiders"), began a series of investigations into busi-

16. Jeffrey M. Berry, *Lobbying for the People* The Political Behavior of Public Interest Groups (copyright © 1977 by Princeton University Press), p. 7. Reprinted by permission of Princeton University Press.
17. Greenwald, *Group Power,* p. 181.
18. Jeffrey M. Berry, *Lobbying for the People,* p. 14.

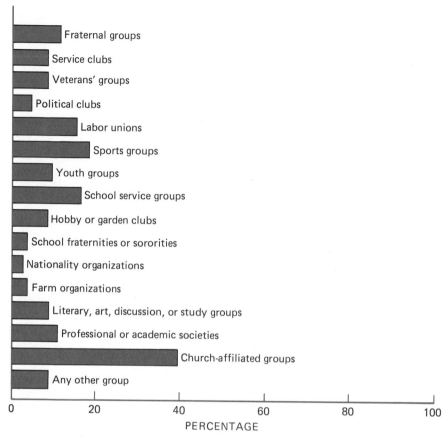

Fraternal groups
Service clubs
Veterans' groups
Political clubs
Labor unions
Sports groups
Youth groups
School service groups
Hobby or garden clubs
School fraternities or sororities
Nationality organizations
Farm organizations
Literary, art, discussion, or study groups
Professional or academic societies
Church-affiliated groups
Any other group

0   20   40   60   80   100

PERCENTAGE

Figure 7.2

Memberships in various organizations. (U.S. Department of Commerce, *Social Indicators 1976.* Washington, D.C.: U.S. Government Printing Office, 1977, p. 535).

ness and consumer affairs. Eventually he established an organization called Public Citizen, Inc., which solicited funds for a mass-based membership and now supports most of the Nader investigations. In all, Nader heads some 15 public interest groups in the areas of consumer affairs, energy, health care, and governmental regulation. Some of the more well known are Congress Watch, which researches, informs about, and lobbies Congress; Critical Mass, devoted to nuclear power concerns, notably safety standards for nuclear power plants; and the Public Interest Research Group, which seeks to establish chapters on college campuses and supports research on public interest issues.

Common Cause is another leading public interest group, founded by former secretary of health, education and welfare John Gardner, in 1970. Its original solicitation for money and members met with success; over 100,000 citizens joined and paid $15 a year in dues. Today Common Cause has a membership over 300,000 and an annual budget of $5 million.[19] Common Cause makes use of a professional staff of lawyers, lobbyists, field organizers, public relations experts, as well as citizen volunteers, to work for reform of the American political system. Major efforts have been directed at the seniority system in Congress, public financing of campaigns, and public disclosure of receipts and expenditures by candidates and lobbyists.

Public interest groups claim to broaden political participation and speak for the national will, but Berry suggests we view them with caution:

> If it is common sense to assume that interest groups are a necessary ingredient of our present political system, it is also common sense to realize that public interest groups are not the savior of that system. Giving the views of public interest groups greater credence, or tailoring public policy more closely to what they advocate, will not necessarily make the governmental decisions more reflective of the national will. Nor is representation through interest groups *per se* an adequate supplement to elected representatives in government. The fact that 30 percent of the public interest groups in the sample have no real membership attests to the problems of organizing individuals around certain interests that they ostensibly share.[20]

Single Interest Groups.   With a factionalizing electorate as party cohesion breaks down, more and more single-minded special interest groups appear and become militant voices. Pro-life forces have become active in the late 1970s opposing abortion and political candidates supporting abortion. Farmers have tractored to Washington to demand higher prices for grain and other farm products. Truckers have blocked gas pumps to dramatize rising fuel costs. And native Americans have camped out at the White House to symbolize the poor treatment given them. ''Gay Rights'' has become a major issue in several American cities, including San Francisco, California, and Dade County, Florida. These single-issue groups have given American politics an increasingly emotional and militant tone.

ETHNIC AND RELIGIOUS GROUPS

Ethnic and religious groups have a long and rich tradition in American politics. One of the major demands of minority groups has been that of economic equality, but ethnic and religious interests transcend economic issues. In America's early development, ethnic groups—Irish, Italian, Polish, Germans, and oth-

19. Ornstein & Elder, *Interest Groups, Lobbying, and Policy Making*, p. 47.
20. From Jeffrey M. Berry, *Lobbying for the People: The Political Behavior of Public Interest Groups*. (Copyright © 1977 by Princeton University Press), p. 291. Reprinted by permission of Princeton University Press.

Single issue politics groups have emerged onto the political scene in the late 1970s as with gay rights groups. (United Press International)

ers—sought to integrate themselves into American society while preserving their cultural heritage. By the twentieth century, black groups began to form to advance the cause of racial equality. The move for the Court's reinterpretation of the Fourteenth Amendment was dramatized in no small measure by the efforts of black civil rights groups. Religious groups, too, have a history of organization and voicing political concerns.[21]

The black movement grew out of white repression after the Civil War. The oldest organization, the National Association for the Advancement of Colored People (NAACP) was formed in 1909. In its earliest years the NAACP avoided

21. There are some interesting studies of ethnic, race and religious groups in politics. See Ronald H. Baylor, *Neighbors in Conflict: The Irish, Germans, Jews and Italians of New York City, 1929–1941* (Baltimore: Johns Hopkins University Press, 1978); Stephen Isaacs, *Jews and American Politics* (Garden City, N. J.: Doubleday, 1974); Richard Kluger, *Simple Justice: The History of Brown* v. *Board of Education* (New York: Knopf, 1975); and Richard Morgan, *The Politics of Religious Conflict* (New York: Pegasus, 1968).

One of the ways American politics—and the American consensus—has changed in recent years is in the rise of single-issue politics. Americans all over the country have banded together not on the basis of class, party, ethnic group, or region, but in support of or in opposition to one particular issue—the environment, nuclear power, control of the schools, urban renewal, the Vietnam war. The kind of consensus that once left individual decisions to government and confined battles over policies to the drafting of party platforms and national political conventions has vanished. The abortion or right to life issue is a good case in point.

On this one issue—whether abortion should be a matter of choice or not—strong forces on both sides have set up national organizations whose supporters may not agree on anything else. Since abortion laws were liberalized in Colorado in 1967, the controversy has gained in momentum: Nine versions of a Human Life amendment to the Constitution are in congressional committees, and seventeen states have requested that constitutional conventions be called. Right to life forces have polled legislators and worked to defeat those who do not hold their view on this one issue. In 1977, the passage of the Hyde Amendment, a rider to the Department of Labor and HEW appropriations bills, aimed to prohibit the use of federal funds for abortion unless the life of the mother was in danger. Prochoice forces challenged the amendment in court. In June 1980, however, the Supreme Court in *Harris* v. *McRae* upheld the constitutionality of the Hyde Amendment. This could mean the end of Medicaid coverage for about 300,000 poor women each year whose abortions have previously been covered.

The result of all this activity and pressure is that politicians, once free to campaign on a general liberal or conservative or middle of the road basis, find themselves forced to pick their way delicately along heavily mined campaign trails. One misstep and a whole bloc of voters is turned away. Parties face the same problem and lose more and more control over candidates and platforms. And the electorate sometimes must make choices on the basis of issues that have nothing to do with the fundamental problems facing American society as a whole. Single-issue politics can be important in solving local problems and in bringing injustices to public attention, but on the national level it can so fragment our society's consensus as to leave us without a common purpose and common goals. After all, if I will not speak to you because you disagree with me over abortion, how are we going to work together to solve the energy crisis, or unemployment, or inflation?

Single-Issue Politics: Public Policy Consumerism

This is the era of single issue politics. Voters with a cause have taken to politics and threatened to take over politics. Commentators have noted well the drama of issue-aroused voters in the late 1970s and 1980s, spurred on by the success of anti-abortion groups and taxpayer revolts. Pro-life forces were credited with unseating liberal Senator Dick Clark of Iowa with a last minute barrage of leaflets. Following California's Proposition 13, in 1978 16 states initiated the placement of limits to taxes and/or government spending on their ballots; all but four passed.

Single-issue politics is emerging as American voters are learning to distrust politics and politicians and are taking politics into their own hands. It represents an effort by interest groups to control the agenda for policy making. It has forced the governmental agenda and taken policy formulation from official policy makers. With the emergent fluidity of issues and the heightened emotionalism, citizens are narrowly focusing on specific issues to achieve policy. Voters treat public policy as a personal business. By analogy, this is public policy consumerism. The increased excitability and instability in the American political process has led citizens to demand that policy achieve specific, often narrowly defined, interest objectives.

A quick survey illustrates the mood and movement of American voters toward single-issue politics—issues range from abortion and taxes to neutering dogs and cats. In 1978 there were nearly 350 issues on ballots in 38 states. Some of the more pertinent single-issue movements are:

Abortion. The Right-to-Life movement has emerged as a potent political force. A CBS poll revealed that 7 percent of Americans would change their vote because of a candidate's stand on abortion, and three-fourths of them opposed abortions.

ERA and women's rights. Several states still have not ratified the ERA or have scheduled votes to rescind ratification; others have placed the issue on the ballot for a referendum. A connected issue is welfare funding for therapeutic abortions.

Nuclear power and the environment. Many of the antiwar protesters turned their attention to nuclear power once the war ended. The accident at Three Mile Island heightened concern for the environment and the effects of nuclear power.

Taxes. Several states have found the issues of limits to taxes or government spending on their ballots. The National Taxpayers Union is pressing for a Constitutional amendment to balance the federal budget.

Homosexual rights. Gay rights has become an increasing issue in areas of the country, notably San Francisco, California, and Dade County, Florida.

For some, single-issue politics is a matter of public interest and public right, and for others it is a mood of frustration and anger as citizens vow to take care of themselves first. Single-issue politics seeks no majoritarian coalition, it chafes at the hint of compromise. The issues have their greatest impact on those citizens who have entered the electorate in the past two and one-half decades. The American people have changed, in some fundamental ways, in their understanding and acceptance of politics.

direct confrontation or mass action, preferring instead to use the courts. Its Legal Defense and Educational Fund developed legal expertise and won many important victories through the years. Even today, the NAACP prefers the marble corridors of the court to the asphalt of the streets. Growing militancy in the 1960s gave rise to newer, mass-based, direct-action organizations. In 1957 Dr. Martin Luther King, Jr., formed the Southern Christian Leadership Conference and successfully used tactics of nonviolent protest. In 1968, the Black Panthers were formed by activists impatient with the results of the other organizations.

Church groups are usually less directly involved in the policy process of government, yet they too have organizations that are occasionally involved in politics. The United States Catholic Conference is the most established Catholic organization. In the 1960s it opposed aid to education that excluded support for parochial schools. There is also the National Conference of Catholic Bishops, which acts, at times, as a voice for Catholic interests. Protestant groups are represented by the National Council of Churches. Their most recent effort was to bring together 25 church groups in support of SALT II.

GOVERNMENT

It may seem unreasonable to include branches of the government as pressure groups, yet congressional committees, caucuses, administrative bureaus, executives, and foreign governments can and do lobby. Government employees are also organized and lobby for benefits and issues of concern to their organization.

A great deal of lobbying revolves around one branch or level of government lobbying another. The Department of Education may lobby for increased educational monies from a House committee on education. During the Watergate years an executive agency, the Office of Economic Opportunity, sued its boss, Richard Nixon, to release impounded funds for the continuation of the agency and its activities. The Executive Office has a legislative relations staff; every department has a congressional liaison or assistant secretary to keep in touch with Congress, key legislators, or committees.

Government pressure groups may take the form of associations such as the National Municipal League, the National Conference of State Legislatures, or the Governors' Conference. Government policymakers at the state and local levels have formed associations to examine common problems and find efficient ways to deal with them. Here governmental organizations are taking policy positions and asking themselves or other branches or levels of government to respond.

The Koreagate scandal illustrated how foreign governments lobby Congress. Most major foreign powers keep lobbyists in Washington to look out for their interests on a number of fronts. Public employees are another potent force. Unionization is growing at the state and local levels, and today some 4 million employees are union members.

GROUPS: LEADERS AND MEMBERS

Why do individuals join interest groups? Studies of political participation reveal that, however widespread, participation in interest groups remains selective. Many Americans do not participate in any interest group. And for those who do, politics may not be the reason. Table 7.2 shows participation in interest groups and the civic concern of the membership. Most groups report a high level of civic involvement and a moderately high concern for political affairs.

Individuals may be motivated to join interest groups for a variety of reasons. Mancur Olson stressed the collective action of a group to provide "benefits" or "rewards" to the indivdual.[22] Olson argued that membership in an interest group is calculated in terms of "costs" and "benefits." Robert Salisbury offered a different explanation. He suggested that a mutual exchange of incentives between members and leaders would support group membership and participation.[23] Salisbury's "exchange theory" focuses on the trading of incentives between members and leaders for a mutually reinforcing incentive for group participation. There were three kinds of incentives: material (tangible rewards such as money), solidary (friendship or community building), and purposive (issue positions or ideology).

SIZE AND COHESION

We normally base our estimate of a group's potential political impact on its size. The size of an interest group is important. For example, the AFL–CIO has 14 million members (and if we count families, almost 50 million) which is over 6 percent of the entire population. By contrast, professional organizations such as the American Medical Association and American Bar Association have much smaller memberships but contain a higher percentage of eligible members. The AMA counts 50 percent of all doctors as members; the Bar Association claims 65 percent of all lawyers. Although size is a factor in the political power of a group, unity is equally important for success. The AFL–CIO may be large, but it does not speak with a united voice on many issues. In fact, the larger the group, the more difficult unity becomes.

People often have overlapping memberships; they belong to more than one interest group. These memberships may be "crosscutting" and lead to a conflict in views or activities. An individual may be a member of a union that supports abortion, a member of the Catholic Church, which opposes abortion, and a member of the Veterans of Foreign Wars, which is more concerned with the Panama

---

22. Mancur Olson, *The Logic of Collective Action: Public Good and the Theory of Groups* (Cambridge, Mass.: Harvard University Press, 1965).
23. Robert H. Salisbury, "An Exchange Theory of Interest Groups," *Midwest Journal of Political Science* (February 1969), 1–32.

Table 7.2
Civic Participation by Members of Voluntary Organizations

Type of organization	Population who report membership (in percent)	Members who report the organizations involved in community affairs (in percent)	Members who report that political discussions take place in the organization (in percent)
Political groups such as Democratic or Republican clubs, and political action groups such as voters' leagues	8	85	97
School service groups such as PTA or school alumni groups	17	82	54
Service clubs, such as Lions, Rotary, Zonta, Jr. Chamber of Commerce	6	81	64
Youth groups such as Boy Scouts, Girl Scouts	7	77	36
Veterans' groups such as American Legion	7	77	56
Farm organizations such as Farmer's Union, Farm Bureau, Grange	4	74	61
Nationality groups such as Sons of Norway, Hibernian Society	2	73	57
Church-related groups such as Bible Study Group or Holy Name Society	6	73	40
Fraternal groups such as Elks, Eagles, Masons, and their women's auxiliaries	15	69	33
Professional or academic societies such as American Dental Association, Phi Beta Kappa	7	60	57
Trade unions	17	59	44
School fraternities and sororities such as Sigma Chi, Delta Gamma	3	53	37
Literary, art, discussion, or study clubs such as book-review clubs, theater groups	4	40	56
Hobby or garden clubs such as stamp or coin clubs, flower clubs, pet clubs	5	40	35
Sports clubs, bowling leagues, etc.	12	28	30

SOURCE: Sidney Verba and Norman H. Nie, *Participation in America: Political Democracy and Social Equality* (New York: Harper & Row, 1972), pp. 178–79. Copyright © 1972 by Sidney Verba and Norman H. Nie.

Canal than abortion. Faced with the "threat" of conflict, individuals may lose interest in politics and the organizations or alter their level of participation. Again, the larger the group, the greater the opportunity for overlapping memberships that can endanger unity.

LEADERSHIP

The task of the interest group leaders is "to maximize the sources of internal group cohesion and act as group spokesman vis-a-vis the outside world."[24] Sinclair holds that effective leadership depends on three factors: (1) communication between leaders and followers, (2) the makeup of the membership, and (3) the distribution of power in the organization.[25]

As Carol Greenwald notes, the internal leadership activity of developing cohesion is directly affected by the size and heterogeneity of the group. More diverse groups, such as national labor unions and federations like the American Federation of Teachers, require a great deal of work to strengthen unity. Time and resources must be expended to mobilize the membership for some political goal. Because of the communication problem, Common Cause, for example, regularly polls its members on items of concern. Leaders of smaller, more homogeneous organizations are more likely to have an agreed upon set of values or goals that allows the leadership to concentrate on strategy and tactics to lobby public officials for the organization.

Internal governance of interest groups is not typically democratic. The president, an executive council, and paid professional staff frequently dominate. They spend full time on organization and goals; members cannot do so. Leaders are the most visible and control the communications process. Although they may be removed or their recommendations challenged, the process is normally not an easy or a likely alternative. National conventions are cumbersome; procedural requirements thwart the unskilled member. Elections have not historically been contested for most organizations.

How representative is the leadership of its members? There is no universal or simple answer; because most organizations are not internally democratic, we cannot conclude that they are unrepresentative. Groups do change and challenge leadership. The United Mine Workers has, in recent years, faced several challenges to its leadership. John Gardner recently stepped aside as president of Common Cause to allow new people to lead the organization. One must measure the responsiveness of leadership by the achievement of goals, the relative satisfaction of the membership, and the opportunity for member participation in the political process.

INTEREST GROUPS IN ACTION

Political pressure groups seek to influence government. Lobbying is a form of communications whereby an interest group interacts with public officials for the purpose of influencing decision making. The federal government defines lob-

24. Greenwald, *Group Power*, p. 48.
25. John E. Sinclair, *Interest Groups in America* (Morristown, N.J.: General Learning Press, 1976), p. 21.

PRACTICING POLITICS   7.2

Lobbying

If you want to influence government directly, one of the best ways is to become a lobbyist. Persuade policy-makers that a certain policy is the right one or that a certain problem needs legislation in order to be solved. Just writing a letter or sending a telegram to a legislator is lobbying. But if you want to work on a broader and more systematic level, you can join an issue group such as Common Cause, which engages in public interest lobbying, or any one of the thousands of organizations listed in the *Washington Information Directory*. This directory is published annually by Congressional Quarterly, Inc., in Washington, and is available in most libraries.

If you work for a group, it is important to plan an effective strategy. Here are two basic steps:

1. Find out what kinds of decisions are needed to reach your goals, and who in government can make them. Don't overlook administrators, who often have much local discretion.
2. Be prepared; understand the political context in which decision-makers work, and draft a policy or a bill so that concrete action can result.

Here are some of the tasks you can perform for your group:

- Research and gather ammunition to support the group's position
- Organize letter-writing campaigns
- Attend hearings to present information or monitor what is being discussed
- Assist in drafting position papers and material to generate publicity
- Organize fundraising activities and events

bying as the solicitation of money for the purpose of influencing congressional legislation. Yet lobbying need not be limited to soliciting money nor to influencing Congress.

Lobbying is the politics of access; groups seek access to public officials who make policy in order to present the group's goals and objectives. Any group may seek to contact a public official, but the effective interest group seeks systematically to communicate its position and maximize its access. Carol Greenwald argues that lobbyist communication is an attempt to affect the behavior of individuals by supplying information. The most effective way, Greenwald suggests, is to influence the official's job security or public image.[26]

26. Greenwald, *Group Power*, p. 63.

THE PROCESS

Access depends on reaching top decision makers at key points in the political process. Generally speaking, interest group activity takes three forms: monitoring political activity, opposing governmental action, and initiating governmental action.[27]

All political interest groups monitor political activity. Significant amounts of any organization's time and resources are put into keeping abreast of legislative proposals, administrative rules and regulations, court cases, and foreign governmental activity. The task is massive. Just reading the *Congressional Record* and the *Federal Register* can be full-time occupations. Yet keeping current is not enough. The earlier one knows what is happening, the quicker one can develop a strategy and gain access. Oftentimes an "early warning system" will allow a group to get access to a key policymaker or mobilize its members before the issue is finalized.

Fighting for the status quo is easier than trying to initiate political change. Many groups spend a good deal of their time opposing governmental action. The oil lobby has worked to prevent the end of the oil depletion allowance. Energy and conservation groups have fought against the deregulation of natural gas or construction of the Alaskan pipeline. Indeed, in a political process such as ours, with its checks and balances, it is easier to block policy at any one point than to initiate and guide new policy through all the steps. People and policymakers are cautious concerning change. And the growing opposition to big government, more regulation, and impersonal or inefficient government all work to facilitate opposing governmental action.

We know, however, that groups can be successful in seeking change. Dam construction along the Tennessee River has been halted and new nuclear power plants have been suspended or postponed as consumer groups lobby the White House or go to court for an injunction. To seek a change in policy is difficult because a group must know exactly what it wishes to achieve and how it can be achieved. Goals must be effectively translated into definite public policy.

INFLUENCE TECHNIQUES

Direct Contact.   Lobbyists consider direct contact most effective. Presenting information or data to an administrator or legislative committee is viewed as the best opportunity to persuade and impress officials: "In direct relationships lobbyists try to become auxiliaries to decision makers, providing information to activate, reinforce, strengthen, and remind the official of his commitment to the issue."[28] This access is difficult to achieve. For the Executive Branch, a visit

---

27. Ornstein and Elder, *Interest Groups, Lobbying and Policy Making*, pp. 54-58.
28. Greenwald, *Group Power*, p. 69.

	Active	Symbolic
Conventional	Voting Writing letters to Congressmen	Fourth of July parades
Nonconventional	Sit-ins	Riots

Figure 7.3

Forms of political participation. (From Bruce A. Campbell, *The American Electorate: Attitudes and Action.* Copyright © 1979 by Holt, Rinehart and Winston. Reprinted by permission of Holt, Rinehart and Winston.)

with a secretary or bureau chief might be the goal; in Congress, direct contact means seeing the members or testifying before a legislative committee.

It is possible to overrate direct contact. Committee hearings generally produce no changes of votes. Speakers are scheduled to testify to dramatize a point more than to present information. Attendance at hearings is spotty at best. Executive contact is also uncertain. Departmental secretaries are not always on top of their organizations; clientele groups may exercise as much influence as the secretary. Presidential politics usually intervene, and the bureaucracy can always plead anonymity or lack of jurisdiction.

Letter Writing.   Almost every group uses letter writing or constituent-initiated contact at some time or other (see Figure 7.3). The intent is to convince public officials that broad support for or opposition against some issue exists. These campaigns also serve to inform the public on an issue of concern for a group and to create a favorable atmosphere of public opinion. Finally, letter writing serves to politicize and satisfy the membership that the organization and its leadership are working to implement the group's goals.

Letter writing campaigns seek to involve the membership to impress upon officials the level of support for a group's position. The National Rifle Association frequently exhorts members to write Congress on pending legislation, even going so far as to include sample letters in its publication, *The American Rifleman.* One drawback of such a technique is that policymakers can usually spot such campaigns and discount much of the activity as inspired by the group's leadership and not representative of the total membership. Only 15 percent of the population engage in letter writing on public issues, and only 3 percent does so on a regular basis.[29] Yet citizens feel letter writing is an effective means of influence. Berry found that 47 percent of the public interest groups surveyed thought letter writing "an effective tool."[30]

Media Campaigns.   Pressure groups also use the media. Television in particular has become a favorite: groups will pay for ads to publicize their positions, to inform the public, and to recruit support. The American Petroleum In-

29. James N. Rosenau, *Citizenship Between Elections* (New York: The Free Press, 1974), p. 209.
30. Berry, *Lobbying For the People,* p. 233.

stitute and the major oil companies have, since 1973, used ads on television to explain the high cost of energy and what the oil industry is doing to combat the problem. Environmentalists have done the same to dramatize pollution and the hazards it poses to life and health. Such campaigns are expensive and require the skills of professionals to be successful.

The media can be effective, if expensive, ways to reach the public, though not necessarily policymakers. The major impact of media campaigns is agenda setting. "Here may lie the most important effect of mass communication, its ability to mentally order and organize our world for us. In short, the mass media may not be successful in telling us what to think, but they are stunningly successful in telling us what to think about."[31]

Direct Action.   A form of influence increasingly in use by at least some interest groups is direct action. We are seeing a tendency on the part of some groups to protest, picket, and even threaten violence as a form of lobbying activity. Direct action has become a useful device for small groups seeking to increase their bargaining ability.[32] Consumer and environmental interest groups have been most prone to boycotts, picketing, and demonstrations. These can be effective techniques to dramatize and crystallize public opinion and force public-policy activity; but there are obvious risks. If the public does not see the actions as legitimate, they invite strong response and may result in a loss of power or prestige for the organization. Such activities are most identified with minorities, the

31. Donald Shaw and Maxwell McCombs, *The Emergence of American Political Issues: The Agenda-Setting Function of the Press* (St. Paul, Minn.: West Publishing Co., 1977), p. 5.
32. See Michael Lipsky, "Protest as a Political Resource," *American Political Science Review* 62 (December, 1968).

Media advertising is one way interest groups work to get their message across. (Stan Wakefield)

Protest action is also a means groups sometimes use to dramatize issues. (United Press International)

disadvantaged, and the poor. When white middle-class protesters engage in direct action, however, such as in the antibusing campaigns, there is less opposition to such techniques.

The evidence collected by Michael Lipsky seems to suggest that protest action does gain media coverage, and that protest can affect policymakers in the political system. The chances for direct action being successful, however, remain slim. Public officials are likely to respond to their traditional publics, not to the protest group.[33]

Social and Technical Services. Lobbyists seek to provide services in order to enhance their standing with policymakers. Much of this activity is legitimate, but some lobbyists feel a need to make their presence known by providing entertainment. In some cases, the services are in the form of gratuities, free theater tickets, or meals. In recent years the threat of conflict of interest has quelled many of the more flagrant forms of gift giving. More common services are those based on friendship and mutual concerns. Lobbyists will trade information, often providing detailed reports based on painstaking research for a public official. Often they will write speeches for a representative or a public official. Information a lobbyist is party to may help an overworked and underinformed bureaucrat or legislator's own career or position vis-a-vis the departmental secretary or committee.

The greater the extent to which any group can be viewed as a source of

33. *Ibid.*, pp. 1157-58.

technical information and expertise on a subject, the greater the reliance on the group by legislators and bureaucrats. Professional groups like the American Medical Association and the American Bar Association traditionally enjoy an advantage. When the American Medical Association comments on health care or the American Bar Association on judicial qualifications, their areas of expertise offer little base for challenge.

Lobbyists may also use social events as opportunities to bring decision makers and lobbyists together. The country club or the cocktail circuit are familiar approaches used by the lobbyist. These are deductible expenses for an organization. President Carter has sought to tighten control over such spending. In fact, reformers urge broader registration laws for lobbyists and more detailed accounting of expenses and activity to assure the public that influence buying does not take place.

Electoral Activities.   Nominally, interest groups maintain a position of political neutrality. Their concern is to influence the policy of government, whether Democrats or Republicans are in control. Group effectiveness, however, is frequently thought to be advanced by electoral activities. The association of the AFL-CIO with the Democratic party is of long standing; the Chamber of Commerce more closely resembles the Republican party in philosophy and outlook.

The extent of electoral activity depends on the resources of interest groups—money and votes. As political parties and political candidates need both, interest groups become a major electoral resource: "Interest groups that are capable of coordinating their members' activities can function alongside the operation of the regular party organization, providing a welcome supplement to the party's activities."[34]

There are several reasons for interest groups to seek an alliance with political parties. Carol Greenwald has noted three. First, party cooperation is another way to ensure access to public officials. Second, groups with sufficient resources (membership or money) can make use of the electoral process to display and maximize these resources. Third, participation in party politics provides an opportunity to shape campaign issues and party platforms in a direction sympathetic with group positions. This forces candidates to take stock of interest group positions and either support them or be cognizant of the consequences of nonsupport.[35]

More recently, some writers on political parties suggest that party organization and traditional support have collapsed. Political parties are only umbrella organizations for interest groups. Interest groups are not uniting and compromising in an alliance, but demanding that the party and candidate move to the group's position. The increasing number of amateurs in politics, including groups seeking

34. Sinclair, *Interest Groups in America*, p. 29.
35. Greenwald, *Group Power*, p. 119.

convention delegates, forces the political parties into a difficult position. They must appeal to interest groups and yet struggle to maintain a majoritarian interest in order to elect candidates to public office.

Campaign Contributions. Elections cost a great deal of money. One of the prime resources an interest group can provide is money. In 1976, congressional campaigns cost $100 million; in 1978 the figure was $155 million. Much of the money comes from interest groups, notably their Political Action Committees (PACs). A political action committee is a legal method for labor unions, professional associations, corporations, or any other organization to solicit funds to be spent for political purposes. In the wake of Watergate and illegal corporate contributions, formation of PACs has given business firms a legal opportunity to solicit employees and stockholders for political contributions. Note Ornstein and Elder:

In 1976—the first year of public financing of presidential campaigns— groups gave nearly $23 million to candidates for Congress. Through their political committees, business groups gave $7 million (up from $2.5 in 1974), labor groups gave more than $8 million (up from $6 million in 1974), health groups, including doctors, gave nearly $3 million (an in-

Table 7.3
1977-1978 PAC Contributions to Federal Candidates
(in millions of dollars)

	Total Contributions	Party Affiliation[a]		Candidate Status[a]		
		Dems.	Reps.	Incumbent	Challenger	Open
Trade, membership, health	$11.5	$ 5.0	$ 6.5	$ 6.7	$2.3	$2.5
Labor	10.3	9.7	0.6	6.1	2.2	2.0
Corporations	9.8	3.6	6.1	5.8	2.0	2.0
No-connected organizations	2.5	0.7	1.9	0.7	1.1	0.7
Cooperatives	0.9	0.6	0.2	0.6	0.1	0.2
Corporations without stock	0.1	0.1	0.0	0.1	0.0	0.0
Total	$35.1	$19.7	$15.3	$19.9	$7.7	$7.4

a. Figures within the party affiliation and candidate status columns do not always equal the total contributions figure because of rounding.

SOURCE: Federal Election Commission. Reported by *Congressional Quarterly* Weekly Report, June 2, 1974, p. 1044.

crease from $2 million two years earlier), and agricultural groups gave $1.5 million (an increase from $360,000 in 1974).[36]

Political Action Committee growth has been phenomenal. In 1970 there were only 90 PACs, in 1974 there were 600, and by 1978 the number had risen to 1,653. Not only has the number of PACs grown, but so has their influence. In 1978 PACs spent a total of $35 million, nearly triple the $12.5 million spent in 1974, and up 50 percent from the $22.6 million raised in 1976. That figure accounts for almost one out of every four dollars spent by a congressional candidate. The prospects for the 1980s are for more money and more activity by PACs. Says the *National Journal,* "You can expect PACs across the board to spend much more money than ever before for the 1980 election. Many PAC managers said they would go into 1980 with comfortable cash balances, and estimates of total receipts frequently are at least double those of two years ago."[37] The lion's share of this money is being contributed to incumbents, whose chances for electoral success are greatest.

Do political contributions produce success? There is no question that more money goes to incumbents and that incumbents very often win reelection. Furthermore, there is recent evidence that money is crucial to the success of any challenger. It is nonincumbents who need the attention of voters, who need recognition. And spending money is the way to achieve recognition: "The more the challenger spends, the smaller the incumbent's victory margins."[38] There is also evidence that contributors, particularly PAC contributors, concentrate on legislators on committees dealing with group areas of interest. Fred Wirtheimer of Common Cause has reported that Representative Blouin of the House Education and Labor Committee, in a tough reelection battle, received campaign gifts from two dozen unions; members on the House Agriculture Committee received large contributions from dairy industry PACs; maritime unions gave extensively to Democrats on the House Committee on Merchant Marine and Fisheries.

REGULATION

In recent years, interest groups increasingly have come under attack. The charges of special interest peddling, capturing public policy, and influence buying are all frequently heard. The word lobbyist connotes sinister motives. In a reform-minded environment, where political scandal and campaign money have worked to erode public trust and confidence, it is not surprising that interest-group regu-

36. Ornstein and Elder, *Interest Groups, Lobbying and Policymaking,* p. 71.
37. *National Journal,* November 24, 1979, p. 1984.
38. Stanton Glantz, Alan Abramowitz and Michael Barkart, "Election Outcomes: Whose Money Matters?" *Journal of Politics* 28 (November 1976), p. 1038. See also Gary Jacobson, "The Effects of Campaign Spending in Congressional Elections," *American Political Science Review* 72 (June 1978).

lation and reform should surface. In 1975, a Harris Poll found three-fourths of the American people agreeing that "Congress is still too much under the influence of special interest lobbies." It is the abuses to the constitutional right under the First Amendment that have led to demands for reform. The 94th and 95th Congresses have struggled with lobby reform, but without much success. Watergate, Koreagate, and the phenomenal rise of political action committees have speeded the pace of reform. Yet Congress is cautious about impinging on the First Amendment or damaging its own basis of support and contributions.

The basic regulations are still those of the 1946 Federal Regulation of Lobbying Act. Passed by Congress as part of the Legislative Reorganization Act of 1946, it was directed toward congressional activity and merely required individuals receiving money from an individual or group for the purposes of lobbying Congress to register with the House and Senate. Lobbyists were required to register, identify their employer, list their general legislative objectives, and file quarterly expense reports, as were the parent groups.

The act contained as many loopholes as it did regulations. It defined lobbying narrowly as the solicitation and collection of money for influencing legislation. Groups or individuals that spent money on their own behalf were exempt from registering. Lobbyists could define for themselves what expenditures were required to be reported as lobbying expenses. Large sums and considerable activity could be excluded at a group's discretion. More critically, the law was specifically directed at individuals and groups making direct contact with legislators for the "principal purpose" of influencing legislation. Groups not making direct personal contact or who could argue their principal purpose was other than lobbying need not register. For 30 years the National Association of Manufacturers did not register, claiming it served numerous purposes other than lobbying.[39] The act specifically exempted testimony before congressional committees and did not cover regulatory agencies or the federal bureaucracy.

In the wake of Watergate, Congress worked on several new versions of lobby legislation. A Senate bill provided for registration based on a definition of one paid officer or employee, and activity, including retaining a law firm or raising $5,000 in solicitations, in order to lobby Congress. This bill applied only to Congress. The Senate bill included far more extensive and detailed reporting requirements. The House passed reform legislation in 1976, but the House bill differed from the Senate bill because it defined a lobbyist as an individual or group spending $1,250 a quarter to lobby and spending 20 percent of an employee's time for lobbying activities. The two chambers could not agree on a compromise so after each chamber had drafted legislation, no new law emerged from the 94th Congress.

The 95th Congress did not prove any more successful, though once again it sought lobby reform legislation. The House Judiciary bill was similar to its predecessor but set the lobbying expense figure at $2,500 a quarter or employing a

39. Ornstein and Elder, *Interest Groups, Lobbying and Policy Making*, p. 104.

person to lobby on 13 or more days in a quarter. It also included a significant disclosure provision for grassroots efforts. The Senate proposed its own version, which was significantly stronger than the House bill; however, Congress adjourned before any joint action could take place.

THE CHANGING NATURE OF GROUP INFLUENCE

Are interest groups too powerful? The American public thinks so; but influence is an elusive quality. It is impossible to pin down. Public opinion and governmental activity are much changed since the writing of Truman's *The Governmental Process,* which described public policy as the result of group interaction. The recent scandals and campaign abuses have caused a cynical and distrustful atmosphere: The reforms proposed in the 1970s would have been labeled un-American during the 1950s.

Government has changed since the 1950s. The federal budget has more than quadrupled. Governmental activity has expanded into new areas. The federal bureaucracy and government regulation are new issues; the characteristic liberal–conservative debate of the 1950s has been transformed into one of economy and efficiency in the 1980s. We now accept as legitimate a range of governmental activity that would have been the source of great ideological concern a few years ago.

In this context, interest groups seek to organize, operate, and compete for access to the decision-making process. To claim they dominate public policy through influence peddling is a naive view of the contemporary political system. As government expanded and increased its efforts, new programs created new clientele groups. This does not make policymaking more difficult; rather, it makes change more unlikely; "The competition of interest groups does not, in the long run, make it more difficult for the government to start doing things, it only makes it difficult for the government to stop."[40]

James Wilson's point was that the expanded scope of government settled the primary issue dividing interest groups. The issue became in the 1970s not the right of government to act but the way in which it would and how much money it would spend. Advocacy of an issue became a matter of public interest. As Wilson put it, "it is difficult to take negative positions on these matters without appearing to defend, out of one's stake and without a philosophical fig leaf, private advantage."[41] This is the atmosphere in which we must confront single-issue politics today.

Single-issue groups are on the rise. The changes in governmental activity and the changes in attitudes among the American people have spawned numerous separate and single-minded groups. Such groups are ideological and politically

40. James Q. Wilson, *Political Organizations* (New York: Basic Books, Inc., 1973), p. 341.
41. *Ibid.,* p. 343.

inflexible; they reject much of the shared consensus and political party activity of the past generation. Single-issue groups take on private and narrow interests, push them on the public agenda, and demand satisfaction as a moral responsibility.

This has some important consequences for interest groups. One such change has been to more closely identify clientele groups with governmental agencies. For example, the Office of Economic Opportunity "lobbied" for welfare rights and benefits. It makes the politicization of any group in terms of group benefits more difficult. A private good is transformed into a public good.

The increased scope of government confers a new legitimacy on interest groups and denies to other groups their traditional legitimacy. Public interest groups have arisen in recent years with the goal of making government accountable. This has provided them with a status and mission that a decade ago would have attracted little interest. Tax reform groups also attract interest in the wake of Proposition 13, the Californian initiated measure to reduce taxes and limit future taxes. By contrast, labor and business groups that have traditionally opposed one another on basic economic terms have suffered. Both labor and business are seen as protected; the public turns to regulation and controlling wages and prices. The traditional issues of free enterprise, collective bargaining, and a minimum wage are seen as "givens." Increased protection for the public via regulation is now more relevant.

The rise of new interest groups in the 1960s and 1970s and the mobilizing of small constituencies has changed expectations. The newer groups carry an ideological commitment in the name of the public. They may act as "veto groups," thereby preventing change. Their support for political parties appears to be waning; alliances have become more difficult to form. The result is that issues get on the public agenda, traditional political practices are criticized, but little change can be produced. Whether or not this is democracy in action is open to debate.

SUMMARY

1. There is no clear-cut evidence on the influence of interest groups on the political process. We know interest groups can exercise considerable power, but all groups are not equal in their ability to be influential. We still do not know how to measure influence carefully.

2. Interest groups are important to the political process because they provide a means of representing individual interest to government. Yet Americans are skeptical about groups and their "influence peddling." Newer issue groups have narrowed their focus, concentrating on single issues.

3. Traditional interests such as business and labor continue to function but are being challenged for influence by the growth of environmental and public interest groups. Many group members find membership valuable for the individual satisfaction of participation and tangible rewards.

4. The success of interest groups depends on the size and cohesion of the group, the skills of the organization's leadership, and the nature of the action required to advance its goals. Generally, groups opposing governmental action are more successful than groups needing to initiate new policies.

5. A key factor in interest-group influence has been the growth in political action committees. PACs have provided a legal means for organizations to contribute money to political campaigns. In recent years PACs have come to dominate the financing of election campaigns. Calls for reform and spending limits are increasingly heard.

TERMS

access   247
alliance   252
cohesion   244
exchange theory   244
faction   227
interest group   229
lobbying   246–47
objective influence   231

occupational group   232
overlapping
  membership   244
Political Action Committee
  (PAC)   253
public interest group   237
reputational
  influence   231

RESEARCH PROJECTS

7.1. Group Lobbying. Select a group in your city or area—labor union, corporation, environmental group, and so on. The telephone book can be of help. Make an appointment and send letters of inquiry regarding their political interest and activity on some issue. You might wish to inquire as to the groups

a. goals—want new legislation, prevent new legislation; involved with regulatory agencies
b. staff—are there full-time, paid personnel employed to lobby
c. budget—how much money of the organization is devoted to lobbying
d. techniques—what kinds of activities do they engage in: testimony, letters, litigation, P.R., and so on.

7.2. Group Testimony. Select a bill before Congress. Go to the *Congressional Record* and review the testimony on the bill in committee. What percentage of the people testifying on the bill represent interest groups? What groups support and oppose the bill? Can you make some assessment of the nature of support and opposition? Finally, make some determination of the quality of the testimony based on facts, thoroughness, and skill of presentation as best you can from the record.

7.3. Interest Profile. Select an issue you are concerned about. How many interest groups exist that are concerned with that issue—nationally and locally? The *Encyclopedia of Associations* will provide the number of national groups and their addresses; the telephone book can help you locally. Maybe you will wish to join one of them.

BIBLIOGRAPHY

Berry, Jeffrey. *Lobbying for the People.* Princeton, N.J.: Princeton University Press, 1977.

The best survey of the growth of "public interest groups" in the political process. The book provides both an overview of characteristics and a detailed discussion of the activity of a few such groups.

Dexter, Lewis A. *How Organizations are Represented in Washington.* Indianapolis, Ind.: Bobbs-Merrill, 1969.

A basic work that surveys representational efforts of groups in Washington D.C. Discusses the means and activities of lobbyists seeking to represent interests before government. Dexter understands representation to be more inclusive than lobbying.

Greenwald, Carol S. *Group Power.* New York: Praeger Publishers, 1977.

The best work to date on interest groups. Provides an excellent overview of interest group activity, resources, and strategies. Spiced with examples.

Milbrath, Lester. *The Washington Lobbyist.* Chicago: Rand McNally, 1963.

A somewhat dated though still basic description of lobbyists. Based on interviews with lobbyists, Milbrath seeks to explain who lobbyists are and how they go about their task.

Ornstein, Norman, and Shirley Elder. *Interest Groups, Lobbying and Policymaking.* Washington, D.C.: Congressional Quarterly, 1978.

An excellent, readable discussion of interest groups lobbying the national government. The book provides a good introduction with theories of group activity and has three case studies illustrating lobbying activity.

Rosenau, James. *Citizenship Between Elections.* New York: Free Press, 1974.

A complex and sophisticated treatment of political participation taking nonelectoral forms. By surveying citizens, Rosenau sought to explain kinds and amount of participation and whether that activity was self-initiated.

Salisbury, Robert H. *Interest Groups in America.* Morristown, N.J.: General Learning Press, 1976.

A collection of essays that run the gamut on interest groups. The articles are written by leading authorities in the field and cover theories of interest groups, organization and leadership, interests and values, and lobbying.

Verba, Sidney, and Norman Nie. *Participation in America*. New York: Harper and Row, 1972.

A most extensive survey of the forms and extent of political participation in America. Makes heavy use of data and becomes technical in places, yet the treatment is thorough and informative on varieties of participation.

Ziegler, L. Harmon, and Wayne Peak. *Interest Groups in American Politics*. Englewood Cliffs, N.J.: Prentice-Hall, 1972.

A basic textbook on interest groups, the authors cover the full array of topics. There are good chapters on the role of interest groups in American politics as well as separate chapters for business and labor groups.

Chapter 8

Political Parties

Nowhere have the changing expectations of American politics been more dramatic than in the case of political parties. American political parties are in a state of decline. For close to two decades, partisan attachment to the two major parties has been weakening. "Strong" Republicans (GOP) and "strong" Democrats have decreased by a third in each party; among the young voters—those under 30—the number of Independents is now greater than that of Democrats and Republicans. National nominating conventions are now dominated by political amateurs motivated by issues or attachment to a candidate, not party loyalty. Ticket splitting has become an increasingly common phenomenon. Writes Everett Ladd, a perceptive student of political parties, "American political parties manifest a diminished institutional presence. As labels, as names on the ballot, they are alive and well, but as organizations they have withered."[1]

Several commentators have noted the impact of contemporary society on political parties, the pressures that have been eroding political party support, and the parties' organizational structures. Figure 8.1 shows the changes in the American electorate. Several important consequences have become visible as a result of changing economic and social relationships in "postindustrial" America. The change to sophisticated technologies, notably com-

1. Everett Carll Ladd, *Where Have All the Voters Gone? The Fracturing of America's Political Parties*, (New York: W.W. Norton & Co., Inc., 1978), pp. xxiii-xxiv.

Getting Younger

(Per cent of voting age population)

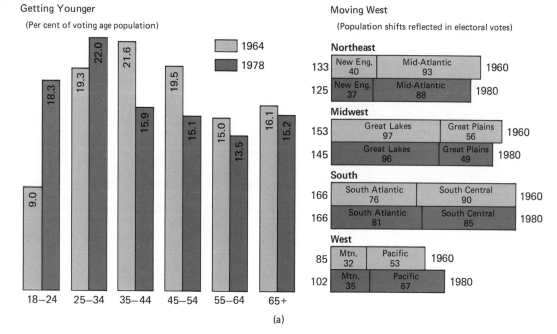

	1964
	1978

Moving West

(Population shifts reflected in electoral votes)

Northeast

| 133 | New Eng. 40 | Mid-Atlantic 93 | 1960 |
| 125 | New Eng. 37 | Mid-Atlantic 88 | 1980 |

Midwest

| 153 | Great Lakes 97 | Great Plains 56 | 1960 |
| 145 | Great Lakes 96 | Great Plains 49 | 1980 |

South

| 166 | South Atlantic 76 | South Central 90 | 1960 |
| 166 | South Atlantic 81 | South Central 85 | 1980 |

West

| 85 | Mtn. 32 | Pacific 53 | 1960 |
| 102 | Mtn. 35 | Pacific 67 | 1980 |

Bar chart values by age group:

	1964	1978
18–24	9.0	18.3
25–34	19.3	22.0
35–44	21.6	15.9
45–54	19.5	15.1
55–64	15.0	13.5
65+	16.1	15.2

(a)

. . . and Becoming More Independent

(Q: "In politics, as of today, do you consider yourself a Republican, Democrat or Independent?")

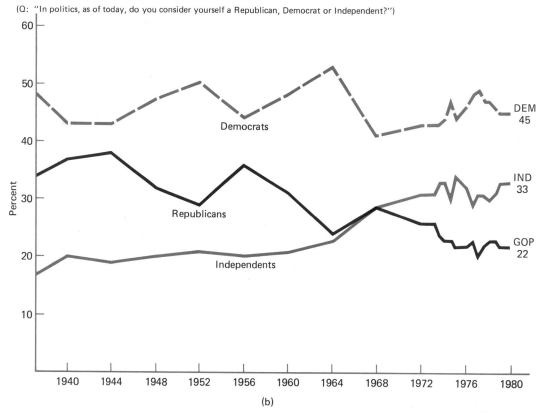
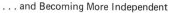

DEM 45

IND 33

GOP 22

Democrats

Republicans

Independents

(b)

Figure 8.1

Profile of the American electorate. (*National Journal,* October 20, 1979. a. Census Bureau; b. Gallup Organization, Inc.)

puter data processing, public polling, and media campaigning, has weakened party control over the electoral process. Candidate and public are now in direct contact. The increasing educational level of the American electorate means that issues become more important. Citizens today are more likely to enter the political process out of a sense of commitment to a candidate or to an issue than at any time in our history. Public interest concerns are replacing the more narrowly defined concerns of interest groups, which once dominated the parties. Labor, for example, no longer dominates the Democratic party. Republicans have become increasingly alarmed over the charge that big business interests dictate their policy. In a political environment where politics is becoming more technologically complicated and the electorate more independent, political parties find a diminished role. ''Anti-partyism'' has become a popular pastime.

THE DECLINE OF THE PARTIES

Three factors play a role in the decline of political parties: weakening party loyalty, changes in campaigning and campaign organizations, and reforms in the nominating process.

PARTY LOYALTY

No factor has received more public attention in the media than the loss of party support among the American electorate. The trend has been continuous since the 1960s. Fewer and fewer voters identify with political parties; the number of citizens who call themselves Independent is growing. There has been a steadily declining number of strong partisan identifiers from both political parties—a drop of 10 percent in strong Democratic identifiers and a 5 percent drop in strong

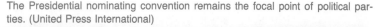

The Presidential nominating convention remains the focal point of political parties. (United Press International)

Republican identifiers. Among voters under 30, a generational split is clearly visible. There, Independents outnumber partisans altogether. Most new voters, in fact, choose to call themselves Independents.

Table 8.1
Party Identification of the Electorate 1960–1980

	1960	1964	1968	1972	1976	1978	1980
Strong Democrats	20%	27%	20%	15%	15%	15%	17%
Weak Democrats	24	25	25	26	25	24	23
Independents	22	22	29	35	36	37	35
Weak Republicans	14	13	14	13	14	13	15
Strong Republicans	15	11	10	10	9	8	8
Apolitical, other	5	2	2	2	1	3	2
Total:	100%	100%	100%	100%	100%	100%	100%

SOURCE: Survey Research Center, University of Michigan.

The declining loyalty to political parties can also be seen in the dramatic rise in ticket splitting, as shown by the increased percentage of congressional districts carried by a presidential candidate and congressional candidates of opposing parties. The rise of ticket splitting parallels the decline in partisan identification. Fifty percent of the voters are not voting for all candidates of one party; they are exercising independent judgment and casting ballots for individual candidates.

Finally, as partisan voting declines, there has been an increase in issue voting. Voters today are much more likely to evaluate candidates and parties in terms of their issue positions and to be influenced by those issue stances. With the decline in party identification, issues have become a far more reliable indicator of a person's vote.[2] According to Nie, Verba, and Petrocik: "Over the two-decade period (1952-1972), party evaluations have come to have less effect on the vote. . . . When it comes to issue evaluations, the increase in their impact on the vote comes from the increased numbers who evaluate candidates in issue terms."[3]

CHANGING CAMPAIGNS

A landmark year for political parties occurred in 1972. In that year both parties faced insurgent or nonparty campaign organizations by candidates for the presidency. George McGovern's supporters used the reform rules of the Demo-

2. Gerald M. Pomper, "From Confusion to Clarity: Issues and American Voters, 1956-1968," *American Political Science Review,* 66 (June, 1972).
3. Norman Nie, Sidney Verba, and John R. Petrocik, *The Changing American Voter* (Cambridge, Mass.: Harvard University Press, 1976), p. 172.

George McGovern accepts the Democratic endorsement for the presidency in 1972, a year that dramatized the changes political parties were undergoing. (United Press International)

cratic party to "capture" a majority of the convention delegates and nominate their candidate. They did so at the expense of the party regulars and partisan support. On the Republican side an incumbent president, Richard Nixon, set up a totally autonomous campaign organization—the Committee to Re-elect the President—to finance and operate his reelection drive. The Republican party was superfluous; the money raised was spent to reelect the president, not to support GOP candidates. Organization staff was drawn from the White House, not the party. In some cases, the Committee supported Democratic candidates considered closer to the president than their Republican challengers.

This trend in campaign has been gaining momentum for some time. Technology has heightened the ability of candidates to forsake political parties. It has accentuated the four M's of politics; mobility, media, money, and machines (computers). With high mobility, Americans now do not have deep-seated loyalties or roots that characterized earlier generations. Attachments to parties cannot develop and grow, so reaction is more to issues and personalities.

Much of a campaign is now conducted through the media, particularly television. It is an instantaneous vehicle for reaching large masses of people. It is also extremely personal: The candidate can speak directly to the people in a setting controlled by the candidate. This accentuates the importance of personality and image. Characteristics such as reliability, honesty, and competence are dramatized, not partisan loyalty. Previously, candidates needed to rely on campaign organizations, door-to-door volunteers, whistle-stop tours, and billboards. Today a candidate needs an advertising specialist, prime time, and money.

Technological sophistication costs money—a great deal of money. The cost of elections has soared. A presidential election (primary contest and general election) costs in excess of $100 million. Congressional races can run into the hundreds of thousands of dollars. Most of the money is used first to poll and analyze issue trends and voting patterns. This has heightened the need for machines—notably computers—to provide detailed, sophisticated data on contemporary electoral behavior. Once the concerns have been targeted, a media campaign is set in motion. Radio, television, and newspaper ads are designed and placed, using the most specialized and effective communication techniques available. There is little need for a political party in the process.

Two important effects of the personal campaign styles are the decline of **presidential coattails** in elections and the advantage of **incumbency** in running for election. Throughout the century, presidential candidates have succeeded in carrying with them congressional candidates of their party. This has been followed in off-year elections by a decline in success for congressional candidates of the president's party. The regularity of this process had been impressive, but now the coattail effect no longer works. Congressional races are becoming insulated from the presidential contest. During the 1930s the average gain or loss for the Democrats was 48 seats.[4] In the 1970s, the net change has been severely diminished. In 1980, however, Reagan's coattails appeared longer. He took thirty-three GOP House members and twelve GOP Senators with him to Washington. The 1976 election saw a shift of only two House seats gained by the Democrats.

Incumbency is an increasing political asset for political candidates. Whether due to ticket splitting, the ability to raise campaign revenue, or the media, it is a political fact that incumbents win reelection and win handily. In the post-World War II years, incumbent candidates to the House of Representatives won 90 percent of their elections; incumbent senators were only slightly less successful, winning approximately 80 percent of their elections. In better than two-thirds of these cases, the results were not even close; the incumbent won with more than 55 percent of the popular vote.

REFORMS OF THE NOMINATING PROCESS

The theme of party reform has been a strong one in the past decade. Since 1968, the Democrats have struggled with internal reforms. The GOP has made less sweeping changes, but has become increasingly concerned about party reform. A longer standing reform has been the use of the primary election as the means of nominating candidates and convention delegates.

---

4. Richard W. Boyd, "Electoral Trends in Postwar Politics," in *Choosing the President,* edited by James David Barber (Englewood Cliffs, N.J.: Prentice-Hall, 1974), p. 187.

DUNAGIN'S PEOPLE

"THE POLLS INDICATE WE COULD END UP WITH TWO CANDIDATES IN NOVEMBER NEITHER OF WHOM CAN BEAT THE OTHER."

Dunagin's People by Ralph Dunagin © 1980 Field Enterprises, Inc. Courtesy of Field Newspaper Syndicate.

Democratic party reforms have opened participation in the party through the open caucus. This has facilitated participation by political activists—the amateurs who come to politics out of an ideological commitment to issues and/or a candidate. The amateur activist is rewarded by party reform and ideological commitment, not party stability. State Soule and McGrath: "The political world of the amateur is defined by internal party democracy, by intense commitment to policies and programs, and by a reluctance to compromise even though the consequences may spell electoral defeat."[5]

Reform of the presidential nominating conventions has meant that three-fourths of Democratic convention delegates are selected by primary elections—as are over two-thirds of Republican delegates.[6] The parties have lost control of the delegate selection process: "Serious candidates have to create elaborate personal organizations to wage the costly and far-flung campaigns that are a precondition of winning."[7] Educated, issue-oriented activists dominate the convention and candidate selection. Party harmony is no longer a concern as the McGovernites showed in 1972 when they refused to compromise on seating delegates and rejected Mayor Richard Daley and the Chicago delegation. And in 1980 several

5. John W. Soule and Wilma E. McGrath, "A Comparative Study of Presidential Nomination Conventions: The Democrats, 1968 and 1972," *American Journal of Political Science* 19 (August 1975), p. 509.

6. From Everett C. Ladd, Where Have All the Voters Gone? The Fracturing of America's Political Parties, W. W. Norton & Co., N.Y., 1978, pp. 56–57.

7. *Ibid.*, p. 57.

Kennedy delegates walked out of the convention or vowed not to support Jimmy Carter when he was renominated for the presidency.

The electoral primary has greatly enhanced this personalized style of campaigning. In 1976, the ''outsider'' to national Democratic politics, Jimmy Carter, benefited directly from the primaries by building upon his success in them to win the Democratic nomination. By 1980 both presidential candidates—Reagan and Carter—came to the convention with primary-selected delegates making the balloting a foregone conclusion, thereby leaving the conventions void of any meaningful choices. Primaries take nominations out of the hands of the party, or at least weaken partisan control in the name of democracy, and place potential candidates directly before the voters. Reliance on the media and appeal to volatile issues enhance candidate success but weaken party responsibility. In 1976 the Democrats started out with 10 candidates for the presidential nomination. Everett Ladd likens the presidential nominee selection process to a flea market:

Candidate Jimmy Carter on the campaign trail. Carter put together a personal organization and succeeded in winning the presidency in 1976. (Jack Knightlinger, The White House)

Thus the U.S. has been reduced in presidential-nominee selection to a system of chaotic individualism. Each individual entrepreneur (the candidate) sets up shop and hawks his wares, that is, himself. The buyers—the voters—do not find the same choice of merchandise in all the states, and one seller, who may attract only a small segment of all the buyers, is finally granted a monopoly. Candidates are able to win, then, because of crowded fields, low turnouts and strategic miscalculations by their opponents, but above all because there is no one in charge. Increasingly there is no formal party mechanism in place with substantial authority to plan for the outcome.[8]

SHAPING THE PARTY SYSTEM

The parties are durable institutions, however; they have survived challenge and change before. In fact, they survive because there is no coherent party organization or clearly identifiable membership. Both parties compete for the same citizen support; both are decentralized coalitions of candidates, interest groups, party activists, and citizen identifiers. They function sporadically—at election time. At the national level, they function once every four years when coalitions must amass to nominate a party candidate for the presidency.

HISTORICAL DEVELOPMENT

The Framers of the Constitution did not foresee the development of parties as we understand them; the Constitution does not even mention political parties. Yet the Framers were well aware of the tendency to associate in groups—"factions" as James Madison called them. His *Federalist No. 10* warned of this tendency to disregard the public good "in the conflicts of rival parties." The convention itself split into two factions over ratification—the Federalists supporting the new Constitution and the anti-Federalists opposed to it. President Washington, in his farewell address upon leaving office, warned the nation against what he viewed as "the baneful effects of the spirit of Party."

Political parties began to take root during Washington's administration (see Figure 8.2). Alexander Hamilton, as Washington's secretary of the treasury, promoted a national banking system and strong, centralized government authority. This drew him the support of bankers, manufacturers, large landholders, and commercial interests. (We often label this group the Whig party.) Alarmed over this aristocratic concentration of power, Thomas Jefferson and James Madison became the spokesmen for a coalition of republican democrats, farmers, trappers, frontiersmen, debtors, and laborers. This was the first Republican party.

These groups, however, remained largely coalitions. The election of 1800 saw the ascendancy of Jefferson and republican democracy. The Republican co-

8. *Ibid.*, p. 69.

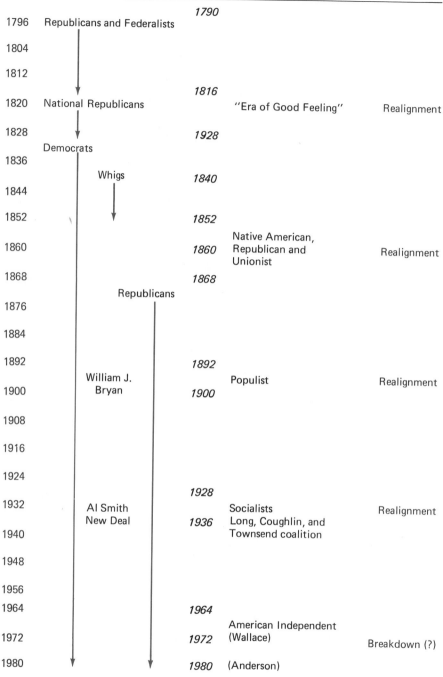

	Major parties		Minor parties and realignments

1790

1796 Republicans and Federalists

1804

1812

1816

1820 National Republicans · · · · · · · · · · "Era of Good Feeling" · · · · · · Realignment

1828 · · · · · · · · · · · · · · · · · · · 1928

Democrats

1836

Whigs · · · · · · · · · · 1840

1844

1852 · · · · · · · · · · · · · · · · · · · 1852

Native American,
1860 · · · · · · · · · · · · · · · · · · · 1860 · · · · · · Republican and · · · · · · Realignment
Unionist

1868 · · · · · · · · · · · · · · · · · · · 1868

Republicans

1876

1884

1892 · · · · · · · · · · · · · · · · · · · 1892

William J. · · · · · · · · · · · · · · · Populist · · · · · · · · · · · · Realignment
1900 Bryan · · · · · · · · · · · · · · · · 1900

1908

1916

1924

1928

1932 Al Smith · · · · · · · · · · · · · · Socialists · · · · · · · · · · Realignment
New Deal · · · · · · · · · · · 1936 Long, Coughlin, and
1940 · · · · · · · · · · · · · · · · · · · Townsend coalition

1948

1956

1964 · · · · · · · · · · · · · · · · · · · 1964

American Independent
1972 · · · · · · · · · · · · · · · · · · · 1972 (Wallace) · · · · · · · · · Breakdown (?)

1980 · · · · · · · · · · · · · · · · · · · 1980 (Anderson)

Figure 8.2

Succession of the two-party system. (Judson L. James, *American Political Parties in Transition*, New York: Harper and Row, 1974. Copyright © 1974 by Judson L. James)

272

alition remained more or less intact until 1824, when competition between factions within the party broke out. One group supported John Quincy Adams, the other supported Andrew Jackson. With the election of 1832, groups of supporters came together to nominate and campaign for a "party" candidate. This was the origin of genuine political parties as we understand them today.

After 1832, the Adams supporters called themselves National Republicans; the Jacksonian backers called themselves Democratic Republicans. From then on, these two parties (the Democratic Republicans dropped the label Republican and called themselves Democrats; the Republicans were replaced by the Whigs in the 1830s, only to be replaced by Republicans in the mid-1850s) nominated, supported, and tried to control candidates running for public office.

From the third decade of the nineteenth century until the present, political campaigning has been dominated by two large coalitions nominating and supporting candidates for public office. In the 1850s and 1860s, slavery and the nature of the Union dominated the parties. A North–South split began to replace the East versus West, urban versus rural divisions. At the turn of the century, populism and reform were gathering momentum. The Democrats nominated William Jennings Bryan in 1896. Theodore Roosevelt led the Republicans in the first decade of the 20th century. World War I shattered America's isolation and the hold of the Democratic Party. The Republicans dominated the 1920s while the economy prospered and big business grew as a result of new mass production techniques for a growing number of consumer products.

The Depression of 1929 and the election of Franklin D. Roosevelt in 1932 brought a critical realignment of the American electorate. Since 1932, there has been a Democratic majority in America. Between 1932 and 1968, there were only eight years of a Republican administration (Eisenhower's); Congress has been in the hands of the Democratic majority for every session except two (1947-48 and 1953-54). Since 1968, the Democrats have continued to control both houses of Congress but held the presidency only with the victory of Jimmy Carter in 1976. Does this mean an emergent Republican majority, as some have suggested, or are political parties diminishing as vehicles? Are presidential races autonomously directed?

This brief historical sketch serves to illustrate the nature of the grand coalitions we have had under the two-party system. Now, the Democratic New Deal coalition of Franklin Roosevelt is breaking apart. When George McGovern challenged the party in 1972, his support differed markedly from the FDR coalition of previous years. Jimmy Carter apparently pieced together enough of the "old coalition," plus the support of blacks and minorities, to gain a narrow victory in 1976. The Republican success at the presidential level has been not with GOP identifiers, but with a Nixon coalition of suburban, white, business, middle-class, employed, and conservative elements of the electorate. Many commentators today suggest that the American electorate is ready for a critical realignment, a refashioning of electoral loyalties due to the breakdown of political party support.

PRACTICING POLITICS   8.1

How to use a voting machine

Some places in this country still use paper ballots and ballot boxes, but most heavily populated areas have switched to voting machines. Here is how to vote by using a voting machine:

1. Make a list of your choices or study the sample ballot at the polling place. You may carry a sample ballot into the voting booth with you.
2. Walk into the booth after you have been checked in the roll book and given a number; move the red handle to the voting position to close the curtains.
3. Move the small black levers next to the names of the candidates you want. As

you move each lever, an "X" will appear beside the name for which you vote. Leave the levers in position.
4. If you have made a mistake or changed your mind, move the small lever back up and press the correct one(s).
5. If you do not like any of the candidates, follow the directions for a write-in vote. Use a ballpoint pen.
6. If you have a problem, do not touch anything; put your head through the curtains and call for help.
7. Check what you have done; then pull the red handle back to the original position. The levers go up and your vote is recorded before the curtains open.

INSTITUTIONAL FACTORS

The American electoral process has been very compatible with the two-party system. Our institutional arrangements have given it support and worked to the disadvantage of minor political parties.

Congressional elections are conducted by districts. We use **single-member districts:** the designated number of representatives for a state are each elected from a separate, single district and the highest vote-getter is elected. So rather than proportional representation, which apportions seats on a proportional basis with each party entitled to a percentage of representatives based on its proportion of the popular vote, we require each party candidate to receive a plurality in each congressional district (in 10 districts, the Democratic candidates may each receive 40 percent of the vote, but if the Republican candidates each receive 60 percent, the Republicans elect 10 representatives to Congress, not six; this is the winner-take-all system). Under such a system, minor parties cannot hope to capture a plurality.

The Electoral College for the selection of the president operates much the same way; a candidate needs a majority of electoral votes to be elected. A state's electoral votes *all* go to the candidate receiving the largest popular vote (a plurality gives unanimous support to a party candidate). To receive that majority, a candidate has to gain pluralities in enough states to receive the necessary number of electoral votes. The more parties there are, the less likely the majority. The dominance of the presidency in American politics keeps the Electoral College coalition alive.

Finally, some commentators have argued that most Americans take a moderate, middle-of-the-road stand on political issues. The American electorate is not ideologically motivated toward politics; people are socialized into a political party, not drawn to it because of issue stands. There is increasing reason to question this today, although the parties do seek majority support. They try to take positions, write platforms, and nominate candidates that will have broad appeal. Our political parties historically have not been ideological parties. They have sought to draw the bulk of their support from the moderate, centrist bulge in the electorate. If parties have to compete for the same, moderate voters, the two-party system is most adaptable to that mission.

POLITICAL PARTY FUNCTIONS

Political parties have served and continue to serve several important functions, though in a diminished capacity. These functions center around one mission—to elect candidates to public office. Everett Ladd has identified three characteristics essential to the success of the party process: competition, representation, and organization.[9]

Competition.   Political parties compete for political power. Successful candidates who assume public office organize and direct the affairs of that office; they formulate, enact, and administer public policy. The party in power knows that if it is unsuccessful, it will be replaced by the other party. A competitive two-party system keeps the party in power attentive to the public interest, responsible in formulating policy, and honest in administration. The challenging party formulates alternative positions and offers criticism so that, at election time, the voter has a choice and a basis on which to evaluate past performance.

Party competition is viewed as compatible with democracy because alternative positions are organized and offered to the citizens. It allows the voters to express their views, and to replace the party in power by peaceful, acceptable means. Party competition seeks to transcend factionalism, sectionalism, and generation as it combines individuals running for office and citizen influence in the political process. Political parties remain the major means of linking together separate electoral contests so that individual citizens can exercise some measure of popular control.

Representation.   Political parties present alternatives both in terms of candidates and in terms of public policy. Parties simplify the issues for the citizen, so that the costs of political activity and support are not greater than the

9. *Ibid.,* p. xvii.

average citizen can afford. Parties afford the opportunity for candidates, interest groups, and citizens to come together to fashion a mutually acceptable set of issues and candidates in return for political support. The fact that American parties are really coalitions has been one of their real strengths. Different people and groups have found support and representation through political parties. Groups have often found their views being adopted by parties and eventually enacted into public policy.

This representational function has offered parties a constant steady stream of potential leaders and candidates. It has kept issues and policy responsibility before the party. By uniting diverse segments of the population, it has played down social conflicts; aspiring leaders have had to prove ready to compromise in order to preserve the coalition.

Organization. Political parties remain the basis for organizing the government. Parties, having competed for public office, having promised to represent interests, have the responsibility for running the government.

It is true that the United States does not have a system of "party responsibility." Parties have little control over their members once they are in power, but they still form the basis for the organization of the government. In Congress, party committees allocate committee assignments for representatives; the president forms an administration largely from party loyalists and advisers.

Political parties are the conduit for public opinion. It is principally through political parties that the mass of citizens can exert influence over the political process and hold public officials accountable. If the control is not direct or always effective, the fundamental premise remains intact: Popular control of policymakers requires organization, and political parties provide a meaningful measure of public control without raising the costs of political participation unrealistically high.

CHANGING FUNCTIONS

The American system places a heavy burden on political parties: they must organize the affairs of government while representing the public interest. This has never been easy or perfectly achieved. To unite millions of people into a coalition and translate their will into public policy is bound to result in distortions. Parties have few mechanisms for insuring partisan loyalty. Responsiveness is sluggish. Yet, in recent years, the functions of political parties have proved even more difficult to carry out. Parties are simply not as strong as they once were.

The Republicans have been relegated to the status of minor party: They have not been in control of the presidency often since 1932 and in control of Congress almost not at all. Today the GOP's strength has dwindled to almost one-fifth of the electorate. Although Republicans made impressive inroads in the 1978 and 1980 elections, it remains to be seen if this can be sustained. The strength of the

Running as an Independent: Elections and Public Policy

In late April 1980 John B. Anderson dropped out of the race for the Republican endorsement for the presidency and became an independent candidate. As an independent candidate Anderson followed an unusual policy in American presidential politics.

In his independent bid for the presidency, Anderson stressed that he was not forming a third party—the routes taken by Bull Moose Theodore Roosevelt in 1912 and American Independent George Wallace in 1968. Although there have been third party candidates on the ballot in several states, such as those in the Socialist Labor Party, the Prohibition Party, and most recently, Lester Maddox as the presidential candidate from Wallace's American Independent Party, Anderson chose to run alone. This was the second presidential election in a row where there was an independent candidate as Eugene McCarthy ran as an independent in 1976.

Essentially, there are three problems of running as an independent for the presidency: ballot access, money, and votes.

The major problem is access to the ballot in the separate states. Each state sets its own laws. First, there are filing dates, and many states have filing dates in May and June. Twenty-one states put the date prior to July 15. Two states—Arkansas and Michigan— have no provision for independent candidates, only for third party candidates. Second are the petitions with signatures for filing as a candidate. For some states, only a minimal number of voter signatures are necessary, but many states require large numbers of votes obtained according to complex rules. California requires

1 percent of all registered voters. Massachusetts requires petitions from individual towns. Other states demand the naming of a vice-presidential running mate or the selection of presidential electors. In 1976 McCarthy could make the ballots in only 27 states, and he started before April.

The problem of money is far less complex but no more pleasing to an independent candidate. Independent candidates for the president are not entitled to public funds from the Federal Election Commission. Anderson's Democratic and Republican counterparts each received $30 million to run their fall contests. So the independent candidate must rely on voluntary private contributions to finance the campaign. The FEC did rule Anderson eligible for retroactive election funding if he achieved 5 percent of the popular vote, which he did achieve.

Voter response is speculative. The history of independents is poor. McCarthy garnered only 1 percent of the popular vote and no electoral votes; Anderson took 7 percent but no state's electoral votes. Most suggest the impact was to rob major candidates of votes. Who did Anderson hurt? Two schools of thought persist: one argument was he hurt Carter as disenchanted liberals voted for Anderson, the other school says he hurt Reagan by siphoning off some of the anti-Carter protest vote. The greatest potential was to deny either major candidate an electoral majority. While this did not happen, it did evidence dissatisfaction with the two party system and encourage Anderson to try for a 1984 bid for the presidency.

Democratic Convention

Photos by Stan Wakefield.

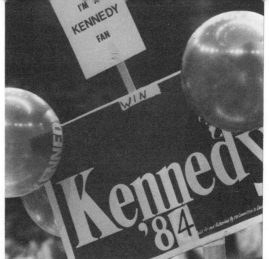

Republican Convention

Photos by Stan Wakefield.

conservative wing of the Republican party further weakens its representatives with the American electorate. Internal competition among the Democrats has created an organizational morass. The New Deal coalition has faced the challenge of young and minority political activists. The party has experienced increasing difficulty in holding the coalition together. Women, Hispanics, young voters, and environmentalists all demand a pivotal place within the party, at the expense of the traditional labor and black partisans.

Party nominations for the presidency have, in recent years, been more ideological and unrepresentative of the people, if election results are any measure (see Figure 8.3). Goldwater in 1964 was able to gather only 38.5 percent of the popular vote for the Republicans. In 1972 McGovern won only 37.5 percent of the vote as the Democratic candidate. Challengers for the nomination are also increasingly ideological: McCarthy in 1968, Reagan and Harris in 1976, Crane and Kennedy in 1980. The breakdown in representativeness is reflected at the polls, and in declining voter identification and negativism toward political parties.

Party organizations have lost control over nominations. Nowhere has the loss of representation and control been more in evidence than in the presidential nominating process. The open caucus and the primary have opened the nomination to a wide spectrum of candidates and groups using the presidential nominating process as a platform or vehicle to dramatize issues. Their concern is less winning than ideological commitment. This has often been the mark of minor or third parties.

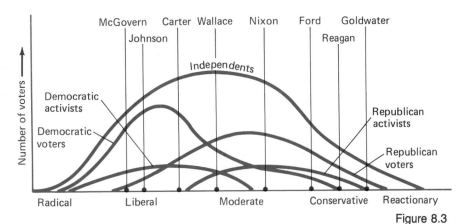

Figure 8.3

Types of and examples of political positions in the United States.

THIRD PARTIES

Third parties are about as old as America. Almost as soon as the Republican-Democrats and Whigs emerged, Americans were given third alternatives: the Anti-Masons (1832), the Know-Nothings (1856), and the Greenbackers (1880). Although none has seriously challenged the two major parties, third parties have been a vehicle for minority viewpoints. Only five times in our political history has a minor party polled over 10 percent of the popular vote; the Know-Nothing party in 1856 got 21.1 percent of the popular vote on an anti-Catholic, anti-Irish platform; in 1860, with the division of the Union, Southern Democrats and Constitutional Unionists combined to take 31 percent of the total vote. In 1912 the Progressive (Bull Moose) party of Theodore Roosevelt won 27.4 percent of the vote; Wisconsin's Robert LaFollette won 16.6 percent of the vote as the Progressive candidate for president in 1924; and in 1968, George C. Wallace, running as the American Independent party nominee, secured 13.5 percent of the popular vote.

V.O. Key has classified minor parties into two broad categories: There are doctrinal parties that profess a particular doctrine and nominate candidates to the presidency over several elections, and then there are transient, short-lived parties that emerge out of economic protest and secessionist movements.[10]

The continuing minor parties are largely unsuccessful in influencing the election results. The Socialist and Communist parties are examples. They continuously nominate candidates for public office, including the presidency, yet they can secure no better than a small fraction of the vote. They survive because of a small band of dedicated supporters. Doctrinal parties exercise little influence on

10. V.O. Key, *Politics, Parties and Pressure Groups,* (New York: Thomas Y. Crowell Co., 1964), p. 255.

FACT FILE

MAJOR MINOR PARTIES

Year	Party	Popular votes (percent)	Electoral votes
1824	Democratic–Republican (Henry Clay)	12.99	37
	Democratic–Republican (William Crawford)	11.17	41
1832	Independent Democrat	0	11
	Anti-Masonic	7.78	7
1836	Independent Democrat	0	11
	Whig (Hugh White)	9.72	26
	Whig (Daniel Webster)	2.74	14
1840	Liberty	0.28	0
1844	Liberty	2.30	0
1848	Free Soil	10.12	0
1852	Free Soil	4.91	6
1856	Whig–American	21.53	8
1860	Southern Democrat	18.09	72
	Constitutional Union	12.61	39
1872	Straight Out Democrat	0.29	0
1876	Greenback	0.9	0
1880	Greenback	3.32	0
1884	Greenback	1.74	0
	Prohibition	1.47	0
1888	Prohibition	2.19	0
	Union Labor	1.29	0
1892	Populist	8.50	22
	Prohibition	2.25	0
1896	National Democrats	0.96	0
	Prohibition	0.90	0
1900	Prohibition	1.50	0
	Socialist	0.62	0
1904	Socialist	2.98	0
	Prohibition	1.91	0
1908	Socialist	2.82	0
	Prohibition	1.70	0
1912	Progressive	27.39	88
	Socialist	5.99	0
1916	Socialist	3.18	0
	Prohibition	1.19	0
1920	Socialist	3.42	0
	Farmer–Labor	0.99	0
1924	Progressive	16.56	13
	Prohibition	0.19	0
1928	Socialist	0.72	0
	Communist	0.13	0
1932	Socialist	2.22	0
	Communist	0.26	0
1936	Union	1.96	0
	Socialist	0.41	0

MAJOR MINOR PARTIES (Continued)

Year	Party	Popular votes (percent)	Electoral votes
1940	*Socialist*	*0.23*	*0*
	Prohibition	*0.12*	*0*
1944	*Socialist*	*0.16*	*0*
	Prohibition	*0.16*	*0*
1948	*States Rights Democrat*	*2.40*	*39*
	Progressive	*2.38*	*0*
1952	*Progressive*	*0.23*	*0*
	Prohibition	*0.12*	*0*
1956	*Constitution*	*0.17*	*0*
	Socialist–Labor	*0.07*	*0*
1960	*Socialist–Labor*	*0.07*	*1 (Harry F. Byrd)*
			15
1964	*Socialist–Labor*	*0.06*	*0*
	Socialist Workers	*0.05*	*0*
1968	*American Independent*	*13.53*	*46*
	Socialist–Labor	*0.07*	*0*
1972	*Libertarian*	*0*	*1*
	American	*1.40*	*0*
	People's	*0.10*	*0*
1976	*Eugene McCarthy, Independent candidate*	*1.00*	*0*
1980	*John Anderson, Independent candidate*	*6.58*	*0*
	Libertarian	*1.04*	*0*

SOURCE: *Guide to U.S. Elections,* Congressional Quarterly, 1975.

the electoral process and in this sense can be said to be outside the system.[11] The rise of the Populists, the Greenback party, and the Progressives of 1924 were all forms of economic protest. Secessionist parties develop by splitting away from one of the major parties. The Progressives of 1912 and the "Dixiecrats" of 1948 are examples of such movements. Minor political parties are not to be judged only by their lack of electoral success. Doctrinal minor parties seek to promote a program that runs counter to those of the major parties. Parties seeking economic reform call attention to new issues and advocate unpopular policies whose time has not yet come. The Progressive party warned of concentration of economic power and the growth of monopolies. The Prohibitionist party continues to struggle for the prohibition of the sale of alcoholic beverages. The impact of minor parties must be judged, in part, by their impact on the major parties. The secessionist parties have alerted the major parties to dissent on public issues. The Dixiecrats of 1948 gave the Democrats warning that the South and civil rights would be controversial and troublesome. The Bull Moose bolt in 1912 was a warning about changing attitudes toward big business.

11. *Ibid.,* p. 255.

The impact of third parties can be to deny the two major parties a majority of electoral votes in a presidential contest. There was much suspicion that the Wallace campaign in 1968 was designed to deny a clear majority to either party and throw the election into the House of Representatives, where some compromise could be fashioned. Some said Eugene McCarthy's bid in 1976 was designed to take electoral votes away from Jimmy Carter.

As much as anything, however, minor parties popularize issues and ideas. They serve as a sounding board for the two major political parties. Their representation functions as a dimension that forces the major parties to adjust, and even to adopt minor party positions in subsequent years. For many third-party supporters, this is reason enough for the existence of a third-party politics.

Yet has the ability of the two major parties to absorb minor party positions diminished? Has the brokerage role of political parties, the ability to accommodate diverse points of view, broken down to a point where political activists, being denied access to the nomination, form their own party? In short, has the decline of parties opened the way for new third-party movements? To date this has not happened, but clearly it becomes an increasing possibility given the reforms to political parties and the unwillingness of aroused delegates to compromise.

What we have seen is the rise of the independent candidate. John Anderson's independent bid for the presidency follows after Eugene McCarthy's 1976 campaign. However, Anderson's 1980 run for the presidency attracted more support and affected partisan voting to a degree which influenced both major political parties.

PARTY MACHINERY

American political parties are decentralized, unlike the Labor and Conservative parties in England and those in West Germany where parties are organized around a parliamentary system of government. Because of the federal nature of our political system, personal candidate organizations, and a once-every-four-year presidential nomination, parties are organized on the state level. As Pendleton Herring noted some time ago, "In the federal sphere, our political parties are temporary alliances of local leaders held together by the hope of winning the Presidency."[12]

State parties vary in organization, structure, and strength. Usually there is a state committee and a state party chair. State committee membership is determined by state party rules; members are usually elected to office by the state convention or in state primary elections. The national party committee and the national chairman try to oversee state party activity, but state committees and chairs are not responsible to the national organization.

12. Pendleton Herring, *The Politics of Democracy: American Parties in Action* (New York: Rinehart & Co., 1940), p. 121.

Mayor Richard Daley of Chicago was one of the last big city "bosses" to control party politics. (Stan Wakefield)

Party organizations at the different levels are independent; the national committee has little control. To the extent that the national organization functions at all, it is largely during presidential election years. Local organizations do not respond well to direction from the state party. Local party chairs and precinct committees become active during elections; they support locally nominated candidates and those state candidates they feel moved to support. The most significant achievement of the local party organization, which may benefit the national and state parties as well as the local party, is to "get out the vote." With this loose organizational structure it is not surprising, then, that local party "bosses" have been able to control political parties in metropolitan areas and that national candidates have set up their own election organizations.

The boss system was maintained in America because the local party organization had control over the nomination of candidates to public office as well as the selection of delegates to the national conventions. There were patronage jobs, in addition, which public officials could pass around to reward loyal support. Typically a **party caucus,** a closed meeting of party leaders, would select the candidates of the party. This small band of local party faithfuls would meet, screen candidates, and produce a slate for the November ballot. This kept the nominating process in the hands of a party elite and brought accusations of back-room deals. Such candidate selections often were not representative of the party membership or the general electorate. Throughout the nineteenth century, however, the party caucus was the preferred method of candidate selection.

State law prescribes the method by which political parties may nominate candidates for public office. In the Populist and Progressive eras, the spirit of reform led to the initiation of the **direct primary** in virtually every state of the Union. By the mid-1920s, popular elections were held to determine party nominees for public office. Party caucus or convention nominees, and any insurgent candidate filing enough signatures on a petition, ran in an election (primary) to secure party endorsement for the general election. Today, primaries are used not only to nominate candidates, but also to select state and national convention delegates and party officers. The primary has become the prinicpal method of nominating candidates to office, and, in the process, weakened party control and effectiveness.

Candidates can direct personal campaign efforts to secure the nomination and win public office, and so candidates have become less dependent on a party for endorsement or support. This has weakened party control. The personalized style of campaigning creates ticket splitting, which further weakens party cohesion. The mood of cynicism and hostility toward parties, combined with ticket splitting and the primary, make it exceedingly unlikely that political parties will become stronger in the near future.

THE NATIONAL PARTY ORGANIZATION

The national party organization is a simple structure consisting of a national committee composed of 50 committeemen and 50 committeewomen elected by the various state committees and conventions, with additional delegates from the District of Columbia, Puerto Rico, and some of the United States territories (Figure 8.4). The national convention elects the national committee members, but this is little more than a formality. The national committee has responsibility for the well-being of the party, but, in fact, it seldom meets and exercises no real authority. Its main task is to set up the process for the national nominating convention.

The national party chairman or chairwoman is selected by the national committee of each party. In fact, he or she is selected by the incumbent president or party presidential nominee at the close of the convention. The position is not one of power; the chair helps to facilitate the presidential campaign, moderates state party disagreements with the national convention, and keeps the peace within the party. The selection of a national chair is usually the product of a compromise with state party leaders. The positions of national party chair and national committeeman and committeewoman change frequently. The chair changes with each new presidential nominee. In 1972, Nixon replaced Robert Dole with George Bush. The Democrats replaced Larry O'Brien with Robert Strauss, a party moderate, in the wake of George McGovern's defeat. In 1980, it was Bill Brock for the GOP and John White for the Democrats.

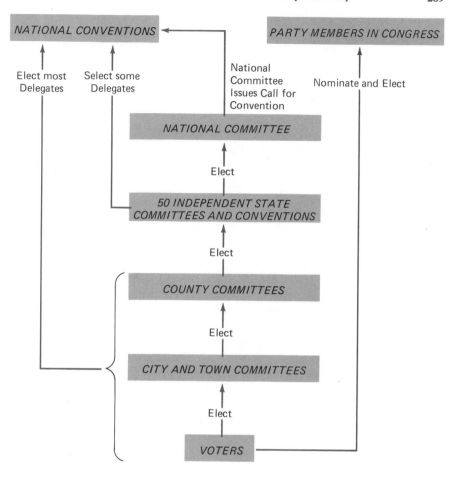

NATIONAL CONVENTIONS   PARTY MEMBERS IN CONGRESS

Elect most   Select some   National
Delegates   Delegates   Committee   Nominate and Elect
                                    Issues Call for
                                    Convention

NATIONAL COMMITTEE

Elect

50 INDEPENDENT STATE
COMMITTEES AND CONVENTIONS

Elect

COUNTY COMMITTEES

Elect

CITY AND TOWN COMMITTEES

Elect

VOTERS

Figure 8.4

Organization of national parties. (Joyce Gelb and Marian Palley, Tradition and Change in American Political Party Politics. New York: Thomas Y. Crowell, 1975. Chart modified from John H. Fenton, *People and Parties in Politics: Unofficial Makers of Public Policy.* Glenview, Ill.: Scott, Foresman, 1966, p. 17)

The national committee officers are not the directors of the presidential campaign. The machinery of the national party is largely ignored. The president or the presidential nominees establish their own organizations, which they run organized around key advisers and supporters who helped launch the nomination drive. Congressional candidates also forsake the national party. Incumbency itself is the major asset. Candidates for the House and Senate also have established personal organizations. They have key backers in their districts, independent access to campaign money, and their own information networks. There are also congressional and senatorial campaign committees created by party members in the House and Senate. These committees campaign for party candidates by raising money, bringing in speakers, providing advice to challengers, and generally supporting party members' bids for reelection.

THE NATIONAL CONVENTION

The crowning achievement of the national party is the national convention. It is the nomination of a presidential candidate and the subsequent campaign that is the essence of the national party. The very existence of the national party is continued by convening to nominate a candidate for the office of the presidency. Although formally the convention has supreme authority for policymaking—it writes the platform, determines rules, elects the national committee, and arbitrates disputes—it exercises little real authority. The four days every four years are a cause of celebration, usually as the party endeavors to keep its national image intact. The days are really designed to achieve one objective: to nominate a presidential candidate. The other items of business—adopting rules, settling delegate seating disputes, and approving the platform—are important, and on occasion they can be dramatic. Take, for example, the rules revisions of the Democrats in 1972, the abortion planks in the party platforms in 1976, and the open convention fight by Kennedy supporters in 1980 to free committed delegates. Yet these areas concern only the activists and party leaders. They are not why a majority of the delegates come to the convention.

And yet the delegates are there because of the rules and reforms to the rules of the delegate selection process. Delegates to the Democratic and Republican conventions are selected according to state law and party rules. Reforming the selection process has become a major concern for both political parties.

DEMOCRATIC RULE CHANGES

The Democrats began to make rule changes in the wake of confrontation in the streets of Chicago in 1968. The McGovern Commission sought to open up the procedures for delegate selection, particularly to "significant groups that have traditionally been identified with the Democratic party." The commission sought to remove control from the party leaders by recommending explicit rules on delegate selection, abolishing the unit rule (which required all delegates to cast their ballots as the majority ruled) establishing affirmative action guidelines to increase representation among youth, women, and minority groups, and requiring all delegates to be selected in the same year as the convention. Although the McGovern Commission did not set quotas as to the number of blacks, women, and youth for each state delegation, the 1972 credentials committee for the convention began establishing them when it was faced with challenges from reform advocates as to the representativeness of state delegations.

The reforms increased the reliance on primaries to select delegates, brought an increase in challenges, and generally radically changed the composition of the delegates. George McGovern was a prime beneficiary of the changes. They allowed the liberal, pro-McGovern activists to capture a majority of the delgate slots and nominate McGovern for the presidency. Due to the ensuing controversy and McGovern's large loss at the polls in 1972, Democratic officials ended the quota system in 1974. New rules for the 1976 convention were drafted. There were affirmative action guidelines, but no quotas. The major change was the establishment of proportional representation: All candidates with 15 percent or more support of delegates at any level would receive proportional support in delegates at the state or national convention. There were to be no state winner-take-all primaries, and 75 percent of all delegates were to be selected at the congressional-district level or lower. The increased emphasis on the primary again provided an easy way to apportion delegates and proved a benefit for Jimmy Carter who did so well in the primary elections in 1976.

For 1980, the Democrats have made further reforms. The proportional representation threshold for eligibility to win delegates would be a sliding scale from the current 15 percent to a high of 25 percent for states that began the delegate selection process later in the year. For 1980, Democrats have banned election of delegates from single-member districts or "loophole," winner-take-all primaries which permitted district level, winner-take-all elections in 1976. They also required the selection of an equal number of men and women delegates from each state. The thrust of the reforms, critics charge, is to make it more difficult for fringe candidates to win convention delegates since candidates need a modest level of support throughout the state to be eligible for delegates under the 1980 rules for apportioning presidential convention delegates.

REPUBLICAN RULE CHANGES

Republican rule changes have been much slower and less dramatic. In 1971, the Ginn Commission (headed by Rosemary Ginn, a committeewoman from Missouri) called for reforms to include open participation, no automatic seating of delegates due to office or party position, no proxies, equal representation of men and women, and proportional representation for persons under 25 years of age. Although the commission's proposals have generally been supported, they have not been made party rules.

A major source of contention within the Republican party is the victory-bonus system, which rewards states with additional delegates if the state voted Republican in the last presidential, congressional, or gubernatorial election. The Ripon Society of liberal Republicans has challenged the system in court, arguing that it rewards small states and thereby denies the one person–one vote equal protection clause of the Fourteenth Amendment. The Supreme Court has refused to hear the case.

The Republican rules-review committee made no major changes for 1980.

Table 8-2
Delegate Selection: Major Party Differences.

Party Rules—With a Difference (the major differences between national Republican and Democratic Party delegate selection rules)		
Issue	*Democratic party rule*	*Republican party rule*
Proportional representation	Required at all levels of the delegate selection process.	Winner-take-all permitted at the statewide and multi-delegate district level.
Open or crossover primaries	Prohibited.	Prohibited unless mandated by state law.
Apportionment of delegates within a state.	A complex formula is used for allocating 75 percent of a state's delegation by district. The rest are to be at large and chosen to satisfy the state's affirmative action goals and to give elected officials and state party leaders at least 10 percent of the delegation.	As determined by the state Republican committee. The rules expressly permit entire delegations to be chosen at large.
Affirmative action	State delegate selection plans must include numerical goals and timetables and specific "outreach" activities. The "goals" are not to be "quotas," except for women, who must make up half the delegation.	"Positive action" is required, but without specific goals, timetables, or plans.
Unit rule	No delegate may be required to cast a vote in accordance wtih a majority at any level of the delegate selection process.	The unit rule is prohibited only for convention voting on presidential and vice presidential nominations
Bound delegates	All delegates are bound for one ballot unless released in writing or chosen as uncommitted delegates.	Delegates must follow state law. A proposed rules change would drop this and let states enforce their own requirements.
Candidate preferences	Pledged delegates must be chosen from a pool of delegates publicly committed to the candidate, who may disavow any delegate.	No comparable rule.

Table 8-2 *(Continued)*

Issue	*Democratic party rule*	*Republican party rule*
Timing	Delegates must be chosen between the second Tuesday in March and the second Tuesday in June. Exceptions may be made for states with earlier or later procedures in 1976 if required by state law.	No specific dates are mentioned. Delegates must be chosen after the call of the convention is published and up to 25 days before the convention.
Compliance review	A state party whose delegate selection procedures have been approved by the party's Compliance Review Commission may be challenged at the convention only for failure to implement an approved plan.	The relative scarcity of national rules leaves little ground for a credentials challenge. But once a challenge is made, no rule grants a state any presumption that it is in compliance.
State laws	Party rules supersede state law. Where the two are in conflict, state parties may be granted exceptions if they have taken "provable positive steps" to have the law changed. No exceptions may be made for states with open primaries.	Deference to state law is written into the party rules.

SOURCE: *National Journal,* October 20, 1979, p. 1743.

Unlike the Democrats, who stressed nationalization of party rules, the Republicans continued to argue for state rules as controlling the delegate selection process. The Republicans are exceedingly aware of their minority status, and they stressed the need for representing youth, minorities, and women at the convention. But to date they have not chosen to mandate this in the form of rules changes.

REFORM RESULTS

What have these reforms accomplished? They have increased reliance on the state presidential primary as a means of selecting convention delegates. They have become the most prevalent way of selecting delegates today. In 1980, approximately two-thirds of all delegates were picked or bound to vote according to

Candidate Ronald Reagan won most state primaries in 1980 and was an easy victor for the party's presidential endorsement. (United Press International)

the results of ballots cast by voters in the primaries. State caucuses or conventions no longer retain the right to nominate or control the balloting of convention delegates. Most state public officials or party officials have no automatic delegate status. As a consequence, the composition of delegates to conventions has changed, at least among Democratic delegates (see Figure 8.5 and Table 8.3).

Table 8.3

Amateurs and Professionals Among Democratic Convention Delegates

Year	Amateur	Semi-professional	Professional	Total
1968 (N = 188)	23%	61%	16%	100%
1972 (N = 314)[a]	51%	22%	27%	100%

a. Delegates do not total 326 due to failure to respond to all the items composing the amateurism-professionalism scale.

SOURCE: John W. Soule and Wilma E. McGrath, "A Comparative Study of Presidential Nominating Conventions: The Democrats 1968 and 1972," *American Journal of Political Science,* Vol. 14, No. 3 (Austin, Tex: University of Texas Press, August 1975).

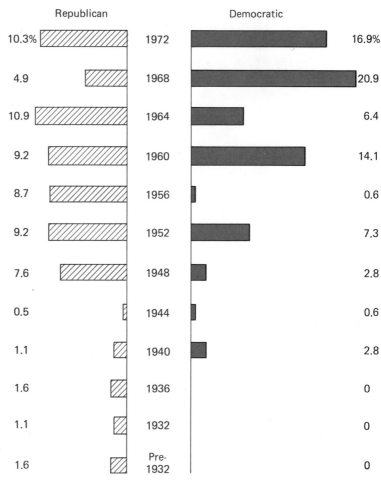

Republican   Democratic

10.3%	1972	16.9%
4.9	1968	20.9
10.9	1964	6.4
9.2	1960	14.1
8.7	1956	0.6
9.2	1952	7.3
7.6	1948	2.8
0.5	1944	0.6
1.1	1940	2.8
1.6	1936	0
1.1	1932	0
1.6	Pre-1932	0

Figure 8.5
Proportion of electoral activists with first experience in presidential campaign years. (John Kessel, *Presidential Campaign Politics.* Homewood, Ill.: Dorsey Press, Inc., 1980, p. 62). Copyright © by John Kessel.

The socioeconomic comparisons in Table 8.4 show that delegates were far more representative of the general public in 1972 and 1976 than they were in 1968. The reform rules are working in this regard. This changed composition also reflects a changed attitude on the part of the delegates. Soule and McGrath noted that the 1972 delegates differed not only in age, sex, and race, but in political orientation as well. The newly enfranchised groups made up the bulk of the political amateurs: "We are left with the tentative conclusion that youth and women, two groups who numerically benefited the most from party reforms, constituted the bulk of political amateurs."[13] These are the persons most committed to reform and issues, and they are least dedicated to party unity or victory.

13. Soule and McGrath, "A Comparative Study of Presidential Nominating Conventions: The Democrats of 1968 and 1972," p. 511.

Table 8.4
Socioeconomic Makeup of Democratic
Convention Delegates

	Women	Blacks	Youth[a]	Other[b]
1968	13%	5.5%	4%	NA
1972	38	15	21	5%
1976	36	7	14	NA
1980	49	15	11	8

a. Eighteen to thirty years of age.
b. Includes delegates of Spanish-speaking or Indian origins; not available for 1968 or 1976.

SOURCE: *The Party Reformed, Final Report of the Commission on Party Structure and Delegate Selection* (Washington, D.C.: Democratic National Committee, July, 7, 1972), pp. 7–8; Congressional Quarterly, *Guide to the 1976 Election;* 1980 data, CBS news survey, in *The New York Times,* August 11, 1980.

Finally, the reliance on primaries and an open delegate-selection process have made the national convention anticlimactic. The distribution of delegates becomes fairly well established before the convention. Rules prohibit the "wheeling and dealing" that marked past conventions. Delegates are bound to candidates for one, two, or even three ballots. Since 1960, no party has used more than one ballot to nominate a presidential candidate. The Ford–Reagan nominating contest was bitterly pursued, but it was still decided on the first ballot. It might also be noted that since 1960, the conventions have been televised nationally. The parties and the candidates are very well aware of the image they convey to viewers and voters; any hint of corrupt politics could be fatal for the election.

The conventions may be anticlimactic because the results are predictable. The new rules may also have changed our expectations regarding the role of the political party:

> This trend may underline the importance of nonparty resources—early candidacy, strong personal organization, money, successful polls and media, political personality—in the contest for nomination. The continuation of these tendencies may lead to a further decline in the role played by party leaders in the presidential nominating process.[14]

POLITICAL PARTIES: A CRITICAL REALIGNMENT

We have been studying the functioning of political parties in a changing environment, a political environment where presidential landslide victories have become commonplace. Equally impressive has been the declining ability of the

14. Joyce Gibb and Marian L. Palley, *Tradition and Change in American Politics* (New York: Thomas Y. Crowell Co., 1975), p. 256.

victorious presidential candidate to translate that vote margin into congressional seats for the party. The argument is commonplace by now: The American electorate has changed its expectations about the political process and the role of political parties within that process. The American electorate may be heading toward a critical realignment. Will the changes result in greater partisan support, or in the dissolution of political parties as we have come to know them? We have seen this realigning cut across traditional partisan affiliation. The consequence has been to accelerate the process of party decomposition. Here is a brief review of the forces working toward realignment.

The parties are operating within a changed environment. The traditional view of centrist, "accommodationist" parties seeking to build a coalition to capture a majority of the electorate, is no longer operative. In the New Deal context, the politics of coalition building kept parties from moving too far from the center, if issues mattered at all. Parties sought to nominate candidates who could appeal to the broad mass of voters and maintain the politics of accommodation and consensus.

Now issues have emerged as an important variable; since 1964, voters have increasingly come to evaluate the parties in terms of their stand on issues. Gerald Pomper has documented this trend of voters to see the Democrats as "liberal" and the Republicans as "conservative."[15] The rise of Barry Goldwater, Eugene McCarthy, George Wallace, George McGovern, and Ronald Reagan are clear indicators of this trend.

Also associated with the rise of issue awareness has been the tendency of voters to choose candidates on the basis of issues. The issue awareness of voters and the rise of ideological candidates have made issues a significant force in determining the presidential vote. Ideological consistency as a basis for voting helps to explain the rise of political activists and the increases in ticket splitting. These are all symptomatic of the current party decline.

We have documented the decline in party identification. There has been a loss of faith among strong party identifiers for both parties. The rise in the number of Independents, particularly among the young, is well known. Harris and Gallop have published polls attesting to the decline in trust and faith in political parties. At the same time that party identification diminishes, there is a rise in ticket splitting. Voters are increasingly likely to vote for candidates of opposing parties. Party labels do not have the force they once had. Almost 50 percent of elections now have split outcomes, where presidential and congressional candidates carrying the district are of differing political parties.

The weakening of party organization also contributes to party decline. Reforms of the delegate selection process have produced a wave of political activists at presidential nominating conventions. These "political amateurs" are ideologues bent on the nomination of their candidate and/or party reform—they are not of a mind to compromise. The democratization of party rules through the use of the

15. Pomper, "From Confusion to Clarity". . . , see also his *Voter's Choice: Varieties of American Electoral Behavior* (New York: Dodd Mead, 1975).

presidential primary has left the party no control over the direction in which presidential nominating conventions will go.

The rise of political amateurs underlines a change in the nature of the groups seeking access to the political parties. New groups, heretofore largely excluded from participation in the party process, have demanded reforms to facilitate their participation in the party system. These groups include blacks, women, youth, and Hispanic Americans. They have become a major force within the Democratic party, and they are also increasingly active as voting blocs within American society.

As a result of these changes—the rise of issues and the decline of party organization—we have a base for critical realignment from party loyalty to a nonparty adherence to issues. "Groups are relocating across party lines, to be sure, in response to new conflict structures. But equally impressive is the movement of voters away from firm partisan ties generally. We are becoming a nation of electoral transients."[16]

PROBLEMS OF REPRESENTATION

Political parties are not representative of the American public. Changes in voter affiliation and organization procedures have left parties weak and disoriented. The electorate voting for a presidential party candidate today is small and unrepresentative of the electorate at large. The new procedures—presidential primaries, proportional representation, and open caucuses—make it increasingly likely that party politics can be captured and dominated by activists seeking reform and ideological candidates. In the words of Ladd and Hadley, we have confused *participation* and *representation* in party politics. Political parties no longer represent large coalitions of people. They no longer have the regulars and

16. Everett Ladd and Charles Hadley. *Transformations of the American Party System,* Second Edition, (New York: W. W. Norton & Co., 1978), p. 320.

the organization to promote compromise and consensus. Those who have spent their lives working for the party are pushed aside to facilitate democratic participation within the party.

What we are not understanding, however, is that open participation is not more representative if we mean that in terms of the general public. Increased participation has democratized political parties, but it has facilitated the demands of new groups of political activists. The nominating process is open to groups and candidates that seek to capture the presidential nomination and use it as a forum to advance their cause or issues. It in no way assures that such groups or candidates represent the American public. If anything, with landslide victories just the opposite is the case. Candidates unacceptable to the American people are succeeding in obtaining party nomination. The ability of the party to appeal to its traditional supporters and identifiers is diminished.

It is not that political parties have ever been perfect instruments for representation. Smoke-filled rooms, political bossism, and closed caucuses have all worked to exclude legitimate interests. There has never been a serious move toward responsible party government in this country. Parties never have exercised control over their elected public officials; party membership always has been loose. Without political parties, however, what is there to provide the representative function? Everett Ladd has noted that political parties have, in the past, made errors and been dishonest but they also have managed to keep the political process together. Can we continue to govern ourselves in an era where political parties have a diminished presence?[17]

SUMMARY

1. Political parties are in a state of decline where politics have become more technologically complicated and the electorate more independent. We see the weakened state of political parties by the decline in party identification, changes in campaigning and campaign organizations, and reforms to the nominating process.

2. While parties have declined, they persist in part because the two parties historically have been grand coalitions, and also because the institutional arrangement of the electoral process works to the disadvantage of third parties.

3. Political parties have served one mission rather well, the election of candidates to public office. From this one mission comes support for the democratic ideas of political competition and representation, which these parties have done less well.

4. Third parties have never been very successful if measured by number of votes. They continue to express minority points of view, however, thereby challenging the two-party structure.

17. Ladd, *Where Have the Voters Gone?*, p. 77.

5. Party machinery is unwieldy and largely irrelevant for the governance of political parties. It functions only for the presidential nominating convention. The direct primary has replaced party organization for control of political parties.

6. Reforms to the presidential nomination process have weakened party control over presidential selection. The delegate selection process has been opened, allowing insurgent candidates significant opportunity to secure the party nomination for president. There remains little party control or responsibility in presidential campaigning.

TERMS

amateur   269
caucus   287
coalition   271
convention   290
critical realignment   273
direct primary   288
doctrinal party   283
endorsement   290
representation   275-76
single-member
   district   274

loophole or winner-take-all
   primary   291
national committee   288
party "boss"   287
platform   290
proportional
   representation   291
quota   290
transient party   283
unit rule   290
victory bonus   291

RESEARCH PROJECTS

8.1 Delegates to Party Conventions. How are political party delegates to conventions selected? Create a flow chart for the political parties in your state—Democrat and GOP—for selecting delegates to local, district, state, and national conventions. When are they selected? Are there caucus or primary elections? Is there a proportional system of representation? Write your state party headquarters and ask for the information. *Congressional Quarterly* and the *National Journal* also carry good overviews on delegate selection.

8.2 Party Platforms. Do a side by side analysis of the party platforms in the 1980 election. List the platforms under major topic headings. Do parties differ significantly in their approach and stand on issues? You can find the platforms in the proceedings of the parties published after each national convention in the presidential election years. There is also a compilation of historical party platforms in a volume by Porter and Johnson, *National Party Platforms* (University of Illinois Press, 1966, with supplement), so you could do this for earlier years as well.

8.3 A National Primary. Write an essay on the concept of a national primary. What are the issues for and against a national presidential primary? What arguments are most convincing to you?

BIBLIOGRAPHY

Broder, David. *The Party's Over: The Failure of Politics in America.* New York: Harper and Row, 1971.

As a journalist Broder senses the problems facing parties and their loss of effectiveness. His solution calls for a revitalization of political parties and the party system.

Burnham, Walter Dean. *Critical Elections and the Mainsprings of American Politics.* New York: W.W. Norton, 1970.

An argument suggesting the decline of political parties and the realignment of the American electorate. Burnham provides insightful historical analysis on the party system and American voting behavior.

Gibb, Joyce, and Marian L. Palley. *Tradition and Change in American Politics.* New York: Thomas Y. Crowell, 1975.

A textbook on political parties with the standard full fare of topics, the authors have managed to capture the sense of change in political parties. The book attempts to look at parties as a response to the environment in which they operate.

Ladd, Everett. *Where Have all the Voters Gone?* New York: W.W. Norton, 1978.

A series of essays by Ladd first appearing in *Fortune,* the volume is a short, but penetrating, analysis of the problems with political parties. Written with wit, Ladd examines the two major parties and the perils of party reform.

Ladd, Everett, and Charles Hadley. *Transformation of the American Party System.* New York: W.W. Norton, 1978.

Looks at the changes in the Democratic and Republican parties since the New Deal. Makes good use of data to explain the breakdown of the old coalition and changed composition of support for political parties.

Maisel, Louis, and Paul M. Sacks. *The Future of Political Parties.* Beverly Hills, Calif.: Sage Publications, 1975.

A collection of essays looking at party decomposition not only in America but also in several states and foreign nations. Some of the articles are specialized and employ technical methods; others, however, give an overview and can be read with greater ease.

Ranney, Austin. *Caring the Mischiefs of Faction.* Berkeley, Calif.: University of California Press, 1975.

The most complete work on reforms to the political parties, with special attention to 1972 in which Ranney had a personal hand. Ranney tries to weigh the relative merits and pitfalls for parties when they undertake internal reform.

Sorauf, Frank. *Party Politics in America*. Boston: Little, Brown, 1976.

A basic text on political parties, with good coverage of the standard topics on political parties—organization, support, electoral performance, and organizing a government. The author sees parties contributing to our notion of representative government.

Sundquist, James. *Dynamics of the Party System*. Washington, D.C.: Brookings Institution, 1973.

A rather extensive and detailed analysis of the history of the party system. Sundquist examines popular support for political parties over time, concluding that party realignment is not likely but parties are not healthy either.

Chapter

9

The Changing American Voter and the Electoral Process

The last two decades of American electoral politics have been characterized by a variety of forces producing change in the system and for the individual voter. Events since our involvement in the Vietnam war have produced a climate of changing expectations. The 1960s saw the rise of civil rights activists and a period of social unrest, with civil disturbances and riots. The Great Society sought to engineer America's resources to solve our social ills. The period of rising entitlements was soon over as we became mired in the conflict in Southeast Asia. The Vietnam war not only drained resources from domestic programs, but became the most unpopular and divisive war in American history. The 1970s brought revelations of political corruption and scandal. Watergate left the nation cynical and uncertain regarding the use of presidential power. In the process Watergate tested the limits of constitutional rule and democratic politics. Economic recession and inflation have emerged as new issues of concern, along with the high cost of government. Issues have become privatized; citizens are turning away from politics and political parties to more personal concerns.

As politics has changed, so has American political behavior. In 1980 the American public was considerably different from the public in 1960. On the eve of John Kennedy's election, the public was little motivated to participate in politics, was content with the political process and the two major political parties, and demonstrated little concern for issues or issue voting. Today the American electorate is defecting from parties, intensely aware of

John Anderson in his independent bid for the presidency in 1980. (Stan Wakefield)

issues as new groups enter the political arena, and showing a strong disaffection for the whole political process.

Change has many dimensions. In this chapter we will attempt to focus on several of these dimensions, particularly those that have had the greatest impact on traditional voting patterns and political behavior. There has been taking place in America a critical realignment of the electorate, as much a result of the changing composition of that electorate as from changes in the attitudes and behavior of citizens already participating in the system.[1]

WHO VOTES

VOTER PARTICIPATION

The basic premise of democracy is citizen participation. A democracy is predicated on the right and ability of a people to choose their own representatives. We frequently evaluate democracy by the extent of the franchise to vote. In the twentieth century, the franchise in America has been extended. The Nineteenth Amendment extended voting rights to women; the 1964 and 1965 Civil Rights

1. Norman Nie, Sidney Verba and John R. Petrocik, *The Changing American Voter* (Cambridge, Mass.: Harvard University Press, 1976), pp. 1–2.

Act, as well as the elimination of the poll tax in the Twenty-fourth Amendment, sought to enforce what the Fifteenth Amendment had established, suffrage for the black American; the Twenty-sixth Amendment lowered the voting age in federal elections to 18 years of age.

Yet it is one of the ironies of American democracy that as we approached universal suffrage in the 1960s, voter participation in elections began to decline. In 1960, a high of 63.1 percent of the eligible voters went to the polls in the presidential election. Since then, there has been a steady and continuous decline. In 1964, 61.8 percent of the voters went to the polls; in 1968, it was 60.7 percent. But in 1972, even with over 7 million new voters added to the electorate, the turnout rate slipped to 55.6 percent; and in 1976 only 54.4 percent came to the polls to choose between Gerald Ford and Jimmy Carter. For 1980 the decline continued as only 52.3 percent cast a vote in the three-way race between Reagan, Carter, and John Anderson.

The decline in voter participation cannot be blamed on the enfranchisement of the 18 to 21 year-old voter. True, their turnout rate is low, but the 6 percent decline over the eight-year period is greater than the youth vote; "at most, the eighteen-year-old vote accounted for less than two percentage points of the decline from 1968 to 1972."[2] The explanation for the declining level of participation must, in part, be that citizens of all ages are making a conscious choice to stay away from the polls. Some citizens have always been indifferent; we know that the lower the concern for the outcome of the election, the less likely a person is to vote. Yet the marked trend in the past two decades suggests that people feel there is little to be gained by political participation. Voter disaffection with the political process, the distrust and cynicism that has emerged, have created a sense of powerlessness and frustration that manifests itself in nonvoting.[3]

We note from Table 9.1 that the nonvoter is more likely to be young, less educated, and of a minority background. These are precisely the groups that have been recently enfranchised. The citizen most likely to turn out to vote is middle-aged, better educated, and white. This may be true for several reasons. The participant is part of the established middle class, which benefits from the system and appears to have greater confidence in the political process. Years ago a study called *The American Voter* established participation rates based on degree of interest in the campaign, concern over the outcome of the election, and sense of political efficacy. Campbell et al. found that the higher the degree of interest, the greater the concern for the outcome, and the greater the sense of political effectiveness on the part of the individual voter, the more likely the citizen was to participate.[4] Those with a stake in the system are more likely to express interest

2. Richard Boyd, "Electoral Trends in Postwar Politics," in *Choosing the President,* edited by James David Barber (Englewood Cliffs, N.J.: Prentice-Hall, 1974), p. 183.
3. See Phillip Converse, "Change in the American Electorate," in *The Human Meaning of Social Change,* edited by Angus Campbell and Phillip Converse (New York: Russell Sage, 1972).
4. Angus Campbell, Phillip Converse, Warren Miller and Donald Stokes, *The American Voter* (New York: Wiley, 1960), Chap. 4.

Table 9.1

Voter Participation in National Elections by Groups[a]

Group Characteristic	1968	Year 1972	1974	1976	1978
Male	69.8	64.1	46.2	59.6	46.6
Female	66.0	62.0	43.4	58.8	45.3
White	69.1	64.5	46.3	60.9	47.3
Black	57.6	52.1	33.8	48.7	37.2
18–20 Years old	—	48.3	20.8	38.0	20.1
21–24 Years old	51.1	50.7	26.4	45.6	26.2
25–34 Years old	62.5	59.7	40.3	55.4	38.0
35–44 Years old	70.8	66.3	49.1	63.3	50.1
45–64 Years old	74.9	70.8	56.9	68.7	58.5
65 and over	65.8	63.5	51.4	62.2	55.9
Residence					
Metropolitan	68.0	64.3	44.7	59.2	
Non-Metropolitan	67.3	59.4	44.7	59.1	
North and West	71.0	66.4	48.8	61.2	48.9
South	60.1	55.4	36.0	54.9	39.6
School year completed					
Grade 8 or less	54.5	47.4	34.4	44.1	34.6
Grade 9 to 12	61.3	52.0	35.9	47.2	35.1
Grade 12	72.5	65.4	44.7	59.4	45.3
More than 12	81.2	78.8	54.9	73.5	57.3

a. Based on estimated population of voting age.

SOURCE: *The Statistical Abstracts of the United States, 1977 and 1979.*

and concern, and to have a sense of efficacy. For the disadvantaged or for newly enfranchised groups there seems to be less direct reward for participation. The political climate of cynicism further discourages participation. Such groups can find no personal meaning or sense of power by participation: "The decline in interest appears to represent more a conscious rejection of politics than a withdrawal into more neutral apathy."[5]

HOW VOTERS DECIDE

Why do citizens vote the way they do? Actually, determining the why of voting is extremely difficult and complex. In the past, we have relied on surveys asking people why they voted as they did, but critics say replies to survey questions do not represent actual behavior. The surveys established the concept of the "normal vote" based on the importance of the long-range effect of party identi-

5. Nie, Verba, and Petrocik, *The Changing American Voter,* p. 280.

The consensus that Roosevelt and the Democratic party built in the 1930s included American minorities; the party sought and depended heavily on the support of blacks and the ethnic groups of the large cities. But with the coming of the civil rights movement in the 1960s, this sense of common purpose began to fade as the minorities, eager to participate more fully in the postwar prosperity, turned to exercising their political power for their own benefit. The result has been similar to that of single-issue politics: Real problems have been brought to public attention and opportunities have been expanded, but the electorate is again fragmented, and parties and politicians are pressured not for general policies, but on specific issues that may then cost them elections.

The newest of these groups is the Hispanic Americans, whose numbers are growing so fast (over 19 million) that they now form the largest single ethnic group after black Americans. They want jobs, education, and better immigration policies. Unlike other earlier immigrants, they are unwilling to submerge themselves in the wider culture. They want education—but bilingual education.

This sounds like a good idea: After all, why not be able to be fluent in two languages? But there are also problems: If Spanish–English bilingual programs are set up, should similar programs be established for every language group? And if people who are already handicapped in a sophisticated, technological society do not learn good English language skills, will they ever be able to compete for jobs and opportunities? If inefficient bilingual programs result in linguistic subcultures, groups may become permanently cut off from the mainstream culture, the basic unity of our society. The fact that we have all, up to now, considered ourselves Americans first and members of an ethnic group second could be weakened and destroyed.

Table 9.2

Voting Pattern by Group in Presidential Elections

Group	1952 Dem.	1952 Rep.	1956 Dem.	1956 Rep.	1960 Dem.	1960 Rep.	1964 Dem.	1964 Rep.
National	44.6%	55.4%	42.2%	57.8%	50.1%	49.9%	61.3%	38.7%
Men	47	53	45	55	52	48	60	40
Women	42	58	39	61	49	51	62	38
White	43	57	41	59	49	51	59	41
Nonwhite	79	21	61	39	68	32	94	6
College education	34	66	31	69	39	61	52	48
High school education	45	55	42	58	52	48	62	38
Grade school education	52	48	50	50	55	45	66	34
Professional and business people	36	64	32	68	42	58	54	46
White-collar workers	40	60	37	63	48	52	57	43
Manual workers	55	45	50	50	60	40	71	29
Union members	61	39	57	43	65	35	73	27
Farmers	33	67	46	54	48	52	53	47
Under 30	51	49	43	57	54	46	64	36
30–49 years	47	53	45	55	54	46	63	37
Over 49	39	61	39	61	46	54	59	41
Protestants	37	63	37	63	38	62	55	45
Catholics	56	44	51	49	78	22	76	24
Republicans	8	92	4	96	5	95	20	80
Democrats	77	23	85	15	84	16	87	13
Independents	35	65	30	70	43	57	56	44

fication, adjusted for short-term deviations due to issues and candidates. As these forces lose their relevance, the notion of a normal vote is less pertinent, although we still find it useful to examine behavior according to various criteria.

One approach is **sociological.** This method focuses on the socioeconomic background of voters and examines voting behavior of citizens according to income, age, race, education, and group affiliations. There continues to be some stability of voting patterns according to sociological variables. The other approach is **psychological.** Instead of stressing group affiliation or socioeconomic background, motives such as party support, issues, or candidate assessment are measured. The psychological approach attempts to explain causality by identifying relevant concerns in the minds of the voters. Great changes appear to be taking place in the psychological motivations influencing voting behavior.

	1968			1972		1976[a]			1980	
Dem.	Rep.	Wallace	Dem.	Rep.	Dem.	Rep.	McCarthy	Dem.	Rep.	Anderson
43.0%	43.4%	13.6%	38%	62%	50%	48%	1%	41%	51%	7%
41	43	16	37	63	53	45	1	37	54	7
45	43	12	38	62	48	51	b	45	46	7
38	47	15	32	68	46	52	1	36	55	8
85	12	3	87	13	85	15	b	82	14	3
37	54	9	37	63	42	55	2	35	51	11
42	43	15	34	66	54	46	b	38	52	8
52	33	15	49	51	58	41	1	46	48	4
34	56	10	31	69	42	56	1	33	56	9
41	47	12	36	64	50	48	2	42	48	8
50	35	15	43	57	58	41	1	46	47	5
56	29	15	46	54	63	36	1	47	44	7
29	51	20	NA[c]	NA[c]	NA[c]	NA[c]	NA[c]	29	66	3
47	38	15	48	52	53	45	1	43	43	11
44	41	15	33	67	48	49	2	38	55	6
41	47	12	36	64	52	48	b	39	54	4
35	49	16	30	70	46	53	b	37	56	6
59	33	8	48	52	57	42	1	40	51	7
9	86	5	5	95	9	91	b	11	84	4
74	12	14	67	33	82	18	b	66	26	6
31	44	25	31	69	38	57	4	30	54	12

a. Figures for some groups do not add to 100% because of the vote for other minor-party candidates.
b. Less than 1.
c. Not available.

SOURCE: Gallup poll, published November 1968, December 1968, December 1972, and December 1976. 1980 data, *New York Times* CBS Poll.

SOCIOLOGICAL FACTORS

Political scientists have studied sociological factors in voting behavior since the 1940s. *The People's Choice* was an early study examining the relationship between class, income, and voting. Said the authors, "social characteristics determine political preference."[6] Out of the New Deal alignment of the electorate there

6. Paul F. Lazarsfeld, Bernard Berelson, and Hazel Gaudet, *The People's Choice* (New York: Columbia University Press, 1944), p. 27

emerged some clear, stable voting patterns by socioeconomic position that were predictable and continuous, interrupted only by short-term conditions that were temporary deviations.

The New Deal patterns of voting behavior from the 1930s through the early 1960s showed distinct social and economic differences. The wealthier, professional, better-educated persons voted predominately Republican. The lower socioeconomic classes, blacks, and union members were largely Democrats. And to a certain degree, these patterns continue to hold true.

Social Class.   Social class can be measured by income and occupation. We see that the upper classes tend to vote Republican, while manual workers are more likely to support the Democratic party. But a word of caution. The trend in America toward continually higher levels of income and education is weakening these traditional patterns. The New Deal distinctions are less relevant. Particularly with the under 30 group, we already know there is a large number of Independents, and these are the people with rising income and educational levels.

Everett Ladd studied changes in social class voting over four presidential elections (1948, 1960, 1968, and 1972).[7] He discovered a dramatic shift in voting patterns since 1948 by socioeconomic group. By 1968 there was a strong tendency for better-educated, high-income people to support Hubert Humphrey, a Democrat. The 1972 election continued the pattern of abandonment of George McGovern by socioeconomic groups. McGovern's support came from the middle-income group. In short, social class continues to demonstrate some differences in preference, but they have significantly narrowed in the last decade as America moves toward becoming a middle-class society.

Race.   Nonwhites have most consistently and dramatically supported the Democratic party. This is the only group to provide a clear majority for the Democratic candidate in *every* presidential election since 1952.

From 1968 to 1972, there was an alarming trend for political parties to be divided on racial lines. In 1972 less than one in three white voters who went to the polls voted Democratic, whereas almost all nonwhites voted Democratic. The 1976 election redressed that balance considerably, although the nonwhite support for the Democratic candidate continued. In fact, many black spokespeople argued that the margin of victory for Jimmy Carter was provided by the overwhelming support of nonwhites for the Democratic nominee: "It is unlikely that Carter would have carried any region, even the South, without black support. Thus, the first true southerner to be elected President since the pre-Civil War period owed his victory to the descendants of the slaves freed in that war."[8]

7. Everett Ladd, "Liberalism Upside Down," *Political Science Quarterly,* Vol. 91, No. 4 (Winter 1976–77).
8. Gerald Pomper and Colleagues, *The Election of 1976,* (New York: David McKay, 1977), p. 62.

Religion.   There continue to be slight differences in preferences by religion. Catholics align themselves more with Democrats, while Protestants are more likely to prefer the Republican party. But these distinctions do not rival the potent force religion was in the 1960 election. John Kennedy was the first Catholic to be elected president. He won 78 percent of the Catholic vote and 38 percent of the Protestant vote. Since that time, however, the effect of religion has moderated a great deal.

Age and Sex.   There do not appear to be any significant differences among men and women in voting patterns. Women voted Republican slightly more than men in the 1950s, but in 1964 and 1968 that was reversed. In 1976, men were slightly more supportive of Carter and women more inclined to Gerald Ford, but the differences cannot be counted as significant.

Age, on the other hand, shows evidence of differences. Young voters find the Democratic party more attractive than the GOP, to the extent that they favor either party. Voters 49 and older show a tendency toward the Republicans, although again we must note that the differences have moderated. Ladd's study concluded that when socioeconomic status is controlled for, voting patterns for persons under 30 show an increasing tendency for the high-status person to vote Democratic, and a lessening tendency for persons under 30 of lower socioeconomic status to vote Democratic.

PSYCHOLOGICAL FACTORS

The chief difficulty with the sociological approach is that the group classifications are associated with voting patterns without attempting to weigh the reasons why people voted as they did. Voting studies conducted during the 1950s attempted to assess why voting patterns were as they were. Angus Campbell, Phillip Converse, Warren Miller, and Donald Stokes, all of the University of Michigan, undertook an examination of voting behavior using the psychological approach. Their *The American Voter* is a landmark study of how citizens perceive politics and act on those perceptions.

The study identified four factors that influence individual political behavior: party identification, group association, issues, and candidate personality. Campbell and his colleagues found that the single most important long-range factor for electoral behavior was party identification. More than anything else, it was partisan attachment that determined how the citizen viewed politics and voted: "We have noted many times that most Americans have an enduring partisan orientation, a sense of party identification, which has wide effects on their attitudes toward the things that are visible in the political world."[9]

9. Campbell, Converse, Miller, and Stokes, *The American Voter*, p. 273.

Party Identification.   *The American Voter* found party identification the single most important determinant of electoral behavior. The coalition fashioned out of the New Deal was a Democratic majority made up of union members, minorities, the disadvantaged, low socioeconomic status persons with lower education and income levels, and manual workers. This pattern prevailed through the 1950s and on into the 1960s. True, there were deviations, as the Eisenhower elections in 1952 and 1956 attested, but Democrats were a two-to-one majority over Republicans. Voting patterns were stable and predictable.

Since 1964, however, party identification has declined as the dominant influence on voting behavior. Party weakness has produced partisan defection. Ticket splitting has reduced partisan support. Issue voting has emerged as a new and powerful determinant of voting behavior (Figure 9.1).

Issues.   Ever since the mid-1960s, issue concern and issue voting have been rising. Conventional wisdom was that the American public conceptualized political issues only dimly, and then with no ideological consistency. That is, the American public understood liberal and conservative policies only in the most

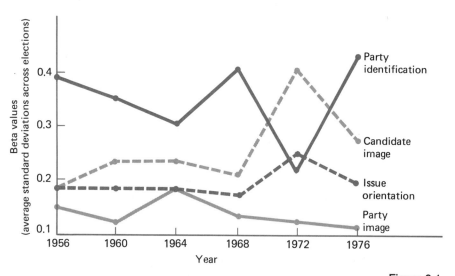

Figure 9.1

Factors influencing presidential voting. (Hill and Luttbeg, Trends in American Electoral Behavior. Itasca, Ill.: F.E. Peacock Publishers, 1980, p. 50. Eugene DeClercq, Thomas L. Hurley, and Norman R. Lutbeg, "Voting in American Presidential Elections," *American Politics Quarterly,* Vol. 3, No. 3, July 1975. Analysis updated through 1976 by Thomas L. Hurley, Department of Political Science, University of Alabama. Data from SRC/CPS Election Studies)

general sense, and people were not consistently liberal or conservative in their positions.

A change began to occur in the early 1960s. Norman Nie discovered that in five areas—social welfare, welfare for blacks, the size of the federal government, school integration, and the cold war—consistent liberal–conservative attitudes were to be found among the general electorate. Issues have become increasingly important to citizens, and they are developing specific positions that are consistent over issues. States Nie: "We argue that the political events of the last decade, and the crisis atmosphere which had attended them, have caused citizens to perceive politics as increasingly central to their lives."[10]

As issues become more important, as voters take clearer and more consistent ideological positions on issues, voting behavior and political campaigns should reflect these changes. And indeed they do. Studies of the 1972 election found that the electorate was polarizing over issues, largely precipitated by the Vietnam war.[11]

Results from the 1976 election indicated a similar if less dramatic pattern. Gerald Pomper stated: "The electorate divided clearly along lines of self-described ideology, three-fourths of the liberals casting ballots for Carter, and seven of ten conservatives choosing Ford."[12] The 1980 election may well signal a turn to the right as voters elected conservative Ronald Reagan and turned out of office several liberal senators and representatives. Those voting for Reagan were more likely to call themselves conservative, oppose increased government spending, and prefer less social welfare legislation. But the major factor for 1980 may well have been candidate personality. Thirty eight percent of Reagan's voters said, "It's time for a change"; Jimmy Carter's weak leadership, notably in controlling inflation, caused many initial defections to Ronald Reagan.

Candidate Personality.   With the decline in partisan loyalty and the rise of ticket splitting, candidate personality is emerging as a major theme in political campaigns.

Candidate personality has always been important. Eisenhower won in 1952 and 1956 largely because voter assessment of his ability to handle the job was stronger and caused defection by Democrats, who could not identify with Adlai Stevenson. But with the rapid changes in the past years and the rise of the media as potent forces in campaigning, personality has emerged in voters' minds as critical.

Admittedly, assessment of candidate personality is a crude measurement of

10. Norman Nie with Kristi Anderson, "Mass Beliefs Systems Revisited: Political Change and Attitude Structure," *Journal of Politics,* Vol. 36, No. 3 (August 1974), p. 571.
11. Arthur H. Miller and Warren Miller, Alden Raine and Thad Brown, "A Majority Party in Disarray: Policy Polarization in the 1972 Elections," *American Political Science Review,* Vol. 70, No. 3 (September 1976), p. 778.
12. Pomper and Colleagues, *The Election of 1976,* p. 74.

the emotional appeal of the candidate. We know that in 1960 Kennedy's youth had greater appeal than Richard Nixon's more "weathered" look. McGovern was perceived as "too radical" by many voters in 1972. And in the 1976 contest Gerald Ford had the reputation of being "clumsy and inept." Clearly voters are making assessments of the ability of candidates to perform the job of president, by whatever standards. And in 1980 personality appeared critical. Many called the election a referendum on President Carter's leadership.

Ticket splitting, voting for candidates of opposing parties, can be directly linked to candidate personality assessment. The ticket splitter is candidate oriented: "Because the ticket splitters are so candidate oriented, it is also necessary to measure in detail their perceptions of the candidate's ability to do the job, his ability to handle specific public problems, and his stand on important issues."[13]

Table 9.3

Partisanship and Opinion Profile of Groups, 1950s and 1970s

	1950s		1970s	
Group	Issues	Party	Issues	Party
Middle and upper status native white southerners	Quite a bit to the right	Strongly Democratic	Move further right	Move away from Democratic party, more Independent
Lower status native white southerners	Moderately right	Strongly Democratic	Move further right	Move away from Democratic party, more Independent
High status northern WASP	Moderately right	Strongly Republican	Move a bit left and splits	Less Republican, more Independent
Middle and lower status northern WASP	Center	Slightly Republican	Move a bit right	More Independent and more Democratic
Blacks	Strongly left	Strongly Democratic	Move even further left	Even more Democratic
Catholics	Moderately left	Strongly Democratic	Move to center	A bit more Independent
Jews	Strongly left	Strongly Democratic	Move further left	A bit more Independent
Border South	Moderately right	Strongly Democratic	Move a bit further right and split a bit	More Independent

SOURCE: Norman Nie, Sidney Verba and John Petrocik, *The Changing American Voter* (Cambridge, Mass: Harvard University Press, 1976).

13. Walter De Vries and V. Lance Tarrance, *The Ticket Splitter: A New Force in American Politics,* (Grand Rapids, Mich.: William B. Eerdmans, 1972), p. 115.

Issues and Party Identification.   The party preferences of groups have changed since the Eisenhower years as the issue concerns of these groups have grown and changed. Voters have become more issue oriented and less party oriented in determining how to vote. Norman Nie, Sidney Verba, and John Petrocik have made an extensive study of the changes in party identification and issue orientation of groups from the 1950s to the 1970s.[14] They found that as a result of the tumultuous events of the 1960s and early 1970s, issues became more relevant and directly of concern to the individual; discrepancies between what the parties professed and what they practiced became apparent. Party affiliation became less meaningful and declined as an explanation for political behavior. Groups stuggled to reconcile their party preferences with the increasing and changing attitude structure: "Groups that have become more liberal since the fifties should have become less Republican and more Democratic. Conversely, groups which have become more conservative should have become more Republican and less Democratic."[15] They note the decline of Democratic strength in the South and the region's movement toward conservatism. Northern Protestants are becoming more liberal and less Republican. Blacks have increased their liberalism and commitment to the Democratic party. For the other groups, attitude changes appear to have produced greater independence rather than partisan attachments.

REDEFINING POLITICAL BEHAVIOR

New groups, new issues, and the decline of partisanship have all produced vast changes in electoral behavior. The continuity of the American system of the 1950s has been broken. Civil rights, the Great Society, Vietnam, Watergate and political scandal, wage and price controls, economic instability, and taxpayer revolt have left profound marks on American citizens. New goups have entered the political process, cutting across the traditional patterns of party alliances. According to Walter Dean Burnham: "The American electorate is now deep into the most sweeping behavioral transformation since the Civil War. It is in the midst of a critical realignment of a kind radically different from others in American electoral history."[16]

FROM PARTY TO ISSUES

The substantial increase in issue concern and voting by the American electorate has not been gradual; it was a marked change that occurred in the late 1960s. Since 1964 presidential campaigns and elections have been characterized

14. Nie, Verba, and Petrocik, *The Changing American Voter,* pp. 267–269.
15. *Ibid.,* p. 267.
16. Walter Dean Burnham, "American Politics in the 1970s: Beyond Party?" in Louis Maisel and Paul M. Sacks, eds., *The Future of Political Parties,* Sage Electoral Studies Yearbook, Vol. 1 (Beverly Hills: Sage Publications, 1975), p. 238.

by ideological and activist participants. Richard Boyd summarizes the central role of issues today as including: (a) issue consistency in attitudes, (b) issue beliefs and partisan loyalties, and (c) issue beliefs and voting.[17]

In the past, surveys revealed an electorate that professed general but confusingly vague attitudes on public affairs. People could be classified ''liberal'' or ''conservative'' by their stands on issues, but there was no real consistency over a series of beliefs. Being liberal on civil rights did not necessarily produce a liberal opinion on foreign relations with Communist nations. People were just as likely to be conservative on one issue and liberal on another. Americans simply were not likely to respond to politics on the basis of issues.

In 1964, however, issues bgan to play a central role and since then the public has developed an issue consistency. Democrats have come to be perceived as ''liberals'' and Republicans as ''conservative'' by voters. An issue polarization has developed between the parties.[18] For the first time, 1964 was an ideological election which challenged the New Deal coalition. The traditional alignments were further decayed in 1972 with the infusion of political activists supporting George McGovern.

Gerald Pomper has documented these changes within the American electorate. Since 1968, on four important issues, the relationship between party identification and issues has crystallized: on all four issues—publicly financed medical care, school integration, federal employment guarantees, and federal aid to education—Democrats were decidedly more liberal than Republicans. On some issues, such as medical care and aid to education, the differences were striking. On others, they were less dramatic but still apparent.[19] The result is an electorate that is gravitating to political parties, or presidential candidates, because of issue stands. We see groups that are liberal over a series of issues—civil rights, welfare, school integration—moving to the Democratic party. Republicans are drawing support from conservative groups—Southerners, business—as a result of the Goldwater and Nixon strategies. Because of these changes, citizens are casting their ballots on the basis of issues and their assessment of a candidate's ability to handle the job.

TICKET SPLITTING

As a result of the decline in party identification and the increasing importance of issues, there has been a dramatic rise in ticket splitting. In recent elections, there has been an increase in split outcomes where the presidential candi-

17. Richard Boyd, ''Electoral Trends in Postwar Politics,'' in *Choosing the President,* edited by James David Barber.
18. Gerald Pomper, ''From Confusion to Clarity: Issues and American Voters, 1956–1968,'' *American Political Science Review,* Vol. 66 (June 1971).
19. *Ibid.,* pp. 418–419.

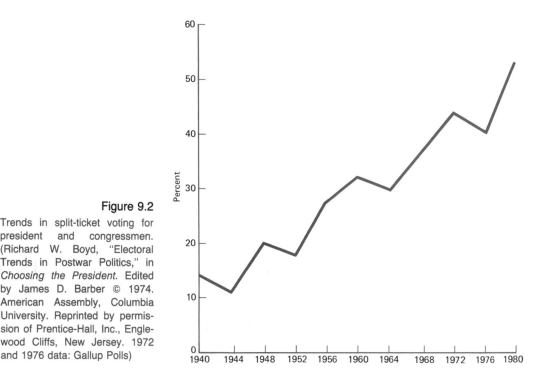

Figure 9.2

Trends in split-ticket voting for president and congressmen. (Richard W. Boyd, "Electoral Trends in Postwar Politics," in *Choosing the President.* Edited by James D. Barber © 1974. American Assembly, Columbia University. Reprinted by permission of Prentice-Hall, Inc., Englewood Cliffs, New Jersey. 1972 and 1976 data: Gallup Polls)

date of one party and the congressional candidate of another party carry the same congressional district (Figure 9.2). There has been a gradual but consistent trend since 1952 for an increased percentage of split outcomes (Figure 9.3). In 1972, the increase was dramatic; there was a 15 percent rise in the level of ticket splitting. We have reached a point where ticket splitting may be greater than straight party voting.

Walter DeVries and V. Lance Tarrance identify the ticket splitter as the new force in American politics. The traditional self-imposed labels of Democrat, Republican, or Independent do not explain how a person actually votes. And when DeVries and Tarrance looked at how people actually had voted, they concluded there was a wide discrepancy between self-perception and actual voting behavior. In 1968, 45 percent of the voters who had identified themselves as Republican split their ticket and voted for at least one Democratic candidate; 47 percent of self-professed Democrats did the same; and 25 percent of Independents reported voting a straight party ballot.[20] In short, it is the traditional party identifier who is exercising independence and voting for the candidates he or she feels are most qualified.

20. DeVries and Tarrance, *The Ticket Splitter,* p. 51.

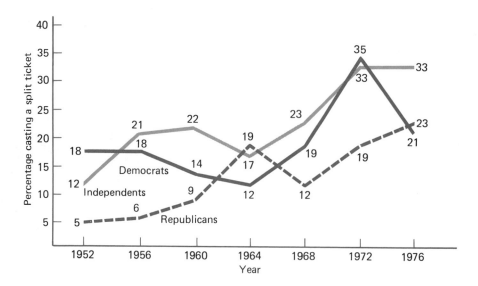

Figure 9.3

Trends in split-ticket voting by party. (H. Asher, *Presidential Elections and American Politics,* Homewood, Ill.: Dorsey Press, 1980, p. 78. SRC/CPS studies of 1952, 1956, 1960, 1968, 1972, and 1976)

Equally as important is that ticket splitters do not rely on political parties and group affiliations in deciding how to cast their ballots. Say DeVries and Tarrance:

> Many voters—principally the ticket splitters, who make up a sizeable portion of the undecided voters in elections—draw their attitudes about candidates and their positions on issues from the media (principally television) and interpersonal relationships (family and friends).
>
> Ticket splitters do not rely on political parties or their affiliations— they rely on the news media for their information about politics and government.[21]

The ticket splitter is more issue oriented. Much of that orientation comes from the ticket splitter's use of the media, especially television. As a result, the ticket splitter does not identify strongly with either political party. And with the voter under 30, who professes a strong propensity to reject partisan labels, we can expect further splitting of ballots between candidates of both parties and a further erosion of political parties.

21. *Ibid.,* p. 115.

VOTER DISAFFECTION

The final emerging theme of voting behavior is one that is well documented
—the growing cynicism and mistrust of government within the American electorate.[22] Voters have become disaffected with the political system; they feel they
have decreasing power and influence over the decision makers they elect to public
office; they feel that politics has become a selfish, corrupt occupation for politicians who look out for themselves. This is understandable in a post-Watergate
environment, but the feelings go much deeper than just Watergate.

The American public is feeling more helpless in influencing the policies of
the federal government. There is a growing sense of powerlessness. Using a "political efficacy" scale to measure the public's feeling about its effectiveness in
influencing the federal government, we can see the rise of a feeling of powerlessness (see Figure 9.4). In response to three items designed to evoke responses of
efficacy, we can see the general decline in efficacy on all three measures.

Throughout the 1950s there was an increase in a sense of effectiveness on
the part of citizens. In response to the events of the 1960s and 1970s, however,
a sense of powerlessness grew: 1976 represented a new low. This sense of powerlessness increased, it must be remembered, in the face of the trend toward a

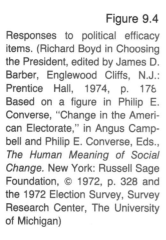

Figure 9.4

Responses to political efficacy
items. (Richard Boyd in Choosing
the President, edited by James D.
Barber, Englewood Cliffs, N.J.:
Prentice Hall, 1974, p. 176
Based on a figure in Philip E.
Converse, "Change in the Ameri-
can Electorate," in Angus Camp-
bell and Philip E. Converse, Eds.,
The Human Meaning of Social
Change. New York: Russell Sage
Foundation, © 1972, p. 328 and
the 1972 Election Survey, Survey
Research Center, The University
of Michigan)

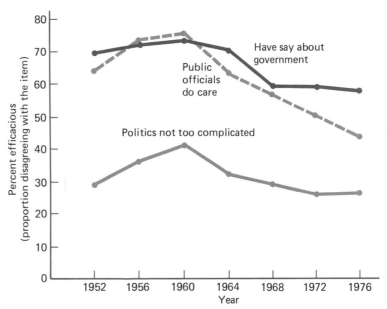

22. See Richard Boyd, "Electoral Trends in Postwar Politics," for an excellent summary treatment of
the trends of voter disaffection.

more educated and informed electorate. One would expect education and information to produce a more skilled and knowledgeable electorate that feels increasingly able to manage or influence political affairs. Yet the trend goes in just the opposite direction.

The rising sense of powerlessness is closely associated with the growing cynicism and mistrust voters have of the political system. This mistrust is not new: There has been a general growth of cynicism and mistrust predating Watergate and beginning in the early 1960s (see Figure 9.5). The rise continued through 1976 due, in part, to the Watergate revelations and the political scandals. This most likely explains the more dramatic jump to 65 percent in the question of trusting government. The equally dramatic rise on the wasting taxes question may be part of the broader issue of economic instability and rising inflation. The American voter is questioning the political process, the integrity of public officials, and their concern for the public interest.

As a result, Americans find politics less and less attractive. As seen in Figure 9.6, turnout at elections has been steadily declining. Every presidential contest since 1960 has attracted fewer voters. The same is true for congressional elections to the House of Representatives. Studies of nonvoters reveal that many

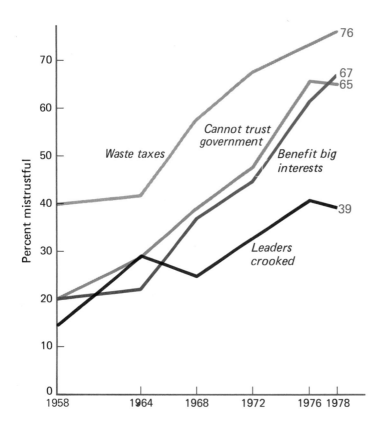

Figure 9.5

Trends in responses to items of trust. (David Hill and Norman Luttbeg, Trends in American Electoral Behavior, Itasca, Ill.: F.E. Peacock, 1980, pp. 114–115. Everett Ladd, "The New Divisions in U.S. Politics," *Fortune,* March 26, 1979)

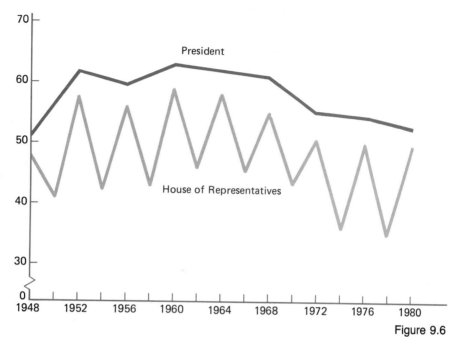

Figure 9.6

Turnout of voters in elections for President and House of Representatives. (Bureau of the Census, Statistical Abstracts, 1962 and 1979)

are "dropouts," persons who voted previously but now find no candidates worth voting for. Lack of political leadership was cited as a primary reason for no voting. The nonvoter frequently gave such cynical responses as "no candidate worth voting for" or "it doesn't make any difference" as an explanation for not voting. This can be all the more alarming as one notes that the turnout rate for young voters is the lowest of all political groupings. We are apparently producing a generation of citizens uncommitted to politics and very skeptical as to its accomplishments.

VOTING PATTERNS

Democratic politics is predicated on the individual citizen exercising the right of decision making in the voting booth. Yet elections are the collective judgment of a people. We have noted the changing expectations of voters as they approach elections and political candidates. The basis for American politcal behavior has changed. And while both political parties can depend on a certain level of public support, the traditional patterns have decayed and eroded. A new independence is dominating voting behavior.

So far we have been reviewing the motivations for electoral behavior. How does this changing pattern of behavior distribute itself on a national level? Even with the changes in individual motivation, we can discern voting patterns that help us to understand a little more clearly how America votes and why citizens vote as they do.

COMPETITIVENESS

One of the more remarkable patterns has been the increase in landslide presidential elections. For national politics, the presidency is the focal point of elections, the office most sought by both parties.

In recent elections, we have vacillated from very close elections to one-sided, landslide victories. The 1960, 1968, and 1976 electoral contests were all very close; the winning presidential candidate had a popular margin of less than 2 percent. By contrast, 1964, 1972, and 1980 were landslide victories: Lyndon Johnson and Richard Nixon each polled over 60 percent of the popular vote. Reagan's 10 percent margin was equally one sided in an election most people said was too close to call.

These results testify to the decline of long-term party loyalties and the emergence of the new politics, in which political activists, issues, and personalities dominate elections. Throughout the 1930s, 1940s, and 1950s, the pattern of competitiveness could be predicted, based on traditional patterns of loyalty; but no more. The old loyalties are dissolving. Landslides and competitiveness alternate, based on short-term factors such as issues and candidate personalities. The media accentuates these factors. The result is that we have nationalized the presidential election, divorcing it from traditional attachments and loyalties. Voters form their impressions and receive their information from the media. This lays the electorate

Table 9.4
Presidential Popular Vote Since 1932

	Democrat	Republican	Other
1932 FDR	57.4%	39.6%	3.0%
1936 FDR	60.8	36.5	2.7
1940 FDR	54.7	44.8	0.5
1944 FDR	53.4	45.9	0.7
1948 Truman	49.5	45.1	5.4
1952 Eisenhower	44.4	55.1	0.5
1956 Eisenhower	42.0	57.4	0.6
1960 Kennedy	49.7	49.5	0.7
1964 Johnson	61.0	38.5	0.4
1968 Nixon	42.7	43.4	13.9
1972 Nixon	37.5	60.7	1.8
1976 Carter	51.0	48.9	0.1
1980 Reagan	41.2	51.0	7.8

SOURCE: Bureau of the Census: Statistical Abstract, 1978.

open to changes and swings on a uniform basis across the nation. Typically, today the presidential ballot is a split ticket with the congressional and state electoral contests.

For congressional contests, the pattern is not altogether different. Table 9.5 shows the pattern of electoral competition for congressional seats from 1966 to 1980. The pattern of noncompetitiveness in the House for four out of five seats has remained fairly stable throughout the whole period. There is greater competition in the Senate, but even here less than half the seats are contested. Most of the uncontested and noncompetitive elections are won by incumbents.

INCUMBENCY

One of the most remarkable patterns in voting behavior is the success of incumbent politicians in being reelected. The American political tradition has a long history of "throwing out the rascals." Yet, either we have no rascals, which current levels of distrust and cynicism would not indicate, or we continue to reelect our politicians for other reasons.

Traditionally, the safest incumbent is the president. Until 1976, when Gerald Ford lost to Jimmy Carter, an incumbent president had not been defeated for reelection since 1932. Since the Civil War, only three incumbent presidents had lost reelection bids until Ford's defeat in 1976. But all that seems to be increasingly changing. While not an elected incumbent, Ford lost to Carter in 1976; Carter in turn, lost to Reagan. Single-term presidents may well become a norm. Since Eisenhower we have not had a president complete a second term in office (though not always due to electoral defeat). Johnson choose not to run for a second term, Ford was defeated in 1976, and Carter was decisively turned back in his 1980 reelection bid.

At the congressional level, Table 9.6 depicts the success of incumbents in winning reelections. In the Senate the numbers are smaller and so is the success ratio, yet two-thirds of incumbent senators win reelection bids.

There are several explanations for the success of incumbents. Because congressional races are less visible and less publicized, the information and visibility advantage rests with the person in office. Incumbents can generally use their office to attract media attention and use the aura of the office to advance their candidacy. The incumbent generally attracts greater sources of funds. This gives the incumbent candidate greater opportunity for exposure. In the absense of any information, notably any negative information, voters appear to go with the trusted, recognized name over the uncertainty and anonymity of a challenger. Ticket splitting is largely done to vote for incumbents. Still others stress that, at the congressional and state levels, party loyalties and alliances are stronger, that the changes in political behavior affect the national contest for the presidency more. Although we have had 16 years of Republican administrations since 1952, there was a Republican majority in Congress for only two years, starting in 1952.

Table 9.5
Electoral Competition for Congressional Seats

	House (%)								Senate (%)							
	1966	1968	1970	1972	1974	1976	1978	1980	1966	1968	1970	1972	1974	1976	1978	1980
Marginal seats (Won with 50% to 55% of the vote)	17	16.6	12.5	14.9	22.2	18.7	17.9	16.8	29.4	48.5	42.4	47.1	39.9	33.3	35.3	56
Safe seats (Won with over 55% of the vote)	72.2	73.3	76.3	75.2	67.4	74.4	71	75	61.8	45.4	57.5	52.9	57.1	60.6	61.8	41
Uncontested	10.8	10.1	11.2	9.9	10.3	6.9	11	8	8.8	6.1	0	0	3	6	3	3

SOURCE: Data compiled from returns reported in *Congressional Quarterly*, 1966-1978.

Table 9-6.
Success of Incumbents Seeking Reelection, 1946-1978

	Senate					House			
Year	Seeking Re-Election	Defeated Pri-mary	Gen-eral	Percent Re-elected	Year	Seeking Re-Election	Defeated Pri-mary	Gen-eral	Percent Re-elected
1946	30	6	7	56.7	1946	398	18	52	82.4
1948	25	2	8	60.0	1948	400	15	68	79.2
1950	32	5	5	68.8	1950	400	6	32	90.5
1952	31	2	9	64.5	1952	389	9	26	91.0
1954	32	2	6	75.0	1954	407	6	22	93.1
1956	29	0	4	86.2	1956	411	6	16	94.6
1958	28	0	10	64.3	1958	396	3	37	89.9
1960	29	0	1	96.6	1960	405	5	25	92.6
1962	35	1	5	82.9	1962	402	12	22	91.5
1964	33	1	4	84.8	1964	397	8	45	86.6
1966	32	3	1	87.5	1966	411	8	41	88.1
1968	28	4	4	71.4	1968	409	4	9	96.8
1970	31	1	6	77.4	1970	401	10	12	94.5
1972	27	2	5	74.1	1972	390	12	13	93.6
1974	27	2	2	85.2	1974	391	8	40	87.7
1976	25	0	9	64.0	1976	384	3	13	95.8
1978	25	3	7	60.0	1978	382	5	19	93.7
1980	29	4	9	55.2	1980	398	6	31	90.7

NOTE: Number seeking reelection is the total number of seats up for election less those where the incumbent was retiring or running for office or where a vacancy existed.

In fact, while Nixon was winning by a landslide in 1972, there was only minimal change in the seats held by the Democrats in Congress. It seems safe to say that the staying power of members of Congress has insulated congressional elections from the presidential contest. We are likely to continue to see minority presidents or even a majority president facing an unsympathetic Congress. President Carter appears to be a case in point.

THE COATTAIL EFFECT

One of the important consequences of the success of incumbents is the decline of the coattail effect in presidential elections, which historically have connected congressional elections to the presidential contest.

A **coattail effect** is the pulling power of a presidential candidate to attract voters so that congressional candidates of the same political party are elected to office. The pattern is simple and consistent. In a presidential-election year there is a net gain in congressional seats for winning presidential party candidates. In off-year elections, congressional candidates of the president's party lose seats to the opposition party. The historical pattern is impressive. Only four times in this century did a presidential candidate fail to add to the congressional seats for his party in Congress. Only once did an off-year election not produce a drop in the number of seats for the president's party.

The regularity of this pattern has been explained by noting the different composition of the electorate at off-year and presidential elections. Angus Campbell suggests that in presidential years, the issues, personalities, and attention to the presidential contest produce a larger turnout by adding peripheral voters who come out only because of the presidential election.[23] These peripheral voters do not normally vote in off-year elections. The short-term factors that brought them to the polls means they are likely to have voted for the winning presidential candidate. The **core voters,** by contrast, vote in presidential and off-years alike. They are the solid partisan loyalists. Peripheral voters are less likely to have a long-standing attachment to a party, but because enough of them vote a straight ticket, the result produces the net gain in congressional seats for the president's party. Then in off-year contests, the core voters are less swayed by short-term factors, and so presidential party candidates cannot count on the added support of peripheral voters.

Table 9.7 reveals that the coattail pattern is diminishing. As issues intruded into elections in the 1960s and 1970s, congressional elections were increasingly insulated from presidential elections. The distinction, based on party identification, of core and peripheral voters is less relevant. The success of incumbent congressional candidates makes their reelection less dependent on presidential election success.

Fewer and fewer seats are being gained by the president; fewer and fewer seats are being lost in the off-year elections. The 1976 change was nearly nonexistent. In fact, in only one state did Carter's popular vote exceed that of the party's senatorial candidate. Stated Charles Jacob: "The clear verdict of 1976 was that widespread voter discrimination by ticket splitting left little room for presidential coattails as a variable to explain the results of Congressional elections."[24] For 1980 coattails reappeared, though some dispute whether Reagan "pulled" congressional candidates or whether a mood of change overwhelmed the electorate. In any case 1980 was a clear victory for Republican candidates in general and the Senate in particular.

SECTIONALISM

America has had a historical pattern of sectional voting. The South was long counted in the Democratic column as the "Solid South." It produced only Democratic congressmen, governors, and state legislatures from the post-Civil War years through the 1960s. Republican strength was in America's heartland and in New England: in the Great Plains, and Maine and Vermont, Republican

23. Angus Campbell, "Surge and Decline: A Study of Electoral Change," in Angus Campbell, *Elections and the Political Order* (New York: John Wiley, 1966).
24. Charles E. Jacob, "The Congressional Elections and Outlook," in Pomper, *The Election of 1976,* p. 92.

Table 9.7

Coattail Effect in Elections, Net Gain or Loss of Congressional Seats for the President's Party

	House		Senate	
	Democrats	Republicans	Democrats	Republicans
	(Number of Seats)		(Number of Seats)	
1950	−29	+28	−5	+5
1952	−23	+22	−2	+1
1954	+21	−18	+1	−1
1956	+1	−3	+1	0
1958	+50	−47	+15	−13
1960	−20	+19	+1	+2
1962	−5	+2	+2	−2
1964	+37	−37	+1	−1
1966	−48	+47	−4	+4
1968	−3	+5	−7	+7
1970	+11	−12	−3	+2
1972	−12	+12	+2	−2
1974	+42	−42	+4	−5
1976	+2	−2	+1	0
1978	−12	−12	−3	+3
1980	−34	+33	−12	+12

SOURCE: Data compiled from election returns reported in *Congressional Quarterly.*

strength could be counted on. Since the New Deal, the Plains states (North Dakota, South Dakota, Nebraska, and Kansas) went Democratic only once, in 1964 for Lyndon Johnson; Maine and Vermont voted Democratic in 1964, Maine in 1968 (Figure 9.7).

Now these patterns are changing. The South voted for Goldwater in 1964, George Wallace in 1968, and Richard Nixon in 1972. Republican senators and governors are also making their appearance in some southern states. The South today is the base for the emerging American conservativism. Rather than support Democrats, southerners are looking for conservative candidates. Nixon made that part of his southern strategy in 1972, though Carter was able to capture the South in 1976. There is much discussion of "Sun Belt politics," the politics of the area from Florida across the Southwest and on into southern California. This area is seen as the new base for conservatives. Reagan made impressive gains in the south in 1980. While the Sun Belt was Carter's stronghold in 1976, he was only able to hold his home state of Georgia in the 1980 election. Otherwise the entire Sun Belt went for Ronald Reagan.

The election of 1976 produced an East–West regional split. Gerald Ford carried every state west of the Mississippi except Texas. Jimmy Carter, on the other hand, showed his strength in the South and the industrial Northeast. Carter succeeded in splitting the Sun Belt, piecing together enough of the old Democratic coalition to seek out a victory. The election was truly a national one, however; the close popular vote margin was consistently true for almost every state.

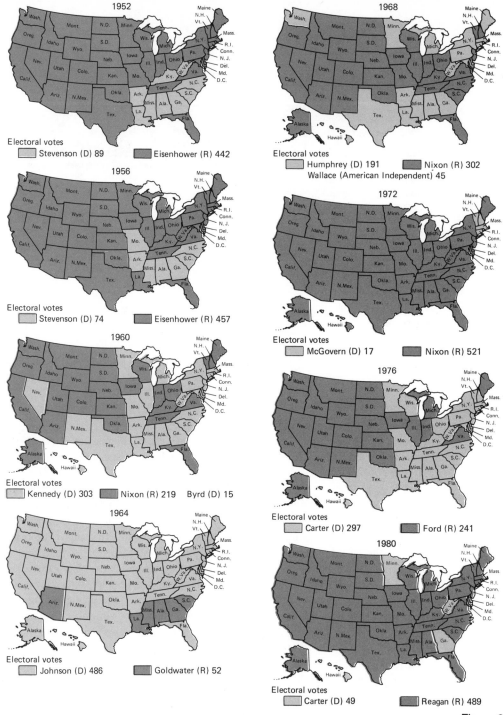

1952

Electoral votes
Stevenson (D) 89   Eisenhower (R) 442

1956

Electoral votes
Stevenson (D) 74   Eisenhower (R) 457

1960

Electoral votes
Kennedy (D) 303   Nixon (R) 219   Byrd (D) 15

1964

Electoral votes
Johnson (D) 486   Goldwater (R) 52

1968

Electoral votes
Humphrey (D) 191   Nixon (R) 302
Wallace (American Independent) 45

1972

Electoral votes
McGovern (D) 17   Nixon (R) 521

1976

Electoral votes
Carter (D) 297   Ford (R) 241

1980

Electoral votes
Carter (D) 49   Reagan (R) 489

Figure 9.7

Presidential election results by states for 1952 to 1976. Notes: 1968—a North Carolina Republican elector cast his vote for George Wallace, making the official count Nixon, 301; Humphrey, 191; Wallace, 46. 1972—A Virginia Republican elector cast his vote for Libertarian candidate John Hospers, making the official count Nixon, 520; McGovern, 17, Hospers, 1. 1976—Republican elector from the state of Washington cast his vote for Reagan, making the official count Carter, 297; Ford, 240; Reagan, 1.

In only 20 states were the two candidates more than 10 percentage points apart.[25] The 1980 election broke the sectional pattern in that Reagan carried almost every state. Yet the South gave Carter his strongest support. In only two southern states did Carter lose by more than 10 percent, he carried Georgia, and lost six southern states by less than two percentage points. Reagan's support was greatest in the West and Midwest. His victory was greater than the national average (Reagan—51 percent; Carter—41 percent) in every state west of the Mississippi except Oregon. In all he carried 27 states with more than a 10 percent difference. Only in the Great Lake states and industrial east was the race less than one-sided.

THE ELECTORAL SYSTEM

Political parties and popular elections are the cornerstones of American democracy. The act of choosing between competing candidates vying for public office is the most basic of political freedoms. And when the voter stands alone in the voting booth, exercising the untrammeled right of free choice, it represents the culmination of a process that is at the heart of democracy. The Constitution, federal and state laws, and political traditions are all at work to ensure an electoral process that gives the American citizen that right. The electoral system is more than ballots and totals, however; it includes nominations and campaigns as well as electoral institutions. And the electoral process has been changing.

We can view the electoral system as three stages, though in fact they are not really so separated. **Nominations** provide for the selection of candidates for public office, the narrowing down of would-be contestants to those who actually are candidates for public office. **Campaigns** provide the most interest and add the most cost to elections. Here candidates seek to get voters to vote for them or would-be candidates campaign for delegates in order to receive a nomination. The **electoral system** is the process of conducting elections, the laws regarding voter registration, balloting, and tallying results.

NOMINATIONS

Basically political parties nominate candidates for public office, although even in nonpartisan elections there must be a process to narrow down the number of contestants. The parties as well as the public require a means of deciding who will run for public office. This is the process of nominations.

The United States Constitution says nothing about nominations; state laws govern this process. The tradition of political parties nominating candidates quickly filled the void. The technique of letting a party caucus nominate candidates gave way in the twentieth century, however, to the more democratic process of letting the voters decide party nominations through the direct primary.

In this country, where we elect a great many public officials, the control of nominations is a considerable power. In several areas where there is no real party

25. Pomper, *Ibid.*, p. 60.

competition, securing the nomination is tantamount to election. Even where real party compeition does exist, selecting the right candidate is important because the choice is primarily between two candidates. Third-party candidates may have an easy time being nominated for office, but rarely are they a potent force in the general election

As a direct result of political reform early in the twentieth century, the voters select party nominees themselves by direct primary. Today every state in the country utilizes the direct primary. The state assumes the burden and cost of conducting these primary elections.

The primary has worked to make the candidate selection process more fair and democratic; but it has also eroded political parties, because they have lost control of nominations. Almost any person who files a petition with the minimum

Jimmy Carter and Walter Mondale receive the endorsement of the Democratic party. (Stan Wakefield)

number of signatures with the secretary of state can be placed on the primary ballot. Neither would-be candidate nor signers of petitions need be party loyalists. Any qualified voter may vote in the primary. While there may be some restrictions on which party contest the voter can vote on, the election is open to all eligible voters.

There are several kinds of direct primary elections. The most common is the **closed primary,** in which voters must make a prior declaration of party affiliation in order to vote in that party's primary. This keeps the primary closed to party loyalists and gives a truer indication of party sentiment. Yet because party loyalties are not strong anyway, the closed primary does not actually exclude people. In an **open primary,** any qualified voter may participate simply by showing up at the polls. No statement of party support is required, the voter is merely asked to choose one party ballot or the other. This allows the voter to "cross over" and vote in the other party's race. If one party has no real contest, voters may be attracted to the other party's contest and vote in it. This primary maximizes freedom of choice, but is not necessarily a true expression of partisan or public support. Two states, Washington and Alaska, now use a **blanket primary,** in which the voter is given both party ballots and can vote back and forth between the parties in choosing nominees for public office. This type of ballot is the most democratic of all, but it further weakens party support, and gives the party little indication of what will happen in the general election.

NOMINATING THE PRESIDENT

Presidential candidates are nominated by party conventions. It is the one occasion for a national political party. Nominally at least, it is the party that controls the nomination for the presidency. Recent reforms in the delegate selection process, however, have weakened party control of the nomination. Candidates now begin to campaign as much as two to three years before the convention to get state delegates by working in state elections, attending fund-raising affairs, and consulting with local party officials. Figure 9.8 shows different paths to the presidential nomination.

The convention process itself is relatively simple: A candidate must receive a majority of delegate votes at the convention in order to secure the nomination. If no candidate receives a majority on the first ballot, the delegates continue to ballot until a majority is achieved for one candidate. Since 1952, however, no party convention has taken more than one ballot to produce a candidate. The delegates come to the convention pledged or with some level of commitment to a candidate.

Each party apportions its delegates differently. The Democrats had 3,331 delegates in 1980. A state's delegates are determined on the basis of population and popular votes cast for Democratic presidential candidates, so the large, populous states have the advantage. The Republicans used 2,259 delegates for 1976. That number resulted from awarding delegates to states that voted Republican in

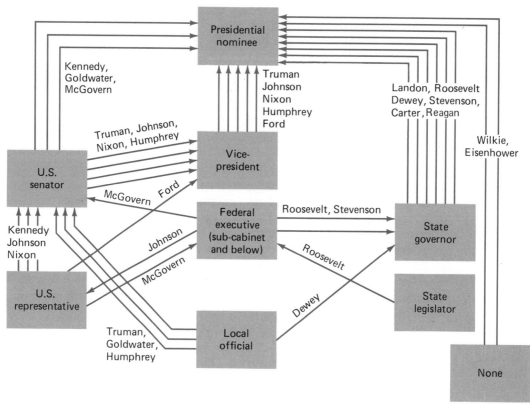

Figure 9.8

Different paths to the presidential nomination. (David R. Matthews, "Presidential
Nominations," in *Choosing the President.* Edited by James D. Barber, © 1974.
American Assembly, Columbia University. Reprinted by permission of Prentice
Hall, Inc. Englewood Cliffs, N.J.)

the previous presidential election and also elected Republican senators, House
members, and governors. This system tends to favor the small states, which have
been the stronghold of Republican strength in the past several years. For 1980 the
Republican's convention delegate count stood at 1,993, with the South losing
delegates due to Carter's victory there and also in four large states: New York,
Texas, Ohio, and Pennsylvania.[26]

Delegate selection processes differ with each state and party. Several delegates are automatically seated, or selected by the party leadership, such as the
congressional delegates, the governor, and state party chairpeople. The Democrats
have proposed abolishing automatic seating. Indeed, the proportions of senators,
House members, and governors as delegates has declined. From 1968 to 1976 the
percentage of senators as delegates declined from 68 to 18 percent, that of House

26. Congressional Quarterly, *Weekly Report* (July 9, 1977), p. 1427.

DUNAGIN'S PEOPLE

3-4

"IF WE DON'T START HAVING SOME LOSERS IN THE PRIMARIES, WE'RE GOING TO WIND UP WITH TOO MANY PRESIDENTS."

Dunagin's People by Ralph Dunagin © 1980 Field Enterprises, Inc. Courtesy of Field Newspaper Syndicate.

members from 39 to 15 percent, and that of governors from 83 to 47 percent.[27] These same figures were generally reflected in the 1980 convention where only 8 of 59 Democratic Senators were delegates to the convention. State conventions may also select delegates. The state convention forms caucuses supporting candidates and chooses delegates for the national convention through majoritarian elections or a proportional distribution. Today the most prevalent method of selecting convention delegates is the presidential primary. Here states may combine the presidential preference test with the delegate selection process.

The number of states using the presidential primary has risen. In 1968 16 states had such a primary; by 1972, 23 states had adopted it; and in 1976 there were 30 states with primaries. In 1980, 33 states held presidential primaries. The use of the primary has facilitated the change from control of nominations by party leaders to direct participation by the electorate. The proportion of convention delegates selected in primaries has now risen to 75 percent of all delegates.

Primary election of convention delegates operates differently in the various states. In some states, voters choose convention delegates directly from among contending slates of delegates. These delegates may or may not be committed to

27. Congressional Quarterly, *Weekly Report,* June 3, 1978, p. 1395.

a candidate, depending on state law. The other basic variation is for the presidential preference primary to bind convention delegates selected by some other means. These two processes are combined in varying fashions:

1. **Presidential preference only.** Delegates are selected by party caucuses, and the presidential preference vote may or may not be binding on the delegates. If the election is binding, the Democratic party requires delegates to be appointed according to a proportional representation formula.
2. **Presidential preference and delegate selection.** One vote for a presidential candidate also elects delegates pledged to or supportive of the presidential candidate. Parties may run unpledged slates of delegates.
3. **Presidential preference and separate election of convention delegates.** Here the voter votes once for a presidential candidate and once for convention delegates. The selected delegates may be bound to the winner according to state law. Some states have an advisory preference vote, with delegates listed as pledged or favoring a candidate. Some states use the mandatory preference, in which case the delegates are required to support that presidential primary winner. Again, proportional representation can be used to apportion delegates if mandatory preference is used.
4. **Delegate selection primary.** Under this format, the voter casts a ballot directly for convention delegates from contending slates. No presidential candidates appear on the ballot, although it is no secret which candidates the various contending slates of delegates prefer.

CAMPAIGNS

With the decline of political parties, the process of conducting campaigns has changed. The nomination of a President has been nationalized, and the new nominating process has changed the approach to and conduct of campaigns. The presidential campaign is now a national campaign.

Political parties as a campaign resource are being replaced by candidate organizations. Since the presidential candidate needed to put together a personal organization to work the states for convention delegates, the same approach is now used for the general election campaign. Candidate organizations are markedly different from the state-oriented groups that dominated the traditional parties. The change began in 1968, when hundreds of out-of-staters converged on New Hampshire and other primary states to work for Eugene McCarthy's challenge to Lyndon Johnson's nomination. They canvassed, knocked on doors, passed out literature, and rasied funds apart from, and often in spite of, the state party organization. In 1972, President Nixon placed all responsibility and resources for his reelection in a Committee to Re-elect the President, thereby bypassing the Republican party altogether. By 1976, the Reagan supporters had become a distinct faction of the GOP party. Carter's support came from campaigners moving from state to state to drum up support for Jimmy Carter. That this approach is so common today, and draws so little criticism, is quiet testimony to the nationalization of presidential campaigns and the erosion of political parties.

As the campaign for the presidency has become nationalized, it has also become subject to new conditions: (1) the national media have become the principal means of campaigning; (2) the cost of campaigning has skyrocketed and requires organizations to seek out sources of funding; and (3) campaign organizations are specialized, professionally staffed organs that plan and execute strategy and tactics with the scientific precision of a modern army.

The Media.   The standing of candidates today is determined not by party support or leadership commitment, but by a handful of reporters and commentators who follow the presidential campaign. The judgment of the media can make or break a candidate. These commentators are well-recognized persons in the field, work for the largest and most prestigious communication firms, and have the trust and confidence of the American public. Candidates direct their campaigns to winning over the press, to getting widespread and favorable attention in the public media.

Since most voters now obtain their political information from the media, concern for one's press is vital. Various tactics can be used to win over the press. With the increased concern for issues, a candidate may stress vital issues, as McGovern did in 1972 with Vietnam. Or a candidate, like Carter in 1976, may seek to take advantage of a public mood—restoring trust and confidence in government, for example. Issue orientation and personality projected have tremendous influence on the voting decisions of the American electorate. The media, not the party, make for campaign success.

Note, for example, the impact of the media in presidential debates. In 1960 John Kennedy successfully projected an image of youthful vigor and ability, while Richard Nixon appeared tired and sullen. Kennedy's phrase ''to get the

Carter and Ford participating in one of their three presidential debates during 1976. (United Press International)

Public Policy and Professional Campaign Managers

Most students of public policy find only an indirect influence on public policy by citizen participation at the polls. Yet democratic public policy requires that citizens select top policy makers. Many feel the importance of elections is not the selection of policy but the choice of policy makers who in turn formulate policy in line with broad programmatic promises made in the campaign (platforms). There is evidence that voters have shaped the direction of public policy by the selection of one party and its platform over another, that critical partisan realignments have resulted in altered national policies, and that voter alignments are organized around substantive issues of policy. "Partisan alignments form the constituent basis for governments committed to the translation of the choices made by the electorate during critical periods into public policy over a relatively long period of time."[1]

A significant policy question to emerge in recent elections, however, is the breakdown of political parties and the management of election by the employment of professional campaign consultants. With the decline of political parties and a rise in the voter's mood of cynicism, political candidates are turning more and more to professional election consultants to manage their campaigns. In such an atmosphere of mechanical, advertised, and impersonal elections, can the electorate's policy role be realistic?

Very few voters understand the involvement and growing importance of professional consultants. These are paid professionals who plan and manage a candidate's campaign. They specialize in almost every facet of an election. Here are just some of the activities for which a candidate can get help.

Overall organization
campaign strategy
campaign management
staff training
counseling
research
fund raising
election day organization
press relations
precinct organization

Specific campaign techniques
polling
electronic media
advertising
mail solicitations
films
voter turnout
graphics
data processing
print media
media time buying

Issues
bonds
women's issues
referendums

Today there are over 200 full-time professional campaign consultants.[2] Theirs is a highly complex and technical business, utilizing the technologies of the computer and electronic media. More often than not the campaign consultants have backgrounds in industries such as media production, advertising, data processing, and polling. They apply their skills and emergent technology to the field of elections.

What are the greater implications of professional campaign consultants? Three implications seem possible, if not evident. The first is for continued antipartyism. The use of consultants is the result of the antiparty feeling in American politics. Personal campaigning and personal campaign organizations feed on this antiparty sentiment and cause it to grow. They place the voter directly before the candidate

and his or her array of consultants. Both become increasingly vulnerable. Second, campaigning is likely to continue to become more specialized. The various facets of the campaign will produce more specialized technologies. This will require close coordination and will make the conduct of elections more complex and costly. Third, there is the implication that elections are subject to manipulation, that elections are not won or lost, they are managed. This can cause the most far-reaching effect if the voter is to continue to have a voice in public policy.

1. Benjamin Ginzberg, "Elections and Public Policy", *American Political Science Review* LXX, March 1976, p. 49.
2. *National Journal,* November 4, 1978, p. 1772.

nation moving again" sounded more attractive to voters with his image from the televised debates. In 1976 both Ford and Carter were media conscious and sought to exploit the other's weaknesses. The three televised debates probably did not have the dramatic impact on voters that the 1960 debate did, but they did succeed in sharpening the differences between the candidates. Gallop Poll results indicated that in the voters' minds, Ford had won the first debate. But by the time of the second debate, public perception of the candidates was changing. Secretary of Agriculture Earl Butz had resigned for his off-color comments about blacks, and in the debate Mr. Ford made his unfortunate statement about no Soviet domination of East Europe. The public gave the second debate to Carter, and Carter's lead over Ford increased. John Anderson knew full well his independent success was linked to being permitted to participate in the 1980 television debates.

The media have the potential to present issues and candidates directly to the people. They reach a wider audience more directly than any party or campaign organization. They can sharpen issues and personality traits, and provide background and comparative analysis. They can give the voter sufficient information and context to make reasoned and informed judgments. But the media also have the capacity for abuse. The selective decisions on what issues or personality features the media concentrate on can distort the image or nature of a campaign. The sensational is too often displayed and emphasized. Since voters are so dependent on media for information, first impressions are critical. Candidates are aware of this and often seek to manipulate the media. Joe McGinniss' *The Selling of the President—1968,* for example, sought to demonstrate how Mr. Nixon used the media in 1968.[28]

28. Joe McGinniss, *The Selling of the President—1968* (New York: Trident Press, 1969).

Professional Organization.   A second campaign technique is the creation of highly specialized, professional campaign organizations.

Public opinion polling is basic to campaign organizations. It helps to identify issues and personality images, and to show the social and political composition of electorates. All presidential candidates employ professional polling firms. Issues and groups are then targeted: those people who are sure to vote for a candidate, those who cannot be won over, and those who are undecided. Then surveys are made to determine what issues are relevant, how people feel, and what the candidate must to do "capture" those blocs of voters. Polls keep the candidate abreast of progress or any changes in voter feelings and concerns. With the aid of computers, samples of voters down to neighborhoods can be analyzed to give voter profiles. Updated information is added and campaign strategies formulated to capitalize on voter thinking. As a result of the scientific polling of voters, a campaign strategy is fashioned. No longer do candidates simply take to the stump, make speeches, shake hands, and eat chicken in union halls. Highly skilled media consultants and advertising firms work with candidates to make use of polling data to present the candidate in a most favorable light.

Professional campaign consultants may not have the ability to make a candidate or create issues, but they do have technical and managerial skills that allow a candidate to present his or her personality and issues in the most efficient and effective manner. They use modern technology—mass media, data processing, direct mail computer systems, and commercial advertising—to win elections. They are specialists in polling, fund raising, advertising, and public relations. Their job is to assist the candidate and the organization from fund raising to precinct organization to election-day voter drives. There are now over 200 such consulting firms in the United States, and most prefer to work for one party or for candidates with a given ideology.[29]

The result of professional technological campaigning had been to destroy traditional campaign techniques. Party workers and organizations are largely superfluous. Many voters are becoming disillusioned and cynical as they are bombarded with slick, Madison Avenue-type political ads.[30] Candidates come to rely heavily on such consultants, particularly candidates who have to run every two years. This has contributed heavily to driving up the cost of campaigning; campaign consultants and media campaigning are extremely expensive.

Campaign Finance.   Whatever the reasons, the American political process has been denigrated by election costs. A recent phenomenon on the political scene has been the rapid growth in costs for conducting political campaigns. Watergate merely illustrated the extent to which money has come to dominate elections. Illegal campaign contributions further erode the confidence the citizen has in candidates and political organizations.

29. *National Journal* (November 4, 1978), p. 1772.
30. *Ibid.,* p. 1776.

The cost of campaigning has risen continuously since 1952, but most dramatically since 1964. The Citizen's Research Foundation estimated that in 1972 a total of $228 million was spent on elections, with 61 percent of the cost going for the presidential campaign (Figure 9.9). The 1976 figures indicate a total of $212 million dollars. The presidential contest cost approximately $115 million, the Senate costs were $38 million, and campaigning for the House cost $61 million. The presidential contest represented a change, as public financing for the first time limited campaign spending. Public funds for presidential campaign costs amounted to $72.3 million in 1976—$43.6 million for the general election, $24.3 million for the primary election (money was distributed to 15 qualifying candidates—13 Democrats and 2 Republicans), and $4.4 million to the political parties to operate the nominating conventions. The escalation of campaign costs slowed down in 1976 as a result of reform efforts: public financing set limits on expenditures; the climate of Watergate made contributors and the public cautious; campaign laws restricted contributions by individual donors; and inflation made political money scarce. The overall rise in costs can be laid directly to increased use

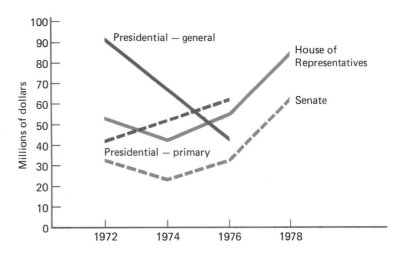

Figure 9.9

Campaign spending in national elections. Note: 1976 total represents public financing limited spending by two major candidates. (Congressional Quarterly, Weekly Report, 1973–1979)

	House	Senate	Presidential		Total
			Primary	General	
1978	88.0	65.5			153.5
1976	60.9	38.1	66.9	45.9	211.8
1974	45.0	28.9			73.1
1972	54.3	35.5	46.6	91.4	227.8

of the mass media and electronic technology. Radio and television costs accounted for one out of every seven dollars spent in the campaign for 1976. Carter spent 40 percent of his general election budge on media costs.

Contributions from large donors have attracted public attention, and up to 1972, the big contributor dominated. More recently, however, reform legislation, bolstered by court decisions, has worked to restrict large contributions and expand the number of small donors. Results of recent polls indicate that 10 to 12 percent of the American public contributes to political campaigns. Herbert Alexander reports that the number of contributors increased during the 1950s and then stabilized:

> 3 million in 1952
> 8 million in 1956
> 10 million in 1960
> 12 million in 1964
> 8.7 million in 1968
> 11.7 million in 1972[31]

This stabilized level of giving stands in spite of the fact that more and more Americans are being solicited for funds. In 1972, 34 percent of the people said they had been asked for political contributions, compared with 20 percent in 1968.

In 1972, $551 million was raised by contributions from persons giving $10,000 or more; they gave 13 percent of all campaign funds and lent another 49 percent of the total.[32] W. Clement Stone, the Chicago insurance executive, was the largest single contributor in 1972, giving $2.1 million to Nixon's reelection campaign and to other GOP candidates. Richard Millon Scaife gave over $1 million to Republican candidates in 1972. The Democrats' largest contributor was Steward R. Mott, who gave in excess of $800,000 to the Democratic coffers in 1972. In all, the largest ten contributors in 1972 gave $7.4 million dollars, the great majority of it to presidential campaigns.[33] Special interest groups and their political action committees are the other sources of large donations. Labor reportedly spent $8.5 million in 1972 for federal campaigns and an examination of 13 business groups revealed they spent $3.3 million for campaigns, 90 percent of the total for Republicans.[34] The rapid rise of **political action committees** (PACs), voluntary political organizations of labor and business that support candidates sympathetic to their goals and ideas, has escalated the cost of elections. PACs have proliferated in the late 1970s. They have also flooded the political process

31. Herbert E. Alexander, *Financing Politics: Money, Elections and Political Reform* (Washington, D.C.: Congressional Quarterly Press, 1976), p. 81.
32. David Adamany, "The Source of Money: An Overview," *Annals of the American Academy of Political and Social Science*, No. 425 (May 1976), p. 20.
33. Alexander, *Financing Politics: Money, Elections, and Political Reform*, pp. 33–34.
34. *Ibid.*, pp. 108–9.

with money. By 1980 PAC receipts were reportedly over $40 million—$18 million for labor PACs and $22 million for corporate PACs.[35]

Small donors are increasing, in part because of the rise of political activists and computer mass-mail solicitations, and in part because of public financing eligibility requirements. The McGovern campaign in 1972 and George Wallace's drive in 1968 are examples of campaigns financed by small contributions. George McGovern reported receiving from 500,000 to a million small donations. One report placed the figure of $100-plus contributors at only 27 percent of total contributors. Wallace backers claimed that 85 percent of the $6.7 million total raised from February to October 1968 was from contributions of less than $100 each.[36] For the 1976 election, House candidates received 36 percent of their money in contributions under $100, while Senate candidates reported 28 percent of their contributions were from donations under $100. But these totals, impressive as they may be, still fall short of a mass-based, grassroots campaign. The totals represent approximately only 1 percent of the voting age population.

Campaign Finance Legislation.   It has been the spiraling costs of elections and the scandals around the 1972 election that spurred the drive for reform. As a result of illegal corporate contributions in the Watergate affair, 21 companies pleaded guilty to illegally contributing over $980,000—most of it to the Nixon campaign. Lack of contribution limits or public disclosure led to charges of influence peddling and buying of public favors.

The Corrupt Practices Act of 1925 sought to restrict campaign spending and provide for public disclosure. The Hatch Act of 1940 set a limit of $5,000 for any person's contribution to a federal candidate or political committee, but there was no limit to the number of committees supporting one candidate to which an individual could contribute. President Johnson labeled the 1925 act "more loophole than law," but it remained the basic election law until 1972.

In 1971 Congress passed the Federal Election Campaign Act. It sought to provide for fuller public disclosure of funding and to draw more donors into politics by allowing a tax credit against a person's federal income tax (50 percent of the contribution up to $25 on a joint return). More specifically, it set limits on media expenditures, placed ceilings on contributions by candidates to their own campaigns, and required reporting and disclosure of expenditures and contributors. Many of these provisions were modified or replaced by the 1974 amendments to the Act. The 1974 amendments came as a direct result of Watergate and produced significant modifications in the 1971 act. They also gave rise to a Supreme Court decision testing the constitutionality of the law.

The 1974 Act had set more restrictive contribution limits. There were also more restrictive limits on campaign spending—$700,000 for congressional candidates and $20 million for each presidential candidate. It established tighter dis-

35. *National Journal,* August 9, 1980, p. 1305.
36. Adamany, "The Sources of Money: An Overview," p. 22.

closure and reporting requirements, and it created a bipartisan Federal Election Commission to oversee enforcement of its provisions. The Act provided for public financing of presidential campaigns, with matching public funds made available to eligible candidates—up to $5 million in the primary election, and total public funding in the general election.

The law was promptly challenged in the courts. A group of plaintiffs composed of conservatives and liberals, including Senator James Buckley (New York-Conservative) and Eugene McCarthy, brought suit arguing that the law violated the First Amendment freedoms of speech and association. They also charged that the Federal Election Commission, with its bipartisan composition, violated the separation of powers by giving Congress a right to appoint members. The Supreme Court, in a landmark case, *Buckley* v. *Valeo*,[37] reviewed the constitutionality of the election law reforms. The court was mixed in its judgment of the 1974 reforms. The court found unconstitutional, as an undue restriction of First Amendment freedoms, limits on political expenditures by a person to promote a political cause or candidacy. The Court also ruled unconstitutional limitations on expenditures by a candidate to further his or her own candidacy. The spending of money to communicate with voters is a form of free speech protected under the First Amendment. But the Court upheld as constitutional limits on contributions to candidates or political organizations. Here the Court sought to draw a distinction between *spending* and *contributing*. Congress could limit contributions in order to equalize influence and prevent the abuses that large contributions brought to the electoral process. And in the presidential contest, if a candidate took public funds, Congress could legitimately limit spending by those candidates as one of the overall conditions for accepting public money. Finally, the Court found the Federal Election Commission illegally constituted, though it upheld the concept of a regulatory commission.

In the wake of *Buckley* v. *Valeo,* Congress quickly adopted new legislation: the 1976 amendments to the Federal Election Campaign Act. The present regulations governing federal elections can be summarized as follows:

1. **Contribution Limits.** Individuals are limited to giving no more than $5,000 a year to a political action committee or a political party. Contributions to any candidate in a primary or general election are limited to $1,000 per candidate per election. The total aggregate contribution limit for an individual is $25,000 a year.

2. **Public Financing.** Matching public funds up to $5 million per candidate are available to eligible presidential candidates for primary elections. To be eligible, a candidate must meet a fund-raising requirement of $100,-000 raised in amounts of $5,000 or more in each of 20 states. Only the first $250 of individual private contributions are matched with public funds. Full public funding, on a voluntary basis, is available for major

37. *Buckley* v. *Valeo,* 424 U.S. 1 (1976).

party presidential candidates in the general election. Minor party candidates are eligible for partial funding if they win 10 percent or more of the vote in two consecutive presidential primaries. If candidates receive full public funding, no private contributions are allowed. Public funding is also available for presidential nominating conventions. Major parties automatically qualify; minor parties would receive a proportion of federal funds based on votes received in the previous election.

3. **Spending Limits.** Presidential candidates who accept public funds may spend no more than $50,000 of their own money. For primaries, presidential candidates accepting public money have state by state spending limits. Candidates may spend an equivalent of 16 cents per voting age resident in each state (adjusted for inflation), with a floor of $264,000 because of New Hampshire's and Alaska's small populations.

4. **Disclosure.** Candidates and committees must file periodic pre- and post-election reports, identifying by name the sources of all contributions totaling over $200 annually and itemizing all expenditures over $200 by name of person or firm paid and purpose of the expenditure.

5. **Enforcement.** The Federal Election Commission has overall responsibility to enforce campaign finance laws and to administer public financing of presidential elections. The six-member bipartisan commission is appointed by the president and confirmed by the Senate.

THE ELECTORAL SYSTEM

Suffrage.   The electoral system centers around the act of voting. The history of the citizen's right to vote—**suffrage**—has been the extension of that right. The extension of the franchise in America has been a long and often controversial process. The nation was founded on the premise that only white, male, 21-year-old property-holding citizens could participate. The history of the American political process has been the democratic erosion of those restrictions to political participation.

Property qualifications were the first to go. Although they did not write it into the Constitution, eighteenth-century thinkers were distrustful of mass citizen participation. The Founding Fathers were inclined to keep from participating those who had no interest or stake in political matters. Gouverneur Morris stated: "Give the votes to the people who have no property and they will sell them to the rich who will be able to buy them." And Roger Sherman declared: "The people immediately should have as little to do as may be about the government." That the states already had laws restricting suffrage seemed adequate to the Framers, and no such prohibitions were added to the Constitution. But by the election of 1832, the mood of the nation had changed. The election of Jackson brought mass campaigning; immigration and the frontier produced a democratization of American life. In short, by the time of the Civil War most states had eliminated property tests for voting.

FACT FILE

QUALIFICATIONS FOR VOTING

State or other jurisdiction	Minimum residence requirement before election days†	Closing date for registration before general election (days)	Cancellation of registration for failure to vote (years)	Registration covers all elections	Who can vote absentee						Other
					Absent on business	Dis-abled persons	Military personnel (including families)	Absent for religious reasons	Students away at school	Temporarily away from polls on election day	
Alabama	10	10	...	★	★	★	★	...	★	★	...
Alaska	30	30	4	★	★	★	★	...	★	★	...
Arizona	50	50	Last general election	★	★	★	★	★	★	★	...
Arkansas	None	20	4	★	★	★	★	★	★	★	(a,b)
California	29	29	...	★	★	★	★	★	★	★	(b)
Colorado	32	32	Last general election	★	★	★	★	★	★	★	(c)
Connecticut	Resident	21	...	★	...	★	★	★	★	★	(d)
Delaware	Resident	3rd Sat. in Oct.	2 consecutive elections	★	...	★	★	★	★	★	...
Florida	None	30	2	★	★	★	★	★	★	★	...
Georgia	Resident	30	3	(e)	★	★	★	★	★	★	(f)
Hawaii	None	30	2	★	★	★	★	★	★	★	(c)
Idaho	Resident	10/5(g)	4	(e)	★	★	★	...	★	★	...
Illinois	30	28	4	★	★	★	★	★	★	★	...
Indiana	30 (in precinct)	29	2	★	★	★	★	...	★	★	...
Iowa	None	10	4	★	★	...	...	...	...	...	(b)
Kansas	Close of registration	20	...	★	★	...	★	★	★	★	...
Kentucky	None	30	4	★	★	★	★	★	★	★	(h,k,u)
Louisiana	Resident	30	4	★	★	★	★	★	★	★	...
Maine	Resident	Election day	...	★	★	★	...	★	...	★	(o)
Maryland	Resident	29	5	(e)	★	...	★	★	★	★	(i)
Massachusetts	Close of registration	28	...	★	...	...	★	★	...	★	...

State											
Michigan	30	30	6	★	★	★	★	★	★	★	(j,k)
Minnesota	20	20(l)	4	(m)	★	★	★	★	★	★	(n)
Mississippi	30	30		★	★	★			★		
Missouri	None	4th Wed. before election		★	★	★	★	★	★	★	(k,n)
Montana	30	30	(p)	★	★	★			★	★	
Nebraska	None	2nd Fri. before election		★	★	★			★	★	
Nevada	30	5th Sat. before election	General election	★	★	★	★	★	★	★	
New Hampshire	10	10		★	★	★	★	★	★	★	
New Jersey	30	29	4	★	★	★	★	★	★	★	
New Mexico	Resident	42	2	★	★	★	★	★	★	★	(k)
New York	30	(w)	2	★	★	★			★	★	
North Carolina	30	21	4	★	★	★	★		★	★	
North Dakota	30	No registration			★	★	★				
Ohio	30	30	4	★	★	★	★	★	★	★	(f,q)
Oklahoma	Resident	10	2	★	★		★		★	★	(c,i)
Oregon	20	8 p.m. election day		★	★	★	★		★	★	(b)
Pennsylvania	30	30	2	★	★	★	★		★	★	
Rhode Island	30	30	5	★	★	★	★			★	(n,r)
South Carolina	Resident	30	2	★	★	★	★	★			
South Dakota	None	15	4	★							(b)
Tennessee	20	29	4, excluding yr. of registration	★	★	★			★	★	(b,f,i,s)
Texas	30	30		★	★	★		★		★	(f,i,k,s)
Utah	30	10		★	★		★	★	★	★	
Vermont	None	17		★	★	★	★	★		★	(a,x)
Virginia	Resident	31	4	★	★	★	★	★	★	★	(a,f,k,u)
Washington	30	30	2	★	★		★				(t)
West Virginia	29	30	2 elections	(v) ★	★	★	★	★	★	★	
Wisconsin	10	2nd Wed. before election (l)		★							(b)

QUALIFICATIONS FOR VOTING

State or other jurisdiction	Minimum residence requirement before election days†	Closing date for registration before general election (days)	Cancellation of registration for failure to vote (years)	Registration covers all elections	Who can vote absentee						Other
					Absent on business	Disabled persons	Military personnel (including families)	Absent for religious reasons	Students away at school	Temporarily away from polls on election day	
Wyoming	Resident	30	General election	★	...	...	...	...	...	...	(t)
Dist. of Col.	30	30	4	★	★	★	★	...	★	★	...
American Samoa	12 months	7	2	★	★	★	★	...	...	★	(y)
Guam	None	30	Last general election	★	★	★	★	...	★	★	(b)
Puerto Rico	120	1st Mon. in July	...	★	...	...	...	...	...	...	...
Virgin Islands	30	30	2 consecutive general elections	★	★	...	★	...	★	★	...

†When law specifies no residence requirement, "none" is listed; when law states only that the voter must be a bona fide resident, "Resident" is listed

(a) Illness.
(b) Unable to get to polls.
(c) More than 10 miles away.
(d) Moved within state.
(e) Registration covers national and state elections; municipal registration is separate.
(f) Election officials.
(g); With precinct registrar 10 days before; with county clerk 5 days.
(h) Spouses of military and students; civilian U.S. employees overseas; religious and welfare organizations with armed forces; university professors.
(i) Emergency ballot issued for illness, injury, or death in immediate family.
(j) Over 60.
(k) In jail but not convicted.
(l) Registration at polls with identification.
(m) All except school elections.
(n) Not absent, but prevented by employment from voting at polling place.
(o) Confinement in a jail or penal institution or lives an unreasonable distance from the polls.
(p) Challenge of qualifications; failure to vote in presidential election.
(q) Over 62; some incarcerated persons.
(r) Work overseas; death in family; on vacation; attending a funeral.
(s) Over 65
(t) Anyone registered.
(u) Merchant marine; citizens working overseas.
(v) In order for permanent registration to be applicable for municipal registration, municipality must pass an ordinance implementing the state law and integrating the city registration with the state law.
(w) Varies according to date set for local registration day.
(x) Injury.
(y) The Election Commissioner disallows absentee ballot voting by residents who have been away from their home district for more than one election (including servicemen & women).

Extending the franchise to black Americans has been a longer and more bitter struggle. The Fifteenth Amendment established the right to vote as a constitutional right for black Americans, but we have seen that the right was ignored and legally circumvented by southern states after the Civil War. Through the use of the white primary, literacy tests, poll taxes, and registration requirements, blacks were prevented from participating. Throughout the late nineteenth century and into the twentieth, federal law and the U.S. courts have worked to eliminate many of the devices used to bar black involvement in the electoral process. The Supreme Court attacked the white primary in 1944, declaring it unconstitutional in *Smith* v. *Allwright*. In 1964 the Court set aside poll taxes in federal election (*Harper* v. *Virginia* thus predated the Twenty-fourth Amendment, which forbade the poll tax in any election). The 1965 Voting Rights Act set aside literacy tests and authorized federal authorities to enter states and register voters. Yet even with the legal barriers overcome, black voting remains low.

The women's suffrage movement leads to passage of the Nineteenth Amendment and the right to vote for women. (United Press International)

The all-male electorate began to be challenged by the turn of the century. Wyoming first allowed women to vote in 1864. By 1900, three additional western states followed suit. From then on, the women's suffrage movement spread and gathered momentum. By 1919 Congress had proposed the Nineteenth Amendment. It was quickly ratified, so that women were able to vote in the 1920 presidential election.

More recent changes have expanded the electorate further. In 1961, the Twenty-third Amendment to the Constitution was ratified, extending suffrage for the presidential contest to the District of Columbia, giving the seat of the government three electoral votes. However, the District of Columbia still has no representation in Congress; it is managed by Congress, although residents pay the same taxes as everyone else. The greatest recent expansion of suffrage came with the addition of the 18 to 21-year-old citizens. In 1970, Congress lowered the voting age to 18 for all elections. The Supreme Court ruled that Congress had power to do so only in federal elections.[38] Some states followed suit, others did not. The Twenty-sixth Amendment, ratified in 1971, extended suffrage rights in all elections to those 18 years of age and older. The Amendment reportedly added 10.5 million Americans to the voting rolls. Yet their record of participation is the lowest of all groups; only half of those who are 18 to 21 do vote.

Reapportionment.   Equally as challenging a concept for democracy as universal suffrage is the notion that every person's vote counts the same as another's. Yet in the twentieth century, while nation and courts were struggling with universal suffrage, there was a growing political imbalance between urban and rural America. State legislatures apportioned electoral districts, which were often drawn on geographical boundaries and favored rural areas. Yet the population explosion and patterns of immigration brought great numbers to urban centers. America was becoming an urban nation, but its legislatures did not reflect the change. By 1960, state legislatures and congressional districts were greatly unbalanced according to population. Many states had districts twice as large as others; California had one district 400 times larger than its smallest.

Legislatures, dominated by representatives benefiting from the system, were reluctant to correct the problem. Representative Emmanuel Celler (Dem.-N.Y.) introduced legislation to require states to reapportion congressional districts so that the population deviance between districts would not be over 15 percent. It failed to muster much congressional support. The courts had also been reluctant to address the issue. In 1946 in *Colegrove* v. *Green,*[39] the Supreme Court ruled that the problem of reapportionment was a "political question." The courts lacked jurisdiction; the issue could properly be settled only by legislatures. But the case had raised an interesting issue. Colegrove had argued that the population variance among legislative districts within a state constituted a state's denial of "the equal

38. *Oregon* v. *Mitchell,* 400 U.S. 112 (1970).
39. *Colegrove* v. *Green,* 328 U.S. 549 (1949).

protection of the laws'' as guaranteed by the Fourteenth Amendment. The Court ruled that Congress alone had the authority to determine fair representation in legislative chambers. But by the 1960s, the Court was of another mind. In 1962, in *Baker* v. *Carr*,[40] the Court ruled that the issue of legislative reapportionment was a justiciable question. In other words, the Court was inviting suits to challenge malapportioned legislative districts. *Baker* v. *Carr* produced a political revolution. It was a landmark case in constitutional law and has dramatically affected the course of American government and politics.

The Court did not have long to wait for suits. In *Wesberry* v. *Sanders* (1964),[41] the Supreme Court ruled that congressional districts had to be apportioned among the states according to population, citing the language of the Constitution in Article 1, Section 2. Said the Court: ''As early as is practical, one man's vote in a Congressional election is to be worth as much as another's.'' In other words, one person, one vote. The same year, in *Reynolds* v. *Sims*,[42] the Supreme Court extended the principle of one person, one vote to cover both houses of state legislatures. The Court relied on the ''equal protection'' clause of the Fourteenth Amendment as the basis for making its ruling. As the court said in *Reynolds*, ''legislators represent people, not trees or acres.'' Legislative districts are to be apportioned on the basis of population: one person, one vote. And if legislatures cannot or will not reapportion, the federal courts will design an acceptable plan for the state.

The 1964 decisions seemed to imply that some population variance would be permissible. Said *Reynolds:* ''Some deviations from the equal-population principle are constitutionally permissible with respect to the apportionment of seats in either or both of the two houses of a bicameral state legislature.'' Just how much remained to be seen. The Court rejected a 6 percent variation for congressional districts in 1969[43] and a 4 percent deviance in 1972.[44] A standard of mathematical exactness was being applied for congressional districts. For state legislatures, greater deviations were being tolerated. In 1973 the Court let stand a Virginia plan that had a 16.4 percent population variation and otherwise permitted a 10 percent variance in a Texas plan.[45] Summarizing its position in *Chapman* v. *Meier*,[46] the Court said: ''As contrasted with congressional districting, where population equality appears now to be the preeminent, if not the sole criterion on which to adjudge constitutionality, . . . when state legislative districts are at issue we have held that minor population deviations do not establish a prima facie Constitutional violation.''

The result of these decisions has been to weaken the political power base of rural areas and strengthen the power base of some urban legislators and members

40. *Baker* v. *Carr*, 369 U.S. 186 (1962).
41. *Wesberry* v. *Sanders*, 376 U.S. 1 (1964).
42. *Reynolds* v. *Sims*, 377 U.S. 533 (1964).
43. *Kirkpatrick* v. *Preisler*, 394 U.S. 526 (1969).
44. *White* v. *Weiser*, 412 U.S. 783 (1973).
45. *Mahon* v. *Howell*, 410 U.S. 315 (1973); *White* v. *Register*, 412 U.S. 755 (1973).
46. *Chapman* v. *Meier*, 420 U.S. 1 (1975).

of Congress. But the real winners have been the suburbs. With the flight from the cities, the real population shifts have occurred in the suburbs. They continue to grow at a rapid rate, much faster than the rest of the nation. Particularly in the North, the Midwest, and the West, suburban communities dominate the political scene. Largely Republican, they are replacing the small town, rural Republican as the backbone of the party. Congress also reflects the rise of the suburban power base. As Richard Lehne points out, the coalition base of the House is likely to change as small-town and big-city representatives, facing similar problems, face the challenge from the newer, still growing suburban communities.[47]

Table 9.8
**Changing Rural-Urban Representation
in Congress**

	1962	1966	1974
Metropolitan Districts	254	264	305
Central City	106	110	109
Suburban	92	98	132
Mixed Metropolitan	56	56	64
Rural Districts	181	171	130
Total	435	435	435

SOURCE: Reprinted from "Suburban Foundations of the New Congress," Richard Lehne, *The Annals of the American Academy of Political and Social Science*, No. 442, November 1975, p. 143. Copyright © 1975.

Registration.   To be eligible to vote in every state but one (North Dakota), a citizen must establish his or her legal qualification to vote. Although the requirements are not great (age and residency), the act of registering is a physical imposition that keeps otherwise eligible voters from participating in elections. In 1976 an estimated 45 million voters were kept from the polls because they were not registered to vote. To combat the issue several states, such as Minnesota, have instituted election-day registration where registration and voting can be done at the same time and in the same place.

Southern states used voter registration to keep blacks off the voter rolls. By moving registration locations or using irregular hours, states kept would-be voters from qualifying and establishing their right to participate. With the 1965 Voting Rights Acts, Congress empowered the Department of Justice to establish registra-

---

47. Richard Lehne, "Suburban Foundations of the New Congress," *Annals of the American Academy of Political and Social Science,* November 1975, p. 150.

How to register to vote

1. In order to vote in any election, you must be registered—that is, you must be entered on the election rolls of your district or area.

2. Regulations on registration differ from state to state according to state law, so you will need to write or call your local Board of Elections, or your county or town clerk. You can seek information from the League of Women Voters of the United States, 1730 M Street NW, Washington, D.C. 20036.

3. In some states you must register in person; others allow mail registration. Generally, for first registration, you need proof of age and residence.

4. When you register you may enroll in a party simply by signing and declaring yourself a member. You may also declare yourself independent, but remember that party enrollment allows you to vote in primary elections.

5. In many states you are permanently registered as long as you vote with a certain frequency (every two years, for example), but check the rules in your state.

6. Usually, residence in a state for 30 to 50 days is sufficient for voting purposes. It is possible to vote in an election in one state and then vote in another election in a different state in the same year, but you will still need to register in both places.

---

tion procedures in areas where blacks had been discriminated against in voting. But President Carter felt this was not good enough; registration provisions still kept too many citizens from participating. Citing the fact that at least 20 other democracies had higher levels of voter turnout, the president proposed a national system of election-day registration. States should be encouraged to adopt such a system, the President noted, for those with election-day registration systems do have higher turnout rates of voting.

A major factor in registration was providing residency. States frequently used a one-year period of residency as a qualification; some states set the time as long as two years. States frequently added county and precinct requirements as well. But the Voting Rights Act of 1970 permitted voting in presidential elections with only a 30-day residency. Then, in 1972, the Supreme Court ruled that no state, for any election, could require more than a 30-day residency.[48] The Court modified the ruling somewhat in 1973, however, by allowing a longer residency in state and local elections—a requirement of 50 days was not unreasonable.[49] But the 30-day limit for voting in presidential elections stood.

48. *Dunn* v. *Blumstein,* 405 U.S. 330 (1972).
49. *Murston* v. *Mandt,* 410 U.S. 679 (1973); *Burns* v. *Forston,* 410 U.S. 686 (1973).

Balloting.   As we walk into the polling place, we probably pay little
ntion to the nature of the ballot or the placement of candidates' names. Yet
:arch has proved that these can affect the outcome. For example, being placed
 on a ballot reduces the number of votes because voters have to "dig" to find
 candidate. Voting machines make writing in names extremely difficult. And
rty column ballot facilitates straight ticket voting.

Whether voting is by machine or paper ballot, two principal forms of ballots
are used. The **party column** (Indiana) ballot lists candidates by parties in straight
columns. This makes party identification considerably easier, and often there is a
single party lever or box to vote for all candidates listed for the party. This ballot
encourages straight party balloting. The **office block** (Massachusetts) ballot lists
candidates by the office sought; all candidates running for president, for example,
are listed under that office. Party affiliation is noted after the candidate, but
straight party voting is made more difficult.

The Electoral College.   In every election except for the presidency,
direct balloting by the people determines the outcome. For the presidency, however, the U.S. Constitution established the Electoral College to mediate between
the people and a legislative election. Electors were to exercise independent judgment.

To be elected president, a candidate must receive a majority of electoral
votes. Each state appoints, as the state legislature may direct, a number of electors
equal to the total number of senators and representatives the state has in Congress.
Normally each party nominates a slate of electors pledged to the party's presidential candidate. Voters in the general election are technically voting not for a presidential candidate, but for a slate of electors, even though the electors' names
may not appear. The presidential candidate winning a *plurality* of the popular
vote receives *all* that state's electoral votes.

Although there is no constitutional requirement that the electors be chosen
by the presidential contest, every state does so. The Constitution says a state
legislature may select electors in such manner as it may direct. The winning electors meet in the state capitol in December, as directed by Congress, and cast their
ballots. Officially they may vote for whomever they feel is most qualified to be
president. In practice, they cast all ballots for the party candidate to whom they
were pledged and who received the most popular votes in the state.

The state transmits the sealed ballots to the president of the Senate. Then,
before the House and Senate in early January, the ballots are opened and counted.
The candidate receiving a majority of electoral votes for president is declared
President-elect. If no candidate receives a majority, the House of Representatives
is directed by the Constitution to choose the president from among the top three
candidates, each state in the House having one vote. If no candidate receives a
majority of electoral votes for vice-president, the Senate must choose from the
top two candidates, a majority of senators determining the winner.

The Electoral College, with its winner-take-all approach, concentrates electoral votes in the heavily populated states: the urban and suburban centered states such as New York, California, Pennsylvania, Ohio, and Texas. Candidates spend their time campaigning in states with the most electoral votes, states where a shift of a few thousand votes can mean an additional 100 or so electoral votes. A presidential candidate needs to carry only twelve states to win a majority of electoral votes, and the candidate needs only a plurality of popular votes to capture all the state's electoral votes. Practically, however, campaign strategy dictates the states to campaign in. Some states are viewed as solid, and only minimal attention is given to campaigning there; others show little likelihood of being carried, so they too are given little campaign effort. The remaining states are the battleground. Some of them are small and receive low priority. Hence, the campaign comes down to the large or medium-size states where campaigning can alter the outcome.

Politically the Electoral College favors the large states; they have the electoral clout, and that is where presidential candidates campaign (Figure 9.10). The votes in larger states swing elections. On the other hand, small states do enjoy a unique status under the Electoral College. Proportionally their share of the elec-

Figure 9.10

Electoral college map of the United States of America. States are drawn in proportion to number of electoral votes, which total 538.

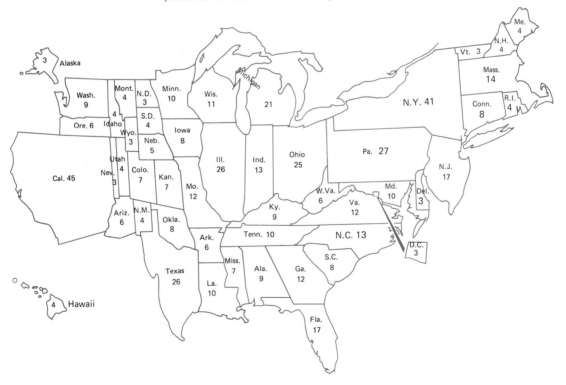

toral vote (because each state has two Senators) is greater than the percentage of the popular vote nationwide. That may be little consolation, but a shift of relatively few votes here and there makes for electoral margins. If the popular vote were used, shifts in the larger states would also count, but with the Electoral College they only increase the margin for winning the same number of electoral votes.

It is precisely because of this electoral distortion, as well as the possibility of defection by electors, that the last decade has seen a rising cry for reform in the Electoral College. In 1960, 1968, and 1976 there were such defections (one each). In 1960 Senator Byrd received one electoral vote that had been won by Kennedy. Wallace received a Republican elector's vote in 1968, and Ronald Reagan received a vote in 1976 from the state of Washington, which voted for Gerald Ford. But the most serious questions arose in 1968, when it was feared that George Wallace's candidacy might deny either major party candidate an electoral majority. (Wallace won 46 electoral votes.) This would have thrown the election into the House of Representatives, where some speculated the candidates might have bargained with state delegations in return for their support. There was some fear that Wallace would ask his electors to vote for Richard Nixon in return for concessions. Obviously, the results made all this speculation irrelevant, but dissatisfaction with the whole Electoral College was enhanced. Again in 1980 John Anderson's bid for the presidency raised the possibility of the House selecting the president. Wild speculation abounds! The House becomes deadlocked; the vice-president serves as president. The Senate refuses to act until the House selects a president; the Speaker of the House serves as acting president. While none of this happened, as in 1968, it created dissatisfaction with the Electoral College.

From time to time various reforms for the Electoral College have been advanced. The reforms may be summarized as follows:

1. *The Automatic Plan.* This would make the least change. It would retain the Electoral College concept and winner-take-all philosophy and merely abolish the selection of electors and their need to vote. Electoral votes are automatically assigned to the winning presidential candidate on the basis of the popular vote in the state. This would eliminate elector defections and the possibility of electoral bargaining as suggested in 1968.

2. *The District Plan.* The Electoral College would be retained, but votes would be awarded on the basis of a plurality of popular votes in each congressional district. Each of the House districts in the state would have one electoral vote to be awarded to the presidential candidate with a plurality of popular votes in that district. The remaining two electoral votes (for the two senators) would go to the statewide popular-vote winner. This plan keeps the electoral structure intact, but would more closely reflect popular-vote trends throughout the county. It would also increase the likelihood of a third-party candidate winning some electoral

votes, and therefore possibly throwing the contest into the House. Some district proposals would alter this feature and have a joint session of Congress, voting as individuals, select the president if no electoral majority was achieved.

3. *The Proportional Plan.* This plan would make the greatest alteration in the Electoral College. It would award electoral votes from a state in direct proportion to the percentage of the popular vote total. So if the two candidates split 52 to 48 percent in the popular vote, the one candidate would be awarded 52 percent of the state's electoral votes (the number of electoral votes determined as now); the other candidate would get 48 percent. This would avoid the present arrangement of winning 52 percent of the popular vote and receiving all the electoral votes. The plan greatly increases the possibility of a fair split and the opportunity for a third-party candidate to throw the election into the House of Representatives.

4. *Direct Election.* The final plan would abolish the Electoral College and let the people elect the president and vice-president through direct popular election. President Carter has advocated such a proposal and has suggested that Congress initiate a Constitutional amendment to that effect. Such proposals have been heard before. In 1969 the House initiated a constitutional amendment calling for the direct election of the president. The plan required the winning candidate to receive at least 40 percent of the popular vote; if no candidate received the requisite minimum, a runoff election would be held between the top two vote getters. The Senate refused to concur, and the proposal died. Carter's plan also seems to be generating little enthusiasm from members of Congress. Opposition to the direct election centers around two arguments: the federal basis of elections, which keeps states with large numbers of electoral votes more influential, and the opportunity for increased fraud and abuse. Voters may be misled or influenced by media campaigns that create a bandwagon effect across the nation.

SUMMARY

1. Elections are the basic means by which the collective judgment of the people is expressed in a democracy. For several decades such judgments were stable and predictable. This has been interpreted to mean satisfaction with the political system. Changes today in voting behavior question those traditional assumptions regarding the electoral process.

2. We are being forced to redefine political behavior. There is considerable movement in the motivation behind voting for candidates. Where party identification once dominated, issues and candidate personality are cited as increasingly important in elections. Issues combine with ticket split-

ting to reduce partisanship, while voter disaffection reduces turnout and commitment to the political process.

3. Recent voting patterns do not speak strongly for the collective judgment of the people. Landslide elections are increasingly common, incumbents win reelection with striking success, and electoral competition is weak. These trends conflict with the rational voter trends where voters exercise independent judgments based on issues and personality assessments.

4. Campaigning for the presidency has become nationalized, heavily dependent on the new technologies such as the media, polling, and fund raising. These have placed the presidential candidates directly before the people. The presidential race is divorced from congressional elections and political parties.

5. Campaign costs have risen rapidly in the past two decades. Because of the cost of campaigning, money has denegrated the electoral process. Reforms in campaign finance have sought to control campaign abuses. The public financing of the 1976 presidential election did succeed in reducing the cost of the presidential campaign.

6. The electoral system has some built-in biases. Many of these preferences have been neutralized as with the case of reapportionment and election day registration. One major remaining issue of electoral bias still unresolved is the Electoral College.

TERMS

9.1. Voter Turnout. What is the voter turnout in your state and city? What are the legal requirements for voting—registration, residency, and balloting? Compare your state and town with others. *The Book of the States* will provide you with legal requirements and restrictions. The *Statistical Abstract* gives turnout by states. Also helpful are the volumes *America Votes* and the *Almanac of Politics* that cover elections by states. You may have to contact your city auditor to determine turnout of eligible voters for your city.

9.2. Popular and Electoral Vote. As you know, presidential elections are determined by the electoral vote, not popular vote. What difference is there between the popular vote and electoral vote? Choose a presidential election, recent or past, possibly compare 1980 with 1960 or 1968 and examine how the electoral vote percentage differed from the popular vote totals. How would a regional or congressional district apportionment of electoral votes alter the results? To find the district vote totals you can go to *Guide to U.S. Elections, America Votes,* or the *Almanac of Politics* for the appropriate years.

9.3. Money and Elections. Select a candidate running for the House of Representatives or the Senate from your state and examine the finance of the campaign. How much money came in on contributions? What is their source? How much money is being spent? In what areas? All federal candidates are required to file periodic and quarterly financial statements as well as a final summary with the Federal Election Commission. These reports are jointly filed with the Secretary of State in the state. They are public records and for a minimal fee you can obtain copies of them.

9.4. Voting and Issues. Numerous commentators on electoral politics have observed the emerging importance of issues in voting behavior. Write an essay describing the change in voting behavior over the past twenty years. What is the changing importance of party identification, group identification, candidate personality, and issues in campaign and voting? There are several excellent works cited in the bibliography for you to consult in writing your essay.

BIBLIOGRAPHY

Agranoff, Robert. *The New Style Election Campaigns*. Boston: Holbrook Press, 1976.

A collection of essays written on campaigns, many by people active in electoral campaigns. Covered are such topics as campaign management, technology use, media, and ethics and reform.

Alexander, Herbert. *Financing Politics: Money, Elections and Political Reform*. Washington, D.C.: Congressional Quarterly, 1976.

The best and most complete source for understanding campaign finance, sources and expenditure of funds, and the impact of campaign reform laws. The book contains up to date data on money and its impact on electoral politics.

Asher, Herbert. *Presidential Elections and American Politics*. Homewood, Ill.: Dorsey Press, 1980.

A text on electoral behavior with excellent coverage of party identification, issues, and the role of the campaign. While the analysis is sophisticated, the book contains a great deal of useful and understandable information.

Campbell, Angus, *et al. The American Voter*. New York: John Wiley and Sons, 1960.

The classic work on voting behavior. Attempts to explain the causes of voting behavior based upon extensive survey of American voters. Party identification is found to be the most powerful cause for voting.

DeVries, Walter, and V. Lance Tarrance. *The Ticket Splitter*. Grand Rapids, Mich.: William Eerdmans, 1972.

The basic work for an understanding of an increasingly common phenomenon. The authors dwell less on self-identification and more on electoral activity to explain electoral behavior. There is good discussion of changing campaign strategies and ticket splitting.

Hill, David, and Norman Luttbeg. *Trends in American Electoral Behavior*. Ithasca, Ill.: F. E. Peacock, 1980.

A very readable summary of electoral trends, including the decline of partisanship and decline of trust in the system. The book makes use of current data but is not technical or difficult to understand. The first chapter has a very good summary of the contemporary debate on stability or change in the American electorate.

Miller, Warren, and Teresa Levitin. *Leadership and Change: Presidential Elections from 1952 to 1976*. Cambridge, Mass.: Winthrop, 1976.

A review of voting behavior from the 1950s to the 1970s, the book explains in great detail the impact of "new politics" of the 1960s on electoral behavior. They conclude the addition of these new groups to the electorate has yet to be fully felt.

Nie, Norman, Sidney Verba, and John Petrocik. *The Changing American Voter*. Cambridge, Mass.: Harvard University Press, 1979.

The new classic on voting behavior. The book seeks to review the change in voting behavior during the 1960s and 1970s. It finds that party identification has declined as an explanation and issues have emerged as increasingly important.

Polsby, Nelson, and Aaron Wildavsky. *Presidential Elections*. New York: Charles Scribner's Sons, 1980.

A basic and first-rate treatment of presidential elections. There is full coverage from securing the nomination to conducting the campaign. Not much on voting behavior.

Pomper, Gerald. *Elections in America*. New York: Dodd, Mead, 1971.

A very good history of elections in America covering such basic topics as the role of elections in a democracy and the right to vote. Gives a good overview of elections in America.

Pomper, Gerald. *Voter's Choice: Varieties of American Electoral Behavior*. New York: Harper & Row, 1975.

A more sophisticated study of voting behavior, Pomper looks at the changing motivation of the American voter. Pomper concludes that voters have become more concerned with issues than was previously the case.

Rae, Douglas. *The Political Consequences of Electoral Laws*. New Haven, Conn.: Yale University Press, 1967.

One of the few books that looks at election laws and the administration of elections for their effect on elections. While sometimes complex, the book is a valuable resource for understanding how the conduct of elections shapes the electoral process.

Chapter
10

The Presidency

"Let us create together a new national spirit of unity and trust." With these words, Jimmy Carter became the thirty-ninth president of the United States. Carter had sensed all during the campaign of 1976 that Americans were looking for the restoration of trust and confidence in government. There was no call to greatness in Carter's inaugural address, for greatness had seemed to wane as a goal in the wake of the unfulfilled promises of the Great Society, the frustrations of Vietnam, and the illegalities of Watergate. Instead Carter promised faith and compassion, and responsive government. The words of President Carter remind us what political scientist James Barber says of the presidency, "For better or for worse, the Presidency remains the prime focus for our political sentiments and the prime source of guidance and inspiration for national politics. . . . If he is lucky and effective, he can call forth from the climate new energies, a new vision, a new way of working to suit a perennially new age."[1]

In the twentieth century, Americans came to see the presidency as the center—the source of public policy and a force for social change. Until 1964, Americans were confident that their president was the right person to lead the nation, that America was prospering, and that it was the president who possessed the knowledge and leadership to lead the nation toward greatness. But the abuses of presidential power in that decade had shaken

1. James David Barber, *The Presidential Character,* Second Edition (Englewood Cliffs, N.J.: Prentice-Hall, 1977), p. 446.

---

the American people. Presidents Johnson and Nixon had pushed presidential power to new limits. The public trust had been abused; the office of the presidency had become mired in illegality and cheap political retribution. The presidency on the eve of Richard Nixon's resignation was isolated and under siege. The people were demanding accountability and responsibility.

Presidential power had grown at the expense of traditional sources of authority: Congress, the bureaucracy, and public opinion. Since Franklin Roosevelt, the president has become our chief policymaker, "the hope of America."[2] The unique blending of foreign and domestic issues after the 1930s produced the unprecedented growth of presidential power. Arthur Schlesinger has observed that

2. Daniel P. Moynihan, White House Press Release, December 21, 1970, p. 11.

President Carter is inaugurated in 1976. (Bill Fitz-Patrick, The White House)

foreign policy put the president in command of the forces of war and peace, the decay of political parties left the president as the premier politician, and the efforts to regulate economic growth placed the president in charge of the economy. Hence, Schlesinger notes, "at this extraordinary historical moment, when foreign and domestic lines of force converged, much depended on whether the occupant of the White House was moved to ride the new tendencies of power or to resist them."[3]

We have created in the presidency what Louis Koenig labels a "Sun King Complex."[4] This is a monarchical tendency to create an office that serves the needs and desires of a single person. "Upon the President is lavished every facility to ease the travail of daily living and to assist his encounters with the 'great issues'."[5] We seek to provide for the president the surroundings and resources fit for a king. And presidents bask in this sunlight of attention and power.

THE ASCENDANCY OF THE PRESIDENCY

The excesses of presidential power brought many Americans to a profound distrust of executive authority, and it produced a sense of outrage against uncontrolled government power in general. Yet the presidency cannot be evaluated only in the light of Vietnam and Watergate. As an institution, it has been growing in power almost since the Constitution was adopted.

CONSTITUTIONAL DIMENSIONS

The Framers of the Constitution were uncertain regarding the presidency. They would not have a monarchy, but the Articles of Confederation had proved the need for an executive. The problem confronting the Framers was to establish an independent and viable executive capable of enforcing the laws and yet not so strong as to overpower the other branches of government.

The Framers quickly settled on a single executive. Randolph had proposed a three-person executive council, but there was strong opposition. Elbridge Gerry felt that in military affairs, a three-person executive would prove indecisive; James Wilson thought a plural executive would not provide "energy, dispatch, and responsibility to the office." The unity of a single executive would be the best safeguard against tyranny. The Framers also rejected election by the legislature, although this proved more troublesome. Direct popular election by the people was unacceptable. The Virginia Plan provided that the president would be chosen by electors selected by Congress, thereby tying the election of the presi-

---

3. Arthur M. Schlesinger, Jr., *The Imperial Presidency* (Boston: Houghton Mifflin Co., 1973), p. 212.
4. Louis Koenig, *The Chief Executive,* 3rd Edition, (New York: Harcourt Brace Jovanovich, 1975), p. 3.
5. *Ibid.*

dent to Congress and ensuring executive accountability. Some delegates proposed that Congress directly select the Chief Executive. Finally, the matter was turned over to a committee that proposed the system we currently have: election by electors equal to the number of senators and representatives and chosen by each state.

These two key convention decisions proved decisive to the establishment and growth of executive power. The decision not to have legislative elections gave the president a national constituency and endowed the chief executive with a status and role unrivaled by any other figure in government. The Electoral College system has not prevented presidents from assuming the mantle of leadership or being the spokesmen for the nation. As E. S. Corwin noted, "The Constitution reflects the struggle between two conceptions of executive power: that it ought to be subordinate to the supreme legislative power, and that it ought to be, within generous limits, autonomous and self-directing."[6]

The Constitution says little regarding executive authority. The power of the presidency is a rich blend of written Constitution, custom, and person (Table 10.1). The powers and responsibilities of presidents have developed as presidents interpreted and fashioned the apparatus of the executive to suit them and the needs of the nation. Yet we insist that this be a presidency within the Constitution, and constitutional provisions have helped to shape the presidency. These are the key provisions:

1. "The president shall be Commander in Chief of the Army and Navy of the United States. . . ." In foreign affairs, no phrase has aided the chief executive more. It has become the basis for the president's "war powers." This would have astonished the Framers, for they viewed the grant of authority as purely supervisory. But from Lincoln on, the commander-in-chief role has grown. It was used by Roosevelt in World War II to set up executive agencies. Aferwards, it sustained justifying rent and price controls as the veterans returned home. Several times presidents have moved, as commander-in-chief, to commit U.S. troops abroad to protect American lives and property. Eisenhower, for example, sent 14,000 troops into Lebanon in 1958 to forestall Communist aggression, and Gerald Ford committed U.S. Marines to free the merchant vessel *Mayaguez,* which had been captured in 1975 by the Cambodians. Two undeclared wars, Korea and Vietnam, are results of presidents exercising their war powers as commander-in-chief. In both cases, Congress acknowledged the president's action as proper under his authority as commander-in-chief.

2. "He shall have Power, by and with the advise and consent of the Senate,

---

6. Edward S. Corwin, *The President: Office and Powers* (New York: New York University Press, 1957), p. 307.

Table 10.1

The Presidential Job Description

Types of Activity	The Subpresidencies		
	Foreign Policy and National Security (A)	Aggregate Economics (B)	Domestic Policy and Programs (C)
Crisis Management	Wartime leadership; missile crisis, 1962	Coping with recessions	Confronting coal strikes of 1978
Symbolic and Morale-building Leadership	Presidential state visit to Middle East or to China	Boosting confidence in the dollar	Visiting disaster victims and morale building among government workers
Priority Setting and Program Design	Balancing pro-Israel policies with need for Arab oil	Choosing means of dealing with inflation, unemployment	Designing a new welfare program
Recruitment Leadership (advisers, administrators, judges, ambassadors, etc.)	Selection of Secretary of Defense, U.N. Ambassador	Selection of Secretary of Treasury, Federal Reserve Board Governors	Nomination of federal judges
Legislative and Political Coalition Building	Selling Panama or SALT treaties to Senate for approval	Lobbying for energy-legislation package	Winning public support for transportation deregulation
Program Implementation and Evaluation	Encouraging negotiations between Israel and Egypt	Implementing tax cuts or fuel rationing	Improving quality health care, welfare retraining programs
Oversight of Government Routines and Establishment of an Early-Warning System for Future Problem Areas	Overseeing U.S. bases abroad; ensuring that foreign-aid programs work effectively	Overseeing the IRS or the Small Business Administration	Overseeing National Science Foundation or Environmental Protection Agency

SOURCE: From Thomas E. Cronin, *The State of the Presidency,* 2nd ed, p. 155. Copyright © 1980 by Thomas E. Cronin. Reprinted by permission of Little, Brown, and Co.

to make treaties, . . ." In recent years, the treaty power, with the requirement of ratification by two-thirds of the Senate, has been supplanted by the use of **executive agreements.** Executive agreements do not require Senate action, but have the same legal standing as treaties. On different occasions Congress has moved, unsuccessfully, to limit the use of executive agreements. The Bricker Amendment in the 1950s would have eliminated executive agreements as a substitute for treaties. In 1972 Congress passed the Case Act, which requires presidents to submit to Congress within 60 days any international agreement concluded with a foreign power. The Act did not, however, limit such agreements.

3. "And he shall nominate, and by and with the advice and consent of the Senate, shall appoint Ambassadors, and other public ministers and consuls, judges of the Supreme Court, and all other officers of the United States, . . ." The appointment power of the chief executive is a perrogative little challenged and interfered with. It is his primary means of establishing a functioning executive branch of government. The only limitation on the executive appointing power is Senate confirmation, and the great majority of presidential appointees are routinely accepted. One area of exception is judicial appointments, where senatorial courtesy functions. And in the case of Supreme Court appointments, judicial qualifications are scrutinized carefully.

The Courts have rejected any effort to restrict or interfere in the appointment power. In *Buckley* v. *Valeo* (1976), the Supreme Court rejected a provision for the Federal Election Commission that allowed congressional officers to appoint some members of the commission. Much earlier, in *Myers* v. *United States* (1926), the Court had rejected any connection between the advice and consent provisions for appointments and removal. The Court held that the Senate could not require

Table 10.2

Treaties and Executive Agreements, 1789 to 1976

Period	Treaties	Executive agreements	Totals
1789–1839	60	27	87
1839–1889	215	238	453
1889–1939	524	917	1,441
1940–1970	310	5,653	5,963
1971–1976	93	1,638	1,731
Totals	1,202	8,473	9,675

SOURCE: *President and Congress,* by Louis Fisher, (New York: Free Press, copyright © 1972), p. 45. By permission of the Macmillan Co. 1971–1976 data from the Congressional Quarterly, *Congress and the Nation,* Vol. IV, p. 865.

presidents to consult the Senate on removing ministerial officers as part of the constitutional advice and consent function.

4. "He shall take care that the Laws be faithfully executed." Perhaps the broadest powers have been derived from this phrase. Not only does it include the laws enacted by Congress, but as interpreted by the Supreme Court in *In re Neagle* (1890), it includes "any obligation fairly and properly inferrible from [the Constitution], or any duty . . . to be derived from the general scope of . . . duties under the laws of the United States." This was interpreted to mean not only enforcement of acts of Congress, but also enforcement of "rights, duties and obligations growing out of the Constitution itself, our international relations, and all the protection implied by the nature of the government under the Constitution." Under this authority, President Cleveland moved to end the long Pullman strike (1894) and President Truman seized the steel mills in 1952. The argument for presidential "implied powers," however, has come under question. In the Pentagon Papers case (*New York Times Co.* v. *United States,* 1971) the Court rejected the claim of inherent power unsubstantiated by statutory approval. It was willing to accept national security claims for confidentiality only if legislatively provided or if it could be demonstrated as causing "irreparable damage to our Nation or its people."

THE GROWTH OF THE PRESIDENCY

The Constitution alone cannot explain the growth of the presidency; at best, it has accommodated change. The growth of the presidency must be accounted for by the changing nature of the Union, the problems confronting the nation, and the nature of those occupying the office. Institution and person have come together to magnify the powers of the modern presidency.

The institution of the presidency has greatly expanded. When George Washington took office in 1789, there were four executive departments: state, war, treasury, and an attorney general. There were approximately 4 million Americans in the thirteen colonies to be governed. Today there are over 4 million Americans on the executive payroll (2.9 million civilians and 2 million in the armed forces). The four executive departments now number thirteen, with an additional host of boards, agencies, and commissions as well as an expanded Executive Office of the President. James Polk wrote in 1848: "I prefer to supervise the whole operations of the government myself." But by the twentieth century the president needed help. The 93rd Congress (1973-74) alone passed 3,088 measures that consumed, in the process, 71,442 pages in the *Congressional Record*. The president now oversees a federal budget that exceeds half a trillion dollars. Washington's first budget called for expending just over $84 million.

The growth of the institution of the presidency has largely been in direct response to issues. As the nation has grown and prospered, new, complex, and pressing issues have thrust the presidency into the forefront of leadership. *War* and *foreign affairs* most plainly have heightened the impact of the presidency. The realization, following World War II, that the globe had shrunk and that no country was immune from nuclear attack made it necessary for presidential power to grow. In foreign relations, the president is the central, dominant policymaker. In an age of computer-deployed multiple warheads (MIRVS) and guerrilla insurgencies, the chief executive has the prime responsibility for protecting the national security of the United States. *Social* and *economic problems* have also broadened the scope and size of the presidency. Beginning with the New Deal, the presidency has become more and more involved in seeking solutions for social and economic problems. Congress has charged the president with maintaining full employment. In 1970, Congress authorized the president to impose wage and price controls in order to stabilize the economy. Lyndon Johnson's Great Society sought massive social reordering of priorities through changed budgetary priorities. There are presidential commissions on civil rights and on the status of women. The executive branch has become a complex of agencies and advisors charged with fashioning alternatives for social and economic problems.

The mass media have also contributed to the expansion of presidential power. Both because of the instantaneous relaying of information on foreign or domestic crises, and because the president is the lone symbol of leadership for

President Theodore Roosevelt popularized the modern presidency and called for strong presidential leadership. (National Archives)

the nation, the media have focused on the presidency. Television and the newspapers cover the slightest move the president makes. Reporters travel with the president across the country or across the seas. To the American people, the president is news. This allows the president to help shape issues and moods. The less attention given to Congress, parties, and interest groups, the more the president can dominate the scene. The third major factor contributing to the growth of the presidency has been personality. The powers of the presidency have been shaped and enlarged due to the nature of the men occupying the office. The particular stamp of individual personalities—how each defined the task and confronted problems—has worked to enlarge the office.

Theodore Roosevelt at the turn of the century made the presidency a "bully pulpit," the object of attention for all within the political arena. His often repeated view of executive authority, the stewardship theory, has become the standard for a strong executive. Roosevelt said:

> My view was that every executive officer, and above all every executive officer in high position, was a steward of the people bound actively and affirmatively to do all he could for the people, and not to content himself with the negative merit of keeping his talents undamaged in a napkin. I declined to adopt the view that what was imperatively necessary for the nation could not be done by the President unless he could find some specific authorization to do it. *My belief was that it was not only his right but his duty to do anything that the needs of the nation demanded, unless such action was forbidden by the Constitution or by the laws.*[7] (Italics added)

Woodrow Wilson, a scholar and educator, dominated the second decade of the twentieth century. Wilson succeeded in getting Congress to pass the Clayton Antitrust Act and in creating the Federal Trade Commission and Federal Reserve System. In foreign affairs, Wilson was the architect of the League of Nations and a world figure. Said Wilson: "The President is at liberty, both in law and conscience, to be as big a man as he can." For greatness and the imaginative use of power, however, Franklin D. Roosevelt stands alone. Elected at the height of the Depression, Roosevelt has become the yardstick for measuring presidential power.[8] His New Deal was a bold design for putting America back on its feet again. When Roosevelt faced opposition for his New Deal program, he took his appeal to the American people. His famous fireside chats rallied public support for his programs. Franklin Roosevelt is also responsible for helping "personalize" the presidency. During the war, Roosevelt kept morale high with his radio broadcasts. FDR was a skilled and astute politician who knew how to use the techniques of leadership and persuasion. John Kennedy also worked

---

7. Theodore Roosevelt, *The Autobiography of Theodore Roosevelt,* ed. Wayne Andrews (New York: Scribner, 1958), pp. 198-199.
8. See Richard Neustadt, *Presidential Power* (New York: John Wiley & Sons, Inc., 1960 & 1980).

PRESIDENTS AND VICE PRESIDENTS OF THE UNITED STATES

President and Political Party	Born	Died	Age at inauguration	Native of—	Elected from—	Term of Service	Vice President
George Washington (F)	1732	1799	57	Va.	Va.	April 30, 1789–March 4, 1793	John Adams
George Washington (F)			61		Va.	March 4, 1793–March 4, 1797	John Adams
John Adams (F)	1735	1826	61	Mass.	Mass.	March 4, 1797–March 4, 1801	Thomas Jefferson
Thomas Jefferson (D-R)	1743	1826	57	Va.	Va.	March 4, 1801–March 4, 1805	Aaron Burr
Thomas Jefferson (D-R)			61		Va.	March 4, 1805–March 4, 1809	George Clinton
James Madison (D-R)	1751	1836	57	Va.	Va.	March 4, 1809–March 4, 1813	George Clinton
James Madison (D-R)			61		Va.	March 4, 1813–March 4, 1817	Elbridge Gerry
James Monroe (D-R)	1758	1831	58	Va.	Va.	March 4, 1817–March 4, 1821	Daniel D. Tompkins
James Monroe (D-R)			62		Va.	March 4, 1821–March 4, 1825	Daniel D. Tompkins
John Q. Adams (N-R)	1767	1848	57	Mass.	Mass.	March 4, 1825–March 4, 1829	John C. Calhoun
Andrew Jackson (D)	1767	1845	61	S.C.	Tenn.	March 4, 1829–March 4, 1833	John C. Calhoun
Andrew Jackson (D)			65		Tenn.	March 4, 1833–March 4, 1837	Martin Van Buren
Martin Van Buren (D)	1782	1862	54	N.Y.	N.Y.	March 4, 1837–March 4, 1841	Richard M. Johnson
W. H. Harrison (W)	1773	1841	68	Va.	Ohio	March 4, 1841–April 4, 1841	John Tyler
John Tyler (W)	1790	1862	51	Va.	Va.	April 6, 1841–March 4, 1845	
James K. Polk (D)	1795	1849	49	N.C.	Tenn.	March 4, 1845–March 4, 1849	George M. Dallas
Zachary Taylor (W)	1784	1850	64	Va.	La.	March 4, 1849–July 9, 1850	Millard Fillmore
Millard Fillmore (W)	1800	1874	50	N.Y.	N.Y.	July 10, 1850–March 4, 1853	
Franklin Pierce (D)	1804	1869	48	N.H.	N.H.	March 4, 1853–March 4, 1857	William R. King
James Buchanan (D)	1791	1868	65	Pa.	Pa.	March 4, 1857–March 4, 1861	John C. Breckinridge
Abraham Lincoln (R)	1809	1865	52	Ky.	Ill.	March 4, 1861–March 4, 1865	Hannibal Hamlin
Abraham Lincoln (R)			56		Ill.	March 4, 1865–April 15, 1865	Andrew Johnson
Andrew Johnson (R)	1808	1875	56	N.C.	Tenn.	April 15, 1865–March 4, 1869	
Ulysses S. Grant (R)	1822	1885	46	Ohio	Ill.	March 4, 1869–March 4, 1873	Schuyler Colfax
Ulysses S. Grant(R)			50		Ill.	March 4, 1873–March 4, 1877	Henry Wilson
Rutherford B. Hayes (R)	1822	1893	54	Ohio	Ohio	March 4, 1877–March 4, 1881	William A. Wheeler
James A. Garfield (R)	1831	1881	49	Ohio	Ohio	March 4, 1881–Sept. 19, 1881	Chester A. Arthur
Chester A. Arthur (R)	1830	1886	50	Vt.	N.Y.	Sept. 20, 1881–March 4, 1885	
Grover Cleveland (D)	1837	1908	47	N.J.	N.Y.	March 4, 1885–March 4, 1889	Thomas A. Hendricks
Benjamin Harrison (R)	1833	1901	55	Ohio	Ind.	March 4, 1889–March 4, 1893	Levi P. Morton

President	Born	Birthplace	Died	Age	State	Term	Vice President
Grover Cleveland (D)	1837		1908	55		March 4, 1893–March 4, 1897	Adlai E. Stevenson
William McKinley (R)	1843	Ohio	1901	54	Ohio	March 4, 1897–March 4, 1901	Garret A. Hobart
William McKinley (R)				58		March 4, 1901–Sept. 14, 1901	Theodore Roosevelt
Theodore Roosevelt (R)	1858	N.Y.	1919	42	N.Y.	Sept. 14, 1901–March 4, 1905	
Theodore Roosevelt (R)				46		March 4, 1905–March 4, 1909	Charles W. Fairbanks
William H. Taft (R)	1857	Ohio	1930	51	Ohio	March 4, 1909–March 4, 1913	James S. Sherman
Woodrow Wilson (D)	1856	Va.	1924	56	N.J.	March 4, 1913–March 4, 1917	Thomas R. Marshall
Woodrow Wilson (D)				60		March 4, 1917–March 4, 1921	Thomas R. Marshall
Warren G. Harding (R)	1865	Ohio	1923	55	Ohio	March 4, 1921–Aug. 2, 1923	Calvin Coolidge
Calvin Coolidge (R)	1872	Vt.	1933	51	Mass.	Aug. 3, 1923–March 4, 1925	
Calvin Coolidge (R)				52		March 4, 1925–March 4, 1929	Charles G. Dawes
Herbert Hoover (R)	1874	Iowa	1964	54	Calif.	March 4, 1929–March 4, 1933	Charles Curtis
Franklin D. Roosevelt (D)	1882	N.Y.	1945	51	N.Y.	March 4, 1933–Jan. 20, 1937	John N. Garner
Franklin D. Roosevelt (D)				55		Jan. 20, 1937–Jan. 20, 1941	John N. Garner
Franklin D. Roosevelt (D)				59		Jan. 20, 1941–Jan. 20, 1945	Henry A. Wallace
Franklin D. Roosevelt (D)				63		Jan. 20, 1945–April 12, 1945	Harry S. Truman
Harry S. Truman (D)	1884	Mo.	1972	60	Mo.	April 12, 1945–Jan. 20, 1949	
Harry S. Truman (D)				64		Jan. 20, 1949–Jan. 20, 1953	Alben W. Barkley
Dwight D. Eisenhower (R)	1890	Texas	1969	62	N.Y.	Jan. 20, 1953–Jan. 20, 1957	Richard M. Nixon
Dwight D. Eisenhower (R)				66	Pa.	Jan. 20, 1957–Jan. 20, 1961	Richard M. Nixon
John F. Kennedy (D)	1917	Mass.	1963	43	Mass.	Jan. 20, 1961–Nov. 22, 1963	Lyndon B. Johnson
Lyndon B. Johnson (D)	1908	Texas	1973	55	Texas	Nov. 22, 1963–Jan. 20, 1965	
Lyndon B. Johnson (D)				56		Jan. 20, 1965–Jan. 20, 1969	Hubert H. Humphrey
Richard M. Nixon (R)	1913	Calif.		56	N.Y.	Jan. 20, 1969–Jan. 20, 1973	Spiro T. Agnew
Richard M. Nixon (R)				60	Calif.	Jan. 20, 1973–Aug. 9, 1974	Spiro T. Agnew 10–11–73 Gerald R. Ford 11–27–73
Gerald R. Ford (R)	1913	Neb.		61	Mich.	Aug. 9, 1974–Jan 20, 1976	Nelson A. Rockefeller
James E. Carter (D)	1924	Ga.		52	Ga.	Jan. 20, 1976–Jan. 20, 1981	Walter F. Mondale
Ronald W. Reagan (R)	1911	Ill.		69	Calif.	Jan. 20, 1981–	George Bush

Key to abbreviations: (D) Democrat, (D-R) Democrat-Republican, (F) Federalist, (N-R) National Republican, (R) Republican, (W) Whig

SOURCE: Joseph Nathan Kane, *Facts About the President*, third edition, 1974.

to personalize the presidency, and Lyndon Johnson sought to capture the spirit of the New Deal with his Great Society. Both saw the office as the seat of leadership and initiative.

PRESIDENTIAL ROLES

Forces in the twentieth century have created for the president several roles that have given the chief executive "an awesome burden." And while these various roles and responsibilities cannot be neatly divided, for presidential activity is what Clinton Rossiter called a "seamless web," it is nonetheless useful to separate out the many and varied roles a president is asked to carry out.

POLITICAL AND POPULAR ROLES

A president comes to Washington a winner. The successful candidate has achieved an electoral victory, millions of Americans voted for the President-elect. This is taken by the incoming president as a mark of confidence from the people, the expression of a political mandate to govern the nation. This is what Richard Pious called the "popular connection." "The President emphasizes a mandate based on an undifferentiated majority—no matter how narrow the victory. The 'voice of the people' may not have offered a mandate on issues in a clearcut campaign, but that does not prevent presidents from claiming to act in the name of the people."[9]

The popular role makes the president an instant superstar. He commands media attention and the public look to the president for leadership. Whatever the president does is of concern to all Americans.

The presidential role of leader is most easily seen as *chief of state*. Here the president combines political leadership with the symbolic, and largely ceremonial, role of head of state. Unlike many countries, where political responsibilities are entrusted to a prime minister and the ceremonial tasks are handled by a monarch or a president, we expect our president to fulfill both functions. There is no clear distinction between ceremonial and political power. It is precisely because the people view the president as head of state that they expect leadership and initiative.

A president is the elected nominee of a political party, and he is expected to play the role of *chief of his party*. As a politician, the president immediately has the advantage, or the disadvantage, of a partisan majority in Congress. A good deal of a president's legislative success depends on partisan ties. With the decline of the coattail effect, presidential campaigning for congressional candidates is less important than it once was. Nonetheless, congressional elections are

9. Richard M. Pious, *The American Presidency,* (New York: Basic Books, 1979), pp. 85–86.

What Happens When You Write to the President

Every piece of mail that comes into the White House is answered—not by the President himself, of course, for no one could read, much less answer, 40,000 to 70,000 letters a week. But every piece of mail is opened, sorted, and analyzed. Then, depending on the content, it is sent to the White House staff, the appropriate government agency, or the Director of Correspondence for a reply. Letters expressing general support or giving views and suggestions receive a reply from the Director of Correspondence. Those containing questions and problems are referred to the appropriate agency or department, and there is an internal followup system to make sure that someone having difficulty with, for example, social security checks receives a reply from the Social Security administration.

Every week information gleaned from the letters is presented to the President and the senior White House staff in a statistical and narrative report summarizing the tone and content of the mail that week. The report is accompanied by a random sample of incoming letters to which the President replies personally. So your letter to the President is not just received and filed: you receive an answer, and what you have to say becomes part of the stream of information that keeps the President and the White House staff informed about what people want and what they are thinking.

Thank you for your letter. It was very thoughtful of you to take the time to share your views with me. Jimmy joins me in sending our best wishes.

Rosalynn Carter

Table 10.3

**Presidents Who Governed
Without Popular Majorities**

Years	President	Percentage of Vote
1825–29	Adams	30.5
1841–45	Tyler	None
1845–49	Polk	49.6
1949–50	Taylor	47.3
1850–53	Fillmore	None
1857–61	Buchanan	45.3
1861–65	Lincoln	39.8
1865–69	Johnson	None
1877–81	Hayes	48.0
1881	Garfield	48.3
1881–85	Arthur	None
1885–89	Cleveland	48.5
1889–93	Harrison	47.9
1893–97	Cleveland	46
1901–05	Roosevelt	None
1913–17	Wilson	41.8
1917–21	Wilson	49.3
1923–25	Coolidge	None
1945–49	Truman	None
1949–53	Truman	49.5
1961–63	Kennedy	49.7
1963–65	Johnson	None
1969–73	Nixon	43.4
1974–77	Ford	None

frequently viewed as an expression of support for presidents and their policies. The decline of parties, however, has caused the distinction between partisan and statesman to become blurred.

DOMESTIC POLICY ROLES

In part because of the popular role of leadership and partisan campaigning and in part because of the tide of rising expectations for domestic policy from the New Deal and Great Society, the president is the initiator of much domestic policy. The president sends up to Congress between 100 and 400 bills annually on domestic issues. Much of the initiative for domestic policy is lodged in the White House today.

Presidents usually enter the White House with a bold design for new directions for America. They then seek to make good on their promises by submitting a legislative program to Congress. The congressional honeymoon generally lasts less than a year. The initially receptive legislature finds that separation of powers gives it ample opportunity to thwart the president's ability to be *chief legislator*. Says Louis Koenig: ''Nowhere else in the Presidential enterprise is there found a greater gap between what the Chief Executive wants to do, what he promises to the electorate in his contest for the office, and what he can do in bringing Congress to enact the laws that alone can give effect to the party program of the previous campaign.''[10]

Twentieth-century presidents have taken lead in proposing legislation. The annual State of the Union message is an ideal way for a president to unveil his legislative program. But a president's rapport with Congress requires more than a program and the support of public opinion to move Congress to action. Successful presidents find it necessary to constantly monitor proposals and consult with legislators (Fig. 10.1).

In his role as legislative leader, a president soon discovers that in this area Congress is endowed with many powers: control of the purse strings, and of legislative calendars, the filibusters, and so on, give Congress ample opportunity to deny a president the laws he wants.[11] In recent years, Republican chief execu-

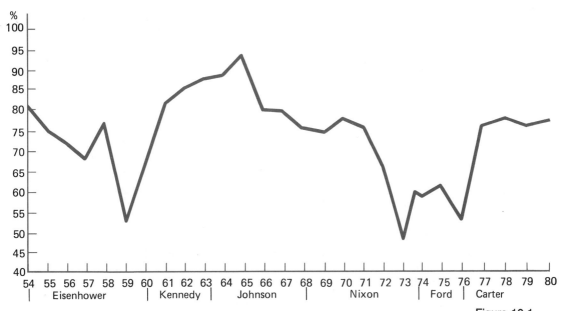

Figure 10.1

Presidential success on measures on which presidents took a position from 1953 to 1978. (*1978 Almanac Quarterly,* 95th Congress, Washington, D.C.: The Congressional Quarterly, 1979, Vol. 34, p. 23c)

10. Louis W. Koenig, *The Chief Executive,* p. 150.
11. George C. Edwards III, *Presidential Influence in Congress* (San Francisco: W. H. Freeman, 1980).

tives have had to face Democratic majorities in Congress. But the president is also not without legislative resources. The most obvious is the veto. The threat of a veto acts as a strong deterrent to legislation the president disapproves. It can also be used to effect compromise. The threat of a veto will often soften Congress and produce a law that has broad support.

After a bill is passed by Congress, the president has ten working days to sign or veto the bill; otherwise it becomes law without his signature. The only exception is the **pocket veto:** If Congress adjourns before the ten-day period, the lack of presidential action effectively kills the bill. In the 1970s President Nixon sought to define the pocket veto to include recess as well as adjournment. The Constitution is not clear on this point but court rulings restrict the pocket veto to formal adjournment of Congress, not a recess. Congress can override a veto by a two-thirds vote of both chambers. But as Table 10.4 illustrates, Congresses have had little success in overriding presidential vetoes.

Another power a president has in his legislative role is **impoundment,** a refusal to spend appropriated funds. Presidents have occasionally used impoundment as an item veto. Since presidents must veto entire legislative acts, they cannot veto particular items or portions of laws, presidents have taken to impounding funds to reject those facets of the legislation they dislike. President Buchanan refused to spend appropriated money for post offices and other public buildings in 1857. Harry S. Truman impounded Air Force funds in 1949 as a means of an item veto, and Richard Nixon in 1972 and 1973 postponed several environmental and housing programs by not spending the appropriated money.[12] In the 1970s, Richard Nixon began a much broader use of impoundment. In fact, he used impoundment to change social policy when he proposed to abolish the Office of Economic Opportunity by refusing to spend the money appropriated for it. Although the Constitution does not require presidents to spend money, federal court decisions on impoundment have taken a narrow view and limited a president's authority to refuse to spend appropriated funds. In 1974 Congress passed the Budget and Impoundment Control Act, requiring a president to spend money appropriated by Congress.

The third power a President may exercise is **executive privilege.** Presidents have at times invoked the privilege of withholding information from Congress. Richard Nixon used this claim broadly to prevent subordinate officers from testifying before Congress. In defense of his position, Nixon cited historical precedent and the constitutional separation of powers. Congress, in turn, cited the need for information in legislating and inquiring after executive administration of congressional laws. At the height of Watergate, the case of executive privilege went before the Supreme Court. The Court recognized the constitutionality of executive privilege, in *U.S.* v. *Nixon,* but refused to accept a blanket claim for such privilege or a president's right to define its use.

12. Louis Fisher, *Presidential Spending Power* (Princeton, N.J.: Princeton University Press, 1975), pp. 165–167.

Table 10.4

Presidential Vetoes, 1789 to 1980

	Regular vetoes	Pocket vetoes	Total vetoes	Vetoes overridden
Washington	2	—	2	—
Madison	5	2	7	—
Monroe	1	—	1	—
Jackson	5	7	12	—
Tyler	6	3	9	1
Polk	2	1	3	—
Pierce	9	—	9	5
Buchanan	4	3	7	—
Lincoln	2	4	6	—
A. Johnson	21	8	29	15
Grant	45	49	94	4
Hayes	12	1	13	1
Arthur	4	8	12	1
Cleveland	304	109	413	2
Harrison	19	25	44	1
Cleveland	43	127	170	5
McKinley	6	36	42	—
T. Roosevelt	42	40	82	1
Taft	30	9	39	1
Wilson	33	11	44	6
Harding	5	1	6	—
Coolidge	20	30	50	4
Hoover	21	16	37	3
F. Roosevelt	372	261	633	9
Truman	180	70	250	12
Eisenhower	73	108	181	2
Kennedy	12	9	21	—
L. Johnson	16	14	30	—
Nixon	24	19	43	5
Ford	44	22	66	12
Carter	11	13	24	2
Total	1373	1006	2378	92

SOURCE: Bureau of the Census, *Statistical Abstract*, 1979. 1980 data, Congressional Record, Jan. 3 and Oct. 2, 1980.

Article II of the Constitution vests "the executive power" in a president of the United States and commands that he "take care that the Laws be faithfully executed." The Constitution does not say how the executive is to go about the task, only that it anticipated the establishment of executive departments to assist the chief executive by allowing the president to require the opinion "of the principal officer in each of the executive departments."

Although much administrative responsibility must be delegated to subordinates, the president is the one charged with final responsibility for *administration of the laws*. The Framers could not possibly have foreseen the enormous growth of government. The growth of the executive branch, in size and function, is unparalleled by the legislative and judicial branches. A vast and complex administrative structure assists the president in taking care that the laws are faithfully executed. There are now 2.9 million employees within executive agencies responsible for spending over $500 billion annually.

The executive branch is divided into 13 executive departments headed by presidentially appointed secretaries. Departments are charged with the implementation of federal programs and with spending appropriated money for such programs. In addition to the cabinet-level departments, there are approximately 60 independent agencies that manage specific areas of concern. These independent agencies are housed within the executive branch but do not fall under the authority of any cabinet department; they are "independent" of executive agencies and independent regulatory agencies. The president retains direct supervisory responsibility for the independent executive agencies; the regulatory agencies exercise their own quasi-executive and judicial powers under broad authority granted by Congress.

Since the tasks of supervision and control are so enormous, presidents have taken to establishing personal lines of information and supervision. In the past two decades, presidents have established personal presidential advisers and an Executive Office within the Office of the President in order to provide more direct and personal kinds of support for the task of managing the affairs of the nation. There has been a rapid growth in the Executive Office of the President. These officers are presidential appointees and have no responsibility other than serving the president.[13] Between 1954 and 1971 the number of presidential advisers grew from 25 to 45, the White House staff from 266 to 600, and the Executive Office staff from 1,175 to 5,395.[14]

Since the New Deal, the president has assumed the major responsibility for *promoting economic growth*. Through his general powers to tax and spend for the general welfare, the president has become the nation's chief economic manager. Legislation has laid economic management squarely at the feet of the president. In 1946, the Employment Act charged the president with maintaining the economy at full employment and submitting to Congress a report on the status of the economic health of the nation. The act empowered the president to control wages, prices, and rents in order to control the economy. This responsibility was extended in 1970 when Congress empowered President Nixon to freeze wages and prices to control inflation.

Much of the executive authority for managing the economy comes from the preparation of the budget. Ever since 1921, the president has had the responsibility for submitting an annual budget to Congress. This gives the president an opportunity to plan, fix priorities, and generally make fiscal policy. In the budget

13. See Thomas Cronin, *The State of the Presidency,* 2nd Edition (Boston: Little, Brown & Co., 1980), especially Chapter 7.
14. Thomas Cronin, *The State of the Presidency,* 1st. Edition, p. 118.

preparation process, new programs may be proposed, domestic spending favored over military defense, or tax cuts initiated. The annual budget is viewed as a statement by the president of his priorities for the coming year.

The president has considerable help in managing the economy. The Office of Management and Budget (OMB) helps prepare the budget. All requests for funding are screened through OMB. The office also monitors the level of spending once the money has been appropriated by Congress. The chief advisers to the president on economic affairs are on his Council of Economic Advisers. They provide information and advice concerning inflation, government spending, and taxation. As of 1974, the Council on Wage and Price Stability monitors the health of the economy with respect to wages, costs, prices, and productivity, and it too is located within the Executive Office of the President.

In recent years, the rate of inflation coupled with high unemployment has meant a rather extensive presidential preoccupation with economic matters, and current problems indicate that this focus will continue.

FOREIGN POLICY AND MILITARY ROLE

There is no area where the power of the President is more virtual and awesome. The president's responsibility in military and foreign policy matters has little challenge. From time to time Congress may check presidential initiative but it rarely, if ever, challenges the authority of the president to conduct foreign relations. It is in the area of foreign affairs that presidential leadership is at its height. Not from any constitutional grant of authority, but from the "silences of the Constitution" the president finds a general power to conduct foreign relations. "The President claims the silences of the Constitution. He finds a general 'power to conduct foreign relations' for the nation. Then he assumes that whatever has not been expressly assigned to Congress is to be exercised by the executive."[15]

Undoubtedly, the most awesome of roles for a president is that of *commander-in-chief* of the armed services. Sitting atop a nuclear arsenal, the president bears the burden for "pushing the button." Although the threat of nuclear warfare makes the role an "awesome burden" there is far more to it. Today the military is a fixed part of American government. Over 2 million Americans serve in the armed forces. In addition, the Defense Department and the branches of the service employ 993,000 civilian employees. The military has a budget of almost $100 billion, one-fifth the entire federal budget.

Donald Robinson has noted that two forces combined to make the commander-in-chief role a prime area of responsibility: "The creation of a massive permanent military establishment, and the negotiation and ratification of a network of treaties, making explicit the responsibility of the United States for security around the world."[16] The president's responsibilities in deploying American

15. Richard Pious, *The American Presidency*, p. 333.
16. Donald L. Robinson, "The President as Commander-in-Chief," in Stanley Bach and George T. Sulzer (eds.), *Perspectives on the Presidency* (Lexington, Mass.: D. C. Heath, 1974), p. 369.

National Security Policy

The National Security of the United States, which guards the nation's physical well being and way of life is protected by two policy areas: foreign policy, whereby we conduct relations with other nations, and military policy, which revolves around the deployment of military forces and weapons to protect U.S. security.

The making of national security policy falls most heavily to the President, although both Congress and the executive branch maintain strong interests in foreign and military policies. But only the President can obtain and analyze the diverse sources of information; only the President can protect the confidentiality of information; and only the President can act swiftly in cases of crisis.

In making national security policy the President relies on a series of formal and informal advisers, which often causes personnel within the White House to rival for power and influence with members of the State Department and Department of Defense. In foreign policies the two major groups of advisers are the National Security Council and the State Department. The National Security Council has acquired great influence ever since the presidency of John F. Kennedy. Composed of the Vice President, Secretary of State, Secretary of Defense, and other personnel designated by the President, the NSC has an expert staff directed by the Special Assistant for National Security Affairs. The Special Assistant has acquired considerable policy influence and advises the President directly on foreign policy. The staff analyzes policy alternatives and forecasts consequences for alternatives. The Secretary of State and the career diplomats who make up the State Department are responsible for implementing the policies adopted by the President. Often their day-to-day operations expertise comes into conflict with the NSC and its more narrow purpose of advising the President.

In military policy there is a more integrated set of policy advisers as the branches of military service within the Department of Defense headed by the Secretary of Defense and Joint Chiefs of Staff are statutory advisers to the National Security Council. Here the technical analysis of defense intelligence combines with NSC staff research to provide the President ready information on military activity around the globe.

The goals of American foreign policy are, broadly, four: (1) national security, (2) international peace and stability, (3) economic assistance, and (4) furthering U.S. interests globally. To this list President Carter had added a fifth, protecting human rights.

Since World War II, the policy objective of national security has been preoccupied with communist containment, although since Vietnam and the late 1970s this objective has lost some of its persuasiveness. The Marshall Plan, NATO, military bases, and military activity— Korea, Vietnam—were all part of a communist containment policy. Even as of 1980, the Olympic boycott and cruise missiles are part of a containment policy. Since Richard Nixon, however, détente (negotiations to reduce tensions and increase trade and cultural exchanges) has indicated a changing policy toward Russia and China. SALT, designed to reduce the number of nuclear weapons and the dependence on military weapons systems for policy, is a result of the changing policy.

The second objective of international peace and stability has meant, most historically, support for the United Nations. It has also involved, more recently, the nuclear nonproliferation treaty (1968), the SALT treaty (1972), and efforts to ratify SALT II. President Carter has added a personal touch with the Camp David Summit (1978), where he brought together Arab and Israeli leaders to secure a peaceful settlement in the Middle East.

Economic assistance has been tied to the first objective by providing economic aid to underdeveloped nations in order to gain their support and loyalty, thereby preventing the spread of communism. Foreign aid is the principal tool of economic assistance. More recently, since the formation of OPEC and the Arab boycott in 1973, the U.S. economic objective has been to maintain a balance of trade, keeping the balance of payments (income from exports less costs from import purchases) from

becoming too great a drain on the economy. President Carter also has resorted to an economic boycott to protest Iran's holding U.S. citizens hostage.

Human rights became a policy objective early in Carter's administration. He declared the protection of human rights in foreign countries to be an aim of U.S. foreign policy. Carter said the United States would use its influence and resources to see that human rights were protected by other governments. The objective has proved difficult to implement, notably where other issues and policy objectives conflict, as with the Soviet Union. But with smaller, friendlier nations, as South Korea and the Phillipines, influence has been exerted to protect human rights.

---

troops and engaging in international negotiations make for a situation where Congress often has no alternative but to yield to the president and support his actions. President Truman, as commander-in-chief, made the decision to drop the first atomic bomb in 1945. John F. Kennedy, after huddling with his advisers, blocked the ports of Cuba to Russian ships in 1962. Lyndon Johnson sent troops into Vietnam to support South Vietnam in 1965, and Richard Nixon personally authorized the bombing of Cambodia in 1970.

Congress has the specific responsibility for declaring war. This has not deterred presidents, however, from making military commitments without congressional approval. In fact, Congress has generally supported presidential action to protect American interests around the globe. Vietnam, however, brought a reexamination of the president's war powers. Congress had passed the Gulf of Tonkin Resolution in 1964 supporting President Johnson's escalation of the war. Johnson, and President Nixon after him, argued that it was all the authorization they needed to take whatever steps they felt necessary to protect the national security of the United States. The secret bombings in Cambodia were more than Congress would tolerate. In 1973 it passed the War Powers Act, aimed at curbing unilateral presidential action. Passed over presidential veto, the act requires the president to inform Congress within 48 hours of committing any armed forces to combat abroad and further provides that such forces must be withdrawn in 60 days unless Congress authorizes their use.

Whether the War Powers Act significantly redresses the balance of power remains to be seen. Generally presidents have enjoyed high public approval for their military actions. And until we seriously redefine America's role in world affairs, there appears little alternative to entrusting the president with broad war powers. As Clinton Rossiter observed, "We have placed a shocking amount of military power in the President's keeping, but where else, we may ask, could it possibly have been placed?"

The *diplomatic role* of the chief executive has always been a source of strength and prestige for the president. It has always been an executive function. Jefferson labeled the making of foreign policy "executive altogether," and Truman brashly declared "I make American foreign policy." While the Constitution does not guarantee executive prerogative and occasionally requires the advice and consent of the Senate, presidents have generally been free to manage foreign affairs. In fact, commentators on the presidency have claimed there ought to be two presidents, one for domestic affairs, and one for defense and foreign policy.[17] It is in the area of foreign affairs that presidents have enjoyed their greatest successes. And although many presidents began with high domestic priorities (Roosevelt and Johnson, for example), their greatest preoccupations were in foreign affairs. In fact, Wildavsky argues: "In the realm of foreign policy there has not been a single major issue on which Presidents, when they were serious and determined, have failed."[18]

The power of a president to act is constitutionally limited to appointing and receiving ambassadors, and to making treaties with the advice and consent of the Senate. But today a president has the ability to commit Americans all across the globe. A network of information and advice coming from the State Department, the Pentagon, intelligence sources such as the CIA, as well as his personal advisers for national security, affords the president knowledge that no other official has. And with the use of executive agreements instead of treaties, the president can enter into commitments that are not easily reversed.

The diplomatic role is most dramatically portrayed by the president's ability to engage the armed forces in war. We have had two "presidential wars" in the recent past: Korea and Vietnam. The president's power in foreign relations can be seen as well by the amount of time and energy he spends on this part of his job and the worldwide effect his actions have. Richard Nixon signaled a turn in American policy toward the Chinese Communists with his visit to Peking in 1971. Jimmy Carter's greatest achievement to date was his personal intervention to bring the Egyptian and Israeli leaders, Anwar Sadat and Menacheom Begin, together for the summit at Camp David in 1978.

The nature of the action taken, or just the posture of the president toward events, shapes American and international policy. He may not be completely at liberty to make foreign policy, but the president has no rival for the role of chief diplomat.

17. See Aaron Wildavsky, "The Two Presidencies," in Stanley Bach and George T. Sulzner (eds.), *Perspectives on the Presidency* (Lexington, Mass.: D. C. Heath, 1974).
18. *Ibid.*, p. 384.

THE EROSION OF THE HEROIC PRESIDENCY

The cumulative effect of the growth of presidential power and of presidential roles has been to create a myth that the president is the hope of American democracy, and indeed the free world. In short we have created a halo for the chief.

Popular opinion, in the decades after the New Deal, supported the growth of presidential power and roles with little dissent. In what Thomas Cronin has labeled the "textbook" or ideal presidency, the growth of presidential resources and responsibilities was not only approved but celebrated: "To the teenager or young adult, textbook discussions of the extensive resources available to the president cannot help but convey the impression that a president must have just about all the inside information and good advice anyone could want. . . . "[19] The textbook presidency celebrated presidential policies and the vast reservoir of thinking and planning that went into these policies. The President's advisory and information networks included the "best and brightest" minds in the nation. The belief was that the president knew best. Cronin summarizes the dimensions of the textbook ideal of the presidency along four exaggerated lines:

Omnipotent–Competent Dimension:

1. The president is the strategic catalyst for programs in the American political system and the central figure in the international system as well.
2. Only the president can be the genuine architect of U.S. public policy, and only he, by attacking problems frontally and agressively and by interpreting his power expansively, can slay the dragons of crisis and be the engine of change to move this nation forward.

Moralistic–Benevolent Dimension

3. The president must be the nation's personal and moral leader; by symbolizing the past and future greatness of America and radiating inspirational confidence, a president can pull the nation together while directing its people toward fulfillment of the American Dream.
4. If, and only if, the right person is placed in the White House, all will be well; and; somehow, whoever is in the White House is the best person for the job—at least for a year or so.[20]

But the textbook ideal has come to a sad end. Public confidence in the presidency began to erode in the mid-1960s and sank to a new low during Watergate. Serious proposals for reform emerged in the wake of Vietnam and Watergate to limit presidential discretion and abuse of power. The very people who cheered the presidency a decade or two earlier have come now to seek ways of

19. From Thomas E. Cronin, *The State of the Presidency*, p. 27. Copyright © 1975 by Little, Brown and Co., Inc. Reprinted by permission of Little, Brown and Co.
20. *Ibid.*, p. 35.

POSITION OF MORAL LEADERSHIP
April 13, 1974

From *Herblock Special Report* (W. W. Norton & Co., Inc., 1974).

checking presidential power. The erosion of the heroic presidency can be traced to four events: Vietnam, the Great Society programs, Watergate, and presidential personality.[21]

Watergate in particular produced demands for weakening the office. Some

21. See Erwin C. Hargrove, *The Power of the Modern Presidency* (New York: Knopf, 1974), pp. 21–28.

Americans wanted retribution for the abuses of presidential power. There were proposals for votes of no-confidence, a plural executive, and reduced responsibilities in several areas. The Vietnam war contributed to the erosion of the presidency in several ways. The process by which America became involved illustrated a lack of planning and sound military advice. All that information and network of advisers at the president's disposal became less reassuring in retrospect as America backed in deeper and deeper. Several commentators suggested that our policy was being dictated by a Cold War attitude of Communist containment that was no longer relevant to the changing world scene. The manner in which presidents conducted the war also produced objections. Had Congress been ''duped'' into passing the Gulf of Tonkin Resolution? American ground forces were introduced into Vietnam purportedly to protect military advisers and American bases of supplies. President Nixon extended the war into Cambodia without public or congressional awareness or approval. The secrecy and high handedness with which Washington executives conducted the war created a storm of protest. We began to hear of a ''credibility gap'' between the presidency and the nation. America's confidence in its leader was shaken.

The Vietnam war probably diverted a good deal of the resources that would have been available for the Great Society, but the programs were already headed for trouble. Passed in the years following Kennedy's assassination, the Great Society legislation promised social reform on a scale unknown since the days of the New Deal. The Great Society was designed to bring the massive resources of the federal government to bear on such problems as poverty, unemployment, poor housing, and social discrimination; and thus to rid the nation of them. But the

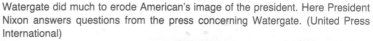

Watergate did much to erode American's image of the president. Here President Nixon answers questions from the press concerning Watergate. (United Press International)

Great Society was fundamentally different from the New Deal. Roosevelt proposed putting people back to work, providing regulation, and underwriting programs. Lyndon Johnson asked for programs that required social engineering—a reordering of goals and priorities to produce massive social change. The goals of the New Deal were relatively easy and manageable; those of the Great Society were not. Lyndon Johnson paid little attention to administering the programs; he appeared more intent on steering legislation through Congress. Many of the programs were hastily drawn, poorly detailed, and impractical: The result was a bureaucratic nightmare. There were overlapping and conflicting bureaucratic jurisdictions. Agencies contended for programs and ended up administering sections of them. There was little evaluation of their effectiveness. In short, the public was bewildered and angry. Promises had been made, government grew, but things did not improve; thus, government became a target.

Watergate caused a rapid decline in support for the presidency. Actually, the term "Watergate" stands for several events rolled into one. There were the campaign abuses such as the break-in at the Democratic headquarters, illegal corporate contributions, and political espionage; there was the misuse of governmental power by involving federal agencies in Watergate (using the CIA to cover up the break-in, asking the IRS to harrass political opponents, and executive personnel refusing to testify or honor subpoenas of congressional committees), and finally the cover-up and obstruction of justice involving not only executive agencies, but the presidency itself. Watergate had cheapened the office of the presidency—Americans expected far more from their chief executive officer. Watergate also illustrated the vast concentration of power in the office of the White House. Mr. Nixon had moved further than any president to centralize authority in the oval office. And along with centralizing control, Mr. Nixon had moved to isolate himself from the traditional constraints in the use of authority. He became virtually inaccessible to public officials. As Watergate grew, he became more removed from politics and relied more heavily on his personal advisers. Watergate demonstrated what could happen when presidential power was isolated from the political arena.

Presidential personality, the final factor producing an erosion of our idyllic view of presidential greatness, may be the sum effect of these three events. All the presidents involved in them made strong efforts to personalize the presidency. Both Lyndon Johnson and Richard Nixon were men of resolve with a sense of mission. They worried over how history would treat them, and they took their appeals to the people. The textbook idea of the presidency had extolled the value of a strong-willed, personal desire for power. It was the skillful crafting of personal policies that produced presidential greatness, whether traditional policymakers were consulted or not. There stood Lyndon Johnson, a man of principle, willing to use power to achieve his goals, frustrated by the insecurities and suspicions generated by his style of leadership. He took to more coercive measures, manipulating people, particularly in foreign affairs, and the result was an erosion of confidence and trust in the leadership of the president. Richard Nixon rode the crest of a great electoral mandate in 1972. He used what he viewed as a personal reaffirmation of his programs and ideology as a vendetta against political enemies. The impoundment of funds, the claim of executive privilege, as well as the conduct of the war in Vietnam, were done in a way that showed disdain for anyone who opposed the Nixon administration. The result was a White House besieged on all sides, and finally Watergate. The presidential styles of Lyndon Johnson and Richard Nixon produced "crises," that were as much self-defined and self-perpetuated as they were real. In their view, the necessity for crisis management left no room for accountability or the more democratic processes of politics.

PRIORITIES, POLICIES, AND PERSONALITY: REDEFINING PRESIDENTIAL POWER

The lack of presidential accountability led Arthur Schlesinger, Jr., to label the Nixon presidency the "imperial presidency."[22] It moved Richard Neustadt to call for the reestablishment of constraints in order to keep the president democratically rooted within the Constitution.[23] Citizens and political scientists alike are rethinking the idea of strong presidential power in the wake of the last decade. Although some reforms would drastically limit or restructure the powers of the office, most serious proposals call for "shared powers." For the post-Watergate presidency, there is increased emphasis on sharing the establishment of priorities. Whether Congress or the president takes the initiative, and the likelihood remains great that the president will continue to exercise considerable initiative, there is little chance that the president can again exert total dominance over public policy: Congress has now imposed many restraints. Yet the tools of presidential power remain substantial. Let us look at the organization of the presidency as it reflects the revised priorities of the post-Watergate presidency.

THE EXECUTIVE OFFICE

As presidential functions and activities increased in the twentieth century, so did the staff serving the president within the Executive Office of the President. In 1939, when the Bureau of the Budget was transferred from the Department of Treasury to the president's Executive Office, it numbered under 50. Today the number of budget examiners and managers approaches 600 and they have a staff of approximately 5,000 employees. The growth of the presidential staff within the Executive Office led Tom Cronin to call the phenomenon the "swelling of the Presidency."[24]

22. Arthur Schlesinger, Jr., *The Imperial Presidency,* especially Chapter 8.
23. Richard E. Neustadt, "The Constraining of the President," in Ronald E. Pynn (ed.) *Watergate and the American Political Process* (New York: Praeger, 1975).
24. From Thomas E. Cronin, *The State of the Presidency,* 1st Edition, Chapter 5. Copyright © 1975 by Little, Brown and Co., Inc. Reprinted by permission of Little, Brown and Co.

Table 10.5
Reorganization of the Executive Office
of the President, 1977

White House Office
Office of the Vice President
Office of Management and Budget
Council of Environmental Quality
Council of Economic Advisers
Office of Science and Technology Policy
Office of the Special Representative for Trade Negotiations
National Security Council
Intelligence Oversight Board
Council on Wage and Price Stability
Domestic Policy Staff
Office of Administration

The burdens on the presidency have brought a demand for swift and decisive action. Most presidents have felt constrained by cabinet secretaries and the bureaucracy. Secretaries are often appointed to appease particular interest groups and settle political debts; the bureaucracy often has a more limited and narrow focus. Hence presidents have preferred to go outside the regular administration for help and advice. The Executive Office staff serves at the pleasure of the president, and its members "speak the President's language."[25]

The executive establishment has grown at the expense of traditional sources of administrative policymaking—the cabinet and the bureaucracy (Figure 10.2). Under Nixon, presidential aides felt free to intrude into departmental affairs, make decisions in the name of the president, and make recommendations for changes in staff or policy. They came to be known as the "palace guard," protecting and isolating the president from administrative and political officials. Said one then close to the presidency: "This represents the greatest of all barriers to Presidential access to reality."[26]

In 1977 President Carter reorganized the Executive Office, eliminating seven offices and cutting back the staff by a third. Carter argued that reorganization would improve efficiency and the quality of the information provided to the president. It would also "strengthen cabinet government." In all, Carter reduced the White House staff from 485 to 351 and eliminated another 250 positions from the Executive Office staff, saving taxpayers a claimed $6 million. The Executive Office of the President can be broken down into six functional areas, reflecting the priorities of the contemporary presidency: (1) national security or foreign affairs, (2) domestic policy, (3) economic affairs, (4) administration or staff management, (5) congressional relations, and (6) public relations.

25. See Stephen Hess, *Organizing the Presidency* (Washington, D.C.: The Brookings Institution, 1976), Chapter 9.
26. George Reedy, *The Twilight of the President* (New York: World Publishing, 1970), p. 98.

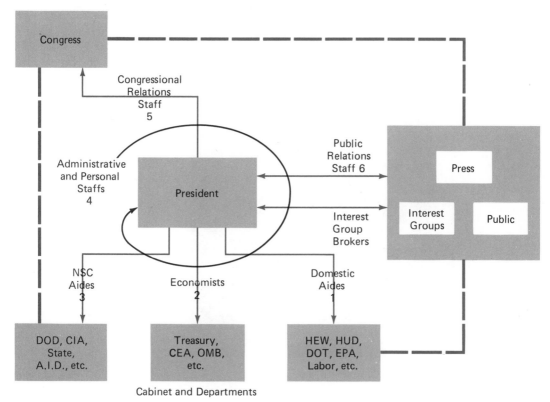

Figure 10.2

Six major staff groups of the White House and the cabinet and its departments. (J.M. Burns, J. Peltason, and T. Cronin, *Government by the People*, 10th edition. © 1978, p. 294. Reprinted by permission of Prentice-Hall, Inc., Englewood Cliffs, New Jersey.

Most contemporary presidents, instead of utilizing the State Department and the advice of secretaries of state, have depended on the National Security Council (NSC) and the presidential assistant for national security affairs. Starting with Eisenhower, the NSC has played an integral part in national defense policy. Kennedy used an executive committee of the NSC during the Cuban missile crisis, and Henry Kissinger's influence in the Nixon administration as national security adviser was due to his dominance of the NSC. As statutory members the National Security Council has the president, vice-president, secretary of state, and secretary of defense. Attached to it as advisers are the director of the Central Intelligence Agency and the chairman of the Joint Chiefs of Staff. Also included in its meetings is the assistant to the president for national security affairs.

In domestic policy there have been some changes. In 1970 Richard Nixon created a Domestic Council in the Executive Office. It was to be the domestic counterpart of the National Security Council in planning strategy and proposing

Henry Kissinger moved from Presidential Assistant for National Security to Secretary of State, combining both roles in the Nixon administration. (United Press International)

public policy across a broad spectrum of issues. John Ehrlichman was its executive director and it included many cabinet officers, but it never seemed to do anything. It met only twice in 1973 and may have been, in part, a casuality of Watergate.[27] Carter abolished the Domestic Council in 1977 and replaced it with the Domestic Policy Staff (DPS). The DPS would report to the assistant to the president for domestic affairs and would work closely with departments and agencies in coordinating information before making recommendations to the president on domestic policy.

The Office of Management and Budget (OMB) and the Council of Economic Advisers are the Executive Office's main resources for economic policy. In President Carter's executive reorganization, the Economic Opportunity Council (its only function of preparing the catalogue of domestic assistance had already been assumed by OMB), the Council on International Economic Policy, and the Energy Resources Council were dropped.

The Office of Management and Budget has become, since its creation by Richard Nixon in 1970, a major executive agency for fiscal and managerial control. Under Nixon, Ford, and Carter, OMB has played a major policy role. In

27. John H. Kessell, *The Domestic Presidency: Decision-Making in the White House* (North Scituate, Mass.: Duxbury Press, 1975), p. 111.

fact, it may very well be the most powerful agency in government today. The main function of OMB is to assist the president in preparing the annual budget. All agency requests for appropriations must be cleared through OMB, and it enforces presidential guidelines in the preparation of recommendations. OMB also acts as a clearinghouse for all proposed legislation from executive agencies; agencies submit proposals to OMB for the president's attention. Finally, OMB plays a major role in developing efficient and effective management techniques. It makes recommendations for implementing programs, administrative reorganization, and reforming the federal bureaucracy.

The Council of Economic Advisers is the other main arm of the president in economic policy. Created after World War II, the council is composed of three members appointed by the president and confirmed by the Senate. It maintains a small but highly technical and competent staff to analyze economic data and trends and to make economic forecasts. The major thrust of the council in recent years has been to advise the president on levels of unemployment, controlling the rate of inflation, and levels of government spending. Of course, the principal weapon is the tax, and the council frequently advises the president on cutting or raising taxes to deal with the cost of living and employment.

A third body, created in 1974 and surviving Carter's reorganization, is the Council on Wage and Price Stability. Its primary mission is to deal with the rate of inflation. The council is to review and appraise federal programs and policies and determine how they contribute to inflation, and to coordinate its activities with those of the Council of Economic Advisers. This council is under the direction of the chair of the Council of Economic Advisers.

President Carter created an Office of Central Administration to provide support for administrative services and to avoid unnecessary duplication and competition among staff. This move was a recognition that the Executive Office of the President had grown over the last few administrations and is now a permanent part of the government. In part, this move was in response to the isolation and autonomy of the presidential staff during the Nixon administration. The "palace guard," as they were known, screened access to the president and moved in his name to implement presidential wishes when agencies balked or were slow to respond. But the move to create this office was also a recognition that any president's time must be managed carefully.

A fifth priority area in the Executive Office is congressional relations. The White House staff for congressional relations seeks to promote the policies supported by the president. Its activities are coordinated by an assistant to the president for congressional liaison, and rise and fall with the particular personal interest each president takes in legislation. White House aides seeking support for a president's policies must deal with congressional committees and their chairs, floor leaders and whips, bill sponsors, and other key figures. One former aide summed up the responsibilities: "We handled the agendas for the Congressional Committees, worked with leaders (like Rayburn and Mansfield), took head counts. We had to hire Congressional liaison people throughout the government, and we would have weekly meetings with them. Then, too, we also had to keep track of all the legislation—track it all down, keep big posters with all the relevant data. We had to work with some task-force people telling them the mood of Congress. We always had to know what was possible.''[28] Legislative responsibilities thus range from public relations to satisfying legislator requests to outright political ''horse trading.''

The final area of concern for the Executive Office can be put in the general category of public relations. The president has a press secretary, and there is a special assistant to the president for media and public affairs and a deputy assistant for public liaison. But all presidential aides are concerned with the president's image and reputation. In the past few administrations, public relations has become a major operation. There are speech writers, media consultants, advance men, and information managers to control the flow of information from the White House. They seek to assess the impact of White House information on the media, the public, Congress, foreign leaders, popularity polls, executive agencies, and others. All recent presidents have been conscious of their reputations and have sought to guard their images with considerable care. This has led to the charge that presidents use their public relations staffs to manipulate public opinion. President Carter was sought to soft-pedal the idea that a president can manipulate and control public opinion. For example, the Office of Telecommunications Policy, so active under Richard Nixon, has been disbanded and many of its functions transferred to an office in the Department of Commerce.

THE CABINET

Every president, beginning with George Washington, has had a cabinet. Today the cabinet includes the president, vice-president, the heads of the 13 executive departments, and other executive branch officials to whom the president accords cabinet rank.

The rise of the White House staff in the Executive Office of the President has meant the decline of the cabinet as a policymaking group. Strong presidents want advice from those who ''speak the President's language'' and will not politically upstage them. The cabinet is not well suited to that role.

A number of criteria go into the selection of cabinet secretaries. First, they are generally prominent politicians and statesmen who will lend credibility to a new administration. Balance and interest representation are also important factors; it is necessary for a president to represent and balance as many interests as possible. Labor is concerned with the appointment of the labor secretary; environmental groups are concerned with the appointment of an interior secretary. There are also other factors to balance: geographic representation, race, and sex. In short, a president ends up with a cabinet he can work with, but often prefers to work without. Although in recent years, Hess notes, the changes in campaigning,

28. As cited in Thomas Cronin, *The State of the Presidency*, p. 135.

The Daily Activities of a President

Photos by Bill Fitz-Patrick, the White House.

Bill Signing

State dinner for King and Queen of Jordan

President Carter with Prime Minister and Mrs. Begin

Cabinet Meeting

Table 10.6

**The President's Cabinet in Order
of Formation**

State	1789
Treasury	1789
Interior	1849
Justice	1870
Agriculture	1889
Commerce	1913
Labor	1913
Defense	1947
Health and Human Services*	1953
Housing and Urban Development	1965
Transportation	1966
Energy	1977
Education[a]	1979

a. The Department of Education was separated
and created from Health, Education and Welfare in 1979; HEW was then renamed Health
and Human Services.

financing politics, and diffusion of power in Congress lessen the traditional constraints on selecting the cabinet. "More than ever before they will be free to
choose their department heads on the basis of ability."[29]

The president–cabinet relationship may be described as feudal. Each secretary has administrative responsibility for a department. Each department has its
interests, including clientele groups, congressional committees, and political
viewpoints. A secretary must balance these against the presidential perspective as
it emerges from cabinet meetings. The result is, as Richard Fenno concluded,
remarkable:

> The extent to which the cabinet concept breaks down in the course of
> the members' activities outside the cabinet meeting. . . . In the day-to-
> day work of the cabinet member, each man fends for himself without
> much consideration for cabinet unity. His survival, his support and his
> success do not depend on his fellow members.[30]

THE VICE-PRESIDENT

"A damned peculiar situation to be in," said Spiro Agnew of the vice-
presidency, "to have authority and a title and responsibility with no real power to
do anything." All vice-presidents have complained that they have no place in the

29. Hess, *Organizing the Presidency,* p. 181.
30. Richard F. Fenno, Jr., *The President's Cabinet* (Cambridge, Mass.: Harvard University Press,
1959), p. 247.

administration; they are outsiders looking in. The office of vice-president is a constitutional anomaly. Its only formal power is to preside over the Senate. Under the Twenty-fifth Amendment, the vice-president, with the concurrence of the cabinet or other body, may declare the president disabled and serve as acting president. If the president dies in office, resigns, or is impeached and removed from office, the vice-president becomes the president and serves for the remainder of the unexpired term of office.

Most presidents, having selected a running mate in the election, have stopped there. They have delegated little responsibility to vice-presidents for fear they might disrupt administration policy, or steal some thunder from a president. So, vice-presidents languish with little to do.

They are shunted off to chair advisory panels and eat chicken dinners at meetings presidents do not wish to attend. Nixon cautioned of turning the vice-president "into merely another bureaucrat—and a secretary of catch-all affairs at that."[31]

Traditionally, vice-presidents have been selected to "balance the ticket" in presidential elections. Lyndon Johnson, a southerner, provided geographical balance by naming Hubert Humphrey of Minnesota his vice-presidential nominee. Nixon selected Agnew to broaden his eastern and southern border states appeal. Carter, a southerner like Johnson, went to the north and nominated Walter Mondale, a liberal. In some cases the choice of vice-presidential running mate can

The issue of the vice presidency was called into question at the 1980 GOP Presidential Convention when Ronald Reagan sought former President Gerald Ford for the second spot. (United Press International)

31. Cited in Stephen Hess, *Organizing the Presidency,* p. 169.

cause serious political difficulties. In 1972 George McGovern selected Thomas Eagleton of Missouri before it was learned that he had been under psychiatric treatment. In 1976 the conservative Ronald Reagan said that if he received the Republican nomination, his running mate would be a liberal senator from Pennsylvania, Richard Schweiker. This alarmed Reagan's conservative backers and brought charges that political expediency had overcome political commitment.

Recent presidents have undertaken to find more active roles and responsibilities for their vice-presidents. Lyndon Johnson used Humphrey as the promoter for the Great Society on Capitol Hill. He also acted as a liaison for urban affairs. Nixon was more inclined to put his vice-presidents, Agnew and Ford, in the front lines of political skirmishes. Each, in his own way, was a partisan campaigner toiling for the Nixon administration and candidates supporting the administration. Ross Baker labeled the use of Spiro Agnew the ''Mario Puzo Theory of the Vice Presidency'': ''The President is the Godfather and the Vice President is his 'button man.' The Vice President is sent to knife, crush and garotte the opponents; after which the President turns up at the memorial services for the victim wearing a carnation.''[32]

President Carter was sought to use Walter Mondale more in a policy role, though the impact of the advice of the vice-president is still not known.

The issue of the vice-presidency has become sensitive in the past two decades. President Kennedy was assassinated in office; there were attempted assassinations of President Ford; two presidential candidates have been shot, and one killed, while campaigning for the presidency. And one president, Richard Nixon, resigned from office rather than face the possibility of impeachment and removal. Many argue that we need strong, capable vice-presidents; and we need a better process for selecting our vice-presidents. Thirteen vice-presidents have become president, six in this century. Both major parties have examined proposals for nominating a vice-president separately and taking control away from the presidential candidate. But nothing has happened yet. Some critics call for abolishing the office altogether. This appears unlikely; most Americans accept and approve of the office. The only other option is to provide some functions for the office, but there seems to be no way to do this without taking something away from the presidency. In Cronin's assessment:

> The verdict of history is harsh on the vice-presidency. The office has done only one thing well, solving our succession problem, and it is open to question whether it has done even that well enough. The vice-presidency in presidential government makes the presidency neither more manageable nor more democratic and accountable. Earl Warren cautioned that alternatives proposed in times of distrust and confusion are likely to develop more problems than they wish to solve.[33]

32. As cited in Stephen Hess, *Organizing the Presidency,* pp. 169–170.
33. Thomas Cronin, *The State of the Presidency,* p. 232.

PRESIDENTIAL PERSONALITY

The heroic presidency sought to merge the office, the powers, and the man into one; the ability to lead and the ability to exercise power were a function of personality. From this attempt Americans are coming to better understand the importance of personality—the presidential character—in presidential success and failure. We are learning that how individual presidents perceive their roles and respond to crisis can have direct effects on each one of us.

Studies of presidential personality seek to explain the crisis of presidential leadership in terms of individual character. One major attempt is James David Barber's *The Presidential Character*.[34] Barber suggests that presidential character is the way a president orients himself toward his office and may be viewed as a function of the person's stance toward experience, his world view, and his style (Figure 10.3). These in turn interact with the situations a president faces—the

Berry's World

"Now, according to our calculations, your popularity and the inflation rate should cross sometime in December."

Reprinted by permission. © 1979 NEA, Inc.

34. James David Barber, *The Presidential Character* (Englewood Cliffs, N. J.: Prentice-Hall, 1972).

Energy level in doing the job

	Positive	Negative
Active	Tends to show confidence, flexibility, a focus on producing results through rational mastery. Examples: Jefferson, Franklin Roosevelt, Truman, Kennedy, Carter	Tends to emphasize ambitious striving, aggressiveness, a focus on the struggle for power against a hostile environment. Examples: John Adams, Wilson, Hoover, Johnson, Nixon
Passive	Tends to show receptiveness, compliance, other-directedness, plus a superficial hopefulness masking inner doubt Examples: Madison, Taft, Harding, Ford	Tends to withdraw from conflict and uncertainty and to think in terms of vague principles of duty and regular procedure Examples: Washington, Coolidge, Eisenhower

Emotional attitude toward the presidency

Figure 10.3

Different types of presidential characters. (Adapted from James D. Barber, *The Presidential Character,* 2nd ed. Englewood Cliffs, N.J.: Prentice-Hall, 1977)

climate of expectation and the power situation he must deal with. Barber contends that there are two dimensions to be looked at: the *degree of activity* a president exerts toward his tasks and the *degree of enjoyment* he receives as a result of his activity. Barber pairs these two dimensions to develop a fourfold classification of presidential character:

Active - Positive: extensive activity and the enjoyment of it; high self-esteem and success in relating to the environment.

Active - Negative: intense effort and low emotional reward for that effort; compulsive, ambitious and power seeking, but self-image is discontinuous and environment is seen as threatening.

Passive - Positive: compliant, cooperative, and agreeable rather than personally assertive; has an optimistic outlook and enjoys the routine of politics and popularity.

Passive - Negative: oriented toward dutiful service; there is limited activity and finds the office frustrating; escapes conflict by emphasizing procedural arrangements.

Says Barber: "*Active-positive* Presidents want most to achieve results. *Active-negatives* aim to get and keep power. *Passive-positives* are after love. *Passive-negatives* emphasize their civic virtue."[35]

35. *Ibid.,* p. 13.

The *active-positive* presidential character most closely fits the image of the strong, dominant leader. Franklin D. Roosevelt and John F. Kennedy are examples. However, Barber notes that some of our recent presidents, such as Lyndon Johnson and Richard Nixon, have been *active-negative* personalities. Such individuals may take driven, uncompromising stands due to their perception of the environment as threatening. These ideas do much to explain the stubborn resistance of the Johnson administration toward criticism of the escalation of the war in Vietnam. They also explain "stonewalling" and "bunker mentality" of the Nixon administration at the height of Watergate.

The ideal would be a presidential personality that accepts a democratic style of authority, a personality with the characteristics of flexibility, tolerance, openness, and persuasiveness. Such a person could accept the idea "that all major policy decisions would be taken openly as shared decisions across President and Congress and that decisions reached through open process of conflict, bargaining, and compromise are likely to be better in quality and more long lasting in their acceptance than those reached in secrecy."[36] We are not, Hargrove argues, yet able to build a comprehensive typology of presidential personalities, but we can note the harmful effects of *active-negatives* on the erosion of democratic norms of government and can see, in general, the criteria needed for a democratic style of authority. Hargrove identifies three minimal qualities:

1. An active, affirmative attitude toward themselves, their work, and life.
2. Evidence that the individual can work in an immediate environment that reflects the norms of equality, respect for a diversity of views, and willingness to face unpleasant truths.
3. Standard political skills to speak, to persuade, to maneuver and manipulate, to structure situations, and to secure agreement in the face of conflict.[37]

If there are a multitude and complexity of issues that tempt our presidents, Bruce Buchanan notes that the office of president has self-destructive tendencies within it. There are forces beyond the control of presidents with which they must contend. Buchanan notes, "The environment delivers the agenda and compels attention to the agenda as delivered."[38] The result is presidents are conditioned by the force and repetition of four compelling psychological encounters - *stress* as a consequence of crisis management, exposure to *deference* as a quality of face-to-face encounters, *dissonance* in translating political promises and preferences into public policy, and *frustration* at meeting resistance to his leadership and policy plans (Figure 10.4).[39]

The consequence of these psychological forces is to impair any president's

36. Erwin C. Hargrove, *The Power of the Modern Presidency*, p. 303.
37. *Ibid.*, p. 78.
38. Bruce Buchanan, *The Presidential Experience: What the Office Does to the Man* (Englewood Cliffs, N. J.: Prentice-Hall, 1978), p. 23.
39. *Ibid.*, pp. 23–25.

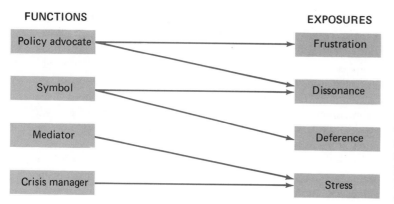

FUNCTIONS

EXPOSURES

Policy advocate

Symbol

Mediator

Crisis manager

Frustration

Dissonance

Deference

Stress

Figure 10.4

Functions of the presidency and resulting exposures. (B. Buchanan, *The Presidential Experience,* What the Office Does to the Man, © 1978, p. 23. Reprinted by permission of Prentice-Hall, Inc., Englewood Cliffs, New Jersey.)

ability to perform effectively. It places a premium on presidential personality. For, as Buchanan notes, the thrust of the exposures on the presidency are to "(1) deplete their physical and emotional energy; (2) nurture systematic distortions in the accuracy with which they perceive themselves and external events; (3) encourage the use of duplicity as an expedient political resource; and (4) erode any values or scruples that interfere with the preservation of presidential power."[40] It is, therefore, all the more incumbent we come to better understand presidential personality and seek those presidents with a democratic style of authority.

TENURE AND SUCCESSION

TENURE

A president, unlike a prime minister, is not selected by a legislature. The president derives the powers of his office from the Constitution; the Constitution also fixes the length of his term. This basic fact is the source of great presidential power: an American president is not obligated to the legislature for his office. Tenure of office is the source of power.

The Founding Fathers worried about the president's term of office, and eligibility for reelection. They wanted an independent executive, but not a dominant authority. The Framers debated a term of seven years with no eligibility for reelection, then a term of six years, and finally the four-year term. The single, longer term of office appeared safest if Congress chose the president, as many delegates preferred. Once the Electoral College was agreed upon, however, the limit on eligibility for reelection was superfluous, and a four-year term was then decided upon.

The two-term presidency quickly became a tradition. The Founders were

40. *Ibid.,* p. 161.

confident that George Washington would be the first president and would serve for the remainder of his years. At the end of his second term, however, Washington declined to be reelected: Two terms were enough. And for half a century, no succeeding president seriously challenged this tradition. Only one president, Franklin D. Roosevelt, served more than two terms, although several presidents in the latter half of the nineteenth century toyed with the prospect of a third term. In fact, in 1875 the possibility loomed large that Ulysses S. Grant would seek a third term. This moved the House of Representatives to pass a resolution suggesting that departure from the two-term tradition would be ''unwise, unpatriotic and fraught with peril to our free institutions.''[41]

In 1951, the Twenty-Second Amendment to the Constitution did what the House of Representatives thought wise in 1875; it limited the presidency to two terms. No person may be elected to the office of the president more than twice. And for those persons succeeding to the presidency during a term of office, like Lyndon Johnson or Gerald Ford, no person ''who has held the office of President, or acted as President, for more than two years of a term to which some other person was elected President shall be elected to the office of President more than once.'' Critics think the amendment unwise and undemocratic. It places too much restraint on executive authority and robs the country of good leadership. On the other side is the argument that a two-term limitation heightens and accelerates presidential power. Knowing that he has but eight years, a president must move quickly and decisively to implement policy. Democratic representation is actually maximized by a president faced with a limited term.

SUCCESSION

Article 2 of the Constitution provides for the vice-president to succeed to the office of president in case of the removal of the president, or on his death, resignation, or disability. But the Constitution leaves it to Congress to provide for succession in the event that both president and vice-president are unable to discharge the duties of the office. Congress has three times enacted legislation for presidential succession. The last, in 1947, provides that in the event both president and vice-president are unable to discharge the duties of president, the office will devolve upon the Speaker of the House, then the president pro tempore of the Senate, followed by the Cabinet members in the order of their establishment. (The first law in 1792 was similar but placed the president pro tem of the Senate first in line; an 1886 law provided for cabinet succession, beginning with the secretary of state and continuing through the cabinet in order of establishment.) The Twenty-Fifth Amendment, passed in 1967, sought to minimize the likelihood of such a double vacancy occurring. It provides for the president, upon a vacancy in the office of the vice-president, to nominate a vice-president who will take office upon confirmation by a majority vote of both Houses of Congress.

41. As cited in Louis Koening, *The Chief Executive*, p. 64.

The Twenty-Fifth Amendment was used in 1973. Vice-President Agnew resigned after pleading guilty to charges of income tax evasion. President Nixon then nominated Gerald Ford, a popular legislative leader, to be vice-president. He was quickly confirmed. In 1974, President Nixon himself resigned rather than face impeachment proceedings. Ford assumed the presidency and again, under the Twenty-Fifth Amendment, with the vice-presidency vacant, nominated Nelson Rockefeller as vice-president. With his confirmation, the nation had a president and vice-president who had both achieved their offices through the Twenty-Fifth Amendment. Neither had been elected; there was no vote of the people and would not be until 1976.

DISABILITY

The Twenty-Fifth Amendment also makes provision for presidential disability. Several times in this century presidents have become disabled, but there have been no provisions for anyone else to assume the duties of the office. Woodrow Wilson was severely incapacitated by a stroke in 1919; Franklin Delano Roosevelt was confined to a wheelchair for the final days of his tenure as president; and President Eisenhower suffered several heart attacks while president. Public concern for the affairs of the office finally culminated in the passage of the Twenty-Fifth Amendment.

This Amendment allows a president to declare his disability by so informing the president pro tempore of the Senate and the Speaker of the House. In such a case, the vice-president becomes the acting president. The president may resume his duties at any time by so declaring to the same two officers of the Senate and House. The Amendment also provides for a president to be declared disabled. The vice-president and a second body—a majority of the cabinet or other body as Congress may provide—may declare the president disabled and unable to discharge the duties of the office. The written declaration is transmitted to the president pro tempore of the Senate and the Speaker of the House and immediately the vice-president assumes all the power and duties of the office as acting president. The president may resume his office with a written declaration that no disability exists. And unless the vice-president and the other body object, he resumes full power and responsibility. If there is disagreement over a continuing disability, the Twenty-Fifth Amendment states that Congress, by a two-thirds vote of both houses, shall determine who shall discharge the duties of the office of president— the president or the vice-president as acting president.

TERMINATING TENURE

There are three ways a president's tenure may be terminated other than electoral defeat at the polls. They are death, resignation, and impeachment.

Table 10.7

Presidents Who Have Died While in Office

William Henry Harrison	1841	
Zachary Taylor	1850	
Abraham Lincoln	1865	Assassination
James A. Garfield	1881	Assassination
William McKinley	1901	Assassination
Warren G. Harding	1923	
Franklin Delano Roosevelt	1945	
John F. Kennedy	1963	Assassination

Death.   Eight presidents have died in office—four of them victims of assassinations.

Resignation.   Only one president, Richard Nixon, has ever resigned from office, although Woodrow Wilson apparently seriously contemplated resigning. By resigning, Nixon was able to retain the benefits extended to all former presidents, namely pension, staff assistance, and secret service protection.

Impeachment.   The nation has twice moved to remove a president by impeachment—Andrew Johnson in the wake of the Civil War and Richard Nixon for the abuses of Watergate.

The Constitution provides that a president may be removed from office for ''treason, bribery, or other high crimes and misdemeanors.'' Under Article II, which lays out the criteria, the House of Representatives is empowered to impeach the president and the Senate, with the Chief Justice of the Supreme Court presiding, removes him. A two-thirds vote of the Senate is necessary for conviction and removal from office. Technically, Andrew Johnson was impeached—the House of Representatives voted eleven articles of impeachment for trial in the Senate. But fortunately for Johnson, the Senate missed conviction by a single vote.

The hue and cry over Andrew Johnson was his firing of his Secretary of War, Edwin Stanton. This violated the Tenure of Office Act, which required that officers appointed with the advice and consent of the Senate be removed only with the consent of the Senate.[42] With Richard Nixon, impeachment centered directly on ''high crimes and misdemeanors.''[43]

President Nixon took the position that a president could be impeached only for specific, indictable criminal acts that were of a ''very serious nature'' and

42. *Myers* v. *U.S.* 272 U.S. 52 (1926) and *Humphrey's Executor* v. *U.S.* 295 U.S. 602 (1935).
43. Raoul Berger, *Impeachment, The Constitutional Problems* (Cambridge, Mass.: Harvard University Press, 1973), especially Chapter 2.

committed in his official capacity as president. This narrow definition, of course, overlooked the Andrew Johnson precedent, which had been blatantly political. Research suggested that political wrongdoing could be an impeachable offense. Ironically, Gerald Ford, Vice President under Nixon, was cited when, as a congressman, he had said the criteria for impeaching Mr. Justice Douglas were "whatever the House [of Representatives] says it is." The House Judiciary Committee took this position when it voted to recommend to the full House three articles of impeachment: obstruction of justice in the Watergate coverup, abuse of power in the misuse of government agencies and violation of the oath of office, and contempt of Congress in willfully disobeying congresssional subpoenas. It was now clear that, for the Judiciary Committee at least, high crimes and misdemeanors were not limited to criminal actions. The nation was spared impeachment proceedings and a trial when Richard Nixon resigned from office in August 1974. Senator Goldwater was said to have reported to Mr. Nixon that there would be no more than 15 votes in the Senate against conviction—well short of the one-third necessary to block conviction.

PRESIDENTIAL RESPONSIVENESS AND RESPONSIBILITY

Changing expectations have put the presidency under considerable stress. Presidential power is great, but presidents are less popular today. If our expectations remain unfulfilled, it is because we have placed unreasonable conditions for leadership on the presidency or because recent presidents have not exercised their power as we wish them to.

The contemporary presidency lacks accountability. To be strong and independent, the president needs autonomy and control. The idea of the heroic presidency led the American people to expect greatness, surely an invitation to excesses of power and lack of accountability. Yet calls for reform do not spark any urgent debate. Proposals for a plural executive or a parliamentary vote of no confidence have little appeal. Ultimately, the restoration of trust and confidence in the chief executive depends on the commitment of the president—and all the institutions of American government—"to reclaim their own dignity and meet their own responsibilities."[44]

"The importance of Presidents," says Aaron Wildavsky, "is a function of the scope of government; the more it does, the more important they become."[45] There is little expectation that government will do less. The problems that face us now leave little opportunity for a diminished presidency. Power has shifted to the presidency as traditional constraints have broken. In foreign policy the need for swift action and secrecy put Congress at a disadvantage. In domestic and economic matters, a decentralized and seniority system kept it on the defensive. The decline of political parties worked to further erode accountability; there are no

44. Arthur S. Schlesinger, *The Imperial Presidency,* p. 418.
45. Aaron Wildavsky, "The Past and Future Presidency," *Public Interest,* No. 41 (Fall 1975), p. 58.

Of all the parts of the American consensus forged under Roosevelt and then carried through after World War II under Truman and Eisenhower, that having to do with America's involvements abroad and the necessity for global defense in order to keep the Soviet Union in line was perhaps the most solid. America sent troops and advisers everywhere: to Europe, the Middle East, Africa, the Far East, South America. For a good many years, there was hardly a portion of the globe, on land or on sea, that did not have its contingent of Americans, civilian and military. And when crises such as that of the 1962 Russian missiles in Cuba came, American presidents rattled rockets, and the world held its breath. But then came Vietnam, and such intelligence agency scandals as that of the covert CIA activities in Chile that led to the downfall of a government and the killing of its leader.

Suddenly all these policies were questionable, and the people began to say loudly and clearly that they did not want so much spent on defense, that they did not want their sons going off to die in jungles and deserts half a world away, that they did not want an intelligence operation that engaged in activities such as murder and assassination. So defense spending came under attack, and Jimmy Carter campaigned on promises to reduce it; the draft was scrapped in favor of an all-volunteer army; we began to shift the emphasis from containment of the Soviet Union to détente; the CIA's wings were clipped and it was made to report to and be under the surveillance of Congress.

Then in 1979, came the Iran crisis and the holding of 50 American hostages by the new Iranian government, plus the invasion of Afghanistan by Soviet troops. By the end of January 1980, President Carter and his advisers had almost reversed all the trends of the previous years. He was calling for increased defense spending and the building of new weapons, as well as for a rapid-deployment force of 100,000 troops for use at crisis points anywhere on the globe. And the United States was again building up allies and agreements for defense: Secretary of Defense Harold Brown went to Peking, and there was talk of eventual arms sales to China; the United States and Egypt conducted joint air exercises in the Middle East; negotiations were under way with African nations for bases and ports; the alliances with Turkey and Pakistan were being shored up. And there was a movement in Congress to repeal the amendment that had stopped secret CIA missions.

There have been objections to these new policies from some of the American public, particularly the young men who may have to serve since the proposal to reinstate the draft has been passed into law, but on the whole the protest has been nothing like that of the 1960s. Has the consensus changed again under the pressure of the energy crisis, inflation, and unemployment, which have damaged the American economy severely and shaken people's faith in the strength of their nation and its ability to deal with problems? It is really too soon to tell, but if attitudes have changed, we may be in for a new era of crisis and confrontation as the nations of the world turn to a "look out for ourselves" policy.

party leaders powerful enough to stand up to a president. The people have come to accept alternative methods of candidate selection that produce weak leaders, and this further erodes party support among the masses. If parties are weak, it is because presidents are strong, and party leaders are powerless to do much about it.

The greatest rival to presidential power turns out to be the bureaucracy. To lead the bureaucracy is to manage the bureaucracy and presidents have been notoriously bad managers. Sheer size and the complexity of the tasks defies management. Not even a president with an enlarged presidential staff can know what takes place every day or what to do about it.

The immediate response of presidents in the wake of Vietnam and Watergate was to take flight. To the immediate criticism that government had grown too large and tried too much, the presidential response was to cut back. The Executive Office staff was reduced. Both Ford and Carter, in differing ways, scaled back on the White House staff. Economy in government has become popular. Presidents support the move as a way to divert criticism of domestic and foreign policy. Economy and efficiency have become surrogates for public policy. Presidents may very well leave the administration of programs to the bureaucracy and the states. In short, presidents will, to use Wildavsky's term, be in "offensive retreat." The presidency came out of the Great Society, Vietnam, and Watergate with almost all the chips of power. Those chips are now being called. Future presidents will have to decide which powers they must retain and how much power they can afford to give away. The future presidency will have to be shared administration; just how much sharing and with whom will be the crucial decisions. As it stands now, suggests Wildavsky, "Presidents, and the governments for which they stand, are either doing too much or too little. They need either to do a great deal more for the people or a great deal less to them. They must be closer to what is happening or much further away. At present, they are close enough to get the blame but too far away to control the result."[46] Presidents are most likely to choose those bases for power that are most strategic but require the least administration. This will remove the president from having to manage. Concludes Wildavsky: "They will be responsible for war and peace abroad, and life and death at home, but not much in between."

SUMMARY

1. The presidency remains the focal point of American politics and America's best hope for leadership. Yet the presidency continues to be an embattled institution struggling to recapture the confidence of the people in the aftermath of Watergate, Vietnam, and the Great Society.

2. Presidential power has been little hampered by constitutional language. The growth of the office has come from pressing social and economic

46. *Ibid.*, p. 73.

problems and, above all, from the strong-willed personalities of the men holding the office. The prevailing view of presidential power makes for executive action. The stamp of each chief executive is indelibly etched into the office by individual style and personality.

3. The growth of presidential power in the twentieth century has led to several important roles for the president. Political and popular roles arose with leadership and a national election for the office; domestic responsibility grew with the economy and the administration of programs; foreign affairs came to the fore with nuclear technology, a shrinking globe, and mass communications.

4. Due to the awesome responsibility entrusted to chief executives, presidents have moved to expand the office and powers—sometimes beyond democratic and constitutional limits. In the last two decades, the heroic view of presidential power has been challenged. Reform and reorganization center on two principal areas: the executive office and presidential personality.

5. The greatest threat to presidential power comes from inappropriate and irresponsible persons occupying the White House. It is incumbent with changing expectations that we redefine the exercise of presidential power. Recent efforts in this direction are encouraging as they focus upon the personality characteristics of presidents and the psychological effects of the experience. Ultimately we need to arrive at a democratic style of leadership that protects the American people but does not inhibit presidential leadership.

TERMS

cabinet 394
disability 404
executive agreement 368
Executive Office 389–390
executive power 379
executive privilege 378
impeachment 405
imperial presidency 389
impoundment 378
item veto 378
"Mario Puzo theory of
  Vice Presidency" 398

pocket veto 378
presidential character
  399–400
stewardship presidency
  371
succession 403
Sun-King complex 365
tenure 402
textbook presidency 385
treaty 366–68
two presidencies 384
veto 378

10.1. Presidential Activity. It is probably impossible to develop a diary on the president's day, but as best you can from newspapers, political magazines, and *Congressional Quarterly* and *National Journal,* try and construct a typical day for the president: Whom did he see, what speeches did he make, what congressional bills did he sign, which administrators did he talk with, and so on? Rather than try to cover each hour, note the particular areas of involvement—Congress, foreign policy, administration, public relations, crisis, and so on.

10.2. Presidential Character. Select a president and attempt to analyze the aspects of that president's character that made him a strong or weak president. What good and bad traits can you list that were relevant to that president's character for being a president of the United States? You may wish to consult James D. Barber's *Presidential Character* (Prentice-Hall) for a fuller treatment of what can be involved. You can also read a biography or two written on the president you have selected. Finally there are ratings of presidents that can help you in your effort. Thomas Cronin has an execellent summary of those ratings in T. Cronin, *The State of the Presidency,* 2nd ed. (Little, Brown, pp. 387–388).

10.3. State of the Union. Select three State of the Union messages from a president having served two terms (one early, say first year; middle just before reelection; and late, last year in office). What are the policy priorities of the president? How do they change over the years with his administration? Do a column by column analysis of the shifting priorities. The State of the Union messages can be found in the *Public Papers of the President* or in *Congressional Quarterly.*

10.4. Cabinet Appointments. Examine the cabinets of one of a few selected administrations. What kinds of people does a president choose to be cabinet secretaries? Note how the members compare and differ on regions of the country, on party, on previous occupation, on political activity prior to appointment, on age, on sex, and so on. A list of cabinet members can most readily be found in the *Congressional Directory,* or *U.S. Government Manual.* The more biographical data can be located in White's *Conspectus of American Biography* and Kane, *Facts about the President.*

BIBLIOGRAPHY

Barber, James D. *The Presidential Character.* Englewood Cliffs, N. J.: Prentice-Hall, 1977.

A major effort to come to grips with personality and its ability for predicting presidential performance. Barber suggests that activity and enjoyment of politics are big factors in understanding presidential character.

Buchanan, Bruce. *The Presidential Experience*. Englewood Cliffs, N. J.: Prentice-Hall, 1978.

A provocative and insightful discussion of the psychological impact of the office and the task upon the person in the White House. Buchanan says the office subjects its occupants to common stresses. How they deal with those stresses determines what kind of president they will be.

Cronin, Thomas. *The State of the Presidency,* 2nd ed. Boston: Little, Brown, 1980.

A leading commentator on the presidency, Cronin explains the relationship and problems between the formal executive government and the White House staff. The book provides good information on the contemporary affairs of the presidency.

Fisher, Louis. *Presidential Spending Power*. Princeton, N. J.: Princeton University Press, 1975.

An important book that examines the history of the presidency in terms of its discretionary spending authority. Much of the book deals with contemporary issues.

Hargrove, Erwin. *The Power of the Modern Presidency*. New York: Alfred A. Knopf, 1974.

A textbook on the presidency that is well written and gives an overview of the presidency. The book centers on the relationship between personality and institutions in the crafting of foreign and domestic policies.

Hess, Stephen. *Organizing the Presidency*. Washington, D. C.: Brookings Institution, 1976.

Looks at staffing the White House from FDR through Richard Nixon. A lively book, Hess provides needed discussion to the quality and utilization of personnel surrounding chief executives.

Koenig, Louis. *The Chief Executive*. New York: Harcourt Brace Jovanovich, 1975.

A good text on the presidency. Koenig sets forth some detailed major roles and responsibilities exercised by the chief executive. The first chapter has a useful perspective on presidential power.

Neustadt, Richard. *Presidential Power*. New York: John Wiley and Sons, 1980.

A classic study on the presidency; widely read and quoted. Neustadt argues that the presidency is what the person makes it, that power depends upon persuasion.

Pious, Richard. *The American Presidency*. New York: Basic Books, 1979.

A major restatement of the presidency. The book is comprehensive in its coverage of the presidency, full of information and examples as it looks at the presidency in the post-Watergate setting.

Chapter
11

Bureaucracy

Government is big business; but unlike most businesses, it does not make money: Government costs more than it takes in—a lot more. Today the public blames the bureaucracy for the cost of government. The bureaucracy is wasteful, inefficient, and enmeshed in red tape. A government study in 1973 found only 16 percent of the American people willing to describe bureaucrats as honest.[1] A 1976 *U. S. News* poll ranked the federal bureaucracy last among 26 institutions in ability to get things done. In 1975 President Carter campaigned by proclaiming: "Our government in Washington now is a horrible bureaucratic mess. It is disorganized, wasteful, has no purpose. . .with little regard for the welfare of the average American citizen."

Attacking the bureaucracy is popular talk for contemporary politicians. All the presidential candidates in 1976 used the theme of bureaucratic cost and inefficiency, but assaults on the bureaucracy come from every quarter. The Boston *Globe* editorialized: "The bureaucratic life rewards conspiracy, sycophancy, ideological conformity, caution, and class solidarity. It punishes innovation, originality and the work ethic."[2] The American public has responded to these attacks with approval and with taxpayer revolts.

1. Subcommittee on Intergovernmental Relations of the Committee on Government Operations, *Confidence and Concern: Citizens View American Government* (Washington, D.C.: Government Printing Office, 1973), p. 310.
2. *National Journal,* September 30, 1978, p. 1540.

Bureaucracy, however, is an indispensable feature of modern government: Administrators possess a great variety of skills essential to the creation of public policy and its implementation. Max Weber long ago recognized the necessary superiority of the bureaucracy: "The decisive reason for the advance of bureaucratic organization has always been its purely technical superiority over any other form of organization . . . the 'political master' finds himself in a position of the 'dilettante' who stands opposite the 'expert,' facing the trained official who stands within the management of administration."[3]

The bureaucracy provides a necessary level of technical expertise to ensure that policy can be formulated and implemented in a competent and rational manner. While presidents and political officials come and go, the bureaucracy remains. The bureaucracy gives the policy process a level of stability and continuity. The expertise of the bureaucracy forms the backbone of American government. This administrative expertise assures the bureaucracy of a role in making public policy.

The actions of the bureaucracy touch the lives of millions of citizens every day in ordinary, and sometimes not so ordinary ways (Figure 11.1). Much of what the bureaucracy does we take for granted: Bureaucrats inspect the foods we eat; they mail out social security checks and process home loans for veterans; they ensure safe and reliable weights and measures for the transaction of business; they run the national parks; forecast the weather; and dredge rivers and harbors.

Changing expectations have made the bureaucracy the target of complaints. Whenever there is a communications breakdown, we blame it on red tape and too much government. Whenever citizen concerns are ignored or denied, we blame it on bureaucratic inefficiency and incompetence. But most bureaucrats insist they are motivated by dedication and commitment to the public trust. Said one Internal Revenue Service employee, "I work with extremely dedicated and competent people. I'd like it if there were more perception of that by the public."[4] Let us take a closer look at who our bureaucrats are.

BUREAUCRATS AND THE CIVIL SERVICE

Approximately 3 million Americans may rightfully be labeled federal bureaucrats. Close to 40 percent of the civilian employees in the federal government work for the Department of Defense and the branches of the services. The next largest employers are the Post Office and the Veterans Administration. Approximately 1.5 million employees work under the civil service system. The median level of employment is GS 7 (the seventh level in the federal schedule, which ranges from GS 1 through GS 18); the pay range for a GS 7 is $11,523 to $14,979

---

3. H. H. Gerth and C. Wright Mills, *From Max Weber: Essays in Sociology* (New York: Oxford University Press, 1946), pp. 214 and 232.
4. *National Journal,* September 30, 1978, pp. 1540–41.

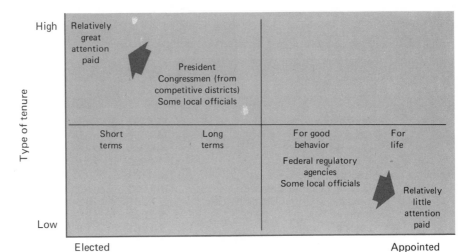

Figure 11.1

The attention public officials pay to demands of the people. (B. Campbell, *The American Electorate: Attitudes and Action* New York: Holt, Reinhart & Winston, 1979, p. 283.) Copyright © 1979 by Holt, Reinhart & Winston. Reprinted by permission of Holt, Reinhart & Winston.

with ten years of experience. There is a wide range in education and skills required. From clerks and typists with a high school education to research analysts with a Ph.D., the bureaucracy is a diverse group of employees. Although Washington, D.C., has the largest concentration of federal employees, 85 percent actually live and work outside Washington in regional and field offices throughout the country.

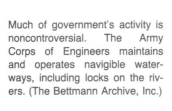

Much of government's activity is noncontroversial. The Army Corps of Engineers maintains and operates navigible waterways, including locks on the rivers. (The Bettmann Archive, Inc.)

Table 11.1

Size of Executive Agencies and Budget Outlays, 1980

	Employees		Budget	
	number	percent	(in billions)	percent
Agriculture	120,150	4.1	23.6	4.2
Commerce	148,002	5.0	3.6	0.6
Defense (civilian)	966,266	32.8	130.6	23.2
Education	17,000	0.6	12.9	2.3
Energy	21,189	0.7	7.7	1.4
Health & Human Services	149,000	5.1	193.7	34.4
Housing & Urban Development	17,581	0.6	11.6	2.1
Interior	80,290	2.7	4.2	0.7
Justice	56,261	1.9	2.6	0.5
Labor	23,901	0.8	27.5	4.9
State	23,745	0.8	2.0	0.4
Transportation	73,075	2.5	17.3	3.1
Treasury	138,146	4.7	75.8	13.4
Other independent agencies				
Postal Service	659,531	22.4	1.7	0.3
Veterans Administration	238,726	8.1	20.7	3.7
Environmental Protection				
Agency	14,300	0.5	5.0	0.9
National Aeronautic and Space				
Administration	23,341	0.8	5.0	0.9
all others	176,633	6.0	18.1	3.2
Total	2,947,137	100	563.6	100

SOURCE: 1980 Budget, Office of Management and Budget; Office of Personnel Management, civilian work force.

THE CIVIL SERVICE

The civil service is based on the premise that similar employees performing like functions should be treated the same and paid the same. Its regulations govern terms of employment and competence, benefits and behavior. The system came into being partly as a result of Charles Julius Guiteau being denied a political patronage job in 1880. He had wanted to be an American consul in France. Such jobs were patronage appointments given for political favors. The denial of the position so angered Guiteau that he took matters into his own hands: He shot and killed President James A. Garfield. Guiteau's action came as there was a rising cry to eliminate the spoils system throughout the federal government. Congress responded; in 1883, the Pendleton Act was passed, creating the civil service system. Patronage was replaced with a nonpartisan, career employment system based on merit. A Civil Service Commission was created to recruit and fill vacancies in employment by open, competitive examinations.

GOOSEMYER   by parker and wilder

Goosemyer by Parker & Wilder. © 1980 Field Enterprises, Inc. Courtesy of Field
Newspaper Syndicate

Now, one century later, President Carter has charged that the civil service
system promotes incompetence and frustrates efficiency. He has proposed a series
of reforms in keeping with his campaign promise to make government more open
and responsive to the people.

THE STRUCTURE OF THE BUREAUCRACY

All the major departments and agencies of the national government—more
than 2,000 agencies, bureaus, commissions, and subunits—are listed in the
United States Government Manual. The introduction says: "Determining what the
Government does and how it affects the individual may not be easy, but it should
not be impossible."

In an earlier chapter, we divided the executive branch into three major
areas: the Executive Office of the President, departments holding cabinet rank,
and independent executive agencies. We will follow this division in the discussion
of bureaucratic organization.

EXECUTIVE OFFICE

We have already dealt with the Executive Office of the President in the
chapter on the presidency. We noted that it has become a permanent bureaucracy
employing some 5,000 people and operates directly out of the Executive Office.
Its personnel are appointed and their function is to serve the president. We have
seen how presidents have come to rely on the National Security Council for advice on foreign affairs and on the Office of Management and Budget in order to
manage the federal bureaucracy. Too often the complaint has been that Executive
Office staff ignore departmental staff, that they formulate advice for the president
without consulting the personnel who will have to administer the policies. Often
they are accused of intruding into departmental affairs when they feel the depart-

mental bureaucracy is too slow or unsympathetic to presidential priorities. One of the major post-Watergate priorities for the bureaucracy is to work out a better and more compatible relationship between the Executive Office of the President and departmental staff.

THE CABINET DEPARTMENTS

Thirteen departments are headed by secretaries appointed by the president; collectively, the secretaries constitute the cabinet. The departments vary greatly in size and prestige: The Department of Labor employs 17,200 people, Defense just under 1 million; Health and Human Service (HHS) employs 140,000.

The organization of departments is similar. Each is headed by a secretary directly responsible to the president. The administrative workload is handled by an under secretary or deputy secretaries, and often there are several assistant deputies or assistant secretaries. In addition, there are staffs to help prepare budgets and to plan and supervise administration. Each department is subdivided into bureaus. The basis for this division differs. The Department of Labor is a *clientele* department, and its bureaus reflect that function: employment and training, labor-management relations, mine safety and health. The Department of State bureaus are divided by *geographical* area. By far the most common division is by work *functions,* such as public health, human development services, and social security.

Departments are the major functional divisions within the bureaucracy by which the executive branch of government administers the laws and carries out the programs established by Congress. Broadly taken, the departments define the executive function today, the primary areas of executive responsibility. Cabinet level departments may be contrasted with executive agencies, which have narrower purposes and greater independence from the chief executive, although such independence may be more fiction than fact. In fact, some cabinet secretaries do carve out considerable autonomy or presidents intrude less in their departmental affairs than in the activity of some executive agencies. The difference between departments and agencies is a matter of status and degree, political reality, and issues often determining the priority they receive.

INDEPENDENT EXECUTIVE AGENCIES

Formally a part of the executive branch, the independent executive agencies are not a part of any cabinet department. They are responsible to the president, but their degree of independence varies with their function and their ties with Congress and groups in the political arena. We can sort these independent executive agencies into four categories.

Independent Agencies.   These agencies function much like departments, but without cabinet status. Their heads, called administrators, operate much like cabinet secretaries. They are appointed by the president (subject to

Senate approval) and are removable by the president. The size and tasks of independent executive agencies vary. The Veterans Administration, for example, is the third largest government agency. Selective Service, all but defunct after Vietnam, once again aids the president in registering and potentially conscripting military personnel. The National Aeronautics and Space Administration administers the space program and research related to space flight. Often because of the services they perform, these agencies are of more interest to Congress and clientele groups than to the president.

Government Corporations. These agencies were designed to be relatively free of presidential control, but still within the executive branch. A cross between a public service and a business enterprise, government corporations like the Tennessee Valley Authority, the Federal Deposit Insurance Corporation, and the U.S. Postal Service seek to provide a commercial service and are organized along the lines of private enterprise. They are governed by a board of directors, appointed by the president (confirmed by the Senate), who have more leeway in making policy than do normal executive agencies. The assumption is that better service can be provided if a board of directors operates the activity using business principles. This was the motivation behind making the Postal Service a government corporation in 1970.

The Independent Regulatory Commissions. Regulatory commissions enjoy a special status within the federal bureaucratic structure. They were created to be independent of the president. Although he appoints members to a commission (subject to Senate approval), he is not free to remove them at will. Terms of office are staggered and often bipartisan appointments are required. The commissions regulate specific activities such as commerce, elections, trade, communications, labor relations, and securities and exchange. They set rules and regulations; they monitor the activity, grant licenses, and administer the policies they set; and they hold hearings, issue fines, and require compliance. In short, independent regulatory commissions exercise legislative, executive, and judicial powers.

The rationale for making these agencies separate is to remove this kind of regulation from politics. The result, however, has been that the regulators have formed a close alliance, and the agencies have been criticized for not regulating but providing a means for special interest groups to protect themselves.

The major independent regulatory agencies include:

1. Interstate Commerce Commission (ICC, 1887). Regulates interstate surface transportation, including trains, trucks, buses, inland waterway and coastal shipping, and freight shippers.
2. Federal Trade Commission (FTC, 1914). Prevents free trade from being stifled by monopoly, price fixing, unfair competition, unfair advertising, or deceptive labeling.
3. Federal Communications Commission (FCC, 1934). Regulates interstate and foreign communications by radio, television, wire, and cable, in-

cluding two-way radio and satellite communications; grants licenses to operate radio and television stations, as well as CB radios.

4. Securities and Exchange Commission (SEC, 1934). Provides information and mandates disclosure for the investing public; regulates all securities markets and stockbrokers.

5. National Labor Relations Board (NLRB, 1935). Administers laws pertaining to labor relations, guaranteeing the employee's right to organize and bargain; also works to prevent and remedy unfair labor practices.

6. Civil Aeronautics Board (CAB, 1938). Regulates civil air transportation within the United States and between the United States and foreign countries; licenses air transportation services and sets rates.

7. Consumer Product Safety Commission (CPSC, 1972). Establishes mandatory safety standards for the design, construction, contents, performance, and labeling of consumer products; requires manufacturers to recall, repair, or replace consumer products that do not comply with standards.

8. Federal Election Commission (FEC, 1974). Formulates policy for federal elections, including disclosure requirements, contribution and expenditure limitations, and public financing of presidential nominating conventions and elections.

9. Federal Energy Regulatory Commission (FERC, 1977). Located within the Department of Energy; regulates the transportation and sale of natural gas, the construction of natural gas pipelines, the transmission and sale of electricity, and the regulation of rates charged for transportation of oil by pipeline.

Service Agencies.   Agencies like the General Services Administration (GSA) and the Office of Personnel Management (formerly the Civil Service Commission) provide services to other agencies within the federal bureaucracy. The GSA is the central purchasing agent for the government, supplying the bureaucracy with its communications, transportation, supplies, and physical facilities. The Office of Personnel Administration acts as the employment agency for the federal government.

THE GROWTH OF THE BUREAUCRACY

Once the federal government had been established, the bureaucracy grew slowly. George Washington's first cabinet consisted of four departments, and the State Department had a total of ten employees, counting the secretary of state. In 1815 the total number of government employees was under 5,000. By the turn of the century the number was still under a quarter of a million, and much of the growth (approximately 85 percent) was attributable to an increase in size of the Post Office. The rapid explosion of federal employees occurred in the twentieth century with World War I, the Depression, World War II, and finally the Great Society programs. The bureaucratic state is a modern phenomenon.[5] The growth of the federal budget is shown in Figure 11.2.

There can be no doubt today of the public's frustration with bureaucracy. Its most outspoken critic, Peter Drucker, states flatly: ''Modern government has become ungovernable.'' Drucker contends that the sheer size and variety of the tasks assigned the bureaucracy make it uncontrollable. No government today controls its bureaucracy and its various agencies. ''Government agencies are all becoming autonomous, ends in themselves, and directed by their own desire for power, their own rationale, their own narrow vision rather than by national policy.''[6] It would be impossible to list all the complaints leveled against the bureaucracy, but we can identify some of the major ones: (a) immunity from popular

Figure 11.2

Growth of the federal budget. Note: Units on vertical scale have been compressed at top of figure because of space limitations. (1790–1970: *Historical Statistics, Colonial Times to 1970.* Washington, D.C., Census Bureau, 1976. 1971–1978: *Statistical Abstract of the United States.* Washington, D.C., Census Bureau, 1976)

5. See Ralph P. Hummell, *The Bureaucratic Experience* (New York: St. Martins, 1977).
6. Peter Drucker, *The Age of Discontinuity* (New York: Harper & Row, 1969), p. 220.

Table 11.2
Growth of the Federal Service

Year	No. of employees	No. of employees as a percent of U.S. population	Percent in agencies other than defense and post office
1816	4,479	0.06	21
1831	11,067	0.08	17
1851	25,713	0.11	15
1871	50,155	0.13	24
1891	150,844	0.24	23
1911	387,673	0.42	30
1931	596,745	0.49	32
1951	2,455,901	1.62	30
1961	2,407,025	1.34	32
1966	2,726,144	1.39	33
1971	2,822,884	1.39	35
1976	2,832,462	1.32	37
1980	2,947,137	1.34	44

SOURCE: *Historical Statistics of the United States; Statistical Abstract,* 1979. 1980 data, U.S. Office of Personnel Management and U.S. Postal Service.

control; (b) giving discretionary authority to public agencies so that the exercise of power is not responsive to the public; (c) preoccupation with routine; and (d) unimaginative or inefficient administration.[7]

The growth of the bureaucracy was intended to promote the efficient administration of public policy in a fair and politically neutral manner. Agencies of administration are structured according to principles common to all large-scale organizations: job specialization, hierarchical authority, a system of rules, and impartial administration.

With large, complex organizations, it is necessary to have job specialization. Each individual in the organization has a specific function to perform. Each task can be identified, the skills necessary to perform the task listed, and persons fitting the skills are recruited to the position. This puts competent persons in place to perform a task required by the organization. Along with the clearly defined authority assigned a position comes the notion of accountability. A hierarchical structure of authority ensures that each specialized task will be coordinated in a coherent way. Each level of work performance is accountable to a higher level of authority and supervision. The result is a pyramidal design: authority flows down from a chief executive to directors to program supervisors to specific employees.

Smooth operation of the organization depends on a system of rules. These

7. See James Q. Wilson, ''The Rise of the Bureaucratic State,'' *Public Interest* 41 (Fall 1975) for a clear statement of the bureaucratic problem.

are written, published rules that govern the day-to-day operation of the organization. They make overall coordination of the organization possible so that the hierarchical control structure can function smoothly. A major reason for the establishment of a set of rules is to ensure impartial administration. Employees are to administer or apply the rules established by the agency; they are not to use their personal standards in applying policy. In other words, personnel are not to let their personal feelings color the way they approach their administrative responsibilities. Policies are to apply to all, without exception.

The problems of bureaucracy begin with the erosion of its principles. The more bureaucracy grows, the greater the specialization, the more difficult control and coordination become. When the federal bureaucracy began, its preeminent function was *service*. There was no controversy, since there was widespread public agreement that the services were necessary and desirable, and could not be provided by private agencies. The services included defense (War Department) diplomacy (State Department), law and prosecutions (Justice), and collecting and dispensing revenues (Treasury).

Throughout the early nineteenth century, government continued to be service-oriented. The postal service was added in 1816. In order to promote and subsidize specific clientele groups, the departments of agriculture, commerce, and interior were established. The railroad industry was helped to establish a nationwide rail network. Road construction and river transportation were promoted to facilitate commerce. Farmers were given land if they would settle and farm it. Protective tariffs kept out imports to protect new, domestic industry. Departmental agencies grew in the first half of the nineteenth century in order to *serve* the growth of the nation and further its productivity.

By late in the century service agencies were being supplemented by *regulatory* activities. The Interstate Commerce Commission was created in 1887; the Federal Trade Commission followed in 1914. Government was now telling private agencies and citizens what they could and could not do. Such regulation came in waves and, as James Wilson observed, each wave left bureaucratic structures that became part of permanent government.[8] The first wave occurred between 1887 and 1890 and was aimed at business monopoly (the Interstate Commerce Act and the Sherman Anti-Trust Act); the second wave, between 1906 and 1915, sought to regulate unfair business practices and strengthen antitrust laws (the Pure Food and Drug Act, the Federal Trade Commission, the Clayton Act); the third wave, during the 1930s, aimed at the concentration of business power and labor-management relations (the Food, Drug and Cosmetic Act, the Securities Exchange Act, the National Labor Relations Act); and the fourth wave, in the 1960s, sought to protect consumers and ensure environmental protection (the Water Quality Act, Clean Air Act, Truth in Lending).

The heavy burden of regulation has vastly increased the size and complexity of the bureaucracy and put a good deal of independent political power in the

8. James Q. Wilson, ''The Rise of the Bureaucratic State,'' p. 96.

FACT FILE

THE REGULATORY ESTABLISHMENT

Agency (in order of creation)	1970	1980
1824　*Army Corps of Engineers*	$ 2	$ 40
1836　*Patent and Trademark Office, Commerce Department*	49	96
1863　*Comptroller of the Currency*	32	190
1871　*Bureau of Fisheries (became Fish and Wildlife Service in 1940)*	NA	20
1887　*Interstate Commerce Commission*	27	80
1903　*Antitrust Division*	9	47
1913　*Federal Reserve Board*	3	11
1914　*Federal Trade Commission*	20	68
1915　Coast Guard	57	368
1916　*Tariff Commission (became International Trade Commission in 1975)*	4	15
1922　*Commodity Exchange Authority, Agriculture Department (became Commodity Futures Trading Commission in 1974)*	—	16
1927　*Customs Service*	20	116
1930　*Federal Power Commission (became Federal Energy Regulatory Commission in 1977)*	18	70
1931　*Food and Drug Administration*	68	317
1932　*Federal Home Loan Bank Board*	21	21
1933　*Employment Standards Administration, Labor Department*	NA	112
1933　*Federal Deposit Insurance Corporation*	39	122
1934　*Federal Communications Commission*	24	71
1934　*Securities and Exchange Commission*	22	68
1935　*National Labor Relations Board*	38	107
1936　*Maritime Administration, Commerce Department (regulatory functions were transferred to the Federal Maritime Commission in 1961)*	4	11
1937　*Consumer and Marketing Service, Agriculture Department (duties were transferred in 1972 to the Agricultural Marketing Service and the Animal and Plant Health Inspection Service; major regulatory duties were transferred from the latter to the Food Safety and Quality Service in 1977)*	197	872
1938　*Civil Aeronautics Board*	48	102
1946　*Atomic Energy Commission (regulatory functions were transferred to the Nuclear Regulatory Commission in 1975)*	12	345
1948　*Federal Aviation Agency (became Federal Aviation Administration in 1967)*	NA	229
1951　*Renegotiation Board*	4	7
1953　*Small Business Administration*	NA	NA
1961　*Agricultural Stabilization and Conservation Service, Agriculture Department*	66	80
1963　*Labor-Management Services Administration, Labor Department*	12	52
1964　*Equal Employment Opportunity Commission*	12	124
1966　*Federal Highway Administration*	NA	29
1966　*Federal Railroad Administration*	4	23
1969　*Council on Environmental Quality*	NA	3
1970　*Cost Accounting Standards Board*	NA	2
1970　*Environmental Protection Agency*	71	1,154
1970　*National Credit Union Administration*	7	17
1970　*National Highway Traffic Safety Administration*	32	132

THE REGULATORY ESTABLISHMENT *(Continued)*

Agency (in order of creation)	1970	1980
1970 *Occupational Safety and Health Review Commission*	—	7
1971 *Farm Credit Administration*	4	12
1972 *Bureau of Alcohol, Tobacco and Firearms, Treasury Department*	NA	137
1972 *Consumer Product Safety Commission*	—	41
1972 *Domestic and International Business Administration, Commerce Department (now the Industry and Trade Administration)*	—	9
1973 *Drug Enforcement Administration*	NA	14
1973 *Federal Energy Administration (became Economic Regulatory Administration in 1977)*	—	156
1973 *Mine Enforcement and Safety Administration, Interior Department (became Mine Safety and Health Administration of the Labor Department in 1977)*	NA	126
1973 *Occupational Safety and Health Administration*	—	173
1974 *Council on Wage and Price Stability*	—	6
1974 *Foreign Agricultural Service, Department of Agriculture*	NA	NA
1975 *Federal Election Commission*	—	9
1975 *National Transportation Safety Board*	5	16
1976 *Federal Grain Inspection Service, Department of Agriculture*	—	25
1977 *Office of Consumer Affairs and Regulatory Functions, Housing and Urban Development Department*	—	21
1977 *Office of Surface Mining Reclamation and Enforcement, Interior Department*	—	148

SOURCE: Center for the Study of American Business, Washington University; published in *National Journal*, January 19, 1980,

hands of the bureaucrat. It has thrust the bureaucrats into close association with the clientele groups being regulated by their agencies. And Congress has delegated more and more regulatory responsibility to the bureaucracy. What this means is that public bureaucracy can no longer be a neutral arena for the administration of public policy. Bureaucrats have become a central force in the political process because they exercise the vast discretionary powers delegated to them by Congress. In the process, they have developed constituencies. So we need to examine the bureaucracy as part of the political process and ask whether it is representative and accountable as a branch of democratic government.

THE POLITICS OF THE BUREAUCRACY

Laws and policies, of necessity, must be general prescriptions for administration. The application of policy to specific circumstances therefore involves interpretation and discretion. Congress has deferred more and more to the bureaucracy the formulation of specific rules and procedures to carry out policies enacted in broad outline form. As a regulatory body, the bureaucracy interacts with any number of political forces, so it must be sensitive to these political forces. Agencies receive their funds from Congress; a congressional inquiry on behalf of a constituent produces a prompt response from the agency. Constituent groups can be mobilized to support the work of an agency or prevent any reduction in funding. Presidential priorities bear on how resources are used. In short, the bureaucracy is enmeshed in the political process. Four parts of this process affect its operation: public opinion, interest groups, Congress, and the executive branch.

PUBLIC OPINION

Many Americans blame the bureaucracy for the problems of government. Bureaucrats are viewed as job-security oriented, unimaginative, and inefficient. In one recent sample, only 30 percent of the people polled thought that government agencies do well in taking care of problems they handle.[9] Yet this general impression is contradicted by people who have had specific encounters with the bureaucracy. Of those surveyed, 80 percent felt they received fair treatment in their contact with government agencies. Yet of these same people, only 42 percent rated government offices in general as being fair: "There seems to be a clear separation of generalized attitudes from the specific attitudes derived from an individual's direct experience."[10]

Table 11.3

Public Satisfaction with Bureaucracy

	Percentage satisfied or highly satisfied	
	General evaluation	Own experience
Overall satisfaction	65	74
Competence	31	72
Fairness	43	82
Consideration	38	77

SOURCE: Robert I. Kahn, Barbara A. Gutek, Eugenia Barton, and Daniel Katz, "Americans Love Their Bureaucrats," Reprinted from *Psychology Today* (June 1975), p. 70. Copyright © 1975 by Ziff-Davis Publishing Company.

Some agencies have been skillful at mobilizing public opinion to support their activities. For years, J. Edgar Hoover maintained a favorable image for the FBI. This allowed the agency great independence within the Department of Justice, produced high morale, and secured Hoover an unassailable position. Only late in Hoover's career, and after his death, did real criticism surface. The Wa-

9. Robert L. Kahn, et al. "Americans Love Their Bureaucrats," *Psychology Today* (June 1975), p. 70.
10. Daniel Katz, Barbara A. Gutek, Robert L. Kahn, Eugenia Barton, *Bureaucratic Encounters* (Ann Arbor, Mich.: Institute for Social Research, 1975), pp. 185–186.

tergate revelations of FBI violations of the law under Hoover did much to erode the popular image of the agency. NASA too enjoyed popularity as it worked to fulfill President Kennedy's promise to put a man on the moon. The strong sense of American mission and competition with the Russians gave NASA status and purpose that it was able to convert into large appropriations and skilled employees.

Agencies are sensitive to public opinion; bureaucrats are aware of the public mood and bewildered by it. Many agencies employ public information specialists to promote communication and good relations between the agency and the public. They know the decline in trust and confidence is affecting their ability to do their job.

INTEREST GROUPS

Much of the apparent criticism of bureaucracy comes from the close affinity between agencies and the groups they serve. The public looks upon these as special interest groups enjoying particular favor with government. Bureaucrats, however, understand that stable political power depends upon building and serving a constituent interest group.

Interest groups and bureaucratic agencies form strong alliances. Often an agency was created to serve a special constituency—the Department of Labor or the Environmental Protection Agency, for example. Interest groups prefer to present their problems to a specific agency charged with monitoring those interests. The sense of shared mutual interest between agency and interest group adds strong emotional and moral overtones to public policy. This was clearly the case when President Nixon sought to abolish the Office of Economic Opportunity by withholding funding for the agency. The agency saw itself as an advocate for disadvantaged groups, and it went to court to have the impounded funds released. Philip Selznick's classic study of the TVA revealed the extent to which a public agency would modify its original objectives in order to gain the support of interest groups in the Tennessee Valley.[11] The agency was willing to give up some autonomy in policy making to buy the support of important local interests. In this way the agency gained an important lobby in support of its primary mission: expanding electric power in the valley.

The strongest alliance is at the middle level of the bureaucracy, where bureau chiefs dominate. Far enough removed from presidential politics, bureau chiefs bargain for political autonomy and power. They are long-term career administrators who develop keen perceptions of the politics within an agency, the groups with which they interact, and the strategic value of issues. Frequently it is to the administrator's advantage to form an alliance with clientele groups.[12] What

11. Philip Selznick, *TVA and the Grass Roots* (Berkeley: University of California Press, 1949).
12. See J. Lieper Freeman, *The Political Process; Executive Bureau–Legislative Committee Relations* (New York: Random House, 1965).

One result of the 1929 Depression was the New Deal idea that the federal government should protect the public interest so that the American people would no longer be at the mercy of big business. This was not a new concept—independent federal regulatory agencies had been established earlier (for example, the Patent Office in 1836)—but the power, scope, and number of those established in the 1930s and since then has been unprecedented. There was the Federal Power Commission in 1930, the Food and Drug Administration in 1931, The Federal Communications Commission and Securities Exchange Commission in 1934. Since 1970 no regulatory agencies were established. The attitude that it was the federal government's job to monitor all commercial and industrial developments affecting the public became firmly established as part of the way business and government interact within our political system. The use of atomic energy for peaceful purposes has, in fact, been under federal control since the first atomic device was tested in the Nevada desert during World War II.

After World War II both political leaders and members of the regulatory agencies followed a policy of encouraging the use of nuclear power to provide energy. By the 1960s the technology seemed sophisticated enough for commercial nuclear power plants, and their development was spurred in the 1970s by the oil and energy crises. The federal Nuclear Regulatory Commission (NRC), whose job it is to license, approve, and supervise safety standards for nuclear plants, began to approve construction plans on a large scale. By early 1979, seventy-two plants were supplying 12.5 percent of our electric power.

But by 1979 there was also entrenched opposition to these plants and especially to the construction of new ones because of grave questions of safety. The Clamshell Alliance, which began as opposition to the construction of a new plant at Seabrook, New Hampshire, became a national movement. And despite a series of incidents, such as the death of three technicians when an experimental reactor exploded at a government test site in 1961 and the partial meltdown at an experimental reactor near Detroit in 1966 the government and industry continued to assure the public that the plants were safe.

None of these incidents, however, received the national attention or approached the potential for disaster of the accident at Three Mile Island in Pennsylvania in April 1979. Although technicians reacted to a valve malfunction within 15 seconds and followed all the correct procedures, what they did was not enough to control a serious leak of radioactive steam and the real possibility of the worst case of all: a meltdown of the core that would have meant danger to thousands of people as many as 20 miles away from the plant. The effect of the incident was intensified by a continuing series of mishaps and the realization that even NRC experts were not sure what had gone wrong, why, and what to do about it quickly and safely. Three Mile Island brought into focus the whole question of a too-close relationship between the regulators and the regulated: Who in fact is regulating whom? And what about the public interest? The aftermath has been not only a halt in the construction of new nuclear power plants, but a definite weakening of the consensus that we can rely on government to put public safety first, no matter what the economic cost might be.

has been called the "iron triangle of politics"—a three-sided symbiotic relation-ship of bureau chief, clientele group, and congressional committee or subcommit-tee—establishes a continual policy process with the bureaucracy at the heart of the decision-making process. There are advantages for the agency administrator since "his organizational independence from both Congressional and Presidential directives is often directly related to his degree of dependence on the interest group clientele that benefits from his decisions. Clientele groups can also increase their bureau's clout with Congress, run interference with OMB for its policy in-terests, rally public opinion behind agency programs, and affect the chances for successful implementation of programs."[13]

In general, the clientele relationship with bureaucratic agencies is a prime source of access for interest groups. A bureau's clientele support can vary widely; not all bureaus have natural constituencies. Groups vary widely in size, cohesive-ness, purpose, and popular support. The more a bureau can build political support among groups and maintain a favorable image within its clientele, the greater the political power of the agency will be.

CONGRESS

Congress and the bureaucracy interact constantly (Figure 11.3): What Con-gress created, it feels free to review and oversee. Congress monitors implementa-tion for several reasons: (1) It is congressional law that bureaucrats administer; (2) it is money appropriated by Congress that is spent; and (3) it is the representatives' constituents who are affected.

Agencies generally establish cordial relationships with congressional com-mittees, particularly committee and subcommittee chairs. For years branches of the military could count on southern Democrats holding powerful seats on appro-priations and armed services committees to fund their budgets or restore money taken out by the administration. Cordial relationships are also important for rep-resentatives. Constituent service is a major element in survival, and this means going to the bureaucarcy for help and answers. A prompt and satisfactory re-sponse is of value to the member of Congress.

A congressional presence in administration is also becoming more common. As more and more discretionary powers are being delegated to the bureaucracy, congressional committees review and monitor the exercise of those powers. Leg-islative clearance for administrative rules and regulations is an increasing phe-nomenon in today's politics. Oversight also provides evidence that Congress is "on the job," watching out for the taxpayer. Generally this is a mutually reward-ing opportunity for both representative and administrator, as each seeks to extend his or her sphere of influence with the other.

This natural tendency to build reliable political support in Congress is most evident in the appropriations process. Agencies seek to maximize their budget

13. Carol Greenwald, *Group Power* (New York: Praeger, 1977), p. 226.

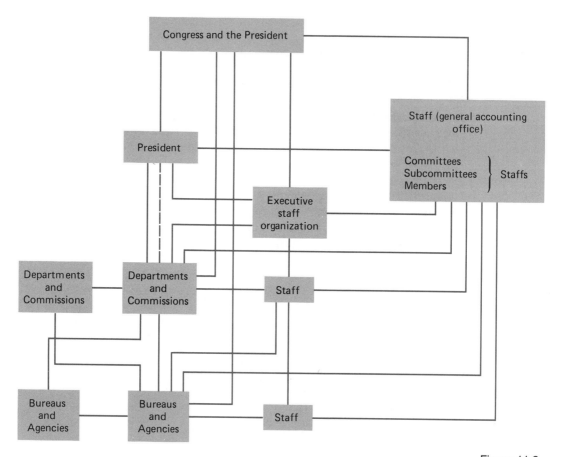

Figure 11.3

Administrative activity in Washington, D.C. (Emmette Redford, *Democracy in the Administrative State,* New York: Oxford University Press, 1969)

requests. The stronger the relationship with Congress, the greater the chance they will get what they requested or, conversely, the smaller the cut. Agencies that produce tangible results—particularly when constituents benefit—have the strongest support with Congress and are more likely to be funded regardless of the president's budget. Congress frequently looks to agencies for support in congressional battles with the executive, and those agencies that provide support fare better at the hands of Congress than at those of OMB or the president.

THE EXECUTIVE BRANCH

The bureaucracy is part of the executive branch, although sometimes only nominally so; presidents have exercised control over the bureaucracy only sporadically and then often with odd results. Presidents usually express frustration with their attempts to manage the bureaucracy and turn to other activities that are more pressing and more personally rewarding. But the attempts at control continue.

One major means of exercising control over the bureaucracy is executive reorganization. After World War II, the Hoover Commission on Organization of the Executive Branch recommended simplifying government and concentrating more power in central authority. President Nixon suggested a radical reorganization of cabinet-level departments to give him more control and provide for rational organization based on pressing problems. The proposal was a victim of Watergate. President Carter was also intent on reorganization. He has already streamlined the White House staff, made reforms in the Civil Service system, and added a Department of Education, but, as of Fall 1980 several other reforms were pending in Congress—consolidation of disaster relief agencies, a natural resources cabinet department, and consolidation of law enforcement agencies. Carter may very well be remembered as the reorganization president.

The president's major resource in controlling the bureaucracy is the Office of Management and Budget (OMB). This office is responsible for the preparation of the budget, monitoring spending, and recommending managerial efficiency. The president can tighten his control by having OMB require agencies to submit budget requests for review. OMB then screens all requests before putting them together for the president to submit as his annual budget. Because of its ability to impose sanctions, OMB is a powerful tool for rewarding and punishing agencies for conforming or not conforming to presidential directives.

The White House staff is a valuable asset for the president. It provides

President Carter consults with his Secretary of Transportation, Neil Goldschmidt. (Karl Schumacher, The White House.)

information unaffected by the politics and intrigues of agency affairs. But presidential staff may also meddle in agency affairs, as in the case of Watergate. On balance, however, the White House staff is an important source of information and ideas for any president seeking to move the bureaucracy.

Bureaucrats find little joy in presidential politics. Too often, presidents seek personal goals in administrative control. There is little attention to administrative procedures within agencies. Cabinet secretaries must balance presidential priorities and agency politics; they cannot advocate a departmental mission to a president whose priorities are turned in another direction, yet they must maintain morale and provide leadership. Agencies see top-level bureaucrats as unsympathetic and unknowledgeable about the problems of administration. Consequently, the bureaucrat turns to Congress, the interest group, or the public for support and rewards (Figure 11.4).

There are considerable restraints on presidential control. First, any president can give administration only limited time. Other roles, with higher political priority, demand attention. Most chief executives are not adept at management; they have neither the background nor the interest in administration. Second, lack of

Figure 11.4

Diagram of bureaucratic activity.

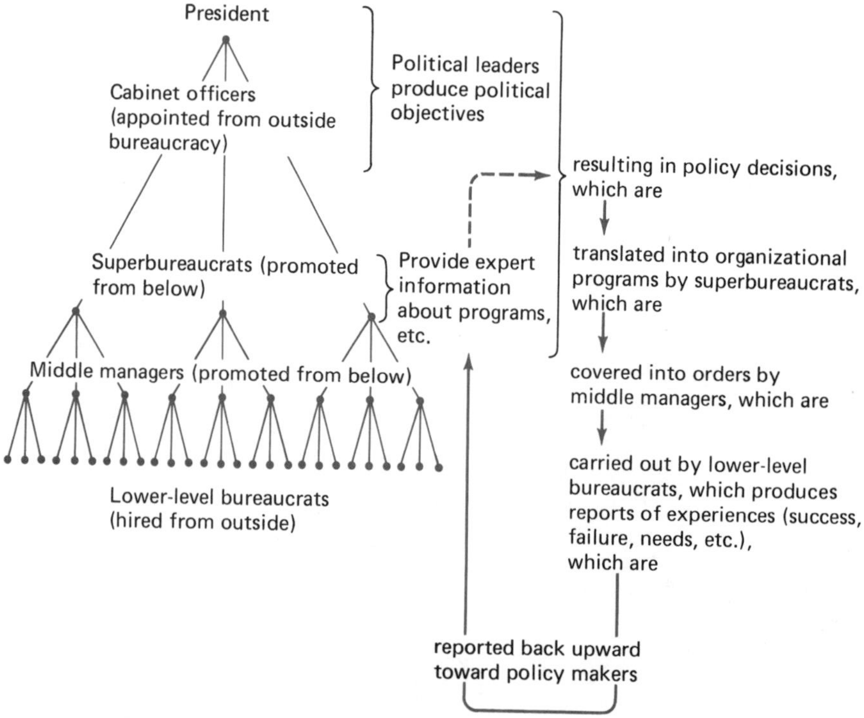

information keeps the president and White House staff from exercising real control. The size and complexity of bureaucracy make it virtually impossible that adequate or timely information will be available. Third, the president must compete with other interested parties, Congress, and constituents for influence. These competitors can work to thwart presidential directives. Congress pulls the purse strings; clients may rally public support and a climate of expectations. This was the case with President Carter's civil service reorganization, when veterans groups resisted abolishing preferences for veterans in employment. As government becomes more complex and multifunctional, with the inclusion of regulatory responsibilities, the decision-making power of the bureaucracy is increased. Let us look at the following patterns in bureaucratic decision-making: rulemaking, rule adjudication, law enforcement, implementation, and policy initiation.

DECISION-MAKING PATTERNS

RULEMAKING

The addition of regulatory responsibility in the twentieth century greatly increased the bureaucracy's power of rulemaking—a quasi-legislative function whereby agency rules have the force of law. Agency lawmaking spells out the public policy Congress has enacted in broad outline. Affected parties must be notified of possible rules, hearings held so the parties may voice their objections, and the final rules published in the *Federal Register*. There are now 17 pages of agency rules published each year for every page of statute law.[14] Critics contend that agency rulemaking has reversed the constitutional order of checks and balances. Congress is to legislate, the executive to veto and administer. Now, critics argue, Congress has deferred to the bureaucracy: Agencies legislate through rulemaking and Congress, using legislative clearance, vetoes or clears the agency rules—a reversal of the constitutional roles.

Rulemaking is a prime responsibility of independent regulatory agencies such as the ICC or FTC, but today all executive agencies make rules. Two examples will illustrate the importance of agency rulemaking. In 1964, after the Surgeon General's report linked cancer to cigarette smoking, the Federal Trade Commission published rules requiring tobacco companies to warn consumers of the health hazards of smoking. The FTC proposed to limit commercial advertising and order the placing of a warning label on cigarette packages. The tobacco industry rallied and succeeded in lobbying Congress to modify and weaken the proposed rules, which went into effect in 1965. In 1974, the Office of Civil Rights of the Department of Health, Education and Welfare gave notice of proposed rules prohibiting sex discrimination in education for the Title IX provision

14. Kenneth J. Meier, *Politics and the Bureaucracy* (North Scituate, Mass.: Duxbury Press, 1979), p. 75.

of the 1972 Educational Amendments. The proposed regulations would terminate federal financial assistance to educational institutions that discriminated on the basis of sex. The rules covered educational programs, housing, employment, admission, and athletics for elementary, secondary, and higher education. It was in college athletics that the greatest controversy emerged. Now women's teams would have to be funded on some equal opportunity basis. Congress and HEW are still wrestling with this issue, while Title IX rules are now law and facilitating greater educational opportunities for women.

RULE ADJUDICATION

Despite the importance of bureaucratic rulemaking, many agencies spend a good deal of their efforts in adjudication of rules: agencies administer the laws by charging persons or organizations suspected with violating rules. They can then apply administrative sanctions to persons or organizations found in violation. Rules of procedure must be followed: notification, evidence, hearings, fairness, and so on. But unlike rulemaking, adjudication applies only to specific parties, or classes of people; it does not establish policy. A widespread practice in bureaucratic agencies, adjudication is a way of enforcing policy by demanding compliance.

The Food and Drug Administration frequently adjudicates when it declares

Auto makers struggle to reduce exhaust emissions. The Environmental Protection Agency has set stiff emission standards for the automobile manufacturers. (United Press International)

drugs unsafe and bans them from the market. The case of the drug laetrile is an example: The FDA demanded evidence of its cancer-curing properties before allowing the drug on the market. The Social Security Administration adjudicates when it passes on disability insurance eligibility. Adjudication is most controversial in the area of environmental protection. Industrial firms have been required by the EPA to install costly pollution abatement devices or be fined. Many proposed projects can be halted or held up until environmental impact statements are adjudicated; damming the Tennessee River, for example, was halted due to the discovery of the impact the dam would have on one species of fish.

LAW ENFORCEMENT

Law enforcement is nothing other than the application of law to specific situations. Discretion is always involved; certain laws are more vigorously enforced than others. The applicability of one law over another must be judged in light of the situation. Bureaucratic agencies make decisions through selective law enforcement. Several federal agencies, such as the FBI, Bureau of Alcohol, Tobacco, and Firearms, the Drug Enforcement Administration, and the Immigration and Naturalization Service, have direct law enforcement responsibilities.

IMPLEMENTATION

When we think of bureaucratic activity, we frequently think of policy implementation: agencies seeking to put into practice the policy established through legislation or executive order. The impact of implementation is seen in the Federal Reserve Board's changing the discount rate or altering the reserve requirement to keep down inflation. The Federal Communications Commission decides how many radio and television stations to license in a given city or area. Another good example of discretion in implementation was the Civil Service Commission's decision to force federal agencies to adopt goals and timetables for hiring minorities as a means of implementing the government policy of nondiscrimination and equal opportunity employment. In 1971, this amounted to a change in policy. Earlier, benign discrimination (the absence of minority employees or applicants) was permitted; now the Civil Service Commission was requiring affirmative action.

One basic issue in policy implementation is whether administrators can use scientific management principles to provide a cost-benefit analysis of program effectiveness. Charles Lindblom has long argued that policymakers actually take an *incremental* approach to policy implementation; that is, bureaucratic momentum produces a sequential process where changes in policy occur in small or marginal amounts that do not disturb or reverse the direction of the initial decision implementing a policy.[15] The fact is we have paid too little attention to imple-

15. Charles F. Lindblom, *The Policy-Making Process* (Englewood Cliffs, N.J.: Prentice Hall, 1968).

Economic Policy

Government policy in economic affairs has two principal objectives: (1) promoting, regulating, or controlling particular forms of economic activity; and (2) controlling levels of economic activity to maintain a healthy and stable economy. While there remains debate over the level of government activity in the economy, events in the twentieth century have prompted a changed public attitude toward favoring increased governmental activity in economics. First, the Great Depression brought massive unemployment and economic stress. Only extensive federal aid brought recovery to the economy. Second, World War II demanded full economic productivity, increased government spending, and, after the war, wage and price controls. Full postwar employment became a chief goal. Third, John Maynard Keynes' *General Theory of Employment, Interest, and Money* was a popular attack on free market economic thinking. He argued the market was not self-regulating, that full employment and prosperity could require government deficit spending to prime economic growth.

Much of the first objective of promoting, regulating, and controlling economic activity is designed to promote the free enterprise, market economy. The first legislation, the Sherman Antitrust Act of 1890, made it a crime to restrain trade or destroy competition in interstate commerce. This was supplemented in 1914 by the Clayton Act designed to insure fair trade by preventing price fixing to eliminate competition. Also created that same year was the Federal Trade Commission, an independent regulatory agency whose responsibility is to maintain free economic competition. There are several means the government utilizes to promote competition and economic activity.[1] Government may employ direct subsidies to encourage business, as with the railroads in the nineteenth century and merchant marine shipping in the twentieth. Promotion of business activity may also use tax policy such as tax exemptions, deductions, credits, lower rates, or selective government expenditures. Other forms of promotion involve loans, public construction projects such as rivers, harbors, and airports, and technical information services.

Business regulation and control began with the Interstate Commerce Commission in 1887 and expanded broadly in the 1930s under the New Deal. Notably in the areas of minimum wages, food, health, and automobiles, regulatory responsibilities were added to department agencies. That is, there were obligations and regulations on the way industries conducted their business. The most recent regulatory additions are in environmental quality, pollution control, and occupational safety. In areas designated as public utilities, economic activity itself is controlled by government. Briefly, public utility regulation involves government sponsorship through licensure to operate, typically as a monopoly. Then a government regulatory commission is established to oversee and promulgate rules for the utility. Standards of service are erected, including the rates charged for service. The government commission also fixes the rate of profit the business may make.

The second broad objective is maintaining economic stability. Since World War II this has meant full employment and steady economic growth, which is achieved through three basic policies: fiscal, monetary, and income.

Fiscal policy involves the taxing and spending power of the federal government to influence economic activity. To stimulate or slow down the economy, government can vary the rate at which it raises or spends money. Government can hold spending constant and increase or decrease taxes or, conversely, government may hold taxes constant and vary the level of spending—deficit spending. There are infinite combinations both of rates of taxing and of spending. The assumption is more money in the economy stimulates economic activity.

Monetary policy is under the direction of the Federal Reserve Board and involves control of the supply of money and credit in the economy. Three basic tools are employed. First, the Federal Reserve Board buys and sells securities on the open market. Buying securities puts additional deposits in member banks, hence allowing them to make loans. Second, the Federal Reserve Board sets the discount rate, which is the interest rate charged by Re-

serve Banks to commercial banks borrowing money from Reserve banks. Higher rates tighten credit and restrict the flow of money. The third tool is the reserve rate, which requires member banks to keep monetary reserves in ratio to their deposits. If the reserve rate is 20 percent then banks must keep 20 percent of the total of loans in reserve in the bank.

Income policy is a more recent addition to government policy for economic stability, coming after World War II and resurfacing again in early 1971. Essentially, it involves setting wage and price guidelines in order to regulate inflation and economic growth. In 1971 President Nixon imposed mandatory wage and price controls. Ended in 1973, this was an unprecedented peacetime use of controls, which previously had been used only during wartime. President Carter has opted instead for voluntary wage–price guidelines to keep down inflationary economic tendencies.

1. J. Anderson, D. Brady, and C. Bullock, *Public Policy and Politics in America,* North Scituate, Mass.: Duxbury Press, 1978, p. 201–204.

---

mentation as a criterion in policy formulation. Two political scientists, for example, have traced the failure of the manpower training program in one city and claim that it failed due to the inadequate attention given program implementation by Great Society architects in Washington, D.C., when the policy was designed.[16] There was effort to involve community groups in the decision-making process of how federal funds would be spent for manpower training. The legislation gave little thought, however, to the "complexity of joint action"—how the groups would come together and agree on the distribution of funds. The result was to set community groups against one another, forcing delays and thereby disrupting program implementation.

POLICY INITIATION

The final area of decision making for the bureaucracy is policy initiation. Long accepted as part of bureaucratic responsibility, **policy initiation** is the suggesting of new policies and programs. In some ways the president and department

16. Jeffrey L. Pressman and Aaron Wildavsky, *Implementation* (Berkeley, Calif.: University of California Press, 1973).

secretaries depend on the agencies for recommendations for new policies or policy changes. Often the agency recommendations may come from client requests or with the prompting of Congress.

The military provides the clearest example: new weapons systems are frequently proposed by branches of the service. Congress often gets in the act because decisions on MIRV missiles or manned bombers affect employment in the states and affect our defense posture with foreign nations. But other agencies also initiate policy. In 1976, for example, HEW began locating fathers of families on welfare (Aid to Families with Dependent Children). The goal was to locate the fathers and force them to support their families, thereby reducing welfare costs. Something as major as America's new policy toward China can result from bureaucratic initiatives. The policy obviously required presidential direction, but the State Department indicated China's readiness to deal with America through small intiatives like cultural exchanges, easing trade restrictions, and permitting scholarly and journalistic trips. Such State Department gestures gave Richard Nixon the opportunity for his reopening talks with the Chinese and his trip to China. These initiatives, then, played a role in the normalization of relations that produced the new China policy.

Policy initiation can be threatening; it can place the agency head in an exposed position and risk rebuke from the president and Congress. Often initiatives are undertaken in clientele-oriented agencies, where a strong constituency can be depended upon for support.

PATTERNS OF CONFLICT

Bureaucracy is perceived as a monolithic structure, an impenetrable maze. Generalizations regarding bureaucracy and administration presume singularity of purpose and attitude that extends to all employees in all executive agencies. There is a certain anonymity and impersonalization to the federal government.

The picture from within the bureaucracy is markedly different. As in any modern, complex organization, there are real persons performing a wide variety of tasks. These people have numerous points of view that can and often do clash. For the serious student of bureaucracy, the stereotype vanishes when the attitudes and behavior of agency personnel are examined. A wide variety of attitudes and responses form patterns of conflict within the bureaucracy.

DEMOCRATIC VALUES

We pay great attention to the democratic values of elected officials, yet very little to the values of the people who administer government programs. If bureaucracy is the fourth branch of government, closest to the public through implementation, then its concern for and commitment to democratic values ought to be of primary concern. This is all the more important because career civil servants are neither elected nor removable by the electoral process.

Bob L. Wynia's study of federal bureaucrats' attitudes toward democracy[17] brought some striking conclusions. Surveying over 400 federal executives from 52 different federal agencies on democratic values—democratic rules for fairness and legal rights, free speech, equality, public interest, and influence—Wynia discovered 60 to 75 percent agreement on items pertaining to democracy. It is significant, however, that approximately one-quarter to one-third do *not* support basic constitutional protections. Said Wynia: "While the overall data lend support to the fact that there is extensive agreement with the democratic philosophy within the bureaucracy, there are many areas of grave and undisputed disagreement on specific applications of democratic principles."[18] When Wynia compared agencies, education of bureaucrats, and years of service, a different picture emerged. Defense agencies tended to draw more "undemocratic types." These individuals were more inclined toward the use of force, toward justifying unfairness in the name of some greater purpose, and scored lowest on equality: "Defense agency executives, for whatever reasons, consistently demonstrate attitudes of an anti-democratic nature, whenever the issue of racial or social equality is raised."[19]

Table 11.4
Bureaucracy Agreement with the Democratic Philosophy

Item	Percentage of bureaucrats who agree with item
There are times when it almost seems better for the people to take the law into their own hands rather than wait for the machinery of government to act.	32
We might as well make up our minds that in order to make the world free a lot of innocent people will have to suffer.	31
We have to teach children that all men are created equal but almost everyone knows that some are better than others.	38
To bring about great changes for the benefit of mankind often requires cruelty and even ruthlessness.	27
The true American way of life is disappearing so fast that we may have to use force to save it.	19

SOURCE: Bob Wynia, "Federal Bureaucrats' Attitudes Toward a Democratic Ideology," Reprinted from *Public Administration Review*. 34 (March/April 1974). Copyright © 1974 by the American Society for Public Administration, 1225 Connecticut Avenue, N.W.; Washington, D.C. All rights reserved.

17. Bob L. Wynia, "Federal Bureaucrats' Attitudes Toward a Democratic Ideology," *Public Administration Review* 34 (March/April 1974), pp. 156–162.
18. *Ibid.*, p. 158.
19. *Ibid.*, p. 161.

Table 11.5

Bureaucratic Agreement with Application of Democratic Values

Item	Percentage of Agrees	Agency			Years of Education			Years in Service			
	Average	Social	Dept. of Defense	Other	0–12	13–15	16+	1–5	6–15	16–25	26+
When the country is in great danger, we may have to force people to testify against themselves even if it violates their rights.	24.6	25.3	30.9	20.4	25.6	26.3	22.5	15.2	23.3	24.6	28.8
Any person who hides behind the laws when he is questioned about his activities doesn't deserve much consideration.	24.8	19.0	29.3	24.4	41.0	26.6	19.1	12.1	16.5	24.6	37.5
We have to teach children that all men are created equal, but almost everyone knows that some are better than others.		34.6	43.9	34.7							
Just as is true of fine race horses, some breeds of people are just naturally better than others.		19.5	28.5	17.3							
Regardless of what some people say, there are certain races in the world that just won't mix with Americans.		13.3	26.0	13.8							

SOURCE: Bob Wynia, "Federal Bureaucrats' Attitudes Toward a Democratic Ideology," Reprinted from *Public Administration Review*, 34 (March/April 1974). Copyright © 1974 by the American Society for Public Administration, 1225 Connecticut Ave., N.W., Washington, D.C. All rights reserved.

Years in service and years of education also seem critical variables in attitude determination and change. Wynia discovered that the less education federal executives had, the more antidemocratic were their attitudes. Formal education apparently is positively correlated with acceptance of basic political and constitutional values of human equality, freedom of speech, and a democratic decision-making process. Also, the longer the time in federal service, the lower the acceptance of a democratic ideology. It is disturbing to note that the "bureaucratic environment" is not conducive to democratic values. The longer one serves in federal agencies, the more one's democratic commitment is eroded.

The results of the study are not altogether encouraging. If we say that bureaucrats have a major responsibility for public policy, then their commitment to democratic values is of some importance. They keep the system going, and they are responsible for keeping it open, responsive to needs, and sensitive to the public.

CHANGE OF ADMINISTRATION

Every four to eight years there is a change in administration. New programs are introduced; priorities change. Elected presidents and political appointees have only a limited time in which to implement their policy. They must contend with a career civil service that is not always loyal or sympathetic to a new administration. Richard Nixon took office in 1969 after a decade of Democratic administra-

"*Think of it! Presidents come and go, but We go on forever!*"

Drawing by Jim Berry. © 1976 NEA, Inc. Reprinted by permission.

tions. His administration had a high level of mistrust toward the career bureaucracy; in short, he and his staff felt that the career civil service was stacked against the administration. A manual for political appointees in the Nixon administration stated: "Because of the rape of the career service by the Kennedy and Johnson Administration . . . this Administration has been left a legacy of finding disloyalty and obstruction at high levels while those incumbents rest comfortably on career civil service status."[20]

Do new administrations face a hostile environment? An unsympathetic and disloyal bureaucracy? Two political scientists set out to discover if Richard Nixon's feeling was warranted: in general, they found that it was. A disproportionate number of Democrats filled key domestic agencies (HEW, HUD and OEO) and directed social services toward partisan constituencies. Moreover, the beliefs of personnel within such agencies evidenced a clear difference with the policies of the incoming Nixon administration. Stated Aberbach and Rockman:

> Our findings document a career bureaucracy with very little Republican representation but even more pointedly portray a social service bureaucracy dominated by administrators ideologically hostile to many of the directions pursued by the Nixon Administration in the realm of social policy. Democratic administrators in the social service agencies were the most hostile to these directions, but even Republican administrators in these same agencies . . . held attitudes that were not wholly sympathetic to the social service retrenchments sought by the Nixon Administration.[21]

Presidential policies are aimed at short-term political goals; bureaucracies are relatively immune from such time pressures. There is also a time lag that thwarts any new administration; it takes a while to change top personnel and get new policies going. And of course any expectation of retrenchment and cost-cutting will meet with bureaucratic resistance.

REFORM AND RESPONSIBILITY

At this point, there is a consensus that the bureaucracy needs reform. Conservatives and liberals alike agree that there is too much government. Presidents have found their goals resisted by an unsympathetic bureaucracy. Citizens feel intimidated by the host of rules and regulations they cannot comprehend but which cost them tax dollars. Reforming the bureaucracy is a high priority in American politics. Recent presidents have been active in suggesting reform measures, thus contributing to the changing climate of attitudes toward the bureaucracy.

20. Cited by Joel D. Aberbach & Bert Rockman, "Clashing Beliefs within the Executive Branch: The Nixon Administration Bureaucracy," *American Political Science Review* Vol. LXX (June 1976), p. 457.
21. *Ibid.*, pp. 466–67.

REORGANIZATION

Richard Nixon was acutely aware of the administrative environment in which his programs were to be carried out. He reformed the old Bureau of the Budget into the Office of Management and Budget, thereby supplanting the primacy of budgetary matters with management concerns. His intent was to provide central direction and coherence for the federal agencies within the executive branch. He also created the Domestic Council where the White House staff could plan and coordinate domestic policy in the same way national security policy was coordinated. Nixon also proposed reform of the cabinet: Six departments would be abolished (Commerce, HEW, HUD, Interior, Labor, and Transportation) and recombined in four departments (Community Development, Natural Resources, Human Resources, and Economic Affairs). Watergate prevented such cabinet reform from receiving serious consideration, and Nixon's efforts to place key political supporters in executive agencies heightened suspicion over his motives for reform.

President Carter campaigned on a platform of reform, and his administration was particularly active in this area. He altered the Executive Office of the President, created the Energy and Education departments with cabinet rank, and pushed through civil service reform. More reforms have been debated; Carter too had proposed cabinet reorganization (Figure 11.5). His proposed Economic Development Assistance Department would have come in large measure from functions presently in Agriculture and Commerce. The Development Assistance Department would have been renamed HUD with increased responsibilities; Agriculture would have been renamed Food and Nutrition; Interior would have become the Department of Natural Resources. Under this proposal, HUD would increase most in responsibility; and Agriculture and Commerce would have stood to lose the most.

CIVIL SERVICE REFORM

Civil Service reform has been Carter's most significant bureaucratic reform. Passed by Congress in October 1978, the Civil Service Reform Act became law with Carter's signature. According to its provisions, the Civil Service Commission has been abolished and replaced with two new agencies: The Office of Personnel Management (OPM) and a Merit Systems Protection Board (MSPB), which became the new board of appeals for employee grievances.

The reform creates a new Senior Executive Service which Jule Sugarman, vice-chairman of the Civil Service Commission, claims "are the most experienced people in government, and collectively they make 90 percent of the decisions in the executive branch—maybe more."[22] This cadre of 9,200 top federal executives can be moved in and out of agencies as "management teams." They will be given annual evaluations by administrators and can be demoted in grade with no

22. *National Journal*, September 30, 1978, p. 1543.

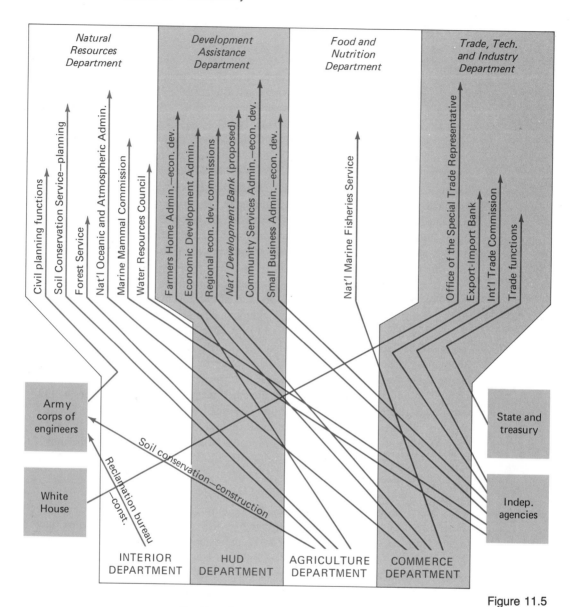

Figure 11.5

President Carter's proposal for cabinet reorganization. (*National Journal,* January 20, 1980, p. 85)

appeal if their performance is not satisfactory. SES employees will not be eligible for automatic, annual pay raises, but will be rewarded by a bonus system for high performance on the job. Managers and supervisors at GS-13 through GS-15 levels will no longer be given automatic pay increases each year; rather, merit pay will be offered these employees based upon an evaluation of their performance.

Table 11.6

Federal Salary Levels[a]

General schedule

GS 1— 7,960– 9,954
GS 2— 8,951–11,265
GS 3— 9,766–12,700
GS 4—10,963–14,248
GS 5—12,266–15,947
GS 6—13,672–17,776
GS 7—15,193–19,747
GS 8—16,826–21,875
GS 9—18,585–24,165
GS 10—20,467–26,605
GS 11—22,486–29,236
GS 12—26,951–35,033
GS 13—32,048–41,660
GS 14—37,871–49,229
GS 15—44,547–50,112
GS 16—50,112
GS 17 and GS 18—50,112

Executive schedule

ES I—52,247
ES II—53,996
ES III—55,804
ES IV—57,637
ES V—59,604
ES VI—61,600

a. The rate of basic pay payable for employees at these rates is limited to the rate payable for level V of the Executive Schedule, which is $50,112.50. Oct. 1, 1980.

The thrust of the reform is to evaluate bureaucrats and reward them for their productivity. The system is designed to stimulate better performance and will greatly increase the ability of cabinet secretaries and other political appointees to manage their agencies by putting together a management team from the top grades of career civil servants.

Critics of the reform fear political intrusion and partisan politics—exactly what the civil service was designed to avoid. They fear that management teams will become political units formed to implement presidential policies.

RATIONAL DECISION MAKING

Although reorganization has been a favored technique for reforming the bureaucracy, in recent years numerous other techniques have been developed in order to make more intelligent decisions and assess agency performance. Often referred to as *rational decision making,* these approaches attempt to make greater use of quantitative data to break out of the incremental mold of decision making. Such techniques borrow heavily from private industry practices. By using system and cost-benefit analysis, it is expected that more efficient management of agency resources will heighten rational control over public policy and increase economy in government. The goal of rational decision making is to provide the capability for arriving at decisions based on hard, scientific data analysis rather than a hunch formed out of past experience.

The new methods were first introduced into the federal government by Defense Secretary Robert McNamara in 1961. In an effort to get a handle on military decision making in the Pentagon, McNamara inaugurated new management tools utilizing computers and quantifiable objectives. The goal was to get some control over the vast sums of money being expended to achieve national defense objectives. The new techniques culminated in a comprehensive budget process called Planning, Programming, Budgeting System (PPB). This process required defense agencies to identify their policy objectives, design programs and alternatives to meet those objectives, and measure the costs for the resources needed. The use of quantified data would allow policymakers to achieve objectives at the lowest cost, but the results were less than encouraging. Most federal agencies were not equipped to measure the "cost effectiveness" of policies. They lacked personnel skilled in the technique. Agencies were also threatened by the perceived control over agency budgets. A mass of paperwork resulted, yet efficiency did not improve. PPB was finally abandoned by the federal government in 1971.[23]

Richard Nixon replaced PPB with a less threatening management system, *Management by Objectives* (MBO). Under MBO, agencies were required to identify short- and long-term objectives and then establish techniques to monitor the achievement of those objectives. Agencies were asked to develop "milestones," actions that aid in realizing the specified objectives. The intent was to dissociate MBO from resource allocation, to take away any perceived threat to the budget resources of an agency, in order to allow agencies to evaluate the achievement of their stated goals.

The implementation of MBO was greeted with mixed reactions. Some agencies, such as the state Department, found the identification of quantifiable objectives and milestones difficult. Bureau chiefs and line managers felt MBO was an effort to control agencies by the President or to criticize agency performance by means of a performance audit. President Nixon took little interest in the imple-

23. See Allen Schick, "A Death in the Bureaucracy: The Demise of Federal PPB," *Public Administration Review,* 33 (March-April 1973), pp. 146–56.

It was the Department of Defense, in 1961, which introduced planning, programming, budgeting systems into government. (The Bettmann Archive, Inc.)

mentation of MBO, and the Office of Management and Budget never became a serious proponent for it. The chief beneficiaries of MBO appear to have been political appointees in departments—secretaries and under secretaries: ''The MBO system provides the secretary with information about the programs for which he is responsible. . . .The MBO system establishes routine reporting mechanisms about major departmental concerns. These objectives are then regularly and consistently monitored in management conferences.''[24]

The most recent technique advocated by President Carter is *Zero Based Budgeting* (ZBB). Zero Based Budgeting puts every agency in the position of justifying its programs and resources annually. As the term implies, each agency starts its budget at zero. Agencies place programs in priority order and provide detailed information justifying the resources needed to operate each program annually. Each agency and department then submits a list of its programs in priority ranking to the president via the Office of Management and Budget. In this way priorities and resource costs can be quickly compared, and weak programs can then easily be weeded out. Costly but low-priority programs can be targeted and resources shifted to more urgent areas. Critics argue that ZBB raises bureaucratic anxiety. Any program receiving a low priority is destined to be eliminated, so the tendency is for agencies to protect their resources and give all programs a high priority. Items given low priority are often those that are favorites of Congress, the agencies knowing full well that Congress will not allow the administration to

24. Richard Rose, *Managing Presidential Objectives* (New York: Free Press, 1976), p. 120.

PRACTICING POLITICS   11.1

How to gain access to government

The federal bureaucracy is huge and some-times seems impossible to penetrate. Here are three sources, found in your local or university library, that can help you begin if you have a problem or want to influence the decisions of an agency.

1. *The Encyclopedia of U.S. Government Benefits* (second edition 1978, published by Wise) tells you how to get small business loans, home mortgages, schol-arships, farm loans, veterans benefits, grants, surplus products, government publications, and valuable free informa-tion.

2. Ralph Nader's Center for the Study of Responsive Law has produced a manual for citizen access to federal agencies called *Working on the System* (published by Basic Books). It is organized by fed-eral agency and gives information sources, agency activities, rules of the game, and how to gain access and par-ticipate.

3. *Protecting Your Right to Privacy: A Di-gest of Systems of Records, Agency Rules, and Research Aids,* has been published by the government to help im-plement the Privacy Act passed in De-cember 1974. It tells you how to find out what, if any, information an agency has about you, who else has regular ac-cess, have errors corrected, and get a copy of your records.

Don't forget your congressman! Congressional offices are prepared to aid constituents with problems in the bureaucracy. Casework on behalf of constituents is a major function of congressional staff, and they are good at it. They *will* and do help citizens with problems with the government. You can also approach one of the many organizations devoted to monitoring government in the public interest. Ralph Nader has founded a number of these: Center for the Study of Responsive Law, PO Box 19367, Washington, D.C. 20036; Con-gress Watch, 133 C Street SE, Washington, D.C. 20006; and Public Citizen, PO Box 19404, Washington D.C. 20036. There are also Common Cause, a national citizen's lobby formed to make government more accountable (2030 M Street NW, Washington, D.C. 20036), and the Center for Federal Policy Re-view, which monitors congressional commit-tees and makes committee members' actions known to their constituents (1509 Sixteenth Street NW, Washington, D.C. 20036).

Some of these are membership organiza-tions; some handle cases; some are sources of information. Check in your community as well; there may be local organizations or groups engaged in lobbying or watchdog activ-ities that could provide you with advice and help.

eliminate them. Supporters of ZBB argue it is a means of restoring efficiency and economy to government. One author, examining the creation of government organizations between 1923 and 1973, discovered that of 175 organizations existing in 1923, no less than 148 were still alive in 1973. In the meantime, no less than 246 new agencies had been created, for a 1973 total of 394.[25]

There is no question that these techniques can generate great quantities of information that serves to clarify program operation and alternatives. But they cannot provide answers for policy choices that are fundamentally political. National health care, welfare for dependent children, parity prices for farmers, or clean water still remain essentially political in nature. No amount of quantitative information can make these hard choices for our representative public officials.

RESPONSIBLE BUREAUCRACY

Running the government is a big business. The administrative apparatus has now become a symbol for corruption and inefficiency, but it was not always so. This is what Kenneth J. Meier had to say in 1979:

> In the United States we are fortunate because the federal bureaucracy is much better than we deserve. Combining the value dimensions of responsiveness and competence, the American federal bureaucracy is clearly the best in the world. No other national bureaucracy has won as many Nobel prizes, and no other bureaucracy responds to as wide an array of interests. These benefits of bureaucracy have come despite numerous obstacles posed by the American people.[26]

But a responsible bureaucracy in the past is no assurance that the federal bureaucracy will always perform responsibly. The bureaucracy is an independent force within American government. It defies control by any of the other branches of government, including the executive. If the bureaucracy has performed competently and responsively, it is not because constitutional checks limit its activities. In an age where regulation, specialization, and complex information are needed, the constitutional branches of government alone cannot meet the challenges government faces. Yet bureaucracy has not escaped the constitutional checks-and-balances system of a democratic political order.

It is precisely because agency administration is a political process that bureaucracy is of interest to Congress, the president, courts, and interest groups. It must compete for power with these other policymakers and share its power with them for the successful implementation of public policy. Congress, the president, and the interest groups ''check'' the bureaucracy because it is an integral part of

25. Herbert Kaufman, *Are Government Organizations Immortal?* (Washington, D.C.: The Brookings Institute, 1976), p. 35.
26. Kenneth J. Meier, *Politics and the Bureaucracy,* p. 204.

our politics. They understand it is not neutral, but subject to political demands from multiple points across our political process. This constant tugging and pulling on the bureaucracy may very well ensure its continuing accountability in American government.

The 1980s will continue to pose new problems. Bureaucracy will become more important, not less. Demands for energy conservation, consumer protection, public interest representation, and public order can be met only through the effective administration of programs. The bureaucracy has forever altered the tripartite constitutional separation of powers. Yet bureaucracy is a constitutional mechanism of government; it conforms to the spirit and law of the Constitution. There may be reason to fear the growth of bureaucratic government, to fear the ability of a bureaucracy to administer the challenges the last years of the twentieth century hold, but there is no reason to fear that the bureaucracy will not operate within constitutional, democratic limits.

SUMMARY

1. The bureaucracy stands at the center of American government, carrying out the programs enacted by Congress and presidents. It receives the brunt of criticism for the cost and inefficiency in government, yet without bureaucrats government service would come to an abrupt halt. Bureaucracy is indispensable to modern government.

2. There is no neat organization for the bureaucracy, with the president at the head as chief manager. Rather, in addition to 13 cabinet departments, there are independent executive agencies, regulatory agencies, and government corporations. The Executive Office of the president, assisting the president in his executive functions, is itself a bureaucracy. Presidents have been notoriously bad managers, little involved with the routine of administration.

3. The stereotype of the anonymous bureaucrat as a neutral administrator impartially following directives is largely a myth. The bureaucracy is enmeshed in the political process. Bureaucratic agencies respond as much to congressional committees and interest groups as they do to presidential policies. Agencies have points of view, little altered by presidential politics during an administration no matter how intent a president is on change.

4. The bureaucracy affords considerable political insulation. Recent presidents have sought reform and reorganization to alter the decision-making patterns of bureaucrats and to make the bureaucracy more manageable. Rational decision-making proposals as well as civil service reforms have proved less than successful to date, but reform will continue.

5. Responsible bureaucracy remains the goal of American government. Despite criticism, Americans have been fortunate in the quality of federal administrators. New regulations and problem areas will make the bureaucracy more important in the future, not less important.

TERMS

bureau 418	management by objectives 446
civil service 416	merit 416
Executive Office 417	Planning, Programming,
fourth branch 438	Budgeting System 446
General Service schedule 445	regulation 433
hierarchy 422	regulatory agency 419
implementation 435	Senior Executive Service 443
incrementalism 435	service agency 420
independent agency 418	specialization 422
iron triangle 429	zero based budgeting 447
clientele group 429	
department 418	

RESEARCH PROJECTS

11.1. Bureaucratic Agencies. How many federal bureaucratic agencies are there in your city and what do they do? Make a list of local federal agencies and what they do. You can get the list by looking under United States Government in the telephone book. To find what they do you can look in the *U.S. Governmental Manual* or the *Washington Information Directory* published by Congressional Quarterly. If you are still not sure what the local agency is responsible for, call them from the number in the telephone book.

11.2. What is a Bureaucracy? The textbook has discussed what a bureaucracy is and the procedures by which it operates. How common is this to any organization? Look at your school or a local corporation and examine the way in which it is a bureaucracy. What similarities and differences do you note in that organization as a bureaucracy from the public bureaucracy?

11.3. Federal Employment. Are you interested in a career with the federal government? What is the civil service? Investigate the procedures and requirements for applying for a job with the civil service of the national government. There is a federal network on job information called Federal Job Information Center, available through the Office of Personnel Management (they have a toll-free number). There are also several commercial guides; a couple are ARCO, *Civil Service Handbook, Complete Guide to U.S. Civil Service Jobs,* and *Pace.*

11.4. Regulatory Agencies. Select an Independent Regulatory Agency; examine its powers and responsibilities. Again, the *U.S. Government Manual* will provide the information as will the *Federal Regulatory Directory* published by Congressional Quarterly. Is there an office in your state or city? Write a brief essay on the major problems or criticisms leveled against that agency. Here you will have to review back issues of newspapers, magazines, or *Congressional Quarterly,* or *National Journal.* The *Reader's Guide* and newspaper indexes will cut down the hunt immeasurably.

BIBLIOGRAPHY

Downs, Anthony. *Inside Bureaucracy.* Boston: Little, Brown, 1967.

An explanation of bureaucratic behavior. Rather comprehensive and complex in its treatment, the book explains how bureaucracies and bureaucrats work.

Fritschler, A. Lee. *Smoking and Politics: Policy-Making and the Federal Bureaucracy.* Englewood Cliffs, N.J.: Prentice-Hall, 1975.

A study of the federal bureaucracy through a case study of the cigarette warning label issue. Much of the book examines policy making within the agency and the pressures the agency was subjected to.

Kaufman, Herbert. *Are Government Organizations Immortal?* Washington, D.C.: Brookings Institution, 1976.

Bureaucratic agencies, like old soldiers, never die. Kaufman provides data and discussion on what happens to public agencies once created. It seems few are ever given burial.

Lindblom, Charles E. *The Policymaking Process.* Englewood Cliffs, N.J.: Prentice-Hall, 1968.

A brief book that attempts to cover the topics involved with public policy making. Lindblom's argument is that public policy ends up being incremental because of the complex environment in which it is made.

Meier, Kenneth. *Politics and the Bureaucracy.* North Scituate, Mass.: Duxbury Press, 1979.

A brief text on the bureaucracy that examines the relationship of the bureaucracy with political institutions. There is a discussion of the interaction of bureaucrats with interest groups and political parties.

Rourke, Francis. *Bureaucratic Power in National Politics*. Boston: Little, Brown, 1978,

A collection of essays on the bureaucracy and bureaucratic power in American government. Some of the useful areas covered are constituencies, expertise, and popular control of bureaucracies.

Seidman, Harold. *Politics, Position, and Power: The Dynamics of Federal Organization*. New York: Oxford University Press, 1975.

An insider's view of the political world of the bureaucracy. Seidman has considerable insight into the struggles of agencies with Congress, the president, and other bureaucratic agencies.

Wildavsky, Aaron. *The Politics of the Budgetary Process*. Boston: Little, Brown, 1974.

A standard work on the budgetary process of the federal government. Wildavsky stresses the political and incremental nature of the process.

Woll, Peter. *American Bureaucracy*. New York: W.W. Norton, 1977.

A basic, readable text on the bureaucracy. Woll gives needed attention to administrative law and the courts. He also covers the bureaucracy's relations with Congress and the Presidency.

Chapter
12

Congress

From the closing days of the 93rd through the 94th Congress (1975–1976), that institution changed and reformed itself. In fact, the 94th Congress enlarged the responsive and representative capacities of the national legislature. The events of the period are significant:

- Impeachment proceedings in the House Judiciary Committee were concluded with the voting of three Articles of Impeachment against the president of the United States (1974).
- Three committee chairs were deposed as both chambers created new methods for the election of committee chairs (1975).
- A "subcommittee bill of rights" sought to distribute the workload and resources in the House of Representatives more evenly and fairly (1973).
- The Senate moved to curb the filibuster as a method of obstructing legislation (1975).
- A new congressional budget procedure and Budget Office were implemented to give back to Congress some of the power lost to the executive (1976).

We are witnessing the resurgence of Congress, an attempt by Congress to reestablish its power and prestige after two decades of decline.

The decline of Congress had been gradual. The public's evaluation in the 1970s has been primarily negative; in 1978 approximately two out of three Americans gave Congress poor marks for the job it was doing.[1] Yet when individuals were pressed to evaluate *their* representative, the response was less unfavorable—fewer people surveyed rated their Congressman negatively. Said Harris: "The prevailing wisdom then is that Congress is worse than the sum of its parts."

The reasons for the decline of Congress over the last two decades are by now standard fare. Power was flowing to the executive. The president was viewed as the representative with a national constituency, the one politician willing to present the issues to all Americans. This built-in electoral advantage gave the presidency a healthy, progressive orientation. The president was expanding the tools of power: staff, impoundment, budget, executive agreement, and so on. The New Deal, the New Frontier, and the Great Society led people to the conclusion that the presidency was the dominant progressive institution, the only real source of new social policy; Congress had become moribund. Concluded Samuel Huntington:

> The loss of Congressional control over the substance of policy is most marked, of course, in the area of national defense and foreign policy. At one time Congress did not hesitate to legislate the size and weapons of the armed services. Now this power—to raise and support armies, to provide and maintain a navy—is firmly in the hands of the executive. . . . In domestic legislation Congress's influence is undoubtedly greater, but even here its primary impact is on the timing and details of legislation, not on the subjects and content of legislation.[2]

Congressional procedures and organization caused dissatisfaction; Congress had become unresponsive and undemocratic. The obstructive power of committee chairs, the House Rules Committee, the filibuster, and the seniority system drew most of the criticism. .Critics argued that undue power was given to unrepresentative minorities—namely conservative, southern Democratic committee chairs. Former U.S. Senator Joseph Clark of Pennsylvania expressed the opinion that "the legislatures of America—local, state, and national—are presently the greatest menace in our country to the successful operation of the democratic process."[3]

In recent years scandal and interest group favors have further eroded Congress's respectability and credibility. First, there was the Wayne Hays (Dem. Ohio) scandal revolving around his staff allowance and fringe benefits. Hays had employed Elizabeth Ray as a $14,000 a year secretary, but the press revealed she was on the payroll primarily to serve as his mistress. Said Miss Ray, "I can't

---

1. The Harris Poll, January 1978.
2. Samuel P. Huntington, "Congressional Response in the Twentieth Century," in David Truman, *The Congress and America's Future* (Englewood Cliffs, N.J.: Prentice–Hall, 1965), p. 24.
3. Joseph S. Clark, *Congress: The Sapless Branch* (New York: Harper and Row, 1964), p. 23.

type, I can't file. I can't even answer the phone." Congressman Robert Sikes (Dem., Fla.) was reprimanded by the House for not revealing financial interests that could cause a "conflict of interest" with his congressional activities. Daniel Flood (Dem., Pa.) was tried (a divided jury could not reach a verdict) on charges of bribery, conspiracy, and perjury stemming from allegations that he used his power in return for bribes. Charles C. Diggs (Dem., Mich.) was convicted on charges of padding his payroll in return for a kickback from employees to pay his personal and business expenses. And in 1979 the Senate "denounced" Herman Talmadge (Dem., Ga.) for financial misconduct. These revelations came on the heels of the Koreagate probe, which revealed that four members and several former members of Congress accepted money from Korean businessman Tongsun Park in return for favorable congressional treatment. And 1980 brought ABSCAM, an FBI undercover probe of eight congressmen who took bribes from FBI agents posing as Arab sheiks or businessmen (hence the name Arab Scam). All these instances reinforced the belief that Congress had been captured by special interest groups.

Changes in the wake of Vietnam and Watergate again make Congress a contender for public policy. The War Powers Act, the Budget and Impoundment Control Act, oversight, legislative clearance, and the Budget Office are all designed to enhance the control of Congress over the priorities of American public policy. Within Congress, there has been a redistribution and widening of power; no longer can a few powerful figures dominate. Removal of power from committees to subcommittees and election of committee chairs have had a tremendous effect on the status and influence of individual legislators. Finally, the scandals and ethics violations that plagued Congress resulted in new, and more stringent, regulations on representatives' outside activities. Codes of ethics and conflict of interest are taken seriously. There have been new limitations on congressional use of the franking (mailing) privilege; outside sources of income have been severely restricted; and new quarterly spending reports are required for staff salaries, travel, postage, and office funds. Congress has been cleaning its own house.

Yet will reform alter Congress? Its role in the democratic political process depends on its ability to resume a major role within a constitutionally divided system of government. Congressional reform must speak to the ability of Congress to fulfill certain roles if the vitality of democracy is to be realized.

The primary function of Congress is *legislation*. Most of the controversy over Congress has been over its ability to legislate, to be innovative and creative to meet the needs of a changing and complex environment. Critics charge that Congress has abdicated its legislative role to the chief executive. Yet nobody has a more elaborate set of procedures or rules designed to facilitate deliberation. The entire congressional process is designed to maximize a deliberated judgment. If properly exercised, the law-making function should lead to effective public policy.

Second, Congress performs a unique *representational* role. The decentralized structure of congressional committees acknowledges a multiplicity of inter-

It is not that there have never been scandals about Congress: a hundred years ago, Mark Twain described the members as a "distinctively native American criminal class." But in the past decade, we have been treated to a constant stream of unsavory revelations. More than thirty members of Congress have been convicted, indicted, or censured for a variety of activities—taking kickbacks, putting mistresses on the payroll, misusing campaign funds, engaging in conflict of interest business deals.

The latest in this long-running serial, following closely on Koreagate, is ABSCAM, the acronym for an FBI "sting" (undercover) operation called "Arab Scam." Eight members of Congress, including three committee chairs, have been named as illegally accepting money from undercover FBI agents posing as wealthy businessmen and Arab sheiks. The original project began in 1978 as part of an operation to lure organized crime suspects into selling stolen securities and objects to undercover agents. The agents used a Washington residence, a yacht, private planes, and thousands of dollars in cash to lure the suspects into criminal activity. As the investigation spread, they approached the eight members of Congress and allegedly offered them substantial amounts of cash and stocks ($25,000 to $50,000) in return for help in establishing residence in the United States, obtaining federal grants and gambling licenses, and making real estate deals. According to the FBI, the legislators were videotaped or taperecorded accepting the bribes.

The ABSCAM investigation was halted prematurely when leaks began appearing in the press in early February 1980, but the uproar has continued not only because of the accusations, but because of the methods used to gather evidence. Criticism of the FBI came, of course, from Congress, but it also came from other sources. The issue is a touchy one: Does government have the right to do anything to see if someone can be tempted into committing a crime? Doesn't government have the duty to investigate any information it receives about wrongdoing? What about the press? Criminal investigations are supposed to be kept secret until a grand jury hands down an indictment. There are those who contend that printing the story violated due process. The press contends that it must serve the public interest, and that the public has a right to know about the conduct of its representatives. Here as in so many areas of American life and politics, there is clearly no consensus.

ests deserving access to the decision-making process. Congress affords legitimate interests an opportunity to help shape public policy. Effective interest representation can result in broad consensus legislation working for shared goals.

Finally, Congress gives the public a direct link with government through *constituency service*. Unlike the other branches, Congress has individual legislators representing specific constituents. Constituency service affords the citizen an opportunity for personal attention in a large, complex political process.

These primary goals are complemented by several other important functions. Increasingly today Congress assumes the function of *administrative oversight* for the executive performance. This role has been heightened by the growth of presidential power since the New Deal and dramatized in importance by events such as Vietnam and Watergate. Another function emerging in importance is that of *informing* the public. Through the use of committee investigations, Congress has informed and even generated public opinion on several important matters of public policy. The Senate Select Committee on Campaign Practices (Ervin Committee) first revealed the breadth and depth of Watergate; congressional committees investigating nutrition, aging, and the environment have revealed to Americans the problems of hunger and malnutrition, growing old and retirement, and pollution. Control of the purse strings gives Congress a marked advantage in *appropriations*. The fact is that all agencies of government must come before Congress annually to have their operating budgets renewed. Frequently Congress can use the role of appropriations to investigate or check executive power. Finally, Congress performs any number of lesser function as a *check and balance* to the other branches of government. With the executive, there is confirmation of major executive appointments, ratification of treaties, determining presidential disability, as well as voting impeachment. With the judiciary, Congress creates judgeships and establishes legal procedures for the courts as well as establishing law and its violations. And with the bureaucracy, Congress is involved with reorganization, clearance for administrative rules, and policymaking.

the small society   **by Brickman**

PRACTICING POLITICS   12.1

How to learn about your congressional representatives

1. Ask your local or university librarian for the current *Congressional Directory*.
2. Locate your district in the maps section.
3. The biographical section, arranged by state and district, will give a brief biographical sketch of your senators and representative, with the electoral history of each and a description of the boundaries of your district.
4. The alphabetical list will give home address, office address, and phone number in Washington.
5. The individual index lists the committees on which senators and representatives serve; check the committee entries to find out what the committee does and where and when it meets.
6. To find your representatives' voting record on important issues, check the *Congressional Quarterly Almanac,* which abstracts voting records from the *Congressional Record*.
7. You may wish to know more about your representatives' position on important issues. Several groups rate members of Congress on their voting records. For example:
   - Americans for Democratic Action (liberal)
   - Americans for Constitutional Action (conservative)
   - AFL-CIO (labor)
   - National Chamber of Commerce (business)
   - Environmental Action (environment)

These are all significant roles for Congress. But reform cannot make Congress into something it is not or was not intended to be:

> Congress is not now and never has been well designed to create its own agenda and then to act on it in a coordinated way to produce a unified domestic and/or foreign policy program. It is particularly well structured to react to many publics (including other governmental institutions) and, in reacting, to criticize, refine, promote alternative proposals, bargain and compromise. Reform directed away from these strengths are unlikely to improve Congress or, in fact, to be taken seriously for very long.[4]

THE LEGISLATORS

The typical image of members of Congress is one of aging politicians waiting for the seniority system to endow them with power. But that stereotyped view is not correct. Senility is not a fault of the contemporary Congress; the average age for representatives has been growing younger over the past 20 years. In 1979

---

4. Charles O. Jones, ''Will Reform Change Congress?'' in Lawrence C. Dodd and Bruce I. Oppenheimer, *Congress Reconsidered* (New York: Praeger Publishers, 1977), p. 250.

the average age went below 50 (49.5) for the first time since World War II, and for the second Congress in a row (95th and 96th Congress) no members of the House of Representatives were over 80 years of age.

The Constitution says little about the qualifications for a representative: the only restrictions are age and residency. Members of the House of Representatives must be twenty-five years of age, citizens of the United States for seven years, and residents of the state from which elected (although the representative need not reside in the district from which elected). Senators must have attained the age of thirty, been citizens for nine years, and be residents of the state electing them. Generally, members have considerable prior political experience; they do not reflect the population as a whole. Legislators have been, and continue to be, predominantly male, white, Protestant, professional, and middle-aged.

Table 12.1

Background Characteristics of the 96th Congress, 1979–1981

	House	Senate
Party		
Democrat	276	59
Republican	159	41
Sex		
Male	419	99
Female	16	1
Age		
Youngest	27	36
Oldest	79	83
Average	48.8	52.7
Minorities		
Black	15	0
Oriental	2	3
Spanish	4	0
Religion		
Protestant	277	73
Roman Catholic	116	13
Jewish	23	7
Mormon	7	4
Other	9	3
Profession[a]		
Lawyers	205	65
Businessmen & Bankers	127	29
Educators	57	7
Farmers	19	6
Journalists	11	2
Public Service/Politics	41	12

a. Some legislators listed more than one profession.

A legal background has traditionally been the most popular route to Congress. In 1979 for the first time, however, the figures showed the lowest percentage of law degrees since records have been kept. Less than half the members of the House of Representatives for the 96th Congress had law degrees. This marked a dramatic decline in the number of lawyers in the House from 1977. As a result of the changing composition, 14 members of the House in 1977 formed a *blue-collar caucus,* representing working-class occupations. Hardly a potent force, its members nonetheless represent a challenge to the traditional image of members of Congress.

Religious affiliations too have shifted. Protestants still predominate, but they have been losing strength since the 1960s to Jews and Roman Catholics. Catholics comprised 20 percent of the membership in the House in 1961, and now comprise 27 percent. In 1961 there were 11 Jewish members of the House; today there are over 20. The Senate's population of Jewish members grew from one to seven.

TENURE AND CAREERISM

As we have already seen, incumbency is a great advantage in running for public office. A majority of the Congressional electoral contests are not close; two-thirds to three-fourths are noncompetitive (the winning candidate received

Figure 12.1

Percent of incumbents seeking reelection who lost. Note: The number of losers is indicated in each bar. (*National Journal,* October 20, 1979)

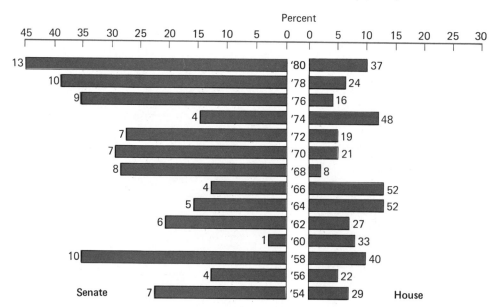

over 55 percent of the popular vote). We call these *safe seats*. It is principally incumbents who win big and enjoy the safe seats. In what David Mayhew entitled the "case of the vanishing marginals," he discovered that the number of incumbent representatives running in the marginal zone (40 to 59.5 percent of popular vote) had roughly halved in the 16 year period from 1956 to 1972.[5] For some reason, it has become considerably easier for incumbent members to poll three-fifths of the vote in November.

This ease of electoral success has helped develop a pattern of careerism in Congress. Throughout the twentieth century, the average number of years in office has increased. By the mid-1960s the average House member had been in office for 11 years or nearly 6 terms, the average Senator for 12 years or two terms, and the percentage of new members entering Congress declined to under 17 percent of the total body. Congress had become an attractive career. By the election of 1979 however, things had changed. By the 96th Congress, 68 percent of the House and 60 percent of the Senate had been elected in 1970 or later. In the 96th Congress, 220 House members have served four years or less; 55 Senators have served six years or less.

There are several explanations for this rapid turnover, and for declining careerism in the 1970s. Reapportionment after the 1970 census contributed to the change, as did the 18-year-old vote. But the main factors appear to be the retirement of veteran representatives and the public mood in the wake of Watergate. During the 1970s, many members who came to Congress after the New Deal or World War II were in their late sixties and seventies. Rather than face stiff challenges, they opted for retirement. The large freshman class elected in 1974 probably reflected the Watergate backlash and the growing public mood of distrust. Republican Congressmen were particularly hurt by electoral defeat in 1974. Another factor is the changing party composition of Congress, which has seen an increase of Democrats. Republican turnover has been almost twice as great as that for Democrats. From 1952 to 1975, GOP turnover has been 59.3 percent, as compared to 35.8 percent for Democrats. And within the Democratic party, turnover has worked to erode the dominance of southern Democrats. The percentage of House Democrats from the South averaged 42 percent in the 1950s, 35 percent in the 1960s, and had further slipped to 28 percent by 1975.

THE LEGISLATIVE ENVIRONMENT

The legislative environment for a member of Congress is one of two worlds. First there is Washington, D.C., and the world of government officials. The other world is the home constituency, where members of Congress must inform and service the public with an eye toward reelection.

Demands on a legislator's time are tremendous; representatives are on the

5. David R. Mayhew "Congressional Elections: The Case of the Vanishing Marginals," *Polity* 6 (Spring 1974), p. 295–317.

go at a frantic pace. Congress is in session nearly year around; between sessions, there are committee hearings, committee reports, party caucuses, office work to do, letters to answer, executive officials to listen to, constituents to see, speeches to make, and trips back home. Some years ago Congressman Clem Miller of California described his typical day. It went as follows:

6:45 A.M.	Rise, read *Washington Post*.
8:00 A.M.	Breakfast with the British ambassador.
8:30 A.M.	Look over mail, dictate replies to important inquiries.
9:00 A.M.	Office appointment with business lobbyist to discuss trade legislation.
10:00 A.M.	Subcommittee hearings on depressed-area bill.
12:00 noon	Attend debate on House floor.
1:00 P.M.	Lunch in office. Read state and local newspapers.
2:00 P.M.	Meeting with Harvard economist John Kenneth Galbraith to discuss tight money and economic policy.
2:45 P.M.	Listen to debate on floor of Congress.
3:30 P.M.	Meeting with a member of the House Appropriations Committee on public works in home district.
5:00 P.M	Sign letters dictated in morning. Go over afternoon mail. Meet with constituents.
6:15 P.M.	Leave for home.
7:15 P.M.	Eat dinner.
8:00 P.M.	Read another newspaper from home district. Go through reports, speeches, and magazines. File material for future speeches.
11:00 P.M.	Read chapter from book.
11:45 P.M.	To sleep.[6]

It is not unusual for a member's average day to be 12 hours long.

Members must keep in touch with their constituencies. It is not enough to answer mail or read local newspapers or deal with constituent problems; members must return to their home constituencies frequently. Reelection is a high priority, and physical presence in the state or district is important. The average representative will make 35 trips home a year and spend an average of 138 days (counting recesses) in the home district.[7]

6. Clem Miller, *Member of the House: Letters of a Congressman* (New York: Charles Scribner & Sons, 1962), p. 66.
7. Richard F. Fenno, Jr., "U.S. House Members in Their Constituencies," *American Political Science Review* 71 (September 1977), pp. 890–897.

PAY AND PERQUISITES

By some standards, members of Congress are well paid. Salaries have risen steadily in the post-World War II years; in 1979, both Senators and Representatives were paid $60,700 a year. But even these salaries are frequently viewed as low compared to private industry. Because the salaries often are not adequate for members to maintain two residences, travel frequently, or live modestly in Washington, most representatives have supplemented their incomes through outside sources—speaking fees and consulting, for example. This has raised serious questions of conflict of interest and resulted, in 1979, in a rule limiting outside income to 15 percent of salary, although the Senate will delay enforcement of the rule until 1983.

Table 12.2
Congressional Allowances, 1970 and 1978

	House		Senate	
	1970	*1978*	*1970*	*1978*
Clerk-hire	$149,292	$273,132	$239,805–401,865	$624,431–1,110,237
Postage	$700	$211	$1,056–1,320	$1,390–1,740
Stationery	$3,500	$6,500	$3,600	$3,600–5,000
Travel (round trips)	12	33	12	40–44
Telephone/telegraph	80,000 units[a]	$5,200 for equipment; 15,000 long-distance minutes	As required	$4,400 plus 15,000–22,500 minutes
District and state offices				
Rental	$2,400	2,500 square feet[b]	?	4,800–8,000 square feet[b]
Furnishings (one-time)	$5,000	$27,000	?	$22,500–$28,500
Expenses	–	–	$1,600	$7,800
Official expenses	$1,200	$7,000	–	–
Constituent communications (begun in 1975)	0	$5,000	Provided at no cost	
Equipment lease begun in 1971	0	$9,000	Assigned at no cost	
Total estimated value	$162,842–180,692	$346,293–399,883	$350,000 plus–411,985 plus	$ 708,121–1,211,077

a. Four units equal one telephone minute; one unit equals one telegram word.
b. The General Services Administration's applicable rates range from $5 to $18 per square foot.

SOURCE: *National Journal,* February 4, 1978, p. 182.

Salaries are supplemented by liberal privileges for travel, postage, and hiring staff employees. These are called **perquisites.**. These have also been a source of trouble for members recently. Frequent trips at taxpayer expense, use of free mailing privileges and office staff funds for reelection activities have caused the public, and Congress, to look carefully at the privileges and their use. House members are allowed 26 free roundtrips home each year; senators receive from 40 to 44 such free trips, depending on the size of the state. Each member of Congress is given a stationery and supplies allotment, telephone allowances, free mailing privileges, and office allowance. All these congressional perquisites have risen significantly in the previous decade. The average allowance in perquisites for a representative nears $500,000 a year and is almost $1 million a year for a senator.

LEGISLATIVE ROLES

The need to keep up in two worlds places inordinate demands on the time and resources of representatives. How they respond to the demands, how they spend their time and resources, determines the kind of legislator they will be. Legislators differ widely in how they spend their time and therefore in the legislative roles they perform.

Members must orient themselves to the work routine of Congress. Thousands of bills and resolutions come before Congress—in committees, before party caucuses, and for floor votes. Different members see their purpose in Congress in different ways. There are **ritualists** who devote themselves to legislative work—committee hearings, learning rules and procedures, and following the progress of legislation. There are **tribunes** who see their role as expressing popular feeling and supporting popular causes. They are the ''show horses'' of Congress; the ritualists are the ''work horses.'' Others view themselves as **brokers;** they facilitate compromise and arbitrate disputes.

In making decisions, representatives respond to differing **constituencies.** Not all members pay equal heed to their home constituency. Some see themselves as free agents, able to decide what a district or the nation needs; they are called **trustees.** A legislator who sees the job as speaking for the district or state that elected him is a **delegate.** A delegate would put aside a personal judgment for what constituents thought best. A **politico** would be more inclined to seek political constituencies, and would concentrate on the political party or caucus within Congress. Politicos combine the trustee and delegate roles. One study of House members found 28 percent of representatives identifying with the trustee role, 23 percent with the delegate role, and a near majority, 46 percent, claiming to be politicos.[8]

Home style[9] expresses the manner in which legislators project themselves in their home states and districts. Members are concerned about their constituen-

8. Roger H. Davidson, *The Role of the Congressman* (New York: Pegasus, 1969), pp. 117–119.
9. This expression is taken from a book by that title, see Richard F. Fenno, Jr., *Home Style* (Boston: Little, Brown, 1978).

cies; they care about getting reelected. Hence they spend a great deal of their time and resources cultivating their constituencies. Richard Fenno measures home style with three dimensions. The first is the allocation of personal and office resources. How much of the scarcest resource, time, is spent back in the district helps show the degree of attention paid to constituents. The other valuable resource is the representative's staff. The greater the number of staff and allocation of their time to constituents, the more focus on constituents. The second ingredient of home style is "presentation of self," the face-to-face contact the legislator has with constituents in explaining and justifying issues and votes. Members return home in order to seek or maintain political support. Finally, Fenno chooses the representative's explanation of his or her Washington activity to illustrate home style. All members relate relevant issues and concerns to district constituencies, and explain their activities on those issues. All claim to be hardworking, diligent supporters of constituent interests. What was surprising, Fenno decided, was the extent to which they all "ran against" Congress: "Differentiating himself or herself from the others in Congress, attacking Congress as an institution, and portraying himself or herself as a fighter against its manifest shortcomings."[10]

Some commentators suggest that these legislative roles can be related back to a single goal—getting reelected. In what David R. Mayhew called the "electoral connection," he argued: "Congressmen are interested in those activities which get them reelected, indeed, interested in nothing else."[11] Mayhew found it useful to view congressional behavior from the vantage point of its serving members' electoral needs. Richard Fenno describes reelection as one of a legislator's three primary goals, the other two being influence within Congress and making good public policy.[12] Whether election plays this pervasive a role or not, the continuing need to go before the people every two or six years is of major importance in the life of a member. "You should say 'perennial' election rather than 'biennial,' said one former Congressman, "it is with us every day."[13]

ORGANIZATION AND POWER IN CONGRESS

Congress is composed of two separate and distinct houses. There is a Senate of 100 with two members from each state; terms are for six years with one-third up for election every two years. The House of Representatives has 435 members, all elected every two years from single-member districts. Each house is responsible for its own organization and operation, sets it own rules, selects committee members, and acts on legislation. All legislation must run the obstacle course of

10. Fenno, *Home Style,* p. 167.
11. David R. Mayhew, *Congress: The Electoral Connection* (New Haven: Conn.: Yale University Press, 1974).
12. Richard F. Fenno, Jr., *Congressmen in Committees* (Boston: Little, Brown and Co., 1973), p. 1.
13. Quoted from Charles L. Clapp, *The Congressman: His Work as He Sees It,* (Washington, D.C.: Brookings Institute, 1963), p. 330.

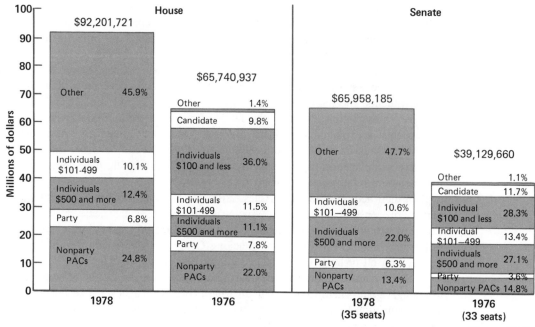

Figure 12.2

Source of receipts for congressional candidates. Notes: Data include only figures for candidates running in general elections. 1978 figures include repaid loans; 1976 figures do not include repaid loans. For 1978, Federal Election Commission did not itemize contributions from individuals of $100 or less or contributions from candidates and loans. 1976 includes loans from candidate to his campaign. Party figures include direct contributions to the candidates and expenditures made on behalf of the candidate by the party. (Federal Election Commission 1976 and 1978 Reports on U.S. Senate and House Campaigns Financial Activity. *Weekly Report,* Washington, D.C.: Congressional Quarterly, Inc., September 29, 1979, p. 2153)

each house and either one has the power to stop action. Yet legislation is a shared function, a power of the whole Congress.

The Founding Fathers had a special concern for legislative power. "In republican government," stated James Madison, "the legislative authority necessarily predominates." The Framers had every intent of ensuring that Congress would dominate policymaking. They took great care in Article I of the Constitution (half of the entire Constitution) to delineate the specific grants of power given this new bicameral legislature. Congress was endowed with a considerable range of fundamental authority:

1. To lay and collect taxes, duties, imports, and excises.
2. To regulate foreign and interstate commerce.
3. To coin money and regulate its value.

4. To establish post offices.
5. To create inferior courts.
6. To declare war.
7. To provide for an army and navy.
8. To make laws necessary and proper for executing its enumerated powers.

The Constitution confers some additional responsibilities on the Senate:

1. To confirm major executive appointments.
2. To ratify treaties.
3. To try all impeachments.

The House also has an additional responsibility: all revenue bills must originate there (but the Senate must approve all bills and is free to amend any revenue bill).

Congress was intended to have major responsibility for policymaking. Yet in our post-Watergate environment there has been much concern that Congress has abdicated its responsibilities in legislation. Not so, says Lewis A. Froman, Jr.: "The United States Congress is probably more powerful as a legislative body vis-a-vis the executive than in any other legislative body in the world. . . . In no other country has the legislature so much capacity for acting independently and for thwarting the will of the executive as in the United States."[14]

The House of Representatives and the Senate are not alike. Each has its own organization, rules, and style of operation. Their interests vary; they serve different constituencies: "We are constituted differently, we serve different purposes in the representative system, we operate differently," claimed former Senator Wayne Morse of Oregon, "why should [the House and Senate] not have different rules."[15] The differences in organization result in a fragmentation of power. Congress is a decentralized organization. Table 12.3 summarizes the major differences between the House and the Senate.

THE LEADERSHIP

Party leadership exerts considerable influence on the legislative process. In 1977, both houses chose new majority party leaders. Thomas P. (Tip) O'Neill, Jr., as Speaker of the House, and Robert C. Byrd as majority leader of the Senate. Both men sought to revive the powers of leadership after a decade of decline. And with GOP control of the Senate in 1981, Howard Baker became majority leader. All arrived at their positions through the typical process of long years of devoted service to the institution of Congress and loyalty to the party.

14. Lewis A. Froman, Jr., *The Congressional Process* (Boston: Little, Brown, 1967), p. 3.
15. Cited in Walter J. Oleszek, *Congressional Procedures and the Policy Process* (Washington, D.C.: Congressional Quarterly Press, 1978), p. 23.

Table 12.3

Major Differences Between the House and Senate

House	Senate
Larger (435)	Smaller (100)
Shorter term of office (2 years)	Longer term of office (6 years)
Less flexible rules	More flexible rules
Narrower constituency	Broader, more varied, constituency
Policy specialists	Policy generalists
Less press and media coverage	More press and media coverage
Power less evenly distributed	Power more evenly distributed
Less prestige	More prestige
More expeditious in floor debate	Less expeditious in floor debate
Less reliance on staff	More reliance on staff

SOURCE: Walter J Oleszek, *Congressional Procedure and the Policy Process.* (Washington, D.C.: Congressional Quarterly Press, 1978), p. 24.

The Office of *Speaker of the House,* the chamber's presiding officer and the majority party's leader, has had a history of strong-willed, dominant occupants. The office had thus become a powerful political post. Between 1890 and 1910, "Czar" Reed and Joe Cannon exercised considerable power in support of the Republican majorities in the House. During the 1940s and 1950s, Sam Rayburn exercised much the same power for the Democrats, bargaining with individuals and applying the rules from the Speaker's chair. But with John McCormack in the 1960s and Carl Albert from 1971 to 1977, the power of the Speaker ebbed. Neither had been aggressive, and when faced with party disunity, preferred not to make arbitrary rulings. Remarked Albert, "I don't want to do anything to offend anyone. I want to be remembered as a Congressman's Speaker, well liked by his colleagues, from whom I am able to get the most cooperation without too much arm-twisting." Tip O'Neill had other aspirations. Elected by the full House in the normal procedure, a straight party vote after being nominated by the party caucus, O'Neill had shown his leadership skills. Elected to the House in 1953, he spent several years in loyal service to the House and the Democratic party, and became a party whip in 1971. Elevated to majority leader in late 1972, O'Neill promised to work for the party but also to be responsive and sympathetic to the members' needs.

The powers of the Speaker of the House are primarily those of personal influence developed through years of service in the House and in lesser leadership posts. The Speaker must be a master of the rules. The Speaker's primary duties are presiding over the House, interpreting the rules and deciding points of order, referring bills and resolutions to committees, scheduling legislation for floor action, and appointing House members of joint and conference committees.

Leadership in the House of Representatives. Former Speaker of the House Thomas "Tip" O'Neill. (United Press International)

The Senate has no formal post comparable to that of the House Speaker. The Constitution makes the vice-president the presiding officer in the Senate. When he is not in attendance, the President Pro Tempore presides. Neither officer has any real political power to compare with that of the Speaker. The real leadership in the Senate is exercised by the *majority floor leader*. The Senate leadership, too, had undergone change with the election of Robert C. Byrd in 1977 as majority leader and GOP Howard Baker in 1981. Elected by the party caucus in the Senate, the majority leader guides party legislation through the Senate. Prior to Byrd, the majority leader for 15 years had been Mike Mansfield, a quiet, scholarly Democrat from Montana. Unlike his predecessor, Lyndon Johnson, who was flamboyant and domineering, Mansfield preferred the quiet and dignity of a low profile.[16] Said Mansfield, "I don't collect any IOU's. I don't do any special favors. I try to treat all Senators alike." Byrd, like his predecessors, was a long-time Senator. He had faithfully served his party in the Senate and had occupied lesser leadership posts before being elected majority leader in 1977. His style was more like Mansfield in that he was quiet and unassuming, but he was intent on leading.

16. Robert Peabody, *Leadership in Congress* (Boston: Little, Brown & Co., 1976), p. 340.

He has developed a complete mastery of Senate rules, and used the prerogative of first recognition to control the agenda in the Senate.

The Senate is a much more informal body; the House is highly structured and governed by formal rules. The Speaker may interpret the rules, but there is little occasion to suspend them. In the Senate, Byrd proceeded most of the time on the basis of "unanimous consent" (one objection can stop a debate or delay a decision). There is little need or occasion to apply formal rules. Byrd defined the role of the majority leader this way: "He facilitates, he constructs, he programs, he schedules, he takes an active part in the development of legislation, he steps in at crucial moments on the floor, offers amendments, speaks on behalf of legislation and helps to shape the outcome of the legislation."

The power of the majority leader is based on the ability to build and maintain a loose alliance of senators to pass or defeat legislation coming before the chamber. The major weapon of the majority leader is influence over the scheduling of action. In the Senate, the majority leader is the ranking official. Neither the President of the Senate nor its President Pro Tempore hold such rank. The majority leader also helps formulate the party's legislative program and priorities. He can nominate members to party committees, suggest assignments for standing committees, and appoint task forces to study and recommend legislation on a wide variety of subjects.

The position of leadership in the House and Senate are important enough that an institutional structure assists the Speaker and majority leader (Figure 12.3). The leadership structure in the two chambers is essentially the same. Each

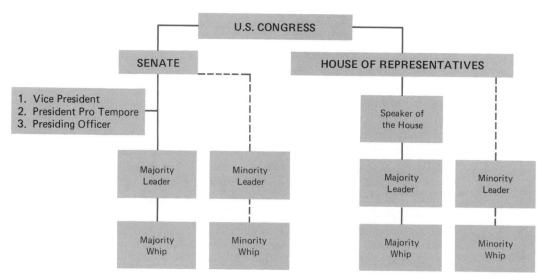

Figure 12.3

Congressional leadership. (Walter J. Oleszek, *Congressional Procedures and the Policy Process,* Washington, D.C.: Congressional Quarterly, Inc., 1978, p. 29)

chamber has a majority and minority floor leader (this is in addition to the Speaker of the House), assistant floor leaders (called whips), several assistants, and a variety of party organizations responsible for formulating the legislative program, steering it through the chamber, and making committee assignments.

The *majority leader* in the House of Representatives is the lieutenant for the Speaker and stands to become Speaker should the present one resign or retire in office. The evolutionary progression to leadership posts in Congress has the earmarkings of an automatic procedure. Whips become majority leaders who, in turn, are selected as Speakers. Majority leaders work to shape and direct party strategy. They have a major responsibility for scheduling legislation and keeping the party together on issues dividing the chamber. Their specific functions are to formulate the party's legislative program, steer the program through the House, monitor committee action on important bills, and schedule appropriate action on matters of legislation.

The *minority leader's* duties are much the same except that the minority leader cannot schedule legislation or depend on a majority to support him. Yet the minority leader acts as party leader for his party in the House or Senate. In the Senate he is consulted by the majority leader on scheduling items of business, and, if the party occupies the White House, acts as the president's spokesman in the chamber. The greatest function the minority leader serves, however, is summarizing minority party criticism of the majority party's legislative performance. But because minority leaders usually end up on the losing side of the aisle, they are more likely to retire voluntarily or be defeated at the polls.[17] As of 1967, only two of twelve majority leaders retired or were defeated. But for 13 minority leaders over time, 5 voluntarily retired and 3 were defeated in reelection bids.

Both parties appoint assistant floor leaders, or *whips,* to assist the majority and minority leaders in carrying out the party's legislative program. In recent years the House Democrats' whip organization has consisted of a chief whip appointed by the floor leader and 15 to 18 assistant whips selected on a regional basis by the state party delegations. In the 96th Congress, the House Republicans had a chief whip, four regional whips, and 15 area whips. The selections are made by the party conference. In the Senate the organization is much the same, although smaller, and the degree of success in the Senate is much less. Senate whips have periodically defied party leadership; senators, in general, have been less amenable to whip pressure to support party preferences.

The prime function of the whip organization is to assist the floor leaders and ensure membership attendance for key action and voting. In a chamber as large as the House of Representatives, it is a major task to keep track of members and ensure their presence on the floor for important votes. In addition to this strategic function, whips are also vital in the communication process between party leadership and members. Whips transmit information. The "whip's package" contains a summary of key legislation and what it would do. It also contains

17. Randall Ripley, *Party Leadership in the House of Representatives* (Washington, D.C.: Brookings Institute, 1967).

a review of the status of all bills, where they are in the process and when action will be taken. The whip's office also writes speeches and provides information to legislators. Whips are instrumental in counting noses for the leadership on close votes, and applying some pressure to keep the party majority intact. Said one Congressman: "The key to effective whip action is timing. The Whip is on the floor surveying the scene and weighing alternatives. . . . If he puts out a call too soon, too urgently, many members will assemble, take a quick look, and then begin to fade until there is a critical deficiency when the vote is taken."[18]

THE PARTY CAUCUS

Party committees are established by both parties in both houses to establish legislative priorities and programs, elect leaders, and approve committee assignments.

The party conference, or *caucus,* consists of all party members in the chamber. Each party has made periodic use of the conference, but it rarely functions as a deliberative body. In the Senate particularly, the caucus has ratified legislative programs and approved party leaders, but has not commanded obedience through binding decisions. The Democratic Conference meets only a few times a year. The Republican Conference meets regularly, frequently weekly, although its actions are not binding for Senate Republicans. In the House, however, the Democratic caucus has become the vehicle for change and reform.

Beginning in the 1960s, newer liberal House Democrats began to seek to revitalize the caucus, their aim being to attack the arbitrary power of conservative committee chairs and the seniority system. They formed a group known as the Democratic Study Group in 1959 and, by 1970, succeeded in securing regular monthly meetings of the Democratic caucus. They sought to unseat John McCormack as Speaker in 1970, but failed. By 1973, these more liberal members had sufficient strength to alter the automatic selection of committee chairs based on seniority. The caucus requires a secret ballot election for the selection of committee chairs. This resulted in 1975 in unseating three long-time committee chairs: Wright Patman (Tex.) of the Banking Committee, F. Edward Hebert (La.) of the Armed Service Committee, and W. R. Poage (Tex.) of the Agriculture Committee. The caucus also made bill-drafting sessions open to the public, created a Steering and Policy Committee under the party leadership to set party and legislative priorities, and gave to this new committee the responsibility for making committee assignments (taking it away from the Ways and Means Committee). The wave of reform has subsided some from the 94th Congress and with it the use of the caucus. Fewer issues are coming before the caucus, and there appears to be less challenge to the power of committee chairs. In the 96th Congress (1979–80), there was only one Democratic challenge to a committee chair (Jamie Whitten, Miss., House Appropriations) and that was unsuccessful.

18. Clem Miller, *Member of the House,* p. 53.

The only organization in Congress is party organization. Party leadership provides a measure of coherence and integration to what is otherwise a decentralized process. They help to shape the environment in which legislators seek to make public policy.

COMMITTEE ASSIGNMENTS

In the House of Representatives, up until the twentieth century, committee assignments were made by the Speaker. Since then, the parties have delegated that responsibility to a special party committee on committees. The Republican committee on committees is composed of a representative from each state with

Table 12.4
Selecting Committee Members

Republicans and Democrats in both chambers abandoned their past adherence to the strict seniority rule. By 1975, all four groups provided some method by which party colleagues could vote on their top-ranking committee member.

House Democrats

Nominations are made by the Steering and Policy Committee, an arm of the leadership. All nominations are voted on individually by secret ballot by Democrats meeting in caucus. Appropriations subcommittee chairmen also are voted on by secret ballot in the caucus.

House Republicans

The GOP committee on committees, composed of one member from each state with Republican representatives, nominates ranking committee members. Party colleagues meeting in caucus (called a conference) vote by secret ballot on each nomination.

Senate Democrats

Nominations are made by the Steering Committee, an arm of the leadership. The list of nominees is given to all Democrats who check off the name of any person on whom they want a separate vote. The lists are returned unsigned to the leadership. If at least 20 percent of the Democrats want a vote on a nominee, it is held by secret ballot two days later.

Senate Republicans

The Republican members of each committee elect their ranking committee member from among their ranks. The choices are subject to a vote of approval in the Republican Conference.

SOURCE: Congressional Quarterly, *Congress and the Nation,* Vol. IV p. 750.

GOP membership, usually the senior member, and is chaired by the House GOP leader. Assignments must be approved by the Republican Conference. The Democrats, beginning in 1974, transferred the assignment power out of the Ways and Means Committee to the newly formed Policy and Steering Committee as a part of the reform drive of the 94th Congress to wrest power from senior members of Congress. The 24-person Policy and Steering Committee is composed of House party leaders, 12 regionally elected members, and 9 members appointed by the Speaker. Its decisions are subject to ratification by the Democratic caucus.

Richard Fenno's study of committee assignments identified three goals that aid in explaining which committees members seek.[19] Committee assignments may be viewed in terms of career and legislative goals. First, assignment to a committee can enhance chances of reelection. Some committees, such as Agriculture, Post Office and Civil Service, or Interior provide an opportunity to perform constituency service and thereby increase a legislator's stock with voters. Second, a committee assignment is a means of maximizing influence over public policy in a given area. Committees such as Education, Foreign Affairs, and Judiciary provide real opportunities for a member to help shape and direct public policy. Third, some committees are highly valued because they provide a means for representatives to maximize their influence within the House or Senate. Because such committees are critical to the operation of Congress, they afford committee members an opportunity to exercise influence over the whole Congress. Some examples are Senate Finance and House Ways and Means (taxes), Appropriations (spending) and House Rules Committee (scheduling).

Since some committees are more desirable than others, competition for seats is keen. Because motivations for seeking a committee may differ, the House of Representatives has designated its committees as *exclusive, semiexclusive,* and *nonexclusive.* Members assigned to an exclusive committee serve on only that committee and on no other standing committee. The exclusive committees are Appropriations, Ways and Means, and Rules. Members assigned to semiexclusive committees, which are the major policy area committees that authorize programs, may serve on one semiexclusive committee and then be assigned to other nonexclusive committees. The nonexclusive committees are viewed as the least attractive, and there are no restrictions on assignments.

The inclination in the past has been for members to gravitate from the nonexclusive to the more exclusive committees as vacancies occurred. New members seeking first committee assignments were rewarded on the basis of their need for reelection help or their ideological stance. Transfer requests were judged on regional balance, party loyalty, and ideological commitment. A recent study of committee assignments in the House concluded, however, that ''freshman representatives who came to the House in recent years were reasonably successful in securing desirable committee assignments, and that most of those who were not so fortunate during the first term transferred to preferred committees during the

19. Richard F. Fenno, Jr., *Congressmen in Committees* (Boston: Little, Brown, and Co., 1973).

second or third term.''[20] Irwin Gertzog calls this the "routinization of committee assignments." Almost all House members were appointed to committees they most preferred by their fifth year in office (two-thirds were granted that preference at once in their first term), and there was little variation in success between Republicans and Democrats.

SENIORITY

One of the major motivations for securing the preferred committee assignment early is seniority. **Seniority** is the practice, in the Senate and the House, of ranking committee members, by party, according to years of continuous service on the committee. The ranking majority party member, the majority party member with the longest consecutive service on the committee, automatically is designated chair of the committee. New members of the committee are added, by party, to the bottom of the list. As vacancies occur, members move up the seniority ladder. When the chair becomes vacant, the next most senior majority party member steps up. Note that seniority specifies *consecutive* service. If a member is defeated and then reelected later, or transfers committees, that person is placed at the bottom of the seniority list.

Seniority encourages a member to make Congress and a committee a career; it discourages committee hopping. Seniority also aids in reinforcing the congressional norms of specialization and institutional loyalty. It provides a measure of stability and continuity in the congressional process. But seniority is also one of the most criticized aspects of Congress. The Ralph Nader task force on Congress called seniority "antiquated," a Darwinian "survival of the survivors."[21] Others have labeled it the bastion of old men, a "senility system" rewarding those who waited out their terms of office in order to accrue the seniority necessary to affirm their power. The chief argument against seniority is that power is not bestowed on the ablest or most effective, only on those who stay the longest. In the past, seniority rewarded conservative southern Democrats with "safe" seats. They were the beneficiaries of the seniority system and they were unrepresentative of a changing America. These committee chairs then used their independent power bases to thwart party programs or presidential initiatives in social welfare, civil rights, and foreign affairs.

By 1970 seniority was under full attack. The House, in the Legislative Reorganization Act of 1970, provided that seniority need not be the sole consideration for the selection of committee chairs. The measure was defeated. Representative Schwengel (R-Iowa) offered a motion providing majority election of chairs by committee vote from the three most senior majority party members. It went down to defeat. But the 1970 Congress did create a committee, headed by Julia

20. Irwin Gertzog, "The Routinization of Committee Assignments in the U.S. House of Representatives," *American Journal of Political Science* 20 (November 1976), p. 698.
21. Mark Green, et al., *Who Runs Congress* (New York: Bantam Books, 1972), p. 58.

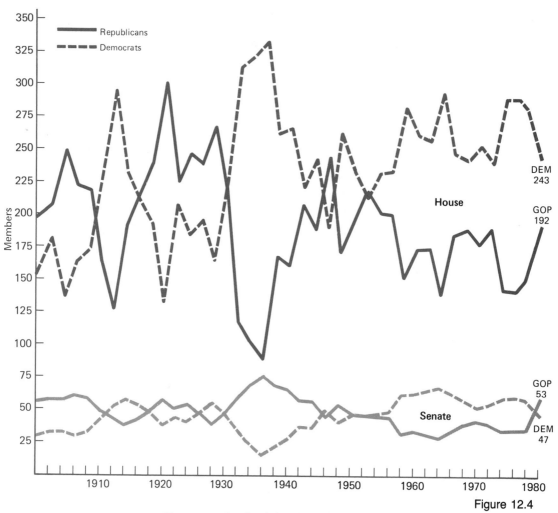

Figure 12.4

The congressional majority: 1900–1978. Source: House of Representatives. (*National Journal,* October 10, 1979, p. 1767)

Butler Hansen (D-Wash.) to study reform of seniority. In 1973 House Democrats approved the Hansen Committee recommendations requiring a caucus vote approving committee chairs. Under the Hansen rule, 20 percent of the party membership could request a secret ballot on committee chairs. The revolt had begun. Although no chairs were rejected in 1973, when Congress convened in 1975, the House Democratic caucus voted to unseat F. Edward Hebert as chair of the Armed Services Committee, W. R. Poage as chair of the Agriculture Committee, and Wright Patman as chair of the Banking Committee. Dissatisfied with a fourth chair, Wilbur Mills of the powerful Ways and Means Committee, caused the caucus to enlarge the Ways and Means Committee by almost 50 percent and remove from it to a newly formed Steering Committee the responsibility for committee assignments. Mills' personal life had achieved notoriety with a series of bizarre incidents including association with a Washington, D.C., striptease dancer who jumped from Mills' car into the water of the Tidal Basin when the car was stopped by police for speeding. As further evidence of House dissatisfaction with seniority, the caucus limited the chair power over subcommittees. A committee caucus would select subcommittee chairs, not the committee chair. A plan was adopted whereby senior committee members could choose two of their current subcommittee positions. Once they had chosen, the more junior members would have free reign to pick the remaining subcommittee slots. Also passed was the "subcommittee Bill of Rights," which forced chairs to respect subcommittee jurisdiction and resources.

Dissatisfaction with seniority had moved Congress to reform, aided, no doubt, by the election to the House of 75 new members in 1974. The moves against seniority, however, reflect a growing trend within Congress. Times had changed since World War II, when safe, conservative southern Democrats occupied the seats of power in Congress; the South has become increasingly competitive, while northern safe seats have increased. As a percentage of overall Democratic membership in Congress, southern power has declined dramatically. The overall percentage of southern representation in the House and Senate went from 49 percent of the 1947 Senate to only 27 percent in the 1979 Senate, and in the House the figures show a decline from 55 percent in 1947 to 27 percent in 1979. That general decline is also reflected in the southerners' diminishing share of committee and subcommittee posts.

The balance of power in Congress has been shifting. There is less tolerance for the "let them wait" attitude. Seniority is less persuasive today than it once was, but it has not been abandoned. One can assume that as northern liberals continue to climb the seniority ladder, challenges to seniority may decrease. The reforms have had two obvious effects. First, House and Senate committee assignments are more democratic; committee chairs and subcommittee posts more broadly reflect the membership. The routinization of committee assignment puts almost everyone where he or she wants to be; caucus decision making ensures sensitivity to party and member needs on the part of chairs. But the democratization of committees has further decentralized legislative decision making. There are more subcommittees than ever. Their jurisdiction and autonomy from the committee and its chair is guaranteed. This places an added burden on party leadership to coordinate and schedule and to provide the integration necessary to produce timely and meaningful public policy.

THE LEGISLATIVE PROCESS

The process of making legislation is basic to our political process, yet the lawmaking process itself is confusing and poorly understood by most Americans. No institution in America receives more recognition than Congress; it conducts

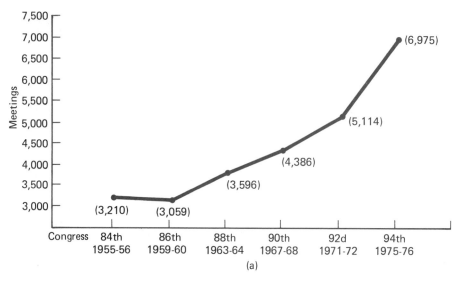

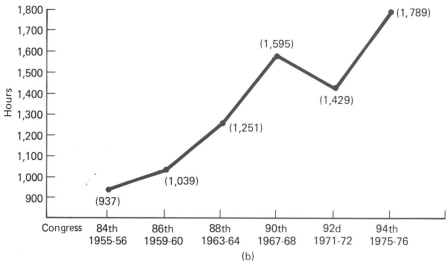

Figure 12.5

The congressional workload. (a) Number of committee and subcommittee meetings 84th–94th Congresses. (b) Number of hours in session. (U.S. House of Representatives, Commission on Administrative Review, *Administrative Reorganization and Legislative Management.* 95th Congress, 1st session, 1977, H. Doc. 95–232, p. 21)

its business in full view of the public, and starting in 1979, before the television cameras. Yet the public often finds Congress undemocratic and slow to respond to public needs.

The legislative process has grown in size and complexity over the years; understanding Congress is no easy task (Figure 12.5). Twenty thousand bills and resolutions are introduced every two years; 2,000 committee reports are filed. The workload of Congress has doubled in the past two decades. The First Congress in 1789 saw only 142 bills introduced and 85 committee reports filed. Today Congress is in session for almost two-thirds of the year, meeting almost 9,000 hours. The increased demands on Congress are due in great measure to the increased complexity and scope of government. Competing demands for resources in the public forum keep Congress deliberative and slow to act.

The legislative process is decentralized. Each bill and resolution must pass both chambers. No bill becomes law without a cumulative, deliberate number of affirmative actions; one negative action in either chamber can kill a bill. Of the 20,000 bills introduced every two years, the vast majority will die in committee for lack of action. For example, in 1975 there were 17,528 measures introduced into Congress, and that year Congress passed 1,443 bills. In fact, no legislation has a serious chance of success without the backing of party leaders or key legislators in the legislative process. The process is much the same in both chambers of Congress (Figure 12.6).

Every bill must be introduced in the House or Senate by a member of the chamber. It is then referred to committee. All bills introduced into Congress are sent to committee. The committee then decides whether or not to consider further action. Usually a subcommittee will hold hearings and do the "mark up" of the

The House of Representatives in session. (Library of Congress Photo)

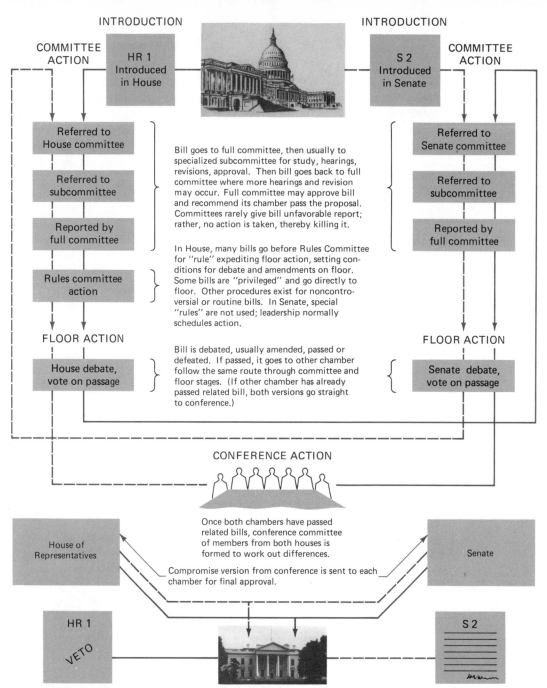

INTRODUCTION   INTRODUCTION

COMMITTEE ACTION   COMMITTEE ACTION

HR 1 Introduced in House

S 2 Introduced in Senate

Referred to House committee

Referred to subcommittee

Reported by full committee

Rules committee action

Referred to Senate committee

Referred to subcommittee

Reported by full committee

Bill goes to full committee, then usually to specialized subcommittee for study, hearings, revisions, approval. Then bill goes back to full committee where more hearings and revision may occur. Full committee may approve bill and recommend its chamber pass the proposal. Committees rarely give bill unfavorable report; rather, no action is taken, thereby killing it.

In House, many bills go before Rules Committee for "rule" expediting floor action, setting conditions for debate and amendments on floor. Some bills are "privileged" and go directly to floor. Other procedures exist for noncontroversial or routine bills. In Senate, special "rules" are not used; leadership normally schedules action.

FLOOR ACTION   FLOOR ACTION

House debate, vote on passage

Senate debate, vote on passage

Bill is debated, usually amended, passed or defeated. If passed, it goes to other chamber follow the same route through committee and floor stages. (If other chamber has already passed related bill, both versions go straight to conference.)

CONFERENCE ACTION

House of Representatives

Senate

Once both chambers have passed related bills, conference committee of members from both houses is formed to work out differences.

Compromise version from conference is sent to each chamber for final approval.

HR 1 VETO

S 2

Compromise version approved by both houses is sent to President who can either sign it into law or veto it and return it to Congress. Congress may override veto by a two-thirds majority vote in both houses; bill then becomes law without President's signature.

Figure 12.6

How a Bill becomes a Law. This diagram shows the most typical way in which proposed legislation is enacted into law. There are more complicated and simpler routes, and most bills fall by the wayside and never become law. The process is illustrated here by two hypothetical bills: House bill No. 1 (HR 1) and Senate bill No. 2 (S 2). Each bill must be passed by both houses of Congress in identical form before it can become law. The path of HR 1 is traced by a solid line and the path of S 2 is traced by a broken line. In reality, most legislation begins as similar proposals in both houses. (*Congress and the Nation*, Vol. IV, p. XXXV, Congressional Quarterly Inc.)

bill. Once the bill has been "marked up" or amended, the full committee votes and makes a recommendation to the full chamber. If the full body, after debating the bill, approves, it is sent to the other house and the process begins all over again. If the two chambers approve the bill, but with differences, a conference committee is created to work out a compromise.

INTRODUCING A BILL

A bill is first drafted in proper form and placed in the "hopper," a box on the clerk's desk. The bill is numbered and labeled with the sponsor's name and then sent to the government printing office, where sufficient copies for study are printed. Bills introduced into the House are prefixed with an "HR" and bills in the Senate with an "S". This format is used whether it is a public bill, resolution, or private legislation. **Resolutions,** subject to the same procedure as other bills, are used for the internal business of either chamber or for expressing the sense of the House or Senate and are passed by that chamber only. **Concurrent resolutions** can affect the internal affairs of Congress, express the opinion of Congress, and require the approval of both the House and Senate. They are not sent to the president for signature, nor do they have the force of law. A **joint resolution,** passed by both chambers, has the force of law and requires the same procedure as bills. **Bills** introduced into Congress can be either *public* or *private*. A private bill deals with individual matters such as claims against the government, immigration, and land titles. Public bills deal with general categories of people on general questions and become public laws if approved by Congress and signed by the president.

The first reading of a bill constitutes its referral to committee, normally a perfunctory task. The presiding officer usually follows the wishes of the bill's sponsor in referring the bill to committee, although tradition and rules do govern. Presiding officers do have a measure of discretion. In cases of new programs or where bills involve overlapping jurisdiction, the presiding officer may select the committee for referral. This happened in 1963, when the civil rights bill was sent to the Senate Commerce Committee instead of the southern-dominated Judiciary Committee. The presiding officer also may split a bill, referring parts of it to different committees.

COMMITTEE ACTION

What happens next is critical to the life or death of a bill. Less than 10 percent of bills referred to committee are never reported out. Often called "little legislatures," committees are the heart and soul of the legislative process. This is where the legislative work is done. Many say that floor debate is for show, but committee action shapes the direction of Congress. Clearly the size of Congress, the number of bills, and time preclude much meaningful floor action, especially

FACT FILE

Résumé of Congressional Activity of the Ninety-Sixth Congress
First Session of the Ninety-Sixth Congress

Data on Legislative Activity
Senate, January 15 through December 20, 1979
House, January 15, 1979 through January 3,1980

	Senate	House	Total
Days in session	167	173	. .
Time in session	1,159 hrs., 01'	974 hrs., 54'	. .
Congressional Record:			
Pages of proceedings	19,560	12,524	32,084
Extension of Remarks	. .	. .	6,398
Public bills enacted into law	60	127	187
Private bills enacted into law	5	38	43
Bills in conference	13	12	25
Bills through conference	22	32	54
Measures passed, total	652	666	1,318
Senate bills	201	86	. .
House bills	146	262	. .
Senate joint resolutions	20	5	. .
House joint resolutions	24	28	. .
Senate concurrent resolutions	19	11	. .
House concurrent resolutions	27	34	. .
Simple resolutions	215	240	. .
Measures reported, total	ª546	ª614	1,160
Senate bills	263	12	. .
House bills	105	376	. .
Senate joint resolutions	19	1	. .
House joint resolutions	9	14	. .
Senate concurrent resolutions	18	1	. .
House concurrent resolutions	8	10	. .
Simple resolutions	219	200	. .
Special reports	41	52	. .
Conference reports	21	65	. .
Measures pending on calendar	70	66	. .
Measures introduced, total	2,712	7,459	10,171
Bills	2,188	6,232	. .
Joint resolutions	132	472	. .
Concurrent resolutions	63	236	. .
Simple resolutions	329	519	. .
Quorum calls	19	86	. .
Yea-and-nay votes	509	359	. .
Recorded votes	. .	313	. .
Bills vetoed	1	. .	1
Vetoes overridden	. .	. .	. .

a. These figures include all measures reported, even if there was no accompanying report. A total of 703 reports have been filed in the Senate, a total of 731 have been filed in the House.

Second Session of the Ninety-Sixth Congress

Data on Legislative Activity
January 3 through September 30, 1980

	Senate	House	Total
Days in session	142	131	. .
Time in session	976 hrs., 53'	768 hrs., 40'	. .
Congressional Record:			
Pages of proceedings	14,253	10,474	24,727
Extension of Remarks	. .	. .	4,833
Public bills enacted into law	74	106	180
Private bills enacted into law	4	13	17
Bills in conference	24	19	. .
Bills through conference	16	22	. .
Measures passed, total	611	617	1,228
Senate bills	199	104	. .
House bills	169	247	. .
Senate joint resolutions	27	20	. .
House joint resolutions	27	31	. .
Senate concurrent resolutions	27	19	. .
House concurrent resolutions	29	40	. .
Simple resolutions	133	156	. .
Measures reported, total	ª591	ª614	1,205
Senate bills	259	34	. .
House bills	110	383	. .
Senate joint resolutions	34	. .	. .
House joint resolutions	16	15	. .
Senate concurrent resolutions	20	4	. .
House concurrent resolutions	8	18	. .
Simple resolutions	144	160	. .
Special reports	23	10	. .
Conference reports	8	21	. .
Measures pending on calendar	130	192	. .
Measures introduced, total	1,421	2,651	4,072
Bills	1,068	2,011	. .
Joint resolutions	77	148	. .
Concurrent resolutions	71	207	. .
Simple resolutions	205	285	. .
Quorum calls	32	71	. .
Yea-and-nay votes	462	369	. .
Recorded votes	. .	168	. .
Bills vetoed	. .	4	4
Vetoes overridden	. .	2	2

a. These figures include all measures reported, even if there was no accompanying report. A total of 462 reports have been filed in the Senate, a total of 712 have been filed in the House.

in the House of Representatives. Congress depends on its committees to get most of the work done. There are 22 standing committees in the House of Representatives, 15 in the Senate, and 356 subcommittees in Congress.

Table 12.5
House and Senate Committees of the Ninety-seventh Congress

Senate Committees	Chairman[a]	State
Agriculture, Nutrition, and Forestry	Jesse Helms	N.C.
Appropriations	Mark O. Hatfield	Ore.
Armed Services	John Tower	Tex.
Banking, Housing, and Urban Affairs	Jake Garn	Utah
Budget	Peter V. Domenici	N.M.
Commerce, Science, and Transportation	Bob Packwood	Ore.
Energy and Natural Resources	James A. McClure	Idaho
Environment and Public Works	Robert T. Stafford	Vt.
Finance	Robert Dole	Kansas
Foreign Relations	Charles H. Percy	Ill.
Governmental Affairs	Williams V. Roth	Del.
Labor and Human Resources	Orrin G. Hatch	Utah
Judiciary	Strom Thurmond	S.C.
Rules and Administration[c]		
Veterans' Affairs	Alan Simpson	Wy.

House Committees	Chairman[b]	State
Agriculture	Thomas S. Foley	Wash.
Appropriations	Jamie L. Whitten	Miss.
Armed Services	Melvin Price	Ill.
Banking, Finance, and Urban Affairs	Henry S. Reuss	Wis.
Budget[c]		
District of Columbia	Ronald V. Dellums	Calif.
Education and Labor	Carl D. Perkins	Ky.
Government Operations	Jack Brooks	Tex.
House Administration	Augustus F. Hawkins	Calif.
Interior and Insular Affairs	Morris K. Udall	Ariz.
Foreign Affairs	Clement J. Zablocki	Wis.
Interstate and Foreign Commerce	John D. Dingell	Mich.
Judiciary	Peter W. Rodino, Jr.	N.J.
Merchant Marine and Fisheries	Walter B. Jones	N.C.
Post Office and Civil Service	William D. Ford	Mich.
Public Works and Transportation	James J. Howard	N.J.
Rules	Richard Bolling	Mo.
Science and Technology	Don Fuqua	Fla.
Small Business	Neal Smith	Iowa
Standards of Official Conduct	Charles E. Bennett	Fla.
Veterans' Affairs	Don Edwards	Calif.
Ways and Means[c]		

a. Because Republicans were in the majority in the Senate during the Ninety-seventh Congress, all committee chairmen were Republicans.
b. Because Democrats were in the majority in the House during the Ninety-seventh Congress, all committee chairmen were Democrats.
c. At time of publication, these chairmanships were still undecided.

Committee members and staff normally have a high degree of expertise in the subject matter within the committee's jurisdiction. The committee has several options with regard to proposed legislation. The first is whether or not to take up the bill in the first place. A committee actually considers only a small fraction of all the bills referred to it. Failure to consider a bill usually kills it. It can also be withdrawn from committee in the House through a **discharge petition,** a petition signed by a majority of the House membership. In the Senate, adoption of a special resolution is necessary. Either attempt rarely succeeds. The other committee options are to adopt the bill, amend it somewhat, or rewrite it entirely.

In the past, committee chairs exercised considerable discretionary power in their committees over what bills would be considered. They still have some power over the workload and set the tone for the committee, but the reforms of the 1970s have moderated their power over bills considerably. The 1960s were known as an era of ''committee government''; the 1970s, the era of ''subcommittee government.'' Between 1971 and 1975, the growing Democratic caucus in the House of Representatives moved to curb the authority of committee chairs and to increase the number and autonomy of subcommittees. By 1975, subcommittees and subcommittee chairs had come to dominate the legislative process. The power of committee chairs was pared in several ways:

1. No House member could hold more than one subcommittee chair (reform adopted 1971). This prevented committee chairs from chairing all subcommittees themselves and opened up opportunities for less senior committee members. In fact, it gave 16 Democrats elected since 1958 their first subcommittee chairs on such key committees as Judiciary; Foreign Affairs; and the Banking, Currency, and Housing Committee.
2. All committees with twenty or more members were required to establish four or more subcommittees (1974). Aimed at the Ways and Means Committee, which had never used subcommittees, this action set a precedent and institutionalized subcommittee government.
3. A subcommittee Bill of Rights established rules for the protection of subcommittees (1973). Caucuses of Democratic committee members were given the authority to select subcommittee chairs, establish subcommittee jurisdictions, set party ratios, and provide adequate budgets for subcommittees. Committee chairs were required to submit bills to subcommittees within two weeks. No longer could a chair kill the bill through delay.
4. Subcommittee chairs and the ranking minority members could hire one staff person each to work directly with them on subcommittee business (1975). This strengthened the resources of subcommittees.
5. Senior Democrats were restricted to membership on two or less subcommittees (1974). Again the Democratic caucus sought to curb the power of seniority, because conservatives were dominating the subcommittees. This measure was aimed primarily at the House Appropriations Committee. The result of the revolt in the House strengthened the jurisdiction

and autonomy of subcommittees. Their workload increased, more hearings were held, and subcommittees began steering bills on to the floor of the House.

In 1977, the Senate also undertook reorganization of its committees. In the new system, no senator can hold more than three committee or subcommittee chairs. It also reduced the total number of standing committees. The Senate has moved to more frequent use of subcommittees, but has never been overwhelmed with the spirit of reform. A Library of Congress study in 1976 found that 28 Senate subcommittees never met in 1975, and 50 percent of all subcommittees held four or fewer meetings that year.

In the House, it is the subcommittee, then, that normally schedules hearings on bills and invites testimony. This creates the public record for a piece of legislation. As a way of gathering information, congressional hearings are a poor procedure; very few minds are changed as a result. At hearings, attendance is haphazard, testimony is frequently prepared and read, and questions are often silly. But it affords interested groups and citizens an opportunity to express their opinion. Committee hearings may also be used to mold public opinion on major topics of concern to Congress. In recent years Congressmen like Senator George McGovern have used committee hearings to focus public attention on the problems of malnutrition and hunger in America. Hearings can also become the launching pad for a national career or a reelection bid.

Most hearings are held in open session; both houses have adopted **sunshine rules** that require open hearings. The House in 1973 and the Senate two years later required all committee meetings to be open to the public unless a majority of the members on a roll call vote close the meeting. Under the rule, a vote to close a meeting can be taken only if public disclosure violates rules or "endangers national security." After conducting public hearings, the subcommittee, or sometimes the full committee, meets to "mark up" the bill. The **mark-up session** is where the committee drafts the bill in the form it wants. Each line is amended or rewritten. Committee members debate and compromise among themselves, with a final vote, and write a report explaining their actions. Under the 1974 reforms, mark-up sessions are open to the public.

The full committee receives the marked up bill from the subcommittee or does the mark up itself, then votes on the bill. It may ratify the subcommittee draft and order the bill reported to the full chamber. Occasionally full committees may report out a bill unfavorably, though it is simpler to not report out such a bill. Often the full committee will consider amendments, frequently from minority members, and the committee must approve, alter, or reject these amendments before the bill can be put to a final vote. The bill is then reported to the full chamber for final disposition. A report of the committee, justifying its actions, accompanies the bill. Dissenting committee members may submit a minority report urging that the reported bill be defeated.

After a bill is reported out of committee, it is placed on a calendar in the

Congressmen in committee where much of the legislative work is done. (Stan Wakefield)

House or Senate. All bills are placed on the calendar in chronological order as they are reported to the chamber. Rarely, however, are bills called up for floor action in that order.

HOUSE FLOOR ACTION

The House of Representatives has five *legislative calendars* to sort out legislative business: **Union** (for revenue and spending bills), **House** (public, controversial bills), **Consent** (noncontroversial bills), **Private** (private relief for individual citizens), and **Discharge** (for petitions to discharge bills from committees). The Union calendar is a privileged calendar, meaning action may be taken without using the Rules Committee when items are placed on it. A few other items are also privileged: conference committee reports, Budget Committee reports, and vetoed bills. These are also considered by the House as they are reported to it. Days of the month are set aside for consideration of the Consent, Private, and Discharge calendars.

The House Rules Committee. Since the calendar system sorts out legislation in the House, with the bulk of controversial issues placed on the House calendar, the House of Representatives needs "rules" to govern floor action on legislation. The House has empowered its Rules Committee to establish rules governing floor consideration of legislation.

As a practical matter, few controversial bills will ever reach the floor of the House without a "rule" from the Rules Committee. A rule may be requested by the chair of the committee reporting the bill. That request is considered by the Rules Committee. The granting of a special rule sets the date, time, and limits for debate on a bill, in effect, removing the bill from the House calendar. The Rules Committee can prohibit amendments from being offered *(a closed rule)* or grant an *open rule,* which permits amendments from the floor. The Rules Committee can also decide whether points of order can be waived for portions of the bill.

The scheduling of legislation makes Rules a powerful House committee. It is the gatekeeper for floor action in the House. By failing to grant a special rule to a bill, the Rules Committee can effectively kill legislation. The threat of withholding a rule has often been cause enough for a committee to delete provisions objectionable to the Rules Committee.

The Rules Committee has therefore been a source of controversy. In the early 1960s conservative southerners led by Rules Chair Howard Smith of Virginia effectively prevented civil rights bills from passing Congress by refusing a rule for such bills. In 1973 reform-minded Democrats allowed House Democrats to refer Ways and Means legislation to the Democratic caucus to instruct the Rules Committee to write an open rule. In 1975 the reform was extended by requiring all Ways and Means revenue bills to receive a rule prior to floor action. Further efforts at reform in 1975 gave the Speaker of the House power to name all Democratic members of the Rules Committee, subject to ratification by the caucus. Said Bruce Oppenheimer: "By gaining full control over the recruitment of Democratic members to the committee and by filling vacancies carefully, the Speaker has turned the [Rules] committee into an arm of the leadership. It can now be relied on to be a traffic cop that serves the leadership instead of one that serves the chairman of the committee."[22]

There are ways of avoiding the Rules Committee, but they are cumbersome and seldom successful. A piece of legislation may be brought to the floor through a suspension of the rules, a discharge petition, or calendar Wednesday. Suspension of the rules require a two-thirds vote of those present; the discharge petition takes a majority of House members' signatures; calendar Wednesday allows committee chairs, in alphabetical order of committees, to call up any of their bills from the House or the Union calendars on Wednesdays. None of these measures are used very often.

22. Bruce I. Oppenheimer, "The Rules Committee: New Arm of Leadership in a Decentralized House," in Lawrence C. Dodd & Bruce I. Oppenheimer, *Congress Reconsidered* (New York: Praeger Publishers, 1977), pp. 113–114.

SENATE FLOOR ACTION

The Senate, being the smaller body, has only two calendars, the **Executive calendar,** for treaties and nominations, and the **Calendar of Business,** where all other legislation is assigned. A bill is brought to the Senate by a call of the calendar or by unanimous consent to take a bill out of order on the calendar. There are no elaborate rules or procedures for bringing a bill to the floor of the Senate, and there is no Rules Committee.

Under Senate rules, any senator at almost any time may ask to bring a bill to the floor. Such a motion is debatable, however, even subject to filibuster, and hence not often used. More often, the majority leader requests unanimous consent of the Senate to remove bills from the Calendar of Business. The practice is for the majority leader, with the aid of the party Policy Committee, and the minority party leader, to schedule debate on agreed-upon legislation by asking the Senate for unanimous consent to schedule and debate those items. This process accommodates individual senators and ensures that important legislation reaches the floor. Majority leader Byrd had used unanimous consent extensively. With it he had controlled the pace of the Senate as well as debate on pending legislation. Senator Byrd had divided the legislative day into blocs, with debate on measures proceeding within defined time limits. Often two or more bills are scheduled for the day. Byrd had achieved the same kind of control over scheduling in the Senate that the Rules Committee exercises in the House of Representatives.

FINAL FLOOR ACTION

Citizens frequently travel to Washington to see Congress in action. Sitting high in the gallery, they expect to hear a spirited debate. Most come away disappointed. Attendance on the floor of Congress is often sparse, action predetermined, and voting routine. Often individual members read remarks into the *Congressional Record,* the daily journal of legislative business, while other members go about the routine of congressional life. The reason for this disappointment is that controversial territory has already been well covered. Committee hearings, the Rules Committee, and consultation with majority and minority leaders provide a relatively clear sense of the issues and their direction. Floor debate, then, is often for show. There are, of course, issues where floor debate is critical, where amendments may be offered, and where the final outcome in doubt. Here supporters and opponents marshal their forces, and whips round up members for quorum calls. But these are infrequent moments of high drama.

The floor action on a bill is directed by the bill's **floor manager,** typically the bill's subcommittee chair or a senior committee member. The ranking minority member on the committee normally leads any opposition to the legislation. Debate in the House is governed by the rule granted from the Rules Committee. When the House debates, the amount of time is determined by the special rule. If there is no rule, each member is allocated one hour for debate. Since the latter is unwieldly, the House may move into a committee of the whole and apportion debate equally between proponents and opponents. Since 1973 the House has used electronic devices to instantly record the votes of members. Members may vote yea (yes), nay (no) or present (abstain). Results are displayed on a large board in the front of the House, where all members may see the results at once.

In the Senate, debate is more commonplace. There are no restrictions on time. Of course, the privilege of unlimited debate can be used to delay legislative action. The **filibuster,** extended debate to prevent a vote, has been used on occasion to prevent a majority from passing legislation. **Cloture** can be invoked to close debate, but this requires a three-fifths vote of the Senate and rarely succeeds.

Voting in the Senate is by voice vote, division (standing), or roll call. The Senate has no electronic equipment. It uses only one method on any given issue. Roll calls are frequent and easily obtained (on request of one-fifth of those present).

Action in the Second Chamber.   Once a bill has passed one house, it must be transmitted to the other house for action, and the process begins all over again.

When the Senate receives a House-passed bill, it is most commonly referred to committee for consideration. On a few occasions the bill may be placed directly on the Senate calendar. A Senate-passed bill received by the House must be referred to committee for action.

The normal procedure for considering legislation is followed. The second chamber's committee will schedule hearings. Amendments may be offered in committee, or from the floor. In the House, a rule from the Rules Committee is likely to be necessary; then follows floor debate and action. If the bill passes both houses with no changes, which is unlikely, it is sent to the president. However, in all likelihood the second chamber has made changes in the bill. The bill is then sent back to the chamber of origin, which may accept the second chamber's amendments or request a conference.

Conference Committee.   Because most controversial legislation has House and Senate differences, it is necessary to call a conference. Senator Bennett Clark of Missouri once suggested, ''all bills and resolutions shall be read twice and, without debate, referred to conference.'' He was, of course, referring to the crucial role conference committees play in the final shape of legislation. Often called the ''third house'' of Congress, conference committees seek to resolve differences between House and Senate versions of a bill. They have the power to rewrite legislation.

Either chamber can request a conference, but both chambers must agree to it. The presiding officers appoint members to a joint House–Senate conference committee. The presiding officers, by tradition, consult with the chairs of the respective committees that considered the bill, then appoint three to twenty members from their house. Typically there will be three to six House members and five to ten Senate members (the Senate routinely sends larger groups than the House). The majority comes from the party in the majority in that chamber. The delegation votes as a unit according to how the majority of that delegation feels. Seniority influences the selection of members. The chairs of the committees and the ranking minority members are usually selected, along with senior committee members. Almost always, members are selected from the standing committee that considered or marked up the bill. The House requires the Speaker to appoint a majority of members ''who generally supported the House position as determined by the Speaker.''

The president signs a bill into law as members of Congress look on. (United Press International)

The conference committee has wide latitude. Until 1974, the sessions were secret and no records were kept. Recent forms require conference hearings to be open to the public unless a majority of either delegation votes to close them. When the conference arrives at an agreement, the bill is reported out to both houses for final disposition. Conference reports are privileged items and do not need to be placed on a calendar or receive a rule. They can and do interrupt most other legislative business. The final bill, as reported by the conference committee, however, may only be approved or rejected; it cannot be amended. It may be remanded back to conference committee on occasion, but the final House and Senate action is an all or nothing proposition.

The Final Step.   Should a bill survive the process in both houses, it is then sent to the White House to await final action by the president.

The president has ten days in which to act, and he has three alternatives. He may sign the bill, thereby indicating approval, and the bill becomes law. If the president does not approve of the legislation, he may **veto** the bill and return it to Congress with a message outlining his objections. If Congress takes no further action, the bill dies. Congress also has an opportunity to override the president's veto. It takes a two-thirds vote of those present in both houses to override a presidential veto. Such action may come at any time during the session after a veto; if successful, the bill becomes law.

The third option for the president is to do nothing. If after ten days the president has not acted, the bill becomes law without his signature. A president may wish to do this for bills he does not strongly support but does not wish to veto. The only exception to a bill becoming a law in ten days without the president's signature is when Congress adjourns before the ten days expire. In this case, we call the bill **pocket vetoed.**

Bills passed by Congress and signed, which then become law, are given a numerical designation. There are two series, one for private law and one for public law. A private law would be Private Law 96-153 (the one hundred fifty-third private law passed by the 96th Congress) and Public Law 218 passed in the 96th Congress would be designated PL 96-218.

CONGRESSIONAL STAFF

The increasing workload of Congress and the increasing complexity of legislation has naturally led to an increase in congressional staff. There has been a marked increase in the number of staff for individual representatives and in the number of staff for committees (Figure 12.7).

Personal staff perform a variety of tasks for the representative. The *administrative assistant* supervises the overall operation of the member's office and is the legislator's right arm. In general, staff answer mail, solve constituent prob-

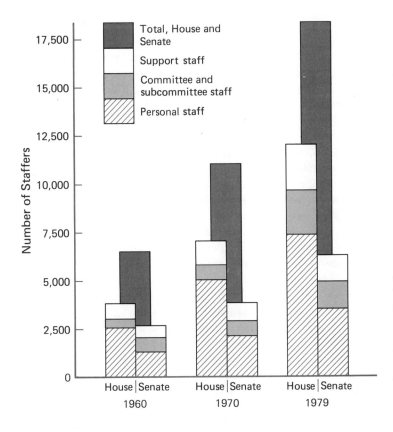

 is the chart. The chart legend and axis:

Number of Staffers

- Total, House and Senate
- Support staff
- Committee and subcommittee staff
- Personal staff

17,500
15,000
12,500
10,000
7,500
5,000
2,500
0

House | Senate — 1960
House | Senate — 1970
House | Senate — 1979

Figure 12.7

Where Hill Staffers Work. Note: The support staff includes employees in offices such as the House clerk, Capitol architect, and sergeants at arms. (House Appropriations Committee, Senate Disbursing Office. *Weekly Report,* Congressional Quarterly, Inc., November 24, 1979, p. 2636)

lems, and keep the representative informed. Staff also research bills, attend committee hearings, and draft reports and speeches.

The rapid expansion of committee staffs reflects the further decentralization of Congress with subcommittee government and the right of majority and minority members of committees to have separate staffs. Committee staffs are instrumental in drafting legislation, conducting investigations, and writing legislative reports. Fox and Hammond's survey indicated that committee staff spent most of their time supplying information, doing legislative research and bill drafting, and engaging in investigations and bureaucratic oversight.[23] Committee staff also work closely with executive agency officials and interest group representatives. They are an important source of contact for both the executive branch and for lobbyists.

Congress has come to depend on staff. Remarked Senator Clark (D. Iowa), "There is no question of our enormous dependency and their influence. In all legislation, they're the ones that lay out the options."

23. Harrison Fox and Susan Hammond, *Congressional Staff* (New York: The Free Press, 1977), p. 119.

SUPPORT AGENCIES

With an increase in staff, Congress has also expanded and upgraded its support agencies. It has upgraded two old agencies, the General Accounting Office and the Congressional Research Service of the Library of Congress, and established two new agencies: the Office of Technology Assessment and the Congressional Budget Office.

The General Accounting Office (GAO) has recently coordinated its activities with those of Congress, though technically it is an independent agency. Its main responsibility is to conduct independent audits of executive agencies, but it also gives legal advice to agencies, reviews management practices, and handles claims and debts against the federal government. The GAO responds to requests from congressional offices and congressional committees. In recent years, the GAO has aided Congress in the performance of its oversight function. The *Congressional Research Service* (CRS) handles legislative requests for information on topics of concern for individual members and congressional committees. It receives over 300,000 requests annually and requires a staff of 800 to field all the requests. Many of the daily requests from representatives concern constituent requests for information, but the CRS has the capacity to provide detailed information on a vast array of complex issues. It does not conduct investigations, but relies on published materials which it pulls together for a legislator or committee. The CRS seeks to be politically neutral and does not advocate policy positions.

The *Office of Technology Assessment* (OTA) was created in 1972 to "provide early indications of the probable beneficial and adverse impacts of the applications of technology." It is governed by a board of six senators and six representatives, divided equally by party. The office has established seven areas for concentration: energy, food, health, materials, oceans, transportation, and world trade. To date it has proved of little utility. Many members do not even know of its existence. In 1977, Republicans charged the OTA was an agency serving Senator Edward Kennedy. The most recent creation of Congress, in 1974, is the *Congressional Budget Office* (CBO). It was designed to generate fiscal analysis in order to rival the president's Office of Management and Budget. The 200 staff members make economic forecasts, summarize cost projections for proposed legislation, and alert Congress to budget targets. The CBO works closely with the newly created House and Senate Budget Committees, as well as the Appropriations and Ways and Means Committee. It aids in implementing the new congressional budget procedure.

LEGISLATIVE DECISION MAKING

The major function of the legislature is lawmaking. The legislative process affords several opportunities for members of Congress to help shape public policies. How they decide what they will do is of considerable importance. What are the factors that influence members' decision making? We will look at a few: the voters, the member's policy position, and their colleagues.

THE VOTERS

Many commentators explain congressional behavior by members' need to be reelected. A good deal of their Washington behavior is dependent on members' perception of their constituencies and how constituents view them. Those who win by close margins pay particularly close attention to the voters in their constituency.[24] Even those with large margins at the polls are likely to maintain they achieve those margins by paying attention to needs of and issues important to the voters.[25] It is David Mayhew's contention that the single-minded attention to re-election explains the activities and goals of Congress.[26] Whether reelection is so pervasive a motive or not, representatives feel constrained to explain their activities to their constituents.

POLICY POSITIONS

Representatives do not come to Washington without having taken any stands on issues. They have basic, fundamental beliefs that shape their orientation toward legislation. They might be liberal, conservative, or moderate. They may oppose greater federal spending or look favorably on domestic welfare programs, but most surely have some personal policy preference.

Aage Clausen studied the voting patterns of members and concluded that they typically vote according to their previously stated position on policies.[27] Most Republicans cluster with other Republicans in opposition to the Democrats. Members will vote with the policy of their party about two-thirds of the time. Although such policy voting was stronger in the nineteenth century, it has become more predominant again in the mid-1970s than it was in the years after World War II. Typically, policy differences are more evident over domestic, welfare, and government management issues than over foreign affairs or civil liberty issues.

COLLEAGUES

With the intense demands on a representative's time and the vast array of legislation, individuals cannot keep informed on every piece of legislation. They must depend on certain colleagues. Most members develop trusted relationships with a few others, often those who think like them. From these trusted colleagues, they receive "cues" for voting. The cue giver may be a respected member of a

24. It was interesting, however, that Richard Fenno could find no connection between electoral margin and attentiveness to the district—trips home or staff resources directed to the district. See Richard F. Fenno, Jr., ''U.S. House Members in Their Constituencies,'' *American Political Science Review* 71, September 1977.
25. John W. Kingdon, *Congressmen's Voting Decisions* (New York: Harper & Row, 1973), p. 31.
26. David R. Mayhew, *Congress, The Electoral Connection.*
27. Aage R. Clausen, *How Congressmen Decide: A Policy Focus* (New York: St. Martins, 1973), p. 213.

committee or a senior member of the state delegation. "[This] makes it possible for the ordinary Congressman both to vote in a reasonably rational fashion and to do so on the basis of exceedingly little information."[28]

A particularly important group of colleagues in the House of Representatives are members of the state delegation. Numerous commentators have examined the state delegation and found it a particularly cohesive body within which members rely heavily upon one another for information.[29] It makes the job of a representative far less hectic.

OTHER INTERNAL INFLUENCES

There are also several informal groups in Congress, predominantly in the House, that perform largely social and informational functions. The freshmen Democrats in the 94th Congress (1975–76) formed a group, even had their own whip organization, and sought to promote unity on a number of issues. From the late 1950s on, House members began to form groups designed to influence policy. They began to bargain with party leaders, committees, and other groups in the House to influence and shape legislative policy.

The oldest and most influential group is the Democratic Study Group. Formed in 1957 by liberal House Democrats, it has evolved into a loose alliance of over 220 House members. Its members pay dues and fund activities out of their staff allowances. Presently it employs a staff of about 25, elects a chair, and has a whip system. Group members form task forces and issue reports on various subjects of relevance for legislation. They put out a weekly "Legislative Report" which summarizes legislative activity for the upcoming week and "fact sheets" analyzing bills of major importance. They were instrumental in the House reforms in the mid-1970s. Members vote together on roll call votes; they form a very cohesive group.[30]

Liberal Republican House members have also formed a policy group known as the Wednesday Group; it was formed in 1963 and meets weekly on Wednesdays. Relatively small (it grew from 14 in 1963–64 to 36 in 1976), it has a small staff and produces issue papers on matters of common concern. Because of its small size, it possesses little power and bargaining advantage with Republican leadership in the House. More recently, conservatives in the House have organized. In 1973 conservative Republicans formed the Republican Study Committee. It has approximately 60 members, and its activity is limited to publishing

28. Donald R. Matthews and James A. Stimson, *Yeas and Nays: Normal Decision Making in the U.S. House of Representatives* (New York: John Wiley & Sons, 1975), p. 45.
29. See John Kessel, "The Washington Congressional Delegation," *Midwest Journal of Political Science,* 8 (February 1964); and Barbara Deckard, "State Party Delegations in the U.S. House of Representatives: A Comparative Study of Group Cohesion," *The Journal of Politics,* 34 (February 1972).
30. Arthur G. Stevens, Jr., Arthur H. Miller and Thomas E. Mann, "Mobilization of Liberal Strength in the House, 1955–1970; The Democratic Study Group," *American Political Science Review* 68 (June 1974).

"fact sheets" for members. Conservative Democrats banded together in 1972 to form the Democratic Research Organization. With about 70 members in 1976, it seeks to counterbalance the liberal Democratic Study Group. It produces legislative "fact sheets" and sponsors speakers to explain conservative positions.

The 1970s have also seen the formation of *issue groups*. There are at least seven such groups in Congress. The oldest, formed in the mid-1960s, is the Members of Congress for Peace. Made up of "doves" on Vietnam, it included both Republicans and Democrats, representatives and senators. In 1976, to provide an alternative to this group, the National Security Research Group formed to provide more conservative, "hawkish" information on national security questions. It has an equal number of Democrats and Republicans among its 25 members. The Environmental Study Conference was formed in 1975 to provide focus and information on environmental issues for 170 House members and 30 senators. It provides weekly bulletins and occasional briefings for members. There is also a Congressional Rural Caucus, with 100 members, dealing with rural development. In 1975, The Congressional Clearinghouse on Women's Rights was formed, with 14 members. It produces a weekly newsletter. There exist, in addition, the Congressional Clearinghouse on the Future and the Blue-Collar Caucus.

The growth of internal groups has also included the emergence of ethnic groups. The Congressional Hispanic Caucus was formed in 1976. The other organization is an older, more recognized force in the House: the Congressional Black Caucus. Formed in 1971, as of 1979 it had 15 members. It acts as a spokesman on leading issues of concern to blacks.

CONGRESSIONAL POWER: SEPARATE BUT EQUAL?

The decade of the 1970s brought changing expectations to what Congress could and should accomplish. Congress has played an important part in shaping governmental response to the decade of change. Basically, two sets of changes have taken place in Congress. First, there has been congressional reform: the legislature has sought to make its lawmaking capacity more democratic and responsive to the changing environment. The second series of changes have occurred in congressional power, largely in the aftermath of Vietnam and Watergate, as Congress sought to redress the balance of power between it and the president.

THE TREND TO REFORM

The first set of changes has been a somewhat contradictory one: there has been further decentralization of power and also centralization of power in the hands of party leadership. The reforms for decentralization occurred early in the decade, occasioned largely by the influx of new members into the House of Rep-

Social Welfare Policy

The welfare state, as we now know our social welfare policies, is a development of the twentieth century. Programs have frequently had presidential sponsorship, but Congress has also taken liberal responsibility for creating welfare programs or altering them to meet constituent and interest group demands. Social welfare has increasingly become the responsibility of the federal government.

Welfare programs date back to 1935 when Aid to Families with Dependent Children (AFDC) was enacted by Congress. Essentially, welfare provides direct cash assistance to persons on a need basis, that is, those who can establish eligibility and a need. AFDC provides support to children without adequate parental support. In 26 states aid is also provided to children in families where the father is unemployed. Benefits are paid to families on the basis of income and number of dependents. As income rises, benefits are reduced. Critics charge that this reduces the incentive to work. The largest category of recipients are female and half are black. In 1980 there were 11 million AFDC recipients costing the federal government $10.5 billion.

The other major welfare program is food stamps. Started as a modest form of nutritional support in 1962, today it is an $8.5 billion component of the welfare system serving some 20 million people. The food stamp program provides coupons (food stamps) to be used in lieu of cash to purchase food (excluding such items as liquor, cigarettes, cleaning supplies). The program is administered by the Department of Agriculture. Again there is an eligibility requirement, but critics charge that enforcement is minimal as striking workers and middle class families have little trouble signing up under the program.

Social welfare programs have changed measurably for those who are employed. Under the New Deal, Social Security and Unemployment Compensation were enacted to prevent economic catastrophe. They are basically public insurance programs whereby individuals and employers contribute to a trust fund. There is no need criterion for participation as these are prevention programs to ensure one a source of income during periods of unemployment or retirement. While the programs have proved popular, Social Security has become controversial in recent years as the fund has become actuarially unsound. The number of contributors has been declining relative to the increase in beneficiaries. Large increases in Social Security taxes have been necessary to keep the program solvent.

The major change occurred with the war on poverty. The New Deal programs were preventive or alleviative, the war on poverty was curative; it sought to brake the cycle of poverty by providing training and jobs. In the mid-1960s youth programs such as Head Start, Neighborhood Youth Corps, and Job Corps attempted to remove children from poverty environments with enrichment programs and employment training, and adult programs as Manpower Development and Training Act sought to give job training. In 1973 Congress added the Comprehensive Employment and Training Act (CETA). CETA created public service jobs for the unemployed and unskilled by making available federal funds to local governments and private groups. In 1979, there were 625,000 public service jobs available as well as another one-half million CETA funded jobs, which cost the federal government $10 billion annually.

Medical care policy is a newer element of

social welfare policy. Passed by Congress in 1965, the two programs are Medicare and Medicaid. Medicare provides limited hospitalization or nursing home care for retired persons receiving Social Security benefits. It is funded from an additional payroll tax collected with the Social Security tax. Participants must enroll in this voluntary program and pay a small monthly fee. Participants must also pay the first $50 for medical services and 20 percent of the cost thereafter. Medicaid acts more like welfare in that free medical care is provided for categoric groups such as AFDC families and states are reimbursed with up to 83 percent of the cost for medical treatment for the poor. States may choose not to participate in the Medicaid program. Since Medicare and Medicaid are limited in scope and some 20 million Americans lack health insurance, the question of national health insurance has become a health care policy issue. Several bills have been introduced in Congress but none have yet to pass. Most proposals call for payroll taxes shared by employees and employers, usually with employers paying the largest share.

A final area of social welfare policy is housing. Originally begun in 1937, housing programs meant grants for the construction of public housing. This served a twofold purpose: reduction of substandard housing and support for the construction industry.[1] Communities were given money to construct low cost, rental housing. In urban areas this meant highrise public housing projects. In the 1960s, as part of the war on poverty, housing programs turned toward subsidized loans to private groups to build and renovate housing, thereby giving the private sector a larger voice in housing programs. In 1968 a rent supplement program was started to aid tenants who paid 25 percent of their income for rent. Today rent subsidies are the backbone of the housing program. Many critics charge that housing is the weak link in the social welfare policy in the United States.

1. J. Anderson, D. Brady, and C. Bullock, *Public Policy and Politics in America,* North Scituate, Mass: Duxbury Press, 1978, p. 115.

---

resentatives. The move toward centralization followed these changes and sought to integrate them to make a more responsive Congress.

The decentralization of Congress was the result of two distinct yet related reforms, the rise of subcommittee government and the attack on committee chairs and their source of power—seniority. The growth of subcommittees comes as a direct result of the recognition of the increasing complexity of legislation and the need for greater specialization. The workload has become just too great for a committee to handle. This was coupled with an influx of new members—80 percent of the House had been elected since 1967—impatient with seniority and committee chairs. Subcommittee government bolsters the forces of decentralization because it fragments control over legislation.

The reforms creating subcommittees were reinforced by the attacks on seniority and committee chairs. As subcommittee autonomy was established, the power of committee chairs was eroded. Conversely, as committee chairs were being challenged, subcommittees inherited decision-making powers. The ad hoc revolts have been led by the revitalized liberal caucus in the House. The requirement that committee chairs be subject to secret ballot by party caucus reflects the unwillingness of these junior representatives to completely erode the position of committee chair; yet they refuse to be tied to seniority. The rejection of three southern committee chairs in 1975 is evidence of the power change in Congress. Yet committee chairs are not without influence. The effort has been to make chairs more solicitous of the committee and party membership that can deprive them of their seat. By depriving chairs of some of their resources they have made the position less valuable and seniority less a factor in achieving it. In order to prevent abuse of power, chairs still control the agenda and set the tone—only now within an environment of sensitivity to members' needs and goals.

The second series of reforms have sought to revitalize party government in Congress, to provide a new set of roles and powers for the party leadership in the House and Senate. In a very real sense, the party caucuses and the power of the leadership have come to be a centralizing force in shaping and influencing decision making in Congress. The emergence of the party caucus served to legitimize the reform proposals; it became the seedbed of renewed activism. By altering the procedure for the selection of committee chairs, the caucus sought to create responsiveness within the House. The creation of the Steering and Policy Committee put committee membership in the control of the party leadership and made it possible for the caucus to influence policy by placing members on committees.

The caucus has been particularly active in restoring trust and confidence to Congress. When the Hays scandal broke out, the House Democratic caucus made it clear they intended to remove him from his influential committees. With Koreagate and the trials of Representatives Diggs and Flood, the caucus renewed its fight for disclosure and limitations on outside income. The caucus has demonstrated its willingness to move quickly and decisively to restore public confidence in Congress and the majority party.

The strengthening of the caucus has meant a renewed strengthening of party leadership posts. Traditionally offices of power, in the 1960s these positions had become weak. The House and Senate were willing to strengthen the positions of party leaders in the 1970s for several reasons. First, the positions were occupied by relatively compliant individuals, Carl Albert in the House and Mike Mansfield in the Senate, who did not oppose reform. Second, there was a divided government. The Democrats held a substantial majority in both the House and Senate, and the White House was occupied by a Republican, at least until 1976. Strong leadership could provide a congressional counterweight to the chief executive. Third, the thrust of reform necessitated protection against disorganization and incoherent policy. The renewal of the caucus afforded an opportunity to enhance leadership authority in tandem with the party caucus.

The increase in power for party leadership came with the 1973 attack on Wilbur Mills and the Ways and Means Committee. The Policy and Steering Committee was created to develop party strategy. By 1975, it also selected committee members. This 24-person committee was dominated by the party leadership: the Speaker, majority leader, chief whip, chief deputy whip, three deputy whips and four members appointed by the Speaker were members of the committee. The power of the party leadership to dominate floor proceedings was also strengthened. In the House, the Speaker's power to refer bills was increased. In the Senate, the majority leader's ability to schedule and control floor debate was the result of reform. With these changes has also come a strengthened whip system. The resources and staff for the whip's office were increased. The new Congressional Budget Office also provides the leadership with information and resources with which to coordinate decision making.

CONGRESSIONAL POWER

The second trend in Congress from the 1970s has been a renewed sense of congressional power. There has been an effort to restore Congress' authority vis-a-vis the executive and to participate more fully as an equal partner in policymaking.

Beginning in 1973 with the Senate Select Committee's hearings into campaign abuses that led to Watergate and subsequently to the impeachment hearings in the House Judiciary Committee, Congress began to look anew at the executive branch and at the use of executive authority. The impeachment proceedings reestablished a sense of authority and challenge to the executive. The House Judiciary Committee refused to be rushed into impeachment, yet moved with reason and determination in voting impeachment.

In foreign policy, Congress was responding to Vietnam and Cambodia. It enacted the War Powers Act in 1973, which limited the power of the president to commit armed forces in any emergency to 90 days. Within 90 days, Congress, by concurrent resolution not subject to presidential veto, may direct the president to disengage such armed forces. It also directed the president to consult the Congress "in every possible instance" before the introduction of forces into combat. Not all supporters of Congress appreciate the War Powers Act. Some argue it gives power away to the chief executive because it recognizes his authority to declare war and encourages short-term intervention. Yet it seeks to redress a real problem. Any future president is obligated to consult Congress, and Congress has the last voice in the commitment of U. S. troops abroad.

In 1974 Congress took similar action on the domestic front with the Congressional Budget and Impoundment Control Act. The nonspending of appropriated funds as a discretionary power of the president has been curtailed. Under the act, the president is obligated to report to Congress any impoundment of appropriated funds. Either chamber, by a resolution, can direct the president to spend any funds temporarily set aside. Should the impoudment be intended as permanent, the action is void unless agreed to by both chambers within 45 days. A court order may be sought for the release of such funds not supported by Congress. This too allows the president some initiative, although it clearly is a reduction in discretion. The same act also created a new budgeting procedure and a Congressional Budget Office. The law gives Congress the resources to combat the presidential resources in fiscal and budgetary affairs.

Finally, Congress has become increasingly active in oversight activities. Through a broad range of devices—committee investigations, confirmation hearings, budget hearings, legislative clearance—congressional oversight of the executive has increased. A 1974 reform in the House required each committee to create an oversight subcommittee or to designate one subcommittee as an oversight committee. In 1977 the Senate reaffirmed its intent to engage in comprehensive oversight. Such devices as **sunset legislation** which fix a time for programs to expire and zero based budgeting are further evidence of the seriousness with which Congress takes examining the operation of the executive branch of government.

CONGRESSIONAL RESPONSIVENESS

There is striking evidence that Congress has been responsive to the changes in societal demands over the decade of the 1970s.

There have been marked changes in five areas of public policy: government management of the economy and national resources, social welfare, civil liberties, agricultural assistance, and international involvement. Aage Clauson and Carl Van Horn's study of political upheaval and congressional voting[31] found that policy positions in Congress, as analyzed through roll call votes, changed markedly on civil liberties and government management issues and that two new issues emerged—the relatively narrow question of agricultural subsidies and the more fundamental issue of national security. On governmental management issues there was a depolarization of parties, and the change in positions on civil rights indicated a lessening of support and increasing similarity in the positions of southern Democrats and Republicans. Said Clausen and Van Horn: "We have found considerable evidence of responsiveness to new conditions and new demands. One form of response has been change in policy positions occurring when continuing members reacted to the disturbing developments in the 1960s and 1970s. . . . Another form of responsiveness evidenced by Congress was the emergence of two new policy dimensions."[32]

Barbara Deckard has argued that these changes in policy positions are the result of a changed agenda for Congress; that although there has been a general decline in party voting, the nature of roll-call voting patterns has changed as the issues have changed.[33] In social welfare there has been a decline in housing programs, social security, and minimum wage issues, and they have been replaced

---

31. Aage R. Clausen & Carl E. Van Horn, "The Congressional Response to a Decade of Change, 1963–1972," *Journal of Politics* 39 (August 1977).
32. *Ibid.*, p. 665.
33. Barbara Deckard, "Political Upheaval and Congressional Voting: The Effects of the 1960's on Voting Patterns in the House of Representatives," *Journal of Politics* 38 (May 1976).

by votes on aid to the poor. For civil rights, the roll call shifted from civil rights for blacks, notably voting rights, to questions on the sale of housing, punishing student protesters, and Washington D.C. home rule. In agriculture Deckard found the agenda changed as well. Farm subsidies dominated the early 1960s, but by the late 1960s a new issue emerged—limiting subsidy payments to farmers. Concluded Deckard: "I would argue that the political upheavals of the 1960s led to a new political agenda in the Congress and that the upheavals, combined with the new agenda, increased the saliency of politics to the mass electorate. Southern Democrats and eastern Republicans responded to the changed political climate by bringing their voting behavior into closer alignment with the perceived preferences of their constituents."[34]

Congress is not perfect, and at times it is slow to respond. But as E. E. Schattschneider said long ago regarding American government, "the struggle for democracy is still going on." We cannot view Congress as either unequal or undemocratic; rather, Congress is a complex, changing organization wrestling with a changing environment.

SUMMARY

1. Congress has struggled with reform throughout the 1970s to reassert itself vis-a-vis the executive and to strengthen its internal procedures for doing business. Yet scandals continue to erode Congress' mature efforts at responsible government.

2. Members of Congress perform many roles. They are provided with considerable resources and staff to assist in these roles. Due to the multiple obligations placed on Congress, the legislative environment is demanding and time consuming. Members of Congress must balance the demands of Capitol Hill with those of the home constituency and reelection.

3. Congress is a decentralized institution where much of the work is done in committees and subcommittees. Party leadership seeks to provide cohesion and direction to this process; both forces have been strengthened by reform. Subcommittees have been increased and strengthened in power. Committee chairmen have been weakened by revitalization of the party caucus, and party leaders have a freer hand in scheduling legislation.

4. The legislative process is complex and burdensome. Reforms have alleviated some obstacles such as seniority, Rules committee, and the Senate filibuster. Yet the process remains serial and suffers under a heavy number of bills and resolutions.

5. Congress enters the 1980s with a renewed sense of power. The major

34. *Ibid.*, p. 345.

questions facing Congress are legislation and representation. Critics wonder if Congress can ever recapture major policy initiative from the executive branch. Supporters stress the democratic character of Congress to represent multiple and diverse interests in society.

TERMS

administrative
    assistant 494
appropriations 459
blue-collar caucus 462
Calendar
    Wednesday 490
careerism 463
casework 459
caucus 474
closed rule 490
cloture 492
committee on
    committees 475
conference
    committee 492
constituency 466
Democratic Study
    Group 498
discharge petition 487
exclusive committee 476

filibuster 492
floor manager 491
home style 466
majority leader 473
mark-up 488
minority leader 473
perquisites 466
pocket veto 494
resolution 483
Rules Committee 489-90
seniority 477
Speaker of the
    House 470
subcommittee bill of
    rights 487
subcommittee
    government 487
sunshine rules 488
unanimous consent 472
whip 473

RESEARCH PROJECTS

12.1. Writing Congressmen. Write your Congressman a letter on some issue before Congress about which you have an interest. You can find out the name and address of Congressmen from the *Congressional Directory* or Congressional Quarterly's *Washington Information Directory*. Does your Congressman have local or regional offices in your area? Finally, look at the response you get back from the Congressman. If several students in class write, compare the results for form and content. Do you think the responses are prepared responses?

12.2. Committee Assignments. Find out what the committee assignments are for your Representative and two Senators. You should look for the following information:

- Committee and subcommittee membership
- Seniority on those committees
- Chairs of committees and/or subcommittees

The best sources for this information are the *Congressional Directory* and Congressional Quarterly *Weekly Report* that list the organization of Congress every two years. Useful material may also be found in *Almanac of American Politics*.

12.3. Roll Call Votes. Select an issue on which the Senate and/or House of Representatives took a roll call vote. Analyze the vote, looking for levels of support by:

a. party

b. region

c. liberals versus conservatives

d. state delegation

Most editions of Congressional Quarterly, *Weekly Report* will have listings for important roll call votes. They also have periodic discussions on voting by party, region, ideology, and so on. You will need to look in the indexes to find these.

12.4. Congressional District. How well does the Congressman reflect the district he or she is elected from? Make a list of Congressmen from your state or describe the history of Congressmen from a district. Develop a set of characteristics from their socioeconomic background—age at election, sex, occupation, race and ethnic origins, income if available. These can be obtained from *Congressional Directories* and the *Almanac of American Politics*. Using census data, compare these characteristics with the dominant characteristics of the district in terms of percentage of people in age, income, occupation, and so on. Is there a similarity between District and Congressman? The best source for Congressional district data is *Congressional District Data Book,* published by the Bureau of the Census.

BIBLIOGRAPHY

Clapp, Charles. *The Congressmen: His Work as He Sees It*. New York: Doubleday, 1964.

Somewhat dated, the book provides a description of congressional life based upon interviews with Congressmen. Gives good and readable coverage to congressional relations, dealings with interest groups and constituents.

Dodd, Lawrence, and Bruce Oppenheimer (eds.) *Congress Reconsidered.* New York: Praeger Publishers, 1977.

Essays on Congress as it has changed in the 1970s. The first essays give an excellent overview while later articles cover specific facets of Congress and its activity with other units of government.

Fenno, Richard F. *Congressmen in Committees.* Boston: Little, Brown, 1973.

The best work on how Congressmen behave in committee. Provides a good discussion of the values and approaches used by different committees to meet their and their members' objectives.

Fenno, Richard F. *Home Style: House Members in Their Districts.* Boston: Little, Brown, 1978.

Fenno traveled with several Congressmen as they returned back home to their districts. What follows is Fenno's account of how Congressmen related their activity to their home constituents.

Fox, Harrison, and Susan Webb Hammond, *Congressional Staffs.* New York: Free Press, 1977.

The only work that covers congressional staffs in detail. Based on surveys and interviews of staff, the volume is a wealth of information and data on the impact of congressional staff on the legislative environment.

Froman, Lewis. *The Congressional Process: Strategies, Rules, and Procedures.* Boston: Little, Brown, 1967.

The most basic and thorough treatment of the rules and procedures of Congress and how they are used. While dated, the book is still basic to understanding the operation of Congress.

Hinckley, Barbara. *Stability and Change in Congress.* New York: Harper and Row, 1978.

A brief and readable overview of Congress. Hinckley gives a nice discussion of the forces of stability and how the roles and norms in Congress mutually reinforce each other to maintain that stability.

Matthews, Donald R. *U.S. Senators and Their World.* New York: Vintage Press, 1960.

Still the best work describing the U.S. Senate and its Senators. While largely dated, the work provides insight on the life and activity of U.S. Senators that remains valid.

Mayhew, David. *Congress: The Electoral Connection.* New Haven, Conn.: Yale University Press, 1974.

Mayhew argues the driving force to Congressional activity is the never ending quest for reelection. Much of what Congress does and what Congressmen do must be so understood, says Mayhew.

Miller, Clem. *Member of the House*. New York: Scribners, 1962.

An amusing and illustrative collection of letters written some time ago by Representative Clem Miller to his constituents. The letters provide useful insight into how Congress operates and what legislators do.

Olesezek, Walter. *Congressional Procedure and the Policy Process*. Washington, D.C.: Congressional Quarterly, 1978.

A newer account of congressional rules and procedures and how they affect the business of Congress. A readable and nontechnical book, Olesezek has included the recent changes and reforms in Congressional procedures.

Peabody, Robert, *Leadership in Congress*. Boston: Little, Brown, 1976.

The most thorough study of Congressional leadership. Peabody focuses on the individuals, their careers, selection, and relations with other Congressmen. Looks at stability and succession of leadership since the 1950s.

Redman, Eric. *The Dance of Legislation*. New York: Simon and Schuster, 1973.

A study of the legislative process, particularly the Senate, as Redman served on the staff of a Senator. Redman gives a lively account following a bill through the Senate, recounting all the political maneuvering and infighting.

Rieselbach, Leroy. *Congressional Reform in the Seventies*. Morristown, N.J.: General Learning Press, 1977.

A brief but good book that examines the efforts at Congressional reform in the 1970s. Provides a summary of reform efforts, but given the criteria Rieselbach establishes, Congressional reform was not too successful.

Ripley, Randall. *Congress: Process and Policy*. New York: W.W. Norton, 1978.

A textbook on Congress by a respected author on Congress. It provides excellent coverage of elections, committees, leadership, Presidential relations, and a typology for policy-making roles.

Chapter
13

The Judiciary

THE FRAMEWORK OF JUDICIAL POWER

An independent judiciary is viewed as one of the basic ingredients of a democratic society. A free people lean heavily upon the judiciary for protection, and this gives the courts great power and responsibility. But this same responsibility subjects judges to certain legal, political, social, and ideological restraints. They are inextricably drawn into political contests when broad issues of social policy call for the reallocation of resources. Judicial power has the capacity to do great good or great evil, depending upon how it is used and controlled.[1]

Clearly the most dramatic source of the Supreme Court's power is **judicial review,** the power of the Court to make authoritative interpretations of federal and state laws and political actions in relation to the United States Constitution. From *Marbury* v. *Madison,* which established the precedent for judicial review, down through *U.S.* v. *Nixon,* the Supreme Court has indefatigably defended "the province and duty of the judicial department to say what the law is."

The need for judicial interpretation is enhanced by the general and brief language employed by the Constitution. Some of the most important

---

1. This section borrows from Walter Murphy's discussion of the framework of judicial power, Walter Murphy, *Elements of Judicial Strategy* (Chicago: University of Chicago Press, 1964), pp. 12–18.

sections of the Constitution talk of "foreign and interstate commerce," "equal protection," "due process," and "the executive power." Nowhere are these spelled out, so that their edification rests less on the meaning of the words themselves than on the policy preferences of the nine men occupying the Supreme Court bench at any given time.

Judicial interpretation, however, is not restricted to Constitutional interpretations. There is equal need to render statutory interpretation. Courts are called on to interpret the meaning and extent of authorizing authority for a good many laws. This can extend from the President's use of war powers to economic regulations and rent and price controls. The judiciary, with its appellate process to the Supreme Court making the final judicial determination of the meaning of law, interprets the language and intent of such laws. This is perhaps inevitable as general laws must be applied to specific circumstances, or because Congress was tentative in defining the scope of law and left it to the courts to resolve the dilemma.

A second source of power is its prestige. The Supreme Court enjoys a moderately high opinion in the minds of the public. This base of public support plays a large role in maintaining the Court's ability to render decisions and obtain compliance.

Since the Court's power is exercised through actual legal suits involving two or more aggrieved parties in a real controversy, another source of judicial power is legitimation of action; that is, through the settlement of a case, one side is interpreted as having acted properly or interpreted the law. In the 1952 *Steel Seizure* case, President Truman was declared to have overstepped his authority and was required to return the steel mills to private ownership. And even though Richard Nixon had to turn over the tapes, the Court did agree to the constitutional doctrine of executive privilege—the first time a court formally acknowledged the principle. In a sense, it legitimized executive privilege for future presidents.

In a democracy there are many modes to legitimizing activity, not the least of which is the ballot box. The law suit is another. By declaring one course of action legitimate, or another unconstitutional, the Court plays a significant part in the legitimation of activity, and the peaceful resolution of conflict in a free society.

In *U.S.* v. *Nixon,* the Supreme Court made clear that no one—not even the president of the United States—is above the law. On this historic commitment to the rule of law rests "the very integrity of the judicial system and public confidence in the system."[2]

Respect for the law is one of the fundamental principles of democratic government; we recognize it as binding on governors and governed alike. It is essential to the equitable and just operation of popular government. Law represents the efforts of a community to establish rules of conduct. Law is an evolutionary, changing process; it is adjusted as the needs of the community change. Law may be enacted by political representatives of the people, codified into statutes, and

---

2. *U.S.* v. *Nixon,* 418 U.S. 683 (1974).

In what seems almost like once upon a time, Americans who lived in urban areas took their services for granted: police, firefighters, sanitation workers, bus drivers, hospital employees, teachers, city hall bureaucrats were all regarded—and regarded themselves—as a special kind of worker. They were employed by the public to provide essential services and they had a special responsibility to keep those services going without interruption. The "job actions," "sickouts," "slowdowns," "blue flu," and strikes that have become all too familiar today were simply unheard of, because there was a consensus that public servants were just that: They had real job security, in return for which they would not strike.

But by the early 1960s this consensus, which had held so strongly since the 1930s, had begun to erode under the pressure of rising prices, inflation, and unsure municipal budgets. Labor unions began to grow and to become more militant. Teachers formed and joined unions, along with clerical employees, police, sanitation workers, and firefighters. And whereas before 1966 there were fewer than 50 strikes a year nationwide, by 1977, 413 walkouts by public employees involved 171,000 workers—despite the fact that in many states strikes by public workers are illegal!

One dramatic instance of this change in consensus was a week-long wildcat strike by police and firefighters in August 1978 in Memphis, Tennessee, the heartland of law and order and patriotism. The dispute was over wages, and in the end the strikers won. But the city had to send for the National Guard and impose a nighttime curfew, and when picketing continued beyond the curfew hour, police officers had to arrest co-workers for breaking the law. The public was divided: People did not want a higher sales tax to pay for the raises, nor did they think public employees should strike. But at the same time there was sympathy for the strikers, because everyone understood the problem of trying to make ends meet in an inflationary economy. Although the mayor threatened to fire every person who went on strike, there were no reprisals. Police and firefighters went back to work with a 6 percent wage increase, a $30 a month raise the following April, and another increase in October 1979.

This is a familiar scenario these days, and the dilemma it reflects is a real one. If the law says a strike by public workers is illegal, shouldn't they be punished if they strike? But what about these workers' right to seek a decent wage? Public employees, who have been losing ground to inflation both in terms of salaries and in terms of mass layoffs because of budget crunches, feel that, having lost whatever advantages they had, they should be treated like any other worker and have the right to strike. In some states they do—but even in states where they do not, judges and city officials have been reluctant to enforce the law because it means alienating a large group of politically powerful people. It is a no-win situation for everyone, and with no general consensus about what is right, both courts and the public vacillate. If applying the law causes those who are sworn to uphold it to become lawbreakers, one of the fundamental pillars of our social consensus seems shaky indeed.

called statutory law. Law also may evolve out of judicial solutions to disputes, when unwritten legal customs and traditions are applied to render justice, as in common law and equity.

COMMON LAW

Common law is judge-made law. Its roots go back to the eleventh century in England. Judges, seeking settlement for disputes, applied prevailing customs to make decisions. Common law is based on precedent; it is a storehouse of custom and principles that informs and binds present decisions. The common law grew through the application of *stare decisis,* which means "to adhere to the decision." Judges look to past decisions, and the reasoning in previous similar cases, to aid in making a decision in the case presently before the bench. As a supplement to common law, Anglo-American law developed **equity.** Sometimes called the "conscience" of the law, equity is also based on stare decisis and is judge-made law. It allows the judge to take action where there is no law. Equity begins where the law ends; equity allows a judge to issue a decree to prevent future wrongs, usually in the form of a writ—an injunction or restraining order— to afford relief that otherwise would be unobtainable. Some states have separate courts of equity; the federal government does not.

STATUTORY LAW

The laws passed by legislative bodies are called statutes and are collectively known as statutory law. They spell out, in writing, and often in great detail, the intent of the law, to whom the law applies, and the penalties to assess when the law is violated. The law is **codified,** written and classified by subject matter. The **United States Code** is the national government's codification of existing statutory law.

When we think of statutory law, we generally distinguish between two types: private law and public law. **Private law** regulates the relationships between private citizens and persons in such areas as marriage, divorce, wills, deeds and contracts. This is often called **civil law.** Although the state is involved in applying and enforcing the statutes, the state is neither the subject of the right nor the object of the obligation. Legal regulations and obligations that apply to public officials, in their capacity as public officials, is known as **public law.** The public law is concerned with the definition, regulation, and enforcement of rights and obligations where the state is the subject of the right or the object of the obliga- tion. It regulates the public order, and includes the **criminal law.** Public law applies to the entire people of the nation, and regulates activity between citizens and government and between branches of the government. The sources of public law are the Constitution, legislative statutes, and administrative regulations. One great branch of public law is **constitutional law.** The Constitution is the source from which all other law is judged. But constitutional law includes not only the document, but all the interpretations of it rendered by the courts. The authoritative interpretation comes from decisions of the United States Supreme Court. Of all public law, the most rapidly expanding area is **administrative law.** With the vast delegation of rulemaking power to agencies of administration in recent decades, judges are frequently asked to review the propriety of those rules and regulations and to determine if fair procedures were followed in their promulgation and application.

Law, then, is the cornerstone of American democracy, the wellspring for a government of law, not persons. It is our nature to turn political issues into legal ones. This is what Alexis de Tocqueville observed a century and a half ago, when he said: "Scarcely any political question arises in the United States that is not resolved, sooner or later, into a judicial question."[3]

JUDICIAL POWER

What do courts do? Article III of the Constitution (Section 2) defines the jurisdiction of the federal judiciary, using the words "cases and controversies," which we have since interpreted to mean actual disputes capable of settlement by judicial means. But Section 2 only gives a brief indication of the scope of judicial activity. A more complete answer is found in the courts' jurisdictional powers; courts, in the American system, perform three functions: they administer law, they resolve conflicts, and they make policy.[4]

ADMINISTRATION OF THE LAWS

The judicial process is viewed as a neutral arena where two contending parties argue their differences in order to establish the culpability of one or other of the parties. In other words, the judicial process is an *adversarial process* to determine the guilt or innocence of the contending parties. Each side argues its side as hard and as best it can; from this presentation of evidence the court is supposedly best able to discover the truth. Law has defined certain acts to be crimes and fixed certain punishments. The court seeks to establish, as a neutral arbitrator, that wrongdoing was done, and then to administer the law and apply the penalty to the wrongdoer. But the court does not *define* the law; it seeks only to establish the facts in order to determine if the law has been violated.

3. Alexis de Tocqueville, *Democracy in America,* ed. Phillips Bradley (New York: Knopf, 1944), p. 280.
4. David W. Rohde and Harold J. Spaeth, *Supreme Court Decision Making,* (San Francisco: W. H. Freeman & Co., 1976), p. 2. This section relies heavily on the discussions in Rohde and Spaeth.

CONFLICT RESOLUTION

Because conflicts arise in every society, there needs to be a way to resolve disputes peacefully. In American society, courts perform this function. The conflict may be between private individuals, or it may involve government itself. Conflict resolution takes place within carefully crafted guidelines. Courts will hear only cases and controversies that are *justiciable,* actual disputes that may be settled by legal methods available to the court. Courts insist there be a case or controversy—a real conflict with injured parties directly affected by the outcome. They will not, for example, entertain ''political questions.''

The courts provide three services for the resolution of conflicts. First, there is the set of procedures and remedies which we call *due process*. Second, judicial settlement provides legitimation. The court resolves that the neighbor owns the land and the fence is permissible, and it rules that the president's claim of executive privilege must give way to the need for evidence in a criminal prosecution. The court puts a seal of approval on one course of action or another, or one interpretation of power over another. The third service in resolving conflict is the grant of governmental power to enforce a decision. The citizen may get a restraining order preventing a neighbor from tearing down the backyard fence, or the landlord secures an eviction notice for a tenant who has not paid rent. This is no different from the district court issuing a subpoena to President Nixon ordering him to deliver the tapes to the Watergate Special Prosecutor.

POLICYMAKING

In administering the laws, and in applying them, the court necessarily is drawn into policymaking. There is a maze of legal rules, contending legislative and executive rules, and constitutional principles to sort through. In finding which rules and procedures to apply to the specific case or controversy before it, the court makes policy. When judges resolve conflict, they legitimize action and create precedent.

Policymaking is rather unique to the American judicial system. We have placed in our courts, the ''least dangerous branch'' of government, the power to make authoritative interpretations on matters of public policy. Because we have a hierarchical structure, in which appellate courts review the decisions of lower courts and the Supreme Court is at the apex of the hierarchy, it is appellate courts, especially the Supreme Court, that are most concerned with matters of public policy. But all courts make policy. There are several reasons for this judicial role in policymaking in the American system:

1. The fundamental law, the Constitution, has been altered little since 1787; yet American society has changed drastically. So the Constitution must be adapted to a changing world.

2. Our distrust of excessive government, which has led us to use the courts to maintain individual liberties.
3. American federalism does not make a clear delineation between the powers state governments may exercise exclusively and the powers to be shared with the national government. The result has been a flood of litigation in which courts, ultimately the Supreme Court, have ruled on a case by case basis.
4. The system of separation of powers, in which the judiciary is the arbiter.
5. The power of judicial review, which provides a means for authoritative interpretation of the law.

JURISDICTION AND STANDING

But judges cannot initiate action; they can only respond to cases brought by others. Nor are courts free to respond to all suits brought before them. Two further conditions must be met: The court must have *jurisdiction,* and the party bringing action must have *standing* to sue.

Jurisdiction.   Jurisdiction is the authority of a court to hear and decide an issue brought before it. In the broadest sense, federal jurisdiction is outlined in Article III of the Constitution. No court can determine for itself its jurisdiction; that is established by the Constitution and law. Only the Supreme Court has power over its appellate jurisdiction. All other courts must receive all cases brought before them when they have jurisdiction.

We can distinguish three kinds of jurisdiction: subject matter, geographic, and hierarchical. Subject matter jurisdiction deals with the nature of the issues brought before the courts. The federal judiciary has general jurisdiction as outlined in the Constitution and law and special jurisdiction on subject matters defined for it by law. The major federal courts (district courts, courts of appeal, and the Supreme Court) have general jurisdiction. There are also courts with special subject matter jurisdiction: the Courts of Claims, the Customs Court, and the Court of Customs and Patent Appeals. States frequently divide subject matter jurisdiction even further into separate civil and criminal courts, which may be further subdivided so that some courts hear only minor (misdemeanor) criminal cases or specific civil cases. Whatever the subject matter jurisdiction of a court, it may hear cases only when one of the parties or the issue being litigated is located within the geographical area for which the court has responsibility. The federal courts use states as their geographical area for which the court has responsibility. The 94 federal district courts are divided into jurisdictional areas within a state. In addition, we distinguish between original jurisdiction and cases heard on appeal (appellate jurisdiction). Trial courts with subject matter jurisdiction try cases (original jurisdiction). On the federal level, these are the district courts. If there is a question over law or fact in rendering the decision, the case may be

Energy and Environmental Policy

By the late 1970s Americans were keenly aware of the need for comprehensive energy and environmental policies. The 1973 OPEC boycott, electrical brown-outs, and high gas and heating fuel bills lead to America's realization of an energy crisis. Fossil fuels were being depleted; America was dependent upon imported oil. Nuclear power raised serious questions for safety, as the Three Mile Island accident reminded people. The disposal of nuclear waste raised environmental concerns. Other forms of energy development either were not commercially feasible or caused environmental problems.

Traditional energy policy has focused on public utility regulation as a means to control production. Government policy has been designed to prevent overproduction of energy in order to stabilize the industry. Government sought to provide for the unlimited consumption of cheap energy and at the same time to guarantee industry a fair rate of profit. Participants in energy policy were limited to the producer groups—oil, coal, natural gas, and nuclear power manufacturers, relevant government agencies, and a few representatives and senators from producer states. Producer groups tended to dominate the policy agenda. But with the emergence of the energy crisis both the issues and the participants in energy policy changed. New groups were politicized into energy policies, consumer and environmental groups became active, western states' Congressmen took a more collective interest, and two new government agencies were established—the cabinet level Department of Energy and the Enviromental Protection Agency.

The reality of the energy crisis had forced public recognition of United States dependence on limited fossil fuels and imported oil. As a result the old energy policy of limited production and cheap energy was yielding to new energy policies. There are three approaches for solving the nation's energy crisis: technical–scientific, economic, and political.[1]

The technological–scientific approach seeks to utilize scientific research and technological applications to increase present energy supplies and create new sources of energy. It looks to past success in technological applications (as space) to increase efficiency and make practical solar, geothermal, wind, and synthetic energy sources. The economic solution demands a better allocation of energy supplies either by a free market mechanism or by government taxation to regulate consumption and revenues generated by the sale of energy. The political solution attempts to find a balance between consumer and producer interests. It tries to maintain supplies at an affordable price while still maintaining producer profitability, keeping both in balance.

These three approaches have produced a changed energy policy, employing in various combinations the three approaches for solving the present energy crisis. The new energy policy is lacking in comprehensiveness but the structure of the new policy is evident.

1. *All out production.* By abandoning the policy of limited production and cheap supplies, government has encouraged producers to expand production and pass the increased costs on to consumers as necessary. Industry is also encouraged to develop marginal sources of energy— strip mining and shale oil—and to explore new sources of fossil fuels—off

shore drilling and natural gas deposits. The policy places a premium on the technological–scientific approach to energy but also requires economic support to make the undertaking economically profitable for producers.

2. *Energy independence.* This policy employs both the technological–scientific and political approaches. It urges conservation techniques by industries and consumers in the use of petroleum while promoting the use of plentiful domestic supplies—coal and nuclear power. The long-term solution depends on technology developing alternative sources of energy as solar, geothermal, wind, and synthetic fuels.

1. J. Anderson, D. Brady, and C. Bullock, *Public Policy and Politics* in America, North Scituate, Mass.: Duxbury Press, 1978, pp. 39–40.

3. *Environmental protection.* The development of energy in either of the two previous policies must acknowledge concern for the environment. A major regulating responsibility of government is the protection of environmental quality. Energy production will be required to protect and to follow closer regulations for nuclear power safety and waste disposal, strip mining of coal, off shore drilling, and pollution.

Courts became an increasing avenue for promoting environmental protection. Already there are several environmental groups going to the courts seeking injunctions or restraints such as the Sierra Club, Ecology Action, Natural Resources Defense Council, Environmental Defense Fund, and public interest lawyers to name but a few.

---

reheard, or appealed to an appellate court that has jurisdiction to review the case. These are the courts of appeal and the Supreme Court.

Standing.   The other limitation to court power in hearing cases is the standing a person has to seek judicial redress. Standing is defined as the interest a person has in the judicial resolution of the conflict. Unlike jurisdiction, where the court has no discretion, the court does have some discretion in interpreting standing. In recent years, the Supreme Court and Congress have greatly liberalized the doctrine of standing, thereby permitting a far wider range of persons to challenge government or corporate interests in the courts.[5]

For standing in the federal courts, a party may file suit where there is a "case" or "controversy." All cases are controversies, but some controversies are not cases. For standing, courts require a real dispute between contending parties whose interests are directly at stake. There can be no friendly suits, cases dreamed up or feigned to render a desirable verdict. The federal courts also do not render advisory opinions.

Standing requires *legal injury*. It is not enough that two parties have a conflict. The conflict must pertain to something that is legally defined, either

5. Karen Orren, "Standing to Sue, Interest Group Conflict in the Federal Courts," *American Political Science Review* 70 (September 1976), pp. 723–41.

public or private. A public injury involves the commission of a crime. A private injury is referred to as a tort. The determination of standing may also be dependent on the finality of action. Courts will not entertain suits unless all nonjudicial remedies have been exhausted first. The issue must be "ripe"; that is, all administrative remedies must have been explored before filing suit. But with the press of certain social issues, normal bureaucratic delays, and agency caution, courts sometimes do not insist on exhaustive nonjudicial remedies before they admit some parties to standing.[6]

There can be no standing when an issue is a political question. What exactly is a political question? There is no clear answer. Any issue may be political if the court decides the matter is better resolved by some other agency or branch of government. The Supreme Court has ruled that the determination of a republican form of government in a state is a political question.[7] So too apparently is the authority to decide if a state has ratified a constitutional amendment.[8] What once was a political question, however, need not remain a political question forever. A classic example is legislative reapportionment. Once it was held to be a political question, but in 1962 the Supreme Court ruled that federal courts have jurisdiction and reapportionment is a justiciable issue. The result was the one person–one vote principle laid down by the Supreme Court in 1964.

THE AMERICAN COURT SYSTEM

The United States is a federal system, so it has a dual court system. The two court systems, national and state courts, exist side-by-side but remain largely separate in jurisdiction (Figure 13.1). The federal courts have no jurisdiction or control over state courts, except when the Constitution or federal law become an issue in a state court. Otherwise state court jurisdiction is fixed by state constitutions and federal court jurisdiction by the national Constitution.

The United States Constitution established only one court, the Supreme Court, and empowered Congress to create inferior courts (Figure 13.2). The very first Congress established the pattern, never seriously disturbed, of creating districts for courts of original jurisdiction and combining those districts into regions for appellate courts. Thus, the hierarchical pattern of the federal judiciary consists of district courts, courts of appeals, and one Supreme Court. There are also special courts and administrative law judges.

DISTRICT COURTS

United States District Courts are courts of original jurisdiction for the federal judiciary. There are 94 district courts, with at least one in each state; larger states have several district courts. One to twenty-seven judges are assigned within

6. *Dombrowski* v. *Pfister*, 380 U.S. 479 (1965).
7. *Luther* v. *Borden*, 7 Howard 1 (1849).
8. *Coleman* v. *Miller*, 307 U.S. 433 (1939).

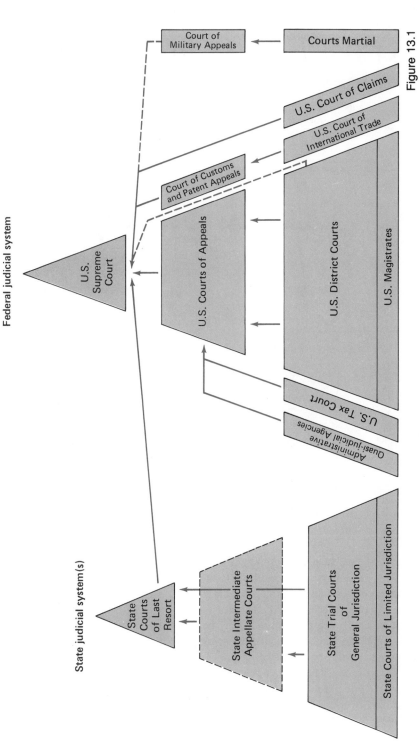

Figure 13.1

Organization of National and State Courts. (Otis Stephens and Gregory Rathjen, *The Supreme Court and the Allocation of Constitutional Power*, San Francisco, Calif.: W.H. Freeman and Company, Copyright © 1980.)

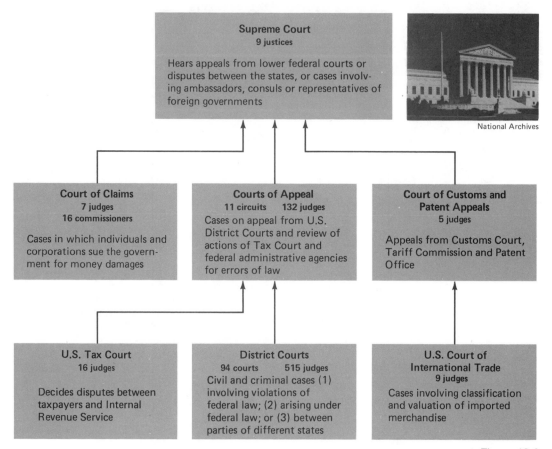

Figure 13.2

Organization of the Federal Courts. (*The Supreme Court Justice and the Law,* 2nd ed. Washington, D.C.: Congressional Quarterly Inc., 1977, p. 5)

each district to hear cases. At present, there are just over 515 permanent federal district court judgeships in the United States. All are appointed by the president of the United States and confirmed by the Senate. And like all federal judges, they hold office for life or good behavior.

District courts are trial courts. They hear almost all the civil and criminal cases arising under federal jurisdiction on original jurisdiction. As trial courts, district courts are the only federal courts to regularly employ *grand* (indicting) and *petit* (trial) juries. They do so in about half the cases they hear. District courts are also required to enforce as well as review administrative orders from executive agencies. Well over three-fourths of the cases filed in district courts are noncriminal. In 1977, 424,000 cases were filed in district courts: 130,567 civil cases,

Federal District Court Judge John J. Sirica. It was Judge Sirica who presided over the initial Watergate trial and who ordered President Nixon to turn over White House tapes. (United Press International)

39,786 criminal cases, and 254,000 bankruptcy cases.[9] There has been an explosion in the workload of the district courts, indeed, of the entire judiciary. The result is delay: The time interval between when a case is filed and when it comes to trial ranged from 4 to 39 months in 1959; from 4 to 49 months in 1965; and from 1 to 52 months in 1972–73.[10]

Because of workload, judges are provided with an array of assistants, all appointed by the judges themselves. There are court reporters, stenographers, clerks and bailiffs, and since 1971, court administrators who relieve the chief judges of administrative and management responsibilities. Most important are United States magistrates. Magistrates, appointed by district court judges for eight-year terms, handle the preliminary steps in the pretrial phase of a case. They can issue arrest warrants, hear evidence to bind an accused over for grand jury indictment, set bail, and try cases for minor federal offenses (with up to six months imprisonment and/or $500 fines).

9. Bureau of the Census *Statistical Abstract of the United States,* 1978, pp. 194 and 582.
10. Henry J. Abraham, *The Judicial Process* (New York: Oxford University Press, 1975), p. 159.

A majority of district court decisions are final. If there is an appeal, in rare instances a decision may be appealed directly to the Supreme Court. The great bulk of district decisions, however, go to the next highest layer in the federal hierarchy, the courts of appeals.

COURT OF APPEALS

Courts of appeals serve as the major appellate courts in the federal judicial system. They review civil and criminal decisions appealed from federal district courts. Additionally, courts of appeals have the responsibility for enforcing and reviewing the activities of executive agencies endowed with quasi-judicial functions, like the Interstate Commerce Commission, the Federal Comunications Commission, and the National Labor Relations Board. In 1977 the records show

"And don't go off whining to some higher court!"
Reprinted by permission of Cartoon Features Syndicate.

that 19,118 cases were filed with the courts of appeals: 4,738 criminal cases; 3,622 civil cases; 7,358 private civil cases; and 2,564 administrative appeals.[11] Approximately 90 percent of the cases end at this level; only a small fraction are appealed to the Supreme Court.

There are eleven federal courts of appeals, ten regional circuits (until 1948 the courts of appeals were known as Circuit Courts) and the eleventh circuit, known as the Court of Appeals for the District of Columbia. Four to twenty-six judges are assigned to each circuit. Because a court of appeals is an appellate court, cases are heard by three- to nine-judge panels. They may sit *en banc;* that is, the entire panel of judges for the court may sit to hear the case, but most often courts of appeal work in three-judge panels because of the increased work-load. They work from the case record of the trial court and only the more significant cases are scheduled for oral arguments. The remainder are judged solely on the basis of briefs and documents submitted to supplement the lower court record. New evidence may not be admitted in appellate proceedings; these courts work from the record established by the trial court of original jurisdiction.

First Circuit:	Maine, Massachusetts, New Hampshire, Rhode Island, Puerto Rico.
Second Circuit:	Connecticut, New York, Vermont.
Third Circuit:	Delaware, New Jersey, Pennsylvania, Virgin Islands.
Fourth Circuit:	Maryland, North Carolina, South Carolina, Virginia, West Virginia.
Fifth Circuit:	Alabama, Florida, Georgia, Louisiana, Mississippi, Texas, Canal Zone.
Sixth Circuit:	Kentucky, Michigan, Ohio, Tennessee.
Seventh Circuit:	Illinois, Indiana, Wisconsin.
Eighth Circuit:	Arkansas, Iowa, Minnesota, Missouri, Nebraska, North Dakota, South Dakota.
Ninth Circuit:	Arizona, California, Idaho, Montana, Nevada, Oregon, Washington, Hawaii, Alaska, Guam.
Tenth Circuit:	Colorado, Kansas, New Mexico, Utah, Oklahoma, Wyoming.

Court of Appeals for the District of Columbia.

THE SUPREME COURT

The Supreme Court is the national symbol of justice. There exists no higher court. The number of justices is fixed at nine by Congress. At times it has had as few as five (1789) and as many as ten (1863), but the number has remained at

11. *Statistical Abstract of the United States,* 1978, p. 194.

nine ever since the time of President Grant in 1869. There are eight associate justices and a Chief Justice.

The Supreme Court has both original and appellate jurisdiction, although its original jurisdiction is rarely exercised. Technically, the Constitution gives the Supreme Court original jurisdiction in four areas: (1) cases between the United States and one of the fifty states; (2) cases between two or more states; (3) cases involving foreign ambassadors, and other foreign public ministers and consuls; and (4) cases begun by a state against citizens of another state or aliens, or against a foreign country.[12] Congress has extended concurrent original jurisdiction to the federal district courts for area (3) and most cases in areas (1) and (4). The only real original jurisdiction exercised by the Supreme Court is in a case or controversy between two or more states. The Court has exercised this jurisdiction only 155 times since its first term back in 1789.

The principal work of the Supreme Court is *appellate*. As an appellate court, it serves as the final arbitrator in disputes, and as the final interpreter of law, including the Constitution of the United States. As an appellate court, the Supreme Court traditionally controls its own docket. Cases may come before the Court on a *writ of appeal,* as a matter of right. This happens when a state supreme court has declared a federal law or treaty unconstitutional, or upheld a state law that conflicts substantially with a federal law or treaty; it also happens when a federal court declares a federal law or treaty unconstitutional in a case in which the United States is a party to the suit. In these cases there is a statutory right of appeal to the Supreme Court. The Court, however, exercises considerable discretion in its "review." Unless a substantial federal question is involved, the Court may reject the appeal. On balance, 85 to 90 percent of such appeals are rejected, and the remaining cases constitute only about 10 percent of the Court's workload. All other cases reaching the Supreme Court come by invitation of the Court. There exists no right of appeal to the Supreme Court. Litigants, however, have the privilege of petitioning the Court to review a case. This is a *writ of certiorari,* meaning literally "making more certain." Of the cases the Supreme Court hears, 90 percent come on grants of writs of certiorari, and these are primarily issues to review the record from courts of appeal. Four Justices must approve before a writ of certiorari can be issued.

Table 13.1
Cases Filed With the U.S. Supreme Court

	1960	1965	1970	1975	1979
Original	0	8	20	14	17
Appellate	1,940	2,766	4,192	4,747	4,714

SOURCE: Statistical Abstract of the United States, 1979; Historical Statistics, Colonial Times to 1970. 1979 data, Office of the Supreme Court.

12. Abraham, *The Judicial Process,* p. 171.

SPECIAL COURTS

In addition to the courts created under Article III of the Constitution, Congress has established special courts, commonly known as *legislative courts* because they were created under Article I, the legislative article. Since their creation, however, Congress has changed the status of the three—the Court of Claims, U.S. Court of International Trade (formerly Customs Court), and the Court of Customs and Patent Appeals—to constitutional courts.

The difference between constitutional and special courts is that the special courts possess nonjudicial functions. They were created to aid Congress in the administration of specific statutes. Nonetheless, their judgments are as legal and authoritative as those of any constitutional court. Judges have been granted the same tenure—life or good behavior—as in the constitutional courts.

The United States Court of Claims.   The Court of Claims, created in 1855, has jurisdiction over property claims against the United States and contract damage suits. It provides relief for the numerous claims arising out of the taking of private property and charges of injury or negligence from a governmental employee. It consists of seven judges and fifteen "commissioners" who travel around the country to assist in gathering evidence.

U.S. Court of International Trade.   With nine judges, the Customs Court is the largest of the special courts. It has jurisdiction to review rulings and appraisals on imports by the collectors of customs, the "dumping" of exports by foreign countries, and decisions by the secretaries of Commerce and Labor for assistance under the Trade Act of 1974, and its decisions may be appealed to the Court of Customs and Patent Appeals.

The United States Court of Customs and Patent Appeals.   With five judges, this court has three primary functions: (1) it reviews decisions of the Customs Court regarding appraisal and duties levied on imported goods; (2) it reviews decisions of the Patent Office regarding the granting of patents and the use of trademarks; and (3) it reviews decisions from the Tariff Commission, which sets tariffs and regulates import practices.

The United States Court of Military Appeals.   More properly called a "legislative" court, this body of three civilian judges applies military law. It is the "civilian supreme court of the military," meaning it offers service personnel a genuine appellate court to interpret and apply military law. This court, at its discretion, reviews courts-martial involving bad conduct discharges and prison sentences of more than one year. It must review courts-martial of generals and admirals, cases where the death penalty was decreed, and cases certified for review by the Judge Advocate General.

The United States Tax Court.   Technically not part of the judiciary, this court is an adjunct of the executive branch, a quasi-administrative agency with independent status in the Internal Revenue Service. Yet its nineteen judges, appointed by the president for twelve-year terms, carry the official designation of judge. The Tax Court reviews IRS deficiency assessments of income, gift, self-employment, and excess profit taxes which have been challenged by the taxpayer. The Commissioner of Internal Revenue is always the defendant in such cases.

ADMINISTRATIVE LAW JUDGES

Sometimes called the "hidden judiciary," administrative law judges now outnumber district and appeals court judges sitting on the federal bench. There were 197 administrative law judges in 1947; in 1979, there were 1,072. Appeals of the rules and regulations promulgated by administrative agencies go to administrative law judges. They review the substance of agency rules, the procedures under which the rules were promulgated, and the fairness with which they are applied. The judges hold hearings, establish a record, and recommend action to agencies or commissions. Decisions can be appealed to the federal courts.

Table 13.2

Administrative Law Judges and Their Functions

Agency	Prime function	Number of Judges
Agriculture Department	Disciplinary proceedings against stockyard owners, produce dealers, brokers and commission merchants	5
Bureau of Alcohol, Tobacco and Firearms, Treasury Department	Permits to import, sell or distill alcoholic beverages	1
Civil Aeronautics Board	Airline route and rate applications, foreign permits and mergers	17
Coast Guard, Transportation Department	Misconduct, negligence and incompetence; narcotics cases	16
Commodity Futures Trading Commission	Suspension or revocation of broker registration	4
Consumer Product Safety Commission	Violations of laws protecting the public from hazardous products	1
Drug Enforcement Administration, Treasury Department	Suspension or revocation of controlled substance registration.	1
Environmental Protection Agency	Permits to discharge pollutants into navigable waters; pesticide registration	6
Federal Communications Commission	Licensing of radio, TV, cable and common carriers	14
Federal Energy Regulatory Commission	Natural gas pipeline construction, abandonment, curtailment and rates; electric rates	23
Federal Labor Relations Authority	Federal employee labor relations	4
Federal Maritime Commission	Investigation and suspension of proposed rates; complaint proceedings for reparations	7

Table 13.2 (Continued)

Agency	Prime function	Number of Judges
Federal Mine Safety and Health Review Commission	Violations of miner health and safety	12
Federal Trade Commission	False or misleading advertising; restraint of trade	12
Food and Drug Administration, Department of Health and Human Services	New drug applications; food standards, color additives	1
Housing and Urban Development Department	Lack of full disclosure in interstate land sales	1
Interior Department	Coal mine health and safety violations, mining claims and grazing rights	8
International Trade Commission	Import law violations	2
Interstate Commerce Commission	Complaints, investigations and applications in the regulation of railroads, motor carriers and water carriers	61
Labor Department	Unfair labor practices; longshoremen compensation claims and rates in government contracts	49
Maritime Administration, Commerce Department	Merchant marine operating differential subsidies; adequacy of U.S. flag service	3
Merit Systems Protection Board	Appeals from disciplinary proceedings against employees of the federal government	1
National Labor Relations Board	Unfair labor practices cases	98
National Transportation Safety Board	Challenges to denial, suspension or revocation of Federal Aviation Administration certification	6
Nuclear Regulatory Commission	Construction permit safety reviews	1
Occupational Safety and Health Review Commission	Employer health and safety violations	47
Postal Rate Commission	Changes in mail classification and rates	1
Postal Service	False representation to obtain money through the mail; second class mail privileges	2
Securities and Exchange Commission	Denial, suspension or revocation of broker-dealer and investment adviser registration	8
Social Security Administration, Department of Health and Human Services	Disability insurance and black lung benefits	660
	Total	1,072

SOURCE: Administrative Conference of the United States, January 1979. Reprinted in National Journal, July 28, 1979.

Slightly more than half of the administration law judges work for one agency, the Social Security Administration, hearing disability cases. Judges are appointed by the agency for which they work. The Office of Personnel Management examines and interviews candidates, and sends the top candidates to the agency for final selection. Administrative law judges have life tenure. President Carter recommended that administration of the judges be shifted from the Office of Personnel Management to the Administrative Conference of the United States, that terms of office be limited to seven years, and that reappointment be dependent on the conference finding judges "affirmatively well qualified."

JUDICIAL ADMINISTRATION

Chief Justice Warren Burger, an outspoken critic of judicial administration, has urged modernization of the federal court system. President Carter, too, proposed reform. Over the years, Congress has aided the process of judicial administration by establishing the Judicial Conference of the United States and the Administrative Office of the United States Courts.

The Judicial Conference, presided over by the Chief Justice of the United States Supreme Court, consists of the chief judge from each of the courts of appeals and one district court judge from each of the eleven circuits. Its function is "to submit to Congress an annual report of the proceedings of the Judicial Conference and its recommendation for legislation." Through the use of committees, the conference studies procedures for the federal courts and formulates recommendations for use by the courts. These recommendations automatically become effective unless rejected by Congress within 90 days. The Administrative Office of the United States Courts handles much of the day-to-day routine for the federal judiciary. It prepares the budgets for the courts, examines dockets, procures supplies, and keeps records.

Because of the workload and the delays, President Carter made a series of recommendations, early in 1979, to lighten the load for the federal judiciary. The proposals included these recommendations:

1. Mandatory court-ordered arbitration at the district court level for tort and contract civil cases that involve only claims of money less than $100,000. Decisions could be appealed.
2. Increased magistrate jurisdiction to allow them to judge criminal misdemeanor and simple civil cases. Consent of both sides would be necessary.
3. Suits between citizens of different states (diversity jurisdiction) where no federal questions of law are involved would be abolished as part of the federal court's jurisdiction.
4. A new national United States Court of Appeals for the Federal Circuit.

This proposal would combine the present Court of Claims with the Court of Customs and Patent Appeals as a single appellate court, retaining the jurisdiction of the present two courts plus adding jurisdiction for patent and trademark appeals.

JUDGES AND JUDICIAL SELECTION

Unlike members of Congress or the president, or most state judges who are elected by the people, federal judges are appointed. The Constitution places in the hands of the president, with the advice and consent of the Senate, the selection of all federal judges.

THE SELECTION PROCESS

The Senate's role is jealously guarded; the practice of "senatorial courtesy" gives a senator veto power over judicial appointments in his or her state, provided the senator is of the same party as the president. The Senate Judiciary Committee sends a "blue slip" to the home state senator asking for an evaluation of the nominee. If the letter is not returned, or returned with objection, the nominee is not even considered. Presidential nominations come before the president upon the recommendation from the attorney general's office, which actively recruits and screens potential nominees to balance the president's interests against judicial qualifications, regional balance, and interest group support for any nominee.

An increasingly important factor, since the Truman administration, is the evaluation of judicial nominees made by the American Bar Association's (ABA) twelve-member Committee on the Federal Judiciary. Over the years it has become an important, influential voice in nominating federal judges, at least below the level of the Supreme Court. President Carter sought to broaden the evaluation process beyond the Senate and the ABA by establishing, through executive order, citizen nominating commissions in the states. Senators must consult these private citizen groups in evaluating judicial qualifications. The order carries no enforcement mechanism, however, so Carter's proposal struck an accommodationist balance between his personal belief and the harsh reality of senatorial politics.

There is also ample evidence that candidates campaign for the federal bench. Interest groups increasingly feel they have a right to make their thoughts known. Judges on the court also campaign. The Chief Justice of the Supreme Court may consult with the president on proposed nominees. The impact of a letter from a Supreme Court justice cannot be dismissed. The selection of federal judges is, and remains, a political process. Every president is keenly aware that the people he places in the federal judiciary, through their decisions, help make public policy.

THE CHARACTERISTICS OF FEDERAL JUDGES

The characteristics of federal judges reflect the considerations that go into the appointment process: political party, ideology, and prior experience.

Political Party.   Party affiliation has always been an important consideration in the selection of federal judges; presidents rarely choose judges from the opposite party. They acknowledge this, but when pressed to divide judgeships between the parties, President Kennedy responded: ''I would hope that the *paramount* consideration in the appointment of a judge would not be his political party but his qualifications. . . .''[13]

Ideology.   Equally important as party is finding a person with the right kind of judicial philosophy. Lincoln expressed this view with his appointment of Salmon P. Chase as Chief Justice in 1864: ''We wish for a Chief Justice who will sustain what has been done in regard to emancipation and the legal tenders.'' Eisenhower bitterly complained that his biggest mistake as president

Table 13.3

Partisan Affiliation of Newly Appointed Federal Circuit and District Judges, 1933-1977

Party affiliation of confirmed judgeship nominees

President (party) years	Democrat	Republican	Percent same as President's party
Roosevelt (D), 1933–45	188	6	97%
Truman (D), 1945–53	116	9	93
Eisenhower (R), 1953–61	9	165	95
Kennedy (D), 1961–63	111	11	91
Johnson (D), 1963–69	159	9	95
Nixon (R), 1969–74	15	192	93
Ford (R), 1974–77	12	52	81
Carter (D), 1977–80	258	6	98

SOURCE: Congressional Quarterly, *Weekly Report,* November 19, 1977. p. 2444. Data for Carter from *U.S. World Report,* October 20, 1980, p. 50.

13. *The New York Times,* August 31, 1960, cited in Harold Chase, *Federal Judges.*

was the appointment of Earl Warren, who became the symbol of a liberal, activist court, as Chief Justice. Richard Nixon pledged to appoint a law-and-order judiciary, and his 207 appointments, including four Supreme Court justices, have had a profound impact on public policy.

The question of ideology is important because judges serve for life; their influence can extend long beyond the tenure of the appointing president. Presidents seek to assess past career performance, public controversies, political activities, as well as recommendations from trusted advisors. One study concluded that presidents are generally successful in appointing judges who conform to their expectations about three-fourths of the time.[14] Conversely, judges contemplating retirement often do so with an eye cast to the White House. Chief Justice Taft refused to retire in 1929. "I must stay on the Court," he stated, "in order to prevent the Bolsheviks from getting control." Justice Douglas tried, unsuccessfully, to delay retirement until a Democrat replaced Gerald Ford as president.

Prior Experience.   The basic prerequisite for judicial appointment is the law degree. Many judges have no or limited prior judicial experience; most, however, have public experience. Since judicial appointments are political appointments, federal judges normally have distinguished themselves in political careers. Approximately one-third of the district court judges served previously as state judges; three in five judges on the court of appeals came with judicial experience, largely as federal district court judges. Carter's record for nominations is somewhat better: 45 percent of district court and appellate court nominations have had prior judicial experience.[15] Of the 102 individual justices appointed as of 1974 to the Supreme Court, 42 had no judicial experience at all, and only 20 percent had ten or more years of previous judicial experience. In fact, many of the eminent names from the roll of Supreme Court Justices are persons with no prior judicial experience.

Carter and Judicial Selection.   Late in 1978, Congress created the largest number of new federal court judgeships ever created by a single act of Congress.[16] President Carter will have had the unique opportunity of filling 117 new district court judgeships and 35 new positions added to the Courts of Appeal. The bill will decrease the caseload of present judges and reduce the backlog of cases; it also gave President Carter the largest block of judicial patronage in our nation's history.

The act contained a provision making the creation of these new judgeships dependent upon the promulgation of merit selection standards and guidelines. President Carter had, on numerous occasions, voiced his support for merit selec-

14. Robert Scigliano, *The Supreme Court and the Presidency* (New York: The Free Press, 1971), p. 146.
15. Congressional Quarterly, *Weekly Report,* October 27, 1979, p. 2419.
16. The Omnibus Judgeship Act, 1978.

FACT FILE

SUPREME COURT NOMINATIONS, 1789–1979

Name	State	Date of birth	Nominated by	To replace	Date of appointment	Confirmation or other action[a]	Date resigned	Date of death	Years service
John Jay	N.Y.	12/12/1745	Washington		9/24/1789	9/26/1789	6/29/1795	5/17/1829	6
John Rutledge	S.C.	1739	Washington		9/24/1789	9/26/1789	3/5/1791	6/21/1800	1
William Cushing	Mass.	3/1/1732	Washington		9/24/1789	9/26/1789		9/13/1810	21
Robert H. Harrison	Md.	1745	Washington		9/24/1789	9/26/1789 (D)		4/20/1790	
James Wilson	Pa.	9/14/1742	Washington		9/24/1789	9/26/1789		8/21/1798	9
John Blair	Va.	1732	Washington		9/24/1789	9/26/1789	1/27/1796	8/31/1800	6
James Iredell	N.C.	10/5/1751	Washington	Harrison	2/8/1790	2/10/1790		10/20/1799	9
Thomas Johnson	Md.	11/4/1732	Washington	Rutledge	11/1/1791	11/7/1791	3/4/1793	10/26/1819	1
William Paterson	N.J.	12/24/1745	Washington	Johnson	2/27/1793	2/28/1793 (W)		9/9/1806	13
William Paterson[c]			Washington	Johnson	3/4/1793	3/4/1793			
John Rutledge[b]			Washington	Jay	7/1/1795	12/15/1795 (R, 10–14)			
William Cushing[b]			Washington	Jay	1/26/1796	1/27/1796 (D)			
Samuel Chase	Md.	4/17/1741	Washington	Blair	1/26/1796	1/27/1796		6/19/1811	15
Oliver Ellsworth	Conn.	4/29/1745	Washington	Jay	3/3/1796	3/4/1796 (21-1)	9/30/1800	11/26/1807	4
Bushrod Washington	Va.	6/5/1762	Adams	Wilson	12/19/1798	12/20/1798		11/26/1829	31
Alfred Moore	N.C.	5/21/1755	Adams	Iredell	12/6/1799	12/10/1799	1/26/1804	10/15/1810	4
John Jay[b]			Adams	Ellsworth	12/18/1800	12/19/1800 (D)			
John Marshall	Va.	9/24/1755	Adams	Ellsworth	1/20/1801	1/27/1801		7/6/1835	34
William Johnson	S.C.	12/27/1771	Jefferson	Moore	3/22/1804	3/24/1804		8/4/1834	30
H. Brockholst Livingston	N.Y.	11/25/1757	Jefferson	Paterson	12/13/1806	12/17/1806		3/18/1823	16
Thomas Todd	Ky.	1/23/1765	Jefferson	New Seat	2/28/1807	3/3/1807		2/7/1826	19
Levi Lincoln	Mass.	5/15/1749	Madison	Cushing	1/2/1811	1/3/1811 (D)		4/14/1820	
Alexander Wolcott	Conn.	9/15/1758	Madison	Cushing	2/4/1811	2/13/1811 (R, 9–24)		6/26/1828	
John Quincy Adams	Mass.	7/11/1767	Madison	Cushing	2/21/1811	2/22/1811 (D)		2/23/1848	
Joseph Story	Mass.	9/18/1779	Madison	Cushing	11/15/1811	11/18/1811		9/10/1845	34
Gabriel Duvall	Md.	12/6/1752	Madison	Chase	11/15/1811	11/18/1811	1/10/1835	3/6/1844	23
Smith Thompson	N.Y.	1/17/1768	Monroe	Livingston	12/8/1823	12/19/1823		12/18/1843	20
Robert Trimble	Ky.	11/17/1776	J. Q. Adams	Todd	4/11/1826	5/9/1826 (27–5)		8/25/1828	2
John J. Crittenden	Ky.	9/10/1787	J. Q. Adams	Trimble	12/17/1828	2/12/1829 (P)		7/26/1863	
John McLean	Ohio	3/11/1785	Jackson	Trimble	3/6/1829	3/7/1829		4/4/1861	32
Henry Baldwin	Pa.	1/14/1780	Jackson	Washington	1/4/1830	1/6/1830 (41–2)		4/21/1844	14
James M. Wayne	Ga.	1790	Jackson	Johnson	1/7/1835	1/9/1835		7/5/1867	32

Name	State	Birth	President	Replaced	Nominated	Confirmed	Vote	Resigned/Retired	Died	Yrs
Roger B. Taney	Md.	3/17/1777	Jackson	Duvall	1/15/1835	3/3/1836	(P)			
Roger B. Taney[c]			Jackson	Marshall	12/28/1835	3/15/1836	(29–15)		10/12/1864	28
Philip P. Barbour	Va.	5/25/1783	Jackson	Duvall	12/28/1835	3/15/1836	(30–11)		2/25/1841	5
William Smith	Ala.	1762	Jackson	New Seat	3/3/1837	3/8/1837	(23–18) (D)		6/10/1840	
John Catron	Tenn.	1786	Jackson	New Seat	3/3/1837	3/8/1837	(28–15)		5/30/1865	28
John McKinley	Ala.	5/1/1780	Van Buren	New Seat	9/18/1837	9/25/1837			7/19/1852	15
Peter V. Daniel	Va.	4/24/1784	Van Buren	Barbour	2/26/1841	3/2/1841	(22–5)		5/31/1860	19
John C. Spencer	N.Y.	1/8/1788	Tyler	Thompson	1/9/1844	1/31/1844	(R, 21–26)		5/18/1855	
Reuben H. Walworth	N.Y.	10/26/1788	Tyler	Thompson	3/13/1844	6/17/1844	(W)		11/27/1867	
Edward King	Pa.	1/31/1794	Tyler	Baldwin	6/5/1844	6/15/1844	(P)		5/8/1873	
Edward King[c]			Tyler	Baldwin	12/4/1844	2/7/1845	(W)			
Samuel Nelson	N.Y.	11/10/1792	Tyler	Thompson	2/4/1845	2/14/1845		11/28/1872	12/13/1873	27
John M. Read	Pa.	2/21/1797	Tyler	Baldwin	2/7/1845		No action		11/29/1874	
George W. Woodward	Pa.	3/26/1809	Polk	Baldwin	12/23/1845	1/22/1846	(R, 20–29)		5/10/1875	
Levi Woodbury	N.H.	12/22/1789	Polk	Story	12/23/1845	1/3/1846			9/4/1851	5
Robert C. Grier	Pa.	3/5/1794	Polk	Baldwin	8/3/1846	8/4/1846		1/31/1870	9/26/1870	23
Benjamin R. Curtis	Mass.	11/4/1809	Fillmore	Woodbury	12/11/1851	12/29/1851		9/30/1857	9/15/1874	5
Edward A. Bradford	La.	9/27/1813	Fillmore	McKinley	8/16/1852		No action		11/22/1872	
George E. Badger	N.C.	4/13/1795	Fillmore	McKinley	1/10/1853	2/11/1853	(P)		5/11/1866	
William C. Micou	La.	1806	Fillmore	McKinley	2/24/1853		No action		4/16/1854	
John A. Campbell	Ala.	6/24/1811	Pierce	McKinley	3/22/1853	3/25/1853		4/26/1861	3/13/1889	8
Nathan Clifford	Maine	8/18/1803	Buchanan	Curtis	12/9/1857	1/12/1858	(26–23)		7/25/1881	23
Jeremiah S. Black	Pa.	1/10/1810	Buchanan	Daniel	2/5/1861	2/21/1861	(R, 25–26)		8/19/1883	
Noah H. Swayne	Ohio	12/7/1804	Lincoln	McLean	1/21/1862	1/24/1862	(38–1)	1/24/1881	6/8/1884	19
Samuel F. Miller	Iowa	4/5/1816	Lincoln	Daniel	7/16/1862	7/16/1862			10/13/1890	28
David Davis	Ill.	3/9/1815	Lincoln	Campbell	12/1/1862	12/8/1862		3/7/1877	6/26/1886	14
Stephen J. Field	Calif.	11/4/1816	Lincoln	New Seat	3/6/1863	3/10/1863		12/1/1897	4/9/1899	34
Salmon P. Chase	Ohio	1/13/1808	Lincoln	Taney	12/6/1864	12/6/1864			5/7/1873	8
Henry Stanbery	Ohio	2/20/1803	Johnson	Catron	4/16/1866		No action		6/26/1881	
Ebenezer R Hoar	Mass.	2/21/1816	Grant	New Seat	12/15/1869	2/3/1870	(R, 24–33)		1/31/1895	
Edwin M. Stanton	Pa.	12/19/1814	Grant	Grier	12/20/1869	12/20/1869	(46–11)		12/24/1869	
William Strong	Pa.	5/6/1808	Grant	Grier	2/7/1870	2/18/1870		12/14/1880	8/19/1895	10
Joseph P. Bradley	N.J.	3/14/1813	Grant	New Seat	2/7/1870	3/21/1870	(46–9)		1/22/1892	21
Ward Hunt	N.Y.	6/14/1810	Grant	Nelson	12/3/1872	12/11/1872		1/7/1882	3/24/1886	9
George H. Williams	Ore.	3/23/1823	Grant	Chase	12/1/1873		(W)		4/4/1910	
Caleb Cushing	Mass.	1/17/1800	Grant	Chase	1/9/1874	1/13/1874	(W)		1/2/1879	
Morrison R. Waite	Ohio	11/29/1816	Grant	Chase	1/19/1874	1/21/1874	(63–0)		3/23/1888	14

Name	State	Date of birth	Nominated by	To replace	Date of appointment	Confirmation or other action[a]	Date resigned	Date of death	Years service
John M. Harlan	Ky.	6/1/1833	Hayes	Davis	10/17/1877	11/29/1877		10/14/1911	34
William B. Woods	Ga.	8/3/1824	Hayes	Strong	12/15/1880	12/21/1880 (39–8)		5/14/1887	6
Stanley Matthews[c]	Ohio	7/21/1824	Hayes	Swayne	1/26/1881	No action			
Stanley Matthews[c]			Garfield	Swayne	3/14/1881	5/12/1881 (24–23)		3/22/1889	7
Horace Gray	Mass.	3/24/1828	Arthur	Clifford	12/19/1881	12/20/1881 (51–5)	7/9/1902	9/15/1902	20
Roscoe Conkling	N.Y.	10/30/1829	Arthur	Hunt	2/24/1882	3/2/1882 (39–12) (D)		4/18/1888	
Samuel Blatchford	N.Y.	3/9/1820	Arthur	Hunt	3/13/1882	3/27/1882		7/7/1893	11
Lucius Q. C. Lamar	Miss.	9/17/1825	Cleveland	Woods	12/6/1887	1/16/1888 (32–28)		1/23/1893	5
Melville W. Fuller[c]	Ill.	2/11/1833	Cleveland	Waite	4/30/1888	7/20/1888 (41–20)		7/4/1910	22
David J. Brewer	Kan.	1/20/1837	Harrison	Matthews	12/4/1889	12/18/1889 (53–11)		3/28/1910	20
Henry B. Brown	Mich.	3/2/1836	Harrison	Miller	12/23/1890	12/29/1890	5/28/1906	9/4/1913	15
George Shiras Jr.	Pa.	1/26/1832	Harrison	Bradley	7/19/1892	7/26/1892	2/23/1903	8/2/1924	10
Howell E. Jackson	Tenn.	4/8/1832	Harrison	Lamar	2/2/1893	2/18/1893		8/8/1895	2
William B. Hornblower	N.Y.	5/13/1851	Cleveland	Blatchford	9/19/1893	1/15/1894 (R, 24–30)		6/16/1914	
Wheeler H. Peckham	N.Y.	1/1/1833	Cleveland	Blatchford	1/22/1894	2/16/1894 (R, 32–41)		9/27/1905	
Edward D. White	La.	11/3/1845	Cleveland	Blatchford	2/19/1894	2/19/1894		5/19/1921	17
Rufus W. Peckham	N.Y.	11/8/1838	Cleveland	Jackson	12/3/1895	12/9/1895		10/24/1909	13
Joseph McKenna	Calif.	8/10/1843	McKinley	Field	12/16/1897	1/21/1898	1/5/1925	11/21/1926	26
Oliver W. Holmes	Mass.	3/8/1841	Roosevelt	Gray	12/2/1902	12/4/1902	1/12/1932	3/6/1935	29
William R. Day	Ohio	4/17/1849	Roosevelt	Shiras	2/19/1903	2/23/1903	11/13/1922	7/9/1923	19
William H. Moody	Mass.	12/23/1853	Roosevelt	Brown	12/3/1906	12/12/1906	11/20/1910	7/2/1917	3
Horace H. Lurton	Tenn.	2/26/1844	Taft	Peckham	12/13/1909	12/20/1909		7/12/1914	4
Edward D. White[b]			Taft	Fuller	12/12/1910	12/12/1910			10[b]
Charles E. Hughes	N.Y.	4/11/1862	Taft	Brewer	4/25/1910	5/2/1910	6/10/1916	8/27/1948	6
Willis Van Devanter	Wyo.	4/17/1859	Taft	Moody	12/12/1910	12/15/1910	6/2/1937	2/8/1941	26
Joseph R. Lamar	Ga.	10/14/1857	Taft	White	12/12/1910	12/15/1910		1/2/1916	5
Mahlon Pitney	N.J.	2/5/1858	Taft	Harlan	2/19/1912	3/13/1912 (50–26)	12/31/1922	12/9/1924	10
James C. McReynolds	Tenn.	2/3/1862	Wilson	Lurton	8/19/1914	8/29/1914 (44–6)	1/31/1941	8/24/1946	26
Louis D. Brandeis	Mass.	11/13/1856	Wilson	Lamar	1/28/1916	6/1/1916 (47–22)	2/13/1939	10/5/1941	22
John H. Clarke	Ohio	9/18/1857	Wilson	Hughes	7/14/1916	7/24/1916	7/18/1922	3/22/1945	6
William H. Taft	Ohio	9/15/1857	Harding	White	6/30/1921	6/30/1921	2/3/1930	3/8/1930	8
George Sutherland	Utah	3/25/1862	Harding	Clarke	9/5/1922	9/5/1922	1/17/1938	7/18/1942	15
Pierce Butler	Minn.	3/17/1866	Harding	Day	11/23/1922	12/21/1922 (61–8)		11/16/1939	17
Edward T. Sanford	Tenn.	7/23/1865	Harding	Pitney	1/24/1923	1/29/1923		3/8/1930	7
Harlan F. Stone	N.Y.	10/11/1872	Coolidge	McKenna	1/5/1925	2/5/1925 (71–6)		4/22/1946	16
Charles E. Hughes[b]			Hoover	Taft	2/3/1930	2/13/1930 (52–26)	7/1/1941		11[b]
John J. Parker	N.C.	11/20/1885	Hoover	Sanford	3/21/1930	5/7/1930 (R, 39–41)		3/17/1958	

536

Name	State	Date of birth	Nominated by	To replace	Date of nomination	Confirmation vote	Date confirmed	Date service terminated	Date of death	Years of service
Owen J. Roberts	Pa.	5/2/1875	Hoover	Sanford	5/9/1930		5/20/1930	7/31/1945	5/17/1955	15
Benjamin N. Cardozo	N.Y.	5/24/1870	Hoover	Holmes	2/15/1932		2/24/1932		7/9/1938	6
Hugo L. Black	Ala	2/27/1886	Roosevelt	Van Devanter	8/12/1937	(63–16)	8/17/1937	9/17/1971	9/25/1971	34
Stanley F. Reed	Ky.	12/31/1884	Roosevelt	Sutherland	1/15/1938		1/25/1938	2/25/1957		19
Felix Frankfurter	Mass.	11/15/1882	Roosevelt	Cardozo	1/5/1939		1/17/1939	8/28/1962	2/22/1965	23
William O. Douglas	Conn.	10/16/1898	Roosevelt	Brandeis	3/20/1939	(62–4)	4/4/1939	11/12/1975	1/19/1980	36
Frank Murphy	Mich.	4/13/1890	Roosevelt	Butler	1/4/1940		1/15/1940		7/19/1949	9
Harlan F. Stone[b]			Roosevelt	Hughes	6/12/1941		6/27/1941		4/22/1946	5[b]
James F. Byrnes	S.C.	5/2/1879	Roosevelt	McReynolds	6/12/1941		6/12/1941	10/3/1942	4/9/1972	1
Robert H. Jackson	N.Y.	2/13/1892	Roosevelt	Stone	6/12/1941		7/7/1941		10/9/1954	13
Wiley B. Rutledge	Iowa	7/20/1894	Roosevelt	Byrnes	1/11/1943		2/8/1943		9/10/1949	6
Harold H. Burton	Ohio	6/22/1888	Truman	Roberts	9/19/1945		9/19/1945	10/13/1958	10/28/1964	13
Fred M. Vinson	Ky.	1/22/1890	Truman	Stone	6/6/1946		6/20/1946		9/8/1953	7
Tom C. Clark	Texas	9/23/1899	Truman	Murphy	8/2/1949	(73–8)	8/18/1949	6/12/1967	6/13/1977	18
Sherman Minton	Ind.	10/20/1890	Truman	Rutledge	9/15/1949	(48–16)	10/4/1949	10/15/1956	4/9/1965	7
Earl Warren	Calif	3/19/1891	Eisenhower	Vinson	9/30/1953		3/1/1954	6/23/1969	6/9/1974	15
John M. Harlan	N.Y.	5/20/1899	Eisenhower	Jackson	1/10/1955	(71–11)	3/16/1955	9/23/1971	12/29/1971	16
William J. Brennan Jr.	N.J.	4/25/1906	Eisenhower	Minton	1/14/1957		3/19/1957			
Charles E. Whittaker	Mo.	2/22/1901	Eisenhower	Reed	3/2/1957		3/19/1957	4/1/1962	11/26/73	5
Potter Stewart	Ohio	1/23/1915	Eisenhower	Burton	1/17/1959	(70–17)	5/5/1959			
Byron R. White	Colo.	6/8/1917	Kennedy	Whittaker	3/30/1962		4/11/1962			
Arthur J. Goldberg	Ill.	8/8/1908	Kennedy	Frankfurter	8/29/1962		9/25/1962	7/25/1965		3
Abe Fortas	Tenn.	6/19/1910	Johnson	Goldberg	7/28/1965		8/11/1965	5/14/1969		4
Thurgood Marshall	N.Y.	6/2/1908	Johnson	Clark	6/13/1967	(69–11)	8/30/1967			
***Abe Fortas**[b]*			Johnson	Warren	6/26/1968	(W)	10/4/1968			
Homer Thornberry	Texas	1/9/1909	Johnson	Fortas	6/26/1968	No action				
Warren E. Burger	Minn.	9/17/1907	Nixon	Warren	5/21/1969	(74–3)	6/9/1969			
Clement Haynsworth Jr.	S.C.	10/30/1912	Nixon	Fortas	8/18/1969	(R, 45–55)	11/21/1969			
G. Harrold Carswell	Fla.	12/22/1919	Nixon	Fortas	1/19/1970	(R, 45–51)	4/8/1970			
Harry A. Blackmun	Minn.	11/12/1908	Nixon	Fortas	4/14/1970	(94–0)	5/12/1970			
Lewis F. Powell Jr.	Va.	9/19/1907	Nixon	Black	10/21/1971	(89–1)	12/6/1971			
William H. Rehnquist	Ariz.	10/1/1924	Nixon	Harlan	10/21/1971	(68–26)	12/10/1971			
John Paul Stevens	Ill.	4/20/1920	Ford	Douglas	11/28/75	(98–0)	12/17/1975			

Boldface - Chief Justice; Italics - Did not serve. D Declined; W Withdrawn; P Postponed; R Rejected a. Where no note is listed, confirmation unrecorded.
b. Earlier court service. See above. c. Earlier nomination not confirmed. See above.
SOURCE: Congressional Quarterly, Inc., *Guide to the U.S. Supreme Court.*

be appointed strictly on the basis of merit without any consideration of political aspects or influence.'' Once in office, Carter proceeded to establish, through executive order, merit selection commissions in the several states making federal district court appointments, and 13 circuit court nominating commissions. The Justice Department has recommended that these panels be composed of lawyers and nonlawyers, with representation of both sexes and minority groups. They are to recommend three to five persons for each vacancy.

The establishment of merit panels has received a mixed reaction. Several states have created such panels. Senator Kennedy is pressing to change the Senate's time-honored practice of senatorial courtesy. Some states and senators have refused to use merit panels, calling them political bodies in disguise. On the other side, the merit panels are criticized by Common Cause and the NAACP's Legal Defense and Educational Fund as not actively recruiting women and minority candidates. One percent of federal judges are women and four percent are black. Former Attorney General Griffin Bell conceded that the panels had not changed the politics of the appointments; only two of the federal judges appointed by Carter have been Republicans.

THE SUPREME COURT

The Supreme Court is more than a legal institution. It serves as our national symbol of justice; and it must resolve questions of national policy. As was the case in *U.S.* v. *Nixon,* and again in *California Regents* v. *Bakke,* the Court was called on to make difficult and profoundly consequential decisions. ''To consider the Supreme Court of the United States strictly as a legal institution is to underestimate its significance in the American political system,'' said Robert A. Dahl, ''for it is also a political institution, an institution, that is to say, for questions of national policy.''[17]

POLITICS, POLICY, AND PUBLIC OPINION

The past three decades have witnessed considerable expansion of judicial activity in the United States. The scope of judicial policymaking has broadened. While judges continue to hear cases long a part of their judicial workload, their activity has expanded into areas once thought unfit for adjudication: welfare administration, prison life, educational policies, road and bridge building, automotive safety standards, and natural resource management.[18] The courts are now actively involved in making social policy.

17. Robert A. Dahl, ''Decision Making in a Democracy: The Role of the Supreme Court as an Internal Policy Maker,'' *Journal of Public Law,* Vol. 6 (1958), p. 279.
18. See Donald L. Horowitz, *The Courts and Social Policy* (Washington, D.C.: Brookings Institution, 1977), p. 4.

The development of judicial activism extends back to the Warren Court and the 1954 school desegregation cases, which signaled a willingness on the part of the courts to test the conventional boundaries of judicial action. Social groups frustrated by the political process now saw the opportunity to use litigation to achieve their goals.

Historically, we might have expected the period of judicial activism to be followed by a period of quietism. This was true in the wake of *Dred Scott* (1857), and in the activities of the Court after overturning New Deal legislation in the 1930s. The Supreme Court has no independent means to enforce its decrees. It must follow the dictates of public opinion, and the president is more in touch with the public than the Court. So a period of activism is usually followed by one of restraint as the president, through the appointive process, redresses the balance. This is the assumed check on judicial power: a Court that goes too far is replaced, through judicial appointment, with a more passive set of justices.

Yet this has not happened in the wake of the Warren Court. The Burger Court, in the main, has continued the policy of judicial activism. The Court has continued to make social policy that has altered American life. It was the Burger Court in 1971 that ordered busing of schoolchildren to overcome segregation in urban cities; the *Roe* v. *Wade* decision permitting abortions is a statement affecting the essence of human rights; and the *Bakke* decision illustrates just how deeply the Court intends to further affirmative action programs. We are in a period of institutionalized activism: "The power of the Court has been exercised so often and so successfully over the last 20 years, and the ability to restrict or control it by either new legislation, Constitutional amendments, or new appointments has met with such uniform failure, that the Court, and the subordinate courts, are now seen as forces of nature, difficult to predict and impossible to control."[19]

INSTITUTIONALIZED ACTIVISM

Judicial activism is now an institutionalized feature of the Supreme Court. In the absence of legislative remedies, the Court has shown a propensity to "take the heat" and involve itself in social policy. Often Congress has built into its programs the opportunity for social groups to seek judicial relief if policies are promulgated without their being consulted or have a negative impact on them. But much of the activity has occurred independently of Congress and the bureaucracy. Courts have ordered special education for disturbed, retarded, or hyperactive students. Courts have struck down residency requirements for eligibility for welfare payments and have established comprehensive programs of care and treatment for the mentally ill in hospitals. And they have done all this by using the traditional judicial powers; these decisions were extensions of regular activities, not departures.

19. Nathan Glazer, "Toward an Imperial Judiciary," *Public Interest,* No. 41, (Fall 1975), p. 110.

Serving on a jury

Some of the regulations for jury service vary from place to place, but everywhere in the United States jury service is the duty of a citizen by law. Your notice to serve is issued in the form of a legal summons; it is not a request, and failure to answer is punishable under the law. Here is how the system generally works.

1. An office of the court designated to handle jurors obtains lists of the names of those residing within a certain area. Voter registration lists are used everywhere; some places also use motor vehicle registration and license lists, data from the Internal Revenue Service, and even names from public utility or telephone company billings.

2. All those who appear on these various lists are sent questionnaires to determine if they are qualified to be jurors. (A juror, for example, must be a citizen of the United States.)

3. The names of those selected as qualified are printed on slips of paper, and the slips placed in a drum. Selection of those to be summoned is done by drawing randomly from the drum, just like in a lottery.

4. The selected persons are sent summonses to appear for jury duty on a certain date. By law, the summons must be answered and the person must serve, but there are, of course, exemptions: a registered nurse, a doctor in private prac-

tice, a lawyer, the sole proprietor of a business, and certain other categories of people may appear before a judge, present their reasons for not wishing to serve, and be exempted.

5. A trial juror serves at least two weeks (maybe more if he or she is chosen to serve on the jury for a lengthy trial). A grand juror (a person chosen to sit on a jury that hears charges to determine whether or not a case should go to trial) must serve at least twenty days.

6. Jurors are paid a daily stipend for serving; the amount varies from locality to locality, but it is usually a token and does not equal the person's regular salary.

7. Being chosen for jury service does not automatically mean that you will be part of a trial. You go to the courthouse each morning, and as cases come up on the calendar, you may be chosen to be among those questioned by the lawyers for each side, and even then you may or may not be selected as a juror. Lawyers, of course, are looking for people they think will render a fair judgment in their particular case and have the right to select jurors.

8. If you are selected, you may be part of the judicial process in anything from a minor traffic accident to a sensational murder, and once on the jury, you serve until the case has been disposed of, whether it is two weeks or a month.

New Areas of Adjudication.   One cause of institutionalized activism is the emergence of new areas of adjudication. For example, housing and welfare rights are the result of litigation, prompted to some degree by congressional legislation. Courts have ordered building programs and decreed that states must "adequately fund" such institutions as mental hospitals and education. In the area of personal freedom, the courts have ruled on marital and cohabitation rights as well as abortion. They have awarded alimony to fathers because of the wife's ability to pay. Courts have equalized school expenditures for teachers' salaries, decreed that bilingual education be provided for Mexican-American children, and suspended the use of National Teacher Examinations by school boards. Courts have required the Farmers Home Administration to restore a disaster loan program, stopped the Forest Services from cutting timber, and told the Corps of Engineers to maintain the nation's non-navigable waterways.[20]

New Litigants with Standing to Sue.   The thrust of the Court into new and broad areas of social policy is, in part, a result of the Court's willingness to broaden standing to initiate litigation to include private litigants, and to permit class action suits.

In the early 1960s, only one such private center, the NAACP Legal Defense Fund, was granted standing. Beginning with the Great Society and the Economic Opportunity Act, however, several poverty law centers were created. As a result of the NAACP precedent, there was a rash of litigation in almost every conceivable area of social policy: welfare, housing, health, education, and penology. New clients—Mexican-Americans, Indians, mental health patients, prisoners, welfare recipients, and women—found the law a potentially quick and effective means to social change.

THE SUPREME COURT IN ACTION

The Supreme Court's term runs from the first Monday in October through the end of June. The Court must narrow down the 5,000 cases filed to a manageable number of cases for the term. The first month or so is spent deliberating over which cases the Court will take. Then the rest of the term, normally through April, is spent calling for briefs and listening to oral arguments. May and June are when the Court renders its verdicts and releases opinions explaining the basis for its decisions.

FILING ON THE DOCKET

To handle the requests for consideration of cases, the Supreme Court has established three dockets. All requests are assigned to one of the three: the original docket contains all cases filed for decision under the Court's original jurisdic-

20. Horowitz, *The Courts and Social Policy,* pp. 4–5.

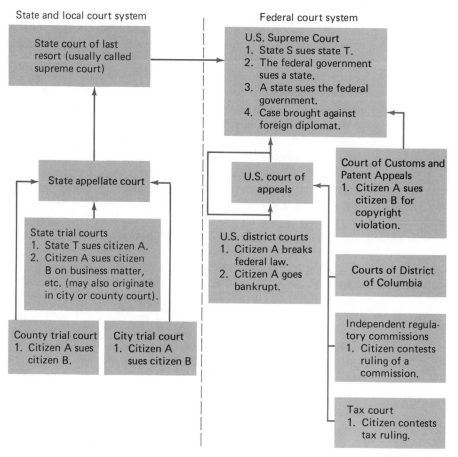

State and local court system

Federal court system

State court of last resort (usually called supreme court)

U.S. Supreme Court
1. State S sues state T.
2. The federal government sues a state.
3. A state sues the federal government.
4. Case brought against foreign diplomat.

State appellate court

U.S. court of appeals

Court of Customs and Patent Appeals
1. Citizen A sues citizen B for copyright violation.

State trial courts
1. State T sues citizen A.
2. Citizen A sues citizen B on business matter, etc. (may also originate in city or county court).

U.S. district courts
1. Citizen A breaks federal law.
2. Citizen A goes bankrupt.

Courts of District of Columbia

County trial court
1. Citizen A sues citizen B.

City trial court
1. Citizen A sues citizen B

Independent regulatory commissions
1. Citizen contests ruling of a commission.

Tax court
1. Citizen contests tax ruling.

Figure 13.3

How cases go through the state and local court systems and the federal court systems to get to the Supreme Court.

tion; the appellate docket contains all the formal appeals from lower court decisions. There are strict rules for filing certiorari writs; in addition, all writs of appeal are put here. The miscellaneous docket contains all the petitions filed *in forma pauperis* (in the manner of a pauper). There is a growing trend for jailhouse lawyers and indigent appellants to use the relaxed standards of the Court to ask for a review of their cases. Requests are often handwritten or typed single-page arguments prepared and researched by the petitioner, using jail libraries and word of mouth advice.

Several times during the term, the justices meet to consider the requests. They discuss and vote on which petitions should be granted. If any four justices approve a petition, it is accepted. Only a small fraction are accepted; less than one in ten cases is accepted for formal legal action. Figure 13.3 illustrates how a case gets to the Supreme Court.

Table 13.4
Disposition of Cases Before the Supreme Court, 1977-1980

| | 1979-1980 | | | 1978-1979 | | | 1977-1978 | | |
| | Cases acted on during term | Cases granted review on merit | | Cases acted on during term | Cases granted review on merit | | Cases acted on during term | Cases granted review on merit | |
		Number	Percent		Number	Percent		Number	Percent
Original	0	0	0	0	0	0	3	0	0
Appellate in forma pauperis	2,249	32	1.4	1,996	19	1.0	1,935	14	0.7
Paid	2,509	199	7.9	2,021	144	7.1	1,946	145	7.5

SOURCE: Office of the Supreme Court.

However, acceptance for review by the Supreme Court does not necessarily mean further briefs or oral argument. Many cases are dealt with *summarily,* they are decided upon on the basis of the information submitted with the request. In 1978-1979 only 168 (3.6 percent) of the 4,731 cases on the docket were accepted for argument; the remainder were dismissed, denied, summarily decided, or carried over (110 or 2.3 percent were by summary judgment; 3,670 or 77.6 percent were denied or dismissed).[21]

ORAL ARGUMENT

The first two weeks of each month the Court listens to oral arguments. The last two weeks are spent behind closed doors discussing the merits of the case and writing opinions.

Before the oral presentation, the lawyers for the contending sides submit *briefs,* lengthy written documents citing law and precedent supporting their position. Forty copies are required! The contending party has 45 days to submit a brief; the answering party, 30 days thereafter. The Court may also invite parties who have an interest in the outcome to prepare *amicus curiae,* or "friend of the court" briefs. Important cases draw numerous *amicus curiae* briefs; the 1954 *Brown* case had 50, and *Bakke* drew 57 such briefs.

At 10 A.M. on the designated day, oral arguments are heard. The black-robed justices file into the marble chamber from behind the velvet curtain. Led by the Chief Justice, Justices sit in order of seniority, faced by the tables for the counselors. Time for oral argumentation is strictly limited and enforced. Each side is allotted one hour, sometimes only a half-hour. Two lights on the lectern inform counsel of time remaining. When a white light flashes, five minutes re-

21. Spaeth and Rhode, *Supreme Court Decision Making,* p. 59.

main; a red light flashes when time has expired, and the counsel must stop immediately.

Oral argument is informal. Reading from the brief is frowned on; Rule 44 of the Court states that "the Court looks with disfavor on any oral argument that is read from a prepared text." The Justices frequently interrupt with questions. In one case several years ago, the Justices interrupted counsel 84 times during two hours of oral argument. In the *Bakke* case, Archibald Cox, representing the Regents of the University of California, was asked the meaning of benchmark ratings, why Asian-Americans were included in the special admissions program, and the relevance of Title VI of the Civil Rights Act. For his part, Reynold Colvin, Mr. Bakke's attorney, got this question from Mr. Justice Powell:

> . . . the University doesn't deny or dispute the basic facts. We are here . . . primarily to hear a Constitutional argument . . . I would like help, I really would, on the Constitutional issues. Would you address that?[22]

Whether oral argument sways the outcome of a case is questionable. Nonetheless, it may have a dramatic impact on the issues before the court. Justice John Harlan thought oral argument critical; he said oral argument "may in many cases make the difference between winning and losing, no matter how good the briefs are."[23]

When the United States is a party to a case before the Supreme Court, the lawyer for the government is the solicitor general of the United States, the third highest ranking official in the Justice Department. The solicitor general oversees all federal appeals in the courts and approves all appeals to the Supreme Court. Archibald Cox, who defended the University of California, Davis, in *Bakke* and who was the first special prosecutor in Watergate, was solicitor general in the Kennedy administration. Before Thurgood Marshall was appointed to the Supreme Court, he served as solicitor general for Lyndon Johnson.

CONFERENCE

Friday is conference day. Approximately 30 times a session, the justices are summoned by a buzzer at 10 A.M. on Friday. They meet in secret to consider requests for petitions and to discuss cases just argued before the Court. Seated around a large U-shaped table, the justices hear the Chief Justice outline the facts and explain his view of how the case should be decided. Each Justice, in terms of seniority, is then expected to present his opinion on the case. When all opinions and arguments have been voiced, a vote is taken. Each Justice votes in reverse order of seniority, with the Chief Justice voting last, and the case is decided.

22. Cited in Allan P. Sindler, *Bakke, De Funis, and Minority Admissions* (New York: Longman, 1978), p. 257.
23. Cited in Spaeth and Rhode, *Supreme Court Decision Making*, p. 60.

The members of the Supreme Court. (United Press International)

The Chief Justice plays a special significant role in the conference. As chair of the conference, he has ample opportunity to influence its agenda. Since he leads the discussion, he can present the facts and precedents that govern much of the discussion. As moderator, he "makes peace" among the several justices. And finally, by voting last, the Chief Justice may be the deciding vote on a controversial case. The Court is noted for its 5 to 4 rulings. On appeal, the decision most frequently is either to affirm a lower court ruling or to reverse that ruling. The reasons for that decision are stated in the opinion of the Court, the official basis for the Court's ruling in a case. Justices who voted with the majority, but for different reasons, may write a separate concurring opinion. Justices in the minority, who opposed the verdict, can write a dissenting opinion.

OPINION WRITING

If a case was relatively simple and commanded a strong majority, the decision may be announced in a *per curium* opinion. Such an opinion is short and unsigned; it simply announces the decision and the facts in the decision. Most cases selected by the Supreme Court, however, require a lengthy, signed opinion.

If the Chief Justice voted in the majority, he can write the opinion or assign it to one of the other Justices in the majority. If the Chief Justice is not among the majority, the task falls to the senior Justice in the majority. The selection of the opinion writer is crucial, as the task of building a majority consensus is difficult. The justice assigned the task of writing the opinion first writes a draft that is circulated to the other members of the Court. His majority members may suggest revisions, and the writer tries to accommodate their suggestions. At this juncture, the other Justices either commit themselves to the opinion or write concurring opinions. In the famous *Bakke* case, there was a total of six opinions for the court.

The opinion is the core of the policymaking role of the Supreme Court. It is the means by which the Court announces its decisions and justifies its reasoning to the world. Through its opinions, the Supreme Court lays down principles that govern future courts and, inevitably, the nation.

MARSHALLING THE COURT

Decision making in the Supreme Court does not just happen. It is the result of a complex, and oftentimes intimately personal, relationship between nine justices.[24] Justices bargain intently with one another to secure a desired point of law or the needed votes to produce a majority. Persuasion and majorities are not automatic, nor do they happen with the voting at the culmination of the conference. Each justice is a distinct personality, intelligent and learned in the law. A justice considers ways to "capture" another justice's vote. "A Justice would have to consider the tactics open to him to carry out his efforts to persuade on the merits of his policy choice, to capitalize on personal regard, to bargain, to threaten, and if possible, to have a voice in the selection of new personnel."[25]

In order to produce a majority on the high court, Justices form blocs and devise strategic plans to trade on the judicial philosophy and professional reputation of other justices. Sections of opinions are written to accommodate judicial positions; drafts of opinions are rewritten to keep a waivering vote. Murphy notes the Justices trade on personal regard to win votes, they selectively vote or withhold votes to gain support, they volunteer to draft opinions in hopes of soothing differences of opinion, they bargain with philosophy and points of law, and they co-opt new members to become part of voting blocs in the Court.[26]

Woodward and Armstrong's *The Brethren* report this intensely political atmosphere to judicial decision making. Votes are often switched on important and

24. For a behind the scenes glimpse of the personal nature of Supreme Court proceedings see Bob Woodward and Scott Armstrong's *The Brethren* (New York: Simon and Schuster, 1979).
25. Walter F. Murphy, *Elements of Judicial Strategy*, p. 43.
26. Walter Murphy, *Elements of Judicial Strategy*, Chapter 3.

sensitive cases. Furthermore, with the Chief Justice voting last, oftentimes reserving his vote, he can command a majority and assign the opinion, thereby influencing the breadth of judicial policymaking.

COMPLIANCE

For all the weight and power attached to Supreme Court decisions, the Court faces important problems in assuring compliance. The Court depends on the interpretation and action of other political institutions and policymakers for compliance. It is by no means automatic—or swift.

In its decisions, the Court is speaking to lower federal courts, state courts, and other political institutions, requiring or forbidding some particular activity, and these institutions and individuals may see or interpret the Court's decisions in different ways. In 1954, reaction to the desegregation decision caused one federal judge to disqualify himself from subsequent desegregation litigation because he opposed the decision. Another federal judge went further; he refused to implement the ruling and declared: "I believe that it will be seen that the Supreme Court based its decision on no law but rather on what the Court regarded as more authoritative, more psychological knowledge."[27]

This does not mean that federal courts can, or do, disregard Supreme Court decisions. By and large there is compliance. Attorneys can appeal, as happened in the example cited above in the desegregation case. The appellate courts overturned the lower court, and compliance with the Supreme Court was effected. In the case of police interrogations and *Miranda* rights, courts will utilize the exclusionary rule and throw out tainted evidence illegally obtained in violation of the guidelines set forth in *Miranda*. Public officials are harder to control, and yet by and large they comply. Richard Nixon publicly stated he would only obey a "definitive decision" regarding release of the Watergate tapes. When the 8 to 0 verdict in *U.S.* v. *Nixon* was handed down, he complied.

LIMITATIONS ON JUDICIAL POWER

For all its power and prestige, the Supreme Court faces the very basic limitation of having to wait for suits to be brought to it. There must be a real case or controversy that is capable of judicial settlement. And there are the numerous "technical" checks that limit judicial power: jurisdiction, standing, a justiciable question, and the rule of precedent.

The Court is also limited by other institutions and courts. It is influenced by Congress and the president as well as by lower court interpretations of Supreme Court decisions.

27. Cited in Henry J. Abraham, *The Judicial Process,* p. 224.

Congress has control of the appellate jurisdiction of the Supreme Court as well as its size. From time to time, it may take issues from the Court's jurisdiction. It may deny funding for the enforcement of decisions it does not like. Congress tried several times to prevent funding for busing to integrate school districts, and there have been attempts to eliminate public funds to pay for legal abortions. Congress always possesses the power to initiate a constitutional amendment to overturn a Court decision. The Sixteenth Amendment for the personal income tax is one example of congressional response to the Court's declaring a law unconstitutional.

The president and the executive branch also limit the Court. The president's appointment power has already been noted. The matter of bringing suit in the first place rests with the solicitor general and the Department of Justice. Whether or not a decision is appealed and ultimately reaches the Supreme Court depends, in part, on the Justice Department's decision. And enforcement of Court decisions depends on the executive branch. The president may press for vigorous enforcement, or he may do so reluctantly, or not at all. When the Court rendered the *Brown* decision in 1954, it was President Eisenhower who sent in the federal marshals to desegregate the University of Mississippi and the Little Rock, Arkansas high school.

Finally there is the limitation judges place upon themselves. Known as *judicial self-restraint,* this doctrine holds that judges should refrain from imposing their own values and policy preferences and decide a case on its merit and according to established legal precedent. For the most part, the Justices exercise their authority with great caution and with careful attention to the weight of legal precedent. They understand that they cannot create solutions to the political controversies that divide a nation, no matter how actively they engage in policymaking.

Courts are limited institutions of power. They are part of the checks and balances process of our governmental scheme, and the constraints on them are severe. Ultimately, the judiciary needs the concurrence of Congress, the president, and the bureaucracy. The ultimate shaping of public policy cannot proceed in a vacuum. For better or worse, the continued existence and strength of democracy rests on our tripartite governmental system. Democracy and the values of freedom and equality are not the sole province of the courts. They are, ultimately, the responsibility of each and every citizen.

The ability of the courts to provide social policy guidance in a period of change is all the more critical when other institutions are groping for direction and purpose, and the Court has responded. The danger comes when we expect too quick a response and too much of a response. What the Court, including the Burger Court, has been doing is not likely to change drastically. We are likely to see further convergence among policymaking institutions, including the Court. Groups are likely to continue to appeal to the courts for social justice. And the Courts will probably throw the questions back to the traditional policy institutions, Congress and the president, but perhaps with a recommendation for action.

SUMMARY

1. American democracy is premised on the notion of a government of law, not men. To the courts fall the prime responsibility of maintaining the rule of law. Judges administer the law, both civil and criminal. They are also charged to interpret administrative rules and regulations as well as the Constitution itself.

2. Judicial power extends far beyond the neutral arena to resolve conflict; courts are actively involved in politics and create policy. There are, however, several technical questions to jurisdiction that the courts maintain, thereby preserving the reputation as a neutral arbitrator.

3. The American court system is a dual-court system. National and state courts exist side by side but have separate jurisdictions. Federal courts include district courts, courts of appeals, and one Supreme Court. In addition there are several special, legislative courts.

4. All federal judges are appointed by the President of the United States. Political party and judicial philosophy are important criteria in the selection of federal judges.

5. The Supreme Court occupies a very special role in American politics. It derives its most important power from its political pronouncements and interpretations on the constitutional powers of other political institutions. The Supreme Court acts as the guardian of the Constitution.

6. Judicial activism has become a permanent feature of the Supreme Court, indeed of all courts. Able to control the cases it hears, the Supreme Court selects only the most important cases that affect American political and social life. The process at arriving at decisions by the Supreme Court is complex and intensely personal among nine individual Justices.

RESEARCH PROJECTS

13.1. Supreme Court Justices. Write a biography of a Supreme Court Justice. Among other things you will want to note:
- education and legal training
- judicial experience
- political reputation and activity
- appointment to the court
- record while on the court
- judicial philosophy

There are several good biographies you can read on the more eminent justices on the high court over the years. You can also go to the major decisions the justice wrote while a member of the court.

13.2. Blocs on the Court. The Court has been noted for its famous 5–4 decisions. Pick one or two years and look at the major decisions of the Court for that year. List the judges who were in the majority and those in the minority. Can you find any pattern of justices consistently voting together? Are there "swing" justices? The easiest way to do this is to go to the *United States Reports* that reports all decisions of the Supreme Court and lists the cases and the voting by the justice, listed by majority or concurring opinions and dissenting opinions.

13.3. Judicial Procedures. Go to a courthouse in your area, either federal or local court. Sit and observe the proceedings. Are these trails, arraignments, bail hearings? You may need a good law dictionary to understand what is going on. Try and make a list of the activities and the procedures employed. You will want to understand two things: (a) much judicial activity taking place is not trial proceedings; and (b) there are many legal procedures involved in the law. When you are done go over the activities and procedures and see if you understand them and why they went together as they did.

BIBLIOGRAPHY

Abraham, Henry. *The Judicial Process*. New York: Oxford University Press, 1975.

An excellent book and the standard for examining the organization and function of the federal judiciary. While there is considerable information, the book gives an overview of law and the courts.

Berger, Raoul. *Government by Judiciary: The Transformation of the Fourteenth Amendment*. Cambridge, Mass.: Harvard University Press, 1975.

Berger provides a historical and scholarly analysis to the origin and transformation of the Fourteenth Amendment. It is Berger's contention that modern jurists have misinterpreted and misused the Amendment.

Chase, Harold. *Federal Judges: The Appointing Process*. Minneapolis, Minn.: University of Minnesota Press, 1972.

The basic work on the process and politics of appointing federal judges. There is considerable historical information and detail from the Kennedy administration in this examination of the prerogative of the president.

Cox, Archibald. *The Role of the Supreme Court in American Government*. New York: Oxford University Press, 1976.

A very brief but insightful discussion of the role of the Supreme Court in modern political events. Cox reacts with some sympathy to the active role of the court in deciding matters of social policy.

Horowitz, Donald. *The Courts and Social Policy*. Washington, D.C. Brookings Institution, 1977.

A very basic work illustrating the active role courts have come to play in determining matters of social welfare. Sometimes technical and often critical, Horowitz provides an essential understanding of what has happened with the courts and social policy.

Jacob, Herbert. *Justice in America*. Boston: Little, Brown, 1978.

A fairly brief but concise book that looks at the role of law and the courts in the political process. Gives a good overview of the functions, participants, and structure of American courts.

Krislov, Samuel. *The Supreme Court in the Political Process*. New York: Macmillan, 1965.

A fine overview of the Supreme Court as it has affected the political process. Krislov makes the case that the Court is enmeshed in politics, discussing judicial appointments, the court's agenda, and decision making.

Murphy, Walter F. *Elements of Judicial Strategy*. Chicago: University of Chicago Press, 1964.

Probably the best and most comprehensive effort to examine how Supreme Court justices reach a verdict. Murphy examines the behavior of judges in seeking to influence one another.

Murphy, Walter, and Herman Pritchett. *Courts, Judges, and Politics*. New York: Random House, 1979.

A rather extensive effort covering the full range of legal politics. A collection of essays and court opinions provide the content covering the role of courts and judges in the American political process.

Rhode, David, and Harold J. Spaeth. *Supreme Court Decision Making*. San Francisco: Freeman, 1976.

An empirical study of decision making in the Supreme Court. A sometimes technical work, the authors seek to examine the variables of decision making—goals, rules, and situations. It contains good discussions of judicial activity and the Supreme Court.

Scigliano, Robert. *The Supreme Court and the Presidency*. New York: Free Press, 1971.

Examines the historical relationships between the president and the Supreme Court. Gives a good account of how presidents have tried to influence the court, including an extensive coverage of judicial appointments.

Woodward, Bob and Scott Armstrong. *The Brethren*. New York: Simon and Schuster, 1979.

A journalistic "behind the scenes" look at the operation of the Supreme Court. Gives an intimate and personal portrayal of the personalities and interactions between the several justices.

Chapter
14

The Future of American Politics

As the decade of the 1970s drew to a close, two-thirds of the American people felt the United States was in deep and serious trouble. Long lines at the gas pumps convinced Americans that the energy shortage was real. Inflation eroded earning power; people complained that they could not keep ahead of it. Changes in the American political process have produced changing expectations of government. The optimism and self-confidence of Americans and their trust in the political system have given way to a fearful mixture of gloom and personal protectionism. The taxpayer revolt hits government's inability to limit spending. Faced with sharply rising gasoline prices, Republicans and Democrats alike blame the administration for not getting tough with the OPEC nations. "The electorate is extremely volatile," says Dubuque University sociologist Wayne Youngquist; "Voters have become like unguided missiles as they try to figure out how to have an effect."[1]

THE REVOLUTION OF FALLING EXPECTATIONS

We remember the late 1950s and 1960s as the era of rising expectations. The changes in our political system since then have produced a revolution of falling expectations.[2] The last two decades have been particularly

1. *Time,* April 30, 1979, p. 20.
2. Irving Louis Horowitz, "The Revolution of Falling Expectations," *Ideology and Utopia in the United States* (New York: Oxford University Press, 1977).

Groups protesting government spending for defense and Congressional salaries while urging money for jobs, education, and energy. (United Press International)

traumatic for American politics. Americans are uncertain of their future; political institutions seem uncertain of how to respond. The traditional assumptions of the 1950s and 1960s were mixed with memories of rice fields in Vietnam, statements about presidential tapes, and double-digit inflation. The old order of things no longer worked.

Post-World War II America promised a generation of citizens upward social mobility and economic security. The 1970s struck a dissonant chord. Three events in particular produced a shift in thinking regarding the future. The Great Society programs raised serious doubts regarding America's ability to engineer its promise of equality and security; Vietnam produced a crisis in priorities and faith in America's leaders; and Watergate further eroded the people's trust and confidence in their public officials' ability to represent and lead. The results have been striking: Americans have become exceedingly weary of government. Citizens think government is oversized and overpowerful and spends to excess. Yet the intervening decades have accustomed citizens to expect government to resolve virtually every public problem they face.

This is an age of finite resources. Americans have come to realize, often in dramatic ways, the limited availability of scarce resources. The need for alterna-

Long lines at the gas pumps like this became common scenes in the 1970s. (United Press International)

tive sources of energy has been recognized, along with the need to manage and control those resources now available, including profits from their sale. Americans are coming to feel more may not necessarily be better. The built-in incentive of progress, of bigger and more, cannot be sustained. Our system has equated progress with freedom; making do with less may become a way of life, but not without some resistance. The tendencies are already there. We see smaller automobiles, home heating conservation, gas station closings, less travel, and more unemployment. In this atmosphere people resist calls for redistribution of wealth. If they must do with less, they do not want government taking even more. Change has been taken out of the people's hands. What people want from government is personal protection from the effects of unintended change. There are two very distinct consequences of this state of confusion. The first is a trend to privatize issues; the other is an extended state of heightened excitability.[3]

This is an age of single-issue politics. The tendency is to blame others for misfortunes and seek government intervention to soften the adjustment and solve the problems. The result has been a turn toward private goals, toward protection and isolation from the unintended consequences of change. This has given rise to a "me first" attitude. The result is excessive and contradictory demands on government. All kinds of groups take their cause to the public, transferring more decision making from the private to the public sector. The heightened excitability

3. See James Q. Wilson, "American Politics, Then and Now," *Commentary* 67 (Fall 1979), 40–46.

this has caused makes groups press their demands before government in ever increasing waves and with ever increasing intolerance.

But government is not without fault either. Programs in the 1960s and 1970s encouraged citizen participation. Newly politicized groups were given veto power over community programs. Politicians continuously campaigned against Congress or the bureaucracy on a pledge to help people avoid government. Every group feels guaranteed a standing of equality before the federal government, in part fostered by the attitude of politicians themselves.

Yet we persist in holding freedom and equality as operative ideals. Expectations continue. The press for equality is legitimate, but what was once largely thought of in economic terms has broadened. We now speak of social and political equality, and we demand that government provide all these equalities for everyone. Here we face the ultimate problem as America enters its third century: can the nation face and solve its problems, and solve them in terms of a democratic political process that many increasingly see as a luxury?

A SECOND REPUBLIC

Theodore Lowi has labeled the condition of America a "Second Republic" because of the changes produced by liberal democratic practices: "During the decade of the 1960's the United States had a crisis of public authority and died.

PRACTICING POLITICS   14.1

Working for the environment

Many national groups now lobby in Washington and across the country for environmental causes. Here are some of the larger and more active ones; write or call for information about activities and membership.

- Environmental Action, 1346 Connecticut Avenue NW, Washington, D.C. 20036
- Environmental Defense Fund, 1525 Eighteenth Street NW, Washington, D.C. 20036
- Friends of the Earth, 620 C Street SE, Washington, D.C. 20003
- National Audubon Society, 1130 Fifth Avenue, New York, New York 10038

- National Parks and Conservation Association, 1701 Eighteenth Street NW, Washington, D.C. 20009
- National Wildlife Federation, 1412 Sixteenth Street NW, Washington, D.C. 20036
- Natural Resources Defense Council, 917 Fifteenth Street NW, Washington, D.C. 20005
- Sierra Club, 530 Bush Street, San Francisco, California 94108
- Wilderness Society, 1901 Pennsylvania Avenue NW, Washington, D.C. 20006

A Second Republic was left standing in its place. We had held no constituent assembly and had written no second Constitution. Yet at some point, beginning in the 1930's and culminating in the 1960's, cumulative changes in national power, national institutions, and in ideology altered our relationship to the Constitution of 1787, making the Second Republic a reality, not a metaphor."[4]

This Second Republic began in earnest during the New Deal. It signaled the growth of government, both in size and in function. But most noteworthy were the changed functions of the federal government. Subsidy policies continued, but increasingly the government was adopting entirely new functions. These were the functions of regulation and redistribution, and they increasingly brought the citizen and coercive power of government together. The institutionalization of the Second Republic occurred in the 1960s when the national government first monopolized a given area of private activity. Such was the case with economic stabilization and wage–price controls as well as with housing, poverty and many of the Great Society programs. Following monopolization, a program was authorized and an administrative agency organized, without legal guidelines, so that the broad area monopolized by the government could be returned piece by piece as a privilege to specific individuals or groups.[5] Or as Lowi puts it, "socialism for the organized, capitalism for the unorganized."

During the 1960s, there were several ways in which the federal government monopolized areas of private activity. There was direct financial domination, as in space, highways, and hospitals where private resources could not compete with the infusion of tax dollars into an area. A second means was to preempt activity through licensing, as in communications, corporate mergers, or wage increases, where activity required permission by the federal government in order to proceed. Finally, the federal government monopolized activity by underwriting risk, thereby guaranteeing activity and established interests. This was the case with the loan to the Lockheed Corporation in 1971. All this was done, Lowi says, "in the name of maintaining public order and avoiding disequilibrium."[6] And so the state grew and the promise of liberal democracy was maintained. But the costs were great. The result of these policies has been, Lowi maintains, to place America in a state of "permanent receivership." Permanent receivership refers to the contemporary method of maintaining social order during a crisis involving the bankruptcy of an individual or enterprise by maintaining the assets in their prebankrupt form and never disposing of them at all, regardless of inequities, inefficiencies, or the cost of maintenance.[7] Permanent receivership assures stability, but stability for established groups and organizations. Policies are discretionary, the work of bargaining for privilege between established interests. The perpetuation of permanent receivership may well mean the end of capitalism, because it uses economic resources

4. Theodore J. Lowi, *The End of Liberalism* 2nd ed. (New York: W. W. Norton and Co., 1979), p. 271.
5. *Ibid.*, p. 278.
6. *Ibid.*
7. *Ibid.*, p. 279.

Perspectives on Public Policy

One of the most basic issues of public policy is who governs. Political scientists are very divided on who, in practice, exercises control over decisions of public policy. They have developed macropolitical approaches to explain political phenomena and control of the policy process: institutional democracy, elitism, interest group pluralism, and systems analysis.

Institutional democracy is the most classical view of power in the policy process. Policy is formulated and adopted by governmental institutions, that is by legislatures, executives, courts, and bureaucracies. These institutional policymakers represent the people, either individually or collectively through the representative institutions of interest groups and political parties. Elections are the means of legitimating one set of policymakers over another. The people hold power and collectively they exercise influence over the policymakers.

While institutional democracy is concerned with formal organizations, legal powers, and procedural process, it does not slight the political realities of power or the informal interaction of participants in the government. Rather it insists that the formal, legal institutions must adopt policies for them to be binding. Policies are legitimate because of the democratic context of policy formulation, both the open context for agenda setting and the control people exercise over official policymakers.

Elitism views public policy from the opposite perspective. Policy reflects the values and choices of a governing elite who are likely not the officially elected representatives and who likely do not reflect the values of the people at large. The core of elitism says that public policy is made by a small number of persons who possess power because of their position and influence in society. Public officials and government agencies implement the policies established by the elite. The people have little influence and less control over the elite's formulation of policy. Policy serves the needs of the elite, not necessarily that of the public welfare, although this cannot be capriciously ignored by the elite.

Interest group pluralism understands public policy as an equilibrium reached between elite dominance of policy formulation and democratic control of policymakers. It contends that policy is the result of interaction among politically active interest groups. Policy at any given instance is the result of the dominance of one or a series of groups; as new groups enter the political arena or as the other groups gain or lose influence, policy shifts to reflect the changed pattern of group influence. The same array of groups is not involved in all issues, hence group activity and influence varies with their interest and effort to influence policy in a given issue. Government strives to moderate the group struggle and responds to the dominant pull of group interests.

The interest group approach assumes that interest group elites vie for policy influence. Individuals may influence policy to the extent they participate in political group affairs. But the struggle for policy takes place between elite representatives of interest groups. At this level there is little individual activity or influence.

System analysis attempts to establish public policy as a political response resulting from demands made in the environment. The political system is made up of identifiable and interrelated institutions and activities that make authoritative decisions. The political system receives inputs from the environment, these being either demands on the system or supports for it. The resulting policy, or outputs, constitute the authoritative decisions. Then the resultant outputs become the substance for new inputs.

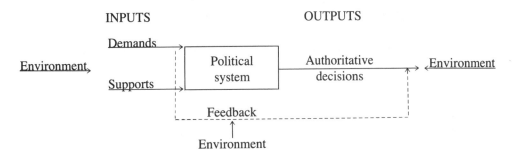

The value of systems analysis is that a wide range of complex data can be related to public policy. It is not limited to political, economic, or even cultural variables. It further illustrates the dynamic nature of the policy process as formulated policies become the agenda (inputs) for future policy adoption. Systems analysis, however, is limited by its very general and abstract nature. It neither specifies how policy is made or who makes it. Rather it provides a framework for the integration of divergent variables.

---

to shore up political and social values; the goal is to maintain the process. There are no ends or direction; maintaining the process is the end.

The American citizen stands today directly before government, unbuffered by the insulation political parties and traditional alliances afford. The instruments of political power have been exposed to the people. Our philosophy of democracy encourages the citizen to use those instruments. And they are, in increasing and conflicting numbers. The 1980s present a new opportunity for the historic and honored principles of liberal democracy. At issue is whether such renewal reestablishes a national vitality and dedication providing national purpose and pride, or whether democracy further fractures our political and social fabric by advancing self-interest. The future will prove just how petty democracy can become or how great democracy is for inspiring dedicated self-government.

FUTURE OF AMERICAN POLITICS

There have never been any easy answers or simple solutions for America's problems. Decision making is necessarily confounded by our historic commitment to the values of liberal democracy. Yet the politics of that order are being attacked. Politics is in a state of disarray; there are changing expectations. Our political institutions struggle to maintain their representative character.

The basic values of democracy—equality, freedom, and individualism—seem more remote today than at any time in our history. The expanded role of government has put the individual in a position of dependence on government. With a budget of over one-half a trillion dollars and increased activity in a myriad of areas, there remains little opportunity for individual self-reliance. Individual freedom and equality depend, in greater and greater degree, upon what government does and does not do.

With the press of issues thrust upon individuals over which they exercise little control, as with inflation and oil prices, citizens turn to government for help. They seek personal security and protection, asking government to protect that which individuals and families have achieved. The result is that issues have become more important to politics. Often this takes the form of single-issue politics as a particular issue drives citizens into the political arena. This has produced increased demands upon government, demands that conflict and produce more strain on the social fabric. As a consequence there is a decline in the traditional loyalties and patterns of behavior. Political party support is declining; there is an erosion of trust in government; public opinion is in disarray.

In this climate of changing expectations the institutions of government— president, Congress and courts—seek to renew and redefine their representational role in a democracy. Congress has acquiesced to the presidency and now struggles to redress the balance. Presidential power has been strained to its limits and now must be limited without losing its vitality of leadership. Courts find the rule of law called upon to settle increasing political disputes. The crisis in confidence is nothing less than a crisis of legitimacy. With expectations changing, constituencies change. As government attempts to respond, there will invariably be greater contest over policies and legitimacy to represent the new priorities of the people.

In the coming decade the greatest test for democracy rests with the institutions shrouding themselves in the abstractions of democratic values without any serious commitment to or conformity with the operative ideals of democratic government. It falls to the citizens to decide if the principles of democracy are worth preserving. Much of what government does will be justified as necessarily compatible with democracy, if only to preserve the present. Only if the people, the citizens, decide that national purpose is worth the struggle can democracy be a valuable form of social organization capable of transcending individual differences.

Appendix A
ANNOTATED DECLARATION OF INDEPENDENCE

(as it reads in the parchment copy.)

THE UNANIMOUS DECLARATION OF THE THIRTEEN UNITED STATES OF AMERICA.

When in the Course of human events, it becomes necessary for one people to dissolve the political bands, which have connected them with another, and to assume among the powers of the earth, the separate and equal station to which the Laws of Nature and of Nature's God entitle them, a decent respect to the opinions of mankind requires that they should declare the causes which impel them to the separation.—We hold these truths to be self-evident, that all men are created equal, that they are endowed by their Creator with certain unalienable Rights, that among these are Life, Liberty and the pursuit of Happiness.—That to secure these rights, Governments are instituted among Men, deriving their just powers from the consent of the governed,—That whenever any Form of Government becomes destructive of these ends, it is the Right of the People to alter or to abolish it, and to institute new Government, laying its foundation on such principles and organizing its powers in such form, as to them shall seem most likely to effect their Safety and Happiness. Prudence, indeed, will dictate that Governments long established should not be changed for light and transient causes; and accordingly all experience hath shewn, that mankind are more disposed to suffer, while evils are sufferable, than to right themselves by abolishing the forms to which they are accustomed. But when a long train of abuses and usurpations, pursuing invariably the same Object evinces a design to reduce them under absolute Despotism, it is their right, it is their duty, to throw off such Government, and to provide new Guards for their future security.—Such has been the patient sufferance of these Colonies; and such is now the necessity which constrains them to alter their former Systems of Government. The history of the present King of Great Britain is a history of repeated injuries and usurpations, all having in direct object the establishment of an absolute Tyranny over these States. To prove this, let Facts be submitted to a candid world.— He has refused his Assent to Laws, the most wholesome and necessary for the public good.—He has forbidden his Governors to pass Laws of immediate and pressing importance, unless suspended in their operation till his Assent should be obtained; and when so suspended, he has utterly neglected to attend to them.—He has refused to pass other Laws for the accommodation of large districts of people, unless those people would relinquish the right of Representation in the Legislature, a right inestimable to them and formidable to tyrants only.—He has called together legislative bodies at places unusual, uncomfortable, and distant from the depository of their public Records, for the sole purpose of fatiguing them into compliance with his measures.—He has dissolved Representative Houses repeatedly, for opposing with manly firmness his invasions on the rights of the people.—He has refused for a long time, after such dissolutions, to cause others to be elected; whereby the Legislative powers, incapable of Annihilation, have returned to the People at large for their exercise; the State remaining in the meantime exposed to all

Philosophy of government

● natural rights
● contract

● rebellion

Cause not entered into lightly

● rules of contract broken

● patient suffering

The Bill of Particulars
● violated self-government thru legislative assemblies

the dangers of invasion from without, and convulsions within.—He has endeavoured to prevent the population of these States; for that purpose obstructing the Laws for Naturalization of Foreigners; refusing to pass others to encourage their migrations hither, and raising the conditions of new Appropriations of Lands.—He has obstructed the Administration of Justice, by refusing his Assent to Laws for establishing Judiciary powers.—He has made Judges dependent on his Will alone, for the tenure of their offices, and the amount and payment of their salaries.—He has erected a multitude of New Offices, and sent hither swarms of Officers to harrass our people, and eat out their substance.—He has kept among us, in times of peace, Standing Armies without the Consent of our legislatures.—He has affected to render the Military independent of and superior to the Civil Power.—He has combined with others to subject us to jurisdiction foreign to our constitution, and unacknowledged by our laws; giving his Assent to their Acts of pretended Legislation.—For quartering large bodies of armed troops among us:—For protecting them, by a mock Trial, from punishment for any Murders which they should commit on the Inhabitants of these States:—For cutting off our Trade with all parts of the world:—For imposing Taxes on us without our Consent:—For depriving us in many cases, of the benefits of Trial by Jury:—For transporting us beyond Seas to be tried for pretended offenses:—For abolishing the free System of English Laws in a neighboring Province, establishing therein an Arbitrary government, and enlarging its Boundaries so as to render it at once an example and fit instrument for introducing the same absolute rule into these Colonies:—For taking away our Charters, abolishing our most valuable Laws, and altering fundamentally the Forms of our Governments:—For suspending our own Legislatures, and declaring themselves invested with power to legislate for us in all cases whatsoever.—He has abdicated Government here, by declaring us out of his Protection and waging War against us.—He has plundered our seas, ravaged our Coasts, burnt our towns, and destroyed the lives of our people.—He is at this time transporting large Armies of foreign Mercenaries to compleat the works of death, desolation and tyranny, already begun with circumstances of Cruelty & perfidy scarcely paralleled in the most barbarous ages, and totally unworthy the Head of a civilized nation.—He has constrained our fellow Citizens taken Captive on the high Seas to bear Arms against their Country, to become the executioners of their friends and Brethren, or to fall themselves by their Hands.—He has excited domestic insurrections amongst us, and has endeavoured to bring on the inhabitants of our frontiers, the merciless Indian Savages, whose known rule of warfare, is an undistinguished destruction of all ages, sexes and conditions. In every stage of these Oppressions We have Petitioned for Redress in the most humble terms: Our repeated Petitions have been answered only by repeated injury. A Prince whose character is thus marked by every act which may define a Tyrant, is unfit to be the ruler of a free people. Nor have We been wanting in attentions to our British brethren. We have warned them from time to time of attempts by their legislature to extend an unwarrantable jurisdiction over us. We have reminded them of the circumstances of our emigration and settlement here. We have appealed to their native justice and magnanimity, and we have conjured them by the ties of our common

● destroyed separation of powers

● tyranny

British lawlessness

kindred to disavow these usurpations, which would inevitably interrupt our connections and correspondence. They too have been deaf to the voice of justice and of consanguinity. We must, therefore, acquiesce in the necessity, which denounces our Separation, and hold them, as we hold the rest of mankind, Enemies in War, in Peace Friends.—

Declaration of Separation

We, therefore, the Representatives of the united States of America, in General Congress, Assembled, appealing to the Supreme Judge of the world for the rectitude of our intentions do, in the Name, and by Authority of the good People of these Colonies, solemnly publish and declare, That these United Colonies are, and of Right ought to be Free and Independent States; that they are Absolved from all Allegiance to the British Crown, and that all political connection between them and the State of Great Britain, is and ought to be totally dissolved: and that as Free and Independent States, they have full Power to levy War, conclude Peace, contract Alliances, establish Commerce, and to do all other Acts and Things which Independent States may of right do.—And for the support of this Declaration, with a firm reliance on the protection of divine Providence, we mutually pledge to each other our Lives, our Fortunes and our sacred Honor.

Signatures

John Hancock.	Fran^s Lewis.
Samuel Chase.	Lewis Morris.
Wm Paca.	Richd Stockton.
Tho. Stone.	Jn° Witherspoon.
Charles Carroll of Carrollton.	Fra. Hopkinson.
George Wythe.	John Hart.
Richard Henry Lee.	Abra Clark.
Th Jefferson.	Josiah Bartlett.
Benj^a Harrison.	Wm Whipple.
Tho. Nelson jr.	Saml Adams.
Francis Lightfoot Lee.	John Adams.
Carter Braxton.	Robt Treat Paine.
Robt Morris.	Elbridge Gerry.
Benjamin Rush.	Step Hopkins.
Benj^a Franklin.	William Ellery.
John Morton.	Roger Sherman.
Geo Clymer.	Saml Huntington.
Ja Smith.	Wm Williams.
Geo. Taylor.	Oliver Wolcott.
James Wilson.	Matthew Thornton.
Geo. Ross.	Wm Hooper.
Caesar Rodney.	Joseph Hewes.
Geo Read.	John Penn.
Tho M: Kean.	Edward Rutledge.
Wm Floyd.	Tho Heyward Junr.
Phil. Livingston.	Thomas Lynch Junr.
Arthur Middleton.	Lyman Hall.
Button Gwinnett.	Geo Walton.

Appendix B
ANNOTATED CONSTITUTION OF THE U.S.

WE THE PEOPLE of the United States, in Order to form a more perfect Union, establish Justice, insure domestic Tranquility, provide for the common defence, promote the general Welfare, and secure the Blessings of Liberty to ourselves and our Posterity, do ordain and establish this Constitution for the United States of America.

ARTICLE I.

Bicameral Congress

SECTION. 1. All legislative Powers herein granted shall be vested in a Congress of the United States, which shall consist of a Senate and House of Representatives.

Election to House of Representatives

SECTION. 2. ¹The House of Representatives shall be composed of Members chosen every second Year by the People of the several States and the Electors in each State shall have the Qualifications requisite for Electors of the most numerous Branch of the State Legislature.

● **qualifications**

²No person shall be a Representative who shall not have attained to the Age of twenty five Years, and been seven Years a Citizen of the United States, and who shall not, when elected, be an Inhabitant of that State in which he shall be chosen.

● **apportionment of seats**

³[Representatives and direct Taxes shall be apportioned among the several States which may be included within this Union, according to their respective Numbers, which shall be determined by adding to the whole Number of free Persons, including those bound to Service for a Term of Years, and excluding Indians not taxed, three fifths of all other Persons.].* The actual Enumeration shall be made within three Years after the first Meeting of the Congress of the United States, and within every subsequent Term of ten Years, in such Manner as they shall by Law direct. The Number of Representatives shall not exceed one for every thirty Thousand, but each State shall have at Least one Representative; and until such enumeration shall be made, the State of New Hampshire shall be entitled to chuse three, Massachusetts eight, Rhode-Island and Providence Plantations one, Connecticut five, New-York six, New Jersey four, Pennsylvania eight, Delaware one, Maryland six, Virginia ten, North Carolina five, South Carolina five, and Georgia three.

⁴When vacancies happen in the Representation from any State, the Executive Authority thereof shall issue Writs of Election to fill such Vacancies.

● **power of impeachment**

⁵The House of Representatives shall chuse their Speaker and other Officers; and shall have the sole Power of Impeachment.

Election to the Senate

SECTION. 3 ¹The Senate of the United States shall be composed of two Senators from each State, [chosen by the Legislature thereof,]* for six Years; and each Senator shall have one Vote.

● **apportionment of seats**

²Immediately after they shall be assembled in Consequence of the first Election, they shall be divided as equally as may be into three Classes. The

NOTE.—This text of the Constitution follows the engrossed copy signed by Gen. Washington and the deputies from 12 States. The superior number preceding the paragraphs designates the number of the clause; it was not in the original.

*The part included in heavy brackets was changed by section 2 of the fourteenth amendment.

Seats of the Senators of the first Class shall be vacated at the Expiration of the second Year, of the second Class at the Expiration of the fourth Year, and of the third Class at the Expiration of the sixth Year, so that one third may be chosen every second Year; [and if Vacancies happen by Resignation, or otherwise, during the Recess of the Legislature of any State, the Executive thereof may make temporary Appointments until the next Meeting of the Legislature, which shall then fill such Vacancies].**

● qualifications

[3]No Person shall be a Senator who shall not have attained to the Age of thirty Years, and been nine Years a Citizen of the United States, and who shall not, when elected, be an Inhabitant of that State for which he shall be chosen.

[4]The Vice President of the United States shall be President of the Senate, but shall have no Vote, unless they be equally divided.

[5]The Senate shall chuse their other Officers, and also a President pro tempore, in the Absence of the Vice President, or when he shall exercise the Office of President of the United States.

● power to try impeachments

[6]The Senate shall have the sole Power to try all Impeachments. When sitting for that Purpose, they shall be on Oath or Affirmation. When the President of the United States is tried, the Chief Justice shall preside: And no Person shall be convicted without the Concurrence of two thirds of the Members present.

[7]Judgment in Cases of Impeachment shall not extend further than to removal from Office, and disqualification to hold and enjoy any Office of honor, Trust or Profit under the United States: but the Party convicted shall nevertheless be liable and subject to Indictment, Trial, Judgment and Punishment, according to Law.

States prescribe Elections

SECTION. 4 [1]The Times, Places and Manner of holding Elections for Senators and Representatives, shall be prescribed in each State by the Legislature thereof; but the Congress may at any time by Law make or alter such Regulations, except as to the Places of chusing Senators.

[2]The Congress shall assemble at least once in every Year, and such Meeting shall [be on the first Monday in December,]*** unless they shall by Law appoint a different Day.

Rules of Organization

SECTION. 5. [1]Each House shall be the Judge of the Elections, Returns and Qualifications of its own Members, and a Majority of each shall constitute a Quorum to do Business; but a smaller Number may adjourn from day to day, and may be authorized to compel the Attendance of absent Members, in such Manner, and under such Penalties as each House may provide.

[2]Each House may determine the Rules of its Proceedings, punish its Members for disorderly Behaviour, and, with the Concurrence of two thirds, expel a Member.

[3]Each House shall keep a Journal of its Proceedings, and from time to time publish the same, excepting such Parts as may in their Judgment require Secrecy; and the Yeas and Nays of the Members of either House on

---

*The part included in brackets was changed by section 1 of the seventeenth amendment.
**The part included in brackets was changed by clause 2 of the seventeenth amendment.
***The part included in brackets was changed by section 2 of the twentieth amendment.

any question shall, at the Desire of one fifth of those Present, be entered on the Journal.

[4]Neither House, during the Session of Congress, shall, without the Consent of the other, adjourn for more than three days, nor to any other Place than that in which the two Houses shall be sitting.

Compensation, Privileges, and Immunities for members of Congress

SECTION. 6 [1]The Senators and Representatives shall receive a Compensation for their Services, to be ascertained by Law, and paid out of the Treasury of the United States. They shall in all Cases, except Treason, Felony and Breach of Peace, be privileged from Arrest during their Attendance at the Session of their respective Houses, and in going to and returning from the same; and for any Speech or Debate in either House, they shall not be questioned in any other Place.

● **no appointive office while serving in Congress**

[2]No Senator or Representative shall, during the Time for which he was elected, be appointed to any civil Office under the Authority of the United States, which shall have been created, or the Emoluments whereof shall have been encreased during such time; and no Person holding any Office under the United States, shall be a Member of either House during his Continuance in Office.

Revenue Bills Originate in House of Representatives

SECTION. 7. [1]All Bills for raising Revenue shall originate in the House of Representatives; but the Senate may propose or concur with Amendments as on other Bills.

Veto and Procedure for Veto Override

[2]Every Bill which shall have passed the House of Representatives and the Senate, shall, before it become a Law, be presented to the President of the United States; If he approve he shall sign it, but if not he shall return it, with his Objections to that House in which it shall have originated, who shall enter the Objections at large on their Journal, and proceed to reconsider it. If after such Reconsideration two thirds of that House shall agree to pass the Bill, it shall be sent, together with the Objections, to the other House, by which it shall likewise be reconsidered, and if approved by two thirds of that House, it shall become a Law. But in all such Cases the Votes of both Houses shall be determined by yeas and Nays, and the Names of the Persons voting for and against the Bill shall be entered on the Journal of each House respectively. If any Bill shall not be returned by the President with ten Days (Sundays excepted) after it shall have been presented to him, the Same shall be a Law, in like Manner as if he had signed it, unless the Congress by their Adjournment prevent its Return, in which Case it shall not be a Law.

● **pocket veto**

Presidential Approval

[3]Every Order, Resolution, or Vote to which the Concurrence of the Senate and House of Representatives may be necessary (except on a question of Adjournment) shall be presented to the President of the United States; and before the Same shall take Effect, shall be approved by him, or being disapproved by him, shall be repassed by two thirds of the Senate and House of Representatives, according to the Rules and Limitations prescribed in the Case of a Bill.

Powers of Congress

SECTION. 8. [1]The Congress shall have Power To lay and collect Taxes, Duties, Imposts and Excises, to pay the Debts and provide for the common Defence and general Welfare of the United States; but all Duties, Imposts and Excises shall be uniform throughout the United States;

● **taxes**

● **borrow money**

[2]To borrow Money on the credit of the United States;

● regulate commerce

● naturalization and bankruptcies

● coin money

● punish counterfeiting

● post offices

● patents

● create inferior courts

● define piracy

● declare war

● raise an army and navy

● nationalize the militia

● authority for District of Columbia

● necessary and proper clause

Prohibition of Powers to Congress

● slave trade

● suspend writ of habeas corpus

[3] To regulate Commerce with foreign Nations, and among the several States, and with the Indian Tribes;

[4] To establish an uniform Rule of Naturalization, and uniform Laws on the subject of Bankruptcies throughout the United States;

[5] To coin Money, regulate the Value thereof, and of foreign Coin, and fix the Standard of Weights and Measures;

[6] To provide for the Punishment of counterfeiting the Securities and current Coin of the United States;

[7] To establish Post Offices and post Roads;

[8] To promote the Progress of Science and useful Arts, by securing for limited Times to Authors and Inventors the exclusive Right to their respective Writings and Discoveries;

[9] To constitute Tribunals inferior to the supreme Court;

[10] To define and punish Piracies and Felonies committed on the high Seas, and Offences against the Law of Nations;

[11] To declare War, grant Letters of Marque and Reprisal, and make Rules concerning Captures on Land and Water;

[12] To raise and support Armies, but no Appropriation of Money to that Use shall be for a longer Term than two Years;

[13] To provide and maintain a Navy;

[14] To make Rules for the Government and Regulation of the land and naval Forces;

[15] To provide for calling forth the Militia to execute the Laws of the Union, suppress Insurrections and repel Invasions;

[16] To provide for organizing, arming, and disciplining, the Militia, and for governing such Part of them as may be employed in the Service of the United States, reserving to the States respectively, the Appointment of the Officers, and the Authority of training the Militia according to the discipline prescribed by Congress;

[17] To exercise exclusive Legislation in all Cases whatsoever, over such District (not exceeding ten Miles square) as may, by Cession of particular States, and the Acceptance of Congress, become the Seat of the Government of the United States, and to exercise like Authority over all Places purchased by the Consent of the Legislature of the State in which the Same shall be, for the Erection of Forts, Magazines, Arsenals, dock-Yards, and other needful Buildings;—And

[18] To make all Laws which shall be necessary and proper for carrying into Execution the foregoing Powers, and all other Powers vested by this Constitution in the Government of the United States, or in any Department or Officer thereof.

SECTION. 9. [1] The Migration or Importation of such Persons as any of the States now existing shall think proper to admit, shall not be prohibited by the Congress prior to the Year one thousand eight hundred and eight, but a Tax or duty may be imposed on such Importation, not exceeding ten dollars for each Person.

[2] The Privilege of the Writ of Habeas Corpus shall not be suspended, unless when in Cases of Rebellion or Invasion the public Safety may require it.

- bill of attainder or ex post facto
- no direct tax
- no state tariff
- no state preference

- no unauthorized expenditure of money

- no titles of nobility

Prohibition of Powers to the States
- no treaties, coin money, bill of attainder, title of nobility

- no duties on imports or exports

- no foreign or interstate compacts, no declaration of war

Executive Power in single President
- term

- electoral college

[3]No Bill of Attainder or ex post facto Law shall be passed.

*[4]No Capitation, or other direct, Tax shall be laid, unless in Proportion to the Census or Enumeration herein before directed to be taken.

[5]No Tax or Duty shall be laid on Articles exported from any State.

[6]No Preference shall be given by any Regulation of Commerce or Revenue to the Ports of one State over those of another: nor shall Vessels bound to, or from, one State, be obliged to enter, clear, or pay Duties in another.

[7]No Money shall be drawn from the Treasury, but in Consequence of Appropriations made by Law; and a regular Statement and Account of the Receipts and Expenditures of all public Money shall be published from time to time.

[8]No Title of Nobility shall be granted by the United States: And no Person holding any Office of Profit or Trust under them, shall, without the Consent of the Congress, accept of any present, Emolument, Office, or Title, of any kind whatever, from any King, Prince, or foreign State.

SECTION. 10. [1]No State shall enter into any Treaty, Alliance, or Confederation; grant Letters of Marque and Reprisal; coin Money; emit Bills of Credit; make any Thing but gold and silver Coin a Tender in Payment of Debts; pass any Bill of Attainder, ex post facto Law, or Law impairing the Obligation of Contracts, or grant any Title of Nobility.

[2]No State shall, without the Consent of the Congress, lay any Imposts or Duties on Imports or Exports, except what may be absolutely necessary for executing it's inspection Laws: and the net Produce of all Duties and Imposts, laid by any State on Imports or Exports, shall be for the Use of the Treasury of the United States; and all such Laws shall be subject to the Revision and Controul of the Congress.

[3]No State shall, without the Consent of Congress, lay any Duty of Tonnage, keep Troops, or Ships of War in time of Peace, enter into any Agreement or Compact with another State, or with a foreign Power, or engage in War, unless actually invaded, or in such imminent Danger as will not admit of delay.

ARTICLE. II.

SECTION. 1. [1]The executive Power shall be vested in a President of the United States of America. He shall hold his Office during the Term of four Years, and, together with the Vice President, chosen for the same Term, be elected, as follows

[2]Each State shall appoint, in such Manner as the Legislature thereof may direct, a Number of Electors, equal to the whole Number of Senators and Representatives to which the State may be entitled in the Congress: but no Senator or Representative, or Person holding an Office of Trust or Profit under the United States, shall be appointed an Elector.

[The Electors shall meet in their respective States, and vote by Ballot for two Persons, of whom one at least shall not be an Inhabitant of the same State with themselves. And they shall make a List of all the Persons voted for, and of the Number of Votes for each; which List they shall sign and

---

*See also the sixteenth amendment.

certify, and transmit sealed to the Seat of the Government of the United States, directed to the President of the Senate. The President of the Senate shall, in the Presence of the Senate and House of Representatives, open all the Certificates, and the Votes shall then be counted. The Person having the greatest Number of Votes shall be the President, if such Number be a Majority of the whole Number of Electors appointed; and if there be more than one who have such Majority, and have an equal Number of Votes, then the House of Representatives shall immediately chuse by Ballot one of them for President; and if no Person have a Majority, then from the five highest on the List the said House shall in like Manner chuse the President. But in chusing the President, the Votes shall be taken by States, the Representation from each State having one Vote; A quorum for this Purpose shall consist of a Member or Members from two thirds of the States, and a Majority of all the States shall be necessary to a Choice. In every Case, after the Choice of the President, the Person having the greatest Number of Votes of the Electors shall be the Vice President. But if there should remain two or more who have equal Votes, the Senate shall chuse from them by Ballot the Vice President.]*

[3]The Congress may determine the Time of chusing the Electors, and the Day on which they shall give their Votes; which Day shall be the same throughout the United States.

● qualifications

[4]No Person except a natural born Citizen, or a Citizen of the United States, at the time of the Adoption of this Constitution, shall be eligible to the Office of President; neither shall any Person be eligible to that Office who shall not have attained to the Age of thirty five Years, and been fourteen Years a Resident within the United States.

● succession

[5]In Case of the Removal of the President from Office, or of his Death, Resignation, or Inability to discharge the Powers and Duties of the said Office,† the Same shall devolve on the Vice President, and the Congress may by Law provide for the Case of Removal, Death, Resignation or Inability, both of the President and Vice President, declaring what Officer shall then act as President, and such Officer shall act accordingly, until the Disability be removed, or a President shall be elected.

[6]The President shall, at stated Times, receive for his Services, a Compensation, which shall neither be encreased nor diminished during the Period for which he shall have been elected, and he shall not receive within that Period any other Emolument from the United States, or any of them.

● oath

[7]Before he enter on the Execution of his Office, he shall take the following Oath or Affirmation:—"I do solemnly swear (or affirm) that I will faithfully execute the Office of the President of the United States, and will to the best of my Ability, preserve, protect and defend the Constitution of the United States."

Power of the President

● commander-in-chief

SECTION. 2. [1]The President shall be Commander in Chief of the Army and Navy of the United States, and of the Militia of the several States, when called into the actual Service of the United States; he may require the Opinion, in writing, of the principal Officer in each of the executive Departments,

---

*This paragraph has been superseded by the twelfth amendment.
†This provision has been affected by the twenty-fifth amendment.

● pardons and reprieves

● treaties and appointment

upon any Subject relating to the Duties of their respective Offices, and he shall have Power to grant Reprieves and Pardons for Offences against the United States, except in Cases of Impeachment.

[2]He shall have Power, by and with the Advice and Consent of the Senate, to make Treaties, provided two thirds of the Senators present concur; and he shall nominate, and by and with the Advice and Consent of the Senate, shall appoint Ambassadors, other public Ministers and Consuls, Judges of the supreme Court, and all other Officers of the United States, whose Appointments are not herein otherwise provided for, and which shall be established by Law: but the Congress may by Law vest the Appointment of such inferior Officers, as they think proper, in the President alone, in the Courts of Law, or in the Heads of Departments.

[3]The President shall have Power to fill up all Vacancies that may happen during the Recess of the Senate, by granting Commissions which shall expire at the End of their next Session.

Legislative Responsibilities

SECTION. 3. He shall from time to time give to the Congress Information of the State of the Union, and recommend to their Consideration such Measures as he shall judge necessary and expedient; he may, on extraordinary Occasions, convene both Houses, or either of them, and in Case of Disagreement between them, with Respect to the Time of Adjournment, he may adjourn them to such Time as he shall think proper; he shall receive Ambassadors and other public Ministers; he shall take Care that the Laws be faithfully executed, and shall Commission all the Officers of the United States.

Impeachable Offenses

SECTION. 4. The President, Vice President and all civil Officers of the United States, shall be removed from Office on Impeachment for, and Conviction of, Treason, Bribery, or other high Crimes and Misdemeanors.

ARTICLE. III.

Federal Courts

SECTION. 1. The judicial Power of the United States, shall be vested in one supreme Court, and in such inferior Courts as the Congress may from time to time ordain and establish. The Judges, both of the supreme and inferior Courts, shall hold their Offices during good Behaviour, and shall, at stated Times, receive for their Services, a Compensation, which shall not be diminished during their Continuance in Office.

Jurisdiction of Courts

SECTION. 2. [1]The judicial Power shall extend to all Cases, in Law and Equity, arising under this Constitution, the Laws of the United States, and Treaties made, or which shall be made, under their Authority;—to all Cases affecting Ambassadors, other public Ministers and Consuls;—to all Cases of admiralty and maritime Jurisdiction;—to Controversies to which the United States shall be a Party;—to Controversies between two or more States;—between a State and Citizens of another State;*—between Citizens of different States,—between Citizens of the same State claiming Lands under Grants of different States, and between a State, or the Citizens thereof, and foreign States, Citizens or Subjects.

---

*This clause has been affected by the Eleventh Amendment.

● original and appellate jurisdiction of Supreme Court

[2]In all Cases affecting Ambassadors, other public Ministers and Consuls, and those in which a State shall be Party, the supreme Court shall have original Jurisdiction. In all the other Cases before mentioned, the supreme Court shall have appellate Jurisdiction, both as to Law and Fact, with such Exceptions, and under such Regulations as the Congress shall make.

● jury trial

[3]The Trial of all Crimes, except in Cases of Impeachment, shall be by Jury; and such Trial shall be held in the State where the said Crimes shall have been committed; but when not committed within any State, the Trial shall be at such Place or Places as the Congress may by Law have directed.

Treason

SECTION. 3. [1]Treason against the United States, shall consist only in levying War against them, or in adhering to their Enemies, giving them Aid and Comfort. No Person shall be convicted of Treason unless on the Testimony of two Witnesses to the same overt Act, or on Confession in open Court.

[2]The Congress shall have Power to declare the Punishment of Treason, but no Attainder of Treason shall work Corruption of Blood, or Forfeiture except during the Life of the Person attainted.

ARTICLE. IV.

Full Faith and Credit

SECTION. 1. Full Faith and Credit shall be given in each State to the public Acts, Records, and judicial Proceedings of every other State. And the Congress may by general Laws prescribe the Manner in which such Acts, Records and Proceedings shall be proved, and the Effect thereof.

Priviliges and Immunities

SECTION. 2. [1]The Citizens of each State shall be entitled to all Priviliges and Immunities of Citizens in the several States.

Extradition

[2]A Person charged in any State with Treason, Felony, or other Crime, who shall flee from Justice, and be found in another State, shall on Demand of the executive Authority of the State from which he fled, be delivered up, to be removed to the State having Jurisdiction of the Crime.

[3][No Person held to Service or Labour in one State, under the Laws thereof, escaping into another, shall, in Consequence of any Law or Regulation therein, be discharged from such Service or Labour, but shall be delivered up on Claim of the Party to whom such Service or Labour may be due.]*

Admission of New States

SECTION. 3. [1]New States may be admitted by the Congress into this Union; but no new State shall be formed or erected within the Jurisdiction of any other State; nor any State be formed by the Junction of two or more States, or Parts of States, without the Consent of the Legislatures of the States concerned as well as of the Congress.

● governing territories

[2]The Congress shall have Power to dispose of and make all needful Rules and Regulations, respecting the Territory or other Property belonging to the United States; and nothing in this Consitution shall be so construed as to Prejudice any Claims of the United States, or of any particular State.

Republican Form of Government

Protect from Domestic Violence

SECTION. 4. The United States shall guarantee to every State in this Union a Republican Form of Government, and shall protect each of them against Invasion; and on Application of the Legislature, or of the Executive (when the Legislature cannot be convened) against domestic Violence.

*This paragraph has been superseded by the Thirteenth Amendment.

ARTICLE. V.

Amending the Constitution

The Congress, whenever two thirds of both Houses shall deem it necessary, shall propose Amendments to this Constitution, or, on the Application of the Legislatures of two thirds of the several States, shall call a Convention for proposing Amendments, which, in either Case, shall be valid to all Intents and Purposes, as Part of this Constitution, when ratified by the Legislatures of three fourths of the several States, or by Conventions in three fourths thereof, as the one or the other Mode of Ratification may be proposed by the Congress; Provided [that no Amendment which may be made prior to the Year One thousand eight hundred and eight shall in any Manner affect the first and fourth Clauses in the Ninth Section of the first Article; and]* that no State, without its Consent, shall be deprived of its equal Suffrage in the Senate.

ARTICLE. VI.

Confederate Debts Valid

[1] All Debts contracted and Engagements entered into, before the Adoption of this Constitution, shall be as valid against the United States under this Constitution, as under the Confederation.

Federal Supremacy

[2] This Constitution, and the Laws of the United States which shall be made in Pursuance thereof; and all Treaties made, or which shall be made, under the Authority of the United States, shall be the supreme Law of the Land; and the Judges in every State shall be bound thereby, any Thing in the Constitution or Laws of any State to the Contrary notwithstanding.

No Religious Tests

[3] The Senators and Representatives before mentioned, and the Members of the several State legislatures, and all executive and judicial Officers, both of the United States and of the several States, shall be bound by Oath or Affirmation, to support this Constitution; but no religious Test shall ever be required as a Qualification to any Office or public Trust under the United States.

ARTICLE. VII.

Ratification of Constitution

The Ratification of the Conventions of nine States, shall be sufficient for the Establishment of this Constitution between the States so ratifying the Same.

DONE in Convention by the Unanimous Consent of the States present the Seventeenth Day of September in the Year of our Lord one thousand seven hundred and Eighty seven and of the Independence of the United States of America the Twelfth IN WITNESS whereof We have hereunto subscribed our Names.

GₒWASHINGTON—
Presid'. and deputy from Virginia.

[Signed also by the deputies of twelve States.]

New Hampshire.

JOHN LANGDON,   NICHOLAS GILMAN.

---

*Obsolete.

Massachusetts.

NATHANIEL GORHAM,   RUFUS KING.

Connecticut.

WM. SAML. JOHNSON,   ROGER SHERMAN.

New York.

ALEXANDER HAMILTON.

New Jersey.

WIL: LIVINGSTON,   WM. PATERSON,
DAVID BREARLEY,   JONA: DAYTON.

Pennsylvania.

B FRANKLIN,   THOMAS MIFFLIN,
ROB^T MORRIS,   GEO. CLYMER,
THOS. FITZSIMONS,   JARED INGERSOLL,
JAMES WILSON,   GOUV MORRIS.

Delaware.

GEO: READ,   GUNNING BEDFORD, jun,
JOHN DICKINSON,   RICHARD BASSETT.
JACO: BROOM,

Maryland.

JAMES MCHENRY,   DAN OF S^T THOS. JENIFER,
DAN^L CARROLL.

Virginia.

JOHN BLAIR   JAMES MADISON Jr.

North Carolina.

WM. BLOUNT,   RICH'D DOBBS SPAIGHT,
HU WILLIAMSON.

South Carolina,

J. RUTLEDGE   CHARLES COTESWORTH PINCKNEY,
CHARLES PINCKNEY,   PIERCE BUTLER.

Georgia.

WILLIAM FEW,   ABR BALDWIN.
Attest: WILLIAM JACKSON, *Secretary.*

RATIFICATION OF THE CONSTITUTION

The Constitution was adopted by a convention of the States on September 17, 1787, and was subsequently ratified by the several States on the following dates: Delaware, December 7, 1787; Pennsylvania, December 12, 1787; New Jersey, December 18, 1787; Georgia, January 2, 1788; Connecticut, January 9, 1788; Massachusetts, February 6, 1788; Maryland, April 28, 1788; South Carolina, May 23, 1788; New Hampshire, June 21, 1788.

Ratification was completed on June 21, 1788.

The Constitution was subsequently ratified by Virginia, June 25, 1788; New York, July 26, 1788; North Carolina, November 21, 1789; Rhode Island, May 29, 1790; and Vermont, January 10, 1791.

ARTICLES IN ADDITION TO, AND AMENDMENT OF, THE CONSTITUTION OF THE UNITED STATES OF AMERICA, PROPOSED BY CONGRESS, AND RATIFIED BY THE LEGISLATURES OF THE SEVERAL STATES PURSUANT TO THE FIFTH ARTICLE OF THE ORIGINAL CONSTITUTION

ARTICLE [I]*

Freedom of religion, speech, press, and assembly

Congress shall make no law respecting an establishment of religion, or prohibiting the free exercise thereof; or abridging the freedom of speech, or of the press; or the right of the people peaceably to assemble, and to petition the Government for a redress of grievances.

ARTICLE [II]

Right to Bear Arms

A well regulated Militia, being necessary to the security of a free State, the right of the people to keep and bear Arms, shall not be infringed.

ARTICLE [III]

Quartering Troops

No Soldier shall, in time of peace be quartered in any house, without the consent of the Owner, nor in time of war, but in a manner to be prescribed by law.

ARTICLE [IV]

Unreasonable Searches and Seizures

The right of the people to be secure in their persons, houses, papers, and effects, against unreasonable searches and seizures, shall not be violated, and no Warrants shall issue, but upon probable cause, supported by Oath or affirmation, and particularly describing the place to be searched, and the persons or things to be seized.

ARTICLE [V]

Grand Jury, Double Jeopardy, Self-incrimination

No person shall be held to answer for a capital, or otherwise infamous crime, unless on a presentment of indictment of a Grand Jury, except in cases arising in the land or naval forces, or in the Militia, when in actual service in time of War or public danger; nor shall any person be subject for the same offence to be twice put in jeopardy of life or limb; nor shall be compelled in any criminal case to be a witness against himself, nor be deprived of life, liberty, or property, without due process of law; nor shall private property be taken for public use without just compensation.

---

*Only the 13th, 14th, 15th, and 16th articles of amendment had numbers assigned to them at the time of ratification.

ARTICLE [VI]

Jury Trial, Know Charges, Confront Witness, and Counsel

In all criminal prosecutions the accused shall enjoy the right to a speedy and public trial, by an impartial jury of the State and district wherein the crime shall have been committed, which district shall have been previously ascertained by law, and to be informed of the nature and cause of the accusation; to be confronted with the witnesses against him; to have compulsory process for obtaining Witnesses in his favor, and to have the assistance of counsel for his defense.

ARTICLE [VII]

Jury Trial in Civil Cases

In Suits at common law, where the value in controversy shall exceed twenty dollars, the right of trial by jury shall be preserved, and no fact tried by a jury, shall be otherwise reexamined in any Court of the United States, than according to the rules of the common law.

ARTICLE [VIII]

Excessive Bail and Cruel and Unusual Punishment

Excessive bail shall not be required, nor excessive fines imposed, nor cruel and unusual punishments inflicted.

ARTICLE [IX]

Unenumerated Rights Protected

The enumeration in the Constitution, of certain rights, shall not be construed to deny or disparage others retained by the people.

ARTICLE [X]

Reserved Powers

The powers not delegated to the United States by the Constitution, nor prohibited by it to the States, are reserved to the States respectively, or to the people.

The first 10 amendments to the Constitution, and 2 others that failed of ratification, were proposed by the Congress on September 25, 1789. They were ratified by the following States, and the notifications of the ratification by the Governors thereof were successively communicated by the President to the Congress: New Jersey, November 20, 1789; Maryland, December 19, 1789; North Carolina, December 22, 1789; South Carolina, January 19, 1790; New Hampshire, January 25, 1790; Delaware, January 28, 1790; New York, February 24, 1790; Pennsylvania, March 10, 1790; Rhode Island, June 7, 1790; Vermont, November 3, 1791; and Virginia, December 15, 1791.

Ratification was completed on December 15, 1791.

The amendments were subsequently ratified by Massachusetts, March 2, 1939; Connecticut, April 19, 1939; and Georgia, March 18, 1939.

ARTICLE [XI]

Federal Court Jurisdiction limited

The Judicial power of the United States shall not be construed to extend to any suit in law or equity, commenced or prosecuted against one of the United States by Citizens of another State, or by Citizens or Subjects of any Foreign State.

The 11th amendment to the Constitution was proposed by the Congress on March 4, 1794. It was declared, in a message from the President to Congress, dated January 8, 1798 to have been ratified by the legislatures of 12 of the 15 States. The dates of ratification were: New York, March 27, 1794; Rhode Island, March 31, 1794; Connecticut, May 8, 1794; New Hampshire, June 16, 1794; Massachusetts, June 26,

1794; Vermont, between October 9, 1794 and November 9, 1794; Virginia, November 18, 1794; Georgia, November 29, 1794; Kentucky, December 7, 1794; Maryland, December 26, 1794; Delaware, January 23, 1795; North Carolina, February 7, 1795.

Ratification as completed on February 7, 1795.

The amendment was subsequently ratified by South Carolina on December 4, 1797. New Jersey and Pennsylvania did not take action on the amendment.

ARTICLE [XII]

Electoral College revised
● **separate balloting**

The electors shall meet in their respective states and vote by ballot for President and Vice-President, one of whom, at least, shall not be an inhabitant of the same state with themselves; they shall name in their ballots the person voted for as President, and in distinct ballots the person voted for as Vice-President, and they shall make distinct lists of all persons voted for as President, and of all persons voted for as Vice-President, and of the number of votes for each, which lists they shall sign and certify, and transmit sealed to the seat of the government of the United States, directed to the President of the Senate;—The President of the Senate shall, in the presence of the Senate and House of Representatives, open all the certificates and the votes shall then be counted;—the Person having the greatest number of votes for President, shall be the President, if such number be a majority of the whole number of Electors appointed; and if no person have such majority, then from the persons having the highest numbers not exceeding three on the list of those voted for as President, the House of Representatives shall choose immediately, by ballot, the President. But in choosing the President, the votes shall be taken by states, the representation from each state having one vote; a quorum for this purpose shall consist of a member or members from two-thirds of the states, and a majority of all the states shall be necessary to a choice. [And if the House of Representatives shall not choose a President whenever the right of choice shall devolve upon them, before the fourth day of March next following, then the Vice-President shall act as President, as in the case of the death or other constitutional disability of the President.]* The person having the greatest number of votes as Vice-President, shall be the Vice-President, if such number be a majority of the whole number of Electors appointed, and if no person have a majority, then from the two highest numbers on the list, the Senate shall choose the Vice-President; a quorum for the purpose shall consist of two-thirds of the whole number of Senators, and a majority of the whole number shall be necessary to a choice. But no person constitutionally ineligible to the office of President shall be eligible to that of Vice-President of the United States.

● **House select from top three for President**

● **Senate choose Vice President from top two**

The 12th amendment to the Constitution was proposed by the Congress on December 9, 1803. It was declared, in a proclamation of the Secretary of State, dated September 25, 1804, to have been ratified by the legislatures of 13 of the 17 States. The dates of ratification were: Vermont, October 28, 1803; North Carolina, December 21, 1803; Maryland, December 24, 1803; Kentucky, December 27, 1803; Ohio, December 30, 1803; Pennsylvania, January 5, 1804; Virginia, February 3, 1804; New York, February 10, 1804; New Jersey, February 22, 1804; Rhode Island, March 12, 1804; South Carolina, May 15, 1804; Georgia, May 19, 1804; New Hampshire, June 15, 1804.

---

*The part included in brackets has been superseded by section 3 of the Twentieth Amendment.

Ratification was completed on June 15, 1804

The amendment was subsequently ratified by Tennessee, July 27, 1804.

The amendment was rejected by Delaware, January 18, 1804; Massachusetts, February 3, 1804; Connecticut, at its session begun May 10, 1804.

ARTICLE XIII

Prohibition on Slavery

SECTION 1. Neither slavery nor involuntary servitude, except as a punishment for crime whereof the party shall have been duly convicted, shall exist within the United States, or any place subject to their jurisdiction.

SECTION 2. Congress shall have power to enforce this article by appropriate legislation.

The 13th amendment to the Constitution was proposed by the Congress on January 31, 1865. It was declared, in a proclamation of the Secretary of State, dated December 18, 1865, to have been ratified by the legislatures of 27 of the 36 States. The dates of ratification were: Illinois, February 1, 1865; Rhode Island, February 2, 1865; Michigan, February 2, 1865; Maryland, February 3, 1865; New York, February 3, 1865; Pennsylvania, February 3, 1865; West Virginia, February 3, 1865; Missouri, February 6, 1865; Maine, February 7, 1865; Kansas, February 7, 1865; Massachusetts, February 7, 1865; Virginia, February 9, 1865; Ohio, February 10, 1865; Indiana, February 13, 1865; Nevada, February 16, 1865; Louisiana, February 17, 1865; Minnesota, February 23, 1865; Wisconsin, February 24, 1865; Vermont, March 9, 1865; Tennessee, April 7, 1865; Arkansas, April 14, 1865; Connecticut, May 4, 1865; New Hampshire, July 1, 1865; South Carolina, November 13, 1865; Alabama, December 2, 1865; North Carolina, December 4, 1865; Georgia, December 6, 1865.

Ratification was completed on December 6, 1865.

The amendment was subsequently ratified by Oregon, December 8, 1865; California, December 19, 1865; Florida, December 28, 1865 (Florida again ratified on June 9, 1868, upon its adoption of a new constitution); Iowa, January 15, 1866; New Jersey, January 23, 1866 (after having rejected the amendment on March 16, 1865); Texas, February 18, 1870; Delaware, February 12, 1901 (after having rejected the amendment on February 8, 1865).

The amendment was rejected by Kentucky, February 24, 1865, and by Mississippi, December 4, 1865.

ARTICLE XIV

Citizenship—U.S. and State

SECTION 1. All persons born or naturalized in the United States, and subject to the jurisdiction thereof, are citizens of the United States and of the State wherein they reside. No State shall make or enforce any law which shall abridge the privileges or immunities of citizens of the United States; nor shall any State deprive any person of life, liberty, or property, without due process of law; nor deny to any person within its jurisdiction the equal protection of the laws.

● **due process**
● **equal protection**

Reduced Representation for Abridging Vote

SECTION 2. Representatives shall be apportioned among the several States according to their respective numbers, counting the whole number of persons in each State, excluding Indians not taxed. But when the right to vote at any election for the choice of electors for President and Vice President of the United States, Representatives in Congress, the Executive and Judicial officers of a State, or the members of the Legislature thereof, is denied to any of the male inhabitants of such State, being twenty-one years of age,* and citizens of the United States, or in any way abridged, except for participation

*See the Twenty-sixth Amendment.

in rebellion, or other crime, the basis of representation therein shall be reduced in the proportion which the number of such male citizens shall bear to the whole number of male citizens twenty-one years of age in such State.

Confederate Officials Denied Federal Office

SECTION 3. No person shall be a Senator or Representative in Congress, or elector of President and Vice President, or hold any office, civil or military, under the United States, or under any State, who, having previously taken an oath, as a member of Congress, or as an officer of the United States, or as a member of any State legislature, or as an executive or judicial officer of any State, to support the Constitution of the United States, shall have engaged in insurrection or rebellion against the same, or given aid or comfort to the enemies thereof. But Congress may by a vote of two-thirds of each House, remove such disability.

Confederate Debts Invalid

SECTION 4. The validity of the public debt of the United States, authorized by law, including debts incurred for payment of pensions and bounties for services in suppressing insurrection or rebellion, shall not be questioned. But neither the United States nor any State shall assume or pay any debt or obligation incurred in aid of insurrection or rebellion against the United States, or any claim for the loss of emancipation of any slave; but all such debts, obligations and claims shall be held illegal and void.

SECTION 5. The Congress shall have power to enforce, by appropriate legislation, the provisions of this article.

The 14th amendment to the Constitution was proposed by the Congress on June 13, 1866. It was declared, in a certificate by the Secretary of State dated July 28, 1868, to have been ratified by the legislatures of 28 of the 37 States. The dates of ratification were: Connecticut, June 25, 1866; New Hampshire, July 6, 1866; Tennessee, July 19, 1866; New Jersey, September 11, 1866 (subsequently the legislature rescinded its ratification, and on March 5, 1868, readopted its resolution of rescission over the Governor's veto); Oregon, September 19, 1866 (and rescinded its ratification on October 15, 1868); Vermont, October 30, 1866; Ohio, January 4, 1867 (and rescinded its ratification on January 15, 1868); New York, January 10, 1867; Kansas, January 11, 1867; Illinois, January 15, 1867; West Virginia, January 16, 1867; Michigan, January 16, 1867; Minnesota January 16, 1867; Maine, January 19, 1867; Nevada, January 22, 1867; Indiana, January 23, 1867; Missouri, January 25, 1867; Rhode Island, February 7, 1867; Wisconsin, February 7, 1867; Pennsylvania, February 12, 1867; Massachusetts, March 20, 1867; Nebraska, June 15, 1867; Iowa, March 16, 1868; Arkansas, April 6, 1868; Florida, June 9, 1868; North Carolina, July 4, 1868 (after having rejected it on December 14, 1866); Louisiana, July 9, 1968 (after having rejected it on February 6, 1867); South Carolina, July 9, 1868 (after having rejected it on December 20, 1866).

Ratification was completed on July 9, 1868.[1]

The amendment was subsequently ratified by Alabama, July 13, 1868; Georgia, July 21, 1868 (after having rejected in on November 9, 1866); Virginia, October 8, 1869 (after having rejected it on January 9, 1867); Mississippi, January 17, 1870; Texas, February 18, 1870 (after having rejected it on October 27, 1866); Delaware, February 12, 1901 (after having rejected it on Febuary 8, 1867); Maryland, April 4, 1959 (after having rejected it on March 23, 1867); California, May 6, 1959.

---

[1]The certificate of the Secretary of State, dated July 20, 1868, was based upon the assumption of invalidity of the rescission of ratification by Ohio and New Jersey. The following day, the Congress adopted a joint resolution declaring the amendment a part of the Constitution. The Secretary of State issued a proclamation of ratification without reservation.

ARTICLE XV

Suffrage for Freed Slaves

SECTION 1. The right of citizens of the United States to vote shall not be denied or abridged by the United States or by any State on account of race, color, or previous condition of servitude.

SECTION 2. The Congress shall have power to enforce this article by appropriate legislation.

The 15th amendment to the Constitution was proposed by the Congress on February 26, 1869. It was declared, in a proclamation of the Secretary of State, dated March 30, 1870, to have been ratified by the legislatures of 29 of the 37 States. The dates of ratification were: Nevada, March 1, 1869; West Virginia, March 3, 1869: Illinois, March 5, 1869; Louisiana, March 5, 1869; North Carolina, March 5, 1869; Michigan, March 8, 1869; Wisconsin, March 9, 1869; Maine, March 11, 1869: Massachusetts, March 12, 1869; Arkansas, March 15, 1869; South Carolina, March 15, 1869; Pennsylvania, March 25, 1869; New York, April 14, 1869 (and the legislature of the same State passed a resolution January 5, 1870, to withdraw its consent to it, which action it rescinded on March 30, 1970); Indiana, May 14, 1869; Connecticut, May 19, 1869; Florida, June 14, 1869; New Hampshire, July 1, 1869; Virginia, October 8, 1869; Vermont, October 20, 1869; Missouri, January 7, 1870; Minnesota, January 13, 1870; Mississippi, January 17, 1870; Rhode Island, January 18, 1870; Kansas, January 19, 1870; Ohio, January 27, 1870 (after having rejected it on April 30, 1869); Georgia, February 2, 1870; Iowa, February 3, 1870.

Ratification was completed on February 3, 1870, unless the withdrawal of ratification by New York was effective; in which event ratification was completed on February 17, 1870, when Nebraska ratified.

The amendment was subsequently ratified by Texas, February 18, 1870; New Jersey, February 15, 1871 (after having rejected it on February 7, 1870); Delaware, February 12, 1901 (after having rejected it on March 18, 1869); Oregon, February 24, 1959; California, April 3, 1962 (after having rejected it on January 28, 1870).

ARTICLE XVI

Income Tax

The Congress shall have power to lay and collect taxes on incomes, from whatever source derived, without apportionment among the several States, and without regard to any census or enumeration.

The 16th amendment to the Constitution was proposed by the Congress on July 12, 1909. It was declared, in a proclamation of the Secretary of State, dated February 25, 1913, to have been ratified by 36 of the 48 States. The dates of ratification were: Alabama, August 10, 1909; Kentucky, February 8, 1910; South Carolina, February 19, 1910; Illinois, March 1, 1910; Mississippi, March 7, 1910; Oklahoma, March 10, 1910; Maryland, April 8, 1910; Georgia, August 3, 1910; Texas, August 16, 1910; Ohio, January 19, 1911; Idaho, January 20, 1911; Oregon, January 23, 1911; Washington, January 26, 1911; Montana, January 30, 1911; Indiana, January 30, 1911; California, January 31, 1911; Nevada, January 31, 1911; South Dakota, February 3, 1911; Nebraska, February 9, 1911; North Carolina, February 11, 1911; Colorado, February 15, 1911; North Dakota, February 17, 1911; Kansas, February 18, 1911; Michigan, February 23, 1911; Iowa, February 24, 1911; Missouri, March 16, 1911; Maine, March 31, 1911; Tennessee, April 7, 1911; Arkansas, April 22, 1911 (after having rejected it earlier); Wisconsin, May 26, 1911; New York, July 12, 1911; Arizona, April 6, 1912; Louisiana, June 28, 1912; Minnesota, July 11, 1912; West Virginia, January 31, 1913; New Mexico, February 3, 1913

Ratification was completed on February 3, 1913.

The amendment was subsequently ratified by Massachusetts, March 4, 1913; New Hampshire, March 7, 1913 (after having rejected it on March 2, 1911).

The amendment was rejected by Connecticut, Rhode Island, and Utah.

ARTICLE [XVII]

Direct Election of Senators

The Senate of the United States shall be composed of two Senators from each State, elected by the people thereof, for six years; and each Senator shall have one vote. The electors in each State shall have the qualifications requisite for electors of the most numerous branch of the State legislatures.

When vacancies happen in the representation of any State in the Senate, the executive authority of such State shall issue writs of election to fill such vacancies: *Provided,* That the legislature of any State may empower the executive thereof to make temporary appointments until the people fill the vacancies by election as the legislature may direct.

This amendment shall not be so construed as to affect the election or term of any Senator chosen before it becomes valid as part of the Constitution.

The 17th amendment to the Constitution was proposed by the Congress on May 13, 1912. It was declared, in a proclamation by the Secretary of State, dated May 31, 1913, to have been ratified by the legislatures of 36 of the 48 States. The dates of ratification were: Massachusetts, May 22, 1912; Arizona, June 3, 1912; Minnesota, June 10, 1912; New York, January 15, 1913; Kansas, January 17, 1913; Oregon, January 23, 1913; North Carolina, January 25, 1913; California, January 28, 1913; Michigan, January 28, 1913; Iowa, January 30, 1913; Montana, January 30, 1913; Idaho, January 31, 1913; West Virginia, February 4, 1913; Colorado, February 5, 1913; Nevada, February 6, 1913; Texas, February 7, 1913; Washington, February 7, 1913; Wyoming, February 8, 1913; Arkansas, February 11, 1913; Maine, February 11, 1913; Illinois, February 13, 1913; North Dakota, February 14, 1913; Wisconsin, February 18, 1913; Indiana, February 19, 1913; New Hampshire, February 19, 1913; Vermont, February 19, 1913; South Dakota, February 19, 1913; Oklahoma, February 24, 1913; Ohio, February 25, 1913; Missouri, March 7, 1913; New Mexico, March 13, 1913; Nebraska, March 14, 1913; New Jersey, March 17, 1913; Tennessee, April 1, 1913; Pennsylvania, April 2, 1913; Connecticut, April 8, 1913.

Ratification was completed on April 8, 1913.

The amendment was subsequently ratified by Louisiana, June 11, 1914.

The amendment was rejected by Utah on Feburary 26, 1913.

[ARTICLE [XVIII]]

Prohibition of Alcohol

[SECTION 1. After one year from the ratification of this article the manufacture, sale, or transportation of intoxicating liquors within, the importation thereof into, or the exportation thereof from the United States and all territory subject to the jurisdiction thereof for beverage purposes is hereby prohibited.

[SECTION 2. The Congress and the several States shall have concurrent power to enforce this article by appropriate legislation.

[SECTION 3. This article shall be inoperative unless it shall have been ratified as an amendment to the Constitution by the legislatures of the several States, as provided in the Constitution, within seven years from the date of the submission hereof to the States by the Congress.]*

The 18th amendment to the Constitution was proposed by the Congress on December 18, 1917. It was declared, in a proclamation by the Acting Secretary of State, dated January 29, 1919, to have been ratified by the legislatures of 36 of the 48 States. The dates of ratification were: Mississippi, January 8, 1918; Virginia, January 11, 1918; Kentucky, January 14, 1918; North Dakota, January 25, 1918; South Carolina, January

---

*Repealed by section 1 of the Twenty-first Amendment.

29, 1918; Maryland, February 13, 1918; Montana, February 19, 1918; Texas, March 4, 1918; Delaware, March 18, 1918; South Dakota, March 20, 1918; Massachusetts, April 2, 1918; Arizona, May 24, 1918; Georgia, June 26, 1918; Louisiana, August 3, 1918; Florida, December 3, 1918; Michigan, January 2, 1919; Ohio, January 7, 1919; Oklahoma, January 7, 1919; Idaho, January 8, 1919; Maine, January 8, 1919; West Virginia, January 9, 1919; California, January 13, 1919; Tennessee, January 13, 1919; Washington, January 13, 1919; Arkansas, January 14, 1919; Kansas, January 14, 1919; Alabama, January 15, 1919; Colorado, January 15, 1919; Iowa, January 15, 1919; New Hampshire, January 15, 1919; Oregon, January 15, 1919; Nebraska, January 16, 1919; North Carolina, January 16, 1919; Utah, January 16, 1919; Missouri, January 16, 1919; Wyoming, January 16, 1919.

Ratification was completed on January 16, 1919.

The amendment was subsequently ratified by Minnesota on January 17, 1917; Wisconsin, January 17, 1919; New Mexico, January 20, 1919; Nevada, January 21, 1919; New York, January 29, 1919; Vermont, January 29, 1919; Pennsylvania, February 25, 1919; Connecticut, May 6, 1919; and New Jersey, March 9, 1922.

The amendment was rejected by Rhode Island.

ARTICLE [XIX]

Women Suffrage

The right of citizens of the United States to vote shall not be denied or abridged by the United States or by any State on account of sex.

Congress shall have power to enforce this article by appropriate legislation.

The 19th amendment to the Constitution was proposed by the Congress on June 4, 1919. It was declared, in a certificate by the Secretary of State, dated August 26, 1920, to have been ratified by the legislatures of 36 of the 48 States. The dates of ratification were: Illinois, June 10, 1919 (and that State readopted its resolution of ratification June 17, 1919); Michigan, June 10, 1919; Wisconsin, June 10, 1919; Kansas, June 16, 1919; New York, June 16, 1919; Ohio, June 16, 1919; Pennsylvania, June 24, 1919; Massachusetts, June 25, 1919; Texas, June 28, 1919; Iowa, July 2, 1919; Missouri, July 3, 1919; Arkansas, July 28, 1919; Montana, August 2, 1919; Nebraska, August 2, 1919; Minnesota, September 8, 1919; New Hampshire, September 10, 1919; Utah, October 2, 1919; California, November 1, 1919; Maine, November 5, 1919; North Dakota, December 1, 1919; South Dakota, December 4, 1919; Colorado, December 15, 1919; Kentucky, January 6, 1920; Rhode Island, January 6, 1920; Oregon, January 13, 1920; Indiana, January 16, 1920; Wyoming, January 27, 1920; Nevada, February 7, 1920; New Jersey, February 9, 1920; Idaho, February 11, 1920; Arizona, February 12, 1920; New Mexico, February 21, 1920; Oklahoma, February 28, 1920; West Virginia, March 10, 1920; Washington, March 22, 1920; Tennessee, August 18, 1920.

Ratification was completed on August 20, 1920.

The amendment was subsequently ratified by Connecticut on September 14, 1920 (and that State reaffirmed on Septeber 21, 1920); Vermont, February 8, 1921; Maryland, March 29, 1941 (after having rejected it on February 24, 1920; ratification certified on February 25, 1958); Alabama, September 8, 1953 (after that State had rejected it on September 22, 1919); Virginia, February 21, 1952 (after rejecting it on February 12, 1920); Florida, May 13, 1969; Louisiana, June 11, 1970 (after having rejected it on July 1, 1920); Georgia, February 20, 1970 (after rejecting on July 24, 1919); North Carolina, May 6, 1971.

The amendment was rejected by South Carolina, January 28, 1920; Mississippi, March 29, 1920; Delaware, June 2, 1920.

ARTICLE [XX]

Terms of Office Changed to January

SECTION 1. The terms of the President and Vice President shall end at noon on the 20th day of January, and the terms of Senators and Representatives at noon on the 3rd day of January, of the years in which terms would have ended if this article had not been ratified; and the terms of their successors shall then begin.

SECTION 2. The Congress shall assemble at least once in every year, and such meeting shall begin at noon on the 3rd day of January, unless they shall by law appoint a different day.

Emergency Succession to Presidency

SECTION 3. If, at the time fixed for the beginning of the term of the President, the President elect shall have died, the Vice President elect shall become President. If a President shall not have been chosen before the time fixed for the beginning of his term, or if the President elect shall have failed to qualify, then the Vice President elect shall act as President until a President shall have qualified; and the Congress may by law provide for the case wherein neither a President elect nor a Vice President elect shall have qualified, declaring who shall then act as President, or the manner in which one who is to act shall be selected, and such person shall act accordingly until a President or Vice President shall have qualified.

SECTION 4. The Congress may by law provide for the case of the death of any of the persons from whom the House of Representatives may choose a President whenever the right of choice shall have devolved upon them, and for the case of the death of any of the persons from whom the Senate may choose a Vice President whenever the right of choice shall have devolved upon them.

SECTION 5. Sections 1 and 2 shall take effect on the 15th day of October following the ratification of this article.

SECTION 6. This article shall be inoperative unless it shall have been ratified as an amendment to the Constitution by the legislatures of three-fourths of the several States within seven years from the date of its submission.

The 20th amendment to the Constitution was proposed by the Congress on March 2, 1932. It was declared, in a certificate by the Secretary of State, dated February 6, 1933, to have been ratified by the legislatures of 36 of the 48 States. The dates of ratification were: Virginia, March 4, 1932; New York, March 11, 1932; Mississippi, March 16, 1932; Arkansas, March 17, 1932; Kentucky, March 17, 1932; New Jersey, March 21, 1932; South Carolina, March 25, 1932; Michigan, March 31, 1932; Maine, April 1, 1932; Rhode Island, April 14, 1932; Illinois, April 21, 1932; Louisiana, June 22, 1932; West Virginia, July 30, 1932; Pennsylvania, August 11, 1932; Indiana, August 15, 1932; Texas, September 7, 1932; Alabama, September 13, 1932; California, January 4, 1933; North Carolina, January 5, 1933; North Dakota, January 9, 1933; Minnesota, January 12, 1933; Arizona, January 13, 1933; Montana, January 13, 1933; Nebraska, January 13, 1933; Oklahoma, January 13, 1933; Kansas, January 16, 1933; Oregon, January 16, 1933; Delaware, January 19, 1933; Washington, January 19, 1933; Wyoming, January 19, 1933; Iowa, January 20, 1933; South Dakota, January 20, 1933; Tennesseee, January 20, 1933; Idaho, January 21, 1933; New Mexico, January 21, 1933; Georgia, January 23, 1933; Missouri, January 23, 1933; Ohio, January 23, 1933; Utah, January 23, 1933.

Ratification was completed on January 23, 1933.

The amendment was subsequently ratified by Massachusetts on January 24, 1933; Wisconsin, January 24, 1933; Colorado, January 24, 1933; Nevada, January 26, 1933; Connecticut, January 27, 1933; New Hampshire, January 31, 1933; Vermont, February 2, 1933; Maryland, March 24, 1933; Florida, April 26, 1933.

ARTICLE [XXI]

Repeal of Prohibition

SECTION 1. The eighteenth article of amendment to the Constitution of the United States is hereby repealed.

SECTION 2. The transportation or importation into any State, Territory, or possession of the United States for delivery or use therein of intoxicating liquors, in violation of the laws thereof, is hereby prohibited.

SECTION 3. This article shall be inoperative unless it shall have been ratified as an amendment to the Constitution by conventions in the several States, as provided in the Constitution, within seven years from the date of the submission hereof to the States by the Congress.

The 21st amendment to the Constitution was proposed by the Congress on February 20, 1933. It was declared, in a certificate of the Acting Secretary of State, dated December 5, 1933, to have been ratified by conventions in 36 of the 48 States. The dates of ratification were: Michigan, April 10, 1933; Wisconsin, April 25, 1933; Rhode Island, May 8, 1933; Wyoming, May 25, 1933; New Jersey, June 1, 1933; Delaware, June 24, 1933; Indiana, June 26, 1933; Massachusetts, June 26, 1933; New York, June 27, 1933; Illinois, July 10, 1933; Iowa, July 10, 1933; Connecticut, July 11, 1933; New Hampshire, July 11, 1933; California, July 24, 1933; West Virginia, July 25, 1933; Arkansas, August 1, 1933; Oregon, August 7, 1933; Alabama, August 8, 1933; Tennessee, August 11, 1933; Missouri, August 29, 1933; Arizona, September 5, 1933; Nevada; September 5, 1933; Vermont, September 23, 1933; Colorado, September 26, 1933; Washington, October 3, 1933; Minnesota, October 10, 1933; Idaho, October 17, 1933; Maryland, October 18, 1933; Virginia, October 25, 1933; New Mexico, November 2, 1933; Florida, November 14, 1933; Texas, November 24, 1933; Kentucky, November 27, 1933; Ohio, December 5, 1933; Pennsylvania. December 5, 1933; Utah, December 5, 1933.

Ratification was completed on December 5, 1933.

The amendment was subsequently ratified by Maine, on December 6, 1933, and by Montana, on August 6, 1934.

The amendment was rejected by South Carolina, on December 4, 1933.

ARTICLE [XXII]

President Limited to Two Terms

SECTION 1. No person shall be elected to the office of the President more than twice, and no person who has held the office of President, or acted as President, for more than two years of a term to which some other person was elected President shall be elected to the office of the President more than once. But this Article shall not apply to any person holding the office of President when this Article was proposed by the Congress, and shall not prevent any person who may be holding the office of President, or acting as President, during the term within which this Article becomes operative from holding the office of President or acting as President during the remainder of such term.

SECTION 2. This article shall be inoperative unless it shall have been ratified as an amendment to the Constitution by the legislatures of three-fourths of the several States within seven years from the date of its submission to the States by the Congress.

The 22d amendment to the Constitution was proposed by the Congress on March 21, 1947. It was declared, in a certificate by the Administrator of General Services, dated March 3, 1951, to have been ratified by the legislatures of 36 of the 48 States. The dates of ratification were: Maine, March 31, 1947; Michigan, March 31, 1947; Iowa, April 1, 1947; Kansas, April 1, 1947; New Hampshire, April 1, 1947; Delaware, April 2, 1947; Illinois, April 3, 1947; Oregon, April 3, 1947; Colorado, April 12, 1947; California, April 15, 1947; New Jersey, April 15, 1947; Vermont, April 15, 1947; Ohio, April 16, 1947; Wisconsin, April 16, 1947; Pennsylvania, April 29, 1947; Connecticut, May 21, 1947; Missouri, May 22, 1947; Nebraska, May 23, 1947; Virginia, January 28, 1948; Mississippi, February 12, 1948; New York, March 9, 1948; South

Dakota, January 21, 1949; North Dakota, February 25, 1949; Louisiana, May 17, 1950; Montana, January 25, 1951; Indiana, January 29, 1951; Idaho, January 30, 1951; New Mexico, February 12, 1951; Wyoming, February 12, 1951; Arkansas, February 15, 1951; Georgia, February 17, 1951; Tennessee, February 20, 1951; Texas, February 22, 1951; Nevada, February 26, 1951; Utah, February 26, 1951; Minnesota, February 27, 1951.

Ratification was completed on Feburary 27, 1951.

The amendment was subsequently ratified by North Carolina on February 28, 1951; South Carolina, March 13, 1951; Maryland, March 14, 1951; Florida, April 16, 1951; Alabama, May 4, 1951.

The amendment was rejected by Oklahoma in June 1947, and Massachusetts on June 9, 1949.

ARTICLE [XXIII]

Electoral Vote for District of Columbia

SECTION 1. The District constituting the seat of Government of the United States shall appoint in such manner as the Congress may direct:

A number of electors of President and Vice President equal to the whole number of Senators and Representatives in Congress to which the District would be entitled if it were a State, but in no event more than the least populous State; they shall be in addition to those appointed by the States, but they shall be considered, for the purposes of the election of President and Vice President, to be electors appointed by a State; and they shall meet in the District and perform such duties as provided by the twelfth article of amendment.

SECTION 2. The Congress shall have power to enforce this article by appropriate legislation.

The 23rd amendment to the Constitution was proposed by the Congress on June 17, 1960. It was declared, in a certificate by the Administrator of General Services, to have been ratified by 38 of the 50 States. The dates of ratification were: Hawaii, June 23, 1960 (and that State made a technical correction to its resolution on June 30, 1960); Massachusetts, August 22, 1960; New Jersey, December 19, 1960; New York, January 17, 1961; California, January 19, 1961; Oregon, January 27, 1961; Maryland, January 30, 1961; Idaho, January 31, 1961; Maine, January 31, 1961; Minnesota, January 31, 1961; New Mexico, February 1, 1961; Nevada, February 2, 1961; Montana, February 6, 1961; South Dakota, February 6, 1961; Colorado, February 8, 1961; Washington, February 9, 1961; West Virginia, February 9, 1961; Alaska, February 10, 1961; Wyoming, February 13, 1961; Delaware, February 20, 1961; Utah, February 21, 1961; Wisconsin, February 21, 1961; Pennsylvania, February 28, 1961; Indiana, March 3, 1961; North Dakota, March 3, 1961; Tennessee, March 6, 1961; Michigan, March 8, 1961; Connecticut, March 9, 1961; Arizona, March 10, 1961; Illinois, March 14, 1961; Nebraska, March 15, 1961; Vermont, March 15, 1961; Iowa, March 16, 1961; Missouri, March 20, 1961; Oklahoma, March 21, 1961; Rhode Island, March 22, 1961; Kansas, March 29, 1961; Ohio, March 29, 1961.

Ratification was completed on March 29, 1961.

The amendment was subsequently ratified by New Hampshire on March 30, 1961 (when that State annulled and then repeated its ratification of March 29, 1961).

The amendment was rejected by Arkansas on January 24, 1961.

ARTICLE [XXIV]

Prohibits Poll Tax

SECTION 1. The right of citizens of the United States to vote in any primary or other election for President or Vice President, for electors for President or Vice President, or for Senator or Representative in Congress, shall not be denied or abridged by the United States or any State by reason of failure to pay any poll tax or other tax.

SECTION 2. The Congress shall have power to enforce this article by appropriate legislation.

The 24th amendment to the Constitution was proposed by the Congress on August 27, 1962. It was declared, in a certificate of the Administrator of General Services, dated February 4, 1964, to have been ratified by the legislatures of 38 of the 50 States. The dates of ratification were: Illinois, November 14, 1962; New Jersey, December 3, 1962; Oregon, January 25, 1963; Montana, January 28, 1963; West Virginia, February 1, 1963; New York, February 4, 1963; Maryland, February 6, 1963; California, February 7, 1963; Alaska, February 11, 1963; Rhode Island, February 14, 1963; Indiana, February 19, 1963; Utah, February 20, 1963; Michigan, February 20, 1963; Colorado, February 21, 1963; Ohio, February 27, 1963; Minnesota, February 27, 1963; New Mexico, March 5, 1963; Hawaii, March 6, 1963; North Dakota, March 7, 1963; Idaho, March 8, 1963; Washington, March 14, 1963; Vermont, March 15, 1963; Nevada, March 19, 1963; Connecticut, March 20, 1963; Tennessee, March 21, 1963; Pennsylvania, March 25, 1963; Wisconsin, March 26, 1963; Kansas, March 28, 1963; Massachusetts, March 28, 1963; Nebraska, April 4, 1963; Florida, April 18, 1963; Iowa, April 24, 1963; Delaware, May 1, 1963; Missouri, May 13, 1963; New Hampshire, June 12, 1963; Kentucky, June 27, 1963; Maine, January 16, 1964; South Dakota, January 23, 1964.

Ratification was completed on January 23, 1964.

The amendment was rejected by Mississippi on December 20, 1962.

ARTICLE [XXV]

Presidential Succession and Disability

SECTION 1. In case of the removal of the President from office or of his death or resignation, the Vice President shall become President.

SEC. 2. Whenever there is a vacancy in the office of the Vice President, the President shall nominate a Vice President who shall take office upon confirmation by a majority vote of both Houses of Congress.

● **declaration of disability**

SEC. 3. Whenever the President transmits to the President pro tempore of the Senate and the Speaker of the House of Representatives his written declaration that he is unable to discharge the powers and duties of his office, and until he transmits to them a written declaration to the contrary, such powers and duties shall be discharged by the Vice President as Acting President.

SEC. 4. Whenever the Vice President and a majority of either the principal officers of the executive departments or of such other body as Congress may by law provide, transmit to the President pro tempore of the Senate and the Speaker of the House of Representatives their written declaration that the President is unable to discharge the powers and duties of his office, the Vice President shall immediately assume the powers and duties of the office as Acting President.

Thereafter, when the President transmits to the President pro tempore of the Senate and the Speaker of the House of Representatives his written declaration that no inability exists, he shall resume the powers and duties of his office unless the Vice President and a majority of either the principal officers of the executive department or of such other body as Congress may by law provide, transmit within four days to the President pro tempore of the Senate and the Speaker of the House of Representatives their written declaration that the President is unable to discharge the powers and duties of his office. Thereupon Congress shall decide the issue, assembling within forty-eight hours for that purpose if not in session. If the Congress, within twenty-one days after receipt of the latter written declaration, or, if Congress is not in session, within twenty-one days after Congress is required to assemble, determines by two-thirds vote of both Houses that the President is unable to discharge the powers and duties of his office, the Vice President shall continue to discharge the same as Acting President; otherwise, the President shall resume the powers and duties of his office.

The 25th amendment to the Constitution was proposed by the Congress on July 6, 1965. It was declared, in a certificate of the Administrator of General Services, dated February 23, 1967, to have been ratified by the legislatures of 39 of the 50 States. The dates of ratification were: Nebraska, July 12, 1965; Wisconsin, July 13, 1965; Oklahoma, July 16, 1965; Massachusetts, August 9, 1965; Pennsylvania, August 18, 1965; Kentucky, September 15, 1965; Arizona, September 22, 1965; Michigan, October 5, 1965; Indiana, October 20, 1965; California, October 21, 1965; Arkansas, November 4, 1965; New Jersey, November 29, 1965; Delaware, December 7, 1965; Utah, January 17, 1966; West Virginia, January 20, 1966; Maine, January 24, 1966; Rhode Island, January 28, 1966; Colorado, February 3, 1966; New Mexico, February 3, 1966; Kansas, February 8, 1966; Vermont, February 10, 1966; Alaska, February 18, 1966; Idaho, March 2, 1966; Hawaii, March 3, 1966; Virginia, March 8, 1966; Mississippi, March 10, 1966; New York, March 14, 1966; Maryland, March 23, 1966; Missouri, March 30, 1966; New Hampshire, June 13, 1966; Louisiana, July 5, 1966; Tennessee, January 12, 1967; Wyoming, January 25, 1967; Washington, Janaury 26, 1967; Iowa, January 26, 1967; Oregon, February 2, 1967; Minnesota, February 10, 1967; Nevada, February 10, 1967.

Ratification was completed on February 10, 1967.

The amendment was subsequently ratified by Connecticut, February 14, 1967; Montana, February 15, 1967; South Dakota, March 6, 1967; Ohio, March 7, 1967; Alabama, March 14, 1967; North Carolina, March 22, 1967; Illinois, March 22, 1967; Texas, April 25, 1967; Florida, May 25, 1967.

ARTICLE [XXVI]

Voting Age Lowered to 18

SECTION 1. The right of citizens of the United States, who are eighteen years of age or older, to vote shall not be denied or abridged by the United States or by any State on account of age.

SEC. 2. The Congress shall have power to enforce this article by appropriate legislation.

The 26th amendment to the Constitution was proposed by the Congress on March 23, 1971. It was declared, in a certificate of the Administrator of General Services, dated July 5, 1971, to have been ratified by the legislatures of 39 of the 50 States. The dates of ratification were: Connecticut, March 23, 1971; Delaware, March 23, 1971; Minnesota, March 23, 1971; Tennessee, March 23, 1971; Washington, March 23, 1971; Hawaii, March 24, 1971; Massachusetts, March 24, 1971; Montana, March 29, 1971; Arkansas, March 30, 1971; Idaho, March 30, 1971; Iowa, March 30, 1971; Nebraska, April 2, 1971; New Jersey, April 3, 1971; Kansas, April 7, 1971; Michigan, April 7, 1971; Alaska, April 8, 1971; Maryland, April 8, 1971; Indiana, April 8, 1971; Maine, April 9, 1971; Vermont, April 16, 1971; Louisiana, April 17, 1971; California, April 19, 1971; Colorado, April 27, 1971; Pennsylvania, April 27, 1971; Texas, April 27, 1971; South Carolina, April 28, 1971; West Virginia, April 28, 1971; New Hampshire, May 13, 1971; Arizona, May 14, 1971; Rhode Island, May 27, 1971; New York, June 2, 1971; Oregon, June 4, 1971; Missouri, June 14, 1971; Wisconsin, June 22, 1971; Illinois, June 29, 1971; Alabama, June 30, 1971; Ohio, June 30, 1971; North Carolina, July 1, 1971; Oklahoma, July 1, 1971.

Ratification was completed on July 1, 1971.

The amendment was subsequently ratified by Virginia, July 8, 1971; Wyoming, July 8, 1971; Georgia, October 4, 1971.

Proposed Amendment

(The amendment proposing that the District of Columbia be treated as a state for purposes of congressional representation and election of president and vice president was proposed by the Ninety-fifth Congress. It passed the House on March 2, 1978, and the Senate on August 22, 1978).

ARTICLE

Proposed Amendment Extending Full Representation to District of Columbia

SECTION 1 For purposes of representation in the Congress, election of the President and Vice President, and article V of this Constitution, the District constituting the seat of government of the United States shall be treated as though it were a State.

SECTION 2 The exercise of the rights and powers conferred under this article shall be by the people of the District constituting the seat of government, and as shall be provided by the Congress.

SECTION 3 The twenty-third article of amendment to the Constitution of the United States is hereby repealed.

SECTION 4 This article shall be inoperative, unless it shall have been ratified as an amendment to the Constitution by the legislatures of three-fourths of the several States within seven years from the date of its submission.

Proposed Amendment

(The amendment relative to equal rights for men and women was proposed by the Ninety-second Congress. It passed the House on October 12, 1971 and the Senate on March 22, 1972.)

ARTICLE

Proposed Amendment Prohibiting Discrimination Based on Sex

SECTION 1 Equality of rights under the law shall not be denied or abridged by the United States or by any State on account of sex.

SECTION 2 The Congress shall have the power to enforce, by appropriate legislation, the provisions of this article.

SECTION 3 This amendment shall take effect two years after the date of ratification.

Ratification deadline extended to June 30, 1982.

Glossary

ABSCAM The 1980 Congressional scandal involving the revelation that FBI agents, posing as Arab representatives, bribed several Congressmen.

access The contact with public officials that forms the basis for lobbying activity. Access depends on reaching key decision-makers at key points in the political process.

adversarial process The judicial process whereby two contending parties argue their differences in order to establish the culpability of one or other of the parties.

affirmative action The policy of providing special assistance to minorities in an effort to equalize results in areas such as education and employment.

agenda setting The identification of important issues. The media performs what is called the agenda-setting function.

amicus curiae "Friend of the court" briefs submitted by interested parties at the invitation of the court.

anti-federalists Individuals who opposed the Constitution, fearing a strong central government.

Appellate Court Intermediate courts and the Supreme Courts in the state and federal court systems that have jurisdiction to review a case.

appropriations A Congressional act authorizing public funds for specific governmental purposes. All agencies of government must come to Congress annually to have their operating budgets renewed.

Articles of Confederation Adopted in 1777, the Articles served as the United States Constitution until replaced by the present Constitution. As a form of government, the Articles granted more power to the individual states than a national government.

badge of slavery Private acts of racial discrimination that violate the Thirteenth Amendment.

bad tendency A test established by the Supreme Court in 1925 to deal with the prohibition of speech threatening the overthrow of the government.

bill of attainder A law declaring a particular individual guilty of a crime and naming the punishment without benefit of trial.

Bill of Rights The first ten amendments to the Constitution. They specify the rights of individuals and the limitations of the national government.

blanket primary A form of direct primary in which the voter is given both party ballots and can vote back and forth between the parties in choosing nominees for public office.

block grant A form of federal aid to state and local governments for broadly defined purposes within which local officials have discretion on the specific programs to be operated.

blue collar caucus A caucus representing working class occupations, formed in 1977 by fourteen members of the House of Representatives.

brief A lengthy written document citing law and precedent, used in court by counsel.

Brown v. Board of Education of Topeka The 1954 Supreme Court decision that declared laws requiring segregation of schools to be unconstitutional.

bureau A subdivision of a bureaucratic department.

busing A court-ordered remedy to overcome intentional discrimination against racial minorities. Students are transported out of their neighborhood to schools some distance from home, if necessary, to break the pattern of segregation.

cabinet Collectively, the thirteen heads of the executive agencies together with the President and Vice-President comprise the Cabinet.

calendar Wednesday A method of avoiding the House Rules Committee by allowing committee chairs, in alphabetical order of committees, to call up any bills from the House or the Union calendars on Wednesdays.

capital punishment The use of the death penalty as a form of criminal punishment.

careerism The tendency for a legislative politician to build a professional career by running for and holding public office.

"cases and controversies" The phrase used in Article III of the Constitution to define the jurisdiction of the federal judiciary. This phrase has been interpreted to mean actual disputes capable of settlement by judicial means.

categorical grant A system of national aid to state and local government for a specific purpose, allowing the recipient little discretion regarding use of the money.

caucus A closed meeting of party leaders.

civil law Private or statutory law regulating the relationships between private citizens.

civil liberties Basic rights and freedoms outside the control of the federal government.

civil service The government employment system based on merit and the premise that similar employees performing like functions should be treated and paid the same.

class action suit A lawsuit brought by a group of persons with a common legal concern, willing to share the costs of bringing suit.

clear and present danger doctrine The test proposed by Supreme Court Justice Holmes for determining when government had the right to restrict free speech. Only when speech provoked a "clear and present danger" were restrictions permissible.

clientele group The natural constituency or consumers of specific government services. The clientele relationship with bureaucratic agencies is a prime source of political power.

closed primary A form of direct primary in which voters must make a prior declaration of party affiliation in order to vote in the party's primary.

closed rule A provision made by the House Rules Committee which prohibits amendments from being offered from the floor.

cloture A Senate procedure invoked to close debate. It requires a three-fifths vote of the Senate.

coattail effect The pulling power of a presidential candidate to attract voters so that congressional candidates of the same party are elected to office.

Committee on Committees A committee of House Republican leaders which assigns House Republicans to committees.

Committee to Re-elect the President (CREEP) The autonomous campaign organization established to finance and operate the 1972 re-election of Richard Nixon.

common law A system of judge-made law based on custom and precedent.

compact colonies Colonies that based their organization on ideas borrowed from religious theory. Government was created out of consent of the governed.

concurrent powers Powers exercised by both national and state governments, such as the power to levy taxes or regulate commerce.

confederation A system of government in which legal authority is held by constituent governments which in turn, may choose to create and delegate authority to a central government. This was the type of government system created by the Articles of Confederation.

conference committee A Congressional committee formed to draft a compromise bill when different versions of a similar bill have been passed by the House and Senate.

contract The idea that government represents a covenant between those who govern and those who are governed. Government power needs the consent of the governed to be legitimate.

cooperative federalism An interpretation of federalism that emerged in the 1930s. This interpretation is characterized by a sharing of governmental powers for the purpose of joint problem-solving.

countercyclical revenue sharing An emergency federal grant program to provide an anti-recessional financial boost to areas facing severe economic and fiscal problems.

critical realignment a long term change in party identification with a relocation of groups across party lines.

cruel and unusual punishment A phrase used in the Eighth Amendment provision intended to regulate the manner and severity of criminal punishment.

democracy Rule by the people.

department The major functional division within the bureaucracy by which the executive branch of government administers the laws and carries out the programs established by Congress.

desegregation Abolishing the practice of racial segregation.

direct primary Popular elections used to determine party nominees for public office and to select state and national convention delegates and party officers.

discharge petition A petition to withdraw a bill from a house committee. It must be signed by a majority of House members.

dissenting opinion A judicial statement explaining the minority justices reasoning for questioning the majority verdict.

doctrinal party A minor political party which professes a particular doctrine and nominates candidates to the Presidency over several elections.

dual federalism A nineteenth century concept of government recognizing a duality of power between national and state governments, each having a distinct sphere of authority and jurisdiction.

due process Legal, constitutional protections of personal rights and liberties.

elastic clause The clause in the Constitution that gives Congress the power to make all laws "necessary and proper" to execute enumerated powers. This clause allowed for the existence of implied powers.

Electoral College The group of electors, appointed by the states, who select the President. To be elected president, a candidate must receive a majority of electoral votes.

elite opinion The opinions of political leaders and media representatives.

enabling act An act of Congress allowing the people of a territory to draft a constitution, preparing the way for statehood.

enumerated powers The powers of the national government specifically provided for and listed in the Constitution.

Equal Rights Amendment A proposed Constitutional Amendment, currently before the states for ratification, that would prohibit sex-based classifications.

equity A legal principle of fairness that allows judges to provide for preventive measures and legal remedies where there is no law applicable.

establishment clause The part of the First Amendment that prohibits the federal government or any state from setting up a church, passing laws to aid any religion, or preferring one religion over another.

Everson v. *Board of Education* The 1947 Supreme Court decision establishing the "wall of separation" doctrine.

exchange theory Robert Salisbury's theory of interest group participation, suggesting that a mutual exchange of incentives between members and leaders supports group membership and participation.

exclusive committee The designation given to the Appropriations, Ways and Means, and Rules Committees of the House of Representatives. Members assigned to an exclusive committee serve on only that committee and no other standing committee.

executive agreements Agreements made by the President which do not require Senate action, but have the same legal standing as treaties.

Executive Office of the President A part of the executive branch appointed to serve the President. It consists of agencies such as the Office of Management and Budget and National Security Council.

executive power The blend of written Constitutional provisions, custom, and person, that constitutes the power of the American Presidency.

executive privilege The power of a President to withhold information from Congress and the judiciary.

Ex Post Facto Law Laws which impose punishment for an act that was not a crime when it was committed.

extradition A Constitutional provision whereby a state shall surrender a fugitive to the state within whose jurisdiction the crime was committed.

fairness doctrine A requirement by the Federal Communications Commission that radio and television broadcasters provide time for replies in cases of personal attack and political editorial.

Federal Election Commission A bipartisan commission which has the responsibility to enforce campaign finance laws and to administer public financing of presidential elections. The six-member commission is appointed by the President and confirmed by the Senate.

federalism A system of government based on a constitutional separation of powers between a national government and component states.

Federalist Individuals who supported the new Constitution and the creation of a strong central authority.

The Federalist A series of articles by Alexander Hamilton, James Madison and John Jay providing a statement of the principles behind the proposed Constitution and urging its adoption.

filibuster Extended debate by a single Senator, or a group of Senators, used to prevent a vote on a piece of legislation.

fiscal federalism Shared responsibility between the national and state (and local) governments for taxing and spending policies.

floor manager The Congressional member responsible for directing the floor action on a bill. Usually the bill's subcommittee chair or a senior committee member acts as floor manager.

free exercise clause The part of the First Amendment that protects the right of individuals to worship as they choose.

full faith and credit A clause in Article IV of the Constitution requiring states to accept the laws, records, and court decisions (in noncriminal cases) of other states.

fungibility The ability to use revenue-sharing money in place of local tax receipts.

gag rule Court orders restricting the printing of information about criminal proceedings in cases where publication might violate the rights of a defendant or prejudice a prospective jury.

Gibbons v. *Ogden* The 1824 Supreme Court decision expanding national authority in interstate commerce.

Gitlow v. *New York* The 1925 Supreme Court decision that for the first time held that a provision of the Bill of Rights could not be impaired by states any more than it could by the national government.

grand jury A jury used by trial courts to investigate accusations against persons charged with crime and indict them for trial.

grant-in-aid A form of money payment from the national (or state) government to state (or local) governments for specified programs, under whatever conditions the granting authority wishes to impose.

great compromise The compromise at the Constitutional Convention that resulted in a two-chamber Congress, with the Senate based on equality of the states and the House of Representatives based on population. Also known as the Connecticut Compromise.

Great Society President Lyndon Johnson's program designed to end poverty and racial injustice through governmental social engineering.

Griswold v. *Connecticut* The 1965 Supreme Court decision recognizing the right to privacy as a constitutionally protected freedom.

Gulf of Tonkin Resolution The 1964 act of Congress authorizing the President to send troops to protect any area seeking American help ''in defense of its freedom.'' This power was used by the Johnson administration to escalate and sustain the war effort in Vietnam.

hierarchy A principle of organizational authority in which direction and orders come from the top down, in a pyramidal design.

horizontal federalism The federal relationship between states, including the obligations imposed by Article IV of the Constitution.

impeachment The Constitutional provision for removing Justices and a President from office. The House of Representatives is empowered to impeach (bring charges against) and the Senate, with the Chief Justice of the Supreme Court presiding, tries the case.

imperial presidency The term used by Arthur Schlesinger, Jr., to describe the Nixon presidency and the lack of presidential accountability associated with it.

implementation The function of bureaucratic agencies involving attempts to put into practice the policies established through legislation or executive order.

implied powers The powers of the national government that can be inferred from enumerated powers.

impoundment Executive refusal to spend funds appropriated by Congress.

incrementalism An approach to policy implementation that involves consideration of only a limited number of alternatives and making

only incremental modifications of past government activities.

In forma pauperis Requests made by indigent appellants using relaxed standards of the Supreme Court to ask for a review of their cases.

inherent powers Powers of the national government that flow not from the Constitution but from the fact that it exists as a government, such as the power to conduct foreign relations.

intensity The strength of the political opinions held by a given individual.

interest group A group of individuals who ban together seeking the support and resources of others to achieve common goals. When the goal becomes to pressure government to enhance the groups objectives, it becomes a political pressure group.

interstate compacts Legal and binding agreements between states made with the consent of Congress.

iron triangle A three-sided symbiotic relationship between bureau chiefs, clientele groups, and Congressional committees and subcomittees. The iron triangle establishes a continual policy process with the bureaucracy at the heart of the decision-making process.

isolationism A theory of foreign policy that opposes international alliances, foreign aid, or trade with communist nations.

issue groups Interest groups that are formed in direct response to a specific public controversy. For example, the Right to Life Association was founded in response to the controversy over the 1973 Supreme Court decision permitting abortions.

item veto The power to disapprove of and block passage of specific parts of a bill. The President does not have this power.

Jim Crow A term used to refer to racial discrimination or segregation.

job specialization The organizational principle that attempts to match competent people with a task required by the organization. Each task must be identified along with the necessary skills before an individual is recruited.

joint-stock colonies Colonies founded as commercial ventures by English trading companies.

judicial activism A judicial style that involves a willingness on the part of the courts to test conventional boundaries of judicial action, playing an active role in shaping public policy.

judicial review The power of the court to make authoritative interpretations of federal and state laws and political actions, in relation to the United States Constitution.

judicial self-restraint A judicial doctrine which holds that judges should restrain from imposing their own values and policy preferences and decide a case on its merit and according to established legal precedent.

jurisdiction The authority of a court to hear and decide an issue brought before it.

justiciable disputes Actual disputes that may be settled by legal methods available to the court. Courts will hear only the cases and controversies that are justiciable.

Keynesian economics The theory that government spending should be used to regulate the economy.

Koreagate A Congressional scandal of the late 1960s and early 1970s involving the testimony of Korean businessman Tongsun Park that he bribed Congressmen for their continued support of U.S. economic and military aid to Korea.

libel Written or spoken statements, known to be false, that defame a person's character or reputation.

lobbying A form of communications whereby an interest group interacts with public officials for the purpose of influencing decision-making.

loophole or winner-take-all primary Presidential primaries in which the winning candidate receives all the state's convention delegates, regardless of how slim the margin of victory.

The Magna Carta An English document, signed in 1215, affirming that the power of the king was not absolute.

majority leader of the Senate The leader of the majority party and the ranking official in the Senate.

majority opinion The judicial statement supporting a decision made by a majority of the justices. If the Chief Justice voted in the majority, he can write the opinion or assign it to one of the other justices in the majority.

management by objectives A management system that requires agencies to identify short- and long-term objectives and then establish techniques to monitor the achievement of those objectives.

mark-up The committee draft of a bill. Each line is amended or rewritten in the form the committee or subcommittee chooses.

McCarran Act A 1950 act of Congress that required communists and communist organizations to register with the Subversive Activities Control Board.

McCulloch v. *Maryland* The 1819 Supreme Court decision affirming that Congress had certain implied powers in addition to those specifically enumerated in the Constitution. This set the stage for expansion of national authority.

Miranda v. *Arizona* The Supreme Court decision that detailed the principles governing police interrogation.

national committee The national party organization responsible for setting up the process for the national nominating convention.

natural rights Inherent, inalienable human rights, such as life, liberty, and property.

new federalism President Richard Nixon's proposal for rebalancing the federal-state relationship, primarily through programs such as revenue sharing.

New Jersey Plan A plan submitted to the Constitutional Convention that differed little from the Articles of Confederation. It called for a plural executive with limited authority and equal representation in Congress for each state regardless of population.

objective influence The ability of an interest group to make good its demands upon government through direct personal contact with political officials.

obscenity A lewd or indecent publication expressing or presenting something offensive, that appeals to the prurient interest.

occupational groups A classification of interest groups by occupation. This typical categorization of interest groups is dominated by business and labor groups.

office block (Massachussetts) ballot A form of ballot that lists candidates by the office sought. Party affiliation is noted after the candidate, but straight party voting is difficult.

open primary A form of political election in which any qualified voter may participate simply by showing up at the polls. No statement of party support is required; the voter is merely asked to choose one party ballot or the other.

operational liberals Persons indicating approval for specific programs involving government policy and power, such as compulsory medical insurance and low-rent housing.

overlapping membership The tendency for individuals to belong to more than one interest group. These memberships may be "crosscutting" and lead to a conflict in views and activities.

party caucus The party conference, consisting of all party members in the legislative chamber.

party column (Indiana) ballot A form of ballot that lists candidates by parties in straight columns.

Pendleton Act The 1883 act of Congress creating the civil service system.

penumbras Zones of privacy emanating from several provisions in the Bill of Rights, particularly the First Amendment. Penumbras were used by the Supreme Court as the basis for its 1965 recognition of the right to privacy as a constitutionally protected freedom.

Per Curium **opinion** A short, unsigned judicial statement of a decision of the Supreme Court, used for relatively simple cases that command a strong majority.

peripheral voters Individuals who come out only because of presidential elections and normally do not vote in off-year elections.

perquisites Allowances for travel, postage, and hiring of staff employees that supplement a legislator's salary.

petit jury A jury used to weigh evidence and decide the issues of a trial in court.

Planning, Programming, Budgeting System (PPBS) A comprehensive budget process that requires federal departments to define their goals precisely and to measure the costs and benefits of alternative programs to achieve those goals.

platform The document, written at the national convention, that specifies a party's position on issues.

Plessy v. *Ferguson* The 1896 Supreme Court decision establishing the separate but equal doctrine.

plurality The largest number of voters.

pocket veto A veto occurring when Congress adjourns within ten days after a bill has been sent to the President and upon which the President takes *no* action.

Policy and Steering Committee A 24-person committee composed of House Democratic leaders. Its primary function is to recommend positions on legislation and assign House Democrats to committees.

political action committees (PACs) A legal method for labor unions, professional associations, corporations, or other organizations to solicit funds to be spent for political purposes.

political amateurs Individuals who are politically motivated by issues or attachment to a candidate, not party loyalty.

political efficacy An individual's attitude about his or her effectiveness in influencing the government.

Presidential Character A study by James David Barber attempting to to explain the crisis of presidential leadership in terms of individual character.

prior restraint The power of government to require prior approval before information can be communicated. In most instances, prior restraint is prohibited under the First Amendment.

private law   Statutory law regulating the relationships between private citizens in such areas as marriage, divorce, wills, deeds, and contracts.

probable cause   The basis upon which a search warrant is issued and, thus, a necessary condition for police searches.

procedural democracy   The process whereby citizens confer legitimacy on public officials. Procedural democracy stresses the importance of the mechanisms for popular government, in particular, the electoral system.

procedural due process   The aspect of due process that refers to the fairness with which laws are enforced.

proprietary colonies   Colonies formed as a royal land grant in which the proprietor obtained complete control.

public interest groups   Interest groups that claim to seek goals that will benefit society in general rather than narrow, special interests.

public law   Legal regulations and obligations that apply to public officials, in their capacity as public officials. The public law is concerned with the definition, regulation and enforcement of rights and obligations where the state is the subject of the right or the object of the obligation.

quota sample   A method used in opinion polling in which members of various groups are surveyed in proportion to their percentage in the population as a whole.

random sample   A method used in opinion polling in which people surveyed are selected completely by chance.

Reed v. *Reed*   The 1971 Supreme Court decision that for the first time offered equal protection guarantees against sex discrimination, under the Fourteenth Amendment.

registration   The physical act of establishing legal qualification to vote. To be eligible to vote a citizen must meet minimum age and residency requirements.

regulatory agency   A government agency specifically designed to regulate some sector of national life while remaining outside executive and congressional control.

republic   A form of government in which people do not govern directly but consent to representatives who make and administer laws for the people.

republicanism   A system of mixed government intended to preclude men from having either an interest or a power to subvert the government.

reserved powers   The term used in reference to state powers. The Tenth Amendment reserved for the states all powers not granted by the Constitution to the national government or prohibited to the states.

resolution   A bill concerned with the internal business of either the House of Representatives or the Senate, and passed by that chamber only.

restitution   The principle of requiring an offender to make reparation to the victim of a crime.

revenue sharing   Returning a portion of the federal tax revenues back to state and local governments to spend as they see fit with no conditions or requirements imposed by the national government.

Roe v. *Wade*   The 1973 Supreme Court decision that extended the right of privacy to include the right to have an abortion.

Roth v. *United States*   The 1957 Supreme Court decision that obscenity is not protected by the First Amendment.

rule adjudication   The power of bureacratic agencies to administer laws by charging persons or organizations suspected with violating rules. They can then apply administrative sanctions to persons or organizations found in violation.

rulemaking   The quasi-legislative function whereby bureaucratic rules have the force of law. Rulemaking is a prime responsibility of independent regulatory agencies.

Rules Committee   The House committee empowered to establish rules governing floor consideration of legislation.

salience   The degree of importance an issue holds for a specific individual.

selective incorporation   The gradual process, whereby Supreme Court decisions have included provisions of the Bill of Rights as applying to limit state governments.

selective perception The tendency of individuals to cognitively screen the contents of the news by focusing on only those issues and facts that support their own concerns and biases.

self-incrimination The Fifth Amendment protection of an individual's right to refuse to bear witness against himself.

seniority The practice of ranking congressional committee members, by party, according to years of continuous service in Congress.

The separate but equal doctrine The doctrine adopted by the Supreme Court in 1896, which affirmed that public accommodations could legally be separate if they were equal.

separation of powers A seventeenth and eighteenth century political theory that was incorporated into the Constitution. To ensure that no single branch of government became too powerful, authority was distributed among the three main branches.

service agency an agency such as the General Services Administration or the Office of Personnel Management which provides services to other agencies within the federal bureaucracy.

single member district The method used in Congressional elections. The designated number of representatives for a state are each elected from a separate, single district.

The Smith Act A law passed by Congress in 1940, making it a crime for anyone to advocate the violent overthrow of the United States government.

Solicitor General The third highest ranking official in the Justice Department. When the United States is a party to a case before the Supreme Court, the Solicitor General acts as the lawyer for the government.

Speaker of the House The leader of the majority party and the presiding officer in the House of Representatives.

stability The resistance to change in a political opinion.

standing The interest a person has in the judicial resolution of a conflict. In recent years, the doctrine of standing has been liberalized, thereby permitting a wider range of people to challenge government or corporate interests in court.

stare decisis A Latin phrase meaning "to adhere to the decision." This principle of looking to past decisions, and the reasoning in previous similar cases, is often used by judges in deciding cases.

statutory law The laws passed by legislative bodies are called statutes and are collectively known as statutory law.

stewardship presidency Theodore Roosevelt's view of executive authority that became the standard for a strong executive. This theory affirmed the president's duty to do anything not illegal that the needs of the nation demanded.

subcommittee bill of rights A measure passed in the 94th Congress that forced committee chairs to respect subcommittee jurisdictions and resources.

substantive democracy The intrinsic values associated with democracy, such as freedom, equality, and individualism.

substantive due process The aspect of due process that deals with the fairness of the law itself.

suffrage The right to vote.

sun belt politics The politics of the area from Florida across the South to the Southwest and on into California; associated with a growing American conservatism.

Sun King complex The term used by Louis Koenig to describe the American tendency to create for the President the surroundings and resources fit for a king.

sunshine rules Rules adopted by both the House and the Senate, intended to minimize the number of closed committee meetings.

symbolic speech Nonverbal behavior generally covered as a form of free expression by the First Amendment.

textbook presidency The theory developed by Thomas Cronin that popular opinion supported the growth of presidential power by extolling the value of a strong-willed, personal desire for power.

ticket splitting   When party identifiers vote for some candidates of the opposing party on the election ballot.

tort   A private injury or wrongful act for which a civil action can be brought.

transient party   A short-lived political party which emerges out of economic protest and secessionist movements.

treaty   A formal agreement between nations. The President has the power to make treaties; however, they require ratification by two-thirds of the Senate.

unanimous consent   The Senate procedure used to call up a bill from the calendar.

uncontrollables   Dedicated and entitled programs that are not subject to annual action by Congress. Presently 75 percent of the federal budget is uncontrollable.

unitary government   A system of government in which all authority is derived from the central government.

unit rule   The rule which required all convention delegates to cast their ballots as the majority ruled.

veto   Executive refusal to sign legislation approved by Congress, thus effectively killing the bill.

victory bonus system   A Republican party convention procedure that rewards states with additional delegates if the state voted Republican in the last presidential, congressional, or gubernatorial election.

video-malaise   A term used by Michael Robinson to describe the growth in negative feelings toward the political system that is attributed to media reporting.

Virginia Plan   Proposed at the Constitutional Convention, it represented a nationalistic plan for establishment of a strong central authority. The plan called for a strong national executive, a national judiciary and the representation in Congress to be based on state population.

wall of separation   The phrase used by the Supreme Court in interpreting the First Amendment prohibition against establishment of a church, thereby preventing public aid or support for religious activity.

Watergate   The term used for the 1972 illegal break-ins at the Democratic National Committee headquarters and the subsequest coverup and conspiracy to obstruct justice leading to the resignation of President Nixon.

whips   Assistant floor leaders who assist the majority and minority leaders in carrying out the party's legislative program.

Writ of Certiorari   A writ that declares the Supreme Court's intention to review a case from a lower court.

zero based budgeting (ZBB)   An approach to budgetary decision making in which each agency must justify all of its programs and resources annually. Each agency starts its budget at zero.

zero population growth   The demographic situation whereby the birth and death rates are balanced, thus there is no net gain in population.

Index